The Modes of Modern Writing

Other books by David Lodge

Criticism:

Language of Fiction (*Routledge & Kegan Paul; Columbia University Press*)
The Novelist at the Crossroads (*Routledge & Kegan Paul; Cornell University Press*)
Graham Greene (*Columbia University Press*)
Evelyn Waugh (*Columbia University Press*)
(*Editor*) Twentieth Century Literary Criticism (*Longman*)
Working with Structuralism (*Routledge & Kegan Paul*)

Novels:

The Picturegoers (*MacGibbon & Kee*)
Ginger, You're Barmy (*MacGibbon & Kee; Doubleday*)
The British Museum is Falling Down (*MacGibbon & Kee; Holt, Rinehart & Winston*)
Out of the Shelter (*Macmillan*)
Changing Places (*Secker & Warburg*)
Small World (*Secker & Warburg*)

The Modes of Modern Writing

Metaphor, Metonymy, and the
Typology of
Modern Literature

David Lodge

The University of Chicago Press

What does literature do and how does it do it. And what does English Literature do and how does it do it. And what ways does it use to do what it does.

Gertrude Stein

The University of Chicago Press, Chicago 60637
Edward Arnold, London
© David Lodge 1977
All rights reserved. Published 1977
University of Chicago Press Edition 1988
Printed in Great Britain
97 96 95 94 93 92 91 90 89 88   5 4 3 2 1

Library of Congress Cataloging in Publication data

Lodge, David, 1935–
    The modes of modern writing : metaphor, metonymy, and the typology of modern literature / David Lodge.
        p.   cm.
    Reprint. Originally published: London : E. Arnold, 1977.
    Bibliography: p.
    Includes index.
    1. Style, Literary. 2. English fiction – 20th century – History and criticism.   I. Title.
PN203.L58 1988
809'.03--dc19
ISBN 0-226-48978-7 (pbk.)   88-10079
                                                                  CIP

Contents

Preface

The first part of this book considers some fundamental questions of literary theory and critical practice, illustrated by reference to a wide range of modern texts; questions such as, what is literature, what is realism, what is the relationship between form and content in literature, and what principles underlie the variety of literary forms, and the changes in literary fashion, in the modern era? To answer such questions, it is argued, we need a comprehensive typology of literary discourse—that is, one capable of describing and discriminating between all types of text without prejudging them. The second part of the book describes and explores a theory of language upon which such a typology may be based—Roman Jakobson's distinction between metaphor and metonymy—and applies it to the analysis of a number of short texts, including those examined in Part One. In Part Three, the theory is applied to a more discursive and historical study of the work of particular writers, or schools and generations of writers, in the modern period.

As is usually the case, the actual genesis of this book was not quite as straightforward as the above summary may suggest. Some years ago I accepted an invitation to contribute to a symposium entitled *Modernism*, edited for Penguin Books by Malcolm Bradbury and James McFarlane. My subject was to be 'The Language of Modern Fiction' and my starting point, in endeavouring to establish some common denominator in the language of novelists who seemed to be such varied and idiosyncratic stylists, was something I had often noticed in casual reading of the 'antimodernist' writers of the 1930s, such as Isherwood, Orwell and Greene, namely their marked preference for simile over metaphor in expressing figures of comparison. In the major modernist novelists such as Joyce, Lawrence and Virginia Woolf, it seemed to me that there was not the same bias, but on the contrary an abundance of metaphor. Some traces of this distinction will be found in what follows, but as my research progressed it was fairly quickly absorbed into what seemed a much more powerful theory.

Like, I suppose, most Anglo-American critics of my generation, I had for some years been making occasional, baffled forays into the foreign territory loosely known as 'structuralism', a word which began to be fashionable in the second half of the 1960s. Here, evidently, was an intellectual movement of rapidly growing influence and prestige, with much to say on the subject of literature and literary criticism. Clearly it could not be ignored. On the other hand, its major texts were difficult to obtain, often available only in a foreign language, and seldom seemed more intelligible when translated into English. Though predisposed to be sympathetic to a formalist and linguistic approach to literary criticism, I found a book like Roland Barthes's *Writing Degree Zero*—one of the first productions of the *nouvelle critique* to be translated—deeply and disturbingly alien in its cryptic, dogmatic style of discussion, unsupported by the kind of close reading which is so characteristic of Anglo-American formalist criticism. The same author's *Elements of Semiology* I found almost incomprehensible (and I wonder how many other readers were misled by that title, invitingly suggestive of a beginner's guide, and put off structuralism for life in consequence?). But I did salvage from that discouraging experience the memory of some allusion to Roman Jakobson's distinction between metaphor and metonymy. In working on my article for the Modernism book, I looked up the source, Jakobson's essay, 'Two Aspects of Language and Two Types of Aphasic Disturbances'. Lightning—and enlightenment—struck. The distinction between metaphoric and metonymic types of discourse not only seemed a much more effective way of distinguishing between the language of modernist and antimodernist fiction than metaphor/simile; it suggested the possibility of an all-embracing typology of literary modes. Jakobson's brief comment on the metonymic character of realistic fiction particularly excited me by its obvious explanatory power. Furthermore, Jakobson's article proved to be the key that unlocked for me some of the sealed doors of structuralism. Pondering it, I began to grasp the principles of, and see the usefulness of, the binary model of language and communication that underlies the whole structuralist enterprise from de Saussure onwards; Roland Barthes's criticism began to make more sense; and I was led back to investigate the origins of the *nouvelle critique* in the work of the Russian Formalists and the Czech Linguistic Circle, discovering the highly suggestive concepts of 'defamiliarization' and 'foregrounding' in the process.

All these ideas, and the whole tradition of thought about language and literature to which they belong, seemed to throw a good deal of light on the problems that had preoccupied me in my previous critical books, *Language of Fiction* (1966) and *The Novelist at the Crossroads* (1971), especially the problem of how to account aesthetically for the realistic novel—how to analyse its formal devices in terms proper to itself and not drawn from drama and poetry. These ideas, and even some of the primary texts in which they first appeared, had of course been available when I was working on those earlier books. René Wellek and Austin Warren refer briefly to the metaphor/metonymy distinction in their *Theory of Literature* (1949), and Roman Jakobson alluded to it in his paper 'Linguistics and Poetics' in the symposium *Language and Style* edited by Thomas A. Sebeok (1960), both of which books I used and referred to in *Language of Fiction*. The ideas were there, under my nose, and yet I did not see them because I was not looking for them. It needed the provocation of the *nouvelle critique* to make them visible to me some years later—and I think my experience has been shared by other English and American critics in the last decade. Although this book is in no sense a systematic introduction to or critique of structuralist criticism (for which the reader is directed to such books as Jonathan Culler's *Structuralist Poetics* (1975), Robert Scholes's *Structuralism in Literature* (1974), Frederick Jameson's *The Prison House of Language* (1972) and Stephen Heath's *The Nouveau Roman* (1972)) it does consciously attempt a synthesis of the two traditions of modern formalist criticism, the European and the Anglo-American. I hope that at least it will serve the function of making some of the concepts of the former tradition better known to exponents of the latter. In particular it seems to me that the importance and possibilities of the metaphor/metonymy distinction have not been adequately recognized even by those English and American critics (such as those named above) who have been most active in studying and disseminating structuralist criticism.*

I have always been a formalist critic, interested in the kind of questions posed by Gertrude Stein in the epigraph to this book, and drawn to the study of the novel partly because of the challenging resistance it seems to offer to formalist criticism. In *Language of Fiction* I took my stand on the axiom that novels are made of words, and argued that since language is self-authenticating in literary discourse in a way that does not apply to nonliterary discourse, all critical questions about novels must be ultimately reducible to questions about language. Though I think it is irrefutable in theory, this argument entailed certain methodological difficulties and

*The only book in English known to me which makes extensive use of Jakobson's theory is *The Story-Shaped World: Fiction and Metaphysics: Some Variations on a Theme* (1975) by my colleague at Birmingham, Brian Wicker, whose application of it is rather different from mine, his book being theological as well as literary in its orientation. I have come across a few articles which use or explore the distinction: Fred G. See, 'The Demystification of Style: Metaphoric and Metonymic Language in *A Modern Instance*' [on W. D. Howells] *Nineteenth Century Fiction* XXVIII (1974) pp. 379–403; Frederick Jameson, 'Wyndham Lewis as a Futurist', *Hudson Review* XXVI (1973) pp. 295–329; and (the most interesting from a theoretical point of view) Roger M. Browne, 'The Typology of Literary Signs', *College English* XXXIII (1971) pp. 1–17. No doubt there are others, but on the whole one is struck by how long it has taken for this idea to work its way into Anglo-American critical discourse. Its application to anthropology is better known, through the work of Edmund Leach, especially *Lévi-Strauss* (Fontana, 1970) and *Culture and Communication* (Cambridge, 1976).

disadvantages. In particular it seemed to entail abstaining from discussing a lot of interesting aspects of novels because they had been pre-empted by content-oriented criticism—or discussing them at the risk of seeming inconsistent. In the working out of the argument, language or style became opposed to such categories as plot and character. The great attraction of the structuralist variety of formalism, it seems to me, is that within its terms of reference this kind of antithesis is dissolved in a more comprehensive theory of literary forms. *Everything* is form, from the individual phrase or sentence, up to the structure of a plot or plot-type; and there is a homology between the smallest structural unit and the largest, because all involve the same basic processes of selection and combination, substitution and deletion. Wherever we cut into the literary text, and in whatever direction, we expose, not 'content', but a systematic structure of signs in which content is made apprehensible.

The *dis*advantage of *this* position, in turn, is that it applies through the whole of culture (i.e. everything that is not nature) and governs nonliterary and indeed nonverbal systems of signs as well as literature. A good deal of the most effective structuralist analysis has been employed upon such areas as fashion, food, advertising, and in the field of literary criticism upon work that would be considered beneath the notice of traditional literary studies, such as thrillers and detective stories. It thus leaves open the question of why we should be interested in literature at all. Structuralist critics, especially the French, have taken a somewhat dismissive stance towards the question of value in literature,* either because they deem it irrelevant to the methodology of formal analysis, or because they are ideologically motivated to undermine the traditional cultural prestige of literature as an institution. Thus, by a curious irony, extreme semiotic formalists and their natural opponents, the content-oriented critics, agree in denying that there is any significant discontinuity between life and art—the former on the ground that life is really no different from art, and the latter on the ground that art is really no different from life.

I suppose I am sufficiently conditioned by the Arnoldian tradition in English studies to feel that any critical method should be able to explain why literature is valued (in other words, what is special about it) as well as how it works. I begin therefore, by addressing myself directly to the question, 'What is Literature?' I fear this chapter may be found dry by some readers, especially if they are unfamiliar with the jargon of modern linguistics and impatient with literary theorizing; but I cannot encourage them to skip, since some basic terms used later are defined here. As soon as possible the theoretical issues are examined in relation to specific texts. It seemed desirable that these

---

*One must make an exception of Roland Barthes's more recent work, *S/Z* (Paris, 1970) and *Le Plaisir du Texte* (Paris, 1973) in which value is defined hedonistically and derived from plurality of signification.

texts should have, for purposes of comparison, a common theme. The choice of capital punishment as that theme was more or less accidental (it began with my noticing first the striking similarities, and then the significant differences, between Michael Lake's account of a hanging in the *Guardian* and Orwell's famous essay); but by the time I had finished the book I had become convinced that the 'condemned prisoner story', as Leonard Michaels calls it (see below, p. 232), has a special fascination for the modern literary imagination. Be that as it may, there is something to be said for testing a formalist critical approach on texts that would appear, more than most, to affect us primarily by virtue of their sombre and highly emotive 'content'.

Part Two is not so much a summary of Jakobson's theory, as a speculative expansion of it, a personal exploration of the hints, possibilities and gaps in that fascinating, cryptic, endlessly suggestive paper referred to above, especially the few densely packed pages headed 'The Metaphoric and Metonymic Poles'. The authors and groups of authors discussed in Part Three were selected with a view to illustrating the relevance of the metaphor/metonymy distinction to as many different types of modern writing as possible. I have not discussed contemporary British fiction at any length, because I have written fairly extensively about it before, but a short chapter on Philip Larkin partly covers the relevant phase of literary history. With the exception of that chapter, the focus of the book is upon prose fiction, because that is the form that interests me most and because to have attempted to do equal justice to poetry and drama would have resulted in an impossibly long book. I hope that the occasional asides and digressions about poetry and drama indicate the relevance of the general approach to these kinds of writing also.

Obviously my chief intellectual debt in the writing of this book has been to the work of Roman Jakobson, albeit to a very small part of it. References to other printed sources from which I have profited will be found in the text and notes. While the book was in preparation I addressed several audiences in England and abroad on aspects of its subject, and benefited from the discussions, formal and informal, that followed. I am especially grateful to colleagues, postgraduate students and undergraduates at the University of Birmingham with whom I have explored many of the ideas and texts discussed below, in seminars and in casual conversation. My research into the background of D. H. Lawrence's story, 'England, My England', was significantly assisted by Gabriel Bergonzi and James Boulton. Mas'ud Zavarzadeh generously kept me supplied with postmodernist texts from America. Finally, I owe a special debt of gratitude to those who read the complete text of this book, at one stage or another of its progress to publication, with eyes alert to errors and obscurities, and who gave me the benefit of their opinions and advice: Park Honan, Deirdre Burton, Helen Tuschling and my wife, Mary.

Parts of the essay in *Modernism*, edited by Malcolm Bradbury and James McFarlane, referred to above, and printed in a slightly different form in the *Critical Quarterly*, are embedded in this book; as are parts of a review-article on Gabriel Josipovici, 'Onions and Apricots; or, Was the Rise of the Novel a Fall from Grace?', also printed in the *Critical Quarterly*. The first chapter of Part One is a condensed version of an essay entitled 'What is Literature? A Despatch From The Front', originally published in *The New Review*.

Prefatory Note to the Second Impression

This Note will probably mean little to readers who are beginning the book for the first time, and they are recommended to turn back to it when they have reached the end of Part Two.

In section 5 of Part Two, entitled 'Poetry, Prose and the Poetic', I suggested that there was a certain discrepancy between two important papers by Roman Jakobson, 'Two Aspects of Language and Two Types of Linguistic Disturbances' (1956) and 'Linguistics and Poetics' (1960), namely, that the later paper defines literariness, or the poetic function of language, in terms ('the poetic function projects the principle of equivalence from the axis of selection into the axis of combination') that correspond to the account of metaphor, but not of metonymy, in the earlier paper.

On further reflection, prompted by Terence Hawkes's discussion of Jakobson in *Structuralism and Semiotics* (1977), and confirmed in conversation with Professor Jakobson himself, I wish to withdraw this criticism. Jakobson sees both metaphor and metonymy as figures of 'equivalence', though generated according to different principles. Thus, to use my own example (in section 1 of Part Two), in the sentence 'Keels ploughed the deep', *ploughed* is a metaphorical equivalent for the movement of the ships, derived from similarity, while *keels* and *deep* are synecdochic and metonymic equivalents for 'ships' and 'sea' respectively, derived from contiguity. The discrepancy of which I accused Jakobson was therefore of my own making, since I treated 'equivalence' and 'similarity' as homologous terms.

I am still of the opinion, however, that Jakobson's discussion of 'literariness' in the influential 'Linguistics and Poetics' is, in effect, biassed towards verse rather than prose, towards dominantly metaphorical writing rather than dominantly metonymic writing; and the celebrated definition itself contains a buried metaphor ('projects') which is more obviously applicable to the formation of metaphor than of metonymy. In my model sentence, *ploughed* violently and illogically forces one context (the earth, agriculture) into another (the sea, navigation); *keels* and *deep* do not have the same effect of transgression and rupture. Therefore, while I was wrong to attribute to Jakobson a theoretical inconsistency, this admission does not, I think, affect the main drift and purpose of this book, which was to redress the balance in literary criticism between analysis of metaphoric and metonymic techniques (something Jakobson himself has called for more than once); nor does it invalidate my own theoretical argument, for this was always closer to Jakobson's than I realised.

Although I did not use Jakobson's term, the underlying argument of the theoretical sections of Part One is that 'equivalence' in the most inclusive sense—repetition, parallelism, symmetry of every kind and on every linguistic level—is what makes a text 'literary', or, alternatively, what a literary reading of a text focusses on. As I try to show in the course of Parts Two and Three, the metonymic mode of writing, typically in the realistic novel, allows a pattern of equivalences to be developed in a text without radically disturbing the illusion of a pseudo-historical reality which is constructed on the axis of combination. There would appear to be two principal ways in which this is done. First, the metonymic signifier foregrounds the signified and thus makes its recurrence and interrelation with other signifieds in the text aesthetically functional: what the Prague School theorists call 'systematic internal foregrounding.' This need not involve actually using the rhetorical figures of metonymy or synecdoche, because a narrative text is always in a metonymic or synecdochic relation to the action it purports to imitate, selecting some details and suppressing (or deleting) many others. We notice and respond to the superintendent's manipulation of his stick in Orwell's 'A Hanging' because, out of all the manifold items of his dress and equipment that might have been described, 'stick' is the only one mentioned in the text. Second, the particular property or attribute of a given signified that is highlighted by a metonymic signifier connotes, by association or similarity, another signified not actually mentioned in the text, thus creating a quasi-metaphorical effect without the use of the rhetorical figure of metaphor. The sexual symbolism of the 'red columns' of the guillotine in Bennett's *The Old Wives' Tale* (III, iii, 4) would be an example. Both kinds of metonymically-generated equivalence are in fact extensively illustrated and discussed in the course of this book, though without being related to Jakobson's theory of literariness as explicitly as I would now wish. The argument advanced in section 8 of Part Two, 'The Metonymic Text as Metaphor', though still, I believe, valid, is not the only way of assimilating the metonymic to the poetic in Jakobson's scheme.

April 1979

Acknowledgements

Grateful acknowledgement is made for permission to quote from the following copyright sources: from *Collected Poems* by W. H. Auden, by permission of Faber & Faber Ltd and Random House Inc.; from *Lost in the Funhouse* by John Barth, by permission of Lurton Blassingame and Secker & Warburg Ltd; from *S/Z* by Roland Barthes, translated by Richard Miller, by permission of Jonathan Cape Ltd and Farrar, Straus, Giroux, Inc. (Translation © 1974 by Farrar, Straus, Giroux Inc. Originally published in France as *S/Z* © 1970 Editions Du Seuil, Paris); from 'Style and Its Image' by Roland Barthes, translated by Seymour Chatman, in *Literary Style* ed. Seymour Chatman, by permission of the translator and Oxford University Press, New York: from *Come Back, Dr Caligari*, by Donald Barthelme, by permission of Little, Brown & Co and A. D. Peters & Co Ltd, and from 'A Film' in *Sadness* by the same author, by permission of Jonathan Cape Ltd and Farrar, Straus, Giroux, copyright © by Donald Barthelme 1970, 1971, 1972 (this story originally appeared in the *New Yorker*); from *More Pricks Than Kicks* (All Rights Reserved. First published by Chatto & Windus, London, 1934), *Murphy*, *Watt* (All Rights Reserved) and *The Unnamable* (from *Three Novels* copyright © 1955, 1956, 1958 by Grove Press, Inc.) by permission of Calder & Boyars Ltd and Grove Press Inc.; from *The Old Wives' Tale* by Arnold Bennett, by permission of Mrs Dorothy Chesterton, Hodder & Stoughton Ltd and Doubleday & Co; from *Trout Fishing in America* by Richard Brautigan, copyright © 1967 by Richard Brautigan by permission of Jonathan Cape Ltd and Delacorte Press/Seymour Lawrence; from *The Naked Lunch*, copyright © 1959 by William Burroughs, by permission of Calder & Boyars Ltd and Grove Press Inc.; from *The Film Sense* by Sergei Eisenstin, by permission of Faber & Faber Ltd and Harcourt Brace Jovanovich, Inc.; from *Collected Poems 1909–1962* by T. S. Eliot, by permission of Faber & Faber Ltd and Harcourt Brace Jovanovich, Inc.; from *Collected Essays* and *The Confidential Agent* by Graham Greene, by permission of the author; from 'The Non-Intervenors' in *Several Observations* by Geoffrey Grigson, by permission of the author; from *Death in the Afternoon* and *Men Without Women* by Ernest Hemingway, by permission of the Executors of the Ernest Hemingway Estate, Jonathan Cape Ltd and Charles Scribner's Sons; from *Goodbye* to *Berlin* and *Lions and Shadows* by Christopher Isherwood, by permission of the Hogarth Press and New Directions Inc. and from *A Single Man* by the same author, by permission of Methuen & Co and Simon & Schuster Inc.; from 'Two Aspects of Language and Two Types of Aphasic Disturbances' and 'Linguistics and Poetics' in *Selected Writings* by Roman Jakobson, by permission of the author; from *The World and the Book* by Gabriel Josipovici, by permission of the author; from *Dubliners*, *A Portrait of the Artist as a Young Man*, *Ulysses* and *Finnegans Wake* by James Joyce, by permission of the Society of Authors, literary representative of the Estate of James Joyce, Jonathan Cape Ltd, The Bodley Head, Viking Press, Inc. and Random House, Inc.; from *The Less Deceived* by Philip Larkin by permission of The Marvell Press, from *The Whitsun Weddings* by the same author, by permission of Faber & Faber Ltd and from *High Windows* by the same author, by permission of Faber & Faber Ltd and Farrar, Straus, Giroux, Inc.; from 'England, My England' in *Collected Short Stories* by D. H. Lawrence and *The Complete Short Stories of D. H. Lawrence* Vol II, copyright 1922 by Thomas B. Selzer, Inc., 1950 by Frieda Lawrence, and from the first version of this story in *The English Review*, October 1915, and from *Women in Love* by the same author, and from a letter from D. H. Lawrence to Catherine Carswell, by permission of Lawrence Pollinger Ltd, Viking Press Inc. and the estate of the late Mrs Frieda Lawrence; the entire text of 'Michael Lake Describes What The Executioner Actually Faces' in *The Guardian* 9 April 1973, by permission of the author; from *Autumn Journal* by Louis MacNeice, by permission of Faber & Faber Ltd and Oxford University Press, New York; from 'In The Fifties' in *I Would Have Saved Them If I Could* by Leonard Michaels, copyright © 1973, 1975 by Leonard Michaels, by permission of the author and Farrar, Straus, Giroux, Inc. (This story first appeared in *Partisan Review*); the entire text of 'A Hanging' in *Shooting an Elephant and Other Essays* by George Orwell, copyright 1945, 1946, 1949, 1950, 1973, 1974, by Sonia Brownell Orwell, also from *Coming Up For Air*, *Keep The Aspidistra Flying* and *Inside The Whale* by the same author, by permission of Mrs Sonia Brownell Orwell, Secker & Warburg Ltd, Brandt & Brandt and Harcourt Brace Jovanovich, Inc.; from *A Hundred Years of Philosophy* by John Passmore, by permission of Duckworth & Co Ltd; from *Le Voyeur* by Alain Robbe-Grillet by permission of Les Editions de Minuit, Paris, and from *The Voyeur* translated by Richard Howard, by permission of Grove Press and Calder and Boyars Ltd; from *The Making of Americans* by Gertrude Stein, by permission of Harcourt Brace Jovanovich, Inc. and from *Look At Me Now And Here I Am* by the same author, by permission of Peter Owen Ltd; from *The Railway Accident and Other Stories* by Edward Upward, by permission of William Heinemann Ltd; from *The Waves*, *To the Lighthouse*, *Jacob's Room* and *Mrs Dalloway*, by Virginia Woolf, by permission of the Hogarth Press and Harcourt Brace Jovanovich, Inc.

Part One

Problems and Executions

1 What is Literature?

We all 'know' what literature is, but it is remarkably difficult to define. When the scholarly journal *New Literary History* recently devoted one of its issues (Autumn, 1973) to the question posed above, the majority of contributors agreed that no abstract, formal definition could be arrived at. Philosophers tell us that such 'essentialist' enquiries are fruitless,[1] that literature, like Wittgenstein's 'games' is a 'family-resemblance concept', the members of the family being linked by a network of overlapping similarities none of which is common to all of them.[2] This latter argument is difficult to refute, and has the attraction, for some, of giving a seal of philosophical approval to theoretical inertia. All games, however, have in common the capacity to be played; and though we lack an equivalent verb in poetics, it seems worthwhile (for reasons suggested in the Preface) enquiring whether there is anything *in* literature that causes or allows us to experience it *as* literature.

Most definitions of literature have, as Tzvetan Todorov observes,[3] been of two kinds: one stating that it is language used for purposes of imitation, that is to say, for the making of fictions, and the other stating that it is language used in a way that is aesthetically pleasing, that calls attention to itself as medium. Todorov attacks modern theorists, such as René Wellek and Northrop Frye, for sliding covertly between these two positions, because, he says, there is no necessary link between them and neither can be a satisfactory criterion for literature alone. I shall argue that there *is* a necessary connection, but it is certainly true that neither definition can stand alone. For, to take the first one, there is literature which is not fiction (e.g. biography) and fiction which is not literature (e.g. advertising in narrative form). Another difficulty with this definition of literature is that the concept of 'fiction' has to be stretched somewhat to cover propositions as well as descriptions, since a good deal of literature (e.g. lyrical and didactic poetry) consists of the former rather than the latter. Recent efforts to apply the speech-act philosophy of J. L. Austin to the theory of literature have enhanced our understanding of what is involved in fictional or mimetic utterance, but have not been able to explain how writing that is factual by intention can acquire the status of literature.[4] It would seem that we can identify literature with fiction only in the weak, negative sense that in the literary text, descriptions and propositions *need* not be put forward or accepted as 'true'.

The other type of definition, literature as language used in a way that is aesthetically pleasing, language that calls attention to itself as medium, has its roots in classical rhetoric, but persists into modern formalist criticism. At its most simple, this theory associates literature with a mere abundance of tropes and figures, and as such is easily refuted. Ruqaiya Hasan, another recent investigator of the problem, observes: 'it is highly doubtful if the frequency of such recognized devices in longer prose works is significantly different from that in, say, a feature article in a quality newspaper.'[5] Nor have the attempts of English and American 'New Critics' to identify literariness with one particular rhetorical device—metaphor, irony, paradox, ambiguity—been conspicuously successful. A more promising approach is the argument of the Czech school of structuralists that literary discourse is characterized by consistent and systematic foregrounding.

'Foregrounding' is the accepted English translation of the Czech word *aktualisace*, which was the central concept of the school of linguistics and poetics that flourished in Prague in the 1930s (to which Roman Jakobson belonged after he left Russia and before he moved to America). In this school of thought, the aesthetic is opposed to the utilitarian. Any item in discourse that attracts attention to itself for what it *is*, rather than acting merely as a vehicle for information, is foregrounded. Foregrounding depends upon a 'background' of 'automatized' components—that is, language used in customary and predictable ways so that it does *not* attract attention. Foregrounding was defined by Jan Mukařovský, the most distinguished of the Czech theorists, as 'the aesthetically intentional distortion of linguistic components'.[6] It is not peculiar to literature—the use of puns in casual conversation is an example of foregrounding; nor does it imply a single linguistic norm, for what is automatized in one kind of discourse will become foregrounded when transferred to another (for example, the use of a technical term in casual conversation). It is not the statistical frequency of foregrounded components that distinguishes literary discourse from nonliterary discourse, but the consistency and systematic character of the foregrounding and the fact that the background as well as the foreground, and the relationships between them, are aesthetically relevant, whereas in nonliterary discourse only the foregrounded components are aesthetically relevant. Furthermore the 'background' of literary discourse is dual: ordinary language ('the norm of the standard language') and the relevant literary tradition.[7]

To this may be added a third type of background: the linguistic norms established by the work itself. Thus, for example, T. S. Eliot's 'Sweeney Among the Nightingales' is foregrounded, first, as poetry against the background of the norms of the standard language, by the presence of metre and rhyme and certain archaic and literary lexical items such as 'the hornèd gate', 'Gloomy Orion', etc. Secondly it is foregrounded as a 'modern' poem against the background of the norms of nineteenth-century English lyric poetry by the inclusion of low subject matter and low diction:

> Gloomy Orion and the Dog
> Are veiled; and hushed the shrunken seas;
> The person in the Spanish cape
> Tries to sit on Sweeney's knees

and by the absence of explanatory links between the various events reported in the poem. And thirdly, the last stanza,

> And sang within the bloody wood
> When Agamemnon cried aloud,
> And let their liquid siftings fall
> To stain the stiff dishonoured shroud

is foregrounded against the background of the rest of the poem by the *absence* of poetic indecorum and by the switch of tense from present to past. At first we are struck by the contrast between the sordid present and the dignified, harmoniously beautiful mythical past to which we are swept by the emphatic 'sang'; then perhaps we recognize that 'liquid siftings' is not after all a metaphor for birdsong but a euphemism for bird-droppings, that the nightingales (representing the natural and aesthetic orders) are as indifferent to Agamemnon as to Sweeney, and that there is not all that much to choose between the two in terms of making a good death. It will be noted that what is foregrounded at one level becomes background at the next.

In the poetics of the Prague school, foregrounding defined in this way is a sufficient criterion of literariness, but Hasan thinks literary foregrounding requires some 'motivation' to explain it. This she finds in the 'unity' of literary texts, a unity of topic or theme that regulates the development of the discourse without being literally present in it:

In literature there are two levels of symbolization: the categories of the code of the language are used to symbolize a set of situations, events, processes, entities, etc. (as they are in the use of language in general); these situations, events, entities, etc., in their turn, are used to symbolize a theme or a theme constellation. I would suggest that we have here an essential characteristic of literary verbal structures. . . . So far as its own nature is concerned, the theme (or regulative principle) of a literary work may be seen as a generalization or an abstraction, as such being closely related to all forms of hypothesis-building. A certain set of situations, a configuration of events, etc. is seen not only as itself (i.e. a particular happening) but also as a manifestation of some deep underlying principle.[8]

This, as Hasan acknowledges, has much in common with Aristotle's definition of the poetic as expressing the universal in the particular. Aristotle, however, equates literature with fiction, to the exclusion of history and philosophy, and so, by implication, does Hasan's theory. It is not immediately obvious how it would, for instance, explain why Boswell's *Life of Johnson* and Pope's *Essay on Man* can be, and are, read as literature, since in these texts there seems to be no second level of symbolization, no second-order theme: Boswell is concerned only with the particular, Pope directly with the universal, and the language of the texts refers us immediately to these regulating themes or topics—Johnson in one case, man's place in the universe in the other. One could get round this difficulty only by saying that Boswell's *Life* is *really* about the nature of genius, or about the problems of writing biography; that the *Essay on Man* is *really* about the terror of the Augustan mind in the face of scepticism or about the problems of fitting philosophical statements into rhyming couplets—finding the regulative principle of the discourse in this kind of motivation. Certainly it is one of the characteristics of a 'literary' reading that we ask what a text is 'about' with the implication that the answer will not be self-evident. We do not merely decode the literary message—we interpret it, and may get out of it more information than the sender was conscious of putting into it. Unfortunately (for the purpose of defining literature) all discourse is open to the same kind of interpretation, as a lot of recent work in linguistics and cultural studies has shown. Roland Barthes's *Mythologies* (Paris, 1957) is a good example of how a second level of symbolization in Hasan's sense can be discovered in journalism, advertising and indeed non-verbal spectacles such as striptease and wrestling.

All one can say to reinforce Hasan's theory is that the literary text *invites* this kind of interpretation, and indeed requires it for its completion, whereas the nonliterary text does not invite it, and is in effect destroyed by it. When Barthes, for example, analyses the contrasting rhetorical strategies used in advertisements for cleaning fluids and detergents ('The implicit legend of [chlorinated fluid] rests on the idea of a violent, abrasive modification of matter; the connotations are of a chemical or mutilating type: the product "kills" the dirt. Powders, on the contrary, are separating agents: their ideal role is to liberate the object from its circumstantial imperfection: dirt is "forced out" and no longer killed . . .'[9]) he renders them impotent: what has been offered as reality is exposed as (in the derogatory sense) a myth. To interpret *Robinson Crusoe* as a myth of bourgeois individualism, however, (as Ian Watt has plausibly done)[10] in no way destroys the power of that story to excite and engage us on the realistic level but explains and enhances it; myth here is used in the honorific sense of a useful fiction, the narrative equivalent of a non-verifiable, non-falsifiable yet valid hypothesis.

We come back to the problem of showing that there is a necessary connection between the fictional and rhetorical definitions of literature. Mukařovský was very insistent that 'the question of truthfulness does not apply in regard to the subject matter of a work of poetry, nor does it even make sense . . . the question has no bearing on the aesthetic value of the work; it can only serve to determine the extent to which the work has documentary value'.[11] The referential dimension of works of literature is regarded by the Prague school as merely a 'semantic component' to be considered by the critic strictly in terms of its structural relationships with other components. The regularizing principle which Hasan looked for in theme or topic is, in their theory, the *dominant*—the component 'which sets in motion, and gives direction to, the relationship of all the other components'.[12] And since literature is not about the real world it must be about itself:

> In poetic language foregrounding achieves maximum intensity to the extent of pushing communication into the background as the objective of expression and of being used for its own sake; it is not used in the services of communication, but in order to place in the foreground the act of expression, the act of speech itself.[13]

A more celebrated and concise formulation of this principle is Roman Jakobson's assertion that the poetic (i.e., literary) function of language is 'the set towards the message for its own sake'. 'Message', here, stands for any act of verbal communication, which Jakobson has analysed in the following terms:

> The ADDRESSER sends a MESSAGE to the ADDRESSEE. To be operative the message requires a CONTEXT referred to . . . a CODE fully, or at least partially common to the addresser and addressee . . . and finally a CONTACT, a physical channel and psychological connection between the addresser and addressee. . . .

Jakobson proposes a typology of utterances according to which of these factors is dominant. Thus, the REFERENTIAL message (e.g. statements of fact) is characterized by the set (*Einstellung*) towards CONTEXT; the EMOTIVE message by the set towards the ADDRESSER (e.g. ejaculations) the CONATIVE message by the set towards the ADDRESSEE (e.g. orders); the PHATIC message by the set towards the CONTACT (e.g. conventional opening exchanges in telephonic communication); and the METALINGUAL message by the set towards the CODE (e.g. definitions of words). The POETIC message is characterized by the set towards the MESSAGE as such, 'for its own sake'.[14]

The usual objections to Jakobson's (and Mukařovský's) definition of the literary are that it is biased towards self-conscious and highly deviant kinds of literature (e.g. the modernist lyric), that it cannot account for kinds of literature in which the referential and communicative element appears to be central (e.g. realistic fiction or autobiography) and that it leads logically to the assertion that the subject matter of a work of literature is merely the pretext for bringing certain verbal devices into play.[15] It is on precisely such grounds that Stanley Fish rejects what he describes as Jakobson's 'message-minus' definition of literature. But he is equally scornful of 'message-plus' definitions that present literature as 'a more effective conveyor of the messages ordinary language transmits', for proponents of this view are 'committed to downgrading works in which the elements of style do not either reflect or support a propositional core'[16]—precisely the kind that are upgraded by the message-minus definition. For Fish and for Todorov, then, available definitions of literature fail because they exclude or downgrade texts pragmatically definable as literature. For Todorov the mistake is to make a dichotomy between literature and non-literature. He argues:

> from a structural point of view, each type of discourse usually referred to as literary has nonliterary relatives which resemble it more than do other types of discourse. For example, a certain type of lyric poetry has more rules in common with prayer than with a historical novel of the *War and Peace* variety. Thus the opposition between literature and nonliterature is replaced by a typology of the various types of discourse.[17]

He does not explain how, lacking a definition of literariness, we may distinguish between literary and nonliterary examples of the same type of discourse—between, say, a prayer that is not literature and a poem by Herbert that is; but he would probably say that this is a 'functional' (as distinct from a structural) distinction that depends upon the cultural values of readers at a particular time. Fish puts it more starkly: 'Literature . . . is an open category . . . definable . . . simply by what we decide to put into it.'[18] For him the mistake is to make a dichotomy between literary language and nonliterary or 'ordinary' language. '*There is no such thing as ordinary language,* at least in the naive sense often intended by that term . . . [T]he alternative view would be one in which the purposes and needs of human communication inform language and are constitutive of its structure.'[19] To deny that there is any difference between literary and nonliterary uses of language has, of course, serious consequences for criticism, for it is then difficult to insist upon the inseparability of form and content in literature.[20] There is, however, a confusion here between the linguistic form of a literary work and the function of its language in the communication of meaning. H. G. Widdowson usefully distinguishes between the two as 'text' and 'discourse', and observes that 'although literature need not be deviant as text it must of its nature be deviant as discourse'.[21] The best term we have for this deviance is, I believe, fictionality, in its most elastic sense. I suggest that literary discourse is either self-evidently fictional or may be read as such, and that what compels or permits such reading is the structural organization of its component parts, its systematic foregrounding. As Widdowson puts it:

> what distinguishes our understanding of literary discourse is that it depends upon our recognizing patterns of linguistic organization which are superimposed as it were on those which the code requires, and our inferring the special values that linguistic items contract as elements in these created patterns.[22]

We must, however, beware of equating literature with 'good literature', as Todorov and Fish do by implication. Another contributor to the *New Literary History* symposium, Dell Hymes, observes:

> there seems to be no special difficulty in categorizing as sculpture works which are great, routine, or amateurishly bad. It is not customary to say that something is not an opera on the ground that it is not great or good. Indeed, of what else except an opera could it be a bad instance? There is no evident reason to be different with regard to literature.[23]

In fact there *is* an evident reason, precisely in that some works of literature can be instances of something else; but Dell Hymes's hint will carry us a long way towards the solution of our difficulties. It is obviously true that 'literature' is a flexible category in that the sum of works included in it will vary from age to age and from person to person. But it is flexible only at its circumference. There are a great many texts which are and always have been literary because there is nothing else for them to be, that is, no other recognized category of discourse of which they could be instances. We may call them *axiomatically literary*. *The Faerie Queen*, *Tom Jones* and 'Among School Children' are examples of such texts; but so are countless bad, meretricious, ill-written and ephemeral poems and stories. These too must be classed as literature because there is nothing else for them to be: the question of their value is secondary. When, however, a text that belongs to another identifiable category of discourse is shifted by cultural consensus into the category of literature, value is the primary criterion. As Todorov says, any text can be given a 'literary reading' (which can only mean the kind of reading appropriate to the texts that are axiomatically literary)—but not all texts will emerge with credit from such a reading. This, however, does not affect the status of texts that are axiomatically literary. *Love Story* is literature whether you like it or not, and would be literature even if nobody liked it. But works of history or theology or science only 'become' literature if enough readers like them for 'literary' reasons—and they can retain this status as literature after losing their original status as history, theology or science. Thus it would be meaningful to say, for example, that a text by Freud is a work of literature as well as a work of science, or to say that even if it isn't acceptable as science it is nevertheless a work of literature; but it would be pointless to criticize it for *not* being a work of literature, because it was intended to be science, and only readers could make it into literature. (It would of course be quite legitimate to criticize *them* for doing so.) The main difference between the two kinds of text is that recognition of 'the set towards the message' is essential to interpretation in the first instance, optional in the second.

Although descriptions and propositions in literature may have the appearance of nonliterary descriptions and propositions, by virtue of sharing a common code, nevertheless the adequacy of what is said in literary discourse 'is not, in any straightforward sense, governed by any state of affairs prior to and independent of what is said'.[24] The systematic foregrounding of axiomatically literary texts often acts in the first place as a sign that this is the case—that the ordinary rules for determining truthfulness do not apply—by foregrounding the text as literature against the background of nonliterature. If such texts are successful, it is because the systematic foregrounding also supplies the place of the absent context of facts and logical entailments which validates nonliterary discourse; one might say that it folds the context back into the message, limits and orders the context in a system of dynamic interrelationships between the text's component parts—and thus contrives to state the universal in the particular, to speak personally to each reader and yet publicly to all, and to do all the other things for which literature has traditionally been valued. If a text which is *not* foregrounded as literature can nevertheless become literature by responding to a literary reading, it can only be because it has the kind of systematic internal foregrounding which makes all its components aesthetically relevant, 'patterns of linguistic organization which are superimposed as it were on those which the code requires'. (We find an intuitive recognition of this by the reading public in the fact noted by Northrop Frye that 'style . . . is the chief literary term applied to works of prose generally classified as non-literary'.[25]) It is this which allows us to read the text 'as if' the criteria of truthfulness did not apply. Boswell's Johnson then becomes something like a fictional character, and his *Life* is read as if it were a kind of novel—though without ceasing to be a biography: we read it on two levels at once, as literature and as history, whereas most other biographies of Johnson are merely history, and conceivably superior as such to Boswell's. Jonathan Culler suggests, in his thoughtful *Structuralist Poetics*, that 'Rather than say . . . that literary texts are fictional, we might cite this as a convention of literary interpretation and say that to read a text as literature is to read it as fiction.'[26]

I would accept this formulation as long as it is recognized that the convention of fictionality derives from texts that *insist* on being read as fiction. The qualification is important because Culler, like Todorov and Fish (though on different grounds), implies that 'literature' is wholly accountable in terms of the reading process—that it is indeed a category of reading procedures, not of the properties of texts. But to stress the dependence of literature upon particular modes of reading is only a half-truth, the other half of which is the dependence of those modes of reading on the existence of literature. The process is dialectical, as Sartre explained in *What is Literature?*

> The operation of writing implies that of reading as its dialectical correlative and these two connected acts necessitate two distinct agents. It is the conjoint effort of author and reader which brings upon the scene that concrete and imaginary object which is the work of the mind.[27]

To accept this version of the literary process does not entail accepting Sartre's prescription of literary *engagement*, because the contractual link between writer and reader which he defines as an appeal to 'freedom' could quite as well be defined as an appeal to something else—to intelligibility, for instance, to use a word Culler himself favours. The important point is that literature is not a body of texts which came into being accidentally, and which we have spontaneously decided to read in a certain way. Most of the discourse we read as literature is on one level the expression of an intentionality to write literature, and it is from such discourse that we derive the conventions of interpretation that Culler calls 'literary competence', which we can then turn experimentally upon discourse that does *not* express such intentionality. Writing requires reading for its completion, but also teaches the kind of reading it requires.

I am therefore accepting that literature is an open category in the sense that you can, in theory, put any kind of discourse into it—but only on condition that such discourse has something in common with the discourse you cannot take out of it: the something being a structure which either indicates the fictionality of a text or enables a text to be read as if it were fictional. I now propose to test this theory on a text chosen deliberately for the resistance it seems to offer to the theory.

2 George Orwell's 'A Hanging', and 'Michael Lake Describes . . .'

George Orwell's 'A Hanging'* is undoubtedly part of 'English Literature', but surely (it may be objected in the light of the preceding discussion) it is a factual document, and to say that it is literature because we can read it as if it were fiction can only deprive it of its main claim to be valued, namely that it is telling the truth, making us 'face the facts' of capital punishment.

*See Appendix A. Figures in square brackets refer to the numbered paragraphs of this text.

When I first read 'A Hanging' I certainly assumed that it was a true story, an eye-witness account. The more I studied it, the more I suspected that Orwell had added or altered some details for literary effect, but I did not doubt that the piece was essentially factual and historical. I think this is probably the response of most readers of 'A Hanging'—certainly nearly all the published commentary on it assumes that it is, like its companion piece 'Shooting an Elephant', a true story based on Orwell's own experience. The exception is the interesting biography of Orwell's early years, *The Unknown Orwell* (1972) by Peter Stansky and William Abrahams. They have interviewed Orwell's friend Mabel Fierz, who was largely responsible for getting *Down and Out in London and Paris* (1933) published and whom he met in 1930. They report:

> he appears to have told her things he told no-one else—from a literary point of view, the most sensational confidence was that his essay 'A Hanging' which came out in the *Adelphi* the next winter* was not, as it purported to be, an eye-witness account but a work of the imagination, for (she remembers him telling her) he had never been present at a hanging.[1]

Stansky and Abrahams have also talked to Orwell's colleagues in the Burmese police force, who agreed that

> It would have been most unusual, though not impossible . . . for him to have been present at a hanging. As Headquarters ASP [Assistant Superintendent of Police] at Insein his duties would not normally require his presence there.[2]

Writing in *The Road to Wigan Pier* (1937) about his experience of administering the British Empire, Orwell says, 'I watched a man hanged once. It seemed to me worse than a thousand murders'[3]— which appears to be a fairly clear reference to, and authentication of, 'A Hanging'. But Stansky and Abrahams show that Orwell, like most of us, did not always tell the strict truth, either in conversation or in print. So there is at least an element of doubt about the eye-witness authenticity of 'A Hanging', a possibility that it is a fiction.

To entertain this possibility may be a shock at first, involving a sense of having been deceived. But on reflection we can see, I think, that the factors which made us read the text as an eye-witness account are mainly *external* to the text. First, most of us read it, no doubt, in a volume of Orwell's essays, a context which implies that is a factual, rather than a fictional account. The volumes of essays in which it appeared, *Shooting an Elephant* (1950) and *Collected Essays* (1961) were, however, posthumous publications: Orwell himself was not responsible for placing 'A Hanging' in this non-fiction context. In his lifetime the piece was published only twice—in the *Adelphi* for August 1931 and in the *New Savoy* in 1946. Secondly, we read 'A Hanging' knowing that George Orwell was a police officer in Burma, a job which

*Actually August 1931.

he grew to detest and repudiate, but one that would plausibly enough involve him in witnessing an execution. We may, indeed, read 'A Hanging' with that reference in *The Road to Wigan Pier* at the back of our minds.

The original readers of 'A Hanging' in the *Adelphi* had no such knowledge of its author. 'Eric A. Blair', as the piece was signed (he did not adopt the name George Orwell until 1933) was known to them only as the author of a few book reviews in the same periodical and of a first-person sketch of a weekend spent in an English workhouse—'The Spike'—published in April 1931, and later incorporated into *Down and Out in Paris and London*. The text of 'A Hanging' itself gives no information about the 'I' figure who narrates: no explanation of why he is present at the hanging, or what his function is supposed to be. This absence would have been more striking to the original readers than it is to us, who read back into the text all the biographical information we have acquired about George Orwell/Eric Blair, much of which he himself supplied in his books from 1936 onwards. Stansky and Abrahams observe the same ambiguity about the 'I' figure in 'The Spike' and in *Down and Out*, which Orwell was writing at about the same time. They argue that the invention of this narrator, originally in 'The Spike', was the crucial technical breakthrough in Eric Blair's early struggles to find a style for himself that was not hopelessly derivative and conventionally 'literary'.

> The material he had accumulated until now had to be reinvented if he was to use it truthfully—which meant not a surface honesty but to get under the surface (any honest reporter could take care of the surface) and get down to the essence of it. He began to write in the first person without intervention: simply, I was there.[4]

But since the focus was to be on '*there*', the personal history of '*I*' had to be rigorously curtailed. (Stansky and Abrahams plausibly suggest that Blair adopted the pseudonym 'George Orwell' when *Down and Out* was published not, as he claimed, because he feared the book would be a failure, but to reinforce the anonymity of the narrator. They also show how he rather clumsily attempted to conceal the fact that he had collected much of the material by deliberately posing as a down-and-out).

It is very unlikely, at this date, that we shall ever be able to establish definitely whether Orwell attended a hanging or not, and more or less impossible that we should ever be able to check the particular circumstances of 'A Hanging' against historical fact. It may be completely factual, it may be partly based on experience, or partly on the reported experience of others, or partly fictional, or wholly fictional—though the last possibility seems to me the least likely. The point I wish to make is that it doesn't really matter. As a text, 'A Hanging' is self-sufficient, self-authenticating—autotelic, to use the jargon word. The internal relationships of its component parts are far more significant than their external references. In fact, when we examine the text carefully we see that these external references—to time, place, history—have been kept down to a minimum. There are no proper names except 'Burma' and the Christian name of the head warder. There are no dates. There is no explanation of the prisoner's crime. And it is because the external references of the text are reduced in this way that the internal relationships of its component parts— what has been referred to earlier as systematic foregrounding or patterns of linguistic organization—are correspondingly important, as I shall show.

'A Hanging' is literature, therefore, not because it is self-evidently fictional, but because it does not need to be historically verifiable to 'work'. Although it is possible, and perhaps natural in some circumstances, to read 'A Hanging' as history, the text will, I believe, survive the undermining of that assumption. It is equally satisfying, equally successful read as a true story or as a fiction or as something in between, and nothing we might discover about its relationship to history will affect its status as literature.

It may seem that I am making too simple a distinction here between fiction and history, and taking a naively positivistic view of the latter. But while it is true that historians construct fictions in the sense that they inevitably select and interpret 'the facts' according to conscious or unconscious ideological predilections, no neutral or total reconstruction of the past being possible, nevertheless history is based on the assumption that there is a body of facts to be selected from and interpreted, and that our understanding of an event can be improved or revised or altered by the discovery of new facts or the invalidation of old ones.[5] There is no way in which our understanding of 'A Hanging' could be improved or revised or altered by the discovery of new facts. In this respect it contrasts instructively with an account of a hanging by Michael Lake that appeared in the *Guardian* for 9 April, 1973 under the title 'Michael Lake Describes What the Executioner Actually Faces'.* This text has many features in common with 'A Hanging', and superficially the same narrative design: the procession to the scaffold, the numbed state of the condemned man, the abrupt operation of the gallows, the whisky and the macabre joking of the officials afterwards, the narrator's residual sense of guilt. 'Michael Lake Describes . . .' seems to me a good piece of journalism, and as a polemic against capital punishment perhaps more effective than Orwell's piece. But it *is* journalism, and remains this side of literature. Its effectiveness depends on our trust that it is historically verifiable. If we discovered that there was no such person as Walter James Bolton, or that Michael Lake had never attended a hanging, the text would collapse, because it would be impossible to read it, as one can read 'A

*See Appendix B.

Hanging', as an effective piece of fiction. Once its external references were cut, the comparative weakness of its internal structure would become all too evident. We should become aware of clichés, opportunities missed, a lack of variety in tempo and in intensity of feeling. Details like 'Mr Alf Addison, an old friend of mine' would no longer have any function and would become irritating irrelevancies. And perhaps we should feel we were being bullied into the desired response by crudely sensationalist means.

Correspondingly, 'A Hanging' has certain qualities which 'Michael Lake Describes . . .' hasn't got: a narrative structure, for instance, that is more than a mere sequence. The structure of Michael Lake's report is a chain of items linked in chronological order and suspended between an opening statement of polemical intent and a closing statement of personal feeling. The structure of 'A Hanging' is also chronological, but it is more complex: the inevitable movement towards the death of the condemned man is deliberately but unexpectedly retarded at two points: first by the interruption of the dog and secondly by the prisoner's invocation of his god. These delays heighten the tension, and they allow the moral protest against capital punishment to emerge out of the narrative instead of being merely signalled at the beginning and end. Another structural difference is that Orwell's piece goes on proportionately longer after the actual execution, enforcing the double concern of the writer: not only with what the execution does to the executed but also what it does to the executioners. In a sense, this extended ending is another form of retardation, since it retards the expected termination of the text.

'Retardation' is one of the basic devices that, according to the Russian Formalist Victor Shklovsky, enable narrative art to achieve the effect of 'defamiliarization' which he held to be the end and justification of all art:

> Habitualization devours objects, clothes, furniture, one's wife and the fear of war. 'If all the complex lives of many people go on unconsciously, then such lives are as if they had never been.' Art exists to help us recover the sensation of life; it exists to make us feel things, to make the stone *stony*. The end of art is to give a sensation of the object as seen, not as recognized. The technique of art is to make things 'unfamiliar', to make forms obscure, so as to increase the difficulty and the duration of perception. The act of perception in art is an end in itself and must be prolonged. *In art, it is our experience of the process of construction that counts, not the finished product.*[6]

Although the last statement leads logically to Shklovsky's celebration of *Tristram Shandy* as the supreme example of narrative art,[7] the quotation in the second sentence is from the diary of Tolstoy, from whom Shklovsky draws several of his illustrations. In other words, there is no incompatibility between the theory of 'defamiliarization' and realistic writing of the kind Orwell practiced—indeed 'A Hanging' illustrates the theory very well, for what Orwell is doing is defamiliarizing the idea of capital punishment—the idea, not the experience of it, since only the first is 'familiar'.

Michael Lake is trying to do the same thing, but by the comparatively crude method of filling out the familiar idea with unfamiliar details. He selects and describes aspects of the event he witnessed which will make us recoil from it: the possibility of Bolton's head being torn off by his own weight, the hypocrisy and/or irrelevance of the chaplain's prayers, the macabre fancy-dress of the executioner's get-up, Bolton's inarticulateness, and so on. But these details belong to quite disparate emotive categories—some are nauseating, some ironic, some pathetic—and Lake makes no attempt to relate them to each other. He fires the details at us on the principle of the shotgun: if a few miss the target, enough will hit it to make the desired effect. It would be difficult to say, on the evidence of the text, exactly what aspect of the proceedings was to him the most significant or indeed what it is, precisely, that makes capital punishment inhuman in his view.

There is no such difficulty in the Orwell text. The central paragraph [10] makes clear what the narrator feels to be wrong about capital punishment (though it is an 'unspeakable wrongness' he in fact proceeds to speak it). Interestingly, it is not the most gruesome or solemn part of the proceedings that provokes this realization, but a gesture so small and ordinary that most people, perhaps including Mr Lake, would never have noticed it (always supposing, of course, that it actually happened): the prisoner side-stepping the puddle. Why is this gesture so pregnant with meaning for the narrator? Because in the context of imminent death, it makes him understand what it is to be alive. Orwell has thus defamiliarized the idea of capital punishment by defamiliarizing something in fact much more familiar, much more veiled by habit: simply being alive. Implicitly the incident reveals that there is all the difference in the world between knowing *that* we shall die and knowing *when* we shall die. Human life exists in an open-ended continuum. We know that we shall die, but if we are healthy our minds and bodies function on the assumption that we shall go on living, and indeed they cannot function in any other way. The man instinctively avoids the trivial discomfort of stepping in the puddle on his way to the scaffold. His nails continue growing even as he falls through the air with a tenth of a second to live. So he is in the intolerable position of having to behave as if he is going to go on living, but knowing that he isn't going to. And the spectator is correspondingly impressed by the grim irony that all present are inhabiting the same continuum of experience, but that for one person it is not open-ended: 'he and we were a party of men walking together, seeing, hearing, feeling, understanding the same world'—the present participles emphasize the notions of continuity and community—'and in two minutes, with a sudden snap, one of us would be gone—one mind less, one world less.'

There is then, in this central paragraph, an emphasis on the idea of time in relation to life and death. 'Time is life, and life is time,' runs the lyric of a modern song.[8] 'Death,' said Wittgenstein, 'is not an event *in* life. We do not live to experience death.'[9] At the level of maximum abstraction that is what 'A Hanging' is about: the paradoxical relationships between the concepts death, life and time, in the context of capital punishment. For capital punishment in a sense seeks to subvert the logic of Wittgenstein's assertion, to force the experience of death into life. That is why it is, or may be held to be, inhuman and obscene. Michael Lake is dimly aware of these paradoxes—at least I think that is why he is shocked and incredulous that the chaplain is reading aloud the Burial Service over the living man. But he hasn't quite worked out what is shocking about it, and without Orwell's piece for comparison we might not have worked it out either.

Throughout 'A Hanging' there are repeated references to the theme of life/death/time which prepare for and sustain the explicit statement of it by the narrator in paragraph 10. In the first paragraph there is the reference to the other 'condemned men due to be hanged in the next week or two'. In paragraph 3, eight o'clock strikes, and the superintendent urges the warders to hurry up: 'The man ought to have been dead by this time. . . .' In paragraph 5 there is the remark that the prisoners can't get their breakfast until the execution is completed—a reference to the continuum of life/time that will go on without the condemned man.

Then comes the intervention of the dog. This of course is the vehicle for several kinds of ironic commentary on the action, but let us just note for the moment that it is a delay, an interruption of the proceedings and duly recorded as such by the narrator: 'It was several minutes before someone managed to catch the dog. Then we put my handkerchief through its collar and moved off once more . . .'[8]. The association of the narrator with the dog through 'my' handkerchief is interesting, perhaps a way of preparing for the narrator's moral recoil from the execution in the next paragraph, in which the personal pronoun 'I' is used for the first time, 'I' becoming distinguished from 'we'. This paragraph ends with the side-stepping of the puddle, which leads to the explicit reflection upon life/death/time in paragraph 10.

In paragraph 12 begins the second interruption or delay: the prisoner's prayer to his god. We are now in a position to appreciate the underlying function of these two delaying or 'retarding' incidents, which as we noted above constitute the main structural feature of the narrative. If the genre were romance, or at least a narrative more overtly fictional and 'literary', these delays might be welcomed by the narrator, and vicariously by the reader, as affording some time in which a reprieve might arrive, or some rescue be effected (one thinks of *The Heart of Midlothian* or *Adam Bede*). But of course no such possibility is hinted at in 'A Hanging'. Although the narrator, in paragraph 10, recognizes the 'unspeakable wrongness' of the execution, he has no intention of trying to stop it, and neither have any of the other people present. Therefore, although for the prisoner every cry is 'another second of life', this only draws out the agony. Since he must die, the quicker the better for everyone's comfort: 'the same thought was in all our minds: oh, kill him quickly, get it over, stop that abominable noise.' [13] To the narrator, the repetition of the god's name is not 'like a prayer or cry for help'—not, that is, like human speech—but 'steady, rhythmical, almost like the tolling of a bell'—in other words, a regular notation of passing time. 'Minutes seemed to pass.' The narrator wonders if the superintendent is allowing the man a fixed number of cries, 'fifty, or perhaps a hundred'. [13]

After the execution is carried out and the body of the man has been inspected, the Superintendent glances at his watch: 'Eight minutes past eight.' [16] In paragraph 17 the procession reverses itself, minus one. There is a reference to the other condemned men waiting to die, a reference to the other prisoners receiving their breakfast—recapitulations of details in the opening paragraphs. Now the unbearable contradictions of life/death/time have been temporarily resolved and an almost hysterical wave of relief and callous good-humour flows over the witnesses, temporarily melting away conventional barriers of caste, status and race. Dialogue—direct speech—suddenly begins to dominate narrative. 'I' is absorbed back into 'we', and the ironies of time are replaced by ironies of space: 'We all had a drink together, native and European alike, quite amicably. The dead man was a hundred yards away.' [24]

One might say that Orwell has achieved the 'defamiliarization' of capital punishment by 'foregrounding' the semantic component of time in his text. There is indeed a close connection between these two concepts—defamiliarization being opposed to habitualization in Russian Formalism as foregrounding is opposed to automatization in the poetics of the Prague school. It is to be noted, however, that the language in which the time motif is reiterated is not itself foregrounded in any obvious way either against the 'norm of the standard' or against the internal norms of the text itself (the nearest equivalent in 'A Hanging' to the foregrounded shift of tense in the last stanza of 'Sweeney Among The Nightingales' is the shift from 'we' to 'I' in paragraph 9).

To sum up the argument so far: 'Michael Lake Describes . . .' is not axiomatically a literary text and could only become one by responding satisfactorily to a 'literary' reading. This, I suggest, it could not do. Whether or not Orwell's 'A Hanging' is axiomatically a literary text is much more problematical and the answer probably depends upon the context in which it is read, and the expectations of the individual reader. It is not foregrounded as literature in any obvious way—indeed it could be said to disguise itself as nonliterature, to merge like a chameleon into the background of writing like 'Michael Lake Describes . . .', though there are certain significant absences in the text which perhaps operate as signs of literariness at an almost subliminal level, and covertly invite a 'literary' reading. That it responds satisfactorily to a literary reading there is no doubt, and I have tried to connect this with certain features of its internal structure. There is a lot more to be said about this text, and we shall return to it in due course. Meanwhile I wish to introduce another text into our discussion which will enable us to test Todorov's hypothesis that 'each type of discourse usually referred to as literary has nonliterary relatives which resemble it more than do other types of literary discourse'.

3   Oscar Wilde: 'The Ballad of Reading Gaol'

Oscar Wilde's poem has a good deal in common with the two prose texts discussed above in respect of subject matter and attitudes. Like them it is about the execution of a certain individual—in this case a trooper of the Royal Horse Guards convicted of murdering his wife or mistress and hanged at Reading Gaol, where Wilde himself was a prisoner at the time. The execution (which takes place at 8 a.m.) is the occasion of mounting horror and intolerable suspense, and there are many references to time:

> So we—the fool, the fraud, the knave—
>   That endless vigil kept,
> And through each brain on hands of pain
>   Another's terror crept.
>
> . . . .
>
> The moaning wind went wandering round
>   The weeping prison-wall
> Till like a wheel of turning steel
>   We felt the minutes crawl . . .
>
> . . . .
>
> We waited for the stroke of eight:
>   Each tongue was thick with thirst:
> For the stroke of eight is the stroke of Fate
>   That makes a man accursed.[1]

The attendant doctor has a watch

>   whose little ticks
> Are like horrible hammer-blows.

There is comment on the paradoxical solicitude of the condemned man's warders:

> Who watch him lest himself should rob
> The prison of its prey

and on the reading of the Burial Service over the living man.

Like 'A Hanging' and 'Michael Lake Describes . . .', 'The Ballad of Reading Gaol' is both didactic and confessional: it seeks to condemn the institution of capital punishment, in which the narrator has no active role, and at the same time confesses his sense of guilt and complicity in the act. Unlike 'Michael Lake Describes . . .', however, and in a much more obvious and unproblematical way than 'A Hanging', 'The Ballad of Reading Gaol' is literature, and would be unhesitatingly identified as such by any reader. It is axiomatically a literary text because there is nothing else for it to be. This is not simply because it is a ballad (the ballad form, though usually a sign of literature, may be applied to nonliterary purposes, e.g. advertising); and certainly not because it is obviously fictional, for it is dedicated to 'C.T.W. Sometime Trooper of the Royal Horse Guards obit. H.M. Prison, Reading, Berkshire, July 7, 1896' and it was public knowledge at the time of publication that Oscar Wilde had been a convicted prisoner in the same gaol. To that extent the poem is more 'historical' than 'A Hanging'. We should be on firmer ground in tracing the poem's literariness to the way it states propositions which do not require our intellectual assent to be effective, for instance:

> For he who sins a second time
> Wakes a dead soul to pain,
> And draws it from its spotted shroud
> And makes it bleed again,
> And makes it bleed great gouts of blood,
> And makes it bleed in vain!

There is indeed in 'The Ballad of Reading Gaol' a heavy loading of religious sentiment, an appeal to transcendental and specifically Christian values (entirely absent from the Orwell and Lake texts) which, though no doubt more immediately accessible and appealing to a Christian reader, are not dependent on the reader's prior belief in or conversion to Christianity for their effectiveness. The poem is, to use I. A. Richards's logico-positivist term, a tissue of 'pseudo-statements'. The sterile and sordid operation of human justice is contrasted with the mysterious mercy and transforming grace of God, and the redemption of the condemned man is affirmed by associating him closely with the passion of Christ: not only by explicit assertion—

> How else but through a broken heart
> May Lord Christ enter in?

—but through an elaborate pattern of symbolism and allusion. The ministry of the prison chaplain is called 'the kiss of Caiaphas'; the last night before the execution is a kind of Gethsemane for the condemned man and for those who watch with him in spirit. There are metaphoric allusions to the Passion like 'And bitter wine upon a sponge/Was the savour of Remorse'; references to cocks crowing, to 'bloody sweats', the 'wounds of Christ' and the Good Thief. The gallows, like the Cross in typological and devotional tradition, is compared to a tree—

> And, green or dry, a man must die
> Before it bears its fruit!

The warders 'strip' and 'mock' the prisoner's corpse. And so on.

Perhaps the most interesting motif is the play on the colour red, and its 'opposite' white.* Northrop Frye, in a brief, brilliant comment on *The Faerie Queen*, has drawn attention to the archetypal and specifically Christian symbolism of these colours:

> St George's emblem is a red cross on a white ground, which is the flag borne by Christ in traditional iconography when he returns in triumph from the prostrate dragon of hell. The red and white symbolize the two aspects of the risen body, flesh and blood, bread and wine, and in Spenser they have a historical connection with the union of red and white roses in the reigning head of the Church. The link between the sacramental and the sexual aspects of the red and white symbolism is indicated in alchemy, with which Spenser was clearly acquainted, in which a crucial phase of the production of the elixir of immortality is known as the union of the red king and the white queen.'[2]

Wilde draws on a surprising number of these associations and combines them skilfully with the given facts of the action he is dealing with—for instance the red uniform of the guardsman:

> He did not wear his scarlet coat,
>   For blood and wine are red,
> And blood and wine were on his hands
>   When they found him with the dead,
> The poor dead woman whom he loved,
>   And murdered in her bed.

Here, in the very first stanza, Wilde introduces one of the keynotes of his poem. Literally the stanza seems to say that the soldier did not wear his scarlet uniform in prison because it would have reminded him of the blood and wine that covered his hands when he committed murder. But this is a slightly fanciful speculation rather than a statement of fact

---

*Archetypally, the opposite of white is black; but red can be opposed to white or black. It has been argued that these are universally the three most common colour terms: i.e. languages with only two basic colour terms have words for black and white, and languages with only three basic colour terms have words for black, white and red. See B. Berlin and P. Kay, *Basic Colour Terms* (Berkeley, 1969); cited by John Lyons, 'Structuralism and Linguistics', *Structuralism: An Introduction* ed. David Robey (Oxford, 1973), p. 16.

(presumably he would not have been allowed to wear his dress uniform in prison anyway). The logical force of 'for' is by no means immediately apparent to the reader, whose attention is more likely to be engaged by the emotive reverberations of the phrase 'blood and wine', which the ballad form permits Wilde to use twice in successive lines. Though the blood and wine are literal facts of the case, the idea of sacramental transubstantiation of one into the other, of the Eucharistic wine into Christ's redemptive Blood, can scarcely be kept out of the reader's mind, and thus the idea of religious transcendence is immanent in the poem from the very beginning. Though there is no mention of whiteness in the stanza it is implicit in the reference to the man's hands and to the woman murdered in her bed (connotations of sheets, nightclothes, naked flesh, death pallor, etc.). Whiteness is *kept* implicit in this way because Wilde wants to use it explicitly later on as an image of grace, redemption, transcendence. For instance, after the fine stanzas describing the burial of the man in quick-lime ('He lies, with fetters on each foot/Wrapt in a sheet of flame') the poet asserts that no seed will be sown on the grave for three years.

> They think a murderer's heart would taint
> Each simple seed they sow.
> It is not true! God's kindly earth
> Is kindlier than men know.
> And the red rose would blow more red,
> The white rose whiter blow.
>
> Out of his mouth a red, red rose!
> Out of his heart a white!
> For who can say by what strange way,
> Christ brings His will to light. . . .

A few lines later, to recall the original symbolism of red = wine = blood, the rose is referred to as 'wine-red'. Towards the end of the poem we return to the image of its opening stanza:

> And with tears of blood he cleansed the hand
> The hand that held the steel:
> For only blood can wipe out blood,
> And only tears can heal:
> And the crimson stain that was of Cain
> Became Christ's snow-white seal.

One does not have to be a stylistician to see that in linguistic form 'A Hanging' is much more like 'Michael Lake Describes . . .' than either is like 'The Ballad of Reading Gaol'. The latter displays a degree of systematization quite absent from the other two texts. In the first place there is the regularity of rhythm and repetition of sounds in rhyme which usually distinguishes verse from prose. And there are other kinds of linguistic schematization which though not peculiar to verse are present here in greater density than one finds in prose: tropes and figures of repetition, equation, symmetry, analogy and contrast. Just looking again at the first stanza, we find repetition of the same sounds in the rhymes *red—dead—bed*, repetition of *blood and wine*, repetition of *dead*, application of two semantically contrasting verbs to the same noun (a kind of zeugma) in the '*woman* whom he *loved*,/And *murdered*', an explicit equation of blood and wine in respect of colour, and an implicit equation of them by allusion to the Eucharist, and an emphatic parallelism of syntactical structure, each line constituting a clause in subject-predicate order and each line being in effect an expansion or explanation of an item in the preceding line. Thus *red* in line 2 explains the significance of *scarlet* in line 1, *on his hands* in line 3 explains the significance of *blood and wine* in line 2, *dead* in line 4 explains *blood* in line 3, *woman* in line 5 explains *the dead* in line 4, and *murdered* in line 6 explains *dead woman* (though not *loved*) in line 5. In these respects, the first stanza (which is also the first sentence) of the poem is a microcosm or model for the whole poem, which is built up in much the same way: the stanzas/sentences (there is always one sentence per stanza) are linked formally by the repetition of verbal formulae and semantically by the expansion of or variation upon the same set of themes.

It would be much more difficult to offer an equivalent account of 'A Hanging' and 'Michael Lake Describes . . .' because there seems to be much less linguistic systematization to get hold of. Indeed one of the first things a critic would probably say about the language of these texts is that on the whole their authors have deliberately *avoided* the various rhetorical devices of which Wilde makes such abundant use, in order to achieve accuracy and authenticity (or the illusion of these qualities). The structure of the discourse, such a critic might suggest, is derived not from rhetoric, not, that is, from the possibilities of linguistic form (e.g. the ballad in Wilde's case) but from reality, the structure of events described. Orwell himself seems to have believed this was indeed how such writing got written:

> What is above all needed is to let the meaning choose the word, and not the other way about. In prose, the worst thing one can do with words is to surrender to them. When you think of a common object, you think wordlessly, and then, if you want to describe the thing you have been visualizing, you probably hunt about until you find the exact words that seem to fit it.[3]

Though revealing about Orwell's literary aims, this description of the compositional process is wholly unsatisfactory. It is based on the fallacy that we can think without using verbal concepts and it therefore ignores the creative function of language in making 'reality' humanly intelligible.

Hangings are highly formalized social rituals and therefore have a more definite structure than most events involving human interaction; and it is certainly the case that both Orwell and Lake have modelled their texts on this structure more closely than Wilde. We have already observed, for instance, that Orwell and Lake follow the chronological order of events, whereas Wilde shifts his narrative about in time a good deal, so that we experience the actual execution not once but many times in the course of the poem. 'A Hanging' and 'Michael Lake Describes . . .' are, however, in no sense totally objective or comprehensive accounts of the events they purport to describe, simply because no such account is possible. There is more order in these texts than in the events they describe because, unlike the events, they are wholly constituted of language, and language is more systematic than nonlanguage. Orwell and Lake have produced their texts by making some selection and organization of the theoretically inexhaustible 'facts' of the events they describe, and it should be possible to analyse how this is done in language more positively than by saying that they have avoided the obtrusive patterning of Wilde's poem. In short, what we need is a definition of the type of discourse to which these texts belong—but a definition that will enable us to explain why one is literature and the other is not. For while Todorov's hypothesis holds good in that 'A Hanging' resembles 'Michael Lake Describes . . .' much more closely than it resembles 'The Ballad of Reading Gaol', the kind of reading which establishes 'A Hanging' as literature, and which (I have suggested) 'Michael Lake Describes . . .' cannot sustain, is essentially the same kind of reading as that which the 'Ballad' naturally invites. A 'literary' reading of the Orwell and Wilde texts alike is essentially a process of identifying and interrelating recurrent features which are thematically significant, the difference being that whereas these features are foregrounded by Wilde's poetic language, they are much less visible in the language of Orwell's text, either because the foreground-background perspective is much shallower or because the thematic motifs are deliberately buried in the background. In this respect, 'A Hanging' is like much realistic fiction. But what is realism?

4   What is Realism?

'Realism' (or 'realistic') is as problematical a term as literature/literary, and for much the same reasons. It is used sometimes in a neutrally descriptive sense and sometimes as an evaluative term; the particular instances to which it is applied will vary from one period to another and from one person to another;[1] and it is not exclusively aesthetic in application. Quite apart from the technical meaning of realism in philosophy, there is an ordinary use of 'realism/realistic' to denote a recognition of facts, usually unwelcome facts, which, though sometimes applied to art, is by no means exclusive to it (e.g. 'The Government had made a realistic assessment of the country's economic situation'). This use of realism usually implies approval and its negative is the disapproving 'unrealistic'. The specifically aesthetic use of 'realism', however, which has the meaning, roughly, of 'truth to life/experience/observation in representation', may be used either evaluatively or descriptively, and has two corresponding negatives, unrealistic and nonrealistic. If we say that a certain text is 'unrealistic' we normally mean that it has tried to be realistic and failed, and if we say that a text is nonrealistic we usually mean that the writer has deliberately chosen to write in the mode of, say, fantasy rather than realism.* But there are many literary texts where the question of realism as an aesthetic category does not seem to arise at all: lyric poetry of a thematic kind, for instance, and even much narrative poetry. It wouldn't make much sense to ask whether 'The Ballad of Reading Gaol' was realistic or not. It has its realistic passages:

> We tore the tarry rope to shreds
>   With blunt and bleeding nails
> We rubbed the doors and scrubbed the floors
>   And cleaned the shining rails:
> And, rank by rank, we soaped the plank,
>   And clattered with the pails

and it has its nonrealistic passages—for example when the 'forms of Fear' and 'Shapes of Terror' are described as dancing and singing through the cells on the eve of the execution:

> With the pirouettes of marionettes,
>   They tripped on pointed tread:
> But with flutes of Fear they filled the ear,
>   As their grisly masque they led,
> And loud they sang, and long they sang,
>   For they sang to wake the dead.

Yet there is no aesthetic conflict between these two very different narrative passages, no problem about accommodating them within the same work, because the 'Ballad' does not demand the kind of assent in which such a conflict could arise. It does not ask (despite the obvious influence of *The Ancient Mariner*) for a willing suspension of our disbelief—the central subject is, after all, a matter of historical fact, and there is no difficulty about accepting it as such. But neither does

*An alternative term, coined by Borges, is 'irrealism'. See, for instance, Tom Samet, 'Contemporary Irrealism', *Novel*, IX (1975) pp. 66–73.

the 'Ballad' ask us to agree, 'Yes, this is how it must have been'—it does not confine itself to historical fact, or make all its details consistent with historical fact, or seek to recreate the experience of historical fact. If Wilde had wanted to do these things he would have written in prose, the natural medium of history. He is not concerned to reconstruct or explain a given event, but to apprehend the event through the attributes and associations which it generates, and for this purpose the highly systematic nature of the ballad form is appropriate.

When applied in the aesthetic sense to nonfictional texts, 'realism' is nearly always an evaluative term which assigns a 'literary' status to the text. To say that 'Michael Lake Describes . . .' is 'realistic' in a neutrally descriptive sense would be a kind of tautology. This kind of writing is either true—true in the sense that the facts given are verifiable—or it is not, in which case it is worthless: nonrealism is not an option for the journalist. Of course, this 'truth' is mainly a matter of conventional trust between reader and writer (or reader and newspaper) but such trust is in part dependent upon the character of the discourse. It is necessary that there should be an absence of logical contradiction because this would throw doubt on the veracity of the report; and some hostages to verifiability must be given in the form of dates, names, etc. Beyond this, we might praise a journalistic report for being 'vivid' or 'sensitive' or 'evocative' or 'revealing', and these would be essentially literary judgments since we are normally in no position to compare a journalistic report with the events it describes (though we can sometimes compare it with other reports) and it is precisely through such judgments that historical or journalistic reports are accorded the status of literature. 'Realistic' is another such word. Consider, for example, Leonard Schapiro's comment on Alexander Solzhenitsyn's *The Gulag Archipelago* (1974):

> The book is shattering in its realism. The horrors, the degradation, the sufferings are described with an actuality which makes one feel that one is oneself present at what is happening. The realism recalls Tolstoy more than any other writer . . .[2]

It is clear from the context, if not from the quotation itself, that this is a literary judgment. In his review Schapiro deals with *The Gulag Archipelago* first as political history, and then as 'a literary work of genius' and it is under the latter heading that he makes the remark about realism. *The Gulag Archipelago*, Schapiro is saying, is history, but it transcends the limitations of historical method by recreating experience in the manner of a novelist (Tolstoy). This does not apparently undermine its status as history (though some historians might think it did).

There is always a suggestion of imagination, of illusion, of the fictive, in the word 'realistic' used as a term of praise, as can be seen by the way Schapiro pays his tribute to the effect: Solzhenitsyn 'makes one feel one is actually present at what is happening'. The writer, by projecting himself into where he is not (and often into where he has never been, because Solzhenitsyn is writing largely about other people's experiences) transports the reader to where *he* is not. This is perhaps the fundamental appeal of all realistic art—and it depends of course on the consumer knowing where he *really* is: reading a book or looking at a picture or watching a film or play. Although in a simple sense realism is the art of creating an illusion of reality, one hundred per cent success in this enterprise equals failure. *Trompe l'oeil* art only becomes art at the moment we recognize how we have been deceived, and it is considered a low form of art precisely because we cannot simultaneously enjoy the illusion and the knowledge that it is an illusion.

For obvious reasons, a verbal text can never be mistaken for the reality it refers to, as an object of visual or plastic art may be mistaken. Writing cannot imitate reality directly (as a film, for instance, can); it can only imitate ways of thinking and speaking about reality, and other ways of writing about it. A working definition of realism in literature might be: *the representation of experience in a manner which approximates closely to descriptions of similar experience in nonliterary texts of the same culture.* Realistic fiction, being concerned with the action of individuals in time, approximates to history: 'history is a novel which happened; the novel is history as it might have happened' as the Goncourt brothers put it.[3] Thus the realistic novel, from its beginnings in the eighteenth century, modelled its language on historical writing of various kinds, formal and informal: biography, autobiography, travelogue, letters, diaries, journalism and historiography.

With respect to fictional texts, then, the term 'realistic' may be used in the neutral, descriptive sense to mean that the discourse is broadly consistent with historical fact as known and mediated by the contemporary historical consciousness. In this sense both Tolstoy and, say, Anthony Powell, are realistic novelists, whereas Lewis Carroll and Thomas Pynchon are not. This realism is a convention which makes possible in the novel the qualitative realism attributed by Schapiro to Solzhenitsyn and Tolstoy, the power of making events, whether invented or factually based, convincingly 'present' to the reader. Paradoxically, whereas realism in the neutral sense indicates a fictional text's approximation to history, realism in the qualitative sense may indicate a historical text's approximation to fiction.

I am conscious here of Hayden White's objection to using an oversimplified concept of history as a route to a definition of realism:

> In my view the whole discussion of the nature of 'realism' in literature flounders in the failure to assess critically what a genuinely 'historical' conception of reality consists of. The usual tactic is to set the 'historical' over against the 'mythical' as if the former were genuinely *empirical* and the latter

were nothing but *conceptual*, and then to locate the realm of the 'fictive' between the two poles. Literature is then viewed as being more or less *realistic*, depending upon the ratio of empirical to conceptual elements contained within it.[4]

I admit to employing this tactic, but I do not see that White offers, in the end, a better one at this level of generality. He does indeed show that 'different historians stress different aspects of the same historical field'[5] because of their different ideological, argumentative, narrative and rhetorical predispositions, and that it is possible to develop a typology of historiography as richly varied as any typology of narrative literature. Nevertheless he concedes that all the varieties of nineteenth-century historiography can be seen as shades within the spectrum of a general professional orthodoxy about the aims and limits of history-writing, an orthodoxy to which only the philosophers of history, Marx and Nietzsche, offered a truly radical challenge. According to this orthodoxy,

> a 'historical account' would be any account of the past in which the events that occupied the historical field were properly named, grouped into species and classes of a distinctively 'historical' sort, and further related by general conceptions of causation by which changes in their relationships could be accounted for.[6]

Such a concept of history will serve as a point of reference for measuring realism in fiction. The radical alternatives proposed by Marx and Nietzsche perhaps correspond, respectively, to the radically nonrealistic fictional modes of metafiction (which destroys illusion by exposing its own structural principles) and mythopoeia (which sacrifices illusion to imagination).

If we hesitate to apply the word 'realistic' to 'A Hanging' it is because the word implicitly raises questions about where the text stands in relation to history and to fiction which, as we have seen, the text seems designed to elude. 'A Hanging' certainly has the effect of making us feel 'one is present at what is happening'. But we cannot be certain whether Orwell is recreating someone else's experience, or creating a fictional experience, or reporting an experience of his own. It purports to be the last of these, and probably most people read it as such: but in that case it would be either redundant or inappropriate to describe it as 'realistic'. What would a truthful account of what the writer actually saw and felt be, but realistic in the neutral sense? And if we say it is realistic in the qualitative sense, doesn't that imply that he has created the *illusion* of his being present at the hanging? I think myself that 'A Hanging' is best classified as an early example of a kind of writing that has been called recently 'the non-fiction novel' or the New Journalism,[7] a kind of writing in which the techniques of realistic fiction, which evolved out of the application of historical narrative methods to fictitious events, are in turn applied to historical events.

This would explain why it so closely resembles realistic fiction in form without being comfortably classifiable as such. To continue the discussion we need a more orthodox example of realistic fiction.

5 Arnold Bennett: 'The Old Wives' Tale'

Pursuing our somewhat morbid theme, let us take as a classic instance of an execution described in a realistic novel, Chapter iii, Book III of Arnold Bennett's *The Old Wives' Tale* (1908), entitled 'An Ambition Satisfied'. This follows closely upon the elopement of Sophia, the more wilful and adventurous of the two sister-heroines, with Gerald Scales, a commercial traveller who has inherited a small fortune, and whose superficial sophistication has dazzled Sophia and blinded her to his essentially weak and coarse-grained character. Scales in fact intended to seduce Sophia and to take her to Paris as his mistress, but when Sophia, sensing danger, insists on being married before proceeding beyond London, Gerald capitulates. The couple spend their honeymoon in Paris and for a while all goes well: Gerald, who is familiar with the country and the language, enjoys showing the worldly, dazzling capital of Louis Napoleon to his innocent and provincial bride, buying her Parisian dresses and taking her to expensive restaurants patronized by the *demi-monde*. Sophia's disillusionment in her husband begins one night when he becomes involved in a drunken quarrel at the Restaurant Sylvain, causing her considerable embarrassment and anxiety (III, ii, 2). However, she rationalizes her criticisms of his conduct, and when the next day he announces his intention of satisfying 'a lifetime's ambition' by witnessing an execution, she agrees to accompany him and his friend Chirac.

> In five minutes it seemed to be the most natural and proper thing in the world that, on her honeymoon, she should be going with her husband to a particular town because a notorious murderer was about to be decapitated there in public. (III, iii, 1)[1].

The town is Auxerre and the condemned is a young man called Rivain, convicted of murdering his elderly mistress: the case had been eagerly discussed at the Restaurant Sylvain, where Gerald met Chirac.

For Sophia the experience is a deepening nightmare. At each stage of the journey she becomes more and more uncomfortably aware of the unpleasant emotion and excitement generated by the impending execution, and of the unsavoury character of those who are attracted by the spectacle. She is in fact being led unawares into a sadistic and sexual orgy. By a series of evasions and subterfuges, Gerald installs her not in the respectable hotel he had promised but in a seedy establishment overlooking the very square where the execution is to take place the next morning, paying for the dingy bedroom a grossly inflated price. (III, iii, 2) At supper that evening, Sophia is alarmed and repelled by the greedy, noisy and licentious behaviour of the company. 'All the faces, to the youngest, were brutalized, corrupt, and shameless.' (III, iii, 3) Gerald, eventually 'somewhat ashamed of having exposed his wife to the view of such an orgy', takes her to the bedroom and leaves her, explaining that he does not intend to go to bed. Sophia lies awake, depressed by the events of the day and disturbed by sounds reaching her from every part of the hotel, some of which are obviously sexual, though with sadistic connotations: 'long sighs suddenly stifled; mysterious groans as of torture, broken by a giggle ....' Suddenly she is startled by a noisy commotion in the square—the first signs of the crowd gathering to witness the execution. Against the promptings of her better self, she 'yielded to the fascination and went to the window'. It is dawn, and the windows of the other buildings around the square are already filled with spectators. 'On the red-tiled roofs, too, was a squatted population.' Down below the police are engaged in pushing back

> a packed, gesticulating, cursing crowd . . . as the spaces of the square were cleared they began to be dotted by privileged persons, journalists or law officers or their friends, who walked to and fro in conscious pride; among them Sophia descried Gerald and Chirac, strolling arm in arm and talking to two elaborately clad girls who were also arm in arm.
>
> Then she saw a red reflection coming from one of the side streets of which she had a vista.

This comes from a lantern on the wagon, drawn by a gaunt grey horse, that brings the components of the guillotine to the square. The crowd bursts into a ferocious chant as the 'red columns' of the guillotine are erected and its mechanism tested;

> *Le voila!*
> *Nicolas!*
> *Ah! Ah! Ah!*

('Nicolas' is evidently a familiar name for the guillotine deriving from its first victim, Nicolas Jacques Pelletier.) To Sophia's dismay the executioner's party retires to the hotel where she herself is situated, and occupies a room on the same floor. The excitement in the square increases.

> In a corner of the square she saw Gerald talking vivaciously alone with one of the two girls who had been together. She wondered vaguely how such a girl had been brought up, and what her parents thought—or knew! . . . Her eye caught the guillotine again, and was held by it. Guarded by gendarmes, that tall and simple object did most menacingly dominate the square with its crude red columns. Tools and a large open box lay on the ground beside it. (III, iii, 4)

She loses sight of Gerald and then, fearing that he might return to the room and find her at the window, she returns to bed, vowing that she will remain there until he comes back. She is awakened from a doze by

a tremendous shrieking, growling and yelling: a phenomenon of human bestiality that far surpassed Sophia's narrow experience. . . . 'I must stay where I am,' she murmured. And even while saying it she rose and went to the window again and peeped out. The torture involved was extreme, but she had not sufficient force within her to resist the fascination. She stared greedily into the bright square. The first thing she saw was Gerald coming out of a house opposite, followed after a few seconds by the girl with whom he had previously been talking. Gerald glanced hastily up at the facade of the hotel, and then approached as near as he could to the red columns . . . the racket beyond the square continued and even grew louder. But the couple of hundred persons within the cordons, and all the inhabitants of the windows, drunk and sober, gazed in a fixed and sinister enchantment at the region of the guillotine, as Sophia gazed. 'I cannot stand this!' she told herself in horror, but she could not move; she could not move even her eyes. . . . Then a gigantic passionate roar, the culmination of the mob's fierce savagery, crashed against the skies. The line of maddened horses swerved and reared, and seemed to fall on the furious multitude while the statue-like gendarmes rocked over them. It was a last effort to break the cordon and it failed.

From the little street at the rear of the guillotine appeared a priest, walking backwards and holding a crucifix high in his right hand, and behind him came the handsome hero, his body all crossed with cords, between two warders, who pressed against him and supported him on either side. He was certainly very young. He lifted his chin gallantly, but his face was incredibly white. Sophia discerned that the priest was trying to hide the sight of the guillotine from the prisoner with his body, just as in the story she had heard at dinner.

Except the voice of the priest, indistinctly rising and falling in the prayer for the dying, there was no sound in the square or its environs. The windows were now occupied by groups turned to stone with distended eyes fixed on the little procession. Sophia had a tightening of the throat, and the hand trembled by which she held the curtain. The central figure did not seem to her to be alive: but rather a doll, a marionette wound up to imitate the action of a tragedy. She saw the priest offer the crucifix to the mouth of the marionette, which with a clumsy unhuman shoving of its corded shoulders butted the thing away. And as the procession turned and stopped she could plainly see that the marionette's nape and shoulders were bare, his shirt having been slit. It was horrible. 'Why do I stay here?' she asked herself hysterically. But she did not stir. The victim had disappeared now in the midst of a group of men. Then she perceived him prone under the red column, between the grooves. The silence was now broken only by the tinkling of the horses' bits in the corners of the square. The line of gendarmes in front of the scaffold held their swords tightly and looked over their noses, ignoring the privileged groups that peered almost between their shoulders.

And Sophia waited, horror-struck. She saw nothing but the gleaming triangle of metal that was suspended high above the prone, attendant victim. She felt like a lost soul, torn too soon from shelter, and exposed for ever to the worst hazards of destiny. Why was she in this strange, incomprehensible town, foreign and inimical to her, watching with agonized glance this cruel, obscene spectacle? Her sensibilities were all a bleeding mass of wounds. Why? Only yesterday, and she had been an innocent, timid creature in Bursley, in Axe, a foolish creature who deemed the concealment of letters a supreme excitement. Either that day or this day was not real. Why was she imprisoned alone in that odious, indescribably odious hotel, with no one to soothe and comfort her, and carry her away?

The distant bell boomed once. Then a monosyllabic voice sounded sharp, low; she recognized the voice of the executioner, whose name she had heard but could not remember. There was a clicking noise. . . .

She shrank down to the floor in terror and loathing, and hid her face and shuddered. Shriek after shriek, from various windows, rang on her ears in a fusillade; and then the mad yell of the penned crowd, which, like herself, had not seen but had heard, extinguished all other noise. Justice was done. The great ambition of Gerald's life was at last satisfied. (III, iii, 4)

It might be felt that in the last paragraph but two in this extract, the one beginning 'And Sophia waited . . .', Bennett has to some extent spoiled his effect by spelling out explicitly and somewhat clumsily what has already been adequately implied. Certainly, any sensitive reader will have apprehended, either analytically or intuitively, that the execution at Auxerre is experienced by Sophia as a violation, both literal and symbolic, of her selfhood, and is therefore an 'objective correlative' for her disillusionment in Gerald as lover and husband. In its way the episode fills up a conspicuously vacant space in the narrative—the absence of any description of Sophia's initiation into sex. In the Restaurant Sylvain, Sophia's face is described as 'so candid, so charmingly conscious of its own pure beauty and of the fact that she was no longer a virgin, but the equal in knowledge of any woman alive'. But the context, contrasting Sophia's 'baby's bonnet' and 'huge bow of ribbon' with the 'violently red lips, powdered cheeks, cold, hard eyes, self-possessed arrogant faces, and insolent bosoms' of the Parisiennes (III, ii, 2) makes it clear that Sophia's 'knowledge' is of a very superficial or self-deceiving kind. Real knowledge comes later, at Auxerre. Or, to put it another way, the execution brings to a crisis Sophia's suppressed suspicions about her husband's weakness of character simultaneously with her suppressed feelings of having been sexually outraged by him. Of course it is not only Sophia who is suppressing these feelings but also Bennett. But it is obvious that if Bennett, in the manner of a present-day novelist, had described the sexual side of the honeymoon in detail, it would have been as trauma for Sophia: everything we are told about her and Scales compels this deduction. The reticence of Edwardian taste, or Bennett's own reticence, led him to transfer this trauma to the execution (though without leaving the bedroom). Possibly this was to the book's advantage.

The expedition to Auxerre is steeped in a thickening atmosphere of sexual licence and degradation from its genesis in the Restaurant Sylvain to its climax in the square, where Gerald is flagrantly unfaithful to his new bride under her very eyes (whether or not Sophia realizes, or allows herself to realize, the full implications of Gerald's emergence from the house opposite with the girl he has picked up in the square is not entirely clear—she reflects later on his 'fatuous vigil of unguessed licence' (III, iii, 5)—but she certainly feels betrayed). It is because she is herself emotionally alienated to an agonizing degree that Sophia is unable to achieve any sympathetic imaginative connection with the prisoner Rivain. Unlike the narrator of 'A Hanging', she is not struck by the poignant contrast between her own freedom and the prisoner's fate. On the contrary, she sees him as 'a doll, a marionette wound up to imitate the action of a tragedy' because she feels herself to be equally deprived of free will, unable (as that antepenultimate paragraph makes clear) to account for her own actions and her own situation. But this does not lead to anything like the penitent and therefore spiritually liberating identification with the condemned man claimed by the narrator of 'The Ballad of Reading Gaol':

> But there were those amongst us all
> Who walked with downcast head,
> And knew that, had each got his due,
> They should have died instead . . .

Interestingly, the colour red, which we traced in its various mutations through 'The Ballad of Reading Gaol' is also a recurrent motif in the Bennett text, though to very different effect. The references to the red rooftiles, the red lantern and the four references to the red columns of the guillotine have already been quoted. One might add that the furnishings of Sophia's hotel bedroom are 'crimson'. Although these references are entirely literal they acquire considerable connotative force, but it is semantically quite remote from Wilde's poem and more deeply buried. Clearly Bennett's 'red' has nothing to do with the redeeming blood of Christ any more than Rivain's 'incredibly white face' has anything to do with the 'white seal' of Christ. There is no possibility of transcendence in Bennett's materialist vision, either for Sophia or for Rivain—who butts the offered crucifix away with his head. Transcendence is hardly present even in a negative or demonic form: though the crowd's roar is 'devilish' we cannot say with much conviction that the red in this scene is the glow of hellfire.

Red is the colour of passion, of sexual love, of sexual sin (the courtesan in the Restaurant Sylvain wears a vermilion cloak in case there should be any doubt that she is a scarlet woman), the colour of blood (which is shed at deflowerings as well as beheadings) and of the erect male sexual organ. We need look no further to explain why Sophia's gaze keeps returning with horrified fascination to the 'red columns' of the guillotine which 'had risen upright from the ground' (as though by their own volition) and beside which she observes 'a large open box'—presumably a receptacle for the head, but also a classic female symbol in Freudian dream analysis. At the climax it is surely not only Rivain's head, but Sophia's maidenhead, and by extension her inviolate self, that lies 'prone under the red column' (*column* now significantly changed from the plural to the singular) 'between the grooves' (the analogy with female genitalia is striking) awaiting the brutal and irreversible stroke. Which she does not in fact see, does not need to see, before she 'shrank down to the floor in terror and loathing, and hid her face, and shuddered'. If there are any doubts about the validity of this reading they should be dispelled when we turn to the next section of the same chapter, where Gerald returns in a state of shock from the execution, and the contempt of Sophia, now beginning to rally, is expressed with veiled allusion to detumescence: 'Not long since he had been *proudly conversing* with impudent women. Now in *swift collapse*, he was as *flaccid* as a sick hound and as disgusting as an aged drunkard' (III, iii, 5, my italics; perhaps it is worth pointing out that 'proud' can mean swollen by sensual excitement and 'conversation' can refer to sexual intimacy).

The search for meaning, the process of interpretation, has taken us along the same path as before: identifying and relating recurrent items of the discourse. It has also led us, apparently, away from our ostensible topic, realism. Phallic guillotines are not the kind of thing we expect to find in realistic fiction, surely? But if there is any truth in the Freudian account of the mind, there is of course no reason why such things should not appear in the literary rendering of 'reality'. The point is simply that in realism we have to look very hard for them, we have to go down very deep to find them, because 'in reality' they are hidden, latent, suppressed. Sophia is not *conscious* of the full significance the 'red columns' have for her, and perhaps Bennett himself is not. Realism is a mode of writing derived from consciousness rather than the unconscious, the daylight rather than the nighttime world, the ego rather than the id: that is why it is such an excellent mode for *depicting* repression.

But in describing *The Old Wives' Tale* as a realistic novel we should be thinking in the first place of the justice it does to the individual experience of a common phenomenal world. In the chapter just reviewed we should be responding to the vivid evocation of the atmosphere in Auxerre on the eve of the execution, the graphic description of the events in the square, and the convincing portrayal of how a young, innocent, provincial English bride reacts to these things—always assuming we considered that Bennett had succeeded in doing what he was trying to do. 'Yes, that's what it would have been like—yes, that's how she would have behaved', is on one important level the kind of response Bennett is seeking to elicit from the reader. As Henry James put it, in discussing this novel:

the canvas is covered, ever so closely and vividly covered, by the exhibition of innumerable small facts and aspects, at which we assist with the most comfortable sense of their substantial truth. The sisters, and more particularly the less adventurous [Constance] are at home in their author's mind, they sit and move at their ease in the square chamber of his attention, to a degree beyond which the production of that ideal harmony between creature and creator could scarcely go, and all by an act of demonstration so familiar and so quiet that the truth and poetry, to use Goethe's distinction, melt utterly together and we see no difference between the subject of the show and the showman's feeling, let alone the showman's manner about it.[2]

In his preface to the novel Bennett makes an observation on the effect of authenticity in the Auxerre episode which bears interestingly on some of the questions raised in our enquiry:

It has been asserted that unless I had actually been present at a public execution, I could not have written the chapter in which Sophia was present at the Auxerre solemnity. I have not been present at a public execution, as the whole of my information about public executions was derived from a series of articles on them which I read in the Paris *Matin*. Mr Frank Harris, discussing my book in *Vanity Fair*, said it was clear I had not seen an execution (or words to that effect), and he proceeded to give his own description of an execution. It was a brief but terribly convincing bit of writing, quite characteristic and quite worthy of the author of *Montes the Matador* and of a man who has been almost everywhere and seen almost everything. I comprehended how far short I had fallen of the truth! I wrote to Mr Frank Harris, regretting that his description had not been printed before I wrote mine, as I should assuredly have utilized it, and, of course, I admitted that I had never witnessed an execution. He simply replied: 'Neither have I.' This detail is worth preserving, for it is a reproof to that large body of readers, who, when a novelist has really carried conviction to them, assert off hand: 'O, that must be autobiography!'

In this last remark we encounter a recognition of the realist's paradoxical situation: that one hundred per cent success in creating an illusion of reality is a kind of failure, in that it denies him a recognition of his artistry. But there is in fact some confusion of categories here. No one could suppose that the Auxerre chapter as presented was 'autobiographical' in the sense that 'A Hanging' might reasonably be supposed to be autobiographical, because this would imply that Bennett was a woman. For the chapter is not really about the execution of Rivain but about Sophia's experience of it, an experience which partly overlaps with the common experience of all those present (the guillotine was red, the gendarmes struggled to control the crowd, the crowd roared the chant about Nicholas, etc.) but is largely peculiar to Sophia, determined by her personality, her physical angle of vision and her emotional situation. In this latter aspect of the experience— what is peculiar to Sophia—we can discriminate between the conscious (e.g. her observation of Gerald's movements) and the unconscious (e.g. the sexual significance of the guillotine) but it is clear that they are connected. Even if Bennett had been present at a guillotining, then, he couldn't possibly have experienced it in the same way as Sophia; whereas it is easy to suppose that if Orwell had been present at a hanging he would have reacted much as the narrator of 'A Hanging'. If Bennett's rendering of Sophia's experience of the event 'carries conviction', therefore, it must be an imaginative achievement on his part. Only the 'public' part of the chapter could possibly be autobiographical—i.e., remembered rather than researched or invented. But there is no way in which a novelist like Bennett can reveal which of these methods he has used at a particular point, no way in which he can indicate the seams joining together recalled, researched and imagined material, without violating the conventions of his mode and destroying his 'realism'.

In the scene that immediately follows the execution, however, Bennett finds a way of drawing attention to the fictiveness of his narrative without violating the illusion of historical veracity he has created. Gerald is brought back to the bedroom by Chirac in a state of shock: 'his curiosity had proved itself stronger than his stomach'. The arrival of the landlady to collect the price of the room, even more inflated than Gerald had admitted, completes Sophia's disillusionment. Surveying Gerald's ignoble, prostrate and dormant figure, she reflects:

> Such was her brilliant and godlike husband, the man who had given her the right to call herself a married woman! He was a fool. With all her ignorance of the world she could see that nobody but an arrant imbecile could have brought her to her present pass.

Sophia's rage gives her the strength to act independently. From this moment begins her recovery from her disastrous elopement with Gerald (a heroic recovery, but also a tragic one, based on the acquisition of money and the denial of eros). She takes from Gerald's coat an envelope containing £200 in English banknotes and sews them into the lining of her skirt, reasoning that he will assume he has lost them.

> With precautions against noise, she tore the envelope and the letter and papers into small pieces, and then looked about for a place to hide them. A cupboard suggested itself. She got on a chair, and pushed the fragments out of sight on the topmost shelf, *where they may well be to this day*. (III, iii, 5, my italics)

What is the force of that last phrase? It seems to claim a kind of verifiability for the narrative which would be appropriate to 'Michael Lake Describes . . .' but which is quite inapplicable to a novel. Of course it is not a serious claim. Only a very naive and muddleheaded reader would have set off to Auxerre in 1908 with any hopes of finding fragments of Gerald's letter and envelope in a hotel room there. The novelist has deliberately overreached himself in his realistic enterprise. By the excessiveness of his claim that Sophia and Gerald belong to real history he reminds us that they belong to fiction. He thus makes explicit what is, according to Roland Barthes, always implicit in the realistic novel: 'giving to the imaginary the formal guarantee of the real, but while preserving in the sign the ambiguity of a double object, at once believable and false.'³ This is very different from the mode of *non*-realism, which we may briefly illustrate with the 'Orgasm Death Gimmick' section of William Burroughs's *The Naked Lunch* (1959).

6   William Burroughs: 'The Naked Lunch'

Burroughs is obviously alluding to this scene* when he says in the Introduction to *The Naked Lunch*:

> Certain passages in the book that have been called pornographic were written as a tract against Capital Punishment in the manner of Jonathan Swift's *Modest Proposal*. These sections are intended to reveal capital punishment as the obscene, barbaric and disgusting anachronism that it is.¹

I have expressed elsewhere some scepticism about this defence:

> It may be that the disgust Mr Burroughs feels for capital punishment has been transferred to the antics of his sexual perverts, but the reverse process which should occur for the reader is by no means to be relied upon. The power of Swift's piece inheres very largely in the tone of calm reasonableness with which the proposal is put forward, so that we feel obliged to supply the emotion which is missing. In *The Naked Lunch*, instead of this subtly controlled irony we have a kinetic narrative style which suspends rather than activates the reader's moral sense, and incites him to an imaginative collaboration in the orgy.²

Although I stand by this comment in general, I am not sure that the final point is entirely fair, and I would certainly acknowledge that Burroughs's writing here is not pornographic. Pornography I define as a type of discourse designed to be used as a substitute for or stimulus to erotic pleasure. (Needless to say, much discourse not so designed can be used for the same purpose.) Like other types of nonliterary discourse (advertising, polemic etc.) pornography can become literary if it responds successfully to a literary reading. What usually prevents it from doing so is that it is *un*realistic rather than nonrealistic: it pretends to a realism it cannot sustain. In its world men are improbably potent, women improbably voluptuous, perfect orgasms are achieved with improbable frequency and sexual encounters are always structured in an order of progressively mounting excitement, novelty and ecstasy. All this bears little resemblance to actual sexual

*See Appendix C.

experience, yet for pornography to be effective in its special function, the fantasy has to be sufficiently realistic for the reader to enter into it imaginatively. This no doubt explains why so many pornographic works from *Fanny Hill* onwards are cast in the form of confession or autobiography, the simplest and most obvious way of giving fiction an appearance of authenticity. If pornographic fiction does not invariably try to be realistic this is because some sexual deviations are inherently fantastic; or, more often, because the use of exotic or fantastic settings legitimizes the pornographic content for the consumer, and perhaps for the guardians of public morality, by providing an alternative, though spurious, focus of attention and by reducing the erotic charge of the action through distancing. The more permissive the moral climate, however, the more realistic pornography tends to be. The soft-core pornography published in contemporary girlie magazines of the *Penthouse* variety, for instance, shows a steady tendency towards pseudo-documentary: stories are illustrated by photographs rather than drawings or paintings, and much space is devoted to letters from readers recounting their sexual experiences, which, whether they come from *bona fide* readers or are in fact written by the magazine's staff, are in most cases fairly obviously erotic fantasies with a 'realistic' dressing. The realistic dressing does not merely contribute to pornography a general air of probability—it also constitutes the only element of variety in the genre, which is otherwise necessarily repetitive, condemned to rehearse again and again the same basic rhythm of excitement and release, the same limited repertoire of physical actions and reactions. This restriction, it should be observed, derives not merely from the sexual possibilities of the human body (e.g. its number of orifices) but also from the tastes of the pornographer's readers, who will usually accept only one particular type of sexual activity—heterosexual *or* homosexual *or* sado-masochistic *or* rubber fetichistic, etc. Only by varying the context of these actions through realistic specificity can the pornographer to some extent disguise their stereotyped character and introduce an element of unpredictability and spontaneity into his narrative, without which the reader could hardly get any satisfaction from it.*

By these criteria, *The Naked Lunch* is not pornographic. Though

---

*In this respect he is not, from a structuralist point of view, very differently situated from any other writer: 'the affectivity which is at the heart of all literature includes only an absurdly restricted number of functions; I desire, I suffer, I am angry, I contest, I love, I want to be loved, I am afraid to die—out of which we must make an infinite literature. Affectivity is banal, or, if you prefer, typical, and this circumstance governs the whole Being of literature; for if the desire to write is merely the constellation of several persistent figures, what is left to the writer is no more than an activity of variation and combination . . .' (Roland Barthes, *Critical Essays*, translated by Richard Howard (Evanston, 1972) pp. xvi–xvii). Arguably, however, pornography does not have the authentic (if banal) affectivity of literature: the pornographer says not, *I* lust, but *you shall* lust.

parts of the passage quoted in the Appendix do, I think, 'incite the reader to an imaginative participation in the orgy' the context is never stable enough for long enough to allow a steady build-up of erotic excitement. The sequence of actions becomes impossible to accept on any kind of 'realistic' level at three points in particular: when Mary eats the corpse of Johnny, when Mark 'turn[s] into Johnny' and when Mark/Johnny leaps out of the room into space. We note, too, that all kinds of sexual behaviour and perversion are mixed up together in this sequence, in defiance of the strict decorum of pornography, just as literary decorum is breached in the mixture of horrific and comic motifs.

The passage in question comes from a chapter entitled *a.j.'s annual party*, and is supposed to be part of a blue movie shown on this occasion. This in a sense 'explains' the non-realistic element in the narrative, since effects and sequences (like the transformation of Mark into Johnny, or the dive through the window into space) that are impossible in actuality can readily be contrived in film.* But such techniques are not generically characteristic of pornographic films, which are as wedded to a surface realism of treatment as pornographic literature, and for the same reasons. The movie in *The Naked Lunch* would be more appropriately described as 'surrealistic'—as is the whole novel. And perhaps here we find the reason why this passage, though not strictly pornographic, is difficult to defend on the grounds advanced by Burroughs himself.

It would seem to be a general rule that where one kind of aesthetic presentation is embedded in another, the 'reality' of the embedded form is weaker than that of the framing form. For instance the presentation of stage action in a film always seems (and is meant to seem) more artificial than the same action would seem as experienced in the theatre, and the same principle applies in reverse to the case of film projection used in a play, even when the film is documentary. The same rule applies when one kind of *writing* is embedded in another, and novelists have exploited this fact from the time of Cervantes. In *Don Quixote* the absurdity of the medieval romances which the hero reads guarantees the reality of the experience that consistently falsifies them, and Gothic romance serves much the same function in Jane Austen's *Northanger Abbey*. But the effect is not inevitably parodic. In *Ulysses*, for example, the surrealistic and dramatic 'Circe' episode is clearly not introduced to guarantee the reality of the framing narrative, but to add another dimension to that reality.

The system of conventions and contrasts between different conventions is much more confused in *The Naked Lunch*. The context in which the passage under discussion is embedded (both the local

---

*Cf. the hospital sequence in Lindsay Anderson's *O Lucky Man*, where the hero discovers another patient who has been surgically transformed into a sheep, and in nausea and horror hurls himself through a high plateglass window—and survives.

context and the whole book) is no more 'realistic' than the passage itself; indeed *it is in many ways less so.* That is to say, although the events reported in this passage are 'impossible', the style in which they are reported is clear, lucid and for the most part of the kind appropriate to descriptions of actuality. Most of *The Naked Lunch*, in contrast, is written in a fluid, fragmentary style of verbal montage, the reader never being quite sure what is happening, or where or when, or why. The justification for this surrealistic method is that the book expresses the consciousness of a drug addict, perhaps one undergoing the agonies of withdrawal; but it means that when we come to the Orgasm Death Gimmick, no norms have been established by which its nauseating grotesquerie can be measured and interpreted in the way intended by Burroughs. Deprived of our bearings in empirical reality, plunged into the ethically uncontrolled world of hallucination and dream, we are in no position to apply the episode (as we apply Swift's Modest Proposal) to the real world and draw an instructive moral.

7   The Realistic Tradition

In *The Old Wives' Tale* the imaginary and the historical, the public and the private, are blended together in a very stable mixture. This rendering of an individual's experience of a common phenomenal world, whereby we share the intimate thoughts of a single character while at the same time being aware of a reality, a history, that is larger and more complex than the individual in the midst of it can comprehend—this is the characteristic achievement of the nineteenth-century realistic novel—the novel of Scott, Jane Austen, Stendhal and Flaubert, to name but four of the novelists whose contribution to the tradition can be clearly discerned in Bennett's novel. From Scott derives the bold, confident handling of the crowd scenes in III, iii (one thinks especially of *The Heart of Midlothian*), the vividly evoked excitement and terror of being caught up in some great and violent public event. The difference between Scott and Bennett is of course that in the former the characters really *are* caught up in history—they are involved in it, made to choose and act in it—they are not (except for the minor characters) mere spectators of it. In the subsequent development of the nineteenth-century realistic novel the main characters are more alienated, their efforts to participate in history are mocked and frustrated (as in Stendhal) or else they are frankly helpless and terrified before it, as Sophia is before the execution of Rivain (she is incapable of mentally integrating her accustomed life in Bursley with her presence at the guillotining: 'either that day or this day was not real') or they are completely indifferent to it, as Sophia is later to the Seige of Paris ('Her ignorance of the military and political situation was complete; the situation did not interest her. What interested her was that she had three men to feed wholly or partially, and that the price of vegetables was rising.')*

The confrontation of private and public experience on the grand scale was beyond Jane Austen's reach and ambition, but she did treat with unsurpassed subtlety the disparities between the inner and the outer life, and the peculiar difficulties of moral judgment in an era of 'secularized spirituality',[1] when manners—the code of external behaviour—constitute a language that simultaneously discloses and disguises the 'reality' within. All the elaborate notation of dress and speech and personal conduct in Bennett's narrative—the *louche* elegance of the Restaurant Sylvain, the hectic, disorganized departure for Auxerre, the increasingly uncomfortable journey, Gerald's incompetent and dishonest management of the matter of hotels, the manners of the other diners at supper, the dress and deportment of the girls in the square—the whole accumulation of clues which gradually inform Sophia that she has been morally and socially compromised and sexually betrayed by her husband—all this is very reminiscent of Jane Austen. She was also perhaps the first novelist to master that judicious blend of authorial omniscience and limited view-point, sliding subtly between direct narrative and free indirect speech, that permits the novelist to command the simultaneous double perspective of public and private experience. It is of course a technique made for irony, for the destruction of illusions, and it is no coincidence that the climaxes of so many realistic novels are ironic discoveries, passages from innocence to experience, the abandonment of convenient fictions and the acknowledgement of harsh reality. This happens to Emma Woodhouse and several other heroines of Jane Austen. But the quality of Sophia's disillusionment, the collapse of all her romantic dreams, the grim irony of her elopement terminating in a sordid hotel room overlooking a public beheading, from which she, who was 'carried away' by Gerald Scales from her safe but dull provincial nest, now longs only to be carried away once more by some other, unspecified, impossible protector—this, and the cool, detached, almost pitiless stance of the implied narrator, remind one strongly of Stendhal and

---

*III, vi, 2. In the Preface, Bennett recalls asking his servant for information relevant to this part of his story. 'I said to the old man, "By the way, you went through the Siege of Paris, didn't you?" He turned to his old wife and said, uncertainly, "The Siege of Paris? Yes, we did, didn't we?" The Siege of Paris had been only one incident among many in their lives. Of course they remembered it well, though not vividly, and I gained much information from them. But the most useful thing which I gained from them was the perception, startling at first, that ordinary people went on living very ordinary lives in Paris during the siege, and that to the vast mass of the population the siege was not the dramatic, spectacular, thrilling, ecstatic affair that is described in history.'

above all Flaubert. The appropriate defence of the somewhat overblown rhetoric of the antepenultimate paragraph of this passage is, therefore, that it is *intended* to jar, to distance the reader, affectively, from Sophia at the very point when the writing, by modulating into free indirect speech ('Why was she in this strange, incomprehensible town . . . ?') penetrates most deeply into her consciousness. Compare *Madame Bovary*:

> What caused this inadequacy in her life? Why did everything she leaned on simultaneously decay? . . . Oh, if somewhere there were a being strong and handsome, a valiant heart, passionate and sensitive at once, a poet's spirit in an angel's form, a lyre with strings of steel, sounding sweet-sad epithalamiums to the heavens, then why should she not find that being?[2]

I am not suggesting that Bennett combined all the virtues of these great novelists—on the contrary, I think he is equal to none of them—but he is clearly writing at the end of a tradition of novel-writing to which they (and of course many others) contributed. It is a tradition which depends upon certain assumptions, especially the assumption that there is a common phenomenal world that may be reliably described by the methods of empirical history, located where the private worlds that each individual creates and inhabits partially overlap. Hence the typical narrative method for this kind of novel is the third-person, past-tense narrative in which, whether the narrator chooses to intervene rhetorically or not, the grammar is a constant sign of his presence, and hence of some context, some reality larger than that defined by the limits of any character's consciousness. As Barthes puts it: 'the discourse of the traditional novel . . . alternates the personal and the impersonal very rapidly, often even in the same sentence, so as to produce, if we can speak thus, a proprietary consciousness which retains the mastery of what it states without participating in it.'[3]

A similar effect can be obtained in first-person narration by opening up and making explicit the distance between the 'I' who narrates and the 'I' who is narrated, making the former supply all the contextual information of which the latter was ignorant or unheeding: but this has the disadvantage of dissipating the immediacy of the narrative preterite, the curious convention by which we experience the story not as a past, but as a continuous present, moving from one unpredictable moment to another into an open-ended future. To the extent that the novelist exploits the superior knowledge of the narrating 'I' over the narrated 'I', he will (as Tristram Shandy discovered) tend to make narration itself the real subject matter of his novel. In most first-person novels the problematical relationship between the two 'I's tends to be suppressed for precisely this reason, though it is apt to become abruptly and awkwardly visible at the very end of the narrative—for example at the end of *Huckleberry Finn*. Yet the first-person method continues to be favoured by realistic novelists throughout the twentieth century. This might be explained by reference to the collapse of confidence in history in our time—confidence in the onward march of progress, in the possibility of reconciling individual and collective aims, in the responsiveness of public events to private actions: a confidence which made possible the ambitious scope and panoramic method of the classic nineteenth-century novel. Total alienation from history leads to solipsism and, in literary terms, the abandonment of realism. 'History,' said Stephen Daedalus, 'is a nightmare from which I am trying to awake', and his creator woke eventually into the mythic dream-world of *Finnegans Wake*. But a less extreme alienation from history leads to the belief that in an absurd or threatening world what the individual sees and feels is real, is alone real: 'I was there.' A good deal of modern realistic fiction is founded on that postulate, on that model—imitating not so much historiography as the documentary sources of historiography: the confession, the traveller's log, the deposition, the case history. Immediately that is said, however, one sees the need to distinguish between writers who use the 'I' as an unqualified sign of authenticity, and those who (like James in 'The Turn of the Screw', Conrad in *Lord Jim*) bracket it within another 'I', and thus draw attention to the inherent ambiguity of all human report, and by inference, to the ultimate impossibility of 'realism'.

8   Two Kinds of Modern Fiction

The Old Wives' Tale was published in 1908. By that time Henry James had published (among other things) *The Ambassadors* (1903) and *The Golden Bowl* (1904), and Conrad *Heart of Darkness* (1902) and *Nostromo* (1904): works beside which, from our present literary vantage-point, Bennett's novel seems technically extraordinarily old-fashioned, so that it is difficult for us to understand James's deference to him in that article, 'The New Novel', from which I have already quoted. Of course, when that article is read in its entirety (it ends with a handsome tribute to Conrad) and read with the care appropriate to James's late style, it is clear that his reservations about Bennett (and Wells) were serious and damaging. Behind the polite compliments, swathed in the veils of James's allusive diction and intricate syntax, there is discernible a fundamental contempt for the way Bennett and Wells practiced the art of the novel. For several decades James had been preaching and striving to put into practice the ideal of organic form in prose fiction—the exquisite adjustment of means to end, without waste, without irrelevance, but with infinite sublety of nuance. Bennett and Wells fell far short of his exacting standards. Of *Clayhanger*, for instance, James says:

> This most monumental of Mr Arnold Bennett's recitals, taking it with its supplement *Hilda Lessways* ... is so describable through its being a monument exactly not to an idea, a pursued and captured meaning, or in short *to* anything whatever, but just simply *of* the quarried and gathered material it happens to contain, the stones and bricks and rubble and cement and promiscuous constituents of every sort that have been heaped in it and thanks to which it quite massively piles itself up. . . . A huge and in its way a varied aggregation, without traceable lines, divinable direction, effect of composition. . . .[1]

Essentially the same ironic judgment is passed on H. G. Wells:

> The more this author learns and learns, or at any rate knows and knows, however, the greater is this impression of his holding it good enough for us, such as we are, that he shall but turn out his mind and its contents upon us by any free familiar gesture and as from a high window forever open—an entertainment as copious surely as any occasion should demand, at least till we have more intelligibly expressed our title to a better.[2]

Why was James's attack so oblique and tentative? Partly, of course, because obliquity and tentativeness were in his nature. Partly because he was genuinely impressed by the extension of subject matter Bennett and Wells had achieved in their novels, and by their comparative freedom from the evasions of Victorian prudery and sentimentality.[3] But the most likely reason for his devious strategy in this essay is that at the time, early in 1914,[4] a direct attack by James on Bennett and Wells would have looked like an instance of sour grapes. James's own literary career was almost over, and it had brought him neither fame nor fortune on any really significant scale. Bennett and Wells were popular, successful and at the same time enjoyed the reputation of being serious artists, advanced thinkers. They were indeed, in James's sardonic but perceptibly envious phrase, 'chin-deep in trophies'.[5] This literary situation had been brought about by the suppression or retardation of the modern movement in England in the first decade of the century. Bennett was a self-conscious disciple of the French realists and naturalists like Zola, the Goncourts and De Maupassant, but he stopped well short of the point at which realism began to turn into symbolism (as it does in, say, *Heart of Darkness*, *The Golden Bowl* and *Dubliners*). The introduction of innovatory ideas from the Continent of Europe initiated by the English Decadents fizzled out in the Edwardian era—it has been suggested, indeed, that the trial of Oscar Wilde provoked a kind of philistine backlash in England against any kind of artistic avant-gardism.[6] Certainly the promise of an English development of *Symbolisme* in poetry was stifled by the supremacy of Kipling, Newbolt and Bridges. Even Yeats seemed discouraged and comparatively unproductive in this first decade of the century. In fiction, James and Conrad were persistently misunderstood, unappreciated and neglected, and Joyce couldn't find a publisher for his work.

When James wrote his article on 'The New Novel' in the *Times Literary Supplement*, this literary situation was about to change for two reasons. The first was Ezra Pound, whose personal mission to make London the centre of a new avant-garde was approaching fruition. It was in 1914 that he made contact with Joyce and met T. S. Eliot, and busied himself promoting their work. Eliot, he observed with awe, had 'modernized himself on his own'. Joyce's prose, he asserted, on the evidence of the first part of *A Portrait of the Artist as a Young Man*, was 'fine stuff, readable as no other recent English prose but James's, Hudson's* and some of Conrad's was readable'.[7] Pound's choice of paragons is interesting, as is his word of commendation: 'readable' was, to most people at the time, precisely what James and Conrad were not. The second reason was the Great War, which at first seemed likely to frustrate Pound's plans—distracting public attention from matters artistic, breaking up the coteries, dispersing the artists and poets, sending many to their deaths on the battlefield—but which eventually ensured the triumph of the modern movement by creating a climate of opinion receptive to artistic revolution. After the convulsion of the Great War the Edwardian certainties and complacencies were unable to reassert themselves, and the stage was set for that astonishing burgeoning of modernism in English literature which saw the appearance, within a few years of each other, of such masterpieces as *Hugh Selwyn Moberly* (1920), *Women in Love* (1920), *The Waste Land* (1922), *Ulysses* (1922), *A Passage to India* (1924) and *Mrs Dalloway* (1925): works beside which the novels of Bennett and Wells suddenly looked what in fact they had always been, distinctly conservative and old-fashioned in form.

Writing in the *TLS* in the spring of 1914, James of course had no knowledge of the war that was coming and the effects it would have on society and culture at large; nor, though he was acquainted with Pound, is it likely that he saw the February issue of a little magazine called *The Egoist* in which, through Pound's offices, the first chapter of *A Portrait of the Artist as a Young Man* appeared. And if he had seen it, would he have recognized its implications for the future of the novel? Probably not. He didn't, after all, appreciate the full significance of *Sons and Lovers*, classifying Lawrence with Compton Mackenzie in 'The New Novel' as a rather wild and undisciplined exponent of the

---

*William Henry Hudson, author of *Green Mansions* (1904). His reputation has not worn well, but he was highly regarded by the literary avant-garde in the early decades of this century. Virginia Woolf, for instance, commends him in her important 1919 essay, 'Modern Fiction'.

same kind of 'saturated' realism as was practised by Bennett and Wells: again, an understandable misjudgment, given the literary moment at which it was made. The whole essay on 'The New Novel' has the defensive, wistful, ironic, gently reproving tone of a master disappointed by the failure of his pupils to profit by his lessons, though compelled to acknowledge that they have achieved some worldly success in their own way. James obviously feels that he represents a certain attitude to the art of fiction—an attitude in which form is accorded maximum importance because 'Form alone *takes*, and holds and preserves, substance'[8]—but an attitude which is out of favour.

How different, how much more confident and aggressive, is the tone of Virginia Woolf's 1919 essay 'Modern Fiction'. Her arguments and her targets are essentially the same as James's in 'The New Novel', but unlike him she writes with buoyant confidence in a nascent literary avant-garde to which she herself and the future of the novel belong. Of Bennett, Wells, Galsworthy she says brusquely: 'the sooner English fiction turns its back on them, as politely as may be, and marches, if only into the desert, the better for its soul.'[9] At first her critique seems to be based on an appeal to content rather than form:

> If we fasten, then, one label on all these books, on which is one word, materialists, we mean by it that they write of unimportant things; that they spend immense skill and immense industry making the trivial and the transitory appear the true and enduring.

But it soon becomes evident that the form, the fictional technique, which Bennett, Wells and Galsworthy are using condemns them to the trivial and transitory content: 'So much of the enormous labour of proving the solidity, the likeness to life, of the story is not merely labour thrown away but labour misplaced to the extent of obscuring and blotting out the light of the conception.' (Compare James on Bennett: 'Yes, yes—but is this *all*? These are the circumstances of the interest—we see, we see; but where is the interest itself, where and what is its centre and how are we to measure it in relation to *that*?')[10] For 'reality', Virginia Woolf substitutes the word 'life'; and 'life', she asserts, is something that traditional realism cannot capture. 'We suspect a momentary doubt, a spasm of rebellion, as the pages fill themselves in the customary way. Is life like this? Must life be like this?' No, 'Life is not a series of gig-lamps symmetrically arranged: life is a luminous halo, a semi-transparent envelope surrounding us from the beginning of consciousness to the end. Is it not the task of the novelist to convey this varying, this unknown and uncircumscribed spirit, whatever aberration or complexity it may display . . .?' As an example of a contemporary novelist who has taken up the challenge she adduces (not without some prim reservations) James Joyce, whose *Ulysses* was then being serialized in the *Little Review*; and she suggests:

For the moderns . . . the point of interest lies very likely in the dark places of psychology. At once, therefore, the accent falls a little differently; the emphasis is upon something hitherto ignored; at once a different outline of form becomes necessary, difficult for us to grasp, incomprehensible to our predecessors . . . there is no limit to the horizon, and . . . nothing—no 'method', no experiment, even of the wildest—is forbidden, but only falsity and pretence.[11]

Virginia Woolf is using the word 'modern' here in a qualitative sense, denying it to novelists (like Bennett) who nevertheless go on writing in the 'modern' age. To distinguish between these two kinds of modern fiction, critics have added a syllable to one of them and called it *modernist*, thus drawing attention to its place in a cosmopolitan movement in all the arts. Modernist fiction is pioneered in England by James and Conrad. It reaches its fullest development in the work of Joyce. Virginia Woolf and Gertrude Stein display some of its most characteristic mannerisms. The late Forster and the early Hemingway, D. H. Lawrence and Ford Madox Ford connect tangentially with this movement. The relationships of alliance and hostility—the traditions which individual talents claimed as their own—were varied and complex. James admired Conrad but not Hardy. Virginia Woolf admired Conrad and Hardy. Lawrence admired Hardy and Conrad but with exasperated reservations; he seems to have had little interest in James and hated Joyce. Joyce hated Lawrence. Everyone except Lawrence seemed to have admired Flaubert. Forster was condescending about James, but admired Lawrence, and of course Virginia Woolf, but was cool about Joyce. Hemingway seems to have admired James, but learned more from Gertrude Stein. Ford collaborated with Conrad, obviously learned much from James, but was among the first to recognize the merit of Lawrence. And so on. Obviously there is no orthodoxy here, no single set of aesthetic assumptions or literary aims; but equally clearly there is a 'family resemblance' between the modernist novelists. There are features which we keep encountering in their work, though they are never found all together or in the same combinations. From these features we can compose a kind of identi-kit portrait of the modernist novel.

Modernist fiction, then, is experimental or innovatory in form, displaying marked deviations from preexisting modes of discourse, literary and non-literary. Modernist fiction is concerned with consciousness, and also with the subconscious and unconscious workings of the human mind. Hence the structure of external 'objective' events essential to traditional narrative art is diminished in scope and scale, or presented very selectively and obliquely, or is almost completely dissolved, in order to make room for introspection, analysis, reflection and reverie. A modernist novel has no real 'beginning', since it plunges us into a flowing stream of experience with which we gradually familiarize ourselves by a process of inference and association; and its ending is usually 'open' or ambiguous, leaving the reader in doubt as to the final destiny of the characters. To compensate for the diminution of narrative structure and unity, alternative methods of aesthetic ordering become more prominent, such as allusion to or imitation of literary models or mythical archetypes, and the repetition-with-variation of motifs, images, symbols—a technique variously described as 'rhythm', 'Leitmotif' and 'spatial form'.[12] Modernist fiction eschews the straight chronological ordering of its material, and the use of a reliable, omniscient and intrusive narrator. It employs, instead, either a single, limited point of view, or a method of multiple points of view, all more or less limited and fallible: and it tends towards a fluid or complex handling of time, involving much cross-reference backwards and forwards across the chronological span of the action.

We have no term for the kind of modern fiction that is not modernist except 'realistic' (sometimes qualified by 'traditionally' or 'conventionally' or 'social'). It makes a confusing and unsatisfactory antithesis to 'modernist' because the modernists often claimed to be representing 'reality' and indeed to be getting closer to it than the realists. Most of them in fact began working within the conventions of traditional realism, and some never made a decisive rupture with it. But the most representative modernist writers (e.g. Joyce, Woolf, Stein) in their pursuit of what they took to be the real found it necessary to distort the form of their discourse until it bore less and less resemblance to the historical description of reality—which, I suggested earlier, provides the principal nonliterary model for literary realism. It is because the norms of the historical description of reality have remained remarkably stable for the last two or three hundred years that I cannot accept the argument that 'realism' is a completely relativistic concept. We can see, for instance, that the characteristic writing of the 1930s in England, which challenged the modernist version of reality, did so *formally* by reverting to norms of nonliterary description of reality not very different from those observed by Bennett and Wells. Of course Orwell, Isherwood and Graham Greene (to name three representative writers of the 1930s) were affected by, and had learned from the modernists; of course they did not merely duplicate the art of the Edwardian realists. The 'materialist' ethos of Arnold Bennett deplored by Virginia Woolf—his acquiescence, one might say, in the values and assumptions of a capitalist class-society— is clearly not embraced by the 1930s novelists; and the informational 'saturation' of the Edwardian novel, wearily acknowledged by James, is replaced in the 1930s by a much more artfully selective use of documentary detail. But there is nevertheless a definable continuity in technique between these two groups of writers, which leads back eventually to classical nineteenth-century realism. The fiction of Orwell, Isherwood, Greene, like the fiction of Bennett, Wells and

Galsworthy, and the fiction of George Eliot, Scott and Jane Austen, is based on the assumption that there is a common phenomenal world that may be reliably described by the methods of empirical history— even if to the later writers in the tradition what this world *means* is much more problematical. From this assumption derives the kind of novel form we have already associated with realism: the blending of public and private experience, inner and outer history conveyed through a third-person past-tense authorial mode of narration or the autobiographical-confessional mode. The tradition continues in the work of many highly regarded English novelists in the next generation or two: Angus Wilson, C. P. Snow, Kingsley Amis, Anthony Powell, Alan Sillitoe, Margaret Drabble, and many others. The post-war period has, indeed, been dubbed an age of reaction against experiment in the English novel,[13] as though the reaction had not occurred much earlier. (Admittedly, there was an interregnum in the 1940s, when modernism enjoyed a qualified revival.)

The politically engagé writers of the 1930s—Auden, Isherwood, Spender, MacNeice, Day Lewis, Upward—criticized the modernist poets and novelists of the preceding generation for their élitist cultural assumptions, their failure or refusal to engage constructively with the great public issues of the time and to communicate to a wide audience. In his Introduction to the anthology *New Signatures* (1932) which launched the poetry of the Auden generation, Michael Roberts had this to say about the previous one:

> The poet, contemptuous of the society around him and yet having no firm belief, no basis for satire, became aloof from ordinary affairs and produced esoteric work which was frivolously decorative or elaborately erudite.[14]

'The poets of *New Signatures*', wrote Louis MacNeice in *Modern Poetry* (1938) 'have swung back to the Greek preference for information or statement. The first requirement is to have something to say, and after that you must say it as well as you can.'[15] In *Lions and Shadows* (1938), Christopher Isherwood described and disowned the artistic assumptions with which he composed his first novel, *All The Conspirators* (1928), when 'experiment' was still a fashionable slogan:

> I thought of the novel (as I hoped to learn to write it) essentially in terms of technique, of conjuring, of chess. The novelist, I said to myself, is playing a game with his reader; he must continually amaze and deceive him, with tricks, with traps, with extraordinary gambits, with sham climaxes, with false directions. I imagined a novel as a contraption—like a motor-bicycle, whose action depends upon the exactly co-ordinated working of all its interrelated parts; or like a conjuror's table, fitted with mirrors, concealed pockets and trapdoors. I saw it as something compact, and by the laws of its own nature, fairly short. In fact my models were not novels at all, but detective stories, and the plays of Ibsen and Tchekhov. *War and Peace*, which I read for the first time a few months later, disarranged and altered all my ideas.[16]

That Isherwood's conversion from this highly formalist view of the art of fiction should have been due to the influence of Tolstoy—that Tolstoy's realism still seemed valid and viable to a young writer in the 1930s—proves that there is consistency and continuity in the concept of literary realism in spite of those critics who consider it to be a totally relative concept.

Formalism is the logical aesthetic for modernist art, though not all modernist writers accepted or acknowledged this. From the position that art offers a privileged insight into reality there is a natural progression to the view that art creates its own reality and from there to the position that art is not concerned with reality at all but is an autonomous activity, a superior kind of game. Russian Formalism began as an attempt to explain and justify early modernist experiment in Russian writing, especially Futurist verse, and the view of the novel which Isherwood derisively summarizes is one that echoes many quite serious statements of the Formalists before Socialist Realism became the Soviet literary orthodoxy. George Orwell, though he dissociated himself from the Marxist or fellow-travelling writers of the 1930s and had little respect for their work, which he considered unlikely to last as well as *Ulysses* or *The Waste Land*, was nevertheless representative of his generation in deploring the indifference to contemporary reality displayed by the writers of the 1920s, and their obsession with form to the neglect of content.

> Our eyes are directed to Rome, to Byzantium, to Montparnasse, to Mexico, to the Etruscans, to the subconscious, to the solar plexus—to everywhere except the places where things are actually happening. When one looks back at the twenties, nothing is queerer than the way in which every important event in Europe escaped the notice of the English intelligentsia. . . . In 'cultured' circles art-for-art's sake extended practically to a worship of the meaningless. Literature was supposed to consist solely in the manipulation of words. To judge a book by its subject matter was the unforgivable sin, and even to be aware of its subject matter was looked on as a lapse of taste.[17]

Graham Greene had little in common ideologically with either the Auden-Isherwood group or with Orwell, but it seemed to John Lehmann, the literary historian of this period in *New Writing in Europe* (1940), that he belonged

> to the movement by reasons of his aims in style and the milieu he chooses . . . as emphatically as Pritchett or Isherwood he has pursued speed in dialogue, simplicity of prose structure, and colloquialism in his diction. He is thus extremely readable and has none of the airs and graces of what Cyril Connolly . . . has called the 'Mandarin style'. And he is as interested as any of the 'Birmingham School' in the ordinary urban and suburban scene of working lives. He has, in fact, exactly the same claim to be called a realist as they—and can make squalor smell as efficiently as Orwell. But *within* that world his preoccupations are entirely different.[18]

These 'preoccupations' were, of course, religious and spiritual—questions of good and evil, salvation and damnation, which are posed with such memorable intensity in relation to small-time gangsters in *Brighton Rock* and priests and peasants in the abandoned Mexico of *The Power and the Glory*. These very personal preoccupations drew Greene into an equally personal definition of the fictional traditions under discussion here. His 1945 essay on Francois Mauriac is particularly interesting in this respect, and worth quoting at length. He begins by recalling—and beautifully characterizing—that essay of Henry James's, 'The New Novel':

After the death of Henry James a disaster overtook the English novel: indeed long before his death one can picture that quiet, impressive, rather complacent figure, like the last survivor on a raft, gazing out over a sea scattered with wreckage. He even recorded his impressions in an article in *The Times Literary Supplement*, recorded his hope—but was it really hope or only a form of his unconquerable oriental politeness?—in such young novelists as Mr Compton Mackenzie and Mr David Herbert Lawrence, and we who have lived after the disaster can realize the futility of those hopes.

For with the death of James the religious sense was lost to the English novel, and with the religious sense went the sense of the importance of the human act. It was as if the world of fiction had lost a dimension: the characters of such distinguished writers as Mrs Virginia Woolf and Mr E. M. Forster wandered like cardboard symbols through a world that was paper-thin. Even in one of the most materialistic of our great novelists—Trollope—we are aware of another world against which the actions of the characters are thrown into relief. The ungainly clergyman picking his black-booted way through the mud, handling so awkwardly his umbrella, speaking of his miserable income and stumbling through a proposal of marriage, exists in a way that Mrs Woolf's Mr Ramsay never does, because we are aware that he exists not only to the woman he is addressing but also in a God's eye. His unimportance in the world of the senses is only matched by his enormous importance in another world.

The novelist, perhaps unconciously aware of his predicament, took refuge in the subjective novel. It was as if he thought that by mining into layers of personality hitherto untouched he could unearth the secret of 'importance', but in these mining operations he lost yet another dimension. The visible world for him ceased to exist as completely as the spiritual. Mrs Dalloway walking down Regent Street* was aware of the glitter of shop windows, the smooth passage of cars, the conversation of shoppers, but it was only a Regent Street seen by Mrs Dalloway that was conveyed to the reader: a charming whimsical rather sentimental prose poem was what Regent Street had become: a current of air, a touch of scent, a sparkle of glass. But, we protest, Regent Street too has a right to exist; it is more real than Mrs Dalloway, and we look back with nostalgia towards the chop houses, the mean courts, the still Sunday streets of Dickens. Dickens's characters were of immortal importance. . . . M. Mauriac's first importance to an English

*Actually, Bond Street.

reader, therefore, is that he belongs to the company of the great traditional novelists: he is a writer for whom the visible world has not ceased to exist, whose characters have the solidity and importance of men with souls to save or lose, and a writer who claims the traditional and essential right of the novelist, to comment, to express his views.[19]

It is not entirely clear whether Greene is presenting James as the last custodian of the religious sense in the English novel or as the novelist who finally killed it. The opening paragraphs (and Greene's essays on James[20]) seem to imply the former, but the passage quoted continues: 'For how tired we have become of the dogmatically 'pure' novel, the tradition founded by Flaubert and reaching its magnificent tortuous climax in England in the works of Henry James. . . . The exclusion of the author can go too far. Even the author, poor devil, has a right to exist and M. Mauriac reaffirms that right.' In fact neither Flaubert nor James excluded the author absolutely, while D. H. Lawrence and E. M. Forster, who exercised the privilege of authorial comment on a large scale in the post-Jamesian period, nevertheless fail to win Greene's approval.

The main source of confusion in this fascinating essay is that Greene has reacted against the modernist or symbolist mode of writing for two quite independent reasons, between which he has tried to establish a causal connection. One reason was literary and was shared in common by most writers of his generation: they deplored the emphasis on individual consciousness and sensibility in modernist writing because it seemed to dissolve and deny the empirical reality of 'the visible world'. ('But, we protest, Regent Street . . . is more real than Mrs Dalloway.' To which protest Virginia Woolf had, of course, already provided an answer in her 1924 essay 'Mr Bennett and Mrs Brown': 'But I ask myself, what is reality? And who are the judges of reality?'[21]). The other set of reasons was moral and religious and was largely peculiar to Greene (though Evelyn Waugh, another Catholic convert, shared them to some extent). He thought the methods of the modernist novel were incompatible with the expression of a Christian world-view. One can see why: Christianity is based on a linear concept of history extending from Genesis to the Last Day, and assumes the unique identity of the individual soul, as the realistic novel is based on the linear plot and the notion of autonomous 'character'; whereas modernist writing is strongly attracted to pagan or neo-Platonic forms of religion, cyclic theories of history and the idea of reincarnation. In fact, however, the realistic novel has much more in common with liberal humanism than it has with either Christian or pagan world views. Certainly there is no necessary connection between an empirical respect for the 'visible world' in literature and a belief in Christianity, though that is what Greene tries to assert.

The introductory part of his essay is designed to set up François Mauriac (and by implication Greene himself, since his technique at this period was similar) as a novelist who has reasserted the great tradition of realistic fiction, but it is a great tradition revised to admit the Christian eschatology which earlier practitioners had tended to exclude from it. It is a commonplace that the most striking thing about the clergymen of Trollope—and for that matter of Jane Austen—is their lack of interest in God; nor does the authorial commentary suggest that God is much interested in them. George Eliot, in that often quoted conversation with Myers in the Fellows' Garden at Trinity, pronounced God inconceivable, immortality unbelievable and only duty peremptory and absolute,[22] and orthodox religion functions in her fiction mainly as a covert metaphor for her own humanistic 'doctrine of sympathy'.[23] The parts of Dickens's novels which invoke a hereafter are the least convincing. In short, although the convention of the omniscient author may derive from the idea of an omniscient deity, and although this narrative method can be used to express a religious world-view, the connection is by no means invariable or even normative. In the realistic novel the third-person omniscient mode is more often used to assert or imply the existence of society, or of history, than of heaven and hell. Indeed, the further the premises of realism are pushed, the more evident becomes their inherent materialism, even atheism, as we see in the French and American naturalists. In England the true successors of Dickens and Trollope were Gissing, Bennett, Wells, and Galsworthy; just as the true successors of James were Virginia Woolf, Ford Madox Ford and E. M. Forster. Neither line of succession is Christian, but surely there is no doubt which of the two is the more 'religious'? The concept of sin is at the heart of Ford's best work; *A Passage to India* is full of the longing for transcendence even if it is ultimately unfulfilled; and was it not for their 'materialism' that Virginia Woolf condemned Bennett, Wells and Galsworthy?

A little later we find C. P. Snow, a novelist much more like Bennett in temper and interests, and certainly in no sense a Christian, taking up essentially the same stance towards the experimental novel as Greene's and forced into a like distortion of literary history:

Looking back, we can see what an odd affair the 'experimental' novel was. To begin with, the 'experiment' stayed remarkably constant for thirty years. Miss Dorothy Richardson was a great pioneer; so were Virginia Woolf and Joyce: but between *Pointed Roofs* in 1915 and its successors, largely American, in 1945, there was no significant development. In fact there could not be; because this method, the essence of which was to represent brute experience through the moments of sensation, effectively cut out precisely those aspects of the novel where a living tradition can be handed on. Reflection had to be sacrificed; so did moral awareness; so did the investigatory intelligence. That was altogether too big a price to pay and hence the 'experimental' novel . . . died from starvation, because its intake of human stuff was so low.[24]

Twenty years on and we find B. S. Johnson, writing shortly before his untimely death, fulminating against writers (among whom Lord Snow would have to be numbered) who continue to practice 'the nineteenth-century novel' in the twentieth century: 'No matter how good the writers are who attempt it, it cannot be made to work for our time, and the writing of it is anachronistic, invalid, irrelevant and perverse.'[25] That sounds very like Virginia Woolf's comment on the Edwardian realists: 'But those tools are not our tools, and that business is not our business. For us those conventions are ruin, those tools are death.'[26] 'Life does not tell stories,' Johnson continues, 'Life is chaotic, fluid, random; it leaves myriads of ends untied, untidily.' Does this sound familiar? 'Life is not a series of gig-lamps symmetrically arranged. . . .'

Wherever we touch down in the twentieth century we seem to find the same argument about the novel going on. Clearly there is no foreseeable end to it, though we might suggest that the pendulum of fashion in its movement between realism and modernism has speeded up to the point where all possible modes of working between the two extremes are now simultaneously available to a single generation of writers (and poets, dramatists, filmmakers, even artists and sculptors, for the same basic issues are raised in all the arts with a mimetic potential). Some writers, perhaps most writers, are unhappy with a tolerant aesthetic pluralism and feel it necessary to take a stand on one side or the other. This is understandable, and perhaps a necessary way of generating creative energy. But there is surely no reason or excuse for literary critics to do the same. As Northrop Frye says, it is not legitimate for the critic 'to define as authentic art what he happens to like and to go on to assert that whatever he happens not to like is, in terms of that definition, not art'.[27] It is necessary, therefore, for criticism of the novel to come to terms with the continuing coexistence of two kinds of modern fiction, with their many sub-species and crossbreeds. But when we look at criticism of the novel we find, more often than not, a repetition of the same polemical and factional spirit as we have found in the *obiter dicta* of practising novelists: a literary politics of confrontation (and in France, lately, of terrorism).

What is needed is a single way of talking about novels, a critical methodology, a poetics or aesthetics of fiction, which can embrace descriptively all the varieties of this kind of writing. The main resistance to the achievement of this aim has been on the side of the realistic novel, which works by concealing the art by which it is produced, and invites discussion in terms of content rather than form, ethics and thematics rather than poetics and aesthetics.

9   Criticism and Realism

> The novel gives a familiar relation of such things as pass each day before our eyes, such as may happen to our friends or to ourselves, and the perfection of it is to represent every scene in so easy and natural a manner, and to make them appear so probable, as to deceive us with a persuasion (at least while we are reading) that all is real, until we are affected by the joys and distresses, of the persons in the story, as if they were our own.[1]

It would be idle to deny that something like the effect described by Clara Reeve in 1785 enters into most people's pleasure in reading realistic fiction, or to pretend that it is limited to the more naive kind of reader, such as the inhabitants of Slough who rang the church bells when the blacksmith's public reading of *Pamela* (1740) reached the heroine's wedding, or the friend of Jane Austen's niece Fanny who wrote of *Emma*: 'I am at Highbury all day, and can't help feeling I have just got into a new set of acquaintances.'[2] 'It is the *point* about the novel that it is interesting' declares the far from naive Professor John Bayley, 'that it is social intercourse by other means. Its unprecedented flux of words is concerned—as Tolstoy said—with questions of how men live and should live. . . . It is a sharing of the commonplace through the medium of the exceptional man, the medium of the artist-novelist.'[3] And a critic writing recently in an academic quarterly commented on *Middlemarch* in terms entirely comprehensible by Clara Reeve's Euphrasia or Fanny Knight's Mrs Cage: 'When we read about the problems of Lydgate's marriage, or about Casaubon's "inward trouble" or about Bulstrode's public fall, it doesn't occur to us that these are *imagined* realities.'[4]

'Speak for yourself,' we may be inclined to respond to Mr Calvin Bedient, who makes this assertion; and indeed all criticism which puts its money on the truthfulness or verisimilitude of fictions is vulnerable to such an objection—all the more because it has usually disarmed itself of any defence based on the formal properties of the fictions concerned. The article by John Bayley from which I quoted is called 'Against a New Formalism'. '*Middlemarch* is rich in reality,' says Mr Bedient, 'It is in effect all vehicle, all medium, all transparency: dead to itself. And this must be said in the face of the vast formal mining to which the novel has been subjected.'[5] The kind of 'formal mining' to which he alludes may be represented by Mark Schorer's analysis of patterns of imagery in *Middlemarch*:

> I should like to suggest a set of metaphorical qualities in *Middlemarch* which actually represents a series apparent in the thinking that underlies the dramatic structure ... metaphors of unification ... of antithesis ... metaphors which conceive things as progressive ... metaphors of shaping and making, of structure and creative purpose; finally there are metaphors of what I should call a 'muted' apocalypse.[6]

It is a common reproach against this kind of critical method that it neglects the human substance of realistic fiction. For example, Malcolm Bradbury complained in 1967,

> We are ... inclined to assume that if we can show that the imagery of cash and legality runs through a Jane Austen novel, or that a whiteness-blackness opposition runs through *Moby Dick*, we can show more about the real being of the book than by showing that it deals with a society, with dispositions of character and relationship, so as to create a coherent moral and social world and an attitude towards it.[7]

Bradbury presents Schorer's kind of approach as a fashionable orthodoxy, which perhaps it was in quarters dominated by the New Criticism in the 1950s and early 1960s; but when Schorer first applied it in the late 1940s he saw it as revolutionary, his task to

> overcome corrupted reading habits of long standing; for the novel, written in prose, bears an apparently closer resemblance to discursive form than it does to poetry, thus easily opening itself to first questions about philosophy or politics, and, traditionally a middle-class vehicle with a reflective social function, it bears an apparently more immediate relation to life than it does to art, thus easily opening itself to first questions about conduct. Yet a novel, like a poem, is not life, it is an image of life; and the critical problem is first of all to analyse the structure of the image.[8]

This of course simply reverses the priorities of Bayley's definition of the novel quoted above—or rather we should say, following chronology, that Bayley is reversing Schorer's priorities. Schorer himself was probably reacting against the vogue for naturalism in the American writing of the 1930s and early 1940s that paralleled developments in England at the same period and had similar sources in political and social consciousness. In 'Technique as Discovery', a companion essay to 'Fiction and the Analogical Matrix', he attacks the reputations of Farrell, Thomas Wolfe, William Saroyan and praises Faulkner, Wescott, and Katherine Ann Porter—inheritors of the modernist or symbolist tradition in fiction. The New Criticism, which was firmly established in America by the time Schorer wrote his article, was itself in large part a product of the modernist-symbolist movement, stemming from the cross-fertilization of the Eliot-Pound literary avant-garde and the Cambridge English School;[9] but the early

New Critics had not concerned themselves much with prose fiction. The originality of Schorer's work was to apply to the novel, and especially to the classic realistic novel (e.g. Jane Austen, George Eliot) critical tools honed and sharpened on poetic drama and lyric poetry. 'Modern criticism,' Schorer declared at the outset of 'Technique as Discovery', 'has shown us that to speak of content as such is not to speak of art at all, but of experience; and that it is only when we speak of the *achieved* content, the form, that we speak as critics. The difference between content, or experience, and achieved content, or art, is technique.'[10] 'It is art that *makes* life, makes interest, makes importance,' wrote Henry James to H. G. Wells, who in turn said (and is condemned by Schorer for saying) 'Literature is not jewellery, it has quite other aims than perfection, and the more one thinks of "how it is done" the less one gets it done. These critical indulgences lead along a fatal path, away from every natural interest towards a preposterous emptiness of technical effort, a monstrous egotism of artistry, of which the later work of Henry James is the monumental warning. "It" the subject, the thing or the thought, has long since disappeared in these amazing works; nothing remains but the way it has been manipulated.'[11]

It will be seen that we are riding the same switchback of attitudes towards the novel that we followed in the preceding chapter. We are also circling back towards the issues raised in the very first chapter. Professor Bayley, for instance, is clearly a 'message-plus' man in Stanley Fish's terms: the novel is 'social intercourse by other means', that is, life as we know it, but rendered more knowable by the mediation of the 'exceptional man', the 'artist-novelist'. Todorov accused modern critics of sliding between imitation and autonomy theories of literature, but Bayley has no hesitation in plumping for the former to the exclusion of the latter, and expressing his preference for writers of the same persuasion:

A writer like Tolstoy whose intention is solely to communicate, to infect us with what he thinks and feels, will be indifferent to any notion of autonomy; all his work will strike us as connected together like our own experience of life, and present us with a complex perspective into which we move as if it were life.[12]

In Henry James and Virginia Woolf, in contrast,

communication is synonymous with the exhibition of an aesthetic object. Their claim to autonomy and the claim to communication in fact coincide, presenting us with a somewhat uneasy amalgam of the two.[13]

The 'new formalists' whom Bayley declares himself 'against' in this essay are principally Frank Kermode and Susan Sontag. The former is reproved for 'attaching far greater weight to the manipulation of the knowingly fictive, the explored illusion, than to the possibility that experience in the novel or poem represents, and joins up with, experience in life. The most enlightened literary artist, according to Kermode, is the one who is most aware that the paradigms of his art are formal, not experiential, and assumes a valid and valuable acquiescence in the fictive, never an attempt at the truth.'[14] Actually this seems to me to misrepresent Kermode's argument in *The Sense of an Ending*.[15] Although Kermode certainly assumes a much less stable 'reality' than Bayley, this does not, as in earlier, more extreme versions of formalism, allow literature the luxury and perhaps irresponsibility of total autonomy, but implicates the writer in a universal human enterprise: understanding a problematical universe. Literature is not the only kind of fiction: history, theology and even physics are also fictions, man-made structures of thought that inevitably distort or misrepresent the brute, irreducible, ineffable 'nature' they grapple with. Literary fictions are special only in being acknowledged as fictions from their inception, but all types of fiction, from predictions of the end of the world to the laws of physics, are subject to obsolescence and replacement. It is true that this theory predisposes Kermode to favour modern novelists who share it, or something like it, but it does not (as Bayley implies) automatically demote writers of the past with a more trusting faith in a stable and knowable reality. On the contrary, Kermode's explanation of the process by which the paradigms of literary fiction are constantly adjusted to take account of changes in public knowledge and consciousness is just about the best model we have to explain in large-scale terms the evolution of the novel, and especially the tendency of major novelists to assert the authenticity of their work by parodic or ironic allusion to the fictive stereotypes they have dispensed with.

Susan Sontag is chiefly interesting as an apologist for postmodernism, and her work need not detain us here. Bayley also glances at the pronouncements of the French *nouveaux romanciers*, like Alain Robbe-Grillet and Michel Butor. But behind the *nouveau roman*, and to some extent behind the criticism of Frank Kermode and Susan Sontag, there is a formidable body of literary theory which, originating in Russian Formalism and structuralist semiotics, has lately dominated literary criticism in France. Bayley does not explicitly refer to the *nouvelle critique* in his article, but it is there, if anywhere, that a 'new formalism' is to be found.

10 The Novel and the Nouvelle Critique

The French *nouvelle critique* has much in common with the Anglo-American New Criticism, and has certainly fought its opponents over many of the same battlefields; but it also has significant differences of origin, principle and practice. Both movements can be traced back to more or less the same source—the ferment of ideas about art and culture generated by early modernism; but whereas the New Criticism was fertilized by the literary avant-garde of Western Europe and America, especially the Pound-Eliot circle, the *nouvelle critique* traces its genealogy back to the creative interaction of Futurist poetry and Formalist poetics in Russia immediately before and after the Revolution. And whereas the New Criticism inherited a theory of language provided by C. K. Ogden and I. A. Richards, the *nouvelle critique* is based on the semiology of Ferdinand de Saussure and the structural linguistics of Roman Jakobson.

The linguistic theory of Ogden and Richards in fact turned out to be limited and incapable of convincing development, while the post-Bloomfieldian linguistics (also, confusingly, called 'structural') which came to dominate language study in the Anglo-American world had little to offer the literary critic. The New Critics—e.g. Empson and the young Leavis in England; Ransom, Tate, Brooks etc. in the United States—though committed in principle to a formalistic view of literature as an art of language, and in practice to the close analysis of texts, of 'the words on the page', had at their disposal a somewhat improvised set of tools with which to carry out their programme: Richards's categories of meaning, his distinction between emotive and referential language, a grammar generally regarded as obsolete by contemporary linguists, and a little traditional rhetoric. On the whole, the work of the New Critics is remarkable for how much they managed to achieve in terms of practical criticism with this limited apparatus, and in spite of (in some cases) a dogmatic hostility to linguistics as a discipline.

The structuralist linguistics of Saussure and the Russian and Czech linguistic circles, largely ignored or undervalued by the Anglo-American academic world until quite recently (Saussure's *Cours de Linguistique Général* (1916), for instance, was first published in an English translation in 1959) has proved immensely more powerful than the linguistic theory of Ogden and Richards who, as John Sturrock has observed,[1] fatefully dismissed Saussure early in *The Meaning of Meaning* (1923). The main puzzle is why the European structuralist tradition of thought about language and literature took so long to make itself felt in the Atlantic cultural hemisphere—for the *nouvelle critique* did not begin to emerge until the 1950s, and in turn made little impact on English and American criticism until the 1960s. Probably the turbulence of European political life in the 1930s and 1940s, which broke up the artistic and scholarly communities of Russia and Eastern Europe, and scattered their participants to the winds, had much to do with it. Many emigrated to America, where they were absorbed and assimilated into the domestic development of the New Criticism, while war-torn Europe itself was hardly a congenial climate in which to work out the implications of semiotic formalism. Although the *nouvelle critique* (unlike the New Criticism) has been associated with the political Left rather than the Right—and, in the case of the critics using the journal *Tel Quel* as their platform, notably Julia Kristeva and Philippe Sollers, with the extreme, Maoist Left—this was a relatively late development which has partly obscured the debt of the movement as a whole to Russian and Czech literary and linguistic theory. The *Tel Quel* group's effort to reconcile Marxism with structuralism has entailed significant revisions of both sides of the equation, and for all the dialectical ingenuity with which it has been pressed,* has met with considerable scepticism from both Left and Right. Certainly structuralism's essential claim would seem to be that it helps us to interpret the world rather than to change it, and initially the *nouvelle critique* (like the *nouveau roman* with which it often acted in partnership) was a schismatic breakaway from the politically committed existentialism of Sartre and Camus that dominated the French literary scene in the immediate post-war era.

The career of the most brilliant of the French new critics, Roland

---

*There seem to be two main lines of argument. One is that the myths about language which structuralist semiology exposes are bourgeois myths (even if unfortunately perpetuated by orthodox communist writers in the form of socialist realism) which must be eliminated before any authentic revolution can take place. The other is that although literature cannot contribute directly to the revolution, because it is an autonomous activity, the effort to establish this autonomy in the practice of writing is in its own terms radically revolutionary and therefore a model for political revolution. Lacan's structuralist reading of Freud is also invoked to forge a link between political revolution and literary innovation; the subject's experience of contradiction, questioning and crisis, leading to new practice, being seen as essential to psychological maturity, political progress and the production of authentic modern literature alike. See David Paul Funt, 'Newer Criticism and Revolution', *Hudson Review* XXII (1969) pp. 87–96 and Graham Dunstan Martin, 'Structures in Space: an account of *Tel Quel*'s Attitude to Meaning', *New Blackfriars*, III (1971) pp. 541–52; and for more sympathetic (indeed fully committed) accounts, Stephen Heath, *The Nouveau Roman* (1972) and John Ellis, 'Ideology and Subjectivity', *Working Papers in Cultural Studies* 9 (Spring 1976) pp. 205–19.

Barthes, shows a steady disengagement from, culminating in a virtual repudiation of, the views of Sartre. In *What is Literature?* Sartre took over Paul Valéry's symbolist distinction between poetry (which is like dancing, an autonomous activity) and prose (which is like walking, purposive and therefore without the grace of art) but reversed the priorities. The poet, locked in his private, magical, incantatory relationship with language is, according to Sartre, plainly incapable of 'engagement' and is therefore respectfully but firmly eliminated from the investigation of *What is Literature?* as early as page 13. 'The art of prose is employed in discourse; its substance is by nature significative; that is, the words are first of all not objects [as in poetry] but designations for objects. . . . In short it is a matter of knowing what one wants to write about, whether butterflies or the condition of the Jews. And when one knows, then it remains to determine how one will write about it.'[2] These assertions (which echo remarks of Orwell and MacNeice quoted earlier) are in due course denied by Barthes and other exponents of the *nouvelle critique*, who argue that what Valéry said about poetry must be true for all literature, and that the 'crisis of language' which Sartre claimed was peculiar to modern poetry, is in fact common to *all* writing in the modern period.

This was Barthes's starting point in *Writing Degree Zero* (1953). The crisis of language is dated somewhere in the middle of the nineteenth century when the failure of the 1848 revolution brought about 'the definitive ruin of liberal illusions',[3] confronting the bourgeois writer with the uncomfortable fact that he was no longer in accord with the inevitable march of history, and that his reality was no longer Reality. Hence the activity of writing, which had hitherto been seen simply as the process by which life was turned into literature through the medium of a classic style accepted and understood by all, now became highly problematical. To justify writing as an activity, it was made an infinitely difficult and complex craft: 'writing is now to be saved not by virtue of what it exists for, but thanks to the work it has cost.'[4] Hence the 'Flaubertization' of literature[5] of which Barthes is particularly contemptuous when it appears in modes of writing that attempt to deny their artificial status and continue to claim some purchase on the authentic 'real'—the naturalism of Zola, De Maupassant and Daudet, or the social realism of later communist writers. *Writing Degree Zero* is a somewhat bleakly determinist book, which appears to see no solution to the modern writer's dilemma apart from *either* ever more desperate experiments with an ostentatiously literary language in the manner of the symbolists and surrealists, leading eventually to incoherence and silence, *or* the effort to achieve a 'degree zero style', neutral, innocent and transparent, of the kind attempted by Camus in *The Outsider*—a Utopia of writing which is no sooner proposed than withdrawn:

> Unfortunately, nothing is more fickle than colourless writing; mechanical habits are developed in the very place where freedom existed, a network of

set forms hem in more and more the pristine freshness of discourse, a mode of writing appears afresh in lieu of an indefinite language. The writer, taking his place as a 'classic', becomes the slavish imitator of his original creation, society demotes his writing to a mere manner, and returns him a prisoner to his own formal myths.[6]

Despite its pessimism, *Writing Degree Zero* is sufficiently historicist in method and Marxist in sympathy to be precariously reconcilable with Sartre's argument in *What is Literature?* It was some time later that Barthes began explicitly to overturn the principles on which Sartre's book was based. In a 1966 paper significantly entitled, 'To Write: an intransitive Verb?' he asserts: 'language cannot be considered a simple instrument, whether utilitarian or decorative, of thought. Man does not exist prior to language, either as a species or as an individual. We never find a state where man is separated from language, which he then creates in order to "express" what is taking place within him: it is language which teaches the definition of man, not the reverse.'[7] The traditional realistic novel is criticized more for its falsification of the relationship between words and things than (as in *Writing Degree Zero*) for its social and political bad faith—politics is now a source of metaphor to describe how language works, rather than the other way round: 'these facts of language were not readily perceptible so long as literature pretended to be a transparent expression of either objective calendar time or of psychological subjectivity, that is to say, as long as literature maintained a totalitarian ideology of the referent, or more commonly speaking, as long as literature was realistic.'[8] The goal of zero degree writing has disappeared to be replaced by something which, though carefully discriminated from the old symbolist modernism diagnosed in *Writing Degree Zero* as suicidal, has obvious continuity with it, and includes several early modernists—Mallarmé, Proust, Joyce—among its exponents:

modern literature is trying, through various experiments, to establish a new status in writing for the act of writing. The meaning or the goal of this effort is to substitute the instance of discourse for the instance of reality (or of the referent) which has been, and still is, a mythical 'alibi' dominating the idea of literature. The field of the writer is nothing but writing itself, not as the pure 'form' conceived by an aesthetic of art for art's sake, but, much more radically, as the only area [*espace*] for the one who writes.[9]

The distinction drawn in that last sentence would not perhaps be visible to a hostile eye. To George Orwell, one of the three genuinely funny jokes produced by *Punch* since the Great War was a cartoon of a literary youth crushing his aunt's innocent question by saying, 'My dear aunt, one doesn't write *about* anything, one just *writes*.'[10] What seemed self-evidently absurd and affected to Orwell, and emblematic of the experimental, aesthetic literary climate of the twenties, is a sign of coming-of-age to Barthes, 'the writer being no longer one who writes *something*, but one who writes, absolutely.'[11]

Barthes's development after *Writing Degree Zero* in the direction of a radical theory of literary autonomy was directly related to his immersion in Saussurian semiology or semiotics (as the 'science of signs' is variously called.) Saussure is fundamental not only to the *nouvelle critique* but to the whole interdisciplinary movement, loosely called structuralism, of which it is a part. In Saussure's semiology, language is taken to be the model for all systems of signs, and it has been used as such in the fields of anthropology, psychology and philosophy as well as literary criticism. The first major product of Barthes's interest in the method was in fact his studies of popular culture and the mass media collected in *Mythologies* (1957).

Saussure defined the verbal sign, or word, as the union of a signifier (i.e. an acoustic image, a sound or symbolization of a sound) and a signified (i.e. a concept) and the relationship between signifier and signified is an arbitrary one. That is, there is no natural or necessary reason why the acoustic image *cat* [kaet] should denote the furry, feline quadruped which it in fact denotes in the English language: it does so by cultural agreement. This nucleus of arbitrariness at the heart of language is an idea of the greatest importance because it implies that it is the relationship *between* words, which means in effect the differences between them, that allows them to communicate, rather than their individual relationships of reference to discrete objects or any (totally illusory) *resemblance* between words and things.* Indeed, in some extreme formulations of the principle, language is seen as only, as it were, accidentally communicative:

> As with most utterances it would seem that the writer's purpose is to communicate a message and make statements, 'to say something'. He tells a story, describes a situation, relates an event, yet, as we know, language communicates only because of a certain number of fundamental properties which make communication possible. Communication is not at the heart of the linguistic act but only an epiphenomenon . . . if literature tells a story, if the author has to use a reference, it is simply a consequence of the fact that he is manipulating a linguistic sign.[12]

The logic of this statement may seem somewhat perverse—why should

---

*This extreme view of the arbitrariness of language has been forcefully challenged by Roman Jakobson in his article 'Quest for the Essence of Language', *Diogenes* LI (1965) pp. 21–37. Drawing on the classification of signs by the pioneering American semiologist Charles Sanders Peirce into icons, indices and symbols, only the last of which are arbitrary, Jakobson argues, with a wide range of illustration, that there is an iconic, or more precisely a *diagrammatic* relationship of resemblance 'patent and compulsory in the entire syntactic and morphological pattern of language, yet latent and virtual in its lexical aspect [which] invalidates Saussure's dogma of arbitrariness'. For example 'in various Indo-European languages the positive, comparative and superlative degrees of adjectives show a gradual increase in the number of phonemes, e.g., *high, higher, highest, altus, altior, altissimus*. In this way the signantia reflect the gradation gamut of the signata'. (p. 29).

we not deduce that language has the 'fundamental properties' it has because it was evolved as a means of communication, and that writers use it because they wish to communicate? Going a stage further, the writers associated with *Tel Quel* have attempted to work out a whole poetics of non-communication, in which 'unreadable' becomes a term of the highest praise, and have themselves produced texts carefully designed to be unintelligible.[13]

It will be obvious how this view of language militates against any mimetic theory of literature and especially against the status of the most mimetic of all the genres, the realistic novel. Not only does semiotic formalism seek to abolish the referential function of language in literary texts, a function in ordinary language on which the novel has always modelled its discourse; it also denies the epistemological validity of empiricism and the concept of the unique, autonomous self-conscious individual, on both of which the novel has usually been seen as founded.[14] Primitive man, Peter Caws explains in a shrewd account of structuralist thinking, 'is in the fortunate position of not knowing that he has a self, and therefore of not being worried about it. And the structuralists have come to the conclusion that he is nearer the truth than we are, and that a good deal of our trouble arises out of the invention of the self *as an object of study*, from the belief that man has a special kind of being, in short from the emergence of humanism. Structuralism is not a humanism, because it refuses to grant man any special status in the world.'[15] But the traditional novel is nothing if not humanistic, and its subject is characteristically a man or a woman worrying like mad about his or her 'self'. In the psychology of Jacques Lacan, 'The subject is an activity, not a thing . . . the subject produces itself by reflecting on itself, but when it is engaged on some other object it has no being apart from the activity of being so engaged.'[16] Hardly the stuff of which 'character' is made.

This radical readjustment of the subject-object relation in structuralist thought does not merely subvert literature of a traditionally mimetic kind, but also the critical procedures which have developed alongside it. If there is no single Truth about the world for the writer to identify and transcribe, then neither is there a single Truth about a text for the critic to identify and transcribe. 'The critic experiences before the book the same linguistic conditions as does the writer before the world,' says Barthes.[17] The task of criticism 'is not to discover forms of truth, but forms of "validity" . . . if there is such a thing as critical proof, it lies not in the ability to *discover* the work under consideration but, on the contrary, to cover it as completely as possible with one's own language'.[18] This in turn leads to a blurring of the conventional distinction between the creative work and the critical commentary on it:

> instead what we have is language and the single problematic it imposes, namely that of interpretation. . . . If, as Derrida puts it, linguistic signs refer

themselves only to other linguistic signs, if the linguistic reference of words is words, if texts refer to nothing but other texts, then, in Foucault's words, 'If interpretation can never accomplish itself, it is simply because there is nothing to interpret.' There is nothing to interpret, for each sign is not itself the thing that offers itself to interpretation but the interpretation of other signs. . . . Interpretation is nothing but sedimenting one layer of language upon another to produce an illusory depth which gives us the temporary spectacle of things beyond words.[19]

As Edwards W. Said has observed, 'Nearly everyone of the structuralists acknowledges a tyrannical feedback system in which man is the speaking subject whose actions are always being converted into signs that signify him, which he uses in turn to signify other signs and so on into infinity',[20] (an impression fostered, one might add, by their habit of quoting each other's aphorisms to rephrase rather than advance the argument, and by their addiction to strings of 'if—' clauses).

All this is profoundly alien and disconcerting to the Anglo-American critical temperament, and is apt to send critics, who in their native intellectual milieu figure as rampant formalists, scurrying for cover behind an old-fashioned, commonsense belief in 'content'. This reaction can be observed in the proceedings of an international conference on the subject of Literary Style, at which Roland Barthes delivered a paper on 'Style and Its Image' that concluded with the following words:

> . . . if up until now we have looked at the text as a species of fruit with a kernel (an apricot, for example) the flesh being the form and the pit being the content, it would be better to see it as an onion, a construction of layers (or levels, or systems) whose body contains, finally, no heart, no kernel, no secret, no irreducible principle, nothing except the infinity of its own envelopes—which envelop nothing other than the unity of its own surfaces.[21]

The editor of the symposium, Seymour Chatman, reports:

> Barthes's final reduction of content to form raised some questions. It was argued that it is one thing to say that even the smallest details of a literary text have a structure, but quite another to say that is all there is, that there is nothing *but* structure. Surely there must be such a thing as the subject of a literary work; that is, it is a meaningful thing to say (for example) that the subject of a story by Hemingway is the sensations of a man returned from the war who finds that even a trout stream seems sinister to him. That is a subject, a choice among other things in the world to write about that Hemingway has made, that is, a content—what Hemingway does with it is the form. How can one reduce the substantive or contentual choice to 'form'? There must remain some pre-existent material which is irreducibly content or subject-matter. Barthes replied that for him 'subject' was an illusory notion. There is no subject expressed by an author; subject is a level in the hierarchy of interpretation.[22]

We observe here the collision of two quite different philosophical traditions, which may be called for the sake of convenience French rationalism and Anglo-Saxon empiricism, and it is difficult to see how the argument could be profitably continued without moving from the area of literature and criticism to that of philosophy. Not all the French new critics are quite so Calvinistically fierce in denouncing empiricism as Barthes. But much structuralist criticism on the typology of narrative in the tradition of Propp[23] leads away from the characteristic concern of Anglo-American criticism with texts. Following Saussure's notion of language as the model for all sign-systems, and his distinction between *langue* (the system, the field of linguistic possibility offered by a given language) and *parole* (the individual utterance, speech act or text) it is argued that there is a homology or fundamental likeness between the structure of sentences and the structure of narrative, so that you can analyse narrative as you can analyse sentences, and you can produce a grammar of narrative which, like ordinary grammar, would show what *paroles* are possible and not possible in the *langue* of narrative. Such criticism need not deal with actual texts at all—indeed Tzvetan Todorov has said, 'The nature of structural analysis will be essentially theoretical and non-descriptive; in other words, the aim of such a study will never be the description of a concrete work. The work will be considered as the manifestation of an abstract structure, merely one of its possible realizations. . . .'[24] This programme has much in common with the anthropology of Lévi-Strauss, for whom all that can be observed of actual societies is 'a series of expressions, each partial and incomplete, of the same underlying structure, which they reproduce in several copies without ever completely exhausting its reality,'[25] and whose work is as disconcerting and challenging to Anglo-American functional anthropology as the *nouvelle critique* is to Anglo-American criticism. Indeed, one of Lévi-Strauss's aphorisms might be nailed to the mast of the entire structuralist enterprise as a message and a warning to the rest of us: 'to reach reality we must first repudiate experience.'[26]

This is a slogan that looks to the novelist about as inviting as the skull-and-crossbones to one of Defoe's merchants. Yet the interesting thing about the *nouvelle critique* is that it has mainly concentrated on the novel—it has pressed its formalism upon precisely the kind of literature that seems most resistant to it. This is another of the significant differences between the *nouvelle critique* and the New Criticism. The latter, as observed earlier, was founded in the first place upon the study of lyric and dramatic poetry, and for a long time the novel was tacitly or explicitly excluded from the general neocritical creed that literary texts are verbal systems in which what is said is indistinguishable from the way it is said—indeed, in many ways it still is excluded, and it may be doubted whether Roland Barthes's paper 'Style and its Image' would have aroused such opposition among its auditors if it had been orientated towards poetry rather than towards prose, and had taken its examples from T. S. Eliot or Valéry rather than Balzac. It is surely significant that the text invoked on that occasion to assert the existence of a content or subject-matter prior to form was a short story by Hemingway ('Big Two-Hearted River', which Philip Young has very plausibly related to the trauma of Hemingway's war wound).[27] It would have been more difficult to make the same point using, say, *The Waste Land* or *Le Cimétier Marin* as examples.

I have no quarrel with the *nouvelle critique*'s insistence on the primacy of language in the creation and criticism of prose fiction, and find the vigour with which the point is pressed exhilarating. But I am less impressed by the polemic against realism that absorbs so much of its energy, since this seems to lead us into the same limiting dichotomy between two kinds of fiction, only one of which we are permitted to admire, that we have already traced in Anglo-American criticism. This tendency can be seen very clearly in one of the first books of criticism published in England to show the influence of the *nouvelle critique*, Gabriel Josipovici's *The World and the Book* (1971). The theory of literary history advanced by this impressively wide-ranging study is a variation on the idea of a Second Fall in consciousness, comparable to T. S. Eliot's idea of a dissociation of sensibility. For Josipovici, as for Eliot, the Second Fall, though long in preparation, occurred decisively round about the seventeenth century; and the dire consequence for literature was realism. It is from literary realism (and all the fallacies about art and reality on which it is, in Josipovici's view, based) that modern fiction has freed us, restoring to us—not the unified and divinely meaningful universe of medieval Christianity, for that is lost for ever, even to Christians—but something equivalently valuable and liberating for modern man: an understanding of the laws of existence, of the nature of human consciousness and human perception, of the inevitable gap between our desires and reality. It is for this reason that he begins with a chapter on Proust and in his second chapter goes back to Dante. For Proust is, in Josipovici's view, the exemplary modern novelist, who makes the uncovering of the 'laws of existence' the aim of his great novel, and Dante the supreme voice of the medieval Christian synthesis. Read correctly, a novel like *A la Recherche du Temps Perdu*

> draws the reader into tracing the contours of his own labyrinth and allows him to experience himself not as an object in the world but as the limits of his world. And, mysteriously, to recognize this is to be freed of these limits and to experience a joy as great as that which floods through us when, looking at long last, with Dante, into the eyes of God, we sense the entire universe bound up into one volume and understand what it is to be a man.[28]

The realistic novel is incapable of producing this liberating effect because while the reader 'is immersed in it . . . there is nothing . . . to falsify what the imagination creates.'[29] 'The act of perception or the act of consciousness is never a neutral one,' says Josipovici. 'Proust and Homer and Virginia Woolf are all aware of this, but the traditional novel appears to ignore it. As a result it implicitly assumes that the world and the world as we are made conscious of it are one.'[30] And: 'to imagine like the traditional novelist that one's work is an image of the real world, to imagine that one can communicate directly to the reader what it is that one uniquely feels, that is to fall into the real solipsism, which is, to paraphrase Kierkegaard on despair, not to know that one is in a state of solipsism.'[31] All this is very reminiscent of Barthes, though Josipovici's wistful and eloquent evocation of an 'unfallen' medieval culture in which the world and the book were one, is not.

Josipovici's discussion of the writers who illustrate his argument positively—Dante, Chaucer, Rabelais, Hawthorne, Proust—is perceptive and persuasive. But his overall thesis, as I have argued at greater length elsewhere,[32] leads to a very selective and narrow concept of the 'modern' and an absurdly reductive caricature of the realistic novel—which in the end Josipovici himself repudiates, citing Proust as follows:

> Genuine art, then, Proust argues, even when it appears to be purely naturalistic fiction, always contains references to that secret world which is the artist's alone and which is normally inaccessible to his or to another's consciousness. . . . This feeling does not attach itself to the overt content of the novel, and it can never be discovered by an analysis of the content, but only by a response to what Proust calls style. This style may be the recurrence of certain images, as in Hardy or Dostoevsky, but it may also manifest itself in the peculiar choice of verbal tense in which the narration is conducted, as Proust noted in Flaubert.[33]

Thus the realistic novel, excluded from the palace of art because of its naive pretensions to represent reality in its content, is finally admitted by the back door when it is acknowledged after all to have a form or 'style'. Something of the same ambiguous redemption of the realistic novel takes place in Roland Barthes's *S/Z* (1970), a line-by-line commentary on a story by Balzac, 'Sarrasine', interspersed with more general explorations of the theory of narrative.

Barthes begins by making a distinction between two kinds of text, that which is *lisible* ('readable') and that which is *scriptible* ('writable'). Richard Miller usefully brings out the meaning of these two terms by translating them as 'readerly' and 'writerly'. The readerly text is based on logical and temporal order; it communicates along a continuous line, we read it one word after another, we consume it, passively. This use of the term overlaps with the usual sense of 'readable' as a term of praise in critical discussion—for instance John Lehmann's description of Graham Greene as 'readable' (see p. 48 above); but when Ezra Pound praised Joyce and James and Conrad for being 'readable' (see p. 43 above) he was thinking of a quality closer to Barthes's *scriptible*. The writerly text makes us not consumers but producers, because we write ourselves into it, we construct meanings for it as we read it, and ideally these meanings are infinitely plural:

> this ideal text . . . is a galaxy of signifiers, not a structure of signifieds; it has no beginning; it is reversible. . . . Systems of meaning may take over this absolutely plural text, but their number is never closed, based as it is on the infinity of language . . . it is a question of asserting the very existence of plurality, which is not that of the true, the probable or even the possible.[34]

Modernist writing aspires to the condition of the *scriptible* (and perhaps in *Finnegans Wake* achieves it) but the classic text (like 'Sarrasine') is a 'multivalent but incompletely reversible system. What blocks its reversibility is just what limits the plural nature of the classic text. These blocks have names: on the one hand truth, on the other empiricism: against—or between them, the modern text comes into being.'[35]

All this seems intended to discredit the classic, realistic, readerly text; but the very extremism of the argument paradoxically works to the latter's advantage. The infinite plurality to which the writerly text aspires renders it ultimately unamenable to analysis, baffling criticism by the plethora of its possible meanings. Of the *scriptible* text, 'there may be nothing to say.'[36] The 'limited plurality' of the classic text is, however, accessible to criticism through the analysis of connotation: the process by which one signified serves as the signifier of something else. This is perhaps the most important single point made (and brilliantly demonstrated) in *S/Z*: that in the literary text, however realistic, nothing is ever merely referential; everything connotes something, and usually several things simultaneously. For example, at one point in 'Sarrasine' the aged Duenna escorts the eponymous hero to a rendezvous with the singer La Zambinella:

> *Elle entraîna le Français dans plusieurs petites rues et s'arrêta devant un palais d'assez belle apparence. Elle frappa. La porte s'ouvrit. Elle conduisit Sarrasine à travers un labyrinthe d'escaliers . . .**

At first sight the two short sentences about knocking on the door seem banal, and, as far as the narrative is concerned, redundant, their function being merely to locate the story in a recognizable world in which houses have doors upon which visitors must knock for admittance. But as Barthes rightly insists, these sentences have literary meanings, 'first because every door is an object of some vague symbolism (a whole complex of death, pleasure, limit, secret, is bound up in it); and next because this door which opens (without a subject) connotes an atmosphere of mystery; last because the open door and the

---

*She led the Frenchman along several back streets and stopped before a rather handsome mansion. She knocked. The door opened. She led Sarrasine along a labyrinth of stairways . . .'

end of the route still remain uncertain, the suspense is prolonged, in other words heightened.'[37] Furthermore, this incident belongs to a series of 'door' motifs which punctuate the story—a story that is itself a delayed disclosure of a mystery, like the opening of a series of doors.

For La Zambinella is in fact a castrato, and Sarrasine the victim of a cruel deception. When he becomes ardent and carries her off to a boudoir, the singer draws a dagger.

> *L'Italienne était armée d'un poignard.—Si tu approches, dit-elle, je serai forcée de te plonger cette arme dans le coeur.**

Barthes discriminates several different interwoven codes in this passage. On the actional or 'proairetic' level it is a recognized stage in the series 'Rape'—the victim's armed defence of her virtue. But since La Zambinella is in fact defending, not 'her' virtue, but a lie, by this gesture, on the hermeneutic level it is a deception—for Sarrasine, and, on first reading, for the reader. On yet another level, the symbolic, the dagger signifies castration, which is the hidden secret and thematic core of the whole tale.[38] When he flourished this example before the Literary Style symposium Barthes mentioned two more codes present in the passage: the French language and the rhetorical code.[39] The rhetorical code (apostrophe, the antonomasia of 'L'Italienne' and the interpolation of an *inquit* into direct speech) confers upon Balzac's use of the French language the status of an *écriture*. It also reinforces the actional code by the somewhat histrionic resonances it imparts to Zambinella's speech and gesture, and at the same time it collaborates with the hermeneutic code, for the use of an epithet, 'L'Italienne', instead of a proper name (like 'le Français' in the previous example) covertly underlines the importance of nationalities in the intrigue (Sarrasine, a recent visitor to Rome, does not know that female roles are always played by castrati in the Papal States at this period).

To Barthes, literature has its very being in this interweaving of multiple codes, none of which has precedence over the rest—certainly not the literal or referential code. 'The literality of the text is a system like any other . . . the meaning of a text can be nothing but the plurality of its systems, its infinite (circular) transcribability.'[40] The infinite transcribability (from one code into another) of the readerly text is presumably different from the infinite plurality of the writerly text; but here and elsewhere Barthes comes close to collapsing his own distinction between the *lisible* and the *scriptible*; and indeed one may wonder whether the distinction is not one of degree rather than essence. Certainly Barthes's commentary impresses one more with the plurality of meanings to be found in 'Sarrasine' than with the limits of that plurality, and thus, against the critic's apparent intention, constitutes a triumphant vindication of the classic text.

*The Italian woman was armed with a dagger, 'If you come any closer,' she said, 'I will be forced to plunge this weapon into your heart.'

Balzac himself, of course, was (to revert to the literary history of *Writing Degree Zero*) writing before the crisis of language hit the bourgeois writer: he was still in good faith in supposing he was describing a stable reality, and it seems that we may legitimately enjoy reading him as long as we do not fall into the same fallacy. The writer, Barthes insists, never applies language to a referent, even if that is what he thinks he is doing; he merely applies one code to another. When he describes a scene, he describes something already organized and framed pictorially.[41] And when he describes a voice, for example in 'Sarrasine'–

> —*Addio, Addio! disait-elle avec les inflexions les plus jolies de sa jeune voix. Elle ajouta même sur la dernière syllabe une roulade admirablement bien exécutée, mais à voix basse et comme pour peindre l'effusion de son coeur par une expression poétique**

Barthes asks:

> What would happen if one actually performed Marianina's '*addio*' as it is described in the discourse? Something incongruous, no doubt, extravagant, and not musical. More: is it really possible to perform the act described? This leads to two propositions. The first is that the discourse has no responsibility vis-à-vis the real: in the most realistic novel, the referent has no 'reality': suffice it to imagine the disorder the most orderly narrative would create were its descriptions taken at face value, converted into operative programmes and simply *executed*. In short (this is the second proposition) what we call 'real' (in the theory of the realistic text) is never more than a code of representation (of signification): it is never a code of execution: *the novelistic real is not operable*. To identify—as it would, after all, be 'realistic' enough to do—the real with the operable would be to subvert the novel at the limit of its genre (whence the inevitable destruction of novels when they are transferred from writing to film, from a system of meaning to an order of the operable).[42]

As so often in reading Barthes, a spasm of empirical doubt intrudes just as one is about to surrender to the energy and eloquence of the argument. Is it really true that novels are destroyed by transference to the cinema screen? One might be more impressed by how *readily* they transfer, compared to poems, plays or *scriptible* prose narratives like *Finnegans Wake*.

What is provocative overstatement in Barthes is apt to become intolerant dogma in his epigones, and this applies particularly to his critique of realism. He is absolutely right to affirm that realism, like any other mode of writing, like any product of culture (this is perhaps the most important single message of structuralism) is a human code, or tissue of codes, not a natural reflection of the Real. But we are not

---

*'Addio, addio,' she said, with the prettiest inflection in her youthful voice. She added to the final syllable a marvellously well-executed trill, but in a soft voice, as if to give poetic expression to the emotions in her heart.

bound to accept the historicist argument that realism ceased to be a valid literary mode by the middle of the nineteenth century. To hold that position entails unwriting (*i.e.* wishing unwritten) a large part of the imaginative effort of the last one hundred years.

11 Conclusion to Part One

In the preceding pages we have surveyed many different issues of literary theory and practice, and considered a variety of texts, writers and schools of criticism. But all of the attitudes and arguments we have reviewed could, I think, be divided into two large and opposing groups according to whether they give priority to content or to form, to the 'what' or the 'how' of literature.

The fundamental principle of one side is that art imitates life, and is therefore in the last analysis answerable to it: art must tell the truth about life and contribute to making it better, or at least more bearable. That is the classical definition and justification of art, which of course covers a considerable diversity and division of opinion about the manner of imitation that is most desirable—for instance whether art should imitate the actual or the ideal. It dominated Western aesthetics from the time of Plato and Aristotle until the beginning of the nineteenth century when it began to be challenged by Romantic theories of the imagination; and by the end of the century it had been turned on its head. 'Life imitates art', Oscar Wilde declared,[1] meaning (a structuralist *avant la lettre*) that we compose the reality we perceive by mental structures that are cultural not natural in origin, and that it is art which is most likely to change and renew those structures when they become tired and mechanical. ('Where, if not from the Impressionists, do we get those wonderful brown fogs that come creeping down our streets, blurring the gas-lamps and changing the houses into monstrous shadows?')[2] What, then, from this point of view does art imitate? The answer is, of course, other art, especially other art of the same kind. Poems are not made out of experience, they are made out of poetry—that is, the tradition of disposing the possibilities of language to poetic ends. T. S. Eliot's 'Tradition and the Individual Talent' is a classic exposition of the idea. It is not so often applied to prose fiction, but novels, too, are demonstrably made out of other novels, and nobody could write one without having read one first. In short, art is autonomous.

The trouble with these two theories of art is that they are equally plausible yet mutually contradictory. It is possible to believe each of them at different times—probably most of us do—but difficult to believe them both simultaneously. As soon as they are brought into the same conceptual space, a battle usually develops. It is a running battle, as I have tried to demonstrate in following the debate about the novel through the twentieth century, and makes a fascinating spectacle; but it does not seem to progress very much. In dialectical terms we observe the clash of thesis and antithesis with little prospect of a synthesis. Since art is supremely the province of forms, and since literature is an art of language, I believe such a synthesis can only be found in linguistic form. But the synthesis must be catholic: it must account for and be responsive to the kind of writing normally approached via content, via the concept of imitation, as well as to the kind of writing usually approached via form, via the concept of autonomy. In the next part of this book I describe a theory of language which offers, I believe, the basis for such a synthesis. It belongs to the European formalist/structuralist tradition, and has therefore entered into the vocabulary of the *nouvelle critique* (notably in the work of Gérard Genette), but as the basis for a poetics it resists the polemical tendency of Barthes and his followers to instate one kind of writing at the expense of another. Of course, the synthesis will only satisfy those who are sympathetic to formalism in the first place. There are an infinite number of possible contents, and many of them are mutually irreconcilable on the level of ethics, ideology, praxis. Content-based criticism cannot be all-embracing by its very nature. But structurally the forms of literature are finite in number. In fact, at a certain level, they can be reduced to two types. If this seems a drastic reduction, it must be remembered that most modern formalist criticism has endorsed only one type.

Part Two

Metaphor and Metonymy

1 Jakobson's Theory

The idea of a binary opposition between metaphor and metonymy can be traced back to Russian Formalism. Erlich observes that Zirmunskij 'posited metaphor and metonymy as the chief earmarks of the Romantic and classic styles respectively' in an essay of 1928.[1] Roman Jakobson records that he 'ventured a few sketchy remarks on the metonymical turn in verbal art' in articles on realism (1927) and Pasternak (1935), and applied the idea to painting as early as 1919.[2] Alluding briefly in their *Theory of Literature* (1948) to 'the notion that metonymy and metaphor may be the characterizing structures of two poetic types—poetry of association by contiguity, of movement within a single world of discourse, and poetry of association by comparison, joining a plurality of worlds', Wellek and Warren refer the reader to Jakobson's essay on Pasternak, Karl Bühler's *Sprachtheorie* (1934) and Stephen J. Brown's *The World of Imagery* (1927).[3] The most systematic and comprehensive (though highly condensed) exposition of the idea, however, and the source most often cited in modern structuralist criticism, is Jakobson's essay 'Two Aspects of Language and Two Types of Aphasic Disturbances', first published in *Fundamentals of Language* (1956) by Jakobson and Morris Halle. In his 'Closing Statement: Linguistics and Poetics' addressed to the 1958 Indiana Conference on Style in Language,[4] Jakobson referred to the same distinction but in a less even-handed way, reinforcing that bias of criticism towards the metaphoric at the expense of the metonymic mode which he had himself diagnosed in the earlier paper. The later one is, however, much better known to English and American critics than the earlier. Perhaps the title, 'Two Aspects of Language and Two Types of Aphasic Disturbances' has not seemed very inviting to literary critics, and a quick glance at the contents of that essay might well discourage further investigation. The seminal distinction between the metaphoric and metonymic poles is compressed into half-a-dozen pages, and seems almost an afterthought appended to a specialized study of language disorders. The theory of language upon which the distinction rests is expounded in a highly condensed fashion, with few concessions to lay readers. In the account of this essay which follows I have tried to make its content and implications (as I understand them) clear by expansions and illustrations which may seem obvious or redundant to readers already familiar with structuralist thinking about language and literature.

Jakobson begins by formulating one of the basic principles of structural linguistics deriving from Saussure: that language, like other systems of signs, has a twofold character. Its use involves two operations—selection and combination:

> Speech implies a selection of certain linguistic entities and their combination into linguistic units of a higher degree of complexity.[5]

This distinction between selection and combination corresponds to the binary oppositions between *langue* and *parole*, between *paradigm* (or *system*) and *syntagm*, between *code* and *message*, in structural linguistics and semiotics. It is perhaps most readily grasped in relation to concrete objects that function as signs, such as clothing, food and furniture. Roland Barthes gives useful illustrations of this kind in his *Elements of Semiology*. For example, to the garment *langue*/paradigm/system/code belongs the 'set of pieces, parts or details which cannot be worn at the same time on the same part of the body, and whose variation corresponds to a change in the meaning of the clothing', while the garment *parole*/syntagm/message is 'the juxtaposition in the same type of dress of different elements'.[6] Imagine a girl dressed in teeshirt, jeans and sandals: that is a message which tells you what kind of person she is, or what she is doing or what mood she is in, or all these things, depending on the context. She has selected these units of clothing and combined them into a garment unit 'of a higher degree of complexity'. She has selected the teeshirt from the set of clothes which cover the upper half of the body, jeans from the set of clothes which cover the lower half of the body and sandals from the set of footwear. The process of selection depends on her knowing what these sets are—on possessing a classification system of her wardrobe which groups teeshirt with, say, blouse and shirt as items which have the same function and only one of which she needs. The process of combination depends upon her knowing the rules by which garments are acceptably combined: that for instance sandals, not court shoes, go with jeans (though the rules of fashion are so volatile that one cannot be too dogmatic in these matters). The combination teeshirt-jeans-sandals is, in short, a kind of sentence.

Consider the sentence, 'Ships crossed the sea'. This has been constructed by selecting certain linguistic entities and combining them into a linguistic unit (syntagm) of a higher degree of complexity: selecting *ships* from the set (paradigm) of words with the same grammatical function (i.e. nouns) and belonging to the same semantic field (e.g. *craft, vessels, boats* etc.); selecting *crossed* from the set of verbs with the same general meaning (e.g. *went over, sailed across, traversed* etc.) and selecting *sea* from another set of nouns such as *ocean, water* etc. And having been selected, these verbal entities are then combined according to the rules of English grammar. To say 'The sea crossed the ships' would be nonsensical, equivalent to trying to wear jeans above the waist and a teeshirt below (both types of mistake commonly made by infants before they have mastered the basic rules of speech and dressing).

Selection involves the perception of similarity (to group the items of the system into sets) and it implies the possibility of substitution (*blouse* instead of *teeshirt*, *boats* instead of *ships*). It is therefore the process by which metaphor is generated, for metaphor is substitution based on a certain kind of similarity. If I change the sentence, 'Ships crossed the sea' to 'Ships *ploughed* the sea', I have substituted *ploughed* for *crossed*, having perceived a similarity between the movement of a plough through the earth and of a ship through the sea. Note, however, that the awareness of *difference* between ships and ploughs is not suppressed: it is indeed essential to the metaphor. As Stephen Ullmann observes: 'It is an essential feature of a metaphor that there must be a certain distance between tenor and vehicle.* Their similarity must be accompanied by a feeling of disparity; they must belong to different spheres of thought.'[7]

Metonymy is a much less familiar term than metaphor, at least in Anglo-American criticism, though it is quite as common a rhetorical device in speech and writing. The *Shorter Oxford English Dictionary* defines metonymy as 'a figure in which the name of an attribute or adjunct is substituted for that of the thing meant, e.g. *sceptre* for *authority*'. Richard A. Lanham gives a slightly different definition in his *A Handlist of Rhetorical Terms* 'Substitution of cause for effect or effect for cause, proper name for one of its qualities or vice versa: so the Wife of Bath is spoken of as half Venus and half Mars to denote her unique mixture of love and strife.' Metonymy is closely associated with synecdoche, defined by Lanham as 'the substitution of part for whole, genus for species or vice versa: "All hands on deck".'[8] The hackneyed lines, 'The hand that rocks the cradle/Is the hand that rules the world' include both tropes—the synecdoche 'hand' meaning 'person' (by inference, 'mother') and the metonymy 'cradle' meaning 'child'. In Jakobson's scheme, metonymy includes synecdoche.

Rhetoricians and critics from Aristotle to the present day have generally regarded metonymy and synecdoche as forms or subspecies

---

*Terms coined by I. A. Richards in *The Philosophy of Rhetoric* to distinguish the two elements in a metaphor or simile. In 'Ships ploughed the sea', 'Ships' movement' is the tenor and 'plough' the vehicle.

of metaphor, and it is easy to see why. Superficially they seem to be the same sort of thing—figurative transformations of literal statements. Metonymy and synecdoche seem to involve, like metaphor, the substitution of one term for another, and indeed the definitions quoted above use the word 'substitution'. Jakobson, however (and there is no more striking example of the advantages a structuralist approach may have over a commonsense empirical approach) argues that that metaphor and metonymy are *opposed*, because generated according to opposite principles.

Metaphor, as we have seen, belongs to the selection axis of language; metonymy and synecdoche belong to the combination axis of language. If we transform our model sentence into '*Keels* crossed the *deep*' we have used a synecdoche (*keels*) and a metonymy (*deep*) not on the basis of similarity but of contiguity. *Keel* may stand for *ship* not because it is similar to a ship but because it is part of a ship (it so happens that a keel is the same shape as a ship, but *sail*, which would be an alternative synecdoche, is not). *Deep* may stand for *sea* not because of any similarity between them but because depth is a property of the sea. It may be objected that these tropes are nevertheless formed by a process of substitution—*keels* for *ships*, *deep* for *sea*—and are not therefore fundamentally different from metaphor. To answer this objection we need to add an item to Jakobson's terminology. In his scheme selection is opposed to combination, and substitution is opposed to 'contexture'—the process by which 'any linguistic unit at one and the same time serves as a context for simpler units and/or finds its own context in a more complex linguistic unit.'[9] But 'contexture' is not an optional operation in quite the same way as 'substitution'—it is, rather, a law of language. I suggest that the term we need is *deletion*: deletion is to combination as substitution is to selection. Metonymies and synecdoches are *condensations* of contexture. The sentence, 'Keels crossed the deep' (a non-metaphorical but still figurative utterance) is a transformation of a notional sentence, *The keels of the ships crossed the deep sea* (itself a combination of simpler kernel sentences) by means of deletions. A rhetorical figure, rather than a précis, results because the items deleted are not those which seem logically the most dispensable. As the word *ship* includes the idea of keels, *keels* is logically redundant and would be the obvious candidate for omission in a more concise statement of the event, and the same applies to *deep*. Metonymy and synecdoche, in short, are produced by deleting one or more items from a natural combination, but not the items it would be most natural to omit: this illogicality is equivalent to the coexistence of similarity and dissimilarity in metaphor.

On a pragmatic level, of course, metonymy may still be seen as a process of substitution: we strike out *ships* in our manuscript and insert *keels*, without consciously going through the process of expansion and deletion described above. This does not affect the fundamental structural opposition of metaphor and metonymy, which rests on the basic opposition between selection and combination.

> Selection (and correspondingly substitution) deals with entities conjoined in the code, but not in the given message, whereas in the case of combination the entities are conjoined in both or only in the actual message.[10]

Ploughed has been selected in preference to, or substituted for, other verbs of movement and penetration (like *crossed, cut through, scored*) which are conjoined in the code of English (by belonging to a class of verbs with approximately similar meanings) but not conjoined in the message (because only one of them is required). *Keels*, on the other hand, is conjoined with *ships* both in the code (as nouns, as items in nautical vocabulary) and in the notional message, *The keels of the ships etc*. The contiguity of *keels* and *ships* in many possible messages as well as in the code reflects their actual existential contiguity in the world, in what linguistics calls 'context', whereas there is no such contiguity between ploughs and ships.

2   Two Types of Aphasia

Impressive evidence for Jakobson's argument that metaphor and metonymy are polar opposites corresponding to the selection and combination axes of language comes from the study of aphasia (severe speech disability). Traditionally aphasia has been studied under the two aspects of sending and receiving the verbal message. Jakobson, however makes his methodological 'cut' in a different dimension, along the line between selection and combination (and again the advantage of a structuralist over an empirical approach to the problem is striking):

> We distinguish two basic types of aphasia—depending on whether the major deficiency lies in selection or substitution, with relative stability of combination and contexture; or conversely, in combination and contexture, with relative retention of normal selection and substitution.[1]

Aphasics who have difficulty with the selection axis of language—who suffer, in Jakobson's terms from 'selection deficiency' or 'similarity disorder'—are heavily dependent on context, i.e. on contiguity, to sustain discourse.

> The more his utterances are dependent on the context, the better he copes with his verbal task. He feels unable to utter a sentence which responds

neither to the cue of his interlocutor nor to the actual situation. The sentence 'it rains' cannot be produced unless the utterer sees that it is actually raining.[2]

Even more striking: a patient asked to repeat the word 'no', replied, 'No, I can't do it'. Context enabled him to use the word that he could not consciously 'select' from an abstract paradigm. In this kind of aphasic speech the grammatical subject of the sentence tends to be vague (represented by 'thing' or 'it'), elliptical or non-existent, while words naturally combined with each other by grammatical agreement or government, and words with an inherent reference to the context, like pronouns and adverbs, tend to survive. Objects are defined by reference to their specific contextual variants rather than by a comprehensive generic term (one patient would never say *knife*, only *pencil-sharpener, apple-parer, bread knife, knife-and-fork*). And, most interesting of all, aphasics of this type make 'metonymic' mistakes by transferring figures of combination and deletion to the axis of selection and substitution:

> *Fork* is substituted for *knife*, *table* for *lamp*, *smoke* for *pipe*, *eat* for *toaster*. A typical case is reported by Head: 'When he failed to recall the name for "black" he described it as "What you do for the dead"; this he shortened to "dead".'
>
> Such metonymies may be characterized as projections from the line of a habitual context into the line of substitution and selection: a sign (e.g. *fork*) which usually occurs together with another sign (e.g. *knife*) may be used instead of this sign.[3]

In the opposite type of aphasia—'contexture deficiency' or 'contiguity disorder'—it is the combination of linguistic units into a higher degree of complexity that causes difficulty, and the features of similarity disorder are reversed. Word order becomes chaotic, words with a purely grammatical (i.e. connective) function like prepositions, conjunctions and pronouns, disappear, but the subject tends to remain, and in extreme cases each sentence consists of a single subject-word. These aphasics tend to make 'metaphorical' mistakes:

> 'To say what a thing is, is to say what a thing is like', Jackson notes. . . . The patient confined to the substitution set (once contexture is deficient) deals with similarities, and his approximate identifications are of a metaphoric nature. . . . *Spyglass* for *microscope*, or *fire* for *gaslight* are typical examples of such quasi-metaphoric expressions, as Jackson christened them, since in contradistinction to rhetoric or poetic metaphors, they present no deliberate transfer of meaning.[4]

This evidence from the clinical study of aphasia is not merely fascinating in its own right and persuasive support for Jakobson's general theory of language; it is, I believe, of direct relevance to the study of modern literature and its notorious 'obscurity'. If much modern literature is exceptionally difficult to understand, this can only be because of some dislocation or distortion of either the selection or the combination axes of language; and of some modern writing, e.g. the work of Gertrude Stein and Samuel Beckett, it is not an exaggeration to say that it aspires to the condition of aphasia. We shall investigate this further in due course; I proceed immediately to consider the final section of Jakobson's paper, 'The Metaphoric and Metonymic Poles', in which he applies his distinction to all discourse, and indeed to all culture.

3   The Metaphoric and Metonymic Poles

The development of a discourse may take place along two different semantic lines: one topic may lead to another either through their similarity or their contiguity. The metaphorical way would be the more appropriate term for the first case and the metonymic for the second, since they find their most condensed expression in metaphor and metonymy respectively. In aphasia one or other of these two processes is blocked. . . . In normal verbal behaviour both processes are continually operative, but careful observation will reveal that under the influence of a cultural pattern, personality, and verbal style, preference is given to one of the two processes over the other.[1]

Jakobson proceeds to classify a great variety of cultural phenomena according to this distinction. Thus, drama is basically metaphoric and film basically metonymic, but within the art of film the technique of montage is metaphoric, while the technique of close-up is synecdochic. In the Freudian interpretation of dreams, 'condensation and displacement' refer to metonymic aspects of the dreamwork, while 'identification and symbolism' are metaphoric.* In painting, cubism 'where the object is transformed into a set of synecdoches' is metonymic and surrealism metaphoric (presumably because it combines objects not contiguous in nature, and selects and substitutes

---

*These are the basic processes by which the latent content of the dream—the real anxieties or desires which motivate it—is translated into its manifest content, the dream itself. Condensation is the process by which the latent content of the dream is highly compressed, so that one item stands for many different dream thoughts, and displacement is the process by which dreams are often differently centred from the anxieties or guilts which trigger them off. Thus something trivial in a dream may have the significance of something important in actuality and the connection between the two can be traced along a line of contiguities by the technique of free association. Dream symbolism is the more familiar process by which, for instance, long pointed objects represent male sexuality and hollow round objects female sexuality.

visual/tactile values on the principle of similarity or contrast.* The two types of magic discriminated by Frazer in *The Golden Bough*, homeopathic or imitative magic based on similarity and contagious magic based on contact, correspond to the metaphor/metonymy distinction. In literature, Russian lyrical songs are metaphoric, heroic epics metonymic. Prose, which is 'forwarded essentially by contiguity' tends towards the metonymic pole, while poetry, which in its metrical patterning and use of rhyme and other phonological devices emphasizes similarity, tends towards the metaphoric pole. Romantic and symbolist writing is metaphoric, and realist writing is metonymic: 'following the path of contiguous relationships, the realistic author metonymically digresses from the plot to the atmosphere and from the characters to the setting in space and time. He is fond of synecdochic details. In the scene of Anna Karenina's suicide Tolstoy's artistic attention is focused on the heroine's handbag. . . .'[2]

'The dichotomy here discussed', says Jakobson, 'appears to be of primal significance and consequence for all verbal behaviour and for human behaviour in general'† and it may be asked whether anything that offers to explain so much can possibly be useful, even if true. I believe it can, for the reason that it is a binary system capable of being applied to data at different levels of generality, and because it is a theory of dominance of one quality over another, not of mutually exclusive qualities.‡ Thus the same distinction can serve to explain

*Cf. Max Ernst: 'One rainy day in 1919, finding myself in a village on the Rhine, I was struck with the obsession which held under my gaze the pages of an illustrated catalogue showing objects designed for anthropologic, microscopic, psychologic, mineralogic, and paleontologic demonstration. There I found brought together elements of figuration so remote that the sheer absurdity of that collection provoked a sudden intensification of the visionary faculties in me and brought forth an illusive succession of contradictory images, double, triple and multiple images, piling up on each other with the persistence and rapidity which are peculiar to love memories and visions of half-asleep.

'These visions called themselves new planes, because of their meeting in a new unknown (the plane of non-agreement).' *Beyond Painting* (New York, 1948), quoted in *The Modern Tradition* (New York, 1965) ed. Richard Ellmann and Charles Feidelson Jr. p. 163.

† And perhaps not only human behaviour. Recent experiments in America in teaching chimpanzees sign-language have made impressive progress. The chimps are able spontaneously to combine the signs they have learned to describe novel situations, and it is reported that one chimp, Washoe, referred to a duck as 'water-bird' and another, Lucy, referred to a melon as 'candy-drink'—metonymic and metaphoric expressions, respectively. 'The Signs of Washoe', *Horizon*, BBC 2, 4 November, 1974.

‡ I think Hayden White fails to appreciate this point about dominance when he describes the metaphor-metonymy distinction as 'dualistic' (*Metahistory*, p. 33n.) He himself follows a more traditional fourfold distinction between the 'master-tropes' of Metaphor, Metonymy, Synecdoche and Irony, which he ingeniously combines with other fourfold classifications of Argument (Formism, Organicism, Mechanism, Contextualism) Emplotment (Romance, Comedy, Tragedy, Satire) and Ideology (Anarchism, Conservatism, Radicalism, Liberalism) to establish a typology of historiography. The symmetry of this apparatus is not without its disadvantages; in

both the difference between category A and category B and the difference between item X and item Y in category A. To make this point clear it is necessary to look more closely at some of Jakobson's pairings of opposites, and to follow up what are no more than cryptic hints in his paper. But first, for convenience of reference, the main points of the paper may be summarized in a schematic fashion by two lists:

METAPHOR	METONYMY
Paradigm	Syntagm
Similarity	Contiguity
Selection	Combination
Substitution	[Deletion] Contexture
Contiguity Disorder	Similarity Disorder
Contexture Deficiency	Selection Deficiency
Drama	Film
Montage	Close-up
Dream symbolism	Dream Condensation & Displacement
Surrealism	Cubism
Imitative Magic	Contagious Magic
Poetry	Prose
Lyric	Epic
Romanticism & Symbolism	Realism

4 Drama and Film

When Jakobson says that drama is essentially 'metaphoric' he is clearly thinking of the generic character of dramatic art as it has manifested itself throughout the history of culture. Arising out of religious ritual (in which a symbolic sacrifice was *substituted* for a real one) drama is correctly interpreted by its audience as being analogous to rather than directly imitative of reality, and has attained its highest achievements (in classical Greece, in Elizabethan England, in neoclassical France) by being poetic, using a language with a built-in emphasis on patterns of similarity and contrast (contrast being a kind of negative similarity). The 'unities' of classical tragedy are not means of producing a realistic

---

particular it entails a strong contrast between synecdoche (seen as essentially integrative, relating part to whole, and thus allied to metaphor) and metonymy (seen as essentially reductive, relating effect to cause, and allied to irony) which tends to blur the meaning of all four terms and thus limit their explanatory power.

D

illusion, but of bringing into a single frame of reference a constellation of events (say, Oedipus's birth, his killing of an old man, solving of a riddle, marriage) that were not contiguous in space or time but combine on the level of similarity (the old man is the same as the father, the wife is the same as the mother, the son is the same as the husband) to form a message of tragic import. Elizabethan drama is more obviously narrative than Greek tragedy (that is, more linear or syntagmatic in its construction) but its most distinctive formal feature, the double plot, is a device of similarity and contrast. The two plots of *King Lear* and the complex pairing and contrasting and disguising of characters in that play is a classic example of such dramatic structure, which generally has the effect of retarding, or distracting attention from, the chronological sequence of events. In the storm scene of *Lear*, for instance—one of the peaks of Shakespeare's dramatic achievement—there is no linear progress: nothing happens, really, except that the characters juggle with similarities and contrasts: between the weather and human life, between appearances and realities. And it is not only in *Lear* that the chain of sequentiality and causality in Shakespearean tragedy proves under scrutiny to be curiously insubstantial. Stephen Booth has convincingly demonstrated how the opening of *Hamlet* plunges us immediately into a field of paradoxes and non-sequiturs which we struggle in vain to unite into a coherent pattern of cause and effect[1] (hence, perhaps, the ease with which Tom Stoppard grafted on to it his more explicitly absurdist and metaphorical *Rosencrantz and Guildenstern Are Dead*). It is demonstrable that the plot of *Othello* allows no time in which Desdemona could have committed adultery with Cassio—but that anomaly doesn't matter, and is indeed rarely noticed in the theatre: the play is built on contrasts—Othello's blackness with Desdemona's whiteness, his jealousy against her innocence, his naivety against Iago's cunning—not cause-and-effect. Othello's self-justifying soliloquy, 'It is the cause, it is the cause, my soul' (V, ii, 1) carries a bitter irony, for there is no cause: not only is Desdemona innocent, but Iago's malice has no real motive (that is why it is so effective).

The naturalistic 'fourth wall' plays which have dominated the commercial stage in our era must be seen as a 'metonymic' deviation from the metaphoric norm which the drama displays when viewed in deep historical perspective. In naturalistic drama every action is realistically motivated, dramatic time is almost indistinguishable from real time, ('deletions' from the chronological sequence being marked by act or scene divisions) and the characters are set in a contextual space bounded and filled with real (or *trompe l'oeil* imitations of) objects—doors, windows, curtains, sofas, rugs—all arranged in the same relations of contiguity with each other and with the actors as they would be in reality. Such naturalism is, arguably, unnatural in the theatre. In reaction against it, many modern playwrights have put an extreme stress on the metaphoric dimension of drama. In Beckett's plays for instance, there is no progress through time, no logic of cause and effect, and the chintz and upholstery of drawing-rooms has given way to bare, stark acting spaces, with perhaps a chair, a row of dustbins and a high window from which nothing is visible (*End Game*). These plays offer themselves overtly as metaphors for the human condition, for on the literal level they are scarcely intelligible. Yet arguably *any* play, however naturalistic in style, is essentially metaphorical in that it is recognized as a *performance*: i.e. our pleasure in the play depends on our continuous and conscious awareness that we are spectators not of reality but of a conventionalized model of reality, constructed before us by actors who speak words not their own but provided by an invisible dramatist. The curtain call at which the actor who died in the last act takes his smiling bow is the conventional sign of this separation between the actors and their roles, between life and art.

The experience of watching a film is entirely different, notwithstanding the superficial similarity of modern theatre and cinema auditoria. There is, for example, no cinematic curtain call. Credits scarcely serve the same function: being written signs in an essentially non-literary medium their impact is comparatively weak, and often considerable ingenuity is used to make it even weaker, distracting our attention from the information the credits convey and integrating them into the film 'discourse' itself (by, for instance, delaying their introduction and/or by superimposing the words on scenic establishing shots or even action shots). Some films do attempt something like a curtain call at the end when they present a series of stills of the main actors with their real names superimposed, but these are invariably stills taken from the film itself, portraying the actor 'in character'—in other words the gap between performance and reality is not exposed.

Of course it is always possible for the film-maker to expose the artificiality of his production—Lindsay Anderson's *O Lucky Man*, for instance, ends with a celebration party on the set for actors and technicians, and Fellini likes to incorporate his cameras and other equipment into his pictures—but this is a highly deviant gesture in film. It is a commonplace that film creates an 'illusion of life' much more readily than drama. We are more likely to feel strong physical symptoms of pity, fear, etc. in the cinema than in the theatre, and this has little to do with aesthetic values. Whereas the play is created before us at every performance, the film is more like a record of something that happened, or is happening, only once. The camera and the microphone are voyeuristic instruments: they spy on, eavesdrop on experience and they can in effect follow the characters anywhere—out into the wilderness or into bed—without betraying their presence, so that nothing is easier for the film-maker than to create the illusion of reality. Of course film is still a system of signs, a conventional language that has to be learned (films are more or less unintelligible to primitive people never exposed to them before).[2] The oblong frame around the image does not correspond to the field of human vision, and the repertoire of cinematic shots—long-shot, close-up, wide-angle, etc.— bears only a schematic resemblance to human optics. Nevertheless, once the language of film has been acquired it *seems* natural: hence the thudding hearts, the moist eyes, in the stalls. We tend to take the camera eye for granted, and to accept the 'truth' of what it shows us even though its perspective is never exactly the same as human vision.

This verisimilitude can be explained as a function of the metonymic character of the film medium. We move through time and space lineally and our sensory experience is a succession of contiguities. The basic units of the film, the shot and the scene, are composed along the same line of contiguity and combination, and the devices by which the one-damn-thing-after-another of experience is rendered more dramatic and meaningful are characteristically metonymic devices that operate along the same axis: the synecdochic close-up that represents the whole by the part, the slow-motion sequence that retards without rupturing the natural tempo of successiveness, the high or low angle shot that 'defamiliarizes', without departing from, the action it is focused on. Consciousness is not, of course, bound to the line of spatio-temporal contiguity, in the way that sensory experience is, but then film does not deal very much or very effectively with consciousness except insofar as it is manifested in behaviour and speech, or can be reflected in landscape through the pathetic fallacy, or suggested by music on the sound track.

This does not mean that film has no metaphoric devices, or that it may not be pushed in the direction of metaphorical structure. Jakobson categorizes montage as metaphoric, presumably because it juxtaposes images on the basis of their similarity (or contrast) rather than their contiguity in space-time. However, the fact that the techniques of cutting and splicing by which montage is achieved are also the techniques of all film editing, by which any film of the least degree of sophistication is composed, creates the possibility of confusion here. John Harrington, for example, in his *The Rhetoric of Film*, defines montage as

> a rhetorical arrangement of juxtaposed shots. The combination, or gestalt, produces an idea by combining the visual elements of two dissimilar images. A longing face, for instance, juxtaposed to a turkey dinner suggests hunger. Or the image of a fox following that of a man making a business deal would indicate slyness. Segments of film working together to create a single idea have no counterpart in nature; their juxtaposition occurs through the editor's imaginative yoke.[3]

The main drift of this definition confirms Jakobson's classification of montage as metaphorical, but the first of Harrington's examples is in fact metonymic or synecdochic in Jakobson's sense: longing faces and turkey dinners *are* found together in nature (i.e. real contexts) and all that has been done in this hypothetical montage is to delete some of the links (*e.g.* a window) in a chain of contiguities that would link the face with the turkey. The fox and the businessman, on the other hand, are not contiguous in nature, but are connected in the montage through a suggested similarity of behaviour, as in the verbal metaphor 'a foxy businessman'. Context is all-important. If the montage of longing face and turkey dinner described by Harrington were in a film adaptation of *A Christmas Carol*, we should interpret it metonymically; if it were interpolated in a documentary about starving animals, it would be metaphoric. Those favourite filmic metaphors for sexual intercourse in the pre-permissive cinema, skyrockets and waves pounding on the shore, could be disguised as metonymic background if the consummation were taking place on a beach on Independence Day, but would be perceived as overtly metaphorical if it were taking place on Christmas Eve in a city penthouse.

Eisenstein himself included in the concept of montage juxtapositions that are metonymic as well as metaphoric:

> The juxtaposition of two separate shots by splicing them together resembles not so much a simple sum of one shot plus another shot—as it does a *creation* . . . each montage piece exists no longer as something unrelated, but as a given *particular representation* of the general theme that in equal measure penetrates all the shot-pieces. The juxtaposition of these partial details in a given montage construction calls to life and forces into the light that *general* quality in which each detail has participated and which binds together all the details into a whole, namely, into that generalized *image*, wherein the creator, followed by the spectator, experiences the theme. . . . What exactly is this process? A given order of hands on the dial of a clock invokes a host of representations associated with the time that corresponds to the given order. Suppose, for example, the given figure be five. Our imagination is trained to respond to this figure by calling to mind pictures of all sorts of events that occur at that hour. Perhaps tea, the end of the day's work, the beginning of rush hour on the subway, perhaps shops closing, or the peculiar late afternoon light. . . . In any case we will automatically recall a series of pictures (representations) of what happens at five o'clock. The image of five o'clock is compounded of all these individual pictures.[4]

Translated into film such a montage of 'five o'clock' would be metonymic or synecdochic rather than metaphorical, representing the whole by parts, parts which are contiguous (because they belong to a larger complex of phenomena taking place at the same time) rather than similar. This is confirmed by Eisenstein's use of the word 'condensation' a few lines later: 'There occurs "condensation" within the process above described: the chain of intervening links falls away, and there is produced instantaneous connection between the figure and our perception of the time to which it corresponds.'[5]

Condensation, it will be recalled, belongs to the metonymic axis in Jakobson's scheme.

Eisenstein was not so much concerned with the difference between metaphoric and metonymic montage as with the difference between montage in general, and what he calls 'representation'—the photographing of an action from a single set-up by a simple accumulation of 'one shot plus another shot'—the cinematic equivalent of non-rhetorical, referential language in verbal discourse. Though celebrated for his daring use of the overtly metaphorical montage (e.g. soldiers being gunned down juxtaposed to cattle being slaughtered, Kerensky juxtaposed with a peacock) Eisenstein was comparatively sparing in his use of the device[6] (*Battleship Potemkin*, for instance, has no fully metaphorical montage though, as Roy Armes points out, the juxtaposition of shots of the three lions, one lying, one sitting and one roaring in the Odessa Steps sequence, creates the impression of a lion coming to life and 'conveyed the idea of protest—with an emotional meaning something like "Even the very stones cried out" '[7]) for the simple reason that if it becomes the main principle of composition in a film, narrative is more or less impossible to sustain. 'Underground' movies define themselves as deviant by deliberately resisting the natural metonymic tendency of the medium, either by a total commitment to montage, bombarding us with images between which there are only paradigmatic relations of similarity and contrast, or by parodying and frustrating the syntagm, setting the naturally linear and 'moving' medium against an unmoving object—the Empire State Building, for instance, or a man sleeping. Poetic drama, as I suggested earlier, is also in a paradoxical sense unmoving, nonprogressive, more concerned with paradigmatic similarities and contrasts than with syntagmatic sequence and cause-and-effect. The peculiar resistance of Shakespearian drama to successful translation into film, despite its superficial abundance of cinematic assets (exotic settings, duels, battles, pageantry etc.) is notorious; and one may confidently assert that the same difficulty would be still more acutely felt in any attempt to film Beckett's plays.* Even modern naturalistic drama (e.g. Albee's *Who's Afraid of Virginia Woolf* or Neil Simon's *The Odd Couple*) seems slightly ill-at-ease in the film medium, and

---

*It is noteworthy that Beckett's one screenplay, for a short film entitled *Film*, made in 1964 with Buster Keaton in the main role, is quite different in structure from his plays, though just as 'experimental' and aesthetically self-conscious. There is plenty of action and no dialogue. Event succeeds event in a logical time/space continuum. The camera follows a man along a street and up some stairs to a room; whenever the camera eye threatens to get a view of the man's face he displays anxiety and takes evasive action. In the room he banishes or covers all objects with eyes—animals, pictures, etc. But while he is dozing the camera eye stealthily moves round to view his face. The man wakes and registers horror at being observed. A cinematic 'cut' identifies the observer as the man himself 'but with a very different expression, impossible to describe, neither severity nor benignity, but rather acute *intentness*'. (Samuel Beckett, *Film* (1972) p. 47.)

most obviously so when it deserts the economical single setting for which it was originally designed, to take advantage of the freedom of location afforded by film. The two media seem to pull against each other. The realistic novel, on the other hand, converts very easily into film—and novelists were in fact presenting action cinematically long before the invention of the moving-picture camera. Consider this passage from George Eliot's first published work of fiction, 'The Sad Misfortunes of Amos Barton':

> Look at him as he winds through the little churchyard! The silver light that falls aslant on church and tomb, enables you to see his slim, black figure, made all the slimmer by tight pantaloons, as it flits past the pale gravestones. He walks with a quick step, and is now rapping with sharp decision at the vicarage door. It is opened without delay by the nurse, cook and housemaid, all at once—that is to say by the robust maid of all work, Nanny; and as Mr Barton hangs up his hat in the passage, you see that a narrow face of no particular complexion—even the smallpox that has attacked it seems to have been of a mongrel, indefinite kind—with features of no particular shape, and an eye of no particular expression, is surmounted by a slope of baldness gently rising from brow to crown. You judge him, rightly, to be about forty. . . .[8]

The passage continues in the same style: Barton opens the sitting-room door and, looking over his shoulder as it were, we see his wife Milly pacing up and down by the light of the fire, comforting the baby. Change George Eliot's 'you' to 'we' and the passage would read not unlike a film scenario. The action certainly breaks down very readily into a sequence of 'shots': *high-angle crane shot of Barton walking through churchyard; cut to door of vicarage opened by Nanny; close-up of Barton's face as he hangs up his hat* . . . and so on. In one respect the passage requires the cinema for its full realization: the charmless, yet human, ordinariness of Barton's physiognomy—the ordinariness which is unloveable yet which (George Eliot insists) we must learn to love—is a quality the cinema can convey very powerfully and immediately, whereas George Eliot can only indicate it verbally by means of negations. There is little doubt, I think, that George Eliot would have been deeply interested in the possibilities offered by the motion-picture camera of capturing the human significance of the commonplace: as it was, she had to appeal, as a visual analogy for her art, to the static pictures of the Dutch painters.[9]

5 Poetry, Prose and the Poetic

Jakobson's characterization of prose as 'forwarded essentially by contiguity' is consistent with the commonsense view that prose is the appropriate medium with which to describe logical relationships between concepts or entities or events. The formal rules of poetry (i.e. verse)—metre, rhyme, stanzaic form etc.—are based upon relationships of *similarity* and cut across the logical progression of discourse. The physical appearance of prose and verse in print illustrates the distinction: the end of a line of prose is arbitrary and of zero significance—the line ends merely so that the text may be accommodated on the printed page (there is no reason other than convenience why prose should not be printed on a continuous strip of paper like ticker tape) and the justification of margins is a visible sign that we should ignore line length in reading prose. The important spaces in the printed prose text are those of punctuation, which are directly related to the sense of the discourse. In verse, on the other hand, the separation of one line from another, made visible on the printed page by the irregular right-hand margin and the capital at the commencement of each new line, is a crucially important component of the discourse, which may be exploited either to support or to contrast with the punctuation according to sense. Jonathan Culler points out that 'If one takes a piece of banal journalistic prose and sets it down on a page as a lyric poem, surrounded by intimidating margins of silence, the words remain the same but their effects for readers are substantially altered.'[1]

The elaborate phonological patterning of poetry, though not in itself semantically motivated, makes metaphor, as Jakobson puts it, 'the line of least resistance' for poetry. Rhyme illustrates the point most clearly, for effective rhyme in poetry, as W. K. Wimsatt observed, consists not in pairing words of similar sound and closely parallel meanings, but in pairing words of similar sound and widely divergent meanings, or with contrasting associations, or having different grammatical functions, e.g. Pope's:

> One speaks the glory of the British Queen,
> And one describes a charming Indian screen.

or

> What dire offence from am'rous causes springs,
> What mighty contests rise from trivial things.[2]

As Roland Barthes puts it: 'rhyming coincides with a transgression of the law of distance between the syntagm and the system (Trnka's law); it corresponds to a deliberately created tension between the congenial and the dissimilar, to a kind of structural scandal.'[3]

Rhyme, in its combination of similarity and dissimilarity, is thus equivalent to metaphor, and is often contrived *by* metaphor, i.e. the two rhyming words are combined through a metaphorical substitution. If we look at the compositional process we can see that the prose writer and the poet are quite differently situated. Both set out to tell a story or expound an argument (all writing must in a sense do one or both of these things) but the poet is constantly diverted from combining items in a natural, logical or temporal succession by the arbitrary demands of the metrical form he has elected to employ. Rhyme, especially, is apt to prevent the poet from saying what he originally intended to say, and to lead him to say something that he would not otherwise have thought of saying. This is well known to anyone who has ever tried to write regular verse, though it is rarely admitted, as though there were something vaguely shameful about it. Of course, if the sense is completely controlled by the exigences of metre and rhyme, doggerel and nonsense result. Successful poetry is that which manages to fulfil all the requirements of a complex, purely formal pattern of sound and at the same time to seem an utterly inevitable expression of its meaning:

> I said, 'A line will take us hours, maybe;
> Yet if it does not seem a moment's thought,
> Our stitching and unstitching has been naught'.[4]

Sometimes this process of stitching and unstitching will lead the poet so far from his original design that the final draft of the poem is unrecognizable from the first; invariably he will be obliged to follow his original line of argument or narrative in an oblique or convoluted fashion, deviating from it and returning to it via metaphorical digression:

> O Wild West Wind, thou breath of Autumn's being,
> Thou from whose unseen presence the leaves dead
> Are driven like ghosts from an enchanter fleeing,
>
> Yellow, and black, and pale and hectic red,
> Pestilence-stricken multitudes! O thou
> Who chariotest to their dark wintry bed
>
> The winged seeds, where they lie cold and low,
> Each like a corpse within its grave, until
> Thine azure sister of the Spring shall blow

Her clarion o'er the dreaming earth, and fill
(Driving sweet buds like flocks to feed in air)
With living hues and odours plain and hill;

Wild Spirit, which art moving everywhere;
Destroyer and preserver; hear, O hear!

Although rhyme is only one of the poetic devices involved here, it is surely doubtful that Shelley's apostrophe would have been so extended or so rich in imagery, or that it would have developed in precisely this way, if it had not been expressed in *terza rima*, in which the second line of each stanza dictates the rhyme of the first and third lines in the next stanza.

The progress and final shape of a prose composition is not necessarily more predictable—one always discovers what it is one has to say in the process of saying it—but this is because of the plurality of contiguities in any given context. In describing a given event (say, a hanging) we cannot record all the relationships between all the items in the context (the context being in any case theoretically infinite); we are obliged to choose at every stage of the discourse to report this detail rather than that, make this connection rather than that. But the combination of discrete items is almost completely under the writer's semantic control—it is not subject to arbitrary and complex phonological requirements as in verse. I say 'almost' because there is, clearly, such a thing as prose rhythm, however difficult to analyse, and other phonological values enter into prose composition and exert some influence over the choice and combination of words (e.g. the obligation to *avoid* rhyming); but it is an infinitely more flexible and less rigorous system of restraints than operates in poetry, where the natural impulse of discourse to thrust onwards and generate new sentences is checked and controlled by the obligation to *repeat* again and again a certain pattern of sounds, syllables, stresses and pauses. The 'poetic function [of language]' Jakobson stated in his paper 'Linguistics and Poetics', 'projects the principle of equivalence from the axis of selection into the axis of combination.'[5]

This is one of Jakobson's most celebrated and often-quoted pronouncements, but there is a difficulty about the word 'poetic' here which has not, I think, been generally recognized: in theory it embraces the whole of literature; in this paper, however, it is applied almost exclusively to verse composition. 'Poetics', Jakobson states at the beginning of his paper, 'deals primarily with the question, *What makes a verbal message a work of art?*' and his answer, already referred to in Part One, is that 'The set (*Einstellung*) towards the MESSAGE as such, focus on the message for its own sake, is the POETIC function of language.'[6] He is quick to point out (following Mukařovský on foregrounding) that the poetic function is not *peculiar* to poetic messages (it occurs in advertising, political slogans and ordinary speech) but is their 'dominant, determining function, whereas in all other verbal activities it acts as a subsidiary, accessory constituent.'[7] How does the poetic function focus attention on the message for its own sake? Jakobson answers with the formula just quoted: 'The poetic function projects the principle of equivalence from the axis of selection into the axis of combination.' He continues:

> Equivalence is promoted to the constitutive device of the sequence. In poetry one syllable is equalized with any other syllable of the same sequence; word stress is assumed to equal word stress, as unstress equals unstress; prosodic long is matched with long, and short with short; word boundary equals word boundary; no boundary equals no boundary; syntactic pause equals syntactic pause, no pause equals no pause. Syllables are converted into units of equal measure, and so are morae or stresses.[8]

While the paper sets out to define 'literariness' in general, this passage seems to identify 'poetry' with metrical composition. Certainly if literature (verbal message as work of art) is characterized by the dominance of the poetic function of language, and the poetic function is dominated by 'equivalence', the whole theory of what constitutes 'literariness' is heavily biased towards verse rather than prose literature. Not surprisingly most of Jakobson's article is taken up with (highly perceptive) analysis of verse writing, with particular attention to phonological patterning. Though he produces examples of the poetic function in nonliterary discourse (e.g. the complex paronomasia of *I like Ike*, and the principle of syllable gradation that makes us prefer 'Joan and Margery to Margery and Joan') he does not face the question of what makes the verbal message in prose a work of art until almost at the end of his paper:

> 'Verseless composition', as Hopkins calls the prose variety of verbal art— where parallelisms are not so strictly marked and strictly regular as 'continuous parallelism' and where there is no dominant figure of sound— presents more entangled problems for poetics, as does any transitional linguistic area. In this case the transition is between strictly poetic and strictly referential language. But Propp's pioneering monograph on the structure of the fairy tale shows us how a consistently syntactic approach may be of paramount help even in classifying the traditional plots and in tracing the puzzling laws that underlie their composition and selection. The new studies of Lévi-Strauss display a much deeper but essentially similar approach to the same constructional problem.
>
> It is no mere chance that metonymic structures are less explored than the field of metaphor. May I repeat my old observation that the study of poetic tropes has been directed mainly towards metaphor, and the so-called realistic literature, intimately tied with the metonymic principle, still defies interpretation, although the same linguistic methodology, which poetics uses when analysing the metaphorical style of romantic poetry, is entirely applicable to the metonymical texture of realistic prose.[9]

This is a puzzling and tantalizing passage. The reference to 'the entangled problems' presented by the 'transitional linguistic area' of prosaic verbal art may seem evasive—or patronizing towards such art. We do not, after all, feel any less confident of classifying *Middlemarch* as literature than *In Memoriam*, and a comprehensive poetics should be able to tell us why. The allusions to Propp and Lévi-Strauss are not really relevant to this problem because these analysts deal with narrative structures abstracted from any particular verbalization, whether in prose or verse. Jakobson seems to acknowledge this lacuna in his argument in the second paragraph, where he invokes his earlier distinction between metaphoric and metonymic writing, but it is a curiously cryptic acknowledgment. Why does realistic literature continue to 'defy interpretation' if metonymy is the key to it? Why doesn't Jakobson himself analyse some examples of this kind of writing in this paper? The answer to these questions is perhaps to be found in the discrepancy between 'Linguistics and Poetics' and the earlier paper on the two aspects of language, namely that the latter implied a concept of literariness ('poetry', verbal message as art) that included *both* metaphoric and metonymic types, but 'Linguistics and Poetics' identifies literariness with only *one* type, the metaphoric. The projection of 'the principle of equivalence from the axis of selection into the axis of combination', offered as a definition of the poetic function in 'Linguistics and Poetics', is in fact a definition of metaphorical substitution according to the linguistic theory of 'Two Aspects of Language'.

Jakobson is more explicit about the problem in the last paragraph of this earlier paper. There he points out that research into poetics has been biased towards metaphor for two reasons. First, the relationship between tenor and vehicle in metaphor is paralleled by the relationship between language and metalanguage, both operating on the basis of similarity. 'Consequently, when constructing a metalanguage to interpret tropes, the researcher possesses more homogeneous means to handle metaphor, whereas metonymy, based on a different principle, easily defies interpretation. Therefore nothing comparable to the rich literature on metaphor can be cited for the theory of metonymy.' The second reason is that 'since poetry is focused upon sign, and pragmatical prose mainly upon referent, tropes and figures were studied mainly as poetic devices' and poetry (i.e. verse) is innately metaphorical in structure. 'Consequently the study of poetical tropes is directed chiefly towards metaphor. The actual bipolarity has been artificially replaced in these studies by an amputated, unipolar scheme which, strikingly enough, coincides with one of the two aphasic patterns, namely with contiguity disorder.'[10] After this laconic observation, it is a little surprising that Jakobson should have perpetuated the 'amputated, unipolar' approach in his later paper on linguistics and poetics.

But one can appreciate the difficulties. To preserve the binary character of the general theory, there ought to be some formula parallel to 'the projection of the principle of equivalence from the axis of selection into the axis of combination' that would describe the *metonymic* aspect of the poetic function. Logically, this ought to be: 'the projection of the principle of contiguity from the axis of combination into the axis of selection'. But if we interpret this formula in the strong sense, as a deviant or foregrounded manoeuvre, we find that it applies to verbal errors characteristic of the similarity disorder, such as saying *fork* for *knife*, *table* for *lamp*, *smoke* for *pipe* etc., of which Jakobson observed, 'Such metonymies may be characterized as projections from the line of a habitual context into the line of substitution and selection.' And if we interpret the formula in the weak sense, to mean simply that contiguity, or context, controls the field of selection, then we have nothing more than a simple description of the way ordinary referential discourse works. This is in fact what we might expect, since literature written in the metonymic mode tends to disguise itself as nonliterature (cf. 'A Hanging') but it does not help us to accommodate such writing in a linguistically-based poetics. On the contrary it would licence us to discuss such literature entirely in terms of its content.

6   Types of Description

I suggested earlier (p. 76) that metonymy and synecdoche, considered as verbal tropes, are transformations of literal kernel statements produced by a process of combination and nonlogical deletion. This would seem to correspond to what we commonly refer to as a novelist's 'selection' of details in narrative description. Such details, E. B. Greenwood claims, 'are surrogates . . . for the mass of observed detail which would have been there in actuality.'* If, then, the appropriate critical response to the metaphoric text is to construct a metalanguage that will do justice to its system of equivalences, the appropriate response to the metonymic text would seem to be an attempt to restore the deleted detail, to put the text back into the total context from which it derives. And indeed the most familiar kind of criticism of the

---

*'Critical Forum', *Essays in Criticism* XII (July 1962) pp. 341–2. Greenwood was contributing to a discussion of F. W. Bateson's and B. Shakevitch's commentary, published in an earlier issue of the same journal, on a story by Katherine Mansfield. Greenwood actually applied the terms metonymy and synecdoche to descriptive detail in realistic fiction, without, it would appear, being aware of Jakobson's theory. I, certainly, was not when I quoted Greenwood's remark in *Language of Fiction* (pp. 43–4).

realistic novel follows precisely this path. The critical commentary is
not so much an analysis of the novel's system as a witness to its
truthfulness, or representativeness, its contribution to, and
consistency with, the sum of human knowledge and human wisdom.
Up to a point such a procedure is natural and indeed inevitable in
discussing realistic fiction, and literary education in schools rightly
begins by teaching students how to do criticism at this level. But such a
procedure can never supply the basis for a 'poetics' of fiction because
its essential orientation is towards content rather than form. At its
worst it merely regurgitates what the novelist himself has expressed
more eloquently and pointedly. Perhaps this is what Jakobson means
when he says that realistic literature 'defies interpretation'.

Characterizing the realistic text as metonymic need not, however,
lead us to adopt such a critical procedure if we remember that
metonymy is a figure of *nonlogical* deletion. This is where we may
locate a specifically literary motivation for the selection of detail. Since
we cannot describe everything in a given context, we select certain
items at the expense of not selecting others: this is true of all discourse.
But in discourse with no 'poetic' coloration at all, (Jakobson's
'pragmatic prose') the selection of items is based on purely logical
principles: what is present implies what is absent, the whole stands for
the part, the thing for its attributes, unless the part or attribute is itself
vital to the message, in which case it is brought into the message as a
whole or thing in its own right. Here, for instance, is an American
desk-encyclopaedia entry on the city of Birmingham, England:

BIRMINGHAM (bur'ming-um) second largest English city (pop.
1,112,340) Warwickshire; a great industrial centre. Covers 80 sq. mi. Has
iron and coal nearby and is noted for metal mfg. Most of Britain's brass and
bronze coins minted here. Utilities and a bank are city owned. Has noted
city orchestra. Site of Anglican and Roman Catholic cathedrals and Univ. of
Birmingham. Heavily bombed World War II.[1]

In reference books of this type, space is at a premium, so abbreviations
and elliptical syntax are used whenever words and letters can be
omitted without causing confusion. This graphological and syntactical
condensation is representative of the way the text is organized
semantically. It does not, for instance, tell us that the skyline of
Birmingham displays many factory chimneys—that is implied by
'great industrial centre'. 'Utilities' includes several agencies and
services, but not banks, so the bank has to be mentioned separately.
Birmingham is not noted for the arts generally, only for its orchestra,
so the orchestra is specified; but we are not told anything about the
orchestra and therefore infer that it is an ordinary symphony
orchestra. In short, the general only yields to the particular when it
does not adequately imply the particular, and the particular never
represents the general—except insofar as the whole catalogue of facts

collectively 'represents' the real city. The text is therefore metonymic only in the sense that it is not metaphoric. It has selected certain details rather than others and combined them together—but any text must do the same. The point is that there is nothing figurative or rhetorical in the mode of selection and combination corresponding to the actual tropes of metonymy and synecdoche. The article is not, of course, a neutral or objective account of Birmingham, just because it *is* selective. But the selection of information, it is safe to assume, is governed by the general conventions and utilitarian purpose of the encyclopaedia rather than by the particular interests and observations of the author, or any design upon the reader's emotions. As a message it is orientated almost entirely towards context; or, in other words, it is referential. Compare this:

> Most students who come to Birmingham are agreeably surprised by their first view of the campus. Steeled to expect an environment of unrelieved industrial sprawl and squalor, they find the University situated on a fine, spacious site, its oddly but interestingly assorted architecture not noticeably stained by soot, surrounded on most sides by the leafy residential roads and green spaces of Edgbaston, a rare example of an inner suburb that has kept its privacy in a modern city.
>
> On one side of the campus, however, the factory chimneys and mean terraced cottages of Selly Oak strike a note more characteristic of 'Brum'. At the Bournbrook gate, indeed, as if by symbolic intent, one small factory (which seems, on acoustic evidence, to be breaking rather than making things) edges right up against the University grounds. Overalled men, stunned by the din inside, emerge occasionally to breathe fresh air, draw on a fag, and stare quizzically at the scholars passing in and out of academe. Whatever illusions life at Birmingham University may foster, the ivory tower mentality is not likely to be one of them.[2]

These are the opening paragraphs of an article published in the *Guardian*, 9 October, 1967, in a series on British Universities entitled 'A Guide for the First Year Student'. It was orientated to a much more specific audience than the encyclopaedia article (not merely Birmingham University first-year students, of course, but *Guardian* readers in general, especially those interested in higher education). And although written by an anonymous 'correspondent', it obviously expressed a more individualized and personal point of view than the encyclopaedia article. Comparing the two texts, one immediately notices how much the *Guardian* article depends on metonymical devices of an overtly rhetorical kind—for example, synecdoche in, 'leafy residential roads and green spaces of Edgbaston' and 'the factory chimneys and mean terraced cottages of Selly Oak'. Parts stand for wholes in these formulations, and they do so with a certain affective and thematic intent. It would have been just as 'true' to the facts to have said, 'the silent streets and hushed houses of Edgbaston' and 'the busy pavements and snug back-to-backs of Selly Oak'; but that would not have served the writer's purpose, which was to set up an opposition between (A) suburban-pastoral and (B) urban-industrial environments. In the first paragraph, the expectation of B is corrected by the experience of A, and in the second paragraph this recognition is in turn corrected by the experience of B: a kind of double peripeteia. The passage reads more smoothly than the encyclopaedia article not simply because it eschews abbreviations and ellipses, but because it combines items in a sequence that both corresponds to their natural contiguity and supports the text's theme. The description in a sense imitates the physical process of exploring the campus, approaching it from the Edgbaston side, and finishing at its border with Selly Oak—where the implied explorer is himself, as it were, observed by the quizzical workers (synecdochically evoked by their overalls and fags). In comparison, the items in the encyclopaedia article are 'contiguous' only in the sense of being connected with the same place—Birmingham. At first unified by what one might call an 'industrial theme', that text quickly disintegrates into a series of heterogeneous facts.

These distinctions are not intended as comparative value-judgments. The two passages have quite different ends in view, and it may well be that the encyclopaedia article does its job better. But there is no doubt, I think, that the *Guardian* piece is more 'literary', and that this is directly traceable to the fact that it exploits metonymic form (both at and above the level of the sentence) for optional, expressive purposes, whereas the encyclopaedia article only uses metonymic procedures inasmuch as it has to, and because it has to.

Am I then claiming that the *Guardian* text is 'literature'? That question could only be answered by putting the passage back into its original context—the entire article, which in fact becomes much more like an encyclopaedia article as it goes on. So my answer would be, no. There is not the kind of systematic internal foregrounding through the whole text which would allow it to sustain a literary reading. Those first two paragraphs do, however, exhibit within themselves a systematic foregrounding of detail, and could conceivably be the opening of a novel, without any revision at all.*

Let us look now at a couple of classic fictional descriptions of cities. They both occur at the beginnings of their respective texts. The first is from E. M. Forster's *A Passage to India*.

Except for the Marabar Caves—and they are twenty miles off—the city of Chandrapore presents nothing extraordinary. Edged rather than washed by the river Ganges, it trails for a couple of miles along the bank, scarcely

---

*The encyclopaedia article could of course also provide the opening to a novel—Kingsley Amis's *The Green Man* (1969) begins with a clever pastiche of an entry in the *Good Food Guide*—but such a novel could not possibly continue for long in the same mode: the encyclopaedia article could only serve as a prelude or foil to the main narrative.

distinguishable from the rubbish it deposits so freely. There are no bathing steps on the river-front, and bazaars shut out the wide and shifting panorama of the stream. The streets are mean, the temples ineffective, and though a few fine houses exist they are hidden away in gardens or down alleys whose filth deters all but the invited guest. Chandrapore was never large or beautiful, but two hundred years ago it lay on the road between Upper India, then imperial, and the sea, and the fine houses date from that period. The zest for decoration stopped in the eighteenth century, nor was it ever democratic. There is no painting and scarcely any carving in the bazaars. The very wood seems made of mud, the inhabitants of mud moving. So abased, so monotonous is everything that meets the eye, that when the Ganges comes down it might be expected to wash the excrescence back into the soil. Houses do fall, people are drowned and left rotting, but the general outline of the town persists, swelling here, shrinking there, like some low but indestructible form of life.[3]

A Passage to India might be described as a symbolist novel disguised as a realistic one, and realistic writing, as we have already seen, tends to disguise itself as nonliterary writing. This opening paragraph certainly achieves its effect of knowledgability and authenticity partly by skilfully imitating the tone and method of the guidebook or travel essay. Yet the passage mentions only three specific topographical items—the Marabar Caves (very deliberately nudged into the prime position by syntactical inversion), Chandrapore itself, and the Ganges. The other substantives are mostly vaguely generalized plurals— bazaars, temples, streets, alleys, fine houses, gardens. There are no overt metonymies and synecdoches of the kind commonly found in travel writing to evoke 'atmosphere' and local colour. The reason for this is obvious: Chandrapore (that is, the original, native city—for the second paragraph goes on to draw a contrasting picture of the suburbs dominated by the British civil station) *has* no local colour, no atmosphere, except that of neglect, monotony and dirt; and to have evoked these qualities by metonymy and synecdoche, to have made them concrete and sensible, would have been to risk making them positive and picturesque. The dominant note of the description is negativity and absence: *nothing extraordinary—scarcely distinguishable . . . no bathing steps . . . happens not to be holy . . . no river front . . . shut out . . . temples ineffective . . . deters . . . never large or beautiful . . . stopped . . . nor was it ever democratic . . . no painting and scarcely any carving . . .* The only overtly metaphorical expressions enforce the same theme: *The very wood seems made of mud, the inhabitants of mud moving . . . like some low but indestructible form of life.**

If the passage has no metonymic and few metaphorical tropes, what

*These are of course similes, not metaphors proper. Although Jakobson does not comment on simile as such it must belong on the metaphorical side of his bipolar scheme since it is generated by the perception of similarity, but it does not involve substitution in the same radical sense as metaphor. For this reason it is more easily assimilated into metonymic modes of writing. For a fuller discussion of this point see below pp. 112–13

is its rhetoric, and why does it remind us of guidebook writing? I think the answer is to be found in the schemes of repetition, balance and antithesis—especially isocolon (repetition of phrases of equal length and usually corresponding construction): *edged rather than washed . . . the streets are mean, the temples ineffective . . . no painting and scarcely any carving . . . The very wood seems made of mud, the inhabitants of mud moving. So abased, so monotonous . . . Houses do fall, people are drowned . . . swelling here, shrinking there . . .* These patterns of words and word order, and the rhythms and cadences they create, are very like the 'figures of sound' that Jakobson analyses in poetry, and they are perhaps the nearest thing in prose to 'the projection of the principle of equivalence from the axis of selection into the axis of combination'. Their familiarity in travelogue and guidebook writing is a good example of the appearance of the 'poetic function' in nonpoetic discourse. In such writing rhetorical patterning provides a certain aesthetic pleasure—the pleasure that inheres in all rhythm—which is supplementary to the interest of the information conveyed and separable from it—in Jakobson's phrase it 'acts as a subsidiary, accessory constituent'.[4] It has a general effect of humanizing the discourse by imparting to it a homogeneous tone of voice and of enabling graceful transitions between discrete facts, thus making the text generally more accessible and assimilable, or in common parlance more 'readable'. The encyclopaedia article on Birmingham could be recast in such a style without any significant modification of the information conveyed (and would indeed have to be so recast if it were an article of any length). But it would be quite impossible to recast Forster's description into the style of the encyclopaedia without loss or change of effect because his tone of voice is inextricably part of the paragraph's meaning. The elegant syntactical inversions, pointed antitheses, delicate cadences, artful repetitions, are not merely wrapping up the facts in a pleasing package, but are at every point organizing and presenting the 'facts' in a way which will emphasize the underlying theme of negativity and absence.

This is still not quite a case of 'projection of the principle of equivalence from the axis of selection into the axis of combination', however. The rhetorical paradigms do not actually intrude into, or divert or frustrate or cut across the syntagmatic continuity of the discourse (in the manner of stanzaic form in poetry)—they collaborate with it. With due respect to Pope, it is in prose not verse that the sound should be an echo to the sense. If this happens consistently in verse, a trite jingle results. Conversely, if phonological patterning is allowed to dominate sense in prose, as in Euphuistic writing, the result is freakish and ultimately self-defeating. Between these two extremes there is plenty of room for verse to shift in the direction of prose norms and vice versa; but the opening of *A Passage to India* is not 'poetic' prose. It is metonymic writing, not metaphoric, even though it contains a few metaphors and no metonymies; it is metonymic in structure, connecting topics on the basis of contiguity not similarity. The description of Chandrapore begins with the river Ganges, then proceeds to the river banks, then to the bazaars which are built along the river banks, then to the streets and alleys that lead away from the river, with the occasional fine houses and gardens. There the description pauses for a brief historical digression (temporal rather than spatial contiguities) before reversing itself and proceeding back from the houses to the bazaars and eventually to the river. Thus the whole paragraph is a kind of chiasmus pivoting on the historical digression, its symmetrical structure duplicating on a larger scale the dominant figures of repetition and balance within individual sentences. Ending, topographically, where it began, it mimics the defeat of the observer's quest for something 'extraordinary' in the city of Chandrapore.

Another example:

London. Michaelmas Term lately over, and the Lord Chancellor sitting in Lincoln's Inn Hall. Implacable November weather. As much mud in the streets, as if the waters had but newly retired from the face of the earth, and it would not be wonderful to meet a Megalosaurus, forty feet long or so, waddling like an elephantine lizard up Holborn Hill. Smoke lowering down from chimneypots, making a soft black drizzle, with flakes of soot in it as big as full-grown snow-flakes—gone into mourning, one might imagine, for the death of the sun. Dogs, undistinguishable in mire. Horses, scarcely better; splashed to their very blinkers. Foot passengers, jostling one another's umbrellas, in a general infection of ill-temper, and losing their foothold at street corners, where tens of thousands of other foot-passengers have been slipping and sliding since the day broke (if this day ever broke) adding new deposits to the crust upon crust of mud, sticking at those points tenaciously to the pavement, and accumulating at compound interest.[5]

This is prose pushed much further towards the metaphoric pole than any of the other examples. The basic structure is a catalogue of contiguous items, but there is a marked tendency for the items to be elaborated metaphorically rather than represented metonymically. The text accelerates rapidly from brief, literal statements to the personification of the November weather ('implacable') then to the fantastic vision of the Megalosaurus and the apocalyptic vision of the death of the sun (metaphorical time-trips to the beginning and end of creation, respectively).* Then the paragraph, so to speak, comes down

---

*The reference to 'waters . . . newly retired from the face of the earth' is ambiguous in that it could allude either to the separation of the waters from the dry land at the Creation (*Genesis* i, 9–10) or to the aftermath of the Flood (*Genesis* viii, 7–17). Verbally the latter passage is more closely echoed, but thematically the other interpretation is more satisfying. In either reading the image yokes together Biblical and modern scientific versions of prehistory in a very striking way, as Mrs J. Politi has observed in a discussion of this passage (*The Novel and its Presuppositions*, Amsterdam, 1976, pp. 201–2). She points to a similar double perspective in the image of the death of the sun, which both echoes Biblical prophecy ('The sun shall be darkened in his going forth'—*Isaiah*, xiii,

to earth again, starts a new sequence of short, literal descriptive details (dogs, horses, umbrellas) but it is not long before the literal mud has generated a new metaphorical excursion. It is perhaps worth comparing this image of the mud 'accumulating at compound interest' with Forster's 'the very wood seems made of mud, the inhabitants of mud moving'. The metaphorical force of the latter is far more muted because of the contextual relationship between tenor and vehicle: with the Ganges present in the scene, mud does not seem an incongruous or unexpected source of analogy. The wood and the people are in fact in physical contact with (contiguous to) the mud with which they are compared. In Dickens, the mud is the tenor of the metaphor, and the vehicle, 'compound interest' has no such physical contiguity with it—and could not have since it is an abstraction. There *is*, however, a contextual relationship of a kind, and one that has been often pointed out; namely, that the setting is the City of London, dedicated to making money ('filthy lucre' in the proverbial phrase) and that the misery caused by the Court of Chancery, which is one of the main themes of the novel, derives from greed for money. Thus, through the conceit, 'accumulating at compound interest', the mud appears to be not merely an attribute of London in November, but an attribute of its institutions: it becomes a kind of metaphorical metonymy, or as we more commonly say, a symbol. The symbolic significance of the mud (as of the fog introduced in the next paragraph) is made explicit a little later in the chapter:

> Never can there come fog too thick, never can there come mud and mire too deep, to assort with the groping and floundering condition which this High Court of Chancery, most pestilent of hoary sinners, holds, this day, in the sight of heaven and earth.[6]

In this opening of *Bleak House*, then, 'the principle of equivalence' has projected into 'the axis of combination' on a considerable scale. Another indication that it belongs to or at least inclines to the metaphoric mode is that any attempt to translate it into film would inevitably rely on the technique of montage: a rapid sequence of juxtaposed shots—panorama of London, the Lord Chancellor in his hall, 'special effect' of a Megalosaurus, smoke lowering down from chimneys, dogs and horses splashed with mud, pedestrians colliding at a street-corner—making up what Eisenstein called a 'generalized *image*, wherein its creator, followed by the spectator, experiences the theme'. No doubt the omission of finite verbs, creating an impression

---

10, 'The sun became black as sackcloth of hair'—*Revelation*, vi, 12) and alludes to the modern geological theory of the gradual cooling of the sun. Mrs Politi plausibly traces the underlying pessimism of the authorial sections of *Bleak House* in part to the troubling impact of biological and geological science upon orthodox belief in the mid-nineteenth century.

of synchrony, the lack of smooth transitions between sentences, and the uniform syntactical structure of sentences, contribute to this montage effect. A film treatment of Forster's opening to *A Pasage to India*, on the other hand, or of the description of Birmingham University and environs, would use a much smoother and less noticeable cutting technique, aiming at a condensed version of a 'natural' visual survey or exploration of the scene. Dickens's verbal montage is, however, more boldly metaphorical than film montage can generally manage to be—and is not, in the last analysis, truly cinematic. The things it makes us 'see' most vividly aren't actually there at all; and what *is* there—muddy dogs and horses, ill-tempered pedestrians—are rather drably and vaguely described. The image of a Megalosaurus waddling down Holborn Hill would be quite difficult to interpret in a film, and might arouse expectations that we were about to see a science-fiction fantasy of the *King Kong* variety. The subtlety of the sootflakes and compound-interest metaphors would be more or less impossible to communicate visually. Quite simply, Dickens's paragraph is not so much a seeing as a saying. It approximates to drama rather than to film inasmuch as the narrator, instead of disguising himself as an eye, a lens, seems to address us as a voice, a histrionic voice (quite different from Forster's relaxed, ruminative voice): the voice of Chorus. He summons up by the power of his eloquence a vision of the familiar, prosaic capital (the technique could hardly work on an *un*familiar city like Chandrapore) strangely denatured and time-warped, fit setting for the tale of twisted motives and distorted values that is to follow. To literal-minded readers, the description will, of course, appear overdone or 'exaggerated'. 'I began and read the first number of *Bleak House*', Henry Crabb Robinson wrote in his diary on 19 March 1852. 'It opens with exaggerated and verbose description. London fog is disagreeable even in description and on the whole the first number does not promise much.'[7]

Bleak House, as Philip Collins observes, 'is a crucial item in the history of Dickens's reputation. For many critics in the 1850s, 1860s and 1870s, it began the drear decline of "the author of Pickwick, Chuzzlewit and Copperfield"; for many recent critics—anticipated by G. B. Shaw—it opened the greatest phase of his achievement.'[8] *Bleak House* marked Dickens's transition from being a humorous, cheerful, essentially reassuring entertainer, who deployed large casts of comic and melodramatic characters against realistic and recognizable backgrounds, to being an ironic and pessimistic critic of what he diagnosed as a sick society,* using symbolist techniques that impart to the physical world a sinister and almost surreal animation; or in our terms, it marked his shift from a metonymic to a metaphoric mode of

---

*H. M. Daleski has drawn attention to the submerged imagery of disease in the opening paragraphs of *Bleak House*: *infection, pollutions, pestilent*. *Dickens and the Art of Analogy* (1970), p. 169.

writing (as far as the authorial chapters are concerned, for Esther's narrative is essentially metonymic, contrasting in this, as in so many other ways, with the author's). The description of London at the beginning of *Bleak House* might be contrasted with the description of Jacob's Island and Folly Ditch in Chapter 50 of *Oliver Twist*, which begins:

> Near to that part of the Thames on which the church at Rotherhithe abuts, where the buildings on the banks are the dirtiest and the vessels on the river blackest with the dust of colliers and the smoke of close-built, low-roofed houses, there exists the filthiest, the strangest, the most extraordinary of the many localities that are hidden in London, wholly unknown, even by name, to the great mass of its inhabitants.[9]

Immediately one notices how much closer this is to the tone of the opening to *A Passage to India*. Like E. M. Forster, Dickens models his discourse on the guide-book: 'To reach this place the visitor has to penetrate through a maze of close narrow streets . . . he makes his way with difficulty . . . Arriving, at length, in streets remoter and less frequented than those through which he has passed. . . .' And so on. There is a profusion of synecdochic detail:

> he walks beneath tottering house-fronts projecting over the pavements, dismantled walls that seem to totter as he passes, chimneys half crushed, half hesitating to fall, windows guarded by rusty iron bars that time and dirt have almost eaten away, every imaginable sign of desolation and neglect.[10]

Although there are metaphorical expressions here (*tottering, hesitating, eaten away*) they are familiar, almost dead metaphors and their impact is relatively weak. Collectively their anthropomorphism invests the environment with a certain quality of menace, but more importantly these architectural details function as indices of (not metaphors for) desolation and neglect. The same strategy is repeated in the following paragraph, which describes the houses on and overlooking Jacob's Island:

> Crazy wooden galleries common to the backs of half-a-dozen houses, with holes from which to look upon the slime beneath; windows, broken and patched, with poles thrust out, on which to dry the linen that is never there; rooms so small, so filthy, so confined, that the air would seem too tainted even for the dirt and squalor which they shelter; wooden chambers thrusting themselves out above the mud, and threatening to fall into it—as some have done; dirt-besmeared walls and decaying foundations; every repulsive lineament of poverty, every loathesome indication of filth, rot, and garbage; all these ornament the banks of Folly Ditch.[11]

This description is clearly a more 'realistic' townscape than that which begins *Bleak House*—which is not to say that *Oliver Twist* as a whole is the more realistic novel. Indeed, one of the signs of its being a relatively immature piece of work is the distance or disparity between its fairy-tale-like plot and the topographical specificity of its London setting. Arguably, Dickens was never an essentially realistic novelist (as, say, George Eliot or Trollope were), and achieved his finest work when he allowed his novels to develop according to metaphorical principles. 'It is my infirmity', he wrote, 'to fancy or perceive relations in things which are not apparent generally.'[12]

These terms—metaphoric, metonymic—are however (it has to be emphasized) relative. Any prose narrative, however 'metaphorical', is likely to be more tied to metonymic organization than a lyric poem. To illustrate the point, and to complete our sample of urban descriptions, we might cite the 'Unreal city' sequence of *The Waste Land*, which, beginning with a deceptively metonymic description of London commuters, in which there is a submerged analogy with Dante's *Inferno*

> Under the brown fog of a winter dawn,
> A crowd flowed over London Bridge, so many
> I had not thought death had undone so many

suddenly explodes into metaphor:

> 'Stetson!
> 'You who were with us in the ships at Mylae!
> 'That corpse you planted last year in your garden
> 'Has it begun to sprout? Will it bloom this year?
> 'Or has the sudden frost disturbed its bed?'

There is no contextual support for these remarks, which would explain them or supply links between them. They are intelligible only as metaphorical articulations of motifs already introduced elsewhere in the poem (e.g. in the very first lines, with their allusions to the distressing burgeonings of spring). *The Waste Land* is indeed a prime example of metaphorical discourse, since it is structured almost exclusively on the principle of similarity and contrast, dislocating and rupturing relationships of contiguity and combination.

7   The Executions Revisited

If we arrange the texts discussed in the preceding section in a horizontal order, thus:

1	2	3	4	5
Encyclopaedia	*Guardian*	*Passage to India*	*Bleak House*	*The Waste Land*

we have a kind of spectrum of discourse extending from the metonymic to the metaphoric poles. Wherever we draw a vertical line between the numbered texts, those on the right of the line will be more 'metaphoric' than those on the left, and those on the left more 'metonymic' than those on the right. The line between literature and nonliterature would go straight through text no. 2, since that is the only one whose status is problematical in this respect.

A similar ordering is possible of the accounts of executions discussed in Part One, thus:

1	2	3	4	5
'Michael Lake Describes . . .'	'A Hanging'	*The Old Wives' Tale*	*The Naked Lunch*	'The Ballad of Reading Gaol'

The two sets do not correspond exactly. There is no equivalent to the encyclopaedia article in the second set, where the line between literature and nonliterature passes through text no. 1. But the comparison of the texts in left-to-right sequence reveals the same basic movement from metonymic to metaphoric dominance. It also confirms and clarifies the distinctions we made between the texts, on other grounds, in Part One; or, to put it another way, our critical reading of these texts confirms the soundness of Jakobson's distinction.

'The Ballad of Reading Gaol', for instance, fully supports the proposition that poetry (as compared to prose) is inherently metaphorical, not necessarily in the quantitative dominance of actual metaphors (though the 'Ballad' is full of them) but in the way the discourse is generated and maintained by 'the projection of the principle of equivalence from the axis of selection into the axis of combination'. Analysis of the complex but highly symmetrical patterning of the first stanza demonstrated this process at work in microscosm, while on the level of the poem's total structure we traced the dominant role, in the development of the poem, of certain thematic and symbolic similarities and contrasts: between human and divine justice, between the condemned man and Christ, between the various connotations of red and white, and so on. This emphasis on metaphorical or paradigmatic relationships in the discourse leads correspondingly to a weakening of metonymic or syntagmatic relationships—i.e. the relationships of contiguity in time and space, and of cause and effect. Whereas all the prose texts, even *The Naked Lunch* passage, keep to a chronological *sequence*, the 'Ballad' is strikingly ambiguous in its handling of time. As we observed, the central act of execution, which is the unique and irreversible climax of the texts by Lake, Orwell and Bennett, seems to occur not once but several times in the course of Wilde's poem—which is to say that it doesn't really 'occur' at all: it is anticipated, recalled and moralized upon, but never presented directly as a single, discrete happening. The structure of the poem is indeed not linear but centripetal—a system of looping digressions from and returns to the central symbolic-thematic core; the subject is not so much unfolded as *rotated* before us. As well as serving the poet's interest in parallels rather than contiguities, the deliberate ambiguity about time makes it difficult and indeed irrelevant to try and distinguish between the real and the imaginary in the poem, so that the question of 'realism' doesn't arise in connection with it.

The distinction is just as difficult to make, but perhaps not quite so irrelevant, in the passage from *The Naked Lunch*. Though this is structured as a sequence, a continuous syntagm, it is unintelligible as such because of logical contradictions between its component parts (e.g. Mark turns into Johnny whom Mary has just eaten). We therefore naturally look for some metaphorical meaning which would 'explain' this impossible combination of events, and Burroughs has told us what it is: the obscenity of capital punishment. If this meaning fails to emerge from the actual reading, it is, I suggested above, because the impossible events are narrated in a style that is more realistic (metonymic in Jakobson's terms) than the surrounding narrative; and it is significant that this style is borrowed from the film medium, which is also metonymic in Jakobson's scheme. The local metaphorical expressions in the Burroughs passage ('scream like a mandrake . . . sound like a stick broken in wet towels . . . one foot flutters like a trapped bird . . . pinwheel end over end and leap high in the air like great hooked fish . . .') do not contribute to the emergence of the moral theme concerning capital punishment, but tend rather to render the actions to which they are applied more physically immediate and credible. And these expressions mostly take the form of simile, which is precisely the form of metaphorical language most amenable to realism because least disturbing to syntagmatic continuity (see below p. 112). If, therefore, this text seems gratuitously obscene, it may be because it displays a fundamental confusion between the metaphoric and metonymic modes of writing: instead of cooperating, the two are pulling in opposite directions.

Jakobson's distinction also enables us to establish why the antepenultimate paragraph of *The Old Wives' Tale*, III, iii, 4, strikes a different note from the rest of the section, and a slightly false one:

> She felt like a lost soul, torn too soon from shelter, and exposed for ever to the worst hazards of destiny. Why was she in this strange, incomprehensible town, foreign and inimical to her, watching with agonized glance this cruel, obscene spectacle? Her sensibilities were all a bleeding mass of wounds. Why?

The metaphors here—vague, 'mixed', rather literary in their derivations—contrast with the essentially metonymic preceding account of the preparations for the execution, and seem comparatively inauthentic beside it. This is not a criticism of Bennett because, as I suggested earlier, he probably intends, in the manner of Flaubert, to hold us back from too ready an identification with Sophia at this point. The whole episode has been narrated from Sophia's point of view, limited to what she could observe from her hotel window, but with a certain detachment which is a function of the impersonal but everpresent narrator: we are always, so to speak, observing Sophia observing the events in the square. Her emotions and sensations are reported to us, or rendered through the convention of monologue (' "I cannot stand this!" she told herself in horror, but she could not move'). In the paragraph under discussion, however, Bennett uses free indirect speech to admit us directly to Sophia's consciousness as her experience reaches its climax. If, verbally, the paragraph seems an *anti*climax, this is appropriate inasmuch as she is unable to cope emotionally with the crisis.

It is noteworthy that the one term significantly absent from the account of the preparations for the execution, which is yet the key to the whole event—blood—finally makes its appearance in this paragraph in the metaphorical 'bleeding'. The guillotining is a ritual of blood: that is what the baying crowd has come to see and that is why the guillotine itself is painted red (though we are not told this and have to infer it). Sophia cannot acknowledge that blood is the source of her appalled fascination by the event, all the more because the shedding of Rivain's blood is identified with the loss of her own virginity. Emotionally paralysed by her unresolved and conflicting feelings about Gerald, she is incapable of a fully human response to the victim Rivain, and her metaphorical claim to be a 'bleeding mass of wounds' seems particularly self-dramatizing and self-pitying in the context of Rivain's literal decapitation.

In general *The Old Wives' Tale* fully exemplifies Jakobson's characterization of literary realism as a metonymic mode: 'following the path of contiguous relationships, the realistic author metonymically digresses from the plot to the atmosphere and from the characters to the setting in space and time. He is fond of synecdochic details.' From its origins in the Restaurant Sylvain to its climax in the hotel bedroom at Auxerre, the story of Sophia's final disillusionment with her husband is woven out of contiguities, which confer plausibility and meaning simultaneously upon the narrative. It is at the restaurant that Gerald first gets interested in the execution and meets Chirac, who offers to conduct him to it; at the same time the *louche* atmosphere of the restaurant (conveyed synecdochically in the 'violently red lips, powdered cheeks, cold, hard eyes, self-possessed arrogant faces and insolent bosoms' clustered about the tables) associates the expedition from its inception with moral corruption, specifically of a sexual character. The description of the journey to

Auxerre mantains the linear continuity of the story but also affords opportunities for thickening the atmosphere of moral and physical degradation: 'Although the sun was sinking the heat seemed not to abate. Attitudes grew more limp, more abandoned. Soot and prickly dust flew in unceasingly at the open window.' Gerald's sexual infidelity just before the execution is coded entirely in terms of contiguity: the presence of two young women in the square at such a time is a sign that they are not respectable; the fact that they are arm-in-arm and talking to Gerald and Chirac who are also arm-in-arm suggests the possibility of an alternative pairing-off, a suggestion which is fulfilled when Gerald is next sighted, 'talking vivaciously alone with one of the two girls who had been together'; and finally the sight of Gerald emerging from a house followed at an interval by the girl is a sign that she is a prostitute and that Gerald has just been her client. Gerald glances up at Sophia's hotel 'hastily'—which we interpret as 'guiltily'. Thus a message is conveyed to the reader through the observations of Sophia, who either does not understand the significance of what she sees, or does not want to understand it, and yet without Bennett's having to intervene as narrator to explain what is happening.

The way in which the guillotine itself is handled in this section is a classic example of how the realistic author can, by selection (or deletion) and repetition within a field of contiguities, construct a metonymic metaphor, or symbol, without disturbing the illusion of reality. The phallic significance of the guillotine is metaphorical, based on similarity, and corresponds directly to the metaphoric aspect of the dreamwork in Freudian analysis (see p. 79n. above). But whereas the mere appearance of a guillotine in a dream would itself in most cases be an enigma demanding interpretation, a vehicle for which we could not but seek a tenor, the appearance of the guillotine in *The Old Wives' Tale* is utterly predictable in context—it is indeed demanded by the context. What makes it capable of bearing a metaphorical meaning as well as taking its place in a natural sequence of contiguities is (a) the prominence it is given by repetition and (b) the synecdochic mode of its presentation, which focuses attention upon two of its properties: its columnar structure and its red colour. If the columns of the guillotine had been mentioned only once, or if the machine had been referred to several times but simply as 'the guillotine' or if it had been exhaustively described in every part and function in the style of Robbe-Grillet, the metaphorical meaning we have attributed to it could not have emerged.

One of the reasons why Orwell's 'A Hanging' reminds us of realistic fiction is the way the participants ('characters' one is inclined to call them) are established and identified by metonymy and synecdoche— e.g. the grotesque moustache of the prisoner, the contrasting toothbrush moustache and gruff voice of the prison superintendent, and the white suit, gold spectacles and black hand of the head jailer. The most interesting detail of this kind is the superintendent's stick, which both represents his authority and expresses his feelings as he manipulates it—moodily prodding the gravel in paragraph 3, slowly poking the ground as the prisoner calls on his god in paragraph 13, making the swift, decisive gesture of command in paragraph 14, poking the corpse in paragraph 16. Through this repetition the stick takes on, like the guillotine in Bennett, the function of a symbol. There is nothing like it in Michael Lake's report. His description of the hangman in paragraph 8 ('He wore a black broad-brimmed hat, a black trench coat, and heavy boots, and he was masked. Only the slit for his eyes and his white hands gleamed in the light') includes too many diverse details to be described as synecdochic, and—more important—none of these details is repeated or echoed subsequently in the text. Compared to 'A Hanging', 'Michael Lake Describes . . .' displays the metonymic mode in an inert, or rhetorically untransformed state. Like the encyclopaedia article on Birmingham (though not quite as starkly) it selects and deletes only because it must, and on pragmatic principles, without any discernible pattern developing through the discourse. The absence of significant repetition from this text is therefore closely related to the absence of any controlling idea comparable to Orwell's life-death-time matrix, and these absences prevent it from satisfying the demands of a 'literary' reading. This instance, at least, would seem to support Ruqaiya Hasan's notion of the kind of 'unity'—'the manifestation of some deep underlying principle'—that distinguishes the literary from the nonliterary text. The only deep underlying principle manifested by 'Michael Lake Describes . . .' is the professional code of the journalist: 'I report what I see, I tell it like it was.' And that is a principle that could be equally well expressed by a report of any event whatsoever. It is not that 'Michael Lake Describes . . .' fails to take up a moral attitude to the execution it describes (in which case it might have acquired the thematic unity of the Absurd). On the contrary it takes up explicit moral attitudes at several points; but these attitudes are not integrated with each other or with the other components of the discourse in any systematic way, such as 'A Hanging' displays under analysis.

8   The Metonymic Text as Metaphor

We observed earlier that even Jakobson himself seemed somewhat baffled by the problem of how to deal, analytically, with the metonymic mode of writing; and we traced the difficulty to the fact that in his scheme the POETIC (i.e. the literary) is homologous with the metaphoric mode, which in turn is opposed to the metonymic mode. How, then, can the metonymic be assimilated to the POETIC?

The solution would seem to lie in a recognition that, at the highest level of generality at which we can apply the metaphor/metonymy distinction, literature itself is metaphoric and nonliterature metonymic. The literary text is always metaphoric in the sense that when we interpret it, when we uncover its 'unity' in Ruqaiya Hasan's sense, we make it into a total metaphor: the text is the vehicle, the world is the tenor. Jakobson himself, as we have already noted, observes that metalanguage (which is what criticism is, language applied to an object language) is comparable to metaphor, and uses this fact to explain why criticism has given more attention to metaphorical than to metonymic tropes. Likewise, at the level of discourse, it is easier to see the entire text as a kind of metaphor applied to reality if it is written in the metaphorical mode than if it is written in the metonymic mode. We are not likely to interpret *King Lear* or *Paradise Lost* as literal reports of the real: at every point these works point to their own status as total metaphors. The human condition, Shakespeare is saying, 'is' *King Lear*; the human condition, Milton is saying, 'is' *Paradise Lost*. The metonymic text however—*Emma*, say, or *The Old Wives' Tale*—seems to offer itself to our regard not as a metaphor but as a synecdoche, not as a model of reality, but as a representative *bit* of reality. Human life 'is like' *Emma*, 'is like' *The Old Wives' Tale*, these authors seem to be saying—the phrase 'is like' denoting, here, a relationship of contiguity rather than similarity, for the writers create the illusion that their stories are or were part of real history, from which they have been cut out and of which they are representative. Taken a little further towards the metonymic pole, such fiction is often described as a 'slice of life'. Yet this phrase, which points to the synecdochic character of the realistic text, is itself a metaphor; and we know that it is not possible for the literary artist to limit himself to merely making a cut through reality, as one might cut through a cheese, exposing its structure and texture without altering it, for the simple reason that his medium is not reality itself but signs. For the same reason, although the metonymic text retards and resists the act of interpretation which will convert it into a total metaphor, it cannot postpone that act indefinitely. As Guy Rosolato puts it:

> The most descriptive or most realistic work culminates in a metaphor which it secretly sustains by the continuity of its narrative, and which is revealed at certain points, notably at its end: metaphor of a 'life', a 'reality', an 'object' thus put into the flow of the work defined by the limits of the book and by the break of its ending.[1]

The truth of this proposition is confirmed by that most characteristic of all gambits in the teaching and criticism of literature: the question, what is the text *about*? Ian Gregor has culled a nice quotation on this subject from Isherwood's novel *A Single Man* (1964) where George, an assistant professor of English at an American college, is discussing a novel by Huxley with his class:

> Before we can go any further, you've got to make up your minds what this novel actually *is* about. . . . At first, as always, there is a blank silence. The class sits staring, as it were, at the semantically prodigious word. *About*. *What* is it about? Well, what does George want them to say it's about? They'll say it's about anything he likes, anything at all. For nearly all of them, despite their academic training, deep deep down still regard this *about* business as a tiresomely sophisticated game. As for the minority, who have cultivated the *about* approach until it has become second nature, who dream of writing an *about* book of their own one day, on Faulkner, James or Conrad, proving definitively that all previous *about* books on that subject are about nothing—they aren't going to say anything yet awhile. They are waiting for the moment when they can come forward like star detectives with the solution to Huxley's crime. Meanwhile let the little ones flounder.[2]

Isherwood, like many creative writers, seems to be deeply suspicious of and hostile to academic criticism, and obviously intends the passage as satire on its procedures. Yet there is no alternative to the 'about game', unless we are to sit before works of literature in dumb silence (which might indicate either admiration or disgust). The most rudimentary exchange of information or opinion about a text ('This is a terrific book'—'Oh, what's it about?') involves the participants immediately in its preliminary moves, and with players of any sophistication the game moves inevitably from mere paraphrase into interpretation. This is just as true of the metonymic text as of the metaphoric. A typical professional critical essay on *Emma* begins:

> The subject of *Emma* is marriage. Put that way the statement seems ludicrously inadequate, for *Emma*—we instinctively feel—is not about anything that can be put into one word. And yet it is as well to begin by insisting that this novel does have a subject. . . .

Emma is about marriage. It begins with one marriage, that of Mrs Taylor, ends with three more and considers two others by the way. The subject is marriage; but not marriage in the abstract. There is nothing of the moral fable here; indeed it is impossible to conceive of the subject except in its concrete expression, which is the plot.[3]

Arnold Kettle's repeated qualifications of his own original proposition indicate his respect for the metonymic structure and texture of the novel, and his anxiety to avoid a reductively 'metaphorical' reading of the text, that would neglect the density and subtlety of detail through which the theme of 'marriage' emerges. Nevertheless, some such reductiveness is inevitable if criticism is going to do more than merely repeat the words of the text. In the metalanguage of criticism, metonymy ultimately yields to metaphor—or is converted into it.

If it is asked why we should value literature written in the metonymic mode, since this mode appears to run against the grain of literature itself (a challenge that has often been directed at the realistic novel) we should probably answer that it is the very resistance which the metonymic mode offers to generalizing interpretation that makes the meaning we *do* finally extract from it seem valid and valuable. No message that is decoded without effort is likely to be valued, and the metaphoric mode has its own way of making interpretation fruitfully difficult: though it offers itself eagerly for interpretation, it bewilders us with a plethora of possible meanings. The metonymic text, in contrast, deluges us with a plethora of data, which we seek to unite into one meaning. Furthermore, it must always be remembered that we are not discussing a distinction between two mutually exclusive types of discourse, but a distinction based on dominance. The metaphoric work cannot totally neglect metonymic continuity if it is to be intelligible at all. Correspondingly, the metonymic text cannot eliminate all signs that it is available for metaphorical interpretation.

9 Metaphor and Context

Apart from the fact that the metonymic text must ultimately submit to a 'metaphoric' interpretation, most such texts, certainly most realistic fiction, contain a good deal of local metaphor, in the form both of overt tropes and of submerged symbolism. And it is not surprising that interpretative critics of a formalist bent (such as Mark Schorer) look with particular attentiveness at this level of the metonymic text. There are however certain controls on the use of metaphoric strategies in realistic fiction, which Jakobson's theory helps to make clear. The basic point is very simple, and has already been touched on in connection with film-montage: it is that, in the metonymic text, metaphorical substitution is in a highly sensitive relation to context or contiguity. The greater the distance (existentially, conceptually, affectively) between the tenor (which is part of the context) and the vehicle of the metaphor, the more powerful will be the semantic effect of the metaphor, but the greater, also, will be the disturbance to the relationships of contiguity between items in the discourse and therefore to realistic illusion. This disturbance can to some extent be muted by using simile rather than metaphor proper, for simile, although it creates a relationship of similarity between dissimilars, spreads itself along the line of combination which metaphor, by its radical strategy of substitution, tends to disrupt. Metaphor, it is sometimes said, asserts identity, simile merely likeness,[1] and perhaps on this account the former trope is usually considered the more 'poetic'.

Northrop Frye, indeed, offers the distinction between metaphor and simile in much the same way as Jakobson offers the distinction between metaphor and metonymy—as models of mythical and realistic literature respectively:

> Realism, or the art of verisimilitude, evokes the response 'How like that is to what we know!' When what is written is *like* what is known, we have an art of extended or implied simile. And as realism is an art of implicit simile, myth is an art of implicit metaphorical identity. The word 'sun-god' with a hyphen used instead of a predicate, is a pure ideogram, in Pound's terminology, or literal metaphor, in ours.[2]

'Like' is an ambiguous word because it can denote either a relationship of similarity between things otherwise dissimilar ('My love is like a red, red rose') or a quality of representativeness deriving from an original contiguity between part and whole or unit and set ('All the roses in the garden are like this one'). I argued in the preceding section that the response to realistic writing, 'How like that is to what we know' is nearer to the second use of *like* than the first; and that it suggests a relationship between the realistic novel and the world that is closer to synecdoche than to simile. This does not, however, entirely invalidate the suggestion that there is some kind of affinity between simile and realism. It is easy to see, for instance, that simile lends itself more readily than metaphor to the empiricist philosophical assumptions that historically underpin realism as a literary mode. When we say that A is like B, we do not confuse what is actually there with what is merely illustrative, but when we say that A in a sense *is* B, the possibility of such confusion is always present, as even the old school text-book examples, 'He fought like a lion' and 'He was a lion in the fight', demonstrate. Aristotle acutely described metaphor as 'midway between the unintelligible and the commonplace';[3]

simile is a little nearer the commonplace, and to common sense.

We may therefore suggest that the difference between metaphor and simile corresponds to the more comprehensive distinction between the metaphorical (which includes simile) and the metonymic poles of language. But two qualifications must be made. First, a writer does not always enjoy freedom of choice between expressing a perceived similarity through metaphor or simile because, as Winifred Nowottny has pointed out, very often the language he is using does not permit him to use the former trope.[4] Graham Greene, for instance, describes an African baby as 'smiling like an open piano',[5] and it is difficult to see how the analogy could be expressed in metaphor proper. Secondly, the factor of 'distance' between tenor and vehicle is more significant than the choice of metaphor or simile. Consider this passage from Virginia Woolf's *The Waves*:

> The sun fell in sharp wedges inside the room. Whatever the light touched became dowered with a fanatical existence. A plate was like a white lake. A knife looked like a dagger of ice. Suddenly tumblers revealed themselves upheld by streaks of light. Tables and chairs rose to the surface as if they had been sunk under water and rose, filmed with red, orange, purple like the bloom on the skin of ripe fruit. The veins of the glaze of the china, the grain of the wood, the fibres of the matting became more and more finely engraved. Everything was without shadow. A jar was so green that the eye seemed sucked up through a funnel by its intensity and stuck to it like a limpet.[6]

This is the metaphoric imagination running riot, and the fact that the vision is expressed sometimes through metaphor proper and sometimes through simile doesn't seem to make much difference.

To sum up the foregoing: we would expect the writer who is working in the metonymic mode to use metaphorical devices sparingly; to make them subject to the control of context—either by elaborating literal details of the context into symbols, or by drawing analogies from a semantic field associated with the context; and to incline towards simile rather than metaphor proper when drawing attention to similarity between things dissimilar. We can observe these principles operating in 'A Hanging', with regard to both symbolism and figurative language.

The superintendent's stick acquires symbolic force by its repeated appearance in the text, associated with a variety of gestures and postures. As an object it is entirely appropriate to its context, and indeed in context it already has a quasi-symbolic function, as a sign of the superintendent's authority. When the superintendent pokes the ground with his stick, and still more when he pokes the corpse of the prisoner, he goes beyond the strictly ritualistic use of his stick and thus reveals the psychological tensions and moral contradictions of his situation. But these violations of decorum are so slight that we scarcely register them as such and the symbolic effect of the stick is almost subliminal. If, however, Orwell's superintendent made much more play with his stick—did much more bizarre and eccentric things with it, e.g. holding it between his legs like a phallus, or aiming it at the prisoner like a gun, then it would become a metaphorical rather than a metonymic symbol. Or suppose Orwell gave the superintendent not a stick but a cricket bat, then the object would become completely metaphorical and not at all metonymic because a cricket bat would be quite out of place in this context. There being no natural contiguity in language or reality between cricket bats and prison superintendents (as there is between sticks and superintendents), we could only interpret the cricket bat on the basis of similarity: between, say, the British colonial prison system and the British public school system; and we should also observe a negative similarity, or contrast, between cricket and executions, generating an irony of a more extreme and overt kind than that which Orwell provides through the appearance of the playful dog. In other words such alterations would transform the text from the metonymic mode of realism or confessional documentary to the metaphoric mode of black comedy or satiric fantasy.

'A Hanging' doesn't use very many metaphors. There is the pathetic fallacy of the *sickly light* in paragraph 1, and the transferred epithet of *desolately thin* in paragraph 3. There are conventional, almost dead metaphors like *toothbrush moustache* and *volley of barks*; and a few other metaphorical expressions that are only a little removed from cliché: *puny wisp of a man* [1], *floated* [3], *gambolled* [8] and *in full tide* [10]. The most obviously metaphorical expressions (i.e. those which draw our conscious attention to a relationship of similarity between dissimilars) are in fact similes:*

Paragraph	1:	like yellow tinfoil
	1:	like small animal cages
	2:	like men handling a fish which is still alive and may jump back into the water
	12:	like the tolling of a bell
	13:	like bad coffee
	15:	dead as a stone

Of these images the most striking, the most 'poetic', is probably the fish simile, and it is also the one that relates most immediately to what I take to be the thematic core of the piece, the life/death/time matrix (because a fish out of water has a short, finite time to live). The comparison of the man to a fish has much more force than the comparison of the prisoners to animals in paragraph 1, implied in *like small animal cages* and reinforced by the reference to *brown silent men squatting*, which without being explicitly metaphorical, irresistibly

---

*I do not classify *not like a prayer or cry for help* [12] and *like a flour bag* [12] as similes, since the word *like* is used in each case not to draw attention to similarity between dissimilars, but to define what is distinctive about something which belongs to a set of things that are axiomatically similar—cries and bags.

evokes the image of animals in a zoo. There is not a great conceptual distance between a cage and a cell, and indeed 'cage' is sometimes used as a kind of dead metaphor in the vocabulary of prisons. Likewise there is an element of contextual appropriateness in the similes, *like the tolling of a bell* and *like bad coffee*: bells often toll to announce a death, and bad coffee is an analogy that comes naturally to mind in a prison at breakfast time. Even *like yellow tinfoil* is naturalized by coming immediately after the reference to Burma, which we associate with yellowish complexions and the saffron robes of Buddhist monks. (The simile would seem more fanciful, more 'poetic' if the text began, 'It was in Africa', or if the simile itself was 'like gold tinfoil'—which would convey the same visual impression.) The fish simile stands out in a way the other similes do not because *there is no sea in the context*: therefore all the semantic impact of the simile is centred on similarity, not contiguity. If there were a great many such similes in 'A Hanging', drawing analogies from sources far removed from the context, the quality of documentary authenticity which it possesses would be dissipated.

This rule does not apply only to writing of a decidedly metonymic bias, like 'A Hanging'. All prose fiction that aims at any degree of realistic illusion will tend to give context a good deal of control over metaphor. Gérard Genette has shown this very perceptively in discussing Proust. *The Remembrance of Things Past* is a book heavily biased towards metaphor: the action of involuntary memory, which is the prime moving force behind the narrative, is a linking of experiences on the basis of their similarity (an irregularity in the paving-stones of Paris, for instance, recalling to Marcel the floor of the baptistery of St Mark's in Venice). But, says Genette, if the initial trigger-mechanism of memory is metaphoric, the expansion and exploration of any given memory (though accomplished with a great display of local metaphor and simile) is essentially metonymic, because of Proust's characteristic tendency towards 'assimilation by proximity . . . the projection of analogical affinity upon relationships of contiguity' and vice versa.[7] One of Genette's examples of this interpenetration of metaphor and metonymy is a comparison of two descriptions of pairs of church steeples. In the first, from *Swann's Way*, the narrator contemplates the plain of Méséglise:

> Sur la droite, on apercevait par-delà les blés les deux clochers ciselés et rustiques de Saint-André-des-Champs, eux-mêmes effilés, écailleux, imbriqués d'alvéoles, guillochés, jaunissants et grumeleux, comme deux épis.*

In the second passage, from *Sodom and Gomorrah*, Marcel, at Balbec, evokes the church of St Mars-le-Vêtu thus:

*'On the right one saw, beyond the corn fields, the two carved and rustic steeples of St André-des-Champs, themselves tapering, scaly, honeycombed, symmetrically patterned as though by an engraving tool, yellowing and rough textured like two ears of corn.'

Saint-Mars, dont, par ces temps ardents où on ne pensait qu'au bain, les deux antiques clochers d'un rose saumon, aux tuiles en losange, légèrement infléchis et comme palpitants, avaient l'air de vieux poissons aigus, imbriqués d'écailles, moussus et roux, qui, sans avoir l'air de bouger, s'élevaient dans une eau transparente et bleue.*

Genette points out that the two pairs of steeples are clearly very similar in appearance, but that the basic analogies in each passage are quite different. Why does Proust compare the steeples in the first passage to ears of corn and those in the second passage to fish? Clearly because of the context of each perception—the cornfields of Méséglise and the sea and bathing of Balbec, respectively.[8]

Genette observes that 'resemblance in an analogy mattered less to Proust than its *authenticity*, its fidelity to relations of spatio-temporal proximity'.[9] In this respect there is a difference between Proust and Orwell. Resemblance *did* matter to the latter—indeed it was the only possible justification for using analogy at all—because his aim was to describe as vividly and accurately as possible some object or event in what he took to be a common phenomenal world. He was always aiming at a historical (or pseudo-historical) 'authenticity'. Proust, on the other hand, was concerned with the authenticity of subjective consciousness. Whereas Orwell's 'I was there' stance implies that if we had been 'there' we should have seen what he saw, Proust implies that no one ever sees the same thing as another: and if we feel that the analogies through which Marcel explores his spatio-temporal context are somewhat extravagant, or tenuous or idiosyncratic, this is entirely appropriate to the whole enterprise of *The Remembrance of Things Past*. The important point to emphasize, however, is that Proust displays the movements of the individual consciousness as it encounters a reality, a context, which is coherent and intelligible to the reader, which is the world that Proust and Marcel and the reader inhabit. This makes *The Remembrance of Things Past* an extension of rather than a deviation from the realistic novel tradition, and entails subordinating analogy to context in the manner analysed by Genette.†
Compare the use of analogy in another modern text concerned to display subjective consciousness:

> Let us go then, you and I,
> When the evening is spread out against the sky
> Like a patient etherized upon a table[10]

---

*'St Mars, whose two antique, salmon-pink steeples, covered with lozenge-shaped tiles, slightly curved and seemingly palpitating, looked, in this scorching weather when one thought only of bathing, like pointed fish of great age that, covered with overlapping scales, mossy and russet, without appearing to move, rose in blue and transparent water.'
† And it is worth noting that the memory-trigger which, in a sense, starts the whole book off, the taste of the madeleine described in the Overture to *Swann's Way*, is metonymic in its operation, recalling experience previously associated with that taste by contiguity.

There is not very much resemblance between an evening sky and a patient on an operating table, and the emotional and semantic distance between these two concepts is very great. The analogy therefore seems highly subjective. Yet we cannot say, as in Proust, that it is authenticated by context, because Prufrock has no associations with medicine, surgery etc., nor is there any other allusion to such things elsewhere in the text. In fact these lines, like so much of Eliot's early verse, turn upon a *violation* of context: an abrupt shift from association of items according to contiguity (first two lines) to association of items according to similarity, (third line) made all the more disconcerting because the perceived similarity is so eccentric and unexpected. The lines also violate poetic decorum in refusing the conventional response to the sunset as something sublime and harmoniously beautiful, and together these violations declare the poem as modernist. The opening lines are representative of the rest of the poem, in which we are given hints about the speaker's spatio-temporal context which we struggle to compose into a coherent 'history' (Prufrock is a middle-aged, middle-class bachelor with cultured and genteel female acquaintance, etc.) but from which the discourse is continually digressing via bizarre analogies ('When I am formulated, sprawling on a pin . . . I should have been a pair of ragged claws . . . though I have seen my head (grown slightly bald) brought in upon a platter . . .') which are far removed from this context.

Like most modernist verse, Eliot's pushes Jakobson's poetic principle to an extreme: substitution not merely projects into, but radically disrupts combination, and the similarities on which substitution is based are often strained or recondite—hence the obscurity of such writing, its (in some cases, to some readers) wilful unintelligibility. A classic instance of such a clash between poet and audience was recorded in the correspondence published in the magazine *Poetry* (Chicago) between the editor, Harriet Monroe, and Hart Crane, concerning one of the latter's poems, 'At Melville's Tomb'. 'Take me for a hardboiled unimaginative unpoetic reader,' Miss Monroe wrote,

> and tell me how *dice* can *bequeath an embassy* (or anything else); and how a calyx (of *death's bounty* or anything else) can give back a *scattered chapter*, *livid hieroglyph*; and how, if it does, such a *portent* can be *wound in corridors* (of shells or anything else).

The first of these queries referred to the lines

> The dice of drowned men's bones he saw bequeath
> An embassy.

Crane replied:

> Dice bequeath an embassy, in the first place, by being ground (in this connection only, of course) in little cubes from the bones of drowned men by the action of the sea, and are finally thrown up on the sand, having 'numbers' but no identification. These being the bones of dead men who never completed their voyage, it seems legitimate to refer to them as the only surviving evidence of certain messages undelivered, mute evidence of

certain things, experiences that dead mariners have had to deliver. Dice as a symbol of chance and circumstances is also implied.

There was more explanation of this kind, but Harriet Monroe was unappeased. 'I think that in your poem certain phrases carry to an excessive degree the "dynamics of metaphor" ' She wrote in her last letter:

> —they telescope three or four images together by mental leaps (I fear my own metaphors are getting mixed!) which the poet, knowing his ground, can take safely, but which the most sympathetic reader cannot take unless the poet leads him by the hand with some such explanation as I find in your letter.[11]

We need not here attempt to adjudicate between the correspondents. Both contributions show that the deviance of modernist poetry consists in emphasizing an existing bias in all poetry towards the metaphorical pole. A different kind of deviance results when the poet, especially the lyric poet, pushes his medium in the opposite direction—when he makes the metaphorical development of his topic subject to the kind of metonymic constraints that the realistic prose writer normally applies. This is a path likely to be followed by a poet reacting against what he feels to be a decadent metaphorical mode—for example, Wordsworth.

Romanticism as a literary movement is classified as 'metaphoric' by Jakobson in relation to realism, and by Zirmunskij in relation to classicism. But the first generation of English romantic poets, at least, thought of themselves as replacing one, inauthentic, kind of metaphorical writing (Coleridge's 'Fancy') with another, more powerful kind ('Imagination') which didn't necessarily express itself through a profusion of metaphorical figures. Certainly the specialized 'poetic diction' of eighteenth-century verse which Wordsworth deplored belonged to a type of poetic discourse that had become compulsive and mechanical in its metaphorizing.

> In vain to me the smiling mornings shine,
> And reddening Phoebus lifts his golden fire:
> The birds in vain their amorous descant join,
> And cheerful fields resume their green attire.[12]

The metaphors click into place as regularly and predictably as the rhymes. Wordsworth's effort to purify the language of English poetry entailed forcing it back towards the metonymic pole: hence his insistence in the Preface to *Lyrical Ballads* that there was no essential difference between poetry and prose, hence his shiftiness about the role of metre in poetry,* hence his determination to 'choose incidents

---

*First he suggests that metre 'superadds' a 'charm' to what otherwise might have been as well said in prose; then that metre makes painful subjects in literature less distressing because of 'the tendency of metre to divest language in a certain degree of its reality';

and situations from common life and to relate or describe them, throughout, as far as was possible in a selection of language really used by men',[13] which makes the preface sound more like the manifesto of a novelist than of a poet. Wordsworth was well aware that readers accustomed to a more ostentatiously metaphoric mode of verse-writing would 'look round for poetry and will be induced to inquire by what species of courtesy these attempts can be permitted to assume that title.'[14] Very little of the vast amount of criticism that has accumulated around Wordsworth's work since then would be of much assistance in answering that question. Wordsworth's greatness as a poet is widely acknowledged, and invoked to justify the detailed explication of his poetry by reference to his life and thought, but rarely demonstrated in formal terms. The reason would seem to be that, as Jakobson says, the verbal analysis of literature is biased towards the metaphoric pole and cannot deal easily with metonymic discourse—all the more when the latter takes the form of verse, where we expect 'equivalence' to dominate 'combination'. How, for instance, does one demonstrate that this is poetry of a high order?

> It is the first mild day of March:
> Each minute sweeter than before,
> The Red-breast sings from the tall Larch
> That stands beside our door.
>
> There is a blessing in the air,
> Which seems a sense of joy to yield
> To the bare trees and mountains bare,
> And grass in the green field.[15]

There doesn't seem to be much here for the usual tools of 'practical criticism' to get a purchase on. Some of the words are arguably metaphorical—*sweeter*, *blessing*, *yield*—but in such a weak, muted degree that we scarcely register them as such. Certainly we should be unlikely to praise these verses (as we might praise the opening of Shelley's *To The West Wind*) for their vivid and striking metaphors. In linking items according to contiguity rather than similarity, the verses conform to the metonymical mode, but they don't exploit the rhetorical figures proper to this mode very extensively either: 'the Red-breast' and 'the green field' are synecdoches even weaker than the weak metaphors just mentioned.

Invoking the theory of the Russian Formalists and Czech structuralists we can say that this extreme simplicity is aesthetically

---

finally he touches on the heart of the matter: 'the pleasure which the mind derives from the perception of similitude in dissimilitude. The principle is the great spring of the activity of our minds and their chief feeder. . . . It would not have been a useless employment to have applied this principle to the consideration of metre. . . .' But unfortunately he excuses himself from doing so.

powerful because it is 'foregrounded' against the background of the highly ornate and highly rhetorical poetic diction of the received poetic tradition, and this is obviously true. But there must be something more than mere abstention to Wordsworth's simplicity if its peculiar effectiveness is to be explained; there must be an art in his apparent artlessness (as in the parallel case of the early Hemingway) which prevents simplicity from degenerating into banality, and which allows us to re-read these lines without feeling that we exhausted their significance on the first reading. In short, he must be *doing something* with the axis of combination which he appears to follow in such a straightforward way. We can begin to see what he is doing by rearranging the words into prose and altering them when logic and clarity require it.

> It is the first mild day of March. The redbreast sings (more sweetly with each minute) from the tall Larch that stands beside our door. There is a blessing in the air which seems to yield a sense of joy to the bare trees and mountains and to the green grass in the field.

This exercise reveals nuances and ambiguities in the original text so slight and subtle as almost to be subliminal in their effects (as are many devices in realistic prose fiction). *Each minute sweeter than before*, though the punctuation indicates that it must describe the birdsong, is likely to be interpreted by the reader, before he gets to the 'Red-breast' as referring back to the March day, partly because of this ordering of information and partly because *sweeter* is more often an adjective than an adverb in English. Likewise the second line of the second stanza, *Which seems a sense of joy to yield* doesn't grammatically require an extension of its predicate, and the subsequent naming of a series of indirect objects to which the sense of joy is yielded comes as a slight surprise. This 'double-take' effect, by which an apparently completed statement turns out to have an unexpected further application is deeply characteristic of Wordsworth, especially in his blank verse poetry, and is usually produced by the subtle and deliberate placing of the line-break in relation to sense and syntax. Christopher Ricks has commented acutely on the importance of the line as a unit, and the relationships between lines, in Wordsworth's verse:

> Life necessitates transitions, indeed it lives on them, but a true transition is one which finds its spontaneity and its surprise somewhere other than in violence. Such transitions and transformations can be set by the poet before your very eyes; they can be the transitions and successions by which a line is taken up by a sequence of lines without being impaired, without ceasing to be itself. In [Donald] Davie's words, 'a little surprise, but a wholly fair one.'[16]

In the poem under discussion, we might suggest that these little surprises, these hesitations of sense between one line and another, contribute to the general idea of the diffusion of the spirit of spring through all creation which is overtly developed later ('Love, now a universal birth/From heart to heart is stealing'); and the same effect is perhaps conveyed by the repeated, redundant *bare* that links the *trees* with the *mountains*, and the displacement of *green* from *grass* (with which it logically belongs) to *field*. Though a Wordsworth poem characteristically follows a linear path (Ricks observes how often the words *line*, *lines* actually occur in his verse) the line of contiguities is always animated by these subtle readjustments of the prosaic syntagm.

In case it should seem that a slight minor poem is being made to bear too much weight in the argument, let us look briefly at a major one, 'Resolution and Independence', of which Coleridge said, 'This fine poem is *especially* characteristic of the author; there is scarce a defect or an excellence of his writings of which it would not present a specimen.'[17] It displays, I think, the characteristic tendencies of metonymic writing in relation to metaphor, summarized earlier: to use metaphorical devices sparingly, to make them subject to context, and to use simile rather than metaphor proper in drawing analogies. The analogies applied to the leech gatherer are all similes:

> As a huge stone is sometimes seen to lie
> Couched on the bald top of an eminence;
> Wonder to all who do the same espy,
> By what means it could thither come and whence;
> So that it seems a thing endued with sense:
> Like a sea-beast crawled forth, that on a shelf
> Of rock or sand reposeth, there to sun itself;
>
> Such seemed this man . . . .
>
> Motionless as a cloud the old man stood,
> That heareth not the loud winds when they call;
> And moveth all together, if it move at all. . . .
>
> But now his voice to me was like a stream
> Scarce heard; . . .

(There are also several comparative formulae which are not quite similes e.g. 'Like one whom I had met with in a dream;/Or like a man from some far region sent'.) Of the similes, the stone, the cloud and the stream are all vehicles taken from the poem's context—the open country. The sea-beast, indeed, is a more exotic analogy, but it is of course applied directly to the stone, and only indirectly to the leech gatherer. Wordsworth himself commented:

> The stone is endowed with something of the power of life to approximate it to the sea-beast; and the sea-beast stripped of some of its vital qualities to assimilate it to the stone; which intermediate image is thus treated for the purpose of bringing the original image, that of the stone, to a nearer resemblance to the figure and condition of the aged Man; who is divested of so much of the indication of life and motion as to bring him to the point where the two objects unite and coalesce in comparison.[18]

From another point of view, however, the *stone* is the intermediate image, since it is more likely to appear in the same context with either *Man* or *sea-beast* than these two things are to appear together in the same context.

It is worth comparing the similes in Lewis Carroll's celebrated parody. They come mainly in the last few lines:

> ... that old man I used to know—
> Whose look was mild, whose speech was slow,
> Whose hair was whiter than the snow,
> Whose face was very like a crow,
> With eyes, like cinders, all aglow,
> Who seemed distracted with his woe,
> Who rocked his body to and fro,
> And muttered mumblingly and low,
> As if his mouth were full of dough,
> Who snorted like a buffalo—
> That summer evening long ago,
> A-sitting on a gate.[19]

From *snow* and *crow*, which belong to the same kind of context as Wordsworth's poem, Carroll turns to analogies that are progressively more remote from the context and progressively more absurd. The absurdity is heightened by the repeated 'O' rhyme—a good example of how doggerel results from allowing equivalence (of sounds) to tyrannize over combination (of sense). Compare, also, Wordsworth's 'his voice to me was like a stream/Scarce heard' with Carroll's deliberately debased and domesticated version:

> And his answer trickled through my head
> Like water through a sieve.

Carroll's poem is not strictly speaking a parody, but a travesty. It treats the same situation as Wordsworth's poem (the poet, burdened with his own anxieties, meets a solitary old man, asks him what he does for a living, only half-listens to the answer because of his own preoccupations, yet is in the end fortified by the encounter) but in a quite different style. In true parody, the style is the object of ridicule which is achieved by exaggerating the mannerisms of the original and/or applying them to incongruous subject-matter; in travesty a change of style is used to ridicule the original subject matter. In the 'White Knight's Song', Carroll systematically violates the metonymic decorum of 'Resolution and Independence'. Whereas Wordsworth's old man gathers leeches, and only leeches—that is why he is encountered beside a moorland pond—Carroll's old man collects (or claims to collect, for he is not likely to collect anything a-sitting on a gate) a preposterous, Dadaist variety of things, most of which do not belong in any way whatsoever to the moors or countryside:

> He said 'I hunt for haddocks' eyes
>   Among the heather bright,
> And work them into waistcoat-buttons
>   In the silent night.
>
> 'I sometimes dig for buttered rolls
>   Or set limed twigs for crabs:
> I sometimes search the grassy knolls
>   For wheels of Hansom-cabs.'

The principal focus of Carroll's satire is the somewhat egotistical preoccupation of the poet in *Resolution and Independence* which seems to prevent him from listening to the answers to his own questions. But whereas Wordsworth's persona is thinking first about poets, who being naturally solitary have some kind of affinity with the leech-gatherer, thinking of them, moreover, sometimes in pastoral terms ('I thought of . . . Him who walked in glory and in joy following his plough, along the mountain side') and then thinking about the leech-gatherer himself ('In my mind's eye I seemed to see him pace about the weary moors continually'), Lewis's White Knight is thinking of subjects both absurd in themselves and absurdly unrelated to anything in the actual situation:

> But I was thinking of a plan
>   To dye one's whiskers green,
> And always use so large a fan
>   That they could not be seen.
> So having no reply to give
>   To what the old man said,
> I cried 'Come, tell me how you live!'
>   And thumped him on the head.

It's not so far removed from the inconsequential ruminations of Eliot's Prufrock:

> Shall I part my hair behind? Do I dare to eat a peach?
> I shall wear white flannel trousers, and walk upon the beach.

I have examined a variety of literary texts in an effort to display, within a brief compass, the possibilities offered by Jakobson's metaphor/metonymy distinction for answering the questions about the ontology and typology of literature raised in Part One. I hope to have indicated that the distinction provides a common descriptive terminology for classifying and analysing types of literary discourse usually seen as based on essentially different and incompatible principles. The theory has been illustrated by comparative analysis of short texts and extracts without much regard to their relative positions in time. It is now appropriate to examine the possibilities of the distinction when applied to more historical concerns of criticism—the discrimination of periods, schools and movements in literature, and the examination of an individual writer's development through his *oeuvre*. In particular we shall see whether Jakobson's scheme enables us to study the differences between modernist and other types of writing in the modern period without being obliged to adopt the partisan and sometimes obfuscating attitudes encountered in Part One.

Part Three

Modernists, Antimodernists and Postmodernists

1   James Joyce

Since orthodox literary history tells us that modernist fiction is in one way or another in reaction against nineteenth-century realism, and deeply influenced by symbolist poetry and poetics, we should expect to find it tending towards the metaphorical pole of Jakobson's scheme. The mere titles of the novels seem to confirm such a classification. The Victorian novelists, and the Edwardian realists who carried on their tradition, tended to use names of persons or places for titles (*David Copperfield, Middlemarch, Barchester Towers, Kipps, Riceyman Steps, The Forsyte Saga*) thus indicating a field or focus of contiguous phenomena as their subject matter. In contrast, the titles of novels in the modernist tradition tend to be metaphorical or quasi-metaphorical: *Heart of Darkness, The Shadow Line, The Wings of the Dove, The Golden Bowl, A Passage to India, The Rainbow, To the Lighthouse, Ulysses, Finnegans Wake* . . .

But not *Dubliners*. *Dubliners* is a synecdochic title implying that the book describes a representative cross-section or sample of the life of the Irish capital. *A Portrait of the Artist as a Young Man* is quasi-metaphorical in that it applies to a work of literature a description that properly belongs to painting, but the word 'portrait' is so common-place in literary discussion as to be an almost dead metaphor. The titles of Joyce's works of prose fiction thus mirror his artistic development from realism to mythopoeia, from (in our terms) metonymy to metaphor.

To be sure, *Dubliners* is not a work of wholly traditional nineteenth-century realism, for the stories do not quite satisfy the criteria of intelligibility and coherence normally demanded of the classic readerly text (as Barthes calls it). In this latter type of text, he observes, 'everything holds together'—every detail, gesture, utterance has several cooperative functions: to forward the action, to explain the action, to describe the setting, and so on—in general to establish the plausibility of the story and protect it from the reader's latent scepticism. 'The readerly is controlled by the principle of non-contradiction, but by multiplying solidarities, by stressing at every opportunity the *compatible* nature of circumstances, by attaching narrated events together with a kind of logical "paste", the discourse carries this principle to the point of obsession.'[1] There may, as in 'Sarrasine', be a mystery or enigma in the story, but the reader knows what the enigma is and confidently awaits its eventual solution. Because of this confidence, he takes pleasure in the delay of the solution (for without this delay there could be no story) and within certain limits will accept authorial evasions or disguisings of the truth to this end. ('The discourse is trying to lie as little as possible,' says Barthes at one point in his commentary, 'just what is required to ensure the interests of reading, that is, its own survival.')[2] The reader who approaches *Dubliners* with expectations derived from such writing is, however, likely to be disappointed and disconcerted. The stories look superficially as if they belong to the classic, readerly, realistic mode: they have the smooth, logical, homogeneous prose style which naturalizes meaning in the readerly text ('the text is replete with multiple, discontinuous, accumulated meanings, and yet burnished, smoothed by the 'natural' movement of its sentences: it is an egg text')[3] yet the reader is likely to find himself forced continually to revise his sense of what any particularly story is 'about'—uncertain therefore what revelation the story is moving towards, and apt to be taken by surprise when it finally comes. The climaxes (epiphanies) of *Dubliners* are mostly anticlimaxes by the criteria of the classic readerly text.

Consider, for example, the first story in the collection, 'The Sisters'. The very title is a stumbling block to the reader, since it suggests the story is going to be 'about' the two sisters, though it proves to be much more concerned with their brother, the old priest, and with the young boy who is the narrator. I say 'young boy' because, despite the maturity of the prose style, we do not have in this story the sense of an adult consciousness *recalling* a boyhood experience. From the very first sentence, with its deictic 'this' (*'There was no hope for him this time: it was the third stroke'*) we are situated in the consciousness and time-plane of the young boy at the time the old priest dies. Perhaps this is what naturalizes the many unresolved enigmas in the narrative, for we experience the events through the consciousness of a young boy struggling to interpret events while being deprived of most of the relevant data by the evasions of the adult world and by his own immaturity. The presentation of action through this limited consciousness justifies (*i.e.* logically explains) the introduction of false clues into the story—for instance, the suggestion that the old priest is guilty of simony. Simony is associated with the old priest in the narrator's mind for purely private and gratuitous reasons:

> Every night as I gazed up at the window I said softly to myself the word paralysis. It had always sounded strangely in my ears like the word gnomon in the Euclid and the word simony in the Catechism.[4]

Later, some fragments of overheard adult conversation imply that there was something corrupt and corrupting about the old priest and this provokes a dream in which the figure of the priest tries to confess to the boy: 'I felt that I too was smiling feebly, as if to absolve the simoniac of his sin.'[5] In fact, as one of the sisters reveals at the end of the story, the dark secret of the priest's past is not simony, not indeed a 'sin' at all, but an accident with the chalice at mass that 'affected his mind': a typical anticlimax.* One night after this mishap he was discovered in his confessional, ' "Wide-awake and laughing to himself. . . . So then, of course, when they saw that, that made them think that there was something gone wrong with him. . . ." '

So the story ends, but the trail of dots must make us wonder whether we have been told the 'whole story' after all. Was it the accident with the chalice that turned the old priest's head, or was the accident itself a symptom of some more deep-seated disease of mind and body—say general paralysis of the insane, as Richard Ellmann hints?[6] Is it fortuitous that running the words *simony* and *paralysis* together produces something close to the word *syphilis*? If this were indeed the real or suspected cause of the priest's death it would explain some of the undertones of the story, the vague suggestions of corruption that are attributed to the priest. But we cannot be at all sure, such is the deliberate ambiguity of the text. It is not, in fact, an 'egg-text': there is a continual leakage of implication and suggestion from its unfinished sentences. The narrator speaks for the reader when he says, 'I puzzled my head to extract meaning from [old Cotter's] unfinished sentences,'—sentences which first introduce the note of mystery and suspicion concerning the old priest:

'I think it was one of those . . . peculiar cases. . . . But it's hard to say. . . .'
'My idea is: let a young lad run about and play with young lads of his own age and not be. . . . Am I right, Jack?
'When children see things like that, you know, it has an effect. . . .'[7]

Cotter is not the only character whose speech has these suggestive lacunae (known to classical rhetoricians as 'aposiopesis'):

My aunt fingered the stem of her wine-glass before sipping a little.
'Did he . . . peacefully?' she asked.
'Oh quite peacefully, ma'am,' said Eliza. You couldn't tell when the breath went out of him. He had a beautiful death, God be praised.'
'And everything . . .?'[8]

These gaps, however, are easy enough to fill, and exemplify a familiar feature of ordinary speech. Mukarovský observes that the automatization of language permits us to communicate in unfinished sentences because it enables us to predict or supply the missing

---

*I do not underestimate the almost superstitious fear and guilt that was attached to any mishap with the consecrated elements in a Catholic culture that took the doctrine of transubstantiation very literally; but it is obviously less serious and less culpable than the selling of sacred offices and objects for gain.

elements. Such fragmentary communication is normal in casual conversation, and a person who always speaks in perfectly formed sentences will in fact be calling aesthetic attention to his speech by foregrounding syntax. In the literary rendering of speech, however— at least in the 'readerly' tradition—the reverse, by convention, is true: characters generally speak in well-formed sentences, and any deviation from *this* norm is foregrounded—for example Miss Bates in *Emma* or Mr Jingle in *Pickwick Papers*. In 'The Sisters' the noncompletion of sentences is not confined (as in Jane Austen and Dickens) to one character, but is common to all the adult characters. It thus tends to be perceived as a general feature of the story, foregrounded against the norm of the tradition (the tradition represented by Jane Austen and Dickens among others), marking an advance towards a greater realism in the literary representation of speech. In fact, as we have just seen, the thematically more significant pattern is the foregrounding of the adults' incomplete sentences against the background of the youthful narrator's completed ones. Aposiopesis is thus disguised as mimesis. One kind of foregrounding (associated with realism) acts as a cover for another kind (associated with thematic patterning).

This was a favourite tactic of those early modernist writers who were concerned to steer naturalistic fiction in the direction of symbolism. We see another example of its operation in the way in which the motif of the Sacrament is cunningly hidden in the realistic texture of 'The Sisters', as in those children's picture-puzzles where the shapes of incongruous objects are hidden in the lines of, for example, wood grain and foliage. For instance, the name of the snuff that the narrator's aunt gives him to take to the priest, 'High Toast', is certainly an irreverent metaphor for (and pun on) 'Host', and the priest's clumsy way of handling it is strikingly parallel to his crucial accident at mass.

> It was always I who emptied the packet into his black snuff-box, for his hands trembled too much to allow him to do this without spilling half the snuff about the floor. Even as he raised his large trembling hands to his nose little clouds of snuff dribbled through his fingers over the front of his coat. It may have been these constant showers of snuff which gave his ancient priestly garments their green faded look, for the red handkerchief, blackened, as it always was, with the snuff grains of a week, with which he tried to brush away the fallen grains, was quite inefficacious.[9]

The gesture of the priest raising his large trembling hands, the decidedly ritualistic associations of the phrase 'ancient priestly garments', help to evoke subliminally the image of the priest celebrating mass, the narrator performing the office of acolyte. 'Inefficacious' is another interesting word, slightly foregrounded because its polysyllabic solemnity seems unwarranted by the comparatively trivial gesture to which it is applied. It is in fact a word favoured by Catholic theological manuals of the relevant period to describe the withholding of sacramental grace due to some irregularity in the administration or reception of the sacraments. The sacrament of penance, for instance, would be 'inefficacious' if the penitent concealed some grave sin from his confessor; and the Eucharist would be inefficacious if received in a state of mortal sin. These are the two sacraments which are central to the story. 'The duties of the priest towards the Eucharist and towards the secrecy of the confessional seemed so grave to me that I wondered how anybody had ever found in himself the courage to undertake them'[10] the narrator reflected after his conversations with the priest; and later Eliza recalls, with reference to her brother, 'The duties of the priesthood was too much for him. And then his life was, you might say, crossed.'[11] This last remark seems to be an allusion to the priest's accident with the chalice (Eucharist) which leads to his being discovered wide-awake and laughing in his confessional (Penance). The anecdote itself is told in the context of a kind of parody Eucharist of sherry and biscuits, served by the two sisters to the narrator and his aunt.

A silence took possession of the little room and, under cover of it, I approached the table and tasted my sherry and then returned quietly to my chair in the corner.[12]

'Approached' is another slightly foregrounded word which has been transferred from the liturgical language of the day (in which communicants always 'approached the altar') to a secular social context. Certainly the parallel between the boy's comportment and that of a communicant in church is very close.

What is the meaning of these and other parallels and allusions to the sacraments? Some are clearly proleptic—like the priest's clumsiness with the High Toast, or the fact that he is seen laid out, 'vested as though for the altar, his large hands *loosely* retaining a chalice'[13] (my italics)—anticipating the revelation of Eliza on the last page. Others can be explained in thematic terms. The parody Eucharist of sherry and biscuits, for instance, might be interpreted as contributing to the theme of failed religion, spiritual paralysis, letter without spirit, ritual without efficacy, which Joyce generally attributed to Irish Catholicism, and of which the priest, last pictured with an 'idle chalice' on his breast, is a personification. The story is, to that extent, precariously contained within the readerly tradition in which 'everything hangs together'. Yet the patterning is in the last analysis in excess of any wholly logical interpretation, and looks forward to the more abundant and playful parallelisms and leitmotifs of *Ulysses* and *Finnegans Wake*, where the perception of similarity is overtly exploited as a comic or magical principle by which the anarchic flux of experience can be ordered and made tolerable. In the remorselessly drab, unredeemed world of *Dubliners* metaphorical similarity is still subordinated to metonymic contiguity: the Eucharist is so plausibly disguised as snuff or sherry and biscuits as scarcely to be perceptible at all, and a story like 'The Sisters' is more likely to be read as a realistic sketch or slice of life than as a symbolist composition of subtly interwoven leitmotifs.

What makes the former response more likely, as I remarked earlier, is the homogeneous 'readerly' prose style, that 'style of scrupulous meanness' as Joyce himself described it, in which all the stories, with the exception of the end of 'The Dead', are written. It was this that made possible the original publication of the 'The Sisters' and two of the other stories in such a middlebrow journal as *The Irish Homestead*; even if the scrupulous meanness of Joyce's observation eventually provoked a backlash from the readership that compelled the editor to ask Joyce not to submit any more, the point is that the subversiveness and originality of the stories was not *immediately* apparent from their verbal form. With *A Portrait of the Artist as a Young Man*, in which Joyce varied his style to imitate various phases of his hero's development, he declared his secession from the fully readerly mode of narrative, and began his career as a fully-fledged modernist writer. Metaphoric similarity is now at certain points given priority over the realistic decorum of metonymic contiguities—in for instance the hero's symbolically appropriate but ethnographically anomalous surname, Dedalus; and although the basic structure of the narrative is linear and chronological, there are gaping holes in the account of Stephen's life, which the discourse makes no attempt to bridge with summary or retrospect, and a corresponding emphasis on thematic echoes and parallels between the different episodes.

The break with the mode of *Dubliners* is not, however, radical. The art of the Christmas Dinner scene, for instance, is entirely continuous with the art of the short stories: here, as in 'The Sisters', we have to make an effort not to be completely hypnotized by the utterly convincing realism of the narration (a fully 'performable' realism, this, even if Balzac's is not) in order to draw out the wealth of connotation buried in the text. Consider, for example, the apparently 'innocent' referential sentence with which this scene begins:

A great fire, banked high and red, flamed in the grate and under the ivytwined branches of the chandelier the Christmas table was spread.[14]

The sentence has a subtle cadence, characteristic of Joyce's writing, which has been produced by a slight modification of the most natural word order, which would have been:

A great fire, banked high and red, flamed in the grate and the Christmas dinner was spread under the ivytwined branches of the chandelier.

That is a straightforward compound sentence formed by linking two parallel subject-predicate clauses; its structure makes clear spatial distinctions between the objects referred to. By rearranging the word order of the second clause Joyce has deliberately created a certain spatial confusion in the reader's mind, and, as it were, pushed the ivytwined branches of the chandelier into closer proximity to the fire. In fact when we read Joyce's sentence we probably run the first clause into the beginning of the second, because the adverbial phrase concerning the chandelier could grammatically qualify *flamed*, thus:

> A great fire, banked high and red, flamed in the grate and under the ivytwined branches of the chandelier.

What is the expressive function of Joyce's syntactical shuffling? It brings into closer juxtaposition the fire (which is red) and the ivy (which is green), and thus strikes a thematic chord which has already been sounded several times in the book, and which is to dominate the scene which follows. The red and the green symbolize the union of socialist and nationalist aspirations in the political movement for Irish independence. On the first page of *A Portrait of the Artist as a Young Man* we learn that:

> Dante had two brushes in her press. The brush with the maroon velvet back was for Michael Davitt and the brush with the green velvet back was for Parnell.[15]

(Michael Davitt was the Catholic leader of the socialist Irish Land League and Parnell, a Protestant, the leader of the Irish Nationalists in Parliament.) The picture of the earth, 'a big ball in the middle of clouds' on the first page of Stephen's geography textbook, has been coloured by another boy, the previous owner, with crayons, 'the earth green and the clouds maroon.' Later Dante tears the backing off her green brush, an incident that marks, domestically, the split in the Irish nationalist movement that occurred when Parnell was cited as co-respondent in a divorce case. Pressure from Davitt and the Catholic bishops wrested political leadership from Parnell and he died, a broken man, in 1891. These events are the main subject of conversation at the Christmas dinner in *A Portrait*, effectively destroying any spirit of Christian fellowship and charity on this occasion—indeed leading to outbursts of violent hatred and anti-Christian sentiment. (That the divorce petition in which Parnell was involved was originally filed on Christmas Eve, 1889, made it perhaps more likely that the wound would be re-opened at this season). Red and green are of course colours traditionally associated with Christmas as well as with Irish political life, so the first sentence of this chapter encapsulates the ironic conflict of political and religious attitudes that is to erupt in the course of the meal. 'Ivy' is particularly notable for a double connotation, being the emblem of the Parnellites (cf. 'Ivy Day in the Committee Room' in *Dubliners*) as well as an evergreen traditionally associated with Christmas (cf. the carol, 'The Holly and the Ivy'). All this weight of suggestion is packed into the sentence without any overt metaphorizing, and with only the subtlest readjustment, through syntax, of the chain of natural contiguities: fire—chandelier—ivy—table.

Later in the novel, in accord with the development of Stephen's romantic, egocentric and literary sensibility, the prose becomes much more 'poetic': metaphor is overt, and the progress of the syntagm is deliberately impeded by repetition of key words and elaborate rhythmical patterning, which together impart a spiralling, rather than a linear movement to the prose, in, for example, the often quoted passage about the girl wading:

> Her bosom was as a bird's soft and slight, slight and soft as the breast of some darkplumaged dove. But her long fair hair was girlish: and girlish, and touched with the wonder of mortal beauty, her face.[16]

or Stephen's reverie about an imagined incestuous love affair:

> The park trees were heavy in the rain and rain fell still and ever in the lake, lying grey like a shield. A game of swans flew there and the water and the shore beneath were fouled by the greenwhite slime. They embraced softly, impelled by the grey rainy light, the wet silent trees, the shieldlike witnessing lake, the swans.[17]

Writing about the composition of *Finnegans Wake*, Richard Ellmann remarks of Joyce: 'He had begun his writing by asserting his differences from other men, and now increasingly he recognized his similarity to them.'[18]

Linguistically, 'difference' belongs to the axis of combination. It is the differences between words that enable them to be combined into syntagms that communicate meaning. One could conceive of a language that consisted of only two words (say, *yes* and *no*) but hardly of a language that consisted of only one. Homophones and homonyms are apt to cause confusion in speech or writing, because they violate this rule of difference. Writing that *emphasizes* the differences between things in the world, that emphasizes the uniqueness of individuals, places, objects, feelings, situations, will tend to operate mainly along the axis of combination or contiguity, in Jakobson's terminology: experience is pictured as an endless mesh of links extending in time and space, each link of which is slightly different from the others; or as a strip of moving-picture film, each frame of which is continuous with yet slightly different from the ones before and after. This way of representing reality can be rhetorically heightened by metonymic devices which delete or rearrange contiguous items, and this is the method of realism, or of symbolism operating under the constraints of realism, as in 'The Sisters' or in the Christmas Dinner scene in *A Portrait*.

Joyce's writing, however, developed steadily in the direction of emphasizing similarity rather than difference—not only psychologically and thematically, but structurally and stylistically. With *Finnegans Wake*, Joyce reached the logical terminus of this artistic development, where similarity is allowed almost total control over the discourse—and thus removed his writing beyond the reach of any criticism oriented to the novel, however elastically conceived. The novel, according to Ian Watt, is well named because of its commitment to imitating individual experience, 'which is always unique and therefore new'.[19] *Finnegans Wake*, however, as Ellmann says,

> is based on the premise that there is nothing new under the sun. . . . In all his books up to *Finnegans Wake* Joyce sought to reveal the coincidence of the present with the past. Only in *Finnegans Wake* was he to carry his conviction to its furthest reaches, by implying that there is no present and no past, that there are no dates, that time—and language which is time's expression—is a series of coincidences which are general all over humanity.* Words move into words, people into people, incidents into incidents, like the ambiguities of a pun, or a dream.[20]

The pun, which is the staple rhetorical device of *Finnegans Wake*, thrives on the abolition of difference and the exploitation of similarity. It seizes on homophones and homonyms, or generates new ones by telescoping two or more different words together. The pun may be considered a special form of metaphor. Metaphor, as we saw in Part Two, consists in substituting for one term another that is grammatically similar and semantically both similar and dissimilar, as when we say 'the ships *ploughed* the sea'. The pun *fuses* two terms that are phonologically or visually similar, but different in meaning, to create a new word in which the two different meanings are present at the same time—as, for instance, the anagrammatic word *cropse* in *Finnegans Wake* which includes *corpse* and *crops*, death and (re)birth; or a context is created in which the double meaning of a word is released, instead of being closed off, as in the very title of Joyce's work, where *Finnegan* contains the double echo of 'finish again' and 'begin again', and *Wake* signifies both death (as a noun) and awakening (as verb).

The ostensible justification of writing in this mode is that *Finnegans Wake* is the account of a dream; but if so, it is humanity that is dreaming. The dreamer in *Finnegans Wake*, Mr Porter, is so heavily disguised by his dreamself, Humphrey Chimpden Earwicker, and *his* innumerable incarnations, (not for nothing do his initials stand for 'Here Comes Everybody') as to be almost invisible. For this reason the metonymic devices of the dreamwork described by Freud are in *Finnegans Wake* thoroughly subordinated to the metaphoric. The suggestion of *earwig* in the name Earwicker, it has been plausibly argued,[21] derives

---

*A sly allusion to the famous last paragraph of 'The Dead', in which the snow that is 'general all over Ireland' is a metonymic symbol for the universality of death.

from a displacement of the taboo word *incest* into *insect*; but the text invites us to take this as a clue not so much to the relationship between Mr Porter and his daughter as to the relationship of all fathers to all daughters. In Freudian theory condensation and displacement operate on a chain of contiguities in the dreamer's experience, and their meaning is recoverable by the dreamer or his analyst by questioning and free association, which reconstitute the original chain (essentially the technique of Sherlock Holmes in dealing with clues). Since we know nothing about Porter except the distorted evidence of the dream itself, this is not a possible way of reading *Finnegans Wake*. We must interpret its condensations and displacements by reference to the history and mythology of the whole human race, which provide a circular field of similarities for Joyce's punning discourse to feed on, 'rounding up lost histereve'.

> Wharnow are alle her childer, say? In kingdome gone or power to come or gloria to be them farther? Allalivial, allalluvial! Some here, more no more, more again lost alla stranger. I've heard tell that same brooch of the Shannons was married into a family in Spain. And all the Dunders de Dunnes in Markland's Vineland beyond Brendan's herring pool take number nine in yangsee's hats. And one of Biddy's beads went bobbing till she rounded up lost histereve with a marigold and a cobbler's candle in a side strain of a main drain of a manzinahurries off Bachelor's Walk.[22]

This meditation on Irish emigration comes from the famous Anna Livia Plurabelle section in which, carrying to its limit the metaphorical principle that one river (the Liffey) stands for/evokes/may be replaced by, all other rivers, some five hundred river names are punningly buried in the discourse (e.g. *yangsee* [yankee] and *manzinahurries* [Manzaranes] in the quotation above) with a distorting and obscuring effect on the syntagmatic sense that has been found by many readers disproportionate to the expressive gain.[23] *Finnegans Wake* is not, indeed, a readerly text. Though short quotations may give delight (who could resist, from 'Anna Livia', 'It's that irrawaddyng I've stoke in my aars. It all but husheth the lethest zswound'?) few have been able to read the book through from beginning to end. Not that it *has* a beginning a middle or an end: the unfinished last sentence joins up with the truncated first sentence—and there you have the problem (for the reader) in a nutshell.

The axis of combination is not wholly neglected in *Finnegans Wake*—if it were, it would be truly unintelligible. Grammar—the code of combination—is still largely intact. If number and concord are not always strictly correct, word-order (the most important single feature of English syntax) is generally regular, as the quotation above shows. But semantically the discourse is developed with scarcely any observance of natural contiguities, of contextual coherence and continuity. As the grammar moves forwards to form predictable combinations of parts of speech the sense jumps sideways or backwards, by means of the pun, in quite *un*predictable ways, to the confusion of the reader who is trying to locate himself on some single narrative line. Narrative depends upon the notion of discrete figures whose fortunes are extended in time. As readers we form certain hypotheses about the future of the plot based on its past and present, and the characteristic affects aroused by narrative—concern, suspense, amusement, wonder, etc.—are achieved by the ways in which these hypotheses or expectations are fulfilled or falsified. But in *Finnegans Wake* the figures are unstable, constantly metamorphosing into each other, or substituted for each other, and the action has no past, present or future, since all events are simultaneously present. The result is a systematic deconstruction of that orthodox historical consciousness on which fictional realism is based, an enterprise strikingly similar to Nietzsche's heretical philosophy of history, characterized by Hayden White as 'metaphorical historiography':

> Just as poetry is itself the means by which the rules of language are transcended, so, too, Metaphorical historiography is the means by which the conventional rules of historical explanation and emplotment are abolished. Only the lexical elements of the field remain, to be done with as the historian, now governed by the 'spirit of music', desires. . . . The historian is liberated from having to say anything *about* the past; the past is only an occasion for his invention of ingenious 'melodies'. Historical representation becomes once more all *story*, no plot, no explanation, no ideological implication at all—that is to say, 'myth' in its original meaning as Neitzsche understood it, 'fabulation'.[24]

Perhaps 'chords' or 'harmonies' would be more appropriate musical terms than 'melodies' to describe Joyce's creative play with the data of history:

> riverrun, past Eve and Adam's [Dublin church on banks of Liffey/Garden of Eden], from swerve of shore to bend of bay, brings us by a commodius [Commodus, Roman Emperor] vicus [Latin, street/Vico, whose cyclic philosophy of history partly inspired *FW*/Vico Rd, Dalkey] of recirculation back to Howth Castle and Environs [HCE].
> Sir Tristram [Tristan and Isolde/Tristram Shandy, hero of another comic experimental novel] violer d'amores [violator/viola] fr'over [rover] the short sea, had passencore [passenger/Fr. *pas encore*= not yet] rearrived from North Amorica on this side the scraggy isthmus of Europe Minor to wielderfight [Germ. *wieder*=again] his penisolate [pen/penis/peninsular] war: nor had topsawyer's [Tom Sawyer's] rocks by the stream Oconee [river in Laurens County, Georgia, USA, on which there is a town called Dublin] exaggerated themselse to Laurens [Cf. Laurence Sterne, author of *Tristram Shandy*] County's gorgios [Romany, *youngsters*] while they went doublin[Dublin/doubling] their mumper all the time: nor avoice from afire bellowsed mishe mishe [Erse, *I am*] to tauftauf [Germ. *taufen*=baptize]thuartpeatrick [Thou art Peter/Patrick/peatrick]: not yet,

though venissoon [venison/very soon/Vanessa, friend of Swift, Dean of St Patrick's Dublin] after, had a kidscad [cadet = younger son = Jacob, disguised in kidskin] buttended a bland old isaac [Isaac, blind father of Jacob/Isaac Butt, ousted from leadership of Irish National Party by Parnell]: not yet, though all's fair in vanessy [Vanessa/Inverness] were sosie sesthers wroth [Susannah, Esther and Ruth/three weird sisters in *Macbeth*] with twone nathandjoe [Jonathan (Swift)/Nathan and Joseph]. Rot a peck of pa's malt had Jhem or Shen [Noah's sons Ham, Shem and Japhet, who saw their father drunk] brewed by arclight and rory end to the regginbrow was to be seen ringsome on the aquaface.[23]

Ulysses, which was originally conceived as a story for *Dubliners*, is situated halfway between the formal extremes represented by that book and *Finnegans Wake*. The title itself is of course metaphoric, pointing to a similarity between dissimilars: Bloom and Odysseus, Stephen and Telemachus, Molly and Penelope, modern Dublin and the Mediterranean of the ancient world. And this is a structural (not a merely decorative) metaphor, in that *it exerts control over the development of the narrative*. Once Bloom has been cast as Odysseus, Stephen as Telemachus and Molly as Penelope, then the story must end with Bloom and Stephen united (however briefly and casually) with Bloom returned (however ingloriously) to his wife (however unfaithful she may have been in his absence). And it is a reasonable assumption that many of the episodes in *Ulysses* were generated by the Homeric model rather than by the modern setting or the psychologies and interrelationships of the modern characters. Bloom's attendance at a funeral was probably suggested to Joyce by the felt obligation to have some contact with the Underworld in his modern epic; the barmaids at the Ormond Hotel, Miss Douce and Miss Kennedy, were no doubt summoned into literary existence by the wish to find some substitute for the Sirens in Bloom's modern Odyssey, and so on.

Joyce did not of course bind himself to a slavish imitation of his Homeric model. Some of the more artificial episodes, like the Oxen of the Sun, are only perfunctorily related to Homer, and, more importantly, a good deal of the material in the book derives from Joyce's own observation and experience, and a felt need to do literary justice to that observation and experience: Joyce's sense of his own youthful self and mature self: his sense of Dublin as a place and as a community; his recollection of that place and community as it was at a particular point in historical time. *Ulysses* thus combines two quite different and (in theory) opposed compositional principles: the realistic and the mythopoeic. On the one hand it is the supreme achievement of the realistic novel tradition. We know these characters with a convincing fullness, an intimacy, an utter candour that was unprecedented in literature before its publication and arguably has never been equalled since. And the milieu in which they move is established with equivalent concreteness and authenticity, achieved, as we know, by amazing feats of recall and patient research. It is all there: the names on the shopfronts, the name of the winner in the day's big race, the architecture of the Bloom's house at 6 Eccles Street. The Dublin of 16 June 1904 lives for ever in the pages of *Ulysses*, immortal and unchanged, consistent with historical fact in almost every detail, and the fictional characters are inserted into it so skilfully that the joins scarcely show: truly a novel that is, in the Goncourts' phrase, 'history as it might have happened.'

And yet: *Ulysses*. We have become so accustomed to that title as to forget its challenging strangeness inscribed above what purports to be a story of Dublin folk one summer day at the beginning of the twentieth century, their trivial, banal, unheroic doings: eating, drinking, excreting, masturbating, copulating, singing, talking, walking, thinking. Without that title, after all, it would be possible (though impoverishing) to read the whole book without realizing that there was a second, mythical dimension to the narrative,* that the actions of Bloom, Stephen and Molly are not merely consistent with and expressive of their individual characters and historical situation, but re-enact (or travesty or parody) the wanderings of Odysseus and the actions of *his* family and acquaintance. And not merely Odysseus, of course: there are many other similarities in the text—Stephen as Hamlet, for instance, or Bloom as 'Ben Bloom Elijah'. The adoption of an overarching metaphorical structure for the book licenses a plurality of other, local substitutions.

Joyce's method of 'manipulating a continuous parallel between contemporaneity and antiquity'[26] greatly excited T. S. Eliot, and probably influenced *The Waste Land*, which was being composed at the time when *Ulysses* was appearing in serial form. When it was complete and published as a book, Eliot saluted Joyce's achievement thus:

> Instead of the narrative method, we may now use the mythical method. It is, I seriously believe, a step toward making the modern world possible for art . . .[27]

What Eliot meant by 'the narrative method' was the method of the classic 'readerly' text: the story that turns upon the solution of an enigma, the disentanglement of an intrigue, or an instructive change of fortune, the story in which 'everything hangs together' in a very obvious way—causality, moralizing, verisimilitude and narrative interest all working together in harness. In the latter part of the nineteenth century, starting perhaps with Flaubert ('The novel ended with Flaubert and with James', Eliot remarked in that same essay on *Ulysses*) this stable synthesis began to show cracks, as a conflict of

---

*Originally, in the serial publication of the novel, Joyce gave to each of the episodes a title drawn from the *Odyssey* (Telemachus, Nestor, Proteus etc.) by which they are still referred to in critical commentary; but he deleted these headings from the text when it was published in book form.

interest between its various elements became evident. For example, the more 'true to life' fiction became, the less likely it was to observe the conventions of the readerly plot. It was the staple complaint of the early modernists against the Edwardian realists that they had not absorbed this lesson, and that their painstaking accumulation of realistic detail was therefore fatally compromised, deprived of authentic 'life'. 'The writer', Virginia Woolf complained in 1919 'seems constrained, not by his own free will, but by some powerful and unscrupulous tyrant who has him in thrall, to provide a plot, to provide comedy, tragedy, love interest, and an air of probability embalming the whole. . . . Is life like this? Must novels be like this?'[28] The modernists found the modes of late Victorian and Edwardian poetry similarly inauthentic in clinging to the myth of a universe that was intelligible and expressible within the conventions of a smoothly homogeneous lyrical idiom. 'We can only say,' T. S. Eliot declared in 1921, 'that it appears likely that poets in our civilization, as it exists at present, must be *difficult*. Our civilization comprehends great variety and complexity, and this variety and complexity, playing upon a refined sensibility, must produce various and complex results. The poet must become more and more comprehensive, more allusive, more indirect, in order to force, to dislocate, if necessary, language into his meaning.'[29]

The modernist enterprise, however, had its dangers and its problems. The logical terminus of their fictional realism was the plotless 'slice of life' or the plotless 'stream of consciousness', and plotlessness could easily become shapelessness, or randomness. 'Difficulty' in poetry could easily become a cover for self-indulgent incoherence. The post-impressionist painters faced the same problem. Glossing Cézanne's celebrated remark that he wanted to paint 'Poussin from nature', E. H. Gombrich says:

> The Impressionists were true masters in painting 'nature'. But was that really enough? Where was that striving for an harmonious design, the achievement of solid simplicity and perfect balance which had marked the greatest paintings of the past? The test was to paint 'from nature', to make use of the discoveries of the Impressionist masters, and yet to recapture the sense of order and necessity that distinguishes the art of Poussin.[30]

Hence the attraction, to Eliot, of Joyce's mythical method, which, so to speak, 'painted Homer from nature'. Eliot's essay is called ' "Ulysses", *Order* and Myth' (my italics) and is concerned to rebut the accusation of Richard Aldington that *Ulysses* was a chaotic, Dadaist work. On the contrary, 'It is . . . a step towards making the modern world possible for art, toward that order and form which Mr Aldington so earnestly desires.'[31] Modern experience, 'the immense panorama of futility and anarchy which is contemporary history'[32] is represented in all its triviality, aimlessness, sordidness, absurdity and contingency, without apparently being tampered with in the interests of plot; yet the representation proves after all to have a structure, a principle of aesthetic order derived from a quite different source (Homer). The representation of a demythologized world, a world 'fallen into the quotidian' (Heidegger's phrase) is thus ingeniously redeemed by allusion to the lost mythical world—aesthetically redeemed by our perception of the structure, and spiritually redeemed by our perception of human continuity between the two worlds.

Ulysses, then, is a realistic or metonymic fiction, (about Bloom, Stephen and Molly) with a mythopoeic or metaphorical structure. As Walton A. Litz has shown in his study of the various drafts of the novel,[33] metaphorical procedures came to predominate as the novel progressed and was progressively revised. The Homeric parallel was of course present from its inception, but the idea of each episode having its own set of leitmotifs—its special art, colour, organ, symbol, 'technic', etc.—was decided at a late stage and the earlier episodes were revised to make them consistent with the later ones. This feature of *Ulysses* must be described as metaphoric in our terms, since it entailed the insertion into the discourse of items on a basis of similarity not contiguity—for instance, allusions to horses, the 'symbol' of 'Nestor', in that episode, or the references to 'heart', the 'organ' of 'Hades', in that episode. These elaborate systems of leitmotifs reinforce the general tendency of *Ulysses* towards an encyclopaedic allembracingness, away from that concern with individual experience that is typical of the realistic novel. If they do not seem intrusively metaphorical—if, indeed, they are seldom consciously perceived by readers without the help of commentators like Stuart Gilbert[34]—it is because what could hardly be contiguous in time or space can very easily be contiguous in a person's 'stream of consciousness'. As Lawrence Sterne had demonstrated in the eighteenth century, the process of association in human consciousness seldom works in a logical, linear fashion, but is characterized by idiosyncratic twists and turns and jumps: the moment of Tristram Shandy's conception was disturbed by Mrs Shandy's untimely enquiry about winding up the clock, 'an unhappy association of ideas which have no connection in nature'.[35] Therefore, under cover of plausibly rendering 'the atoms as they fall upon the mind in the order in which they fall . . . [tracing] the pattern, however disconnected in appearance, which each sight or incident scores upon the consciousness'[36] (as Virginia Woolf put it) Joyce could smuggle into his discourse items drawn from the most heterogeneous contexts to make up other, quite artificial patterns, unrelated to the individual psychologies of his characters. Ignoring the signal of the title, it is possible to read the first few episodes of *Ulysses* (up to and including 'Hades') merely as realistic fiction equipped with psychological hi-fi. It is only with the pastiche headlines of 'Aeolus' that the discourse openly, verbally, displays its plurality of reference (in this case to journalism as an institution as well as to the Dublin *Evening Telegraph*). As the novel progresses, the use of parody and pastiche, which place the discourse at some aesthetic distance from the material it is mediating, becomes more and more pronounced, culminating in the virtuoso feats of 'The Oxen of the Sun' (based on a metaphorical equation between the evolution of English prose and the development of the foetus in the womb) and Circe (with its profusion of surrealistic substitutions and transformations). Joyce can afford these metaphoric flights because the metonymic base of his work is so secure; and in the closing episodes he returns us to that base. In *Ulysses*, the metonymic mode is transformed and enriched but not (as in *Finnegans Wake*) obliterated by the metaphoric.

One of the great achievements of this novel, unmatched by other exponents of the stream of consciousness technique, is the way Joyce discriminates stylistically between the consciousnesses of his main characters. It is noteworthy that this, too, is achieved by varying the proximity of the discourse to the metaphoric and metonymic poles. Stephen's consciousness is essentially metaphoric—he is constantly transforming what he perceives, the world of contiguities, of *nacheinander* (one thing after another) and *nebeneinander* (one thing next to another)[37] into other images and concepts drawn from his reading, on the basis of some perceived similarity or ironic contrast. The more insistently he does this—the more substitutions he makes— the weaker becomes the chain of combination and the more difficult it is for the reader to follow the discourse. Thus 'Proteus', in which Stephen is actively pondering the metaphorical processes of the mind (and stepping up their power artificially by closing his eyes and shutting off one sensory channel to the world of contiguities) is the most 'difficult' of the first three episodes. And all these episodes are more difficult than any of the episodes pertaining to Bloom.

For Bloom's stream of consciousness is by comparison essentially metonymic. We are always much more aware of what he is doing— where he is situated in time and space—because there is a more direct connection between what he is thinking and what he is doing. When his consciousness digresses from what he is doing, his associations still connect items that are contiguous rather than similar. The difference between Stephen and Bloom in this respect may be illustrated by comparing the responses of each to the perception of a female figure. This is Stephen, on Sandymount strand, catching sight of the midwife, Mrs Florence MacCabe:

> Mrs Florence MacCabe, relict of the late Patk MacCabe, deeply lamented, of Bride Street. One of her sisterhood lugged me squealing into life. Creation from nothing. What has she in the bag? A misbirth with a trailing navelcord, hushed in ruddy wool. The cords of all link back, strandentwining cable of all flesh. That is why mystic monks. Will you be as

gods? Gaze in your omphalos. Hello. Kinch here. Put me on to Edenville. Aleph, alpha: nought, nought, one.

Spouse and helpmate of Admon Kadmon: Heva, naked Eve. She had no navel. Gaze. Belly without blemish, bulging big, a buckler of taut vellum, no, whiteheaped corn, orient and immortal, standing from everlasting to everlasting. Womb of sin.[38]

What is significant here is not the mere profusion of metaphors ('hushed', 'cable of all flesh', 'buckler', 'whiteheaped corn' etc.) but that the interior monologue *proceeds* by a series of perceived similarities and substitutions. It is the perception of similarity between a telephone cable and the umbilical cord that leads Stephen's thought from the midwife to Eve, from his own birth to the birth of the race, drawing in other similarities and contrasts: the cords that monks wear around their waists (symbols of chastity and also of being joined together in the Mystical Body of Christ) the navels contemplated by oriental mystics, the navelless belly of Eve which reminds Stephen of the 'whiteheaped' bosses (*omphaloi*, the same word meaning 'navels' also) on the Achaean shields in the *Iliad*, of the Song of Songs ('Thy belly is like a heap of wheat set about with lilies' vii, 2) and of Thomas Traherne's vision of Paradise ('The corn was orient and immortal wheat, which never should be reaped, nor was ever sown. I thought it had stood from everlasting to everlasting').[39]

Compare Bloom, also looking at a woman: his neighbour's servant girl, who is just ahead of him at the counter of the pork butcher:

A kidney oozed bloodgouts on the willowpatterned dish: the last. He stood by the nextdoor girl at the counter. Would she buy it too, calling the items from a slip in her hand. Chapped: washing soda. And a pound and a half of Denny's sausages. His eyes rested on her vigorous hips. Woods his name is. Wonder what he does. Wife is oldish. New blood. No followers allowed. Strong pair of arms. Whacking a carpet on the clothes line. She does whack it, by George. The way her crooked skirt swings at each whack.

The ferreteyed porkbutcher folded the sausages he had snipped off with blotchy fingers, sausagepink. Sound meat there like a stallfed heifer.[40]

Bloom's perception of the girl herself is very strikingly synecdochic— he sees her in terms of her chapped hands, vigorous hips, strong arms and skirt: parts standing for the whole. Also his thought *proceeds* by associating items that are contiguous rather than (as in the case of Stephen) similar. The girl is linked with her master (Woods), the master with the mistress, the age of the mistress with the youth of the girl, the youth of the girl with the jealousy and repressiveness of the mistress who forbids her to have male visitors. In the second paragraph we appear to have metaphor rather than metonymy: *ferreteyed, sausagepink, like a stallfed heifer*. But is is significant how heavily these similitudes depend upon contiguity and context. The physical juxtaposition of the butcher's fingers and the sausages he is handling provides Bloom with the readymade metaphor *sausagepink*.

The comparison of the butcher to a stallfed heifer makes a substitution from the same vocabulary area of meat, butchery etc., and even *ferret* is associated with the killing of animals for human consumption. These are all, in fact, weakish metaphors or similes precisely because, in each case, the two terms of the figure, the tenor and the vehicle, are drawn from essentially the same context, not from 'different spheres of thought', in Ullmann's phrase,[41] as are, for instance, the umbilical cord and the telephone cable in the passage just quoted from 'Proteus'.

Molly Bloom's stream of consciousness is still more 'metonymic' than her husband's, inasmuch as she seldom makes *any* metaphorical connections between items. Such metaphors and similes as occur in her discourse are rarely coined by her, but are colloquial or proverbial clichés. She is very literalminded, pragmatic, down-to-earth. Bloom's speculative, whimsical thought is as far removed from hers as Stephen's complex, ironic and cultured intelligence is from Bloom's. Molly is always asking Bloom to explain words to her, but is dissatisfied with his answers because they refer the question of meaning to the system of language rather than to reality.

> —Metempsychosis?
> —Yes. Who's he when he's at home?
> —Metempsychosis, he said, frowning. It's Greek: from the Greek. That means the transmigration of souls.
> —O, rocks! she said. Tell us in plain words.[42]

This exchange in 'Calypso' is recalled in Molly's soliloquy at the end of the novel:

> Arsenic she put in his tea off flypaper wasnt it I wonder why they call it that if I asked him he'd say its from the Greek leave us as wise as we were before[43]

She is correspondingly contemptuous of the prurient periphrases of the priest hearing her youthful confession of petting:

> he touched me father and what harm if he did where and I said on the canal bank like a fool but whereabouts on your person my child on the leg behind high up was it yes rather high up was it where you sit down yes O Lord couldn't he say bottom right out and have done with it[44]

'Bottom', as Stuart Gilbert has pointed out, is one of the keywords of the 'Penelope' episode, which mark transitions in Molly's consciousness from one train of thought to another.

> The movements of Molly Bloom's thoughts in this episode appear, at first sight, capricious and subject to no law. But a close examination shows that there are certain words which, whenever they recur, seem to shift the trend of her musings, and might be called the 'wobbling points' of her monologue. Such words are 'woman', 'bottom', 'he', 'men'; after each of these there is a divigation in her thoughts, which, as a general rule, revolve about herself.[45]

Gilbert ingeniously compares this process to the movement of the earth through space. Molly (an Earth-mother figure) revolves on her own egocentric axis, but is subject to other forces in the planetary system to which she belongs. Another way of putting it would be to compare Molly's monologue to a long-playing gramophone record to which we, as readers, are listening, each track or band of which is concerned with a particular phase of her life and usually with a particular man. There is the track about the young Leopold and his courtship of her, the track about their married life, the track about her youth in Gibraltar and her lover Lieutenant Gardiner, and the more recently recorded tracks concerning her sexual encounter with Blazes Boylan the previous afternoon and Leopold's behaviour since returning to the house with Stephen in the early hours of the morning. The stylus or pick-up arm of Molly's consciousness, as she lies half-awake in bed, does not follow these tracks in chronological order, but jumps backwards and forwards across the surface of the disc. It will be following one track and then provoked by some psychic vibration (usually marked by one of the key words) suddenly 'skate' across to settle in the grooves of another track. When we first tune into her thoughts she is thinking about Bloom's behaviour on coming to bed, asking to have his breakfast in bed the next morning:

> Yes because he never did a thing like that before as ask to get his breakfast in bed with a couple of eggs

As becomes clear later, Molly suspects that Leopold has had some sexual encounter during the day which has given him an appetite (hence the 'Yes because') but the image of Bloom having breakfast in bed jogs the pick-up and sends it skipping back to an episode much earlier in their married life:

> since the *City Arms* hotel when he used to be pretending to be laid up with a sick voice doing his highness to make himself interesting to that old faggot Mrs Riordan that he thought he had a great leg of and she never left us a farthing all for masses for herself and her soul greatest miser ever was actually

The transition of thought here from the present to the past is triggered by a perceived similarity between Bloom having breakfast in bed the next morning and Bloom having breakfast in bed in the past, but this is not a metaphorical kind of similarity. The two events belong to the same order of reality, the married life of the Blooms; one occasion on which Bloom orders breakfast in bed reminds Molly of another. That is in fact all the events have in common, since the earlier breakfast in bed had nothing to do with sexuality at all. Molly's 'because' in the first line of her monologue is therefore characteristically lacking in any real logical force. Her memory plays over Mrs Riordan's character, but always egocentrically:

she had too much old chat in her about politics and earthquakes and the end of the world let us have a bit of fun first God help the world if all the women were her sort down on bathingsuits and lownecks of course nobody wanted her to wear I suppose she was pious because no man would look at her twice I hope I'll never be like her a wonder she didn't want us to cover our faces but she was a well educated woman certainly and her gabby talk about Mr Riordan here and Mr Riordan there I suppose he was glad to get shut of her and her dog smelling my fur and always edging to get up under my petticoats especially then still I like that in him polite to old women like that[46]

The recollection of Bloom 'pretending to be laid up with a sick voice' leads to rumination on his tendency, representative of his sex, to make a great fuss when ill:

when he cut his toe with the razor paring his corns afraid hed get blood poisoning but if it was a thing I was sick then wed see what attention only of course the woman hides it not to give all the trouble they do

and the word 'woman' jolts the pick-up again:

yes he came somewhere Im sure by his appetite anyway love its not or hed be off his feed thinking of her . . . .[47]

Which is 'where we came in.'

2   Gertrude Stein

Our examination of Joyce's work, particularly of *Ulysses*, shows that, while the general tendency of modernist writing is towards metaphoric structure and texture, there are modernist versions of the metonymic mode: the interior monologues of Bloom and Molly are almost as 'modernist' in verbal form (i.e. as strikingly foregrounded against the norms of the fictional tradition) as that of Stephen. The most obviously foregrounded feature is the incompletion of sentences (given additional emphasis by the elimination of punctuation in the case of Molly)—a kind of grammatical synecdoche by which the rapid and erratic shifts of consciousness from one topic to another are imitated. This suggests that modernist prose writing may be characterized by a radical shift towards the metonymic pole of language to which prose naturally inclines anyway, as well as by a displacement towards the metaphoric pole. In this connection it is interesting to look at the work of Gertrude Stein, for her writing oscillated violently between the metonymic and metaphoric poles, pushing out in each direction to points where she began to exhibit symptoms of Jakobson's two types of aphasia.

It is not surprising that most readers find Gertrude Stein's work (apart from the relatively readerly *Autobiography of Alice B. Toklas* [1932]) intolerably monotonous and/or impenetrably obscure. She was one of those rare artists whose work was 'experimental' in a sense genuinely analogous to scientific experiment: a series of artificial and deliberate experiments designed to test some hypothesis about language, or perception, or reality, or about the relations between these things. Its interest and value is therefore largely theoretical, rather than particular and concrete, and can best be appreciated in the context of her own theoretical glosses upon it, in essays and lectures. Not that Gertrude Stein herself would have accepted this limiting definition of her artistic endeavours. She thought of herself, like other early modernists, as an artist who was adapting her medium, literary language, to communicate a new perception of reality, a personal vision of the world which was yet publicly valid, if only the public would wake up and recognize that perception and experience had changed.

> The only thing that is different from one time to another is what is seen and what is seen depends upon how everybody is doing everything. This makes the thing we are looking at very different and this makes what those describe it make of it, it makes a composition, it confuses, it shows, it is, it looks, it likes it as it is, and this makes what is seen as it is seen.[1]

Gertrude Stein's own view of reality and our experience of it has been traced back, in part, to the philosophy of William James, who was her tutor at Harvard, and of Henri Bergson, whom James acknowledged as an independent precursor of his own 'radical empiricism'. Certainly John Passmore's summary of salient points in the thought of these two philosophers, though written without any regard to Gertrude Stein, seems acutely relevant to her work:

> Bergson . . . contrasts time as we think about it and time as we experience it. Conceptually considered, he says, time is assimilated to space, depicted as a straight line with 'moments' as its points, whereas experienced time is *duration*, not a succession of moments—it flows in an invisible continuity. This flowing quality, according to Bergson, is characteristic of all our experience: our experience is not a set of 'conscious states' clearly demarcated. Its phases 'melt into one another and form an organic whole'. . . . Our language consists of distinct words with well-defined outlines; this same distinctiveness we are misled into ascribing to the world we symbolize in language. . . . This is extraordinarily similar to James's account of experience in his *Principles of Psychology* (1890) as a 'stream of consciousness'. James there drew attention to what he took to be the central error of traditional empiricism—that, for it, experience consists of isolated 'impressions' or 'sensations'. 'Consciousness does not appear to itself chopped up into bits,' he protested, 'it is nothing jointed, it flows.' From the beginning, according to James, our experience is of the related—a fact

which escapes our notice only because for practical reasons we have so strong a tendency to seize upon the 'substantive' parts of our experience at the expense of the 'transitive parts'.[2]

The first thing that happens when these ideas (which appealed to a great many writers besides Gertrude Stein) are applied to literature, is the diminution and eventual disappearance of story, for story depends upon the conventional 'spatial' conception of time as a series of discrete moments. 'A thing you all know is that the three novels written in this generation that are important things written in this generation, there is, in none of them a story,' Gertrude Stein declared. 'There is none in Proust in *The Making of Americans* or in *Ulysses*.'[3] This is an overstatement, of course, but less so with respect to Gertrude Stein's own book than in relation to the others.

To be sure, *The Making of Americans* (composed 1906–8) looks superficially like a story, a family saga, an ambitious extension of the classic realistic novel of the nineteenth century—truer, more historical:

> not just an ordinary kind of novel with a plot and conversations to amuse you, but a record of a decent family progress decently lived by us . . . and so listen while I tell you all about us, and wait while I hasten slowly forwards, and love, please, this history of this decent family's progress.[4]

'History' is constantly appealed to as the aim of the writing:

> some time there will be a history of every kind and every one of such of them . . .[5]
> Some time then there will be a history of all women and all men . . .[6]
> Some time then there will be every kind of a history of everyone who ever can or is was or will be living.[7]

The Making of Americans, then, seems to be offered as a fragment of some huge universal history or chronicle. Starting with the Hersland family, it aims to fan out and describe all the ramifications of their relationships—not merely their marriages into other families but the governesses and seamstresses they employed and *their* families and marriages—and then move out further to cover the whole field of human contiguities that makes up recorded history:

> Sometime there will be written a long book that is a real history of everyone who ever was or are or will be living from their beginning to their ending.[8]

Yet the discourse is very unlike what we expect from history or chronicle, still less from the realistic novel. To begin with, there are almost no events, and such events as are described are fairly trivial, e.g. the episode of Martha and the umbrella:

> This one, and the one I am now beginning describing is Martha Hersland, and this is a little story of the acting in her of her being in her very young

living, this one was a very little one then and she was running and she was in the street and it was a muddy one and she had an umbrella that she was dragging and she was crying. 'I will throw the umbrella in the mud,' she was saying, she was very little then, she was just beginning her schooling, 'I will throw the umbrella in the mud,' she said and no one was near her and she was dragging the umbrella and bitterness possessed her, 'I will throw the umbrella in the mud,' she was saying and nobody heard her, the others had run ahead to get home and they had left her, 'I will throw the umbrella in the mud', and there was desperate anger in her; 'I have throwed the umbrella in the mud,' burst from her, she had thrown the umbrella in the mud and that was the end of it all in her. She had thrown the umbrella in the mud and no one heard her as it burst from her, 'I have throwed the umbrella in the mud,' it was the end of all that to her.[9]

This is vivid and expressive, but instead of describing other such events Gertrude Stein repeats this one several times, with additions and variations of detail. Such episodes are in any case few and far between, and the text consists mainly of discourse about the processes of composition and the nature of psychological being.

In 'Portraits and Repetition' Gertrude Stein remarks:

I said in the beginning of saying this thing that if it were possible that a movement were lively enough it would exist so completely that it would not be necessary to see it moving against anything to know that it is moving. This is what we mean by life and in my way I have tried to make portraits of this thing have tried always may try to make portraits of this thing.[10]

In orthodox narrative, events are the points of reference by which we register that the story is 'moving', they correspond to the points on a line in the conventional conceptualization of time as characterized by Bergson. Gertrude Stein virtually eliminated events from *The Making of Americans* because she was more interested in capturing the Bergsonian *durée*, ('not a succession of moments, it flows in an invisible continuity') or what she herself called 'a continuous present':

A continuous present is a continuous present. I made almost a thousand pages of a continuous present. Continuous present is one thing and beginning again and again is another thing. These are both things. And then there is using everything.[11]

These are the three staple devices of Gertrude Stein's early narrative work, *Three Lives* (composed 1903–4), *The Making of Americans* and *A Long Gay Book* (composed 1909–12). 'Using everything' is the ostensible aim of writing a history of everybody; 'beginning again and again' is the device of reverting to the same episode (such as Martha and the umbrella) instead of describing fresh ones: and the 'continuous present' is the evocation of a sense of movement that is not measured on an orthodox chronological scale. These three interrelated devices are all experiments along the metonymic axis of discourse. 'Using everything', the megalomaniac desire to cover, eventually, the whole field of human contiguities with language, defies the practical necessity to *select*, and insists on the essential uniqueness or 'difference' of each human being underlying their superficial similarity or 'resemblance' to each other. Since the enterprise of using everything is actually impossible, Gertrude Stein doesn't actually attempt it; she merely *promises* it, while in fact 'beginning again and again'. As readers we are tantalized by a story that is always being promised but never actually materializes and teased into attending to another kind of movement that is not progressive in the same way as a story: the 'continuous present' of existence.

Stylistically, the continuous present is characterized above all by the domination of verbs and gerunds over nouns, of the 'transitive' over the 'substantive' in William James's terminology. This is a marked deviation from the stylistic norm of nineteenth-century realistic fiction, which was generally notable for nominalization, the appropriate vehicle of its heavy freight of specificity and local colour.[12] But it is not (as in most early modernist writing) a deviation away from the metonymic pole towards the metaphoric. The concrete nouns, the substantives, are not, as in Henry James for example, removed from the descriptions of external reality merely to reappear in metaphorical rendering of inner psychological processes:[13] they simply, in Gertrude Stein, *disappear*. In this, and in some other respects, the style of *The Making of Americans* corresponds to the speech of aphasics suffering from what Jakobson calls similarity disorder or selection deficiency, which he places on the metonymic side of his linguistic scheme. This type of aphasic, it will be recalled, has great difficulty in naming things. Shown a pencil, for instance, he is likely to define it metonymically by reference to its use: 'to write'. In his speech main clauses disappear before subordinate clauses, subjects are dropped or replaced by a repeated all-purpose substitute word (like *one*, *it*, or *thing*) while the words 'with an inherent reference to the context, like pronouns, pronominal adverbs, words serving merely to construct the context, such as connectives and auxiliaries, are particularly prone to survive.'[14] Compare Gertrude Stein in 'Poetry and Grammar':

> A noun is the name of anything, why after a thing is named write about it. A name is adequate or it is not. If it is adequate then why go on calling it, if it is not then calling it by its name does no good. . . . Adjectives are not really and truly interesting . . . because after all adjectives affect nouns. . . . Verbs and adverbs are more interesting. In the first place they have one very nice quality and that is they can be so mistaken. It is wonderful the number of mistakes a verb can make and that is equally true of its adverbs. . . . Then comes the thing that can of all things be most mistaken and they are prepositions. Prepositions can live one long life being really nothing but mistaken and that makes them irritating if you feel that way about mistakes but certainly something that you can be continuously using and everlastingly enjoying. I like prepositions the best of all. . . . Then there are

articles. . . . They are interesting because they do what a noun might do if a noun were not so unfortunately so completely unfortunately the name of something. . . . Beside that there are conjunctions, and a conjunction is not varied but it has a force that need not make anyone feel that they are dull. Conjunctions have made themselves live by their work. . . . So you see why I like to write with prepositions and conjunctions and articles and verbs and adverbs but not with nouns and adjectives. If you read my writing you will see what I mean.[15]

Thus Gertrude Stein's refusal to use nouns, her deliberate preference for those parts of speech most likely to generate 'mistakes', results in a style that has much in common with aphasics who make mistakes involuntarily because they *cannot* use nouns. This sort of style:

Each one is mostly all his living all her living, a young one, an older one, one in middle living, an old one to themselves, to any one, to some one. That is to say not any one is all his living all her living to anyone, that is to say not any one, that is to say not any one hardly is feeling another one being a young one and then an older one and then an old one. It is a very strange thing this thing and an interesting thing that almost not any one is to any one is to themselves inside them one having been in all parts of being living.[16]

It is difficult to convey by quotation the effect of this kind of writing sustained over 'a thousand pages'. To many readers it will seem—has seemed—merely perverse, yet behind it there was a thoroughly coherent and consistent artistic and epistemological theory. Gertrude Stein was seeking 'to make a whole present of something that it had taken a great deal of time to find out'—that is, to capture the living quality of a character or an experience that she had observed or brooded on for a long period, but without giving the impression of *remembering* it and thus destroying its existential presentness:

We in this period have not lived in remembering, we have living in moving being necessarily so intense that existing is indeed something, is indeed the thing that we are doing.[17]

Gertrude Stein described her literary development as a process of liberating herself from 'remembering' in order to capture the quality of existing:

When I first began writing although I felt very strongly that something that made that some one be some one was something that I must use as being them, I naturally began to describe them as they were doing anything. In short I wrote a story as a story, that is the way I began, and slowly I realized this confusion, a real confusion, that in writing a story one had to be remembering, and that novels are soothing because so many people one may say everybody can remember almost anything. It is this element of remembering that makes novels so soothing. But that was the thing that I was gradually finding out listening and talking at the same time that is realizing the existence of living being actually existing did not have in it any element of remembering and so the time of existing was not the same as in the novels that were soothing. . . . I wondered is there any way of making what I know come out not as remembering. I found this very exciting. And I began to make portraits.[18]

The Making of Americans is a text which purports to be a story but turns into a series of portraits, and these portraits are composed not, like traditional 'character-sketches', out of details but out of inner rhythms. 'I conceived what I at that time called the rhythm of anybody's personality,'[19] she said in 'Portraits and Repetition', and this was how she described her method in *The Making of Americans* itself:

> Some slowly come to be repeating louder and more clearly the bottom being that makes them. Listening to repeating, knowing being in every one who ever was or is or will be living slowly came to be in me a louder and louder pounding. Now I have it to my feeling to feel all living, to be always listening to the slightest changing, to have each one come to be a whole one to me from the repeating in each one that sometime I come to be understanding.[20]

The technique, then, entailed a close attention to repetition in others, and an elaborate use of repetition in verbal description. Yet Gertrude Stein later denied that it *was* repetition, strictly speaking, because of the 'slightest changing' that was always involved. Interestingly, she compared her technique to the (metonymic) technique of film, then in its infancy as a medium:

> Funnily enough the cinema has offered a solution of this thing. By a continuously moving picture of any one there is no memory of any other thing and there is that thing existing. . . . I was doing what the cinema was doing, I was making a continuous succession of the statement of what that person was until I had not many things but one thing. . . . In a cinema picture no two pictures are exactly alike each one is just that much different from the one before, and so in those early portraits there was . . . as there was in *The Making of Americans* no repetition . . . anything one is remembering is a repetition, but existing as a human being, that is being listening and hearing is never repetition. It is not repetition if it is that which you are actually doing because naturally each time the emphasis is different just as the cinema has each time a slightly different thing to make it all be moving.[21]

Gertrude Stein abandoned *A Long Gay Book* (the sequel to *The Making of Americans*), in which she intended to 'go on describing everything',[22] when she realized that the logic of her literary development made it necessary to dispense with even the pretence of story. She turned to the writing of portraits detached from any narrative context, for example the 'Picasso' of 1909, which begins:

> One whom some were certainly following was one who was completely charming. One whom some were certainly following was one who was charming. One whom some were following was one who was completely charming. One whom some were following was one who was certainly completely charming[23]

and continues in the same style of repetition with minimal variation. The next stage in Gertrude Stein's development was to eliminate the human altogether, because the human carried with it ineradicable vestiges of time as a continuum rather than as a continuous present:

> in regard to human beings looking inevitably carries in its train realizing movements and expression and as such forced me into recognizing resemblances, and so forced remembering and in forcing remembering caused confusion of present with past and future time.[24]

Gertrude Stein thus followed the aesthetic path later traced by Ortega y Gasset in *The Dehumanization of Art* (1948) with an unflinching resolve only equalled by the post-impressionist painters whose work she collected. The next stage was in fact to make portraits of inanimate objects that have been compared to the 'still-lives' of Picasso and Matisse.

> I began to make portraits of things and enclosures that is rooms and places because I needed to completely face the difficulty of how to include what is seen with hearing and listening and at first if I were to include a complicated listening and talking it would be too difficult to do. That is why painters paint still lives.[25]

But this phase in her development led to a radical reversal of direction in her verbal style.

The discourse of *The Making of Americans* was essentially an *extended* discourse: length and continuity were of the essence, for only in this way could Gertrude Stein's conception of human existence as an un-segmented flow, a play of secret rhythms, be rendered. Like the selection-deficiency aphasic, the narrator of her book does not readily switch from one topic to another, or stop and start a fresh line of discourse. New paragraphs frequently begin with the self-cueing phrase, 'as I was saying' which keeps the discourse tied to the same context for page after page. Punctuation which would disturb and interrupt the continuous present is avoided:

> When I first began writing, I felt that writing should go on, I still do feel that it should go on but when I first began writing I was completely possessed by the necessity that writing should go on and if writing should go on what had colons and semi-colons to do with it, what had commas to do with it, what had periods to do with it what had small letters and capitals to do with it to do with writing going on . . .[26]

The same contempt was extended to question marks and inverted commas to indicate direct speech. The only punctuation Gertrude Stein was prepared to admit at this stage were the full stop and the paragraph break—the sentence and the paragraph constituting in her mind natural units in prose writing (corresponding roughly, one might say, to the shot and the scene in cinematic discourse). In the transition from human portraits to still lives, however, she switched from length to brevity, from verbs to nouns, from prose to poetry and (in our terms) from metonymic to metaphoric experiment.

> But after I had gone as far as I could in these long sentences and paragraphs that had come to do something else I then began very short things and in doing very short things I resolutely realized nouns and decided not to get around them but to meet them, to handle, in short to refuse them by using them and in that way my real acquaintance with poetry was begun.[27]

The reference here is to the short prose-poems describing objects, food and rooms, collected in *Tender Buttons* (1911). Some examples:

A CARAFE, THAT IS A BLIND GLASS

A kind in glass and a cousin, a spectacle and nothing strange a single hurt colour and an arrangement in a system to pointing. All this and not ordinary, not unadorned in not resembling. The difference is spreading.

A BOX

Out of kindness comes redness and out of rudeness comes rapid same question, out of an eye comes research, out of selection comes painful cattle. So then the order is that a white way of being round is something suggesting a pin and it is disappointing, it is not, it is so rudimentary to be analysed and see a fine substance strangely, it is so earnest to have a green point not to red but to point again.

A CUTLET

A blind agitation is manly and uttermost.

A COLD CLIMATE

A season in yellow sold extra strings makes lying places.

APPLE

Apple plum, carpet steak, seed clam, coloured wine, calm seen, cold cream, best shake, potato, potato and no gold work with pet, a green seen is called bake and change sweet is bready, a little piece a little piece please. A little piece please. Cane again to the presupposed and ready eucalyptus tree, count out sherry and ripe plates and little corners of a kind of ham. This is use.[28]

This mode of writing, following the lead of Gertrude Stein herself, has been called the literary equivalent of cubism in painting. But it is in fact much closer to surrealism than to cubism, since it does not confine itself to merely changing the relationships of contiguous planes and of parts to wholes as they are in nature (as does for instance the Picasso 'Woman in an Armchair' that decorates the cover of the Penguin selection of Gertrude Stein) but presents an object in terms of other objects often far removed from it and from each other in context. The very title *Tender Buttons* is a surrealist metaphor, reminding one of the soft treatment of hard objects (melting watches etc.) in the painting of

Salvador Dali. Since buttons cannot be literally tender, 'Tender Buttons' must be a metaphor. For what? Nipples have been suggested, but without a context there is in fact no way of knowing what an expression like 'tender buttons' might mean, and this is generally true of the whole collection.

In 'Portraits and Repetition', Gertrude Stein described how, at this stage in her development, she was excited by the discovery that the words that made 'what I looked at be itself' were not the words that belonged to conventional description, that made the object merely 'look like itself'.[29] In 'Poetry and Grammar' she described her technique in *Tender Buttons* as 'looking at anything until something that was not the name of that thing but was in a way that actual thing would come to be written.'[30] *Tender Buttons* she described as 'poetry', and 'Poetry is concerned with using with abusing, with losing with wanting, with denying with avoiding with adoring with *replacing* the noun.'[31] (my italics). This is clearly a type of metaphorical writing based on radical substitution (or replacement) of referential nouns. But the perception of similarity on which metaphor depends is in this case private and idiosyncratic to a degree that creates almost insuperable obstacles to understanding.* Correspondingly, the axis of combination which should link the various substitutions together into an intelligible chain, is radically disturbed and dislocated. The result is a kind of discourse that has something in common with the speech of aphasics suffering from contiguity disorder or contextual deficiency, in which Jakobson says:

> The syntactical rules organizing words into a higher unit are lost; this loss, called agramatism, causes the degeneration of the sentence into a mere 'word-heap'. . . . Word order becomes chaotic, the ties of grammatical coordination and subordination whether concord or government, are dissolved. As might be expected, words endowed with purely grammatical functions, like conjunctions, prepositions, pronouns and articles, disappear first, giving rise to the so-called 'telegraphic style'. . . .[32]

The analogy is not exact. Word order, for instance, is still basically regular in *Tender Buttons*, and it is possible to construct perfectly intelligible sentences on the model of, for example 'A season in yellow sold extra strings makes lying places' e.g. 'A backstreet in the city, given appropiate markings, provides parking places')—the problem with the original sentence here is not so much syntactical as lexical or semantic. But there are some items (e.g. 'APPLE') where grammar has disintegrated to the point where 'word-heap' seems an appropiate description of the end result.

Superficially, Gertrude Stein's writing in *Tender Buttons* resembles the experiments of the Dadaists and their successors in aleatory art.

---

*See Allegra Stewart's heroic effort to explicate 'A CARAFE' in *Gertrude Stein and the Present* (Cambridge, Mass., 1967) p. 87ff.

Tristan Tzara composed poems by shredding his own writing and other miscellaneous texts, shaking up the pieces in a bag, and transcribing them in the order in which he plucked them out, one by one. William Burroughs has used a similar technique in some of his novels, cutting up and splicing together heterogeneous texts on an (allegedly) random basis. *Tender Buttons* looks as if it might have been composed in the same way. But whereas the aim of these other writers has been to affront human rationality and/or to demonstrate the capacity of nature (represented by the word-heap) to generate its own meanings independently of human intervention—essentially a postmodernist enterprise—Gertrude Stein maintained the traditional stance of the artist as one who by the exercise of a special gift or skill was seeking to bring her medium into closer and closer proximity to her perceptions. She would have heartily endorsed Ortega's words:

> There is no difficulty in painting or saying things which make no sense whatever, which are unintelligible and therefore nothing. One only needs to assemble unconnected words or draw random lines. But to construct something that is not a copy of 'nature' and yet possesses substance of its own is a feat which presupposes nothing less than genius[33]

This was precisely what Gertrude Stein admired in Picasso and Matisse, and what she aimed at in her own work. If *Tender Buttons* fails it is perhaps because it attempts something that violates the very essence of her medium, language: the combination axis of language cannot be so brutally dislocated without defeating the system's inherently communicative function. *Tender Buttons* is a feat of *de*creation: the familiar tired habits of ordinary discourse are shaken off by 'jolting words and phrases out of their expected contexts'[34] and this is certainly exhilarating, but the treatment is so drastic that it kills the patient. A new creation does not transpire. But it is important to recognize that Gertrude Stein hoped it would. She was a modernist, not a postmodernist* 'I had to feel anything and everything that for me was existing so intensely that I could put it down in writing as a thing in itself without at all necessarily using its name.' This is essentially the Symbolist poetic, expounded by Mallarmé in terms of evocation and suggestion:

> It is not description which can unveil the efficacy and beauty of monuments, seas or the human face in all their maturity and native state, but rather evocation, allusion, suggestion ... out of a number of words, poetry

---

*Since writing this I have come across Neil Schmitz's article 'Gertrude Stein as a Post-Modernist: The Rhetoric of *Tender Buttons*' (*Journal of Modern Literature* III (1974) pp. 1203–1218), which contains some ingenious readings of *Tender Buttons* but does not convince me that the aesthetic principles on which that work was based were postmodernist. But there is, of course, some continuity between modernism and postmodernism, and I would not deny that it is particularly visible in the work of Gertrude Stein.

fashions a single new word which is total in itself and foreign to the language—a kind of incantation[35]

by Ezra Pound in terms of the image:

An 'Image' is that which presents an intellectual and emotional complex in an instant of time[36]

and by Eliot in terms of the 'objective correlative' and his catalytic model of poetic composition.[37] These were all poets speaking of poetry, or poetic drama, and Gertrude Stein herself regarded *Tender Buttons* as poetry. Yet the general aim behind all her writing is the same: to render the elusive quality of 'existence' as it is truly perceived when we shed the habits of an obsolete epistemology. In most of the early modernists this enterprise entailed a radical questioning of the conventional notion of time in relation to experience: a conversion of the dynamic or kinetic into the static, of the temporal into the spatial, of successiveness into simultaneity;[38] and on the whole this process could be taken furthest in lyric poetry, with its natural emphasis on paradigmatic similarity rather than in prose with its natural emphasis on syntagmatic continuity. Yet in her experimental metonymic writing, like *The Making of Americans*, Gertrude Stein showed how far prose might go in the same direction, by the artful use of repetition with variation; and it was this aspect of her work, rather than her experiments in the metaphoric mode, that had the most creative influence on other writers, in particular Ernest Hemingway.

3 Ernest Hemingway

Hemingway met Gertrude Stein in the early 1920s when he was living in Paris and struggling to establish himself as a writer. He became well acquainted with her work, especially *The Making of Americans*, which he persuaded Ford Madox Ford to print in the *Transatlantic Review* and which he proofread for the author. The friendship was always precariously dependent upon Hemingway's willingness to play the part of pupil to master, and in due course the inevitable breach occurred; but looking back on that period of his life in *A Moveable Feast* (1964), Hemingway acknowledged her importance as a literary innovator: 'She had . . . discovered many truths about rhythms and the use of words in repetition that were valid and valuable and she talked well about them.'[1]

Hemingway wanted to be both a realist and a modernist: the ambition is implicit in his trinity of 'good' American writers—Mark

Twain, Stephen Crane and Henry James.[2] A newspaper reporter himself, he was seeking to combine the truthfulness of good journalism with the intensity and permanence of great imaginative writing. Speaking of the time when he knew Gertrude Stein, Hemingway recalled:

> I was trying to write then and I found the greatest difficulty, aside from knowing what you truly felt, rather than what you were supposed to feel, and had been taught to feel, was to put down what really happened in action: what the actual things were which produced the emotion that you experienced. In writing for a newspaper you told what happened and, with one trick and another, you communicated the emotion aided by the element of timeliness which gives a certain emotion to any account of something that has happened on that day; but the real thing, the sequence of motion and fact which made the emotion and which would be valid in a year or in ten years, or, with luck and if you stated it purely enough, always, was beyond me and I was working very hard to try and get it.[3]

It was essentially a problem of style, though Hemingway tended to formulate it in terms of existential authenticity (the passage quoted is part of an explanation of why he studied bullfighting). Hemingway's vision of life, tempered by the experience of war, was bleakly materialistic, in the philosophical sense: positivist, anti-metaphysical, stoical; though by temperament he was highly sensitive, superstitious and sentimental. It is the tension between these two sets of qualities— the latter battened down under a style derived from the former—that accounts for the extraordinary power of his best work.

The logical medium for Hemingway's materialism was a style scrupulously restricted to denotation, as he himself suggested in one of the most celebrated passages of *A Farewell to Arms*:

> There were many words that you could not stand to hear and finally only the names of places had dignity. Certain numbers were the same way and certain dates and these with the names of the places were all you could say and have them mean anything. Abstract words such as glory, honour, courage or hallow were obscene beside the concrete names of villages, the numbers of roads, the names of rivers, the numbers of regiments and the dates.[4]

The banishment of abstraction is of course a rhetorical illusion: 'dignity' is allowed to stand in this passage and is indeed a concept absolutely central to Hemingway's vision of life. In the same way he purged his style of metaphor but contrived to retain in it the emotive resonance of metaphorical writing.

Overt metaphor, in the earlier (and better) Hemingway is invariably a sign of falsity and illusion. The story 'Hills Like White Elephants' is worth glancing at in this connection since its title draws ironic attention to the one overtly metaphorical expression in the text. The story begins in Hemingway's characteristic denotative mode: 'The hills across the valley of the Evro were long and white.' A young man and woman are sitting on a railway platform facing the hills, drinking and bickering as they wait for a train. They quarrel about the girl's observation that the hills 'look like white elephants'. Gradually it becomes clear to the reader that the man is trying to persuade the girl to have an abortion. Through trivial, banal, repetitious talk—the story consists almost entirely of dialogue—Hemingway communicates with wonderful exactness the feeling of a relationship that has reached that stage where the two people involved are disenchanted with each other yet frightened at the prospect of a crisis and separation. The action is minimal: they order drinks, get up, walk about, sit down. The conversation builds small reconciliations which immediately break down. The last words of the story are the girl's: 'I feel fine.' But we don't believe her. The white hills, fancifully transformed by the girl's simile, stand for impossibility: the recovery of innocence and the first careless rapture of love, freedom from the contingencies of the flesh. (In its French translation the story is entitled '*Paradis Perdu*'.) 'If I do it,' says the girl, referring to the abortion, 'then it will be nice again if I say things like white elephants and you'll like it?' 'I'll love it,' he replies. 'I love it now but I just can't think about it.'[5]

By denying himself metaphor, Hemingway was of course deliberately cutting himself off from the symbolist tradition which directly or indirectly nourished most of the early modernist prose writers—James, Conrad, Ford, Joyce, Virginia Woolf. Most of these authors shared the view that God (at least the God of orthodox Christianity) was dead and that the world was a wasteland, a place of meaningless suffering, unsuccessful communication and shattered illusions. Hemingway had no quarrel with them there. But in the exercise of their craft, which they invested with a quasi-religious solemnity, these writers found some relief or release from a nihilistic *Weltanschauung*. Writing itself, especially through metaphorical devices, turned life into art, made art into an alternative reality, luminous, harmonious, immutable and transcendent, and this was often accomplished by the invocation and reworking of old myths. Hemingway wanted nothing of that kind; yet he shared the same basic ambition of the modernists: to translate raw experience into immortal form by renewing the means of expression. It could only be done, therefore, by working on the metonymic axis of his medium, and this was where the precept and example of Gertrude Stein was probably crucial, in showing what might be done in prose by rhythm and repetition.

Repetition is a characteristic of vernacular speech, because most speakers of any language use a very limited vocabulary, and because speech (compared to writing) encourages a good deal of redundancy in the interests of communication (too high a ratio of information to lexical units puts great strain on the receiver of the message and makes the message vulnerable to interruption or interference from other sources). Now the characteristic mode of American realistic fiction is a narrative voice based on the vernacular. It was because Mark Twain showed how this could be done that Hemingway accorded him a prime place in American literary history ('All modern American literature comes from one book by Mark Twain called *Huckleberry Finn*'[6]). Hemingway had absorbed this lesson long before he met Gertrude Stein. A story written when he was seventeen includes the following paragraph:

> Yes, he was a bad Indian. Up on the upper peninsular he couldn't get drunk. He used to drink all day—everything. But he couldn't get drunk. Then he would go crazy; but he wasn't drunk. He was crazy because he couldn't get drunk.[7]

Here we see in embryo some of the characteristic devices of Hemingway's mature style: the short simple sentences, the refusal to avoid an awkward echo (*up on the upper*), the repetition and permutation of word and phrase, eschewing elegant variation. By conventional literary standards this is clumsy and tautologous writing, but it expresses quite powerfully a baffled and desperate state of mind. It hasn't, however, got much resonance, it is not particularly haunting or memorable, it doesn't have the purity of expression Hemingway described as his aim in the passage quoted earlier from *Death in the Afternoon*. It's the kind of thing Sherwood Anderson did well, but that was so far from (or so dangerously near to) what Hemingway was aiming at that he had to exorcise Anderson's influence in *The Torrents of Spring* (1926). What Hemingway learned from his exposure to modernist literary theory and practice and from his own trials and errors in the crucial Paris years, was to refine and complicate the basic devices of vernacular narration so as to give his writing something of the magical, incantatory quality of symbolist poetry, without losing the effect of sincerity, of authenticity, of 'the way it was'—in short to combine realism and modernism in a single style. Consider the opening paragraph of his story 'In Another Country':

> In the fall the war was always there, but we did not go to it any more. It was cold in the fall in Milan and the dark came very early. Then the electric lights came on, and it was pleasant along the streets looking in the windows. There was much game hanging outside the shops and the snow powdered in the fur of the foxes and the wind blew their tails. The deer hung stiff and heavy and empty, and small birds blew in the wind and the wind turned their feathers. It was a cold fall and the wind came down from the mountains.[8]

This perfectly illustrates Jakobson's account of the realistic author's metonymic method: 'Following the path of contiguous relationships, the realist author metonymically digresses from the plot to the atmosphere and from the characters to the setting in space and time.

He is fond of synecdochic details.' Hemingway's narrator digresses from the 'plot' (the situation of wounded soldiers receiving treatment—though the fact that the digression occurs so soon, before the situation has been properly explained, is of course a deviation from the procedures of classical realism) to the atmosphere (the cold autumn evenings) and the setting, Milan, which is presented synecdochically (the city represented by its shops, the shops by the game shops, the game by certain animals, and the animals by certain parts of their bodies—fur, tails, feathers). In this way the paragraph moves along a straight line of contiguity. But there is another system of relationships at work in the writing based on the repetition of certain words and grammatical structures and rhythmical patterns, which has the opposite effect, drawing our attention (if only subliminally) to similarities rather than contiguities, keeping certain words and concepts echoing in our ears even as our eyes move forward to register new facts. In particular the reader will be affected by the repetition of the words *fall*, *cold* and *wind*. Though *fall* and *cold* are paired together in the second sentence, all three words are combined together only once, in the last sentence—which is why it has a finality and resonance not easy to account for in logical or semantic terms. This last sentence clinches a network of association between the season and the emotions of the wounded soldiers. As the carefully arranged words of the opening sentence intimate, and the story goes on to make explicit, the war is always with the soldiers, in their minds and in their wounds (those who are cured will be returned to the front to face violent death again, and those who will not go to war again will not have lives worth living). The war is going on in the mountains; the wind comes from the mountains; *cold* and *fall* are connected obviously enough with death. In the context of these reverberating repetitions, the synecdochic details of the game hanging outside the shops inevitably function as symbols of death and destruction, though there is nothing figurative about the manner of their description, just as there is no pathetic fallacy in the description of the weather. In this way—by carefully disguising the 'projection of the principle of equivalence from the axis of selection into the axis of combination'—an apparently metonymic style is made to serve the purposes of metaphor.

4　D. H. Lawrence

Like Hemingway, D. H. Lawrence was obliquely connected to the modernist movement, sharing some of its aims and assumptions (e.g. the need to innovate, to revolutionize the traditional forms) but rejecting others (e.g. the tendency inherited from Symbolism to set art against life as an alternative and superior kind of order). Both Lawrence and Hemingway believed strongly in maintaining a vital connection between art and experience—but of course for very different reasons and to very different literary effects. Where Hemingway worked hard to disguise his artfulness as naive truthtelling, and strove for economy and understatement, Lawrence wrote throughout his career with unrestrained (and often uncontrolled) lyrical or prophetic exuberance, and responded with notable enthusiasm to those early American writers whom Hemingway rejected because of their artificial literary language.[1] Where Hemingway's style abstained as far as possible from abstraction and metaphor, Lawrence's revelled in both. Yet Lawrence cannot be classified, any more than Hemingway, as a 'metaphoric' writer in the same sense as we have applied that term to Joyce or T. S. Eliot. Similarity (and contrast) never, in Lawrence, control the development of the discourse as in the 'mythical method' of *Ulysses* or *The Waste Land*. Continuity was more important to Lawrence than irony. 'Flow' was one of his favourite words to express the quality he looked for in authentic living and authentic writing:

> It is the way our sympathy flows and recoils that really determines our lives. And here lies the vast importance of the novel, properly handled. It can inform and lead into new places the flow of our sympathetic consciousness, and it can lead our sympathy away from things gone dead.[2]

It is consistent with this concern for 'flow' that Lawrence rarely indulges in those deviations from chronological sequence that are generally typical of the modernist novel (though he is, significantly, vaguer about *dates* than the traditional realistic novelist*). And his

---

*Frank Kermode has commented on this feature of *Women in Love*, comparing it to George Eliot's *Middlemarch*, in 'D. H. Lawrence and the Apocalyptic Types', *Continuities* (1968), p. 149.

narrative voice, however much it varies in tone, from the shrewdly down-to-earth to the lyrically rhapsodic, and whatever character's consciousness it is rendering, is always basically the same, unmistakeably Lawrentian. Not for him the mimicry, the pastiche, the rapid shifts of voice and linguistic register, that we encounter in Joyce and Eliot. What we know about the compositional habits of these writers confirms the distinction. Joyce revised his work by making innumerable insertions and substitutions, often as late as proof stage. Lawrence, as is well known, to revise a novel had to write it all out from the beginning; he had to reactivate the basic continuity and rhythm of the discourse in order to make any changes in it. Whereas Joyce (and perhaps Eliot, if we judge by the evidence of *The Waste Land* manuscript) saw the text as a kind of *space*, a verbal object the components of which might be juggled about, replaced, added to and subtracted from, Lawrence seems to have regarded it as a *sound*, a 'tremulation on the ether' to use his own phrase:[3] an utterance that, like the oral epic, could only be modified in the act of recitation.

This concern for flow, for continuity, meant that Lawrence's style had to be essentially metonymic in structure, forwarded by contiguity, though the meanings he groped after could only be expressed metaphorically. As in Hemingway, therefore, though to totally different effect, repetition both rhythmical and lexical is exploited to shift an ostensibly metonymic style in the direction of metaphor. Here is a typical passage from *Women in Love*, just after Gudrun and Ursula have witnessed Gerald Crich ruthlessly subduing his horse which is panic-stricken by the passing of a colliery train:

> The man [i.e. the gatekeeper of the level-crossing] went in to drink his can of tea, the girls went on down the lane, that was deep in soft black dust. Gudrun was as if numbed in her mind by the sense of the indomitable soft weight of the man bearing down into the living body of the horse: the strong, indomitable thighs of the blond man clenching the palpitating body of the mare into pure control: a sort of soft white magnetic domination from the loins and thighs and calves, enclosing and encompassing the mare heavily into unutterable subordination, soft-blood-subordination, terrible.[4]

In this short, two-sentence paragraph there is a remarkable amount of repetition—lexical repetition (*soft, indomitable, man, body, thighs, mare, subordination*) and rhythmical repetition, produced by syntactical parallelism. The long second sentence consists of a main clause ('Gudrun was as if numbed in her mind by the sense of . . .') followed by three participial phrases, each of which is an expansion of the preceding one. The parallelism of syntactical structure can be shown by laying out the three phrases in columns, thus:

| 1 the indomitable soft weight of the man | bearing down into the living body of the horse |

| 2 | the strong indomitable thighs of the blond man | clenching the palpitating body of the mare |
| 3 | a sort of soft white magnetic domination from the loins and thighs and calves | enclosing and encompassing the mare heavily into unutterable subordination, soft-blood-subordination, terrible. |

Of particular interest in this paragraph is the behaviour of the word *soft*. 'Soft black dust' in the first sentence is a straightforward referential use of the adjective. 'Soft weight' in the next sentence is foregrounded by being a little paradoxical. It is not quite an oxymoron, for some things can be heavy *and* soft, but it doesn't seem to be particularly appropiate, in the circumstances, to Gerald, whose physical contact with the horse seems rather to be 'hard'. One might almost suspect that Lawrence lazily wrote '*soft* weight' simply because he had just written '*soft* black dust' and the word was in his head. Yet 'soft weight' does, of course, make a kind of metaphorical sense, because Gerald, the colliery owner, is associated with the soft black dust that covers the countryside, and this chapter is in fact called 'Coal-Dust'. A kind of equation is implied—Gerald:mare as colliery:countryside. The next use of *soft* is explicitly metaphorical: 'a sort of soft white magnetic domination' (a phrase that echoes an earlier description of Gerald on the horse: 'Gerald was heavy on the mare, and forced her back. It seemed as if he sank into her magnetically, and could thrust her back against herself.'[5]). Again, *soft* seems to be used here more as a purely formal repetition rather than for any descriptive aptness, but again under examination the word proves to contribute a new meaning. For the repetition of *soft* is now linked with the inversion of *white* (for *black*) and Gerald is, of course, associated throughout the novel with whiteness as well as blackness in his fair physique (here indicated by *blond*) and in the 'soft white' snow in which he meets his death. 'Soft-blood-subordination', in which *soft* appears for the fourth and last time in this paragraph, is another mysteriously metaphorical expression, with yet another shade of meaning. Exactly what meaning it is not possible to say with any precision. We are told elsewhere in *Women in Love* that 'words themselves do not convey meaning, that they are but gestures we make, a dumb show like any other,'[6] and the passage under discussion contains its own reminder to this effect in 'unutterable'. But clearly the fourth use of *soft* would be quite incomprehensible without the other three. We can in fact say with reasonable confidence that the whole passage is a premonition of the ultimately destructive sexual relationship that is to develop between Gerald and Gudrun. That Gerald's horse is a mare rather than a stallion is not, of course, fortuitous. Gudrun sees in his domination of the mare a type of sexual possession which both appalls and fascinates her. Certainly much of the language, from 'the soft weight of the man' to 'soft-blood-subordination', which seems odd as a description of a man trying to control a horse, becomes more intelligible when applied to a man making love to a woman or (to be more exact) when applied to a woman's imagining what it would be like to be made love to by a certain type of man. In short, the passage would seem to conform, at its deepest level of meaning, to Jakobson's metaphoric category, in that it turns on Gudrun's perception of a similarity between herself and the mare, and an emotional substitution of herself for the mare. Yet this substitution is never made explicit: it emerges out of an intense dwelling on the literal event.

Lawrence's writing in this passage appears to be 'forwarded by contiguity' in the sense that each clause or phrase takes its impetus from an item in the preceding one, the repeated words knitting the units together on the pattern of Ab Bc Cd De etc. Yet the effect of progression and continuity this produces is a kind of illusion: the discourse is not really moving forward to encompass new facts, but unfolding the deeper significance of the same facts. The passage develops a more and more psychological, a less and less referential, presentation of the event by a gradual accretion of vague metaphorical meaning, which does not interrupt or break the continuity of the discourse. In this process the repetition of *soft* plays a crucial role, for it is a metonymic attribute of the context at the beginning of the passage and a metaphorical vehicle for the sexual mysticism at its conclusion. In this respect the passage is a kind of microcosm of the process by which *Women in Love* as a whole grew out of the *ur*-novel 'The Sisters' and separated itself from *The Rainbow*; and a microcosm, too, of the way *The Rainbow* developed from its family-saga beginning to its visionary conclusion, and of the way Lawrence developed, in the writing of these paired novels, away from the more conventional realistic fiction of *Sons and Lovers*.

The same tendency may be observed in the three versions of *Lady Chatterley's Lover*[7] through which Lawrence's revisions transformed an initially realistic love story (in which an idyllic love affair between an aristocratic lady and her gamekeeper is tested against the harsh realities of a society in which class-differences and class-antagonisms threaten the permanence of the relationship) into a didactic pastoral romance in which the love idyll is allowed an easy victory over circumstances and offered as a type of redemption from the sickness of modern society. Pastoral is, in our terms, a 'metaphorical' genre: it does not pretend to describe agrarian society realistically, but offers an imaginative model of, or metaphor for, the good life. In literary tradition it often involves educated, genteel characters pretending, voluntarily or by force of circumstances, to be unsophisticated country folk. Lawrence's Connie and Mellors are both refugees from a corrupt and decadent world of civilization, from a countryside ravaged by industry, from a social and cultural life eaten away by greed, pseudo-sophistication and class antagonism; they plunge into the woods, throw off their clothes, decorate each other's bodies with flowers, use rude and dialect words (a feature of pastoral as far back as Theocritus) and make uninhibited love in the open air. It is true that pastoral elements were present in *The First Lady Chatterley*, but they were very much subdued in comparison with *John Thomas and Lady Jane* and *Lady Chatterley's Lover*. In these two revisions Lawrence made a crucial readjustment of the structural balance of the story: in the first version the love affair begins early in the narrative and dominates the first half of the book; the second half is concerned with the problems of fitting this relationship into society. In the second and third versions the initial meeting between Connie and Mellors is much delayed to allow an extensive treatment of Connie's sexual repression and alienation from her social milieu. The love affair, with its greatly expanded descriptions of sexual intercourse, thus dominates the *second* half of the final *Lady Chatterley's Lover*, and this has the effect of making it seem a solution to the problems raised in the first half. It is quite consistent with this move towards a more schematic pastoral treatment of the story that Mellors should be more educated (an ex-officer who can speak standard English if he wants to) than his precursor Parkin. Lawrence did not, however, solve all the problems of reader-response raised by his revisions, and left the final version vulnerable to complaints that it is often absurd, unconvincing and doctrinaire. *The First Lady Chatterley* is certainly the most aesthetically unified version of the three, but it is the least ambitious—almost a throwback to the Lawrence of *Sons and Lovers*.

To examine the dynamics of Lawrence's writing in some detail, especially the way in which he seems, as it were, to feed metaphorically upon his own metonymies, working himself up from shrewd observation of social and environmental realities into a poetic, prophetic mode of utterance, it is more convenient to look at one of his short stories than at the long, complex novels. 'England, my England' is not perhaps among his greatest stories, but it is a very powerful one, and belongs to the most important phase of his literary career. First written in the crucial year of 1915, when *The Rainbow* was completed and *Women in Love* begun, it was substantially revised and expanded in 1921, by which time Lawrence had not only made considerable progress in working out his 'metaphysic' but also achieved greater poise and confidence in expressing his ideas through narrative. He evidently considered the revised version of 'England, My England' to be important enough to stand as the title-story of a collection he published in 1922.

The second version of the story, in bare outline, is as follows: Egbert and Winifred are a young married couple, passionately in love, who occupy an old cottage on the edge of a common in Hampshire. The cottage is a gift from Winifred's father, Godfrey Marshall, a strong-willed, self-made man, who has settled several of his children in the same way on his estate. Egbert is handsome, charming, well-bred, but without a profession or ambitions, so the young couple are increasingly dependent upon the largesse of the father when they start a family. This dependence begins to come between them. Their eldest child cuts her leg on a sickle left lying in the garden by Egbert and, due to the incompetence of the local doctor, is eventually crippled by the accident. Winifred's response to this crisis, conditioned by her religious upbringing (the Marshalls are Catholics), is a deliberate frigidity towards her husband. The First World War begins and Egbert, who is unaffected by vulgar patriotism, hesitates about enlisting. He asks his wife's advice and she refers him to her father. Marshall advises him to join up. Egbert does so, and after some months' service is killed by a German shell. The last few pages of the story, describing this incident, contain heavy hints that Egbert expected, and in a sense willed, this death.

The first, much shorter version of the story has essentially the same narrative line, with the following important exceptions: the main character (called Evelyn) is in no way responsible for the accident to his daughter, and, at the end of the story, in his mortally wounded state he manages to shoot three German soldiers dead before he is killed and horribly mutilated by a fourth. (This version was never reprinted after its appearance in *The English Review*, October 1915, and is little known.)

In both versions the story poses obvious problems of interpretation. Egbert's death is presented not, as in most modern war literature (Hemingway's, for example) as something absurd and pitiful in its randomness and pointlessness, but as something profoundly meaningful and indeed inevitable, an appropiate termination of a futile life. But who, or what, is responsible for the futility? Is it Egbert himself, because of his fundamental decadence and lack of purpose? Is it his father-in-law who patronized him? Is it his wife who deliberately denied him her love? Or senseless circumstance that crippled his daughter and thus made him an outcast from his own family? Like so much of Lawrence's writing, 'England, My England' was partly inspired by real people and events, and it is tempting to look to these sources for a key to its enigmas, as does Harry T. Moore in his biography, *The Intelligent Heart*. In the first half of 1915, Lawrence and Frieda were loaned Viola Meynell's cottage on the family estate of Wilfred Meynell at Greatham, Sussex. Another cottage belonged to Wilfred Meynell's daughter Madeline and her husband Percy Lucas, brother of the man-of-letters E. V. Lucas. The Percy Lucases had three daughters, the eldest of whom, Sylvia, was crippled as the result of an injury to her leg caused by a sickle carelessly left lying in the grass outside the cottage (though *not* by her father). According to Moore,

Lawrence tutored this little girl for a while, but took a dislike to her father:

> he saw Percy Lucas as a loafer, dependent upon the bounty of Wilfred Meynell and leaning for spiritual support upon Madeline; these things Lawrence put into the cruel portrait of Percy, as Egbert, parasitic dweller at Godfrey Marshall's family colony at Crockham in 'England, My England'. Yet, for all its meanness, the portrait did not completely lack sympathy: the Egbert of the story was really a victim of the ostensibly benevolent paternalism that dominated the colony.[8]

Moore's account has been challenged on a number of points by Percy Lucas's daughter Barbara.[9] She states that Lawrence did not tutor Sylvia, but a cousin of hers, and that Sylvia, her mother and her sisters were in London throughout the Lawrence's stay at Greatham, except for a short visit in the Easter holidays; while Percy, who had volunteered for military service in 1914, would necessarily have been absent from the estate at this period except for the occasional brief leave. Barbara Lucas believes that Lawrence and the Lucas family met, in fact, on only one occasion, during those Easter holidays of 1915.[10] Lawrence's correspondence, however, suggests a closer acquaintance than that.

The story written in 1915 and published in October of the same year in *The English Review* proved cruelly prophetic when Percy Lucas died of wounds received in the battle of the Somme in July 1916. Even Lawrence, never overscrupulous about using friends and acquaintances as models for his characters, felt a pang of remorse. He wrote to Catherine Carswell on 16 July 1916:

> It upsets me very much to hear of Percy Lucas. I did not know he was dead. I wish that story at the bottom of the sea, before ever it had been printed. Yet, it seems to me, man must find a new expression, give a new value to life, or his women will reject him, and he must die. I liked Madeline Lucas the best of the Meynells really. She was the one who was capable of honest love: she and Monica. Lucas was, somehow, a spiritual coward. But who isn't?
>
> I ought never, never to have gone to live at Greatham. Perhaps Madeline won't be hurt by that wretched story—that is all that matters. If it was a true story, it shouldn't really damage.[11]

After continuing the letter on other topics, Lawrence added a characteristic postscript:

> No, I don't wish I had never written that story. It should do good in the long run.

It is not clear whether by 'true story' Lawrence meant, true to the facts of the Lucas marriage, or true in some wider, more representative sense. As Emile Delavenay has pointed out[12], the second version of the story is in several respects much more faithful to its sources in real life than the first version. For example, Godfrey Marshall, a Quaker in the first version, is made a Catholic in the second, (Meynell himself was a Catholic convert who had originally been a Quaker); and the whole account of the cottage and the 'Crockham' estate (unnamed in the first version) seems, to judge by Barbara Lucas's evidence, much more specifically evocative of Greatham in the second version. This seems a somewhat callous proceeding on Lawrence's part in view of his earlier misgivings about Madeline's possible response, unless he thought that by making the story more literally true to the facts he would make it somehow more acceptable. But in that case, why did he deliberately depart from the facts by making Egbert responsible for the accident—a suggestion that could only cause offence to the dead man's family? My own opinion is that by the time he came to revise the story, living in Sicily, far away from England, Lawrence was no longer interested in or bothered by the possible private repercussions of the story and that the specific details about Greatham came into the story almost accidentally, along with a great deal of 'doctrine' that has little to do with Greatham, in the process of revision, as Lawrence strove to give the story more depth and concreteness. Moore's description of 'England, My England' as a 'story *à clef*' is not only limiting, but misleading, based on a reading of the second version of the text in the light of Lawrence's comments on the first. Even of this first version Lawrence, describing it, at the time of publication. as 'a story about the Lucases', immediately went on to say, 'The story is the story of most men and women who are married today—of most men at the War, and wives at home.'[13] To Catherine Carswell the following year he was more specific about the theme: 'a man must find a new expression, give a new value to life, or his women will reject him and he must die.' And behind that theme is a still larger one: the idea that death and dissolution may be the route to a new creation, and that there may be a kind of heroism in following it, even at the cost of one's own extinction. I shall try to show how these ideas find expression in a mode of writing that is continually turning its realistic particulars into symbols and its descriptive metaphors into thematic ones. This process is observable both in the differences between the two versions and in the development of the second version itself. The evolution of the story, in short, was always in the direction of the metaphorical pole.

I observed above that Lawrence's novels are invariably chronological in structure, but the compression required by the short-story form sometimes led him to depart from this norm, as in 'England, My England'. The first version of the story is in the form of an extended retrospect in the hero's mind at the time of his mortal wounding. The second version begins on the day of the accident to the daughter, then looks back on the history of the marriage, then returns to the time of the opening paragraphs to describe the accident; the remainder of the narrative proceeds chronologically. The opening pages describe Egbert working, rather unsuccessfully, on the edge of the common, extending the garden path that leads from his 'Hampshire cottage that crouched near the earth amid flowers blossoming in the bit of shaggy wilderness round about.'[14] In the opening description of the setting a long historical perspective is introduced:

> The sunlight blazed down upon the earth, there was a vividness of flamy vegetation, of fierce seclusion amid the savage peace of the commons. Strange how the savage England lingers in patches: as here, amid these shaggy gorse commons, and marshy, snake infested places near the foot of the south downs. The spirit of place lingering on primeval, as when the Saxons came, so long ago. Ah, how he had loved it! The green garden paths, the tufts of flowers, purple and white columbines, and great oriental red poppies with their black chaps and mulleins tall and yellow, this flamy garden which had been a garden for a thousand years, scooped out in the little hollow among the snake infested commons. He had made it flame with flowers, in a sun-cup under its hedges and trees . . . . The timbered cottage . . . belonged to the old England of hamlets and yeomen . . . it had never known the world of today. Not till Egbert came with his bride. And he had come to fill it with flowers.[15]

The corresponding passage in the first version is as follows:

> The sunlight blazed down on the earth; there was a vividness of flamy vegetation and flowers, of tense seclusion amid the peace of the commons. The cottage with its great sloping roofs slept in the for-ever sunny hollow, hidden, eternal. And here he lived, in this ancient, changeless hollow of flowers and sunshine and the sloping-roofed house. It was balanced like a nest in a bank, this hollow home, always full of peace, always under heaven only. It had no context, no relation with the world; it held its cup under heaven alone, and was filled for ever with peace and sunshine and loveliness.
>
> The shaggy, ancient heath that rose on either side, the downs that were pale against the sky in the distance, these were the extreme rims of the cup. It was held up only to heaven; the world entered in not at all.[16]

The timelessness of the cottage's setting, here associated with a vaguely Christian 'eternity', is in the second version given a distinctly primitive or 'savage' note, further emphasized by the mention of snakes (which are wholly absent from the first version). The description of the flowers in the second version is more detailed and more lyrical, and they are associated metonymically with Egbert because he planted and tended them. As the second version continues, Winifred and her family are associated metaphorically with bushes and trees, especially the hawthorn:

> She moved with a slow grace of energy like a blossoming, red-flowered bush in motion. She, too, seemed to come out of the old England, ruddy, strong, with a certain crude, passionate quiescence and a hawthorn robustness.[17]

The image is reiterated after the introduction of Godfrey Marshall, and the association of Egbert with flowers shifts from the metonymic to the metaphoric:

> The girls and the father were strong-limbed, thick-blooded people, true English, as holly-trees and hawthorn are English. Their culture [*i.e.* their high cultural interests] was grafted on to them as one might perhaps graft a common pink rose on to a thorn-stem. It flowered oddly enough, but it did not alter their blood. And Egbert was a born rose.[18]

Apart from a comparison of Winifred to 'a blossoming tree in motion' in the first version[19], all these metaphors of vegetation were added in the second version.

At first the marriage is a success, based on strong physical passion. 'Ah, that it might never end, this passion, this marriage! The flame of their two bodies burnt again in that old cottage, that was haunted already by so much by-gone, physical desire. . . . They too felt that they did not belong to the London world any more.'[20] But this feeling of having dropped out of the modern world is an illusion paid for by Godfrey Marshall's fortune, made in the industrial North and maintained in the City of London.

> They drew the sustenance for their fire of passion from him, from the old man. It was he who fed their flame. He triumphed secretly in the thought. And it was to her father that Winifred still turned, as the one source of all security and support. . . . For Egbert had no ambition whatsoever. . . .[21]

Then the first child is born. A fair, delicate-limbed child, Joyce takes after her father and is thus associated like him with flowers—'a wild little daisy-spirit . . . this light little cowslip child.'[22] But Joyce requires a Nanny and this entails further financial dependence on Godfrey. Furthermore, maternity makes sexual love less important to Winifred and cements her bond to the real provider and protector of her offspring.

> Her child seemed to link her up again in a circuit with her own family. Her father and mother, herself, and her child, that was the human trinity for her. Her husband? Yes, she loved him still. But that was like play. Till she married, her first human duty had been towards her father: he was the pillar, the source of life, the everlasting support. Now another link was added to the chain of duty: her father, herself, her child.[23]

The image of the father as a pillar is given an interesting Biblical association a little later:

> She began to resent her own passion for Egbert . . . he was charming, he was lovable, he was terribly desirable. But—but—oh, the awful looming cloud of that *but!*—he did not stand firm in the landscape of her life like a tower of strength, like a great pillar of significance.[24]

The close juxtaposition of *cloud* and *pillar*, though they are in fact metaphors applied to different things, evokes the image of the pillar of the cloud in Exodus, in which the patriarchal God of the Old Testament hid himself. And the image of Egbert as a flower also acquires Biblical associations:

> What did she want—what did she want? Her mother once said to her, with that characteristic touch of irony: 'Well, dear, if it is your fate to consider the lilies, that toil not, neither do they spin, that is one destiny among others, and perhaps not so unpleasant as most.' ... Winifred was only more confused. It was not a question of lilies. At least, if it were a question of lilies, then her children were the little blossoms. They at least *grew* ... as for that other tall, handsome flower of a father of theirs, he was full grown already, so she did not want to spend her life considering him in the flower of his days.[25]

The pillar-image returns in the form of a modified cliché: 'Why wasn't he like Winifred's father, a pillar of society, even if a slender, exquisite column?'[26]

Thus the marriage approaches deadlock. Egbert's basic desire was to 'hold aloof' from the world, but Winifred 'was not made to endure aloof. Her family tree was a robust vegetation that had to be stirring and believing.'[27] The dead metaphor 'family tree' is thus revived, and developed further in the next paragraph in respect of Marshall: 'In a dark and unquestioning way, he had a sort of faith: an acrid faith like the sap of some not-to-be-exterminated tree.'[28] This leads, *via* the repetition of 'acrid', into a disquisition on Marshall's potency as an Old Testament father-figure:

> He had a certain acrid courage, and a certain will-to-power ... he had kept, and all honour to him, a certain primitive dominion over the souls of his children, the old, almost magic prestige of paternity. There it was, still burning in him, the old smoky torch of paternal godhead . . .. Here was a man who had kept alive the old red flame of fatherhood that had even the right to sacrifice the child to God, like Isaac.[29]

The association of Marshall with the God of the Old Testament, only hinted subliminally in the juxtaposition of *cloud* and *pillar*, now becomes more explicit. And the potent image of 'flame', originally attributed to the relationship between Egbert and Winifred, is now transferred to her father, its red glow contrasted with the 'hard white light of our fatherless world'.[30] Having 'once known the glow of male power [Winifred] would not easily turn to the hard white light of feminine independence,'[31] but her attempts to bring up her own children 'with the old dark magic of paternal authority' are neutralized by Egbert's passivity.[32]

With this passage, in which Lawrence's own voice, and opinions, dominate the discourse, (and which belongs exclusively to the second version) the long retrospect ends; and the story proceeds to narrate, in a vivid, dramatic style, the accident to Joyce and its painful aftermath. When Joyce proves to be irremediably crippled Winifred interprets the tragedy as a judgment on her own sensual indulgence, and becomes frigid towards her husband. Medical treatment for the child requires a move to London, but Egbert, driven away 'like Ishmael'[33] by self-reproach and his wife's hostility, spends much time alone in the cottage:

> with the empty house all around him at night, all the empty rooms, he felt his heart go wicked. The sense of frustration and futility, like some slow, torpid snake, slowly bit right through his heart. Futility, futility: the horrible marsh-poison went through his veins and killed him. . . .
>
> He was alone. He himself cleaned the cottage and made his bed. But his mending he did not do. His shirts were slit on the shoulders, when he had been working, and the white flesh showed through. He would feel the air and the spots of rain on his exposed flesh. And he would look again across the common, where the dark, tufted gorse was dying to seed, and the bits of cat-heather were coming pink in tufts, like a sprinkling of sacrificial blood.
>
> His heart went back to the savage old spirit of the place: the desire for old gods, old, lost passions, the passion of cold-blooded, darting snakes that hissed and shot away from him, the mystery of blood sacrifices, all the lost, intense sensations of the primeval people of the place, whose passions seethed in the air still, from those long days before the Romans came. The seethe of a lost, dark passion in the air. The presence of unseen snakes.[34]

This is an obscure passage, partly because the connotations of 'snakes' are so ambiguous. There are no references to snakes in the first version, but several in the second. On the first page the already isolated and resentful Egbert, working on the edge of the common, hears his children's voices from the cottage:

> high, childish voices, slightly didactic and tinged with domineering: 'If you don't come quick, nurse, I shall run out there to where there are snakes.' And nobody had the *sangfroid* to reply: 'Run then, little fool.' It was always, 'No darling. Very well, darling. In a moment, darling. Darling, you *must* be patient.'[35]

It is hard to say whether this is the author's reflection, or the character's. But if the latter's it certainly seems to have the author's support. Graham Hough, quoting this passage, comments:

> Only a fragment, and a fragment chosen probably in resentment at the contrast between this kind of childhood and [Lawrence's] own; yet a sharp, prying little searchlight on to a whole ethos.[36]

Fair enough. But the fragment is not merely a bit of shrewd social observation. The child's threat of running out 'to where there are snakes' is repeated some fifteen pages later as a cue to the reader that the narrative, after the long retrospect, has returned to the opening scene. After a brief silence Egbert hears a shriek: Joyce has run into the garden and cut her leg on a sickle that Egbert has carelessly left lying on the grass. Does that imply that he, in effect, willed the accident ('Run then, little fool'), his sickle substituted for the snake? We may be reminded of a strange episode in the preceding account of the early days of the marriage:

> One day Winifred heard the strangest scream from the flower-bed under the window of the living room: ah, the strangest scream, like the very soul of the dark past crying aloud. She ran out and saw a long brown snake on the flower-bed, and in its flat mouth the one hind leg of a frog was striving to escape, and screaming its strange, tiny, bellowing scream. She looked at the snake, and from its sullen, flat head it looked at her, obstinately. She gave a cry and it released the frog and slid angrily away.[37]

Is this a proleptic allegory of Winifred's child being injured in the leg through an accident caused by Egbert's carelessness, the 'obstinate' Egbert whom she finally drives away, Egbert who planted the flower bed? If not, it is hard to see what the episode means and why it is given such prominence. Much later in the story Egbert is indeed compared to a snake, but a harmless one:

> As soon as sympathy, like a soft hand, was reached out to touch him, away he swerved, instinctively, as a harmless snake swerves and swerves and swerves away from an outstretched hand.[38]

And in the passage I started with, in this survey of the snake motif, Egbert is the *victim* of a metaphorical snake-bite.

As Frank Kermode has observed[39], the snake was for Lawrence an emblem of corruption—a vital, possibly redemptive corruption. In *The Crown*, that strange, prophetic Bestiary written in the same year as the first 'England, My England', the snake is described as 'the spirit of the great corruptive principle, the festering cold of the marsh. This is how he seems, as we look back. We revolt from him, but we share the same life and tide of life as he.'[40] In the same place we find the identical story of the screaming frog discovered in the jaws of a snake on a flower-bed outside a cottage—obviously the incident had happened to the Lawrences at Greatham. Afterwards, Lawrence says, when the snake had slipped 'sullenly' away:

> We were all white with fear. But why? In the world of twilight as the world of light, one beast shall devour another. The world of corruption has its stages, where the lower shall devour the higher, *ad infinitum*.[41]

Lawrence is saying that we should try to overcome the natural revulsion we feel for the snake and recognize the promise of new life that is in him: 'under the low skies of the far past aeons, he emerged a king out of chaos, a long beam of new life.'[42] In the beast-symbolism of *The Crown* he is contrasted with the vulture, who represents a static, negative kind of corruption. Lawrence was brooding, at this time, on the idea that corruption carried to extremes, the vital kind of corruption represented by the snake, might be the only way for both the individual and civilization at large to achieve rebirth and renewal. 'In the soft and shiny voluptuousness of decay, in the marshy chill heat of reptiles, there is the sign of the Godhead . . . decay, corruption, destruction, breaking down, is the opposite equivalent of creation.'[43] The idea is discussed at some length by Birkin and Ursula in the 'Water-Party' chapter of *Women in Love*, where, as Kermode points out, the same emblems, including the snake and the marsh, are invoked.

It is difficult to see how the uninstructed reader could perceive all this occult doctrine in 'England, My England', but it is perhaps clear enough that Egbert's longing to seek relief or release from his intolerable marital situation in some kind of primitive, instinctual blood-letting is expressed symbolically by associating him with the snakes on the common before it is fulfilled literally by his participation in the Great War. In the corresponding scene in the first version, war has already been declared, there are no references to snakes or the primeval past, and Egbert's motivation is more obvious: 'Egbert as he worked in the garden . . . felt the seethe of the war was with him'[44] rather than feeling 'the seethe of a lost, dark passion in the air.' And in the second version Egbert is much more hesitant about joining in the war when it is declared—a point made by reverting to the flower-metaphor:

> He was a pure-blooded Englishman, perfect in his race, and when he was truly himself he could no more have been aggressive on the score of his Englishness than a rose can be aggressive on the score of its rosiness.[45]

The question for Egbert is not (as it was for most of his generation) one of patriotic duty, but of whether or not to seek his own annihilation:

> And yet, war! Just war! Not right or wrong, but just war itself. Should he join? Should he give himself over to war? The question was in his mind for some weeks. Not because he thought England was right and Germany wrong. Probably Germany was wrong, but he refused to make a choice. Not because he felt inspired. No. But just—war.[46]

We are told that 'What Egbert felt subtly and without question, his father-in-law felt also in a rough, more combative way. Different as the two men were, they were two real Englishmen, and their instincts were almost the same.'[47] Lawrence adds, a little inconsistently, that Godfrey Marshall supported English 'industrialism' against German 'militarism' as the lesser of two evils; but the point has been made that both men dissociated themselves from the patriotic emotion evoked by the title:

> What have I done for you,
>   England my England?
> What is there I would not do,
>   England my own?

. . . .

> Ever the faith endures,
> England, my England:—
>
> Take and break us: we are yours,
> England my own![48]

'England, my England' was a phrase Lawrence was to invoke again in a famous elegiac passage in *Lady Chatterley's Lover*, where Connie drives through a Midlands landscape, the pastoral beauty and historical landmarks of which have been horribly disfigured by the ugly encroachments of modern industrial 'civilization'. Perhaps this association has encouraged critics to interpret the short story as also being an elegy for England—for example Stephen Spender:

> 'England, My England' is Lawrence's English elegy. Not that he sympathizes much with Egbert. Let the dead bury their dead, is his motto. For probably England is dead. Sometimes Lawrence thinks he is the only Englishman alive. But Egbert is nobler than the other characters in this story because, like Mrs Wilcox in *Howards End*, he lives and dies for a past which he symbolizes. And like Forster's heroine he does not resist death. It is the realization in him of the fate of English consciousness.[49]

This reading has elements of truth, but ignores the narrator's insistence throughout the story that there is something dilettante and superficial about Egbert's cult of the English past ('his old folk songs and Morris dances'[50]); and ignores, also, the very considerable respect that is accorded to Godfrey Marshall, in whom an equally authentic Englishness is combined with an ability to survive in the modern world (the flower/tree imagery enforces this distinction). In familial relationships Godfrey exerts far more power (a power specifically invested with ancient, primitive associations) than Egbert, who is defeated in his marriage long before he falls in battle. So far from being an admirable trait, Egbert's nostalgic cult of 'old England' (which should not be confused with the 'savage', 'primeval' snake-infested common) is a sign of his decadence and impotence. 'A man must find a new expression, give a new value to life, or his women will reject him and he will die,' Lawrence wrote to Catherine Carswell; and his writing of the war-time and post-war period, both fictional and non-fictional, shows him obsessed with these two, linked ideas: the definition of a healthy relationship between the sexes and the apocalyptic-utopian idea of a brave new world being born out of the painful dissolution of the old. Egbert, having (unlike, say, Birkin) no new value to offer, is rejected by Winifred and must die in the Great War which Lawrence was inclined to see as the death-throes of an exhausted culture, and perhaps the birth-pangs of a new one. 'The war is one bout in the terrific, horrible labour, our civilization labouring in child-birth and unable to bring forth.'[51]

Only in this way can we account for the curious tone of the ending of the story—especially the disconcerting lack of pity (conventional emotion of elegy) in the powerful description of Egbert's death—and for the apocalyptic imagery that permeates it. Egbert is doomed as soon as he enlists. 'At the end of the summer he went to Flanders, into action. He seemed already to have gone out of life, beyond the pale of life. He hardly remembered his life any more, being like a man who is going to take a jump from a height, and is only looking to where he must land.'[52] The story moves quickly to its dénouement. Egbert is manning one of three 'machine-guns' (so called by Lawrence, though they appear to be field-guns), behind the front line. 'The country was all pleasant, war had not yet trampled it. Only the air seemed shattered and the land awaiting death.'[53] Mention of gorse, and of Egbert's shirt slit on the shoulders, reminds us of him working at Crockham and brooding on primitive blood-sacrifice, but Egbert's own mind is almost blank: 'So many things go out of consciousness before we come to the end of consciousness.'[54] He mans the guns with brisk efficiency: 'Pure mechanical action at the guns. It left the soul unburdened, brooding in dark nakedness. In the end, the soul is alone. brooding on the face of the uncreated flux, as a bird on a dark sea.'[55]

This last image is very striking because it is not, like the imagery of flowers and trees and snakes, drawn from the realistic context, nor is it, like the earlier Biblical imagery, developed gradually through puns, clichés and progressive shifts of meaning. The image of a bird on a dark sea is remote from the context of an artillery battle, and signals the movement of the discourse into a new register, the extension of the author's imagination into a realm beyond the reach of empirical experience: death itself. Not that Lawrence dispenses with symbolism drawn from the context. Apocalyptic motifs are, for instance, neatly camouflaged in the next paragraph of description:

> Nothing could be seen but the road, and a crucifix knocked slanting and the dark autumnal fields and woods. There appeared three horsemen on a little eminence, very small, on the crest of a ploughed field. They were our own men. Of the enemy, nothing.[56]

The three horsemen presumably correspond to those seen by the author of Revelation before the appearance of the fourth horse, the pale horse with the rider that is Death;[57] for when Egbert finally dies on the last page of the story it is described as a hallucinatory vision of a mounted German soldier: 'What was that? A light! A terrible light! Was it figures? Was it the legs of a horse colossal—colossal above him: huge, huge?'[58]

To return to the earlier point in the story: a shell falls and the explosion makes a 'twig of holly with red berries fall like a gift on to the road below'—a poignant reminder of Egbert's severance from the Marshall family, and of the domestic fate that has brought him to this situation. Two more shells fall and then a third, which mortally wounds Egbert. This shell, by a now familiar rhetorical device, is metaphorically fused with the soul as bird:

into the silence, into the suspense where the soul brooded, finally crashed a noise and a darkness and a moment's flaming agony and horror. Ah, he had seen the dark bird flying towards him, flying home this time. In one instant life and eternity went up in a conflagration of agony, then there was a weight of darkness.

When faintly something began to struggle in the darkness, a consciousness of himself, he was aware of a great load and a changing sound. To have known the moment of death! and to be forced, before dying, to review it. So, fate, even in death.[59]

In Egbert's last agony his own longing for oblivion is developed into an apocalyptic vision of civilization itself desperately seeking its own dissolution; and there can be no doubt that as a character he has been deprived of all conventional, *dulce-et-decorum-est-pro-patria-mori* motivation so that he may witness more effectively to the truth of Lawrence's prophecies:

Death, oh, death! The world all blood, and the blood all writhing with death. The soul like the tiniest little light out on a dark sea, the sea of blood. And the light guttering, beating, pulsing in a windless storm, wishing it could go out, yet unable.

There had been life. There had been Winifred and his children. But the frail death-agony effort to catch at straws of memory, straws of life from the past, brought on too great a nausea. No, No! No Winifred, no children. No world, no people. Better the agony of dissolution ahead than the nausea of the effort backwards. Better the terrible work should go forward, the dissolving into the black sea of death, in the extremity of dissolution, than that there should be any reaching back towards life. To forget! To forget! Utterly, utterly to forget, in the great forgetting of death. To break the core and the unit of life, and to lapse out on the great darkness. Only that. To break the clue and mingle and commingle with the one darkness, without afterwards or forwards. Let the black sea of death itself solve the problem of futurity. Let the will of man break and give up.[60]

As Lawrence wrote in *The Crown*: 'the act of death may itself be a consummation and life may be a state of negation.'[61] In his recognition of that Egbert achieves a kind of heroism of the spirit, which we feel the more strongly in the second version of the story because he does not perform the superficially heroic action of the first (killing the three German soldiers).

5   Virginia Woolf

In the modernist writers discussed so far we have observed a general
tendency to develop (either within the individual work, or from one
work to another) from a metonymic (realistic) to a metaphoric
(symbolist or mythopoeic) representation of experience. Virginia
Woolf exemplifies this tendency very clearly. The essential line of her
literary development may be traced through the following novels: *The
Voyage Out* (1915), *Jacob's Room* (1922), *Mrs Dalloway* (1925), *To The
Lighthouse* (1927) and *The Waves* (1931) (her other books being, most
critics agree, diversions, digressions or regressions from this line).
And surveying these five novels rapidly in the order in which they were
written, flicking the pages, as it were, rapidly before our eyes so that
the changes in narrative form are speeded up and 'animated' in the
fashion of a child's cartoon book, it is obvious how the structure of the
traditional novel, with its rounded characters, logically articulated
plot, and solidly specified setting, melts away; how the climaxes of plot
are progressively pushed to the margins of the discourse, mentioned in
asides and parentheses; how the author's voice, narrating, explaining,
guaranteeing, fades away as the discourse locates itself in the minds of
characters with limited knowledge and understanding; how the unity
and coherence of the narratives comes increasingly to inhere in the
repetition of motifs and symbols, while the local texture of the writing
becomes more and more densely embroidered with metaphor and
simile. The distance in technique between *The Voyage Out* and *The
Waves* is almost as great as that between *Dubliners* and *Finnegans
Wake*. But although the two writers travelled, formally, in the same
general direction, they were driven by very different sensibilities
working on very different experience, and Virginia Woolf's
metaphorical mode is correspondingly different from Joyce's. It might
be said that whereas his writing aspired to the condition of myth, hers
aspired to the condition of lyrical poetry.

Essentially her writing does not so much imitate experience as
question it. It is no exaggeration to say that all her important books are
concerned with the question that opens the third section of *To The
Lighthouse*: 'What does it mean, then, what can it all mean?'[1] 'It', of
course, is life. And the question of the meaning of life is intimately tied

up with the fact of death. For if life is, in itself, held to be good, it is always threatened by death and is therefore (if, like Virginia Woolf, you are an agnostic with no faith in an afterlife) tragic. On the other hand, if life is not held to be good, there is no point in living it and one might as well kill oneself. We hardly commit a critical indecorum by invoking biographical data at this point and remarking that Virginia Woolf's early life was darkened by a series of deaths in her immediate family, especially by the unexpected and premature deaths of her mother, her half-sister Stella and her brother Thoby; that immediately after her mother's death, and intermittently throughout her life, Virginia suffered acutely from depressive mental illness, and that eventually she committed suicide. A shrewd psychoanalyst might deduce as much from an examination of the novels listed above, for they are all explicitly concerned with the question of the 'meaning of life', and all involve the sudden, premature deaths of one or more of the major characters: Rachel Vinrace in *The Voyage Out*, Jacob in *Jacob's Room*, Septimus Smith in *Mrs Dalloway*, Mrs Ramsay and her children Andrew and Prue in *To The Lighthouse*, Percival and Rhoda in *The Waves*.

Either life is meaningless, or death makes it so: Virginia Woolf's fiction is the trace of her efforts to extricate herself from that existential double-bind, to affirm the value of life in the teeth of disappointment and death. Her answer, fragile enough, but delivered with eloquent intensity, was to invoke those privileged moments in personal, subjective experience when the world seems charged with goodness and joy—harmonious, unified and complete. Here is Mrs Ramsay at such a moment, presiding over her dinner table, and planning a match between Lily Briscoe and William Bankes:

> Foolishly, she had set them opposite each other. That could be remedied tomorrow. If it were fine, they should go for a picnic. Everything seemed possible. Everything seemed right. Just now (but this cannot last, she thought, dissociating herself from the moment while they were all talking about boots) just now she had reached security; she hovered like a hawk suspended; like a flag floated in an element of joy which filled every nerve of her body fully and sweetly, not noisily, solemnly rather, for it arose, she thought, looking at them all eating there, from husband and children and friends; all of which rising in this profound stillness (she was helping William Bankes to one very small piece more and peered into the depths of the earthenware pot) seemed now for no special reason to stay there like a smoke, like a fume rising upwards, holding them safe together. Nothing need be said, nothing could be said. There it was all around them. It partook, she felt, carefully helping Mr Bankes to an especially tender piece, of eternity; as she had already felt about something different once before that afternoon; there is a coherence in things, a stability; something, she meant, is immune from change, and shines out (she glanced at the window with its ripple of reflected lights) in the face of the flowing, the fleeting, the spectral, like a ruby; so that again tonight she had the feeling she had had

once today already, of peace, of rest. Of such moments, she thought, the thing is made that remains for ever after. This would remain.[2]

The experience described here has something in common with Joyce's 'epiphanies' ('the sudden "revelation of the whatness of a thing", the moment in which "the soul of the commonest object . . . seems to us radiant" ')[3], with Yeats's images of 'unity of being' and with T. S. Eliot's 'still points' redeemed from time in *Four Quartets*. But in Virginia Woolf the moment is not, as in Joyce, a kind of sacramental transubstantiation of the commonplace achieved by art: though sought by artists in her fiction, the privileged moment is not exclusive to them, and their attempts to fix it in words or paint are generally unsuccessful. Nor is it, as in Yeats and Eliot, attached to a particular metaphysic, guaranteed by Revelation, orthodox or heterodox. Lily Briscoe undoubtedly speaks for the author when she reflects: 'The great revelation had never come. The great revelation perhaps never did come. Instead there were little daily miracles, illuminations, matches struck unexpectedly in the dark.'[4] The privileged moment is, then, transitory and recognized as such by those that experience it ('this cannot last, she thought'), and yet it transcends time: 'It partook . . . of eternity . . . of such moments, she thought, the thing is made that remains for ever after.'

Thus a kind of immortality is asserted and death apparently defeated. But what kind of immortality? What is 'the thing that remains for ever after'? When Mrs Ramsay dies, the memory of this moment dies with her; for although she is as a person remembered with love and sympathy by her family and friends, they do not remember the particular moments that meant so much to her. In fact, at the very instant when Mrs Ramsay is looking fondly at Lily Briscoe and planning to marry her to William Bankes, Lily is consumed with a hopeless passion for Paul Rayley who has just engaged himself to Minta Doyle; and looking back on this meal many years later she remembers only the pain of Paul's rebuff, and the folly of Mrs Ramsay's matchmaking plans. The privileged moment Lily recalls in Part III in connection with Mrs Ramsay, 'which survived, after all these years, complete, so that she dipped into it to refashion her memory of her, and it stayed in the mind almost like a work of art', occurred on the beach with the usually unamiable Charles Tansley— 'Mrs Ramsay bringing them together; Mrs Ramsay saying, "Life, stand still here"; Mrs Ramsay making of the moment something permanent'[5]—a 'little miracle' of which Mrs Ramsay herself was quite unconscious. In short, Virginia Woolf's modernist insistence on the relativity and subjectivity of experience undermines the redeeming power of the privileged moment, because the moment is never shared.

As an answer to the fundamental problems of life and death, then, the privileged moment does not stand up to very close logical scrutiny; but it is intimated, and celebrated, in a cunningly woven web of verbal nuances which deliberately keeps the reader's analytical intelligence at bay. The long quotation above shows the different ways in which the writing accomplishes this feat: the paratactic syntax, adding clause to clause in the loosest fashion, seems perpetually to postpone the moment when the sentence will commit itself to something final (note the preference for semi-colons over full-stops). The parenthetic references to banal events outside consciousness ('It partook, she felt, carefully helping Mr Bankes to a specially tender piece, of eternity') break into the stream of reflection, mitigate the tendency to metaphysical pretentiousness and make the point that the miraculous joy of the moment arises out of the commonplace, not from some transcendental source. And the figurative expressions are dealt out in such profusion, withdrawn and substituted with such rapidity ('like a hawk . . . like a flag . . . like a smoke . . . like a fume . . . like a ruby') that we take from the passage a hazy, synaesthetic impression rather than any precise image.

Virginia Woolf's mature novels—*Mrs Dalloway, To The Lighthouse* and *The Waves*—are all about sensitive people living from one privileged moment to the next, passing through intervening periods of dissatisfaction, depression and doubt. For this reason, they are essentially plotless. Their endings are false endings, or non-endings, which leave the characters exactly where they have always been, living inside their heads, doomed to oscillate between joy and despair until they die. Virginia Woolf closes each book on an affirmative up-beat—'For there she was', 'I have had my vision', 'Against you I will fling myself, unvanquished and unyielding, O Death!'—but the cut-off point is essentially arbitrary, and it is clear that if the text were to continue another down-beat must inevitably follow. It is not fortuitous that the presiding symbols of the two later novels—the lighthouse with its pulsing beam, and the waves breaking on the shore—have this same regular, oscillating rhythm, and are susceptible of bearing multiple and contradictory meanings. Arguably this oscillating psychological rhythm makes Virginia Woolf's work ultimately unsatisfying because the affirmation of the value of life so often uttered is never really made to stick. It certainly makes her writing liable to seem monotonous, especially in *The Waves*, where there is no variety in the verbal texture either—each character's consciousness being rendered in interior monologues of uniform style. It is this drastic subordination of *difference* to *similarity* in *The Waves* that makes it the most 'poetic' (or in our terms, metaphoric) of Virginia Woolf's novels. As in *Finnegans Wake*, the boundaries of individual character are dissolved, though it is a mystical impersonality rather than Joyce's mythic polysemy that dissolves them. 'And now I ask, "Who am I?"' Bernard says, in his long, remarkable final monologue:

> 'I have been talking of Bernard, Neville, Jinny, Susan, Rhoda and Louis. Am I all of them? Am I one and distinct? I do not know. We sat here

together. But now Percival is dead, and Rhoda is dead; we are divided; we are not here. Yet I cannot find any obstacle separating us. There is no division between me and them. As I talked I felt "I am you". This difference we make so much of, this identity we so feverishly cherish, was overcome.'[6]

Although *The Waves* was the logical terminus of Virginia Woolf's artistic development, most readers will probably prefer *To The Lighthouse* or *Mrs Dalloway* (as they prefer *Ulysses* to *Finnegans Wake*)—novels in which lyrical intensity is combined with a lively, though distinctively modernist, mimesis of social and personal life.

I propose to examine in more detail the stages by which Virginia Woolf detached her writing from the formal constraints of the traditional novel, up to and including the writing of *Mrs Dalloway*. Her thematic preoccupation with the meaning of life and death was of course there from the beginning. 'And life, what was that?' wonders Rachel Vinrace, the heroine of *The Voyage Out*. 'It was only a light passing over the surface and vanishing as in time she would vanish, though the furniture would remain.'[7] And much later, looking at her fiancé reading as she writes letters, and struck by her ignorance of what is passing through his head and by the gap between her perceptions and what she is writing, she asks herself: 'Would there ever be a time when the world was one and indivisible?'[8]. Just when it looks as if there might be, for her, in her marriage, she is struck down by a fatal illness. The suddenness, the cruel arbitrariness of this death is very powerfully conveyed (it surely had its source in the death of Thoby Stephen) and implies that no affirmation of the value of life that is projected into future time is to be relied upon, because it is at the mercy of death. This ending inverts (as the match between Susan Warrington and Arthur Venning parodies) the endings of nineteenth-century novels in which the union of hero and heroine is an assurance of the possibility of a happy life extended in time and lived out in a world of meaningful social relationships. Indeed, *A Voyage Out* in many ways resembles a well-built Victorian novel the foundations of which are sinking into the morass of modern scepticism, causing the fabric to warp, crack and in places collapse. It has a huge cast of characters, most of them hit off with admirable wit and perception; but whereas the classic nineteenth-century novel accounted for all its characters (however implausibly) in terms of the plot, thus conveying the sense of society as something that was, however corrupt, ultimately intelligible and therefore redeemable, most of Virginia Woolf's characters drift in and out of focus in a curiously random way, and the plot that might unite them into a single pattern never transpires. Since the action takes place on a cruise and in a South American resort town, the random collision of disparate characters is 'realistic' enough, but what they are all doing in the book, apart from demonstrating the infinite variety of human nature, is not easy to say, since for a large part of the time they are not even under the observation of the heroine whose quest for the meaning of life is the ostensible subject of the novel. Chapter Nine, set in the hotel at San Marina, comes I think as a surprise to the reader, introducing, as it does, a whole crowd of new characters at a fairly late stage of the novel; and the manner of their introduction is interesting. The authorial narrator moves invisibly from one room to the next, fascinated by the contiguity of their forty or fifty varied inhabitants, whose interests, desires, and fears are totally disparate. Terence Hewet, Rachel's fiancé and an aspirant novelist, is similarly fascinated and baffled by the same phenomenon: 'I've often walked along the streets where people live all in a row, and one house is exactly like another house, and wondered what on earth the women were doing inside.'[9] The narrative of *The Voyage Out*, then, is forwarded by contiguity in the sense that it pursues a chain of events, a series of encounters between people brought into chance contact, but for the most part these contiguities resist any attempt at integration into a world 'one and indivisible'.

Virginia Woolf's critics usually describe *Jacob's Room* as her first truly experimental novel, which it was. They also describe it as experimenting with the stream of consciousness, which it hardly does to any significant extent, most of the text being authorial narration or dramatic presentation. Virginia Woolf left a vivid record of the book's genesis in her diary:

> . . . having this afternoon arrived at some idea of a new form for a new novel. Suppose one thing should open out of another—as in an unwritten novel— only not for 10 pages but 200 or so—doesn't that give the looseness and lightness I want; doesn't that get closer and yet keep form and speed, and enclose everything, everything? My doubt is how far it will enclose the human heart—Am I sufficiently mistress of my dialogue to net it there? For I figure that the approach will be entirely different this time: no scaffolding; scarcely a brick to be seen; all crepuscular, but the heart, the passion, humour, everything as bright as fire in the mist.[10]

The phrase 'an unwritten novel' refers to a short story of that title first published in *The London Mercury* in July of the same year (1920). In it, the narrator scrutinizes a woman seated opposite her in a railway carriage and tries to compose a novel about her, struggling to extract an imaginative truth from the clues of her appearance and deportment (the metonymic or synecdochic indices of character in realistic fiction). At the end of the journey the woman, whom the narrator has cast as a repressed spinster, is met by her son, and the fiction collapses:

> Well, my world's done for! What do I stand on? What do I know? That's not Minnie. There never was Moggridge. Who am I? Life's bare as a bone.[11]

This metafictional vein is continued, less archly, in *Jacob's Room*. The novel is really about the difficulty of writing a novel, of truly representing a person in the written word: 'It is thus that we live, they say, driven by an unseizable force. They say that novelists never catch it.'[12] Virginia Woolf does not deny the failure, but affirms the novelist's compulsion to keep trying:

> But though all this may very well be true—so Jacob thought and spoke—so he crossed his legs—filled his pipe—sipped his whisky, and once looked at his pocket-book, rumpling his hair as he did so, there remains over something which can never be conveyed to a second person save by Jacob himself. Moreover, part of this is not Jacob but Richard Bonamy—the room; the market carts; the hour; the very moment of history. . . . Even the exact words get the wrong accent on them. But something is always impelling one to hum vibrating, like the hawk moth, at the mouth of the cavern of mystery, endowing Jacob Flanders with all sorts of qualities he had not got at all—for though, certainly, he sat talking to Bonamy, half of what he said was too dull to repeat; much unintelligible (about unknown people and Parliament); what remains is mostly a matter of guess work. Yet over him we hang vibrating.[13]

The author's omniscience is, then, strictly limited. She rarely enters Jacob's mind to report what he is thinking, and when she does so her interpretation of his thoughts is uncertain. In interpreting his external behaviour she is little wiser than his friends and family: 'But whether this is the right interpretation of Jacob's gloom as he sat naked, in the sun, looking at the Land's End, it is impossible to say; for he never spoke a word. Timmy sometimes wondered (only for a second) whether his people bothered him. . ..'[14]

Although, as always with Virginia Woolf, there is a great deal of metaphor and simile in the local texture of the writing, structurally *Jacob's Room* belongs in the metonymic category. Its experimentalism is all performed on the chain of combination—the chain of contiguous events that is Jacob's life—and consists mainly in cutting away huge sections of this chain and viewing the remainder from odd angles and perspectives. As readers we are rushed from one brief, fragmentary scene to the next ('one thing open[ing] out of another', as Virginia Woolf noted in her diary) without explanation or preparation. We come into ongoing coversations, hear a few scraps of dialogue and try to guess what is being talked about, before we are whisked on to another scene. Essentially *Jacob's Room* is a conventional *Bildungsroman* speeded up and subjected to drastic 'cutting' of a cinematic kind. Its experimentalism is a technique of radical and stylish *deletion* ('no scaffolding, scarcely a brick to be seen'), and deletion, as I argued earlier, is the operation by which metonymic devices are produced. The most daring deletion of all is Jacob's death in the Great War. This death, which is proleptically figured in his surname, Flanders (a metaphoric device, this, a kind of pun, but a discreet one) is crucial to *Jacob's Room* because it invests with a deep pathos the self-confessed failure of the novelist (and of the other characters) to understand Jacob or penetrate the mystery of his being, expressing the baffled grief of all those whose sons, brothers and lovers were killed before they were really known. Yet this death is not described, or even referred to directly. It is represented in the most oblique way, by metonymy and synecdoche—the sound of guns across the sea[15] and Jacob's empty room and empty shoes:

> Listless is the air in an empty room, just swelling the curtains; the flowers in the jar shift. One fibre in the wicker armchair creaks, though no one sits there.
>
> Bonamy crossed to the window, Pickford's van swung down the street. The omnibuses were locked together at Mudie's corner. Engines throbbed, and carters, jamming the brakes down, pulled their horses up sharp. A harsh and unhappy voice cried something unintelligible. And then suddenly all the leaves seemed to raise themselves.
>
> 'Jacob! Jacob!' cried Bonamy, standing by the window. The leaves sank down again.
>
> 'Such confusion everywhere!' exclaimed Betty Flanders, bursting open the bedroom door.
>
> Bonamy turned away from the window.
>
> 'What am I to do with these, Mr Bonamy?'
>
> She held out a pair of Jacob's old shoes.[16]

This is a beautifully judged conclusion, poignant, without the least sentimentality. But one can't help feeling that elsewhere in the novel Virginia Woolf used the technique of deletion as a means of evasion as well as expression—evasion of things she couldn't really handle. Sex, for instance: the stylish indirection with which Jacob's sexual life is represented doesn't quite conceal the essentially sentimental stereotypes to which it conforms. And the 'new form' she heralded in her diary did not take her any further than the form of *The Voyage Out* in vindicating life against death. The next, decisive step was taken with *Mrs Dalloway*.

Virginia Woolf had an interesting correspondence about aesthetics with the painter Jacques Raverat at the time when she was working on this novel. He suggested that writing, as an artistic medium, was limited by being 'essentially linear', unable therefore to render the complex multiplicity of a mental event, which he compared to a pebble cast into a pond, 'splashes in the outer air in every direction. and under the surface waves that follow one another into forgotten corners.'[17] Virginia Woolf replied that it was precisely her aim to go beyond 'the formal railway line of the sentence' and to disregard the 'falsity of the past (by which I mean Bennett, Galsworthy and so on) . . . people don't and never did think or feel in that way; but all over the place, in your way.'[18] As Quentin Bell remarks, 'it is possible to find in *Mrs Dalloway* an attempt of this nature.'[19] In our terms, the novel marks the transition in Virginia Woolf's writing from the metonymic to the metaphoric mode. Instead of lineality, simultaneity ('If *Jacob's Room* shows cinematic cutting and fading, *Mrs Dalloway* borrows from montage and superimposed frames,' Carl Woodring has shrewdly commented[20]). Instead of different people in the same place at the same time (e.g. the hotel at Santa Marina) different people in different places at the same time, (time marked by the chimes of Big Ben) perhaps looking at the same thing (the aeroplane in the sky). Instead of a life, or a voyage, a single day. Instead of authorial narration, the stream of consciousness in which events (i.e. thoughts) follow each other on the principle of similarity as much as contiguity—a June morning in Westminster, for instance, reminding Clarissa of mornings in her youth because a simile of children on a beach seems to her equally applicable to both:

> And then, thought Clarissa Dalloway, what a morning—fresh as if issued to children on a beach.
>   What a lark! What a plunge! For so it had always seemed to her when, with a little squeak of the hinges, which she could hear now, she had burst open the French windows and plunged at Bourton into the open air. How fresh, how calm, stiller than this of course, the air was in the early morning; like the flap of a wave; the kiss of a wave; . .[21]

Joyce, no doubt, had shown Virginia Woolf the way, though, as I observed earlier, there is no equivalent in *Mrs Dalloway* to the mythical subtext of *Ulysses*. Structurally, Virginia Woolf's novel resembles the 'Wandering Rocks' episode of *Ulysses*, in which a variety of Dublin characters are observed perambulating the city at the same time, thinking their own thoughts, crossing each other's paths, or linked by the throwaway leaflet, 'Elijah Comes' that is floating past them down the Liffey.

Virginia Woolf's abandonment of a linear narrative structure and her plunge into the stream of consciousness can be related readily enough to the avant-garde *Zeitgeist*. But it was also related to her personal concern with testing the meaning of life against the fact of death; for the privileged moment which she was to offer as a kind of answer to the problem could be only given proper emphasis in a novel of the new kind, in which the causal or chronological ordering of events was subordinated to rendering the impression they made on the individual consciousness, showing, in Lily Briscoe's words, 'how life, from being made up of separate little incidents which one lived one by one, became curled and whole like a wave which bore one up with it and threw one down with it, there, with a dash on the beach.'[22] Going out to order flowers for her party, Mrs Dalloway feels that life is good. She loves 'life; London; this moment of June'.[23] Walking towards Bond Street she is troubled by the thought of death: 'did it matter that she must inevitably cease completely: all this must go on without her;'[24] but consoles herself with a vague myth of immortality: 'somehow in the streets of London, on the ebb and flow of things, here, there, she survived, Peter survived, lived in each other, she being part, she was positive, of the trees at home;. . . part of people she had never

met; being laid out like a mist between the people she knew best . . .'[25]
In fact, it is not so much the prospect of her own physical death that
disturbs Clarissa as the death-in-life that overcomes her at moments of
negativity, hatred and self-loathing, and that (we infer later) has
tempted her to suicide. These moments are antithetical to the
privileged moments of joy and love by which she lives, and both can be
provoked by the most trivial stimuli. Coming back to her house from
shopping, for instance, she feels blessed:

> It was her life, and, bending her head over the hall table, she bowed beneath
> the influence, felt blessed and purified, saying to herself, as she took the pad
> with the telephone message on it, how moments like this are buds on the tree
> of life . . .[26]

But when the message proves to be one that injures her vanity and
separates her from her husband (Lady Bruton has asked him to lunch
without her) her love of life drains away and she feels herself 'suddenly
shrivelled, aged, breastless'.[27] She goes up to her room ('There was an
emptiness about the heart; an attic room') where she usually sleeps (or
rather reads, late into the night) apart from her husband. This leads to
a depressed meditation on her sexual frigidity which in turn yields to a
reviving memory of privileged moments when, through intimacy with
other women, she obtained an insight into erotic rapture:

> Only for a moment; but it was enough. It was a sudden revelation, a tinge
> like a blush which one tried to check and then, as it spread, one yielded to its
> expansion, and rushed to the farthest verge and there quivered and felt the
> world come closer, swollen with some astonishing significance, some
> pressure of rapture, which split its thin skin and gushed and poured with an
> extraordinary alleviation over the cracks and sores. Then for that moment,
> she had seen an illumination; a match burning in a crocus; an inner meaning
> almost expressed. But the close withdrew; the hard softened. It was over—
> the moment.[28]

The psychological rhythm of Peter Walsh is very similar, alternating
between love and aggression, optimism and pessimism, life and death.

> As a cloud crosses the sun, silence falls on London; and falls on the mind.
> Effort ceases, time flaps on the mast. There we stop; there we stand. Rigid,
> the skeleton of habit alone upholds the human frame. Where there is
> nothing, Peter Walsh said to himself; feeling hollowed out, utterly empty
> within. Clarissa refused me, he thought. He stood there thinking, Clarissa
> refused me.
>
> Ah, said St Margaret's, like a hostess who comes into her drawing room
> on the very stroke of the hour and finds her guests there already. I am not
> late . . .—like Clarissa herself, thought Peter Walsh, coming downstairs on
> the stroke of the hour in white. It is Clarissa herself, he thought, with a
> deep emotion, and an extraordinary clear, yet puzzling recollection
> of her, as if this bell had come into the room years ago, where they sat

at some moment of great intimacy, and had gone from one to the other and had left, like a bee with honey, laden with the moment. But what room? What moment? And why had he been so profoundly happy when the clock was striking? Then, as the sound of St Margaret's languished, he thought, she had been ill, and the sound expressed languor and suffering. It was her heart, he remembered; and the sudden loudness of the final stroke tolled for death that surprised in the midst of life, Clarissa falling where she stood, in her drawing room. No! No! he cried. She is not dead! I am not old, he cried, and marched up Whitehall, as if there rolled down to him, vigorous, unending, his future.[29]

Septimus Smith, however, has decided that life is not worth living. Traumatized by the horrors of the Great War, he sees the world as an evil place from which he is anxious to escape, and he does so by committing suicide. Through the coincidence of his consultant Sir William Bradshaw's being a guest at Clarissa's party that evening (it is the only vestige of 'plot' in the novel), this stranger's death comes to her attention:

A young man had killed himself. And they talked of it at her party—the Bradshaws talked of death. He had killed himself—but how? . . . He had thrown himself from a window . . . She had once flung a shilling into the Serpentine, never anything more. But he had flung it away. They went on living . . . They (all day she had been thinking of Bourton, of Peter, of Sally), they would grow old. A thing there was that mattered; a thing, wreathed about with chatter, defaced, obscured in her own life, let drop every day in corruption, lies, chatter. This he had preserved. Death was defiance. Death was an attempt to communicate, people feeling the impossibility of reaching the centre which, mystically, evaded them; closeness drew apart; rapture faded; one was alone. There was an embrace in death.

But this young man who had killed himself—had he plunged holding his treasure? 'If it were now to die, 'twere now to be most happy,' she had said to herself once, coming down, in white.[30]

It will be noted that this passage echoes words and ideas in the two long quotations preceding: the moments of 'close' intimacy, of rapture, that Clarissa has fleetingly experienced with other women, and Peter's memory of Clarissa coming downstairs in a white dress. Peter had then a vision of Clarissa 'falling dead where she stood in her drawing room'. But it is Septimus who, in a sense, dies in her drawing room (' "A young man had killed himself." Oh! thought Clarissa, in the middle of my party, here's death')[31] And Clarissa feels that Septimus has in a sense *died in her place*. For she has felt the same terror of life ('She had felt it only this morning . . . the terror; the overwhelming incapacity, one's parents giving it into one's hands, this life, to be lived to the end . . . there was in the depths of her heart an awful fear . . .') but she has been sufficiently protected, especially by her husband, from seeking the final remedy. 'She had escaped. But that young man had killed himself.' Paradoxically she feels her survival as 'Somehow . . . her disaster—her disgrace. It was her punishment to see sink here a man, there a woman, in this profound darkness, and she forced to stand here in her evening dress. She had schemed, she had pilfered. She was never wholly admirable.'[32] Thus Clarissa accepts her own failure, and acquires a new tranquility and peace. 'Odd, incredible, she had never been so happy. Nothing could be slow enough, nothing last too long.'[33] Yet at the same time 'she felt somehow very like him—the young man who had killed himself. She felt glad that he had done it, thrown it away while they went on living.'[34] This is the real climax of the novel: a moment of perceived similarity and spiritual substitution. And, as we know, it had an exact analogue in the genesis of the novel, for in Virginia Woolf's original design there was no Septimus character, and Clarissa was 'to kill herself, or perhaps merely to die at the end of the party'.[35]

6   In the Thirties

He went out into Oxford Street: there was no hurry now: nothing to be done until he saw Lord Benditch. He walked, enjoying the sense of unreality—the shop windows full of goods, no ruined houses anywhere, women going into Buzzard's for coffee. It was like one of his own dreams of peace. He stopped in front of a bookshop and stared in—people had time to read books—new books. There was one called *A Lady-in-Waiting at the Court of King Edward*, with a photograph on the paper jacket of a stout woman in white silk with ostrich feathers. It was incredible. And there was *Safari Days*, with a man in a sun helmet standing on a dead lioness. What a country, he thought again with affection. He went on. He couldn't help noticing how well clothed everybody was. A pale winter sun shone and the scarlet buses stood motionless all down Oxford Street: there was a traffic block. What a mark, he thought, for enemy planes. It was always about this time that they came over. But the sky was empty—or nearly empty. One winking, glittering little plane turned and dived on the pale clear sky, drawing in little puffy clouds, a slogan: 'Keep warm with Ovo.' He reached Bloomsbury—it occurred to him that he had spent a very quiet morning: it was almost as if his infection had met a match in this peaceful and preoccupied city.[1]

This passage from Graham Greene's *The Confidential Agent* (1939) contains within it a parodic allusion to Virginia Woolf. The traffic jam in the West End, the sky-writing aeroplane, are details taken from *Mrs Dalloway*, and the very structure of some sentences imitates Virginia Woolf's characteristic cadences ('What a mark, he thought, for enemy planes.'). But the centre of consciousness in Greene's passage is a visitor from a European country (not named, but obviously modelled on Spain) in the throes of civil war, and what seemed reassuringly normal in the London scene to Clarissa Dalloway seems to him extraordinary. Looked at in the perspective that he is familiar with, the red buses are potential bombing targets, and the single aeroplane in the sky is chiefly notable for its innocuousness. England seemed sunk in a bourgeois dream of peacefulness and stability. The character, 'D', feels its appeal, but judges it to be ultimately a dangerous illusion, hiding political tensions and injustices that are being openly fought over in his own country. The Bloomsbury he is walking towards is not Virginia Woolf's home ground, a region of high culture and discreetly unconventional *mores*, but a Bloomsbury of disconsolate foreigners and seedy hotels, in one of which D's political collaborators are planning to double-cross him, and where his only ally is the pathetic fourteen-year-old chambermaid, Else, whose best prospect of escape from drudgery is to become a prostitute's maid:

> Fourteen was a dreadfully early age at which to know so much and be so powerless. If this was civilization—the crowded prosperous streets, the women trooping in for coffee at Buzzards, the lady-in-waiting at King Edward's court, and the sinking, drowning child—he preferred barbarity, the bombed streets and the food queues: a child there had nothing worse to look forward to than death.[2]

The preference expressed here for 'barbarity' over 'civilization' strikes a characteristically Greeneian note of gloomy antihumanism, one which he sounded most emphatically in his African travel book *Journey Without Maps* (1936). But Greene was certainly not alone in thinking that there was something unreal about the surface tranquillity of English life in the 1930s. Reality, the young writers of the period felt, was elsewhere—especially in Germany or Spain—and was creeping upon England in the form of impending war. George Orwell's heroes can imagine as easily as D the English sky filled with bombing planes—and do so with a certain apocalyptic relish, a disgust with a modern 'civilization' and its fruits, which is not so very different from Greene's. Consider Gordon Comstock, for instance, in *Keep the Aspidistra Flying* (1936), enraged and nauseated by advertisements, especially one for Bovex ('Corner Table enjoys his meal with Bovex'):

> The sense of disintegration, of decay, that is endemic in our time, was strong upon him. Somehow it was mixed up with the ad-posters opposite. He looked now with more seeing eyes at those grinning yard-wide faces. After all, there was more there than mere silliness, greed and vulgarity. Corner Table grins at you, seemingly optimistic, with a flash of false teeth. But what is behind the grin? Desolation, emptiness, prophecies of doom. For can you not see, if you know how to look, that behind that slick self-satisfaction, that tittering, fat-bellied triviality, there is nothing but a frightful emptiness, a secret despair? The great death wish of the modern world. Suicide pacts.

Heads stuck in gas ovens in lonely maisonettes. French letters and Amen pills. And the reverberations of future wars. Enemy aeroplanes flying over London; the deep threatening hum of the propellers, the shattering thunder of bombs. It is all written in Corner Table's face.[3]

Although Orwell, consistent with his own humanist convictions, makes his hero ultimately renounce this alienated state of mind, the conversion is unconvincing and certainly lacks the rhetorical force of the earlier despair. A later hero, George Bowling, maintains his pessimism to the end:

It's all going to happen. All the things you've got at the back of your mind, the things you're terrified of, the things that you tell yourself are just a nightmare or only happen in foreign countries. The bombs, the food-queues, the rubber truncheons, the barbed wire, the coloured shirts, the slogans, the enormous faces, the machine-guns squirting out of bedroom windows.[4]

We have already glanced, in Part One, at the shift in literary taste and literary aims that characterized the new writers of the 1930s: their attacks on the obscurity, allusiveness and élitism of the modernist-symbolist tradition, and their call for a more politically aware and openly communicative approach to the practice of writing. 'Realism' came back into favour. Stephen Spender published a pamphlet called *The New Realism* in 1939, in which he said that:

there is a tendency for artists today to turn outwards to reality, because the phase of experimenting in form has proved sterile. If you like, the artist is simply in search of inspiration, having discovered that inspiration depends on there being some common ground of understanding between him and his audience about the nature of reality, and on a demand from that audience for what he creates.[5]

The reversal of modernist assumptions about art could scarcely be more clearly stated. In 1937 Spender, with Storm Jameson and Arthur Calder-Marshall, had founded a left-wing monthly review called *Fact*. It was short lived, but the title was symptomatic of a general appetite for and reliance upon empirical fact among literary intellectuals in the 1930s. It was the decade of the Left Book Club ('built on documents and the proposition that facts were knowledge'[6]) and of Mass Observation, an experiment in amateur sociology which had thousands of people all over the country writing reports of everything they saw and experienced in their ordinary lives on one day in every month (Graham Greene ingeniously introduces a Mass Observer into *The Confidential Agent* to incriminate the murderers of Else). History was no longer a nightmare from which the writer was struggling to awake but an enterprise in which he was keen to participate ('history forming in our hands' as John Cornford wrote)[7] and imaginative literature tended to model itself on historical types of discourse—the autobiography, the eye-witness account, the journal. *Journey to a War*, *Letters from Iceland*, *The Road to Wigan Pier*, *Journey Without Maps*, *Autumn Journal*, 'Berlin Diary', are some characteristic titles of the period. The result was the formation of a very distinctive and homogeneous period-style, or *écriture*, underlying the surface idiosyncracies of personal styles. In our terms there was a pronounced swing back from the metaphoric to the metonymic pole of literary discourse. One obvious trace of this can be seen in the quotations from Greene and Orwell above: the use of synecdochic detail to evoke a scene and to symbolise an abstraction at the same time. In the second quotation from *The Confidential Agent* Greene recapitulates in a condensed form details from his own previous descriptions—details which are now made to 'stand for' two contrasting cultural and political situations. Orwell uses a similar technique: 'Corner Table' (itself a metonymic expression) stands for a whole debased universe of discourse, the money-world of a capitalist class-society—and triggers in the observer's imagination a montage of images of modern death, spiritual and physical. The montage is metonymic, not metaphorical, for the various items in it belong to the same general context of modern urban life. The same is true of George Bowling's prophecy of totalitarian terror engulfing England: it is like a newsreel, cutting from one representative scene or close-up to another.

It is interesting to compare *Coming Up For Air* with *A la Recherche du Temps Perdu*. George Bowling's reminiscent evocation of his past is triggered (as Marcel's memory is often triggered) by a chance similarity: a newspaper headline, 'KING ZOG'S WEDDING POSTPONED' revives an echo of Og the king of Bashar in the psalm and transports George mentally back to the church services he attended as a child. But whereas Proust's evocations of the past are drenched in metaphor, George's are catalogues of literal facts, with little or no figurative elaboration:

> How it came back to me! That peculiar feeling—it was only a feeling, you couldn't describe it as an activity—that we used to call 'Church'. The sweet corpsy smell, the rustle of Sunday dresses, the wheeze of the organ and the roaring voices, the spot of light from the hole in the window creeping slowly up the nave.[8]

The same metonymic technique is used throughout the book. Boyhood, for instance, is evoked thus:

> It's a kind of strong, rank feeling, a feeling of knowing everything and fearing nothing, and it's all bound up with breaking rules and killing things. The white dusty roads, the hot sweaty feeling of one's clothes, the smell of fennel and wild peppermint, the dirty words, the sour stink of the rubbish dump, the taste of fizzy lemonade and the gas that made one belch, the stamping on the young birds, the feel of the fish straining on the line—it was all part of it.[9]

Obviously one of the reasons for Orwell's avoidance of metaphor is that he is using as his narrator an 'ordinary' sort of man to whom any fine writing of the Proustian kind would be quite inappropriate—'It's not that I'm trying to put across any of that poetry of childhood stuff' George assures us, 'I know that's all baloney.'[10] The choice of such a narrator, and the deliberate acceptance of the stylistic limitations entailed, is deeply characteristic of the period.

There *is* in fact a mythopoeic, metaphorical level in *Coming Up For Air*, but it is very thoroughly buried under the ordinary prosaic surface. As a child, George tells us, he had a passion for fishing, a pursuit which for him symbolizes the healthier state of culture and society in those pre-World-War-I days: 'fishing is somehow typical of that civilization'[11]. In the neglected garden of the local mansion, Binfield House, the young George discovered a pool filled with carp of prodigious size:

> It was a wonderful secret for a boy to have. There was the dark pool hidden away in the woods and the monstrous fish sailing round it—fish that had never been fished for and would grab the first bait you offered them. . . . But as it happened I never went back. One never does go back. . . . Almost immediately afterwards something turned up to prevent me, but if it hadn't been that it would have been something else. It's the way things happen.[12]

'The way things happen' sums up the rueful, shrugging, stoical pessimism of George Bowling's (and Orwell's?) attitude to life, one that the realistic novel is well adapted to express: life as a sequence of accidents, a plot without a Providence directing it, a chain of local cause-and-effect, the general pattern of which can only be seen in retrospect, when it is too late to do anything about it. Four years later George takes his girl friend into the grounds of Binfield House:

> Now I was so near, it seemed a pity not to go down to the other pool and have a look at the big carp. I felt I'd kick myself afterwards if I missed the chance, in fact I couldn't think why I hadn't been back before. I actually started wandering along the bank in that direction, and then when I'd gone about ten yards I turned back. It meant crashing your way through a kind of jungle of brambles and rotten brushwood, and I was dressed up in my Sunday best. Dark-grey suit, bowler hat, button boots, and a collar that almost cut my ears off. That was how people dressed for Sunday afternoon walks in those days. And I wanted Elsie very badly.[13]

George returns to Elsie and they have sex for the first time. 'So that was that. The big carp faded out of my mind again, and in fact for years afterwards I hardly thought about them.' When he goes back to Lower Binfield some twenty-five years later, hopefully carrying a newly purchased fishing rod, he finds that the grounds of the old house have been turned into a middle-class housing estate and that the carp pond has become a rubbish tip. 'I'd learned the lesson all right. Fat men of forty-five can't go fishing. That kind of fishing doesn't happen any longer, it's just a dream, there'll be no more fishing this side of the grave.'[14]

Behind this story there is detectable the faint outline of the Edenic myth: the carp-filled pool in the heart of the wilderness is a kind of Paradise, sacred and innocent, from which the hero is expelled by a double fall into social conformity (the Sunday best) and sexuality (Elsie), a Paradise which (since there is no Redemption in the Orwellian world) he is unable to regain. But the magical-mythical associations of fish and fishing (which Eliot, for example, exploits in 'The Waste Land') are not invoked. On the contrary, George attributes historical, not mythical connotations to fishing—'the very idea of sitting all day under a willow tree beside a quiet pool . . . belongs to the time before the war, before the radio, before aeroplanes, before Hitler'—and finds his poetry in the mere denotative names of fish:

> There's a kind of peacefulness even in the names of English coarse fish. Roach, rudd, dace, bleak, barbel, bream, gudgeon, pike, chub, tench. They're solid kind of names.[15]

I compared George Bowling's nightmare visions of the totalitarian future to a newsreel. Film (a metonymic mode in Jakobson's scheme) was a major source of inspiration for many of the 1930s writers. It was a period in which British documentary film-makers achieved great distinction, notably in the work of John Grierson's GPO Film Unit, and in an issue of *Fact* devoted to the theory of revolutionary writing, Storm Jameson explicitly recommended documentary writers to study the film medium:

> Perhaps the nearest equivalent of what is wanted exists already in another form in the documentary film. As the photographer does, so must the writer keep himself out of the picture while working ceaselessly to present the *fact* from a striking (poignant, ironic, penetrating, significant) angle.[16]

Perhaps Christopher Isherwood was thinking of snapshots rather than moving pictures when he compared his stance as narrator to a camera—'I am a camera with its shutter open, quite passive, recording, not thinking'—[17] but in his lightly fictionalized autobiography, *Lions and Shadows* (1938), he makes quite clear how deeply influenced he was, as a writer, by film—and incidentally confirms the close affinity between cinematic and literary realism:

> I had always been fascinated by films . . . I was a born film fan. Chalmers [Edward Upward] was inclined to laugh at my indiscriminate appetite for anything and everything shown on a screen. . . . I was, and still am, endlessly interested in the outward appearance of people, their infinitely various ways of eating a sausage, opening a paper parcel, lighting a cigarette. The cinema puts people under a microscope. You can stare at them, you can examine them as though they were insects. . . . Viewed from this standpoint, the

stupidest film may be full of interesting revelations about the tempo and dynamics of everyday life: you see how actions look in relation to each other; how much space they occupy and how much time . . . if you are a novelist and want to watch your scene taking place visibly before you, it is simplest to project it on to an imaginary screen. A practised cinema-goer will be able to do this quite easily.[18]

There are two aspects to the connection Isherwood makes here between film and novel. One is the use of metonymic and synecdochic detail (detail of appearance, behaviour, dress, possessions etc.) as a way of identifying and defining character. One thinks, for instance, in Isherwood's own work, of Mr Norris's wig in *Mr Norris Changes Trains* (1935) and Sally Bowles's green-painted finger-nails ('a colour unfortunately chosen, for it called attention to her hands, which were much stained by cigarette smoking and dirty as a little girl's').[19] This kind of selective detail is, as we have seen, a staple device of realism and predates the motion-picture camera, but it is used by the writers of the 1930s with an economy and visual flair developed by their acquaintance with the cinema—and perhaps by the decade's enthusiam for sociological rapportage. When Graham Greene's D evades pursuit by breaking into a basement flat in central London, his eyes pan round the room to note the furnishings from which the character of the occupier is confidently deduced:

> a divan covered with an art needlework counterpane; blue-and-orange cushions; a gas fire. He took it quickly in to the home-made watercolours on the walls and the radio set by the dressing-table. It spoke to him of an unmarried ageing woman with few interests.[20]

This woman never appears in the novel, but her character, and the context of furnishings from which it is inferred, contribute to the subsequent development of the story in a way which, if we follow it, illustrates the second aspect of Isherwood's comment—the cinematic construction of scene.

D breaks into the flat a second time, bringing with him, at gunpoint, the agent K who has double-crossed him and who has been partly responsible for the murder of Else. D intends to execute summary justice by shooting K, but has some difficulty in screwing himself up to do the deed. K frantically appeals to context:

> 'This is England!' the little man shrieked as if he wanted to convince him-self. . . . Certainly it was England—England was the divan, the waste paper basket made out of old flower prints, the framed Speed map and the cushions: the alien atmosphere plucked at D's sleeve, urged him to desist. He said furiously, 'Get off that divan.'[21]

D forces K into the bathroom, shuts his eyes and pulls the trigger, missing his target by a foot. There is a ring at the front door, D shuts the bathroom door and goes to answer the bell. On the previous occasion when he broke into the flat a policeman had called, so we expect that the caller at this inopportune moment is another policeman. It is in fact D's girl, Rose: he had given her the address of his hideaway, but forgotten that he had done so (so have we). D tells Rose that he tried to shoot K but failed. When he opens the bathroom door, however, K pitches forward into the room—dead from heart failure. They lay him out on the divan and there is another knock on the door. This time it is a young man called Fortescue, a neighbour. D and Rose pretend that they are friends of the flat's rightful occupier, a Miss Glover, who has loaned them the place for a party and that K is drunk. Given the character of Miss Glover and the absence of any signs of a party such as bottles and glasses, this is a highly implausible story, but Fortescue, though puzzled, is too innocent to guess the truth. 'His young-old face was like a wide white screen on which you could project only selected and well-censored films for the family circle. . . . They watched him climbing up the area steps into the safe familiar reassuring dark. At the top he turned and waved his hand to them, tentatively.'[22] This sequence, as they say in the trade, 'shoots itself'. All the dynamics of its narrative interest—the suspense, the surprise, the irony—are highly cinematic, generated and expressed through contiguities of space and time: doors opening on the unexpected, crisis following crisis without respite or relaxation.

Graham Greene was himself a professional film critic in the 1930s, and the cinematic quality of his writing has often been commented upon. Richard Hoggart, for instance, observes of *The Power and the Glory*:

> Throughout, the eye shifts constantly, without explanatory links. In the first paragraph the solitary figure of Mr Tench is picked up crossing the hot deserted square; a few vultures look down at him; he tosses something off the road at them and one rises; with it goes the camera and introduces us to the town, the river, the sea.[23]

There are, of course, purely verbal ironies in the opening paragraph of *The Power and the Glory* (e.g. 'over the tiny plaza, over the bust of an ex-president, ex-general, ex-human being') for which it would be difficult to find visual equivalents. But the general strategy of the description, the kind of spatial relationships it establishes between the human figure and his environment, and in particular the way the focus of the description, following the flight of the vulture, pulls up and away to widen our perspective, is indeed all very cinematic in feeling. As Hoggart observes, 'Greene can assume an audience familiar with unusual camera angles and quick fadings in and out, and uses both with great skill.'[24]

Verse in the 1930s exhibited the same tendency as narrative prose to rely heavily on metonymic and synecdochic devices. The structure of

Auden's 'Spain', for example, a classic example of its period, is composed of three contrasting catalogues representing, respectively, the historical past in which civilization painfully evolved:

> Yesterday the assessment of insurance by cards
> The divination of water; yesterday the invention
>   Of cartwheels and clocks, the taming of
> Horses. Yesterday the bustling world of the navigators

—the utopian future that will follow a successful revolution:

> Tomorrow the rediscovery of romantic love
> The photographing of ravens; all the fun under
>   Liberty's masterful shadow;
> Tomorrow the hour of the pageant-master and the musician

—and the present, with its commitment to 'struggle'

> Today the deliberate increase in the chances of death,
> The conscious acceptance of guilt in the necessary murder;
>   Today the expending of powers
> On the flat ephemeral pamphlet and the boring meeting.[25]

This last stanza provoked a famous attack from George Orwell:

> The . . . stanza is intended as a sort of thumbnail sketch of a day in the life of a 'good party man'. In the morning a couple of political murders, a ten-minute interlude to stifle 'bourgeois' remorse, and then a hurried luncheon and a busy afternoon and evening chalking walls and distributing leaflets. All very edifying. But notice the phrase 'necessary murder'. It could only be written by someone to whom murder is at most a *word*. Personally I would not speak so lightly of murder. It so happens that I have seen the bodies of a number of murdered men. . . . Therefore I have some conception of what murder means—the terror, the hatred, the howling relatives, the post-mortems, the blood, the smells.[26]

Orwell's rebuke was deserved and Auden acknowledged as much by subsequently revising the stanza (to read, 'the *inevitable* increase in the chances of death' and 'the *fact* of murder') and eventually repudiated the entire poem. What is interesting from our point of view, however, is that Orwell turns against Auden the very same 'thumbnail sketch' technique that the poet himself had used, filling out the abstract concept of 'murder' with a catalogue of metonymic and synecdochic details, just as Auden had filled out the abstract concept of the revolutionary struggle.

The prevalence of the definite article in 1930s verse, statistically measured by G. Rostrevor Hamilton in *The Tell-tale Article* (1949) and recently discussed by Bernard Bergonzi in an article on 'Auden and the Audenesque'[27] is a natural concomitant of this metonymic technique. In itself it is not of course peculiar to 1930s verse—as Hamilton discovered, the ratio of definite articles tends to be as high in descriptive poetry of the eighteenth century—but in 1930s verse it is often further emphasized by the deletion of finite verbs. This is the case in 'Spain'; and also in Geoffrey Grigson's poem 'The Non-Interveners', written in the same year (1937) as Auden's, and based on essentially the same antithesis as *The Confidential Agent*:

> In England the handsome Minister with the second
> and a half chin and his heart-shaped mind
> hanging on his thin watch-chain, the Minister
> with gout who shaves low on his holly-stem neck.
>
> In Spain still the brown and gilt and the twisted
> pillar, still the olives, and in the mountains
> the chocolate trunks of cork trees bare from
> the knee, . . .
> . . . and also the black slime under
> the bullet-pocked wall, also the arterial blood
> squirting into the curious future, . . .[28]

Louis MacNeice remembered Spain in the same fashion, as a collection of verbal snapshots:

> With writings on the walls—
>   Hammer and sickle, Boicot, Viva, Muerra;
> With *café au lait* brimming the waterfalls,
>   With sherry, shellfish, omelettes.
> With fretted stone the Moor
>   Had chiselled for effects of sun and shadow;
> With shadows of the poor,
>   The begging cripples and the children begging.[29]

Deletion or avoidance of finite verbs is the main deviation from conventional grammar in 1930s verse, and it is not, of course, one that causes much difficulty for the reader. On the whole, 1930s writing in verse and prose emphasized syntagmatic connections between verbal items, reflecting grammatically the empirical connections between entities in the observable world. The complex, self-embedding syntax of James and Conrad was as unfashionable as the fragmentary, dislocated, allusive language of Eliot, Pound, and Joyce, the mystical metaphorical flights of Lawrence, or Virginia Woolf's paratactic lyricism. Sentences in 1930s verse, like the plots of 1930s novels, have a clearly recognizable and intelligible structure. The tone of Audenesque lyric poetry is either hortatory:

> And throw away
> beginning from today
> the eau de Cologne which disguised you, the stick which propped,
> the tennis racquet, the blazer of the First Fifteen[30]

—or conversationally relaxed:

> About suffering they were never wrong,
> The Old Masters: how well they understood
> Its human position: how it takes place
> While someone else is eating or opening a window
> or just walking dully along;[31]

This last, much anthologized poem, Auden's 'Musée des Beaux Arts', is not topically political in theme, but it belongs to the 1930s and it is, significantly, an explicit inquiry into, and celebration of, the aesthetics of realism, emphasizing the cardinal importance of contingent contiguity in such art:

> How, when the ages are reverently, passionately waiting
> For the miraculous birth, there must always be
> Children who did not specially want it to happen, skating
> On a pond at the edge of a wood.[32]

'In general', Bernard Bergonzi writes in the article mentioned above, 'the characteristics of the Audenesque in syntax and diction seem to me to be ... copious use of the definite article, unusual adjectives and adjectival phrases, and surprising similes, which have a reductive or trivializing effect; and personified abstractions.'[33] The prevalence of the definite article we have already accounted for as an inevitable feature of a nominalizing style, and the other features are obvious ways of rhetorically heightening and varying such a style, preventing it from degenerating into mere catalogues of data. If a style emphasizes nouns, particularity must be conveyed through adjectives, or adjectival phrases, or through analogies, as the language of nineteenth-century realistic fiction shows. The use of personified abstractions is more distinctive, and no doubt derives from the writers' sense of being caught up in the tide of history, having important moral and political messages to deliver. 'History', indeed, was itself one of their favourite abstract words. Samuel Hynes remarks that Auden revised the line, 'And called out of tideless peace by a living sun' in the 'Prologue' of 1933 to read, in 1936, 'And out of the future into actual history.'[34] Bergonzi quotes the famous conclusion to 'Spain':

> History to the defeated
> May say alas but cannot help or pardon

and juxtaposes a passage from Edward Upward's story 'Sunday' in which the same abstraction is tied to a typical synecdochic catalogue:

> History is here in the park, in the town. It is in the offices, the duplicators, the traffic, the nursemaids wheeling prams, the airmen, the aviary, the new viaduct over the valley. It was once in the castle on the cliff, in the sooty churches, in your mind; but it is abandoning them, leaving with them only the failing energy of desperation, going to live elsewhere.[35]

As Bergonzi remarks, the Marxist implications in this invocation of 'History' are obvious enough; but the peculiar stylistic *frisson* which the writers of the 1930s derived from clamping together huge abstractions with particular concrete details of ordinary life was not confined to Party members or to fellow-travellers. Graham Greene does the same with metaphysical and theological concepts like good, evil, faith:

> It isn't a gain to have turned the witch or the masked secret dancer, the sense of supernatural evil, into the small human viciousness of the distinguished military grey head in Kensington Gardens with the soft lips and the eye which dwelt with dull lustre on girls and boys of a certain age.[36]

> Good and evil lived in the same country, came together like old friends, feeling the same completion, touching hands beside the iron bedstead.[37]

> He was aware of faith dying out between the bed and the door.[38]

I have already commented, especially in connection with Orwell's 'A Hanging', on the preference of the realistic writer for simile rather than metaphor and his tendency to draw the vehicles of such similes from the literal context of the narrative. I commented in the same place on the ambivalence of the word *like*, which may indicate a synechochic relationship derived from contiguity as well as a relationship based on similarity. Both these points are well illustrated by the opening of Christopher Isherwood's 'A Berlin Diary (Autumn 1930)' in *Goodbye to Berlin* (1939):

> From my window, the deep solemn massive street. Cellarshops where the lamps burn all day, under the shadow of topheavy balconied facades, dirty plaster frontages embossed with scroll-work and heraldic devices. The whole district is like this: street leading into street of houses like shabby monumental safes crammed with the tarnished valuables and second-hand furniture of a bankrupt middle class.[39]

The first two sentences present the scene as a catalogue of selected details and attributes, the main verbs of these sentences being characteristically deleted. The third sentence uses the word *like* to stress the synecdochic character of the street: all streets in the district are like this one. Then *like* is used again to construct a simile: 'houses like monumental safes'. But the vehicle of this simile is taken from the context, and thus serves to reinforce our sense of the context rather than to introduce some other, quite different field of reference. For these houses almost certainly *contain* safes, safes very probably crammed with tarnished valuables (it was a period of chronic inflation and financial instability). That, at least, is the impression the sentence leaves us with—the simile is, as it were, simultaneously a synecdoche.

On the next page of the same text Isherwood describes the interior of his lodgings:

> The extraordinary smell in this room when the stove is lighted and the

window shut; not altogether unpleasant, a mixture of incense and stale buns. The tall, tiled stove, gorgeously coloured, like an altar. The washstand like a Gothic shrine. The cupboard also is Gothic, with carved cathedral windows: Bismark faces the king of Prussia in stained glass. My best chair would do for a bishop's throne. In the corner, three sham medieval halberds (from a theatrical touring company?) are fastened together to form a hatstand. Frl. Schroeder unscrews the heads of the halberds and polishes them from time to time. They are heavy and sharp enough to kill.

Everything in the room is like that: unnecessarily solid, abnormally heavy and dangerously sharp. Here, at the writing table, I am confronted by a phalanx of metal objects—a pair of candlesticks shaped like entwined serpents, an ashtray from which emerges the head of a crocodile, a paperknife copied from a Florentine dagger, a brass dolphin holding on the end of its tail a small broken clock. What becomes of such things? How could they ever be destroyed? They will probably remain intact for thousands of years: people will treasure them in Museums. Or perhaps they will merely be melted down for munitions in a war. Every morning, Frl. Schroeder arranges them very carefully in certain unvarying positions: there they stand, like an uncompromising statement of her views on Capital and Society, Religion and Sex.[40]

Here the similes, 'like an altar', 'like a Gothic shrine' introduce a different context, but they do so reductively, to ironic effect. The anticlimactic collocation 'incense and stale buns' ensures that no transcendental glamour will attach itself to the ecclesiastical look of the furniture. The simile construction, pivoting on the word *like*, maintains a clear distinction between what these things are and what they suggest, and the gap between the two serves as an index of bourgeois pretentiousness. When the narrator says that everything in the room was 'like' the mock halberds, 'unnecessarily solid, abnormally heavy and dangerously sharp', he uses the word *like* differently, to establish a 'real', i.e. synecdochic, relationship between the halberds and the other furnishings. The bric à brac described in the second paragraph of the passage is mocked for its iconic metaphorizing, the surrealism of *kitsch* (the serpentine candlesticks, crocodile ashtray etc.). The last use of *like* in this paragraph is particularly interesting. Although it seems to connect two parts of a simile, there is in fact no *similarity* between tenor and vehicle. There is no such thing as a statement of Frl. Schroeder's views on Capital and Society, Religion and Sex—and if there were, it would in no sense *resemble* a pair of candlesticks, an ashtray, a paperknife and a broken clock, however fantastically ornamented these things may be. One might say that the possession of these objects is congruous with the possession of those views, or even that in some sense the possession of those views *caused* the acquisition of these objects. Thus a synecdochic or metonymic relationship has been presented as if it were metaphorical.

Graham Greene uses simile in a similar, but more flamboyant way:

1 Congratulate me, he seemed to be saying, and his humorous friendly shifty eyes raked her like the headlamps of a second-hand car which had been painted and polished to deceive.[41]
2 Virginity straightened in him like sex.[42]
3 He felt anger grinding at his guts like the tide at the piles below.[43]
4 Evil ran like malaria in his veins.[44]
5 She carried her responsibilities carefully like crockery across the hot yard.[45]
6 He drank the brandy down like damnation.[46]

The analogy in (1) tells us little about the appearance of Anthony Farrant's eyes, but it reinforces the moral judgment of his character as 'shifty' by evoking the social context to which he belongs—one in which the buying and selling of deceptively shiny secondhand cars would be not uncommon. The similes in (3), (4) and (5) are all drawn from the character's immediate context—the sea and Brighton pier in (3), the disease-ridden Mexican climate in (4) and Coral's domestic role in (5). All yoke abstract and concrete violently together in a way that (as Richard Hoggart has observed)[47] is very characteristic of Graham Greene, but which is also, as we have seen, a common feature of 1930s writing generally. The contextual appropriateness of these similes helps to accommodate their abrupt leaps from abstract to concrete within a generally realistic or prosaic account of experience. Examples (2) and (6) also depend upon a kind of fusion, or confusion, of metaphorical similarity with metonymic contiguity. 'Virginity' and 'sex' are existentially, physiologically connected: this simile is not so much a comparison between two different but similar things as a comparison between the positive and negative sides of the same thing. Brandy is not 'like' damnation in any definable sense, but the priest is thinking about his own unworthiness for salvation while drinking brandy, and bargaining for some bottles of the liquor which he will pay for with the hard-won offerings of the pious peasantry who want their children baptized. His addiction to brandy, in short, brings him close to committing the sin of simony, and brandy could therefore be said to be his 'damnation' (as gin is jocularly and proverbially said to be 'mother's ruin') by a metonymic substitution of effect for cause.

I alluded briefly in Part One to Christopher Isherwood's account, in *Lions and Shadows*, of his early literary development—of how he weaned himself, partly under the influence of Tolstoy's realism, from what he came to regard as a shallow and trivializing experimentalism in his first attempts at writing fiction. He also describes in the same book the parallel case of his friend Edward Upward (referred to as 'Alan Chalmers'), a case that, traced through Upward's own early writings,[48] throws vivid light upon the motivation of that generation of writers in their quest for a more realistic and historically responsible *écriture* than that of the modernist tradition, and upon the kind of stylistic choices and sacrifices this quest entailed. The characteristic trend of formal development in the major modernist writers, as we have seen, was from a metonymic type of writing in their early work to a metaphorical mode in their mature and late work. Upward's development was exactly the reverse. And it should be remembered that although he now seems a comparatively minor figure, he enjoyed a legendary reputation in left-wing literary circles in the 1930s, and exerted a powerful influence on writers who became more famous than himself—not only Isherwood, but Auden and Stephen Spender among others.[49] For these reasons I propose to examine Upward's early writing in some detail.

Isherwood's relationship with Upward began at school: 'Never in my life have I been so strongly and immediately attracted to any personality, before or since. Everything about him appealed to me. He was a born anarchist, a born romantic revolutionary.'[50] The two youths went up together to Cambridge, where, as a form of escape from, or defence against, the various psychological pressures commonly experienced by clever, rebellious undergraduates, they began to invent a fictitious, surrealistic alternative world, known at first as the 'Old Town'. Isherwood describes a typical moment in the formation of this fantasy:

> One evening, I happened to read aloud the name under a fluttering gas-lamp: 'Garret Hostel Bridge'. 'The Rats' Hostel!' Chalmers suddenly exclaimed. We often conversed in surrealist phrases of this kind. Now we both became abnormally excited: it seemed to us that an all-important statement had been made. At last, by pure accident, we had stumbled upon the key-words which expressed the inmost nature of the Other Town.[51]

Later the Other Town was displaced by a mythical village called Mortmere, which the two young men gradually populated with a large cast of characters. From merely talking about it, they progressed to writing about it—Upward in particular seems to have written a great many Mortmere stories. Only the last of these survives: 'The Railway Accident', written in 1928, after Upward had left the University. Isherwood describes it as 'a farewell to Mortmere which left Chalmers free to develop his extraordinary technique in other, more fruitful directions. Nevertheless, Mortmere was the mad nursery in which Chalmers grew up as a writer.'[52] Comparison with the Angria and Gondol sagas of the Brontë children is irresistible. Like the Brontës, Upward and Isherwood came to see that they must disengage themselves from the mythology of their immature work in order to develop as artists. But in Upward's case, at least, the imaginative cost of the renunciation was great, and it is open to question whether the promise of 'The Railway Accident' was ever fulfilled.

This story begins with the narrator, Hearn, being seen off by the officious Gunball from an unidentified railway terminus on a journey to Mortmere. As the train leaves, he is joined by Gustave Shreeve, also bound for Mortmere, where both are to participate in a Treasure Hunt organized by the vicar, the Rev. Welken. Shreeve's remarks (disturbed by terrific noise emanating from a party of territorial soldiers in an adjoining carriage) recall a railway accident on the route to Mortmere caused by a collapsing tunnel, and hint that the accident may recur. The train indeed swerves on to the branch line that leads to the blocked and disused tunnel. Hearn and Shreeve manage to jump clear, but an express train follows closely behind at high speed with catastrophic results. The scene shifts to Mortmere and the Treasure Hunt, which ends in angry accusations of cheating and a duel fought with pea-shooting pistols. One of the pistols proves to be loaded with real ammunition and wounds one of the duellists. The story ends with the news that Harold Wrygrave, the Mortmere architect and builder of the tunnel, has been arrested on a charge of trainwrecking.

The mode of 'The Railway Accident' is best described as surrealistic. When Isherwood applies this term in *Lions and Shadows* to his and Upward's fantasy world he comments: 'I use the term "surrealism" simply for the purpose of explanation: we had, of course, no idea that a surrealist movement already existed on the Continent.'[53] Surrealism did not really make a full impact upon the English cultural scene until the International Surrealist Exhibition of 1936, but its roots were in the modernist 1920s. The first Surrealist Manifesto was published in 1924, and André Breton defined the period of 1912–1923 as 'the heroic epoch of surrealism'.[54] As the European literary and artistic *avant garde* became more politically conscious, some attempt was made by Breton and others at a synthesis of surrealism and Marxism on the flimsy ground that both were revolutionary movements, but by the time of the London Surrealist Exhibition the idea was beginning to look increasingly implausible. A writer in the *Left Review* at the time summed up the attitude of politically orthodox literary intellectuals: 'Surrealism is not revolutionary, because its lyricism is socially irresponsible. . . . Surrealism is a particularly subtle form of fake revolution.'[55] It is indeed difficult to see how the principles and methodology of Marxist-Leninism could be reconciled with Breton's definition of surrealism as 'Pure psychic automatism through which one seeks to express . . . the absolute functioning of thought . . . in the absence of all rational control and apart from any ethical or moral considerations . . . a belief in the supreme quality of certain forms of association heretofore neglected: in the omnipotence of dream, in the disinterested play of thought.'[56] The influence of surrealism on the writing of the 1930s was therefore either superficial or confined to writers who were not representative of the main literary current of the period, especially the poets sometimes referred to as the New Apocalypse school—David Gascoyne, George Barker, Dylan Thomas and others. Certainly by 1936, the year of the Surrealist

Exhibition, Upward and Isherwood had already weaned themselves from their own privately generated surrealistic world of Mortmere.

Surrealist painting, it will be recalled, is classified as metaphoric by Jakobson, and opposed to the metonymically experimental art of cubism. Surrealism is in fact a particularly radical metaphorical mode, the force of which is as much negative as positive. By this I mean that what strikes one about the juxtaposition of items in surrealist art (visual, or verbal) is in the first place not so much any similarity between them as their incongruity—the violation of natural relationships of contiguity entailed in the juxtaposition. The shock to the perceiver's expectations and habits, derived from the rational, empirical world-view of common sense, frees his mind and sensibility to play over the juxtaposition, and perhaps discover metaphorical meanings in it. The point may be illustrated from Magritte's painting 'Time Transfixed' which most appropriately decorates the cover of the Penguin edition of *The Railway Accident*. This interior, painted with Magritte's characteristic hardedged naturalism, depicts a fireplace with marble mantelpiece bearing a clock and two candlesticks and surmounted by a large mirror. The fireplace is boarded or walled up and from a point in this vertical plane, just under the mantelshelf, in the position where one might expect a stove to be connected by a flue to the chimney, there projects into the room a steam locomotive with smoke issuing from its funnel, drastically reduced in scale, though perceptively larger than the usual model train. The scale is very important: if the locomotive were big enough to fill the fireplace we would have an obvious and quickly exhausted visual joke based on the similarity between a tunnel and a fireplace (a kind of pictorial equivalent to the comic song, 'The railroad came through the middle of the house'). If the scale were smaller it would suggest a toy which had been eccentrically mounted in this position. But as it is, the locomotive looks like a real locomotive which has been subjected to some strange enchantment, shrunk in size, its weight still more drastically reduced (it gives the impression of floating two or three feet above the ground rather than being supported by a bracket) and its movement (the smoke is streaming backwards, indicating speed) frozen. In short, there is no possible logical, rational explanation for the contiguity of the engine and the fireplace, though the scrupulous naturalism of the treatment teasingly invites us to seek one. Defeated in our attempt to interpret the picture according to contiguity, we are, in our contemplation of it, led eventually to perceive various relationships of similarity, both visual and semantic, among its components. The lines of the floorboards look like railway lines, and are the right 'gauge' to accommodate the locomotive. Both a fireplace and an engine burn coal.[57] The circular face of the locomotive's boiler is the same size as the clock-face, and the reflection of the clock in the mirror, lengthening its shape by replication, emphasizes the formal symmetry between these two objects, both of which are in the centre of the picture, and project forward from the predominantly vertical planes of the wall, mantelpiece and mirror. The clock face shows the time as seventeen minutes to one. The hands of the clock may be moving, but there is no way of showing this in a painting: in the painting the time is always seventeen minutes to one. To paint a clock *is* to 'transfix time', but without the locomotive we should not be aware of this—we should interpret the clock face as a synecdoche for the progress of time. Unlike a clock, a locomotive can be painted in motion (by the treatment of the smoke). Because the locomotive in the picture is so obviously and strangely arrested in full career—spellbound, one might say—we are made to appreciate that the clock's movement is also spellbound by pictorial representation.

The railway train, it may be suggested, is an inherently metonymic product of technology. In form it is a kind of syntagm, a combination of units (locomotive, carriages, guard's van) in a prescribed order. Its progression is linear, unidirectional and highly predictable, like orthodox prose (we recall Virginia Woolf's wish to go beyond 'the formal railway line of the sentence'). Ships and aeroplanes lend themselves readily to metaphorical transformation, but trains, except in the rather strained anthropomorphism of children's stories, are likely to become realistic 'symbols' rather than metaphors: symbols of Progress, Energy, Industrialism, or whatever. Thus any radically metaphorical treatment of the railway train, any striking disturbance of its contextual norms, is likely to make a strong impact— as we see in 'The Railway Accident'.

At the beginning of the story, Hearn, waiting for his train to depart, is puzzled by the appearance of another train drawn up on the other side of the platform:

> My impression of most details in the design of this train were that they were unnecessary or, if necessary, belonging to a world in which I should have felt as wholly disorientated as though, suffering from amnesia after an accident, I had found myself among hoardings bearing futurist German advertisements.[58]

In fact, this *is* exactly how Hearn (and the reader) feels as the story develops. Gunball, who is seeing him off, disconcerts him by remarking:

> 'So I suppose this one will go there too . . .'
> 'Where? Which one?'
> 'The train you're leaning out of at this moment. To Mortmere. But I was just saying I'd noticed that the other one certainly does.'[59]

It is too late for Hearn to change trains. Gunball shouts, 'Anyway, your train will arrive somewhere'—a patently absurd remark, since railway journeys are always made with a specific destination in view— and the train pulls out of the station. 'The first gasometers, restful, solemn, like stumps of semi-amputated breasts, curved past the window in frost-bright air. . . . Now for many months of complete summer I should idle in gardens warm with croquet and the tinkling of spoons. . . .'[60] The grotesquely vivid simile of the semi-amputated breasts is typically surrealistic (they *displace* rather than define the gasometers in our mind's eye) as is the impossible confusion of seasons. The railway accident itself is described with a fine profusion of varied metaphors and similes:

> Coaches mounted like viciously copulating bulls, telescoped like ventilator hatches. Nostril gaps in a tunnel clogged with wreckage instantly flamed. A faint jet of blood sprayed from a vacant window. Frog-sprawling bodies fumed in blazing reeds. The architrave of the tunnel crested with daffodils fell compact as hinged scenery. Tall rag-feathered birds with corrugated red wattles limped from holes among the reeds.[61]

W. H. Sellers seems to me wrong in suggesting that 'what gives the story its bizarre quality is that, from beginning to end, the incidents that occur do so only in the deranged mind of the narrator'.[62] On the contrary, the story is bizarre precisely because the text contains no normative reality against which we can measure Hearn's perceptions and declare them deranged. It is dreamlike, but he (and we) do not awake from the dream. The dream is, to quote André Breton, 'omnipotent'.

But Upward—and Isherwood—eventually came to feel that they must awake from the dream of Mortmere. By 1928, Isherwood comments,

> Mortmere seemed to have brought us to a dead end. The cult of romantic strangeness, we both knew, was a luxury for the comfortable University fireside; it could not save you from the drab realities of cheap lodgings and a dull underpaid job. . . . Chalmers . . . was to spend the next three years in desperate and bitter struggles to relate Mortmere to the real world of the jobs and the lodging houses; to find the formula which would transform our private fantasies and amusing freaks and bogies into valid symbols of the ills of society and the toils and aspirations of our daily lives. . . . And Chalmers did at last find it . . . quite clearly set down, for everybody to read, in the pages of Lenin and of Marx.[63]

Upward represented this quest in his novella *Journey to the Border* (1938), a work in which we can see the metaphorical mode of 'The Railway Accident' being subordinated to an allegorical purpose and finally crushed. Allegory is a metaphorical device, of course, but its exploitation of similarity is very rigidly controlled in the interests of a didactic message and it can be easily combined with an essentially metonymic type of narrative. For example, George Orwell's *Animal Farm* is based on a system of similarities between the story of the animals and the history of the Russian Revolution, but the narrative is quite intelligible without the application of this code, and is enjoyed as such by children. When the 1930s writers did not use documentary or realistic modes of writing, when they wrote in an overtly fictive, metaphorical mode, it was usually in forms of allegory—sometimes referred to, in the criticism of the period as 'fable', 'myth' and 'parable'.[64] Reviewing the Auden–Isherwood play, *The Ascent of F6*, and the first issue of *New Writing*, Stephen Spender noted in the former, 'the rhythmic contrast which the writers maintain between two entirely different methods of presentation: firstly, realistic scenes of political reportage; secondly fables'; and of the latter he observed: 'the best stories in the volume are either very realistic fragments of actual life ... or they are allegories.'[65] Other examples of the allegorical mode in the period would be the early poetic works of Auden and Day Lewis—*The Witnesses, The Orators, The Magnetic Mountain*—and the novels of Rex Warner—*The Professor, The Aerodrome.* It must always be remembered that these writers had grown up under the influence of the modernist movement of Eliot, Pound and Joyce, and never entirely repudiated its aesthetics even if they rejected its politics and philosophy. Most of them hoped that writing could continue to be 'modern' while at the same time being committed, and the allegorized myth or fantasy was one appealing way of making the metaphorical imagination historically responsible. In practice, the most successful efforts in this direction were ideologically ambiguous, while the felt obligation to deliver a politically 'orthodox' message was apt to deprive the fable of imaginative life. This was very much the problem that preoccupied Edward Upward, for of the Auden group he was the only one who could be said to be a fully committed Marxist, but it can hardly be said that he solved it. *Journey to the Border* is an allegory the message of which leads ultimately to a renunciation of its own imaginative devices.

The hero, referred to throughout, with the anonymity typical of allegory, as 'the tutor', is employed by a wealthy businessman (representing Capitalism) to coach his son. The action takes place on a day when the tutor is compelled against his inclinations to accompany father and son to a horse-race meeting. During the day, the tutor, who is in a state of barely controlled hysteria, undergoes various trials and temptations. His grip upon reality is insecure, and at the racecourse he is subject to strange visions and hallucinations, centering on a large marquee. When he first glances inside this erection he has an impression of luxury which he recalls with disgust 'tempered by a certain ... half-ashamed desire' as a profusion of surrealistically incongruous objects.[66] But when he eventually enters the marquee,

The scene was reassuringly normal. Small tables covered with white cloths and surrounded by green iron chairs occupied the central area of uncarpeted grass, and he saw no Nubian statue, no chenille-hung buffalo head.[67]

Journey to the Border thus differs crucially from 'The Railway Accident' in that the hero's subjective distortion of reality is explicitly revealed and framed by a 'normal' version of the same objects and events. What is interesting from our point of view is that illusion and reality are explicitly equated with the metaphorical and metonymic modes, respectively. For example:

> Why shouldn't he dare to give free play, within sane limits, to a happiness which was no longer based on fantasies but on the actual possibilities of his real surroundings? . . . The marquee was not like a racing yacht in full sail, it was not like a white-walled aerodrome from which he could instantly fly to any part of the world, it was not like a crowded flutter of girls' frocks along the esplanade, was not like a mansion with circular mansard windows and broad white pillars and porticoes and gilded urns, not like a cool place for the protection of art and learning, not like a white balcony from which he could look at mountains through a powerful brass telescope. It was like an ordinary marquee, white and rather large. It was like the actual destination towards which a slowly moving car was taking the tutor.[68]

This destination *is* the marquee, so the opposition between similarity and contiguity could scarcely be more emphatic. However it must be pointed out that the tutor's rejection, here, of fanciful imagery is compromised by the fact that the 'actuality' he seeks to embrace is politically corrupt. Inside the marquee all his fear and loathing erupt again in a conversation with a sadistic young colonial administrator. The tutor proves susceptible to the indoctrination of a psychologist called Mavors who preaches a gospel of instinctual liberation and unreason. He lapses back into the language of surrealistic free association, and a seductive girl reminds him of a romantic encounter they had at Cambridge: 'You talked about pergolas and about fountains. I had never heard that sort of language before, but I knew at once that I had always wanted to hear it. I remember one phrase especially: "Rubber statuary in gardens of ice-cream roses".'[69] Erotically excited, the tutor proposes to elope with her, but the frightening spectacle of a kind of fascist rally in the marquee forestalls him and he runs off in a panic.

The tutor's problem is explained to him by another girl (his 'good angel') Ann: 'you see quite clearly what is wrong with the system in which you are living. . . . But you take no action. You are content to hate and despise your life.'[70] Alienated from the real world, but unwilling to transform it morally by political action, he falls back upon private, surrealistic transformations of the world which correspond to the clinical symptoms of schizophrenia. The solution is therefore twofold: first he must abandon illusion and recognize reality. Then he must commit himself to changing reality. All this is explained in a long dialogue between the tutor and his own political conscience. Again it is fascinating to see how the argument conforms to the rhetorical opposition between metaphor and metonymy. The tutor defends his fantasies as having some basis in reality: 'even the maddest fantasies must fetch their materials from real life'. But his *alter ego* retorts:

> 'How far do your thoughts give a true picture of the relations actually existing among things? You might think of a man with wings. The man might be real, a friend of yours, and the wings might have belonged to a real swan you had seen in a public park, but the combination in your mind would be nothing more than a contemptible fantasy, a myth.'[71]

Whether intentionally or not, there is a fitting irony in the fact that the metaphorical birdman, the myth so contemptuously dismissed here, is the Icarus figure central to the imagination of the greatest modernist writer, James Joyce. The *alter ego* relentlessly orders the tutor to 'Look around you. Become aware of your real situation . . . what do you think you will see next?'

> 'The races will come to an end. People will begin to disperse. Some of them will go towards the car park. That's where I shall go. I shall see the car which brought me here. I shall see Mr Parkin and the boy.'
> 'Fine. Now you're facing it. And the next?'
> 'The return. The house with the four lawns. Bed. Tomorrow. The window and the treetops. Rooks. Beer. Latin and Scripture. The day after tomorrow and the days after that.'
> 'That's your real situation.'[72]

The world is thus reduced to chronological sequence, spatial contiguities, synecdochic detail. But the tutor protests that he cannot 'stand' this world—he would rather return to his delusions. *The alter ego* says that there is 'another way . . . the way of the workers. You must get in touch with the workers' movement'.[73]

This answer may seem rather facile, and hardly acquires more plausibility in the sequel, when the tutor hesitatingly strikes up acquaintance with a 'worker' on the racecourse—a naively handled episode in which a politically motivated encounter is invested with all the emotion of a sexual adventure ('Already the tutor had begun to feel interested and a little excited. A worker was looking at him. The tutor was pleasantly excited. Stop it at once. Try to feel indifferent').[74] But that is the didactic conclusion of the story. It is *Journey to the Border* rather than 'The Railway Accident' that was Upward's 'farewell to Mortmere', for the fantasies that the tutor tries unsuccessfully to defend against the criticism of his *alter ego* clearly recall the myth of Mortmere. 'Dreams of escape. Twisted fantasies. Unhealthy substitutes for the action you ought to have taken,' the *alter ego* calls them.

> 'Quite true. But they were something more than that. They may have been a substitute for action, but at the same time they were themselves a form of action. They may have been fantastic but at the same time they contained within them elements of something other than fantasy. . . . They were my attempts to find a significance in the life I was leading, to build up my experiences into a coherent, a satisfying pattern.[75]

H

In spite of this eloquent defence of imagination, the *alter ego* wins the debate, and the tutor, having resolved to join the workers' movement, rejoices, in the last lines of the story, at having 'come out of the cloud of his cowardly fantasies'.[76] Reading this dialogue of the mind with itself I was strongly reminded of Keats's *The Dream of Hyperion*, in which the poet first defends himself against, and then finally pleads guilty to, Moneta's accusation that he is 'a dreaming thing' incapable of benefiting 'the great world'. More ominously one may be reminded of the Moscow Trials which were taking place at about the time *Journey to the Border* was being written, and of the 'confessions' that were extracted from the accused on those occasions.

Edward Upward himself joined the Communist Party, and became one of the most uncompromising Marxist literary intellectuals of the 1930s. George Orwell quotes him, in 'Inside the Whale', as stating flatly that 'no book written *at the present time* can be "good" unless it is written from a Marxist or near-Marxist viewpoint'.[77] Upward's own career, however, seems to confirm Orwell's judgment that total commitment to any ideological orthodoxy is inimical to literary creation. Upward published only one short piece after *Journey to the Border* appeared in 1938, and from 1942 onwards he was totally silent. In 1948 he left the Party, and has since published two novels, conventionally realistic in technique, about the internal conflicts in the British Communist Party: *In the Thirties* (1962) and *The Rotten Elements* (1969).

In this chapter I have used the terms 'writers of the 1930s', '1930s writing', in a sense quite familiar to literary historians. It is not implied that *every* writer of that time shared the same aims and technical predilections; but looking back on the period we are probably more struck by the homogeniety than by the variety of its literary output. There is, I think, only one indisputably major writer belonging to that generation (the generation, roughly speaking, who were still at school when World War I ended) who has not been mentioned so far, and that is Evelyn Waugh. There are several reasons why his work does not fit neatly into the general characterization I have attempted of the *écriture* of the 1930s. Politically, he was a kind of conservative anarchist, and more sympathetic, therefore, than his left wing contemporaries to the pessimism, and despair of secular 'progress', that underlay so much modernist writing. I have attempted to show elsewhere how potent in Waugh's work was the 'myth of decline' which Northrop Frye has identified as central to T. S. Eliot's imagination.[78] Where Waugh parted company with the great modernists was in renouncing their 'subjectivity'—which as far as prose fiction was concerned meant renouncing the limited point of view or the stream of consciousness technique. His model was not Henry James or James Joyce, but Ronald Firbank.[79] The disorderliness, the contingency, the collapse of value and meaning in contemporary life, are rendered dramatically through conversational nuances and ironic juxtapositions; narratively through the elimination or parody of cause-and-effect. But the implied author mediating this vision of comical anarchy, this farcical Wasteland, remains objective—morally, emotionally and stylistically. He does not, except in passages of obvious pastiche, bend his verbal medium to fit the contours of his characters' sensibilities, nor dissolve the structure of formal English prose to imitate subconscious or unconscious processes of the mind. He retains always a classical detachment, lucidity and poise, and often makes his authorial presence felt as much by his abstention from comment as by what he actually says. This is the source of Evelyn Waugh's distinctive tone, and of his most characteristic comic effects; it is also what has troubled critics who accuse him of being cruel, snobbish and nihilistic. In the 1930s, when compassion, moral indignation and democratic sentiment were at a premium in the literary world, he was an isolated figure.

Nevertheless his style of writing was, in its own way, as 'readerly' as the other 1930s writing we have looked at; and although it seems misleading to describe Waugh as a 'realist' in the same sense as Isherwood, Greene and Orwell, because of the element of extravagant farce and caricature in his work, there is no doubt about his interest in and feeling for the signs and indices of social class, status and style in speech, dress and behaviour. In this regard he made extensive use of metonymic and synecdochic detail (consider, for example, the important function of architecture, furnishings and fittings in *A Handful of Dust* (1935)), while being very sparing of metaphorical figures.[80] It is vital to the effect of Waugh's novels that the absurd and outrageous is presented very literally. One might say that the technique of the early novels is metonymic in an experimental way—like Virginia Woolf's *Jacob's Room*, but applying the method she used to the purposes of comedy. Waugh deletes from and rearranges the contiguous elements of his subject to produce absurd and ironic incongruities—Agatha Runcible coming down to breakfast at No. 10 Downing St. dressed in a Hawaiian grass skirt, for instance; or Basil Seal unwittingly eating his girlfriend Prudence at a cannibal feast; or Tony Last reading Dickens aloud at gun-point in the depths of the South American jungle. But the imaginative idea which lies behind and unifies the narrative is often quasi-metaphorical in a way that reminds us of modernist writing. The title *Decline and Fall* (1928) hints at an analogy between modern Western society and the late Roman Empire; *Black Mischief* (1932), *A Handful of Dust* and *Scoop* (1938) all turn upon ironic parallels between civilization and barbarism—the social jungle of London compared with the real jungle of South America or tropical Africa. Ironic comparisons and cross-references between these different milieux are accomplished by a cinematic technique of cross-cutting between short scenes often occurring simultaneously in different places—like Greene and Isherwood, Waugh was deeply influenced by the cinema.[81]

In *Work Suspended* (1942), and still more obviously in *Brideshead Revisited* (1945), Waugh made a radical change in his technique. His style became heavily metaphorical, given to long, elaborate analogies, but at the same time the narrative itself became more conventional in structure, following the fortunes of a group of interrelated characters as they unfolded in time and space. The resemblance to Proust suggested by the retrospective stance of the narrator, and by the lush nostalgia of his reminiscence, is only skin deep: there is no questioning of the nature of perception and consciousness such as we find in *La Recherche du Temps Perdu*. Later, in the *Sword of Honour* trilogy, Waugh trimmed the self-indulgent metaphorizing from his writing and returned to a modified form of his earlier technique, with happy results. But his efforts to revise *Brideshead Revisited* (1960) in the same spirit were less successful: it was too much a product of its period, of the partial, somewhat phoney revival of modernism in the 1940s.

7   Philip Larkin

1930s writing was, characteristically, antimodernist, realistic, readerly and metonymic. In the 1940s the pendulum of literary fashion swung back again—not fully, but to a perceptible degree—towards the pole we have designated as modernist, symbolist, writerly and metaphoric. Sooner or later the leading writers of the 1930s became disillusioned with politics, lost faith in Soviet Russia, took up religion, emigrated to America or fell silent. Christianity, in a very uncompromising, antihumanist, theologically 'high' form, became a force in literature (the later Eliot, the Charles Williams–C. S. Lewis circle, the 'Catholic novel' of Greene and Waugh). Bourgeois writers no longer felt obliged to identify with the proletariat. Bohemian, patrician, cosmopolitan attitudes and life-styles became once more acceptable in the literary world. To say that the English novel resumed experimentalism would be an overstatement; but 'fine writing' certainly returned and an interest in rendering the refinements of individual sensibility rather than collective experience. There was a revival of Henry James, and many people saw Charles Morgan as his modern successor. Fantasy such as Upward and Isherwood had felt obliged to purge from their work was luxuriated in by Mervyn Peake. There was great excitement at an apparent revival of verse drama, principally in the work of T. S. Eliot and Christopher Fry. Perhaps the movement of the pendulum was most evident in the field of poetry. The reputations of Eliot and Yeats triumphantly survived the attacks launched against them in the 1930s, and the most enthusiastically acclaimed younger poet was Dylan Thomas, a 'metaphoric' writer if ever there was one.

In the middle of the 1950s, a new generation of writers began to exert an opposite pressure on the pendulum. They were sometimes referred to as 'The Movement' (mainly in the context of poetry) and sometimes, more journalistically, as the 'Angry Young Men' (mainly in the context of fiction and drama). Some of the key figures in these partially overlapping groups were: Kingsley Amis, Philip Larkin, John Wain, D. J. Enright, Thom Gunn, Donald Davie, Alan Sillitoe, John Osborne, Arnold Wesker. Others who shared the same general aims and assumptions as these writers, or contributed to the formation of a distinctively 1950s *écriture*, were William Cooper, C. P. Snow and his wife Pamela Hansford Johnson, Colin McInnes, Angus Wilson, John Braine, Stan Barstow, Thomas Hinde, Keith Waterhouse, David Storey and, in precept if not in practice, Iris Murdoch.* The 1950s writers were suspicious of, and often positively hostile to the modernist movement and certainly opposed to any further efforts at 'experimental' writing. Dylan Thomas epitomized everything they detested: verbal obscurity, metaphysical pretentiousness, self-indulgent romanticism, compulsive metaphorizing were his alleged faults. They themselves aimed to communicate clearly and honestly their perceptions of the world as it was. They were empiricists, influenced by logical positivism and 'ordinary language' philosophy. The writer of the previous generation they most respected was probably George Orwell.† Technically, the novelists were content to use, with only slight modifications, the conventions of 1930s and Edwardian realism. Their originality was largely a matter of tone and attitude and subject matter, reflecting changes in English culture and society brought about by the convulsion of World War II—roughly speaking, the supersession of a bourgeois-dominated class-society by a more meritocratic and opportunistic social system. The poets dealt with ordinary prosaic experience in dry, disciplined, slightly depressive verse. In short, they were antimodernist, readerly, and realistic, and belong on the metonymic side of our bi-polar scheme.

The most representative writers of this generation were Kingsley Amis and Philip Larkin (significantly they were close friends at Oxford). I have written elsewhere of Amis's work and its relation to modernist writing,[1] so I shall confine myself here to Philip Larkin. That he is an antimodernist scarcely needs demonstration. To find his

*See her essay 'Against Dryness', *Encounter* XVI (January 1961, pp. 16–20).
†In his introduction to the first important Movement anthology, *New Lines* (1956) Robert Conquest named Orwell as a major influence on these poets. Orwell's influence is even more evident in the fiction and criticism of the 1950s writers, especially John Wain's.

own poetic voice he had to shake off the influence of Yeats that pervades his first volume of poems *The North Ship* (1945); and he has made no secret of his distaste for the poetics of T. S. Eliot which underpins so much verse in the modernist tradition. 'I . . . have no belief in "tradition" or a common myth-kitty, or casual allusions in poems to other poems or poets,' he has written;[2] and, 'Separating the man who suffers from the man who creates is all right—we separate the petrol from the engine—but the dependence of the second on the first is complete.'[3] Like Orwell (see p. 21 above) Larkin believes that the task of the writer is to communicate as accurately as he can in words experience which is initially non-verbal: poetry is 'born of the tension between what [the poet] non-verbally feels and what can be got over in common word-usage to someone who hasn't had his experience or education or travel-grant.'[4] Like most writers in the antimodernist, or realist or readerly tradition, Larkin is, in aesthetic matters, an antiformalist: 'Form holds little interest for me. Content is everything.'[5]

It would be easy enough to demonstrate abstractly that the last-quoted assertion is an impossibly self-contradictory one for a poet to make. A more interesting line of enquiry, however, is to try and define the kind of form Larkin's work actually has, in spite of his somewhat disingenuous denials. (He has claimed, characteristically, that the omission of the main verb in 'MCMXIV',[6] which so powerfully and poignantly creates the sense of an historical moment, poised between peace and war, arrested and held for an inspection that is solemn with afterknowledge, was an 'accident'[7]—as if there could be such a thing in a good poem.) My suggestion is that we can best accomplish this task of defining the formal character of Larkin's verse by regarding him as a 'metonymic' poet.

Poetry, especially lyric poetry, is an inherently metaphoric mode, and to displace it towards the metonymic pole is (whether Larkin likes it or not) an 'experimental' literary gesture. Such poetry makes its impact by appearing daringly, even shockingly unpoetic, particularly when the accepted poetic mode is elaborately metaphoric. This was true of the early Wordsworth, as I argued in Part Two, and it was certainly true of Philip Larkin in his post-*North Ship* verse: nothing could have been more different from the poetry of Dylan Thomas and the other ageing members of the 'New Apocalypse'. Larkin, indeed, has many affinities with Wordsworth (in spite of having had a 'forgotten boredom' of a childhood)[8] and seems to share Wordsworth's 'spontaneous overflow' theory of poetic creation, which T. S. Eliot thought he had disposed of in 'Tradition and the Individual Talent'. 'One should . . . write poetry only when one wants to and has to,' Larkin has remarked; and, 'writing isn't an act of the will.'[9] His poetic style is characterized by colloquialism, 'low' diction and conscious cliché:

Coming up England by a different line
For once, early in the cold new year,
We stopped, and, watching men with number-plates
Sprint down the platform to familiar gates,
'Why, Coventry!' I exclaimed. 'I was born here.'[10]

                                                    I lie
Where Mr Bleaney lay, and stub my fags
On the same saucer, and try

Stuffing my ears with cotton-wool, to drown
The jabbering set he egged her on to buy.
I know his habits—what time he came down,
His preference for sauce to gravy, why

He kept on plugging at the four aways—[11]

When I see a couple of kids
And guess he's fucking her and she's
Taking pills or wearing a diaphragm,
I know this is paradise

Everyone old has dreamed of all their lives—[12]

With Wordsworth, Larkin might claim that his 'principal object . . . was to choose incidents and situations from common life, and to relate or describe them, throughout, as far as was possible in a selection of language really used by men, tracing in them truly, though not ostentatiously, the primary laws of our nature,'[13] though it is from common urban-industrial life that he usually chooses them—shops, trains, hospitals, inner-city streets and parks. The gaudy mass-produced glamour of chain store lingerie—

Lemon, sapphire, moss-green, rose
Bri-Nylon Baby-Dolls and Shorties

provides the occasion for a tentative, uncondescending meditation on the mystery of sexual allure:

How separate and unearthy love is,
Or women are, or what they do,
Or in our young unreal wishes
Seem to be: synthetic, new,
And natureless in ecstasies. [14]

The topic of death is handled in contexts where modern urban folk face it, the ambulance and the hospital:

                        All know they are going to die.
Not yet, perhaps not here, but in the end,
And somewhere like this. That is what it means,
This clean-sliced cliff; a struggle to transcend
The thought of dying, for unless its powers
Outbuild cathedrals nothing contravenes
The coming dark, though crowds each evening try

With wasteful, weak, propitiatory flowers.[15]

Larkin is a declared realist. 'Lines on a Young Lady's Photograph Album', strategically placed at the beginning of his first important collection, *The Less Deceived* (1955), is his 'Musée des Beaux Arts', taking not Flemish painting but snapshots as the examplary art form:

> But o, photography! as no art is,
> Faithful and disappointing! that records
> Dull days as dull, and hold-it smiles as frauds,
> And will not censor blemishes
> Like washing lines and Hall's Distemper boards,
>
> But shows the cat as disinclined, and shades
> A chin as doubled when it is, what grace
> Your candour thus confers upon her face!
> How overwhelmingly persuades
> This is a real girl in a real place,
>
> In every sense empirically true![16]

Like a realistic novelist, Larkin relies heavily on synecdochic detail to evoke scene, character, culture and subculture. In 'At Grass', the past glories of race horses are evoked thus:

> Silks at the start: against the sky
> Numbers and parasols: outside,
> Squadrons of empty cars, and heat,
> And littered grass: then the long cry
> Hanging unhushed till it subside
> To stop-press columns on the street.[17]

In Hull

> domes and statues, spires and cranes cluster
> Beside grain-scattered streets, barge-crowded water,
> And residents from raw estates, brought down
> The dead straight miles by stealing flat-faced trolleys,
> Push through plate-glass swing doors to their desires—
> Cheap suits, red kitchen-ware, sharp shoes, iced lollies,
> Electric mixers, toasters, washers, driers—[18]

After the Agricultural Show

> The carpark has thinned. They're loading jumps on a truck.
> Back now to private addresses, gates and lamps
> In high stone one-street villages, empty at dusk,
> And side-roads of small towns (sports finals stuck
> In front doors, allotments reaching down to the railway);[19]

To call Larkin a metonymic poet does not imply that he uses no metaphors—of course he does. Some of his poems are based on extended analogies—'Next, Please', 'No Road' and 'Toads', for instance. But such poems become more rare in his later collections. All three just mentioned are in *The Less Deceived*, and 'Toads Revisited' in

The Whitsun Weddings (1964) makes a fairly perfunctory use of the original metaphor. Many of his poems have no metaphors at all—for example, 'Myxomatosis', 'Poetry of Departures', 'Days', 'As Bad as a Mile', 'Afternoons'. And in what are perhaps his finest and most characteristic poems, the metaphors are foregrounded against a predominantly metonymic background, which is in turn foregrounded against the background of the (metaphoric) poetic tradition. 'The Whitsun Weddings' is a classic example of this technique.

> That Whitsun, I was late getting away:
>   Not till about
> One-twenty on the sunlit Saturday
> Did my three-quarters-empty train pull out,
> All windows down, all cushions hot, all sense
> Of being in a hurry gone. We ran
> Behind the backs of houses, crossed a street
> Of blinding windscreens, smelt the fish-dock; thence
> The river's level drifting breadth began,
> Where sky and Lincolnshire and water meet.

This opening stanza has a characteristically casual, colloquial tone, and the near-redundant specificity ('One-twenty', 'three-quarters-empty') of a personal anecdote, a 'true story' (compare Wordsworth's 'I've measured it from side to side,/'Tis three feet long, and two feet wide'). The scenery is evoked by metonymic and synecdochic detail ('drifting breadth', 'blinding windscreens' etc.) as are the wedding parties that the poet observes at the stations on the way to London, seeing off bridal couples on their honeymoons:

> The fathers with broad belts under their suits
> And seamy foreheads; mothers loud and fat;
> An uncle shouting smut; and then the perms,
> The nylon gloves and jewellery substitutes,
> The lemons, mauves and olive-ochres that
>
> Marked off the girls unreally from the rest.

Apart from the unobtrusive 'seamy', there are no metaphors here: appearance, clothing, behaviour, are observed with the eye of a novelist or documentary writer and allowed to stand, untransformed by metaphor, as indices of a certain recognizable way of life. There *is* a simile in this stanza, but it is drawn from the context (railway stations) in a way that, we have seen in other chapters, is characteristic of realistic writers using the metonymic mode:

> As if out on the end of an event
>   Waving goodbye
> To something that survived it.

As the poem goes on, Larkin unobtrusively raises the pitch of rhetorical and emotional intensity—and this corresponds to the

approach of the train to its destination: the journey provides the poem
with its basic structure, a sequence of spatio-temporal contiguities (as
in 'Here'). Some bolder figures of speech are introduced—'a happy
funeral', 'a religious wounding'; and in the penultimate stanza a
striking simile which still contrives to be 'unpoetic', by collapsing the
conventional pastoral distinction between nasty town and nice
country:

> I thought of London spread out in the sun,
> Its postal districts packed like squares of wheat.

It is in the last stanza that the poem suddenly, powerfully, 'takes off',*
transcends the merely empirical, almost sociological observation of its
earlier stanzas and affirms the poet's sense of sharing, vicariously, in
the onward surge of life as represented by the newly wedded couples
collected together in the train ('this frail travelling coincidence') and
the unpredictable but fertile possibilities the future holds for them.

> We slowed again,
> And as the tightened brakes took hold, there swelled
> A sense of falling, like an arrow-shower
> Sent out of sight, somewhere becoming rain.[20]

This metaphor, with its mythical, magical and archaic resonances, is
powerful partly because it is so different from anything else in the
poem (except for 'religious wounding', and that has a tone of
humorous overstatement quite absent from the last stanza).

Something similar happens in Larkin's most famous poem, 'Church
Going',[21] where the last stanza has a dignity and grandeur of diction—

> A serious house on serious earth it is,
> In whose blent air all our compulsions meet,
> Are recognized, and robed as destinies

which comes as a thrilling surprise after the downbeat, slightly ironic
tone of the preceding stanzas, a tone established in the first stanza:

> Hatless, I take off
> My cycle-clips in awkward reverence.

That line-and-a-half must be the most often quoted fragment of
Larkin's poetry, and the way in which the homely 'cycle-clips' damps
down the metaphysical overtones of 'reverence' and guarantees the
trustworthy ordinariness of the poetic persona is indeed deeply typical
of Larkin. But if his poetry were limited to merely avoiding the pitfalls
of poetic pretentiousness and insincerity it would not interest us for
very long. Again and again he surprises us, especially in the closing
lines of his poems, by his ability to transcend—or turn ironically

---

*Larkin instructed Anthony Thwaite, then a radio producer, that the poem should be
read holding a carefully sustained note until the very end, when it should 'lift off the
ground', according to David Timms. *Philip Larkin* (1973) p. 120.

upon—the severe restraints he seems to have placed upon authentic expression of feeling in poetry. Sometimes, as in 'The Whitsun Weddings' and 'Church Going', this is accomplished by allowing a current of metaphorical language to flow into the poem, with the effect of a river bursting through a dam. But quite as often it is done by a subtle complication of metre, line-endings and syntax. For example, the amazing conclusion to 'Mr Bleaney':

> But if he stood and watched the frigid wind
> Tousling the clouds, lay on the fusty bed
> Telling himself that this was home, and grinned,
> And shivered, without shaking off the dread
>
> That how we live measures our own nature,
> And at his age having no more to show
> Than one hired box should make him pretty sure
> He warranted no better, I don't know.[22]

Syntactically this long periodic sentence is in marked contrast to the rest of the poem, and marks a reversal in its drift: a shift from satiric spleen vented upon the external world—a Bleaney-world to which the poetic persona feels superior—to a sudden collapse of his own morale, a chilling awareness that this environment may correspond to his own inner 'nature'. This fear is expressed obliquely by a speculative attribution of the speaker's feelings to Mr Bleaney. The diction is plain and simple (if more dignified than in the preceding stanzas) but the syntax, subordinate clauses burgeoning and negatives accumulating bewilderingly, is extremely complex and creates a sense of helplessness and entrapment. The main clause so long delayed—'I don't know'—when it finally comes, seems to spread back dismally through the whole poem, through the whole life of the unhappy man who utters it.

Many of Larkin's most characteristic poems end, like 'Mr Bleaney', with a kind of eclipse of meaning, speculation fading out in the face of the void. At the end of 'Essential Beauty' the girl in the cigarette ad becomes a Belle Dame Sans Merci for the 'dying smokers' who

<blockquote>

sense
Walking towards them through some dappled park
As if on water that unfocussed she
No match lit up, nor drag ever brought near,
Who now stands newly clear,
Smiling and recognizing, and going dark.[23]
</blockquote>

We

> spend all our life on imprecisions
> That when we start to die
> Have no idea why.[24]

Death is, we can all agree, a 'nonverbal' reality, because, as Wittgenstein said, it is not an experience *in* life; and it is in dealing with death, a topic that haunts him, that Larkin achieves the paradoxical feat of expressing in words something that is beyond words:

> Life is slow dying . . .
> And saying so to some
> Means nothing; others it leaves
> Nothing to be said.[25]

The same theme, I take it, forms the conclusion to the title poem of Larkin's most recent collection, *The High Windows*. The poet compares his generation's envy of the sexual freedom of the young in today's Permissive Society to the putative envy of older people of his own apparent freedom, in his youth, from superstitious religious fears.

> And immediately
> Rather than words comes the thought of high windows:
> The sun-comprehending glass,
> And beyond it, the deep blue air, that shows
> Nothing, and is nowhere, and is endless.[26]

8 Postmodernist Fiction

The history of modern English literature, it has been suggested in the foregoing chapters, can be seen as an oscillation in the practice of writing between polarized clusters of attitudes and techniques: modernist, symbolist or mythopoeic, writerly and metaphoric on the one hand; antimodernist, realistic, readerly and metonymic on the other. What looks like innovation—a new mode of writing foregrounding itself against the background of the received mode when the latter becomes stale and exhausted—is therefore also in some sense a reversion to the principles and procedures of an earlier phase. If the critical pronouncements associated with each phase tend to be somewhat predictable, the actual creative work produced is not, such is the infinite variety and fertility of the human imagination working upon the fresh materials thrown up by secular history. But the metaphor/metonymy distinction explains why at the deepest level there is a cyclical rhythm to literary history, for there is nowhere else for discourse to go except between these two poles.

There is, however, a certain kind of contemporary avant-garde art which is said to be neither modernist nor antimodernist, but postmodernist; it continues the modernist critique of traditional mimetic art, and shares the modernist commitment to innovation, but pursues these aims by methods of its own. It tries to go beyond modernism, or around it, or underneath it, and is often as critical of modernism as it is of antimodernism. In the field of writing such a phenomenon obviously offers an interesting challenge to the explanatory power of the literary typology expounded above. The object of this chapter, then, is to attempt a profile of postmodernist fiction and to test the relevance of the metaphor/metonymy distinction to it. Postmodernism has established itself as an *écriture*, in Barthes's sense of the word—a mode of writing shared by a significant number of writers in a given period—most plausibly in the French *nouveau roman* and in American fiction of the last ten or fifteen years, and I shall be concerned here chiefly with the latter. But I shall make reference to texts by British writers where these seem relevant, and I begin with Samuel Beckett, who has a strong claim to be considered the first important postmodernist writer.

Beckett served his literary apprenticeship in the shadow of classical modernism. His earliest publications in prose were a contribution to a symposium on Joyce (1929) and a study of Proust (1930). The opening story, 'Dante and the Lobster', in his first book of fiction, *More Pricks than Kicks* (1934), shows him just beginning to detach himself from the modernist tradition, especially from the technique of Joyce, with whom, of all the modernist writers, Beckett has the closest affinity (and for whom he worked, for a time, as secretary). As it happens, this story deals with the same theme of life/death/time as the texts discussed in Part One. Belacqua, a Dublin student, performs various banal tasks in his day—makes himself a sandwich of burnt toast and gorgonzola cheese for his lunch, attends an Italian lesson, collects a lobster from the fishmonger for his aunt's and his own supper. Among the miscellaneous pieces of information that impinge on his consciousness is the fact that a convicted murderer is to be hanged the next day. Spectacles of pain and misery in the streets on his way home, combined with inner musings on Dante, especially the line from the *Inferno*, '*qui vive la pietà quando è ben morta*',* provoke Belacqua to ask, 'Why not piety and pity both, even down below?', to pray for 'a little mercy in the stress of sacrifice' and to extend his compassion to the convicted murderer:

> Poor McCabe, he would get it in the neck at dawn. What was he doing now, how was he feeling? He would relish one more meal, one more night.[1]

This mood is, however, exposed as a sentimental illusion, for what really shocks Belacqua into a true awareness of pain and death is the discovery that the lobster is still alive and must be boiled in that state so that he may eat it.

> 'Christ!' he said 'it's alive.'
> His aunt looked at the lobster. It moved again. It made a faint nervous act of life on the oilcloth. They stood above it, looking down on it, exposed

*'Here pity lives when it is virtually dead.' Belacqua remarks that there is a 'superb pun' on pity/piety.

cruciform on the oilcloth. It shuddered again. Belacqua felt he would be sick.

'My God' he whined 'it's alive, what'll we do?' . . .

'You make a fuss' she said angrily 'and upset me and then lash into it for your dinner.'

She lifted the lobster clear of the table. It had about thirty seconds to live.

Well, thought Belcqua, it's a quick death, God help us all.

It is not.[2]

This conclusion to the story (which I have much abridged) takes place in the aunt's kitchen which, like Dante's Hell, is in 'the bowels of the earth'. The *Divine Comedy* seems to function in Beckett's story much as Homer's *Odyssey* does in *Ulysses*. Belacqua's name (as improbable as Dedalus) derives from *Purgatory*; at the opening of the story he is wrestling with the interpretation of a difficult passage in *Paradise*; and his conversation with his Italian teacher touches on 'Dante's rare movements of compassion in Hell'.[3] The story seems to indicate the ultimate irrelevance of the Christian metaphysic (supremely articulated by Dante) to the problem of suffering and death. It thus reverses the message of Oscar Wilde's 'The Ballad of Reading Gaol'; but Christian symbolism and allusion, especially to the Passion, permeate the climax of the story even if largely disguised under 'low' diction ('Christ!' 'cruciform' 'My God' 'lash into'), evidently to underline the horror of the world when recognized for what it is, a place where one creature lives by the cruel sacrifice of another, right along the chain of being. The identification of the lobster with Christ is clearly signalled earlier in the story when Belacqua, talking to a French teacher, is obliged to use the word *poisson*. 'He did not know the French for lobster. Fish would do very well. Fish had been good enough for Jesus Christ, Son of God, Saviour. It was good enough for Mlle Glain.'[4] Even the hilarious business of Belacqua's lunch fits into the same thematic scheme, inasmuch as Belcaqua's toasting of the bread till it is black, and his handling of the cheese, are portrayed as violent actions perpetrated upon innocent living matter:

> He laid his cheek against the soft of the bread, it was spongy and warm, *alive*. But he would very quickly take that fat white look off its face . . .[5] [my italics]

> He looked sceptically at the cut of cheese. He turned it over on its back to see was the other side any better. The other side was worse. . . . He rubbed it. It was sweating. That was something. He stooped and smelt it. A faint fragrance of corruption. What good was that? He didn't want fragrance, he wasn't a bloody gourmet, he wanted a good stench. What he wanted was a good green stenching rotten lump of Gorgonzola cheese, *alive*, and by God he would have it.[6] [my italics]

The handling of the cheese is proleptic of the aunt's treatment of the lobster at the end of the story: 'She caught up the lobster and laid it on its back. It trembled. "They feel nothing" she said.'[7]

Up to a point, then, 'Dante and the Lobster' responds to the same kind of reading as an episode of *Ulysses*, as a narrative of modern life which alludes to a prior myth that is in some sense a key to its meaning, and in which a superficially gratuitious sequence of banal events is guided towards a final thematic epiphany by discreetly planted *leitmotifs*. But there is a good deal in the text that is not accountable in these terms. The manic, obsessional and eccentric behaviour of the hero, for instance (a long way from the endearing whims and fetishes of Bloom) is in no sense 'explained' by the story. It is funny, but it is also disconcerting. So is, in a different way, the last line of the story: 'It is not.' This is not the first occasion on which the author who 'speaks' the narrative is distinguishable from Belacqua, through whose eyes it is mainly seen, but it is certainly the most emphatically foregrounded— being, in effect, not merely a comment, but a flat contradiction and dismissal of the hero and his hollow epiphany. The author, as it were, scuttles his story in its last line, and this prevents the reader from leaving its uncomfortable implications safely enclosed within the category of 'literature' or 'fiction'. These are features which become progressively more marked in Beckett's fiction (and in postmodernist writing generally), while the 'mythical method' (exemplified by the Dantean parallels) 'of ordering, of giving a shape and significance to the immense panorama of futility and anarchy that is contemporary history' (as T. S. Eliot said of Joyce)[8] disappears, is displaced by a growing insistence that there is no order, no shape or significance to be found anywhere.

Beckett's next work of fiction, *Murphy* (1938) begins:

> The sun shone, having no alternative, on the nothing new. Murphy sat out of it, as though he were free, in a mew in West Brompton . . . He sat naked in his rocking-chair of undressed teak, guaranteed not to crack, warp, corrode or creak at night. It was his own, it never left him. The corner in which he sat was curtained off from the sun, the poor old sun in the Virgin again for the billionth time. Seven scarves held him in position. Two fastened his shins to the rockers, one his thighs to the seat, two his breast and belly to the back, one his wrists to the strut behind. Only the most local movements were possible. Sweat poured off him, tightened the thongs. The breath was not perceptible. The eyes, cold and unwavering as a gull's, stared up at an irridescence splashed over the cornice moulding, shrinking and fading.[9]

This discourse raises a lot of questions in the reader's mind. Some are answered: for instance, Murphy constrains his body in this eccentric manner in order to live more completely in his mind—he is a dedicated solipsist. But how does Murphy manage to tie himself up unassisted? and where is the seventh scarf? More fundamentally, whose voice are we listening to? Who takes pity on 'the poor old sun', and who compares Murphy's eyes to a gull's, and what is the import of these tropes? It is difficult to answer these questions.

If 'Dante and the Lobster' reminds one of Joyce, *Murphy* is Beckett's '1930s' novel. Its drab, historically precise setting (London,

1935), and its subject matter (penniless, alienated young man having difficulties in finding acceptable employment and keeping his girlfriend) have certain affinities with the novels of Isherwood and Orwell (especially *Keep the Aspidistra Flying*) but the experience of reading it is very different. While renouncing the mythic parallelism of Joyce's treatment of Dublin, it also ignores or ridicules the conventions of realism adopted by the representative novelists of the 1930s. There is no local colour in *Murphy*, no evocative synecdochic detail in the descriptions of places and people. The opening of Chapter 2, describing Celia in a list of facts and figures—

Age	Unimportant
Head	Small and round
Eyes	Green
Complexion	White
Hair	Yellow
Features	Mobile
Neck	$13\frac{3}{4}''$

etc.—mocks the conventional novelistic description of physical appearance, as the description of Murphy's grotesque green suit parodies the realistic novelist's reliance on the code of clothing as an index to character.[10] The narrator is for the most part impersonal and aloof, but given to disconcerting interventions, addresses to the reader ('gentle skimmer') and metafictional comments ('Celia, thank God for a Christian name'. . . . 'The above passage is carefully calculated to deprave the cultivated reader'). The predictability of the style and development of the action is extremely low, and although it is a very funny book it is not at all easy to read for this reason. It *resists* reading by refusing to settle into a simply identifiable mode or rhythm, thus imitating, on the level of reading conventions, the resistance of the world to interpretation.

The latter idea becomes explicit in the next novel *Watt* (1953— composed 1942–3), supremely in the episode of the Galls, who appear at the door of the house where Watt is working as a servant to Mr Knott:

> We are the Galls, father and son, and we are come, what is more, all the way from town, to choon the piano.
> They were two, and they stood, arm in arm, in this way, because the father was blind, like so many members of his profession. For if the father had not been blind, then he would not have needed his son to hold his arm, and guide him on his rounds, no, but he would have set his son free, to go about his own business. So Watt supposed, though there was nothing in the father's face to show that he was blind, nor in his attitude, either, except that he leaned on his son in a way expressive of a great need of support. But he might have done this, if he had been halt, or merely tired, on account of his great age. There was no family likeness between the two, as far as Watt could make out, and nevertheless he knew he was in the presence of a father and son, for

had he not just been told so. Or were they not perhaps merely stepfather and stepson. We are the Galls stepfather and stepson—those were perhaps the words that should have been spoken. But it was natural to prefer the others. Not that they could not very well be a true father and son, without resembling each other in the least, for they could.[11]

Uncertainty spreads like the plague through the world of *Watt*. 'The incident of the Galls father and son,' observes the narrator, 'was followed by others of a similar kind, incidents that is to say of great formal brilliance and indeterminable purport. . . . And Watt could not accept them for what they perhaps were, the simple games that time plays with space . . . but was obliged, because of his peculiar character, to enquire into what they meant. . . . But what was this pursuit of meaning, in this indifference to meaning? And to what did it tend? These are delicate questions.'[12] Indeed—but questions absolutely fundamental to Beckett's work. The often-asserted resistance of the world to meaningful interpretation would be a sterile basis for writing if it were not combined with a poignant demonstration of the human obligation to attempt such interpretation, especially by the process of organizing one's memories into narrative form. In the next stage of Beckett's narrative writing, the trilogy of *Molloy* (1951), *Malone Dies* (1951) and the *Unnamable* (1953) (all of which first appeared in French) the impersonal, erratically intrusive and rhetorically unpredictable narrator of the earlier fiction is displaced by a series of first-person narrators, increasingly isolated and deprived of sensory stimuli, desperately trying to make sense of their experience by recalling it. The contradiction between the futility of the effort and the compulsion to make it produces a longing for extinction and silence, which in turn provokes fear and a frantic clinging to the vestiges of consciousness—which is intolerable.

> . . . if only there were a thing, but there it is, there is not, they took away things when they departed, they took away nature, there was never anyone, anyone but me, anything but me, talking to me of me, impossible to stop, impossible to go on, but I must go on, I'll go on, without anyone, without anything, but me, but my voice, that is to say I'll stop, I'll end, it's the end already, shortlived, what is it, a little hole, you go down into it, into the silence, it's worse than the noise, you listen, it's worse than talking, no, not worse, no worse, you wait, in anguish, have they forgotten me, no, yes, no, someone calls me, I crawl out again, what is it, a little hole, in the wilderness. It's the end that is the worst, no, it's the beginning that is the worst, then the middle, then the end, in the end it's the end that is the worst, this voice, that, I don't know, it's every second that is the worst . . .[13]

It would be quite false to suggest that all postmodernist writers share Beckett's particular philosophical preoccupations and obsessions. But the general idea of the world resisting the compulsive attempts of the human consciousness to interpret it, of the human predicament being in some sense 'absurd', does underlie a good deal of postmodernist writing. That is why it seeks to find formal alternatives to modernism as well as to antimodernism. The falsity of the patterns imposed upon experience in the traditional realistic novel is common ground between the modernists and the postmodernists, but to the latter it seems that the modernists, too, for all their experimentation, obliquity and complexity, oversimplified the world and held out a false hope of somehow making it at home in the human mind. *Finnegans Wake* (to take the most extreme product of the modernist literary imagination) certainly 'resists' reading, resists interpretation, by the formidable difficulty of its verbal style and narrative method, and perhaps it has yet to find that 'ideal reader suffering from ideal insomnia' for whom, Joyce said, it was designed. But we persist in trying to read it in the faith that it is ultimately susceptible of being understood—that we shall, eventually, be able to unpack all the meanings that Joyce put into it, and that these meanings will cohere into a unity. Postmodernism subverts that faith. 'Where is the figure in the carpet?' asks a character in Donald Barthelme's *Snow White* (1967), alluding to the title of a story by Henry James that has become proverbial among modern critics as an image of the goal of interpretation; but he adds disconcertingly: 'Or is it just ... carpet?'[14] A lot of postmodernist writing implies that experience is 'just carpet' and that whatever patterns we discern in it are wholly illusory, comforting fictions.

The difficulty, for the reader, of postmodernist writing, is not so much a matter of obscurity (which might be cleared up) as of uncertainty, which is endemic, and manifests itself on the level of narrative rather than style. No amount of patient study could establish, for instance, whether the man with the heavy coat and hat and stick encountered by Moran in *Molloy* is the man Molloy designated as C, or Molloy himself, or someone else; and Hugh Kenner's description of Beckett 'filling the air with uncertainty, the uncertainty fiction usually dissipates',[15] will apply to a lot of postmodernist writers. We shall never be able to unravel the plots of John Fowles's *The Magus* (1966) or Alain Robbe-Grillet's *Le Voyeur* (1955) or Thomas Pynchon's *The Crying of Lot 49* (1966), for they are labyrinths without exits. Endings, the 'exits' of fictions, are particularly significant in this connection. Instead of the closed ending of the traditional novel, in which mystery is explained and fortunes are settled, and instead of the open ending of the modernist novel, 'satisfying but not final' as Conrad said of Henry James,[16] we get the multiple ending, the false ending, the mock ending or parody ending.

The classic type of the 'closed' ending is that of the crime story in which the detective solves the mystery, reduces to meaningful order the apparently meaningless confusion of clues, and ensures that justice is done. Muriel Spark parodies this convention, and implicitly criticizes the presumption of those (novelists as well as policemen) who play the part of Providence, in novels which disconcertingly readjust the roles of criminal, victim and witnesses. Thus in *The Driver's Seat* (1970) Lyse scatters across Europe in the days before her death a trail of clues which make no sense at all until we grasp that she is in a sense the plotter as well as the victim of the crime. In the same author's *Not to Disturb* (1971) the servants in a luxurious villa on Lake Geneva make their arrangements to profit by a *crime passionelle* which has not yet occurred. Journalists are alerted, statements prepared, contracts negotiated by transatlantic telephone, interviews recorded on tape and film, while the husband, wife and lover are still arguing in the library. The suave butler, Lister, who presides over the whole operation, observes of his employers that 'They have placed themselves, unfortunately, within the realm of predestination.'[17] He excludes two people from the house 'because they don't fit into the story' and the weather (always ready to cooperate with gods and novelists) obligingly eliminates them with a thunderbolt.

In *The French Lieutenant's Woman* (1969) John Fowles presents alternative endings to his story and invites the reader to choose between them. John Barth floats a whole series of possible endings to the title story of his collection *Lost in the Funhouse* (1968), but rejects them all except the most inconclusive and banal. Another story, 'Title', perceptibly influenced by Beckett, contrives not to end at all:

> It's about over. Let the dénouement be soon and unexpected, painless if possible, quick at least, above all soon. Now now! How in the world will it ever[18]

Richard Brautigan adds to the ending of *A Confederate General From Big Sur* (1964) 'A SECOND ENDING', then a third, a fourth and fifth.

> Then there are more and more endings: the sixth, the 53rd, the 131st, the 9,435th ending, endings going faster and faster, more and more endings, faster and faster until this book is having 186,000 endings per second.[19]

The same author concludes the penultimate chapter of *Trout Fishing in America* (1967), entitled 'PRELUDE TO THE "MAYONNAISE" CHAPTER': 'Expressing a human need I always wanted to write a book that ended with the word Mayonnaise.'[20] And accordingly the last chapter consists of the transcript of a letter written in 1952 from 'Mother and Nancy' to 'Florence and Harv' which has the P.S., 'Sorry I forgot to give you the mayonaise [sic].'[21] There is the additional joke that this whimsical human need could have been fulfilled without the last chapter, since the penultimate chapter also ends with the word 'mayonnaise', and the 'MAYONNAISE CHAPTER' is no less arbitrary a way of ensuring that the book ends on that word, since the letter in no way relates to anything that has gone before. Indeed, insofar as the P.S. misspells the word, Brautigan has cheated himself of his intention by transcribing it.

Critical opinion varies about how significantly *new* postmodernism really is. Leslie Fiedler, for instance, thinks it is genuinely revolutionary;[22] Frank Kermode, on the other hand, thinks that it has achieved only 'marginal developments of older modernism'.[23] Both opinions are tenable—both are in a sense 'true'. It depends upon what you are looking for and where you are standing when you are looking. Fiedler is mainly concerned with American literature and culture (in the anthropological sense); Kermode with the international avant-garde in all the arts. Fiedler defines postmodernism primarily as a very recent 'posthumanist' phenomenon, hostile or indifferent to traditional aesthetic categories and values, offering a polymorphous hedonism to its (largely youthful) audience, and unamenable to formalist analysis. Its art is anti-art, and demands 'Death-of-Art criticism'.[24] Kermode, on the other hand, approaches postmodernism as a historian of art and aesthetics and has little difficulty in tracing its theoretical assumptions back to either classical modernism or to the Dadaist schism that developed as long ago as 1916; and he sees the latter tradition as an essentially marginal one, its products more akin to jokes than art, 'piquant allusions to what fundamentally interests us more than they do.'[25] The aim of this chapter is not to try and settle the disagreement, but to try and throw light on the formal principles underlying postmodernist writing.

If Jakobson is right, that all discourse tends towards either the metaphoric or the metonymic pole of language, it should be possible to categorize postmodernist writing under one heading or the other. The theory (crudely summarized) states that all discourse connects one topic with another, either because they are in some sense similar to each other, or because they are in some sense contiguous with each other; and implies that if you attempt to group topics according to some other principle, or absence of principle, the human mind will nevertheless persist in trying to make sense of the text thus produced by looking in it for relationships of similarity and/or contiguity; and insofar as a text succeeds in defeating such interpretation, it defeats itself. It would, I believe, be possible to analyse postmodernist writing in these terms, but perhaps not very profitable. For if we extend the term 'postmodernist' to cover all the writers to whom it seems applicable, we might identify them individually as either metaphoric or metonymic, but it would be difficult to show that their work, considered *collectively*, has any bias towards one pole or the other. Rather it would seem that we can best define the formal character of postmodernist writing by examining its efforts to deploy both metaphoric and metonymic devices in radically new ways, and to defy (even if such defiance is ultimately vain) the obligation to choose between these two principles of connecting one topic with another. What other alternatives might there be? The headings below are intended to indicate some of the possibilities.

Contradiction

> But what is the good of talking about what they will do as soon as Worm sets himself in motion, so as to gather himself without fail into their midst, since he cannot set himself in motion, though he often desires to, if when speaking of him one may speak of desire, and one may not, one should not, but there it is, that is the way to speak of him, as if he were alive, as if he could understand, as if he could desire, even if it serves no purpose, and it serves none.[26]

This passage from *The Unnamable* cancels itself out as it goes along, and is representative of a text in which the narrator is condemned to oscillate between irreconcilable desires and assertions. Famously, it ends, 'you must go on, I can't go on, I'll go on.' If that were rearranged slightly to read, 'I can't go on, you must go on, I'll go on', it would not be at all self-contradictory, but a quite logically motivated and 'uplifting' sequence of despair followed by self-admonishment followed by renewed resolve. As it stands, each clause negates the preceding one. Leonard Michaels approaches this radically contradictory basis for the practice of writing when he says in 'Dostoevsky', 'It is impossible to live with or without fictions.'[27] The religion of Bokonism in Kurt Vonnegut's *Cat's Cradle* (1963) is based on 'the cruel paradox of . . . the heartbreaking necessity of lying about reality and the heartbreaking impossibility of lying about it.'[28]

One of the most emotively powerful emblems of contradiction, one that affronts the most fundamental binary system of all, is the hermaphrodite; and it is not surprising that the characters of postmodernist fiction are often sexually ambivalent: for example, Gore Vidal's sex-changing Myra/Myron Breckinridge,[29] and the central character of Brigid Brophy's *In Transit* (1969), who is suffering from amnesia in an international airport and cannot remember what sex he/she is (the narrator cannot examine his/her private parts in public, but cannot retreat to the privacy of a public convenience without knowing what she/he desires to find out). Henry, the hero of the postmodernist half of Julian Mitchell's duplex novel *The Undiscovered Country* (1968)* is transformed into a woman, and then into a hermaphrodite, and is engaged in the pursuit of a beautiful creature of equally uncertain sex. At the climax of John Barth's allegorical fabulation *Giles Goat-boy* (1966) the caprine hero and his beloved Anastasia survive the dreaded inquisition of the computer WESCAC when, locked together in copulation, they answer the question 'ARE YOU MALE OR FEMALE?' with two simultaneous and contradictory answers, 'YES' and 'NO'.[30]

---

*The other half is realistic or autobiographical in mode. I have written about this work at some length in *The Novelist at the Crossroads* pp. 26–32.

Permutation

Both metaphoric and metonymic modes of writing involve selection, and selection involves leaving something out. Postmodernist writers often try to defy this law by incorporating alternative narrative lines in the same text—for example John Fowles' *The French Lieutenant's Woman* and John Barth's 'Lost in the Funhouse', already cited, Robert Coover's 'The Magic Poker' and 'The Babysitter' in *Pricksongs and Descants* (1969) and Raymond Federman's *Double or Nothing* (1971). This procedure is another kind of 'contradiction', though in practice we are usually able to resolve it by ranking the alternatives in an order of authenticity. A more radical way of denying the obligation to select is to exhaust all the possible combinations in a given field. In the imaginary world of 'Tlön, Uqbar, Orbis Tertius', one of the fables of Jorge Luis Borges that have exercised a potent fascination over many American postmodernist writers, 'Works of fiction contain a single plot, with all its imaginable permutations';[31] and the labyrinthine novel of Ts'ui Pen in Borges' 'The Garden of the Forking Paths' is constructed on similar principles:

> In all fictional works, each time a man is confronted with several alternatives, he chooses one and eliminates the others; in the fiction of Ts'ui Pen, he chooses—simultaneously—all of them. *He creates*, in this way, diverse futures, diverse times which themselves also proliferate and fork. Here, then, is the explanation of the novel's contradictions. Fang, let us say, has a secret; a stranger calls at his door; Fang resolves to kill him. Naturally, there are several possible outcomes: Fang can kill the intruder, the intruder can kill Fang, they both can escape, they both can die, and so forth. In the work of Ts'ui Pen, all possible outcomes occur; each one is the point of departure for other forkings.[32]

By plausibly imagining the impossible, Borges liberates the imagination. Beckett uses permutation in a more limited way and to more depressive effect:

> As for his feet, sometimes he wore on each a sock, or on the one a sock and on the other a stocking, or a boot, or a shoe, or a slipper, or a sock and boot, or a sock and shoe, or a sock and slipper, or a stocking and boot, or a stocking and shoe, or a stocking and slipper, or nothing at all. And sometimes he wore on each a stocking, or on the one a stocking and on the other a boot, or a shoe, or a slipper, or a sock and boot, or a sock and shoe. . . .[33]

and so on, for a page and a half. There are several similar passages in *Watt*, in which every possible combination of a set of variables is exhausted. Probably the most famous example of permutation in Beckett, however, is in *Molloy*, where the eponymous hero wrestles with the problem of distributing and circulating his sixteen sucking stones in his pockets in such a way as to guarantee that he will always suck them in the same order.[34] Beckett's characters seek desperately to impose a purely mathematical order upon experience in the absence of any metaphysical order. In *Murphy* the hero, making his lunch from a packet of mixed biscuits, is torn between his weakness for one particular kind of biscuit and the possibility of total permutability:

> were he to take the final step and overcome his infatuation with the ginger, then the assortment would spring to life before him, dancing the radiant measure of its total permutability, edible in a hundred and twenty ways![35]

When reduced to only two variables, permutation becomes simply alternation and expresses the hopelessness of the human condition. ' "For every symptom that is eased, another is worse," ' opines Wylie in *Murphy*. ' "The horse leech's daughter is a closed system. Her quantum of wantum cannot vary ... Humanity is a well with two buckets ... one going down to be filled, the other coming up to be emptied." '[36] In Joseph Heller's *Catch 22* (1961) there is a wounded soldier in the hospital entirely swathed in bandages and connected to a drip-feed bottle and a bottle for waste fluid:

> When the jar on the floor was full, the jar feeding his elbow was empty, and the two were simply switched over quickly so that the stuff could drip back into him.[37]

Discontinuity

One quality we expect of all writing is continuity. Writing is a one-sided conversation. As every student, and every critic, knows, the most difficult aspect of composing an essay or thesis or book is to put one's scattered thoughts into an ideal order which will appear to have a seamless logical inevitability in its progress from one topic to another, without distorting or omitting any important point. This book itself contains innumerable sentences and phrases included not primarily to convey information but to construct smooth links between one topic and another. In fiction, metonymic writing offers a very obvious and readily intelligible kind of continuity based on spatio-temporal contiguities; the continuity of metaphorical writing is more difficult, but not impossible to identify. And as it is by its continuity that a discursive text persuades the reader, implying that no other ordering of its data could be intellectually as satisfying, so it is by its continuity that a work of fiction, if successful, imposes its vision of the world upon the reader, displaces the 'real world' with an imagined world in which the reader (especially in the case of realistic fiction) lives vicariously. Postmodernism is suspicious of continuity. Beckett disrupts the continuity of his discourse by unpredictable swerves of tone, metafictional asides to the reader, blank spaces in the text, contradiction and permutation. Some recent American writers have gone a step further and *based* their discourse upon discontinuity. 'Interruption. Discontinuity. Imperfection. It can't be

helped,' insists the authorial voice of Ronald Sukenick's *98.6*[38]
98.6 illustrates the most obvious sign of discontinuity in
contemporary fiction—the growing fashion for composing in very
short sections, often only a paragraph in length, often quite disparate
in content, the breaks between sections being sometimes further
emphasized by capitalized headings (as in Richard Brautigan's *In
Watermelon Sugar* [1968]), numbers (as in Robert Coover's 'The
Gingerbread Man') or typographical devices (like the arrows in
Vonnegut's *Breakfast of Champions* [1973]). Vonnegut's later novels
and all of Brautigan's are built up in this way, out of sections too short
to be recognized as conventional chapters. Donald Barthelme uses
bizarre illustrations to break up the text of some of the pieces in *City
Life* (1971), and Raymond Federman ingeniously varies the
typographical layout of *Double or Nothing*, using techniques borrowed
from concrete poetry to avoid the odium of

a very direct form of narration without any distractions
without any obstructions just plain

normal
regular
readable
realistic
leftoright
unequivocal
conventional
unimaginative
wellpunctuated
understandable
uninteresting
safetodigest
paragraphed
compulsive
anecdotal
salutory
textual

PROSE　　prose　　　　prose　　　boring
PROSE　　　PROSE　　prose　　　　PROSE plain　PROSE[39]

Leonard Michaels has recently developed what is virtually a new
genre: the cluster (it is precisely *not* a sequence) of short passages—
stories, anecdotes, reflections, quotations, prose-poems, jokes—each
with an individual title in large type. Between these apparently
discontinuous passages the bewildered but exhilarated reader bounces
and rebounds like a ball in a pinball machine, illuminations flashing on
and off, insights accumulating, till the author laconically signals
TILT. One such cluster, 'I Would Have Saved Them If I Could', is
concerned with the same life/death/time theme in the context of capital
punishment—'the condemned prisoner story', Michaels calls it—that

we have encountered several times already in this study, but it is quite distinctive in form. It consists of seventeen sections: *Giving Notice*, a brief, bitter comedy of Jewish American life, turning on a son's loss of faith; *A Suspected Jew*, an interpretation of Borges's story 'The Secret Miracle' about a Jewish writer Jaromir Hladik, executed by the Gestapo, who was allowed by God enough time between the firing of the bullets and death to mentally complete his unfinished masterpiece; *The Subject at the Vanishing Point*, a memoir of the narrator's—and author's?—grandfather, a refugee from Polish pogroms; *Material Circumstances*, a hostile vignette of Karl Marx roused to historical wrath by a landlord's insolence; *Business Life*, a wry anecdote of the narrator's uncle who runs successful beauty parlours; *Shrubless Crags*, a quotation from Byron's *The Prisoner of Chillon* about a condemned prisoner; *Song*, a three-line gag about Russian folksongs; *Blossoms*, about the terrifying early experiences of the uncle in Europe; *The Screams of Children*, about Jesus, Hladik, Kafka, the Final Solution; *Heraclitus, Hegel, Giacometti, Nietzsche, Wordsworth, Stevens*, on philosophical systems; *Alienation*, about the relation of Marxism to Christianity; *Lord Byron's Letter*, the transcription of a letter in which the poet gives an eye-witness account of three criminals being guillotined ('the second and third (which shows how dreadfully soon things grow indifferent) I am ashamed to say, had no effect on me as a horror, though I would have saved them if I could'); *Species Being*, a critique of the letter; *Dostoevsky*, a brief account of Dostoevsky's story of being reprieved from sentence of death; *The Night I Became a Marxist*, a mock-Pauline account of conversion; and *Conclusion*, which points out that 'from a certain point of view [that of the dead] none of this shit matters any more'.[40] After several readings a kind of thematic coherence does begin to emerge from this textual collage, epitomized by the sentence quoted earlier from Dostoevsky, 'It is impossible to live with or without fictions.' Fictions, whether literary, theological, philosophical or political, can never make death acceptable, or even comprehensible, yet in a world 'incessantly created of incessant death' (*Conclusion*) we have no other resource. There are degrees of authenticity (Byron's honest exactitude is preferred to Borges's whimsy or Marx's theorizing) but in the end it makes no difference. Such a paraphrase, however, is more than usually misleading, since it is only in the actual reading experience, in the disorientation produced by the abrupt and unpredictable shifts of register from one section to another, that the effects of bafflement, anguish, contradiction are felt. Michaels's exploitation of discontinuity can be more conveniently illustrated by quoting the opening lines of a less complex story, 'In the Fifties':

> In the fifties I learned to drive a car. I was frequently in love. I had more friends than now.
> When Krushchev denounced Stalin my roommate shit blood, turned yellow and lost most of his hair.

I attended the lectures of the excellent E. B. Burgum until Senator McCarthy ended his tenure. I imagined NYU would burn. Miserable students, drifting in the halls, looked at one another.

In less than a month, working day and night, I wrote a bad novel.

I went to school—NYU, Michigan, Berkeley—much of the time. I had witty, giddy conversation, four or five nights a week, in a homosexual bar in Ann Arbor.

I read literary reviews the way people suck candy.

Personal relationships were more important to me than anything else.

I had a fight with a powerful fat man who fell on my face and was immovable.

I had personal relationships with football players, jazz musicians, ass-bandits, nymphomaniacs, non-specialized degenerates, and numerous Jewish premedical students.

I had personal relationships with thirty-five rhesus monkeys in an experiment on monkey addiction to morphine. They knew me as one who shot reeking crap out of cages with a hose.[41]

The 'story' (hardly the right word, but there is no other) continues in the same mode: bald statements of fact which appear to have nothing to connect them except that they belong to the life of the narrator in the 1950s, and seem to have been selected at random from his total experience. There is a kind of recurrent theme—the political impotence of the 1950s—but most of the statements made have nothing to do with it. It's a very risky procedure, but it works because of the casual brilliance of the writing and because the writer persuades us that the discontinuity of his text *is* the truth of his experience. 'I used to think that someday I would write a fictional version of my stupid life in the fifties,' says the narrator at one point, and the implication is that the raw ingredients of that life heaped in front of us constitute a more authentic record than would be any well-made novel.

In the work of Donald Barthelme the principle of *non-sequitur* governs the relationships between sentences as well as between paragraphs. 'Edward looked at his red beard in the tableknife. Then Edward and Pia went to Sweden, to the farm.'[42] The purely temporal continuity of these actions is overwhelmed by the huge difference in scale between them and the absence of any causal connection.

From his window Charles watched Hilda. She sat playing under the black pear tree. She bit deeply into a black pear. It tasted bad and Hilda looked at the tree inquiringly. Charles started to cry. He had been reading Bergson. He was surprised by his own weeping, and in a state of surprise, decided to get something to eat.[43]

This passage begins with a kind of logical continuity of motivation, but frays out into disparate reactions of Charles—weeping, reading Bergson, feeling hungry—which have nothing to do with Hilda or with each other. One of Barthelme's favourite devices is to take a number of interrelated or contiguous characters, or consciousnesses or conversations, and scramble them together to produce an apparently random montage of bizarrely contrasting verbal fragments ('fragments are the only forms I trust,' a Barthelme character observes).[44] For example, 'The Viennese Opera Ball':

> It is one of McCormack's proudest boasts, Carola heard over her lovely white shoulder, that he never once missed having dinner with his wife in their forty-one years of married life. She remembered Knocko at the Evacuation Day parade, and Baudelaire's famous remark. Mortality is the final evaluator of methods. An important goal is an intact sphincter. The greater the prematurity, the more generous should be the episiotomy. Yes, said Leon Jaroff, Detroit Bureau Chief for *Time*, at the Thomas Elementary School on warm spring afternoons I could look from my classroom into the open doors of the Packard plant. Ideal foster parents are mature people who are not necessarily well off, but who have a good marriage and who love and understand children. The ninth day of the ninth month is the festival of the crysanthemum (Kiku No Sekku) when *sake* made from the crysanthemum is drunk.[45]

Randomness

The discontinuity of the discourse in Brautigan, Michaels, Barthelme, often looks like randomness, but it would be more accurate to say these writers compose according to a logic of the absurd. The human mind being what it is, true randomness can only be introduced into a literary text by mechanical means—for instance the cut-up method of William Burroughs. As he says, 'You cannot will spontaneity. But you can introduce the unpredictable spontaneous factor with a pair of scissors.'[46] The writer cuts up pieces of different texts, including his own, sticks them together in random order and transcribes the result. A similar method of introducing an element of genuine randomness into literature is to issue books in loose-leaf form, the reader being invited to shuffle the sheets to produce his own text (for example B. S. Johnson's *The Unfortunates* [1969]). Such experiments seem to me the least interesting, because most mechanical, way of trying to break out of the metaphor/metonymy system; and I have nothing to add to what I have already said about them elsewhere.[47]

Excess

Some postmodernist writers have deliberately taken metaphoric or metonymic devices to excess, tested them, as it were, to destruction, parodied and burlesqued them in the process of using them, and thus sought to escape from their tyranny. Thomas Pynchon's *Gravity's Rainbow* (1973), for example, takes the commonplace analogy between rocket and phallus and pursues its ramifications relentlessly and grotesquely through the novel's enormous length, while the V motif in the same author's first novel *V* (1963) mocks interpretation by the plurality of its manifestations. Donald Barthelme practices metaphoric overkill more locally, for example in this absurd cadenza of comparisons for the collection of moonrocks in the Smithsonian Institute:

> The moon rocks were as good as a meaningful and emotionally rewarding seduction that you had not expected. The moon rocks were as good as listening to what the members of the Supreme Court say to each other, in the Supreme Court Locker Room. They were as good as a war. The moon rocks were better than a presentation copy of the Random House Dictionary of the English Language signed by Geoffrey Chaucer himself. They were better than a movie in which the President refuses to tell the people what to do to save themselves from the terrible thing that is about to happen, although he knows what ought to be done and has written a secret memorandum about it. The moon rocks were better than a good cup of coffee from an urn decorated with the change of Philomel, by the barbarous king. The moon rocks were better than a ¡huelga! led by Mongo Santamaria, with additional dialogue by St. John of the Cross and special effects by Melmoth the Wanderer.[48]

Richard Brautigan's *Trout Fishing in America* is notable for its bizarre similes, which are based on very idiosyncratic perceptions of resemblance and which frequently threaten to detach themselves from the narrative and develop into little self-contained stories—not quite like a heroic simile, because they are not returned to the original context at their conclusion. For example:

> The sun was like a huge fifty-cent piece that someone had poured kerosene on and then lit with a match and said, 'Here, hold this while I go get a newspaper' and put the coin in my hand, but never came back.[49]

> Eventually the seasons would take care of their wooden names [on grave markers] like a sleepy short-order cook cracking eggs over a grill next to a railroad station.[50]

> my body was like birds sitting on a telephone wire strung out down the world, clouds tossing the wires carefully.[51]

> His eyes were like the shoelaces of a harpsichord.[52]

> The light behind the trees was like going into a gradual and strange department store.[53]

> The creek was like 12,845 telephone booths in a row with high Victorian ceilings and all the doors taken off and all the backs of the booths knocked out.[54]

> The streets were white and dry like a collision at high speed between a cemetery and a truck loaded with sacks of flour.[55]

If these similes strain the principle of similarity to breaking point, the title of the book is used to take the principle of substitution to excess. Trout Fishing in America can be a person:

> And this is a very small cookbook for Trout Fishing in America as if Trout Fishing in America were a rich gourmet and Trout Fishing in America had Maria Callas for a girlfriend and they ate together on a marble table with beautiful candles.[56]

a corpse:

> This is the autopsy of Trout Fishing in America as if Trout Fishing in America had been Lord Byron and had died in Missolonghi, Greece, and afterwards never saw the shores of Idaho again[57]

or the name of a hotel

> Half a block away from Broadway and Columbus is Hotel Trout Fishing in America, a cheap hotel. It is very old and run by some Chinese.[58]

Trout Fishing in America receives letters, and sends replies signed 'Trout Fishing in America'. Trout Fishing in America can be an adjective:

> THE LAST MENTION OF TROUT FISHING IN AMERICA SHORTY[59]
> WITNESS FOR TROUT FISHING IN AMERICA PEACE[60]

Trout Fishing in America can be a pen nib:

> I thought to myself what a lovely nib trout fishing in America would make with a stroke of cool green trees along the river's shore, wild flowers and dark fins pressed against the paper.[61]

Trout Fishing in America, in short, can be anything Brautigan wants it to be.

One equivalent, on the axis of combination, to this excess of substitution, would be the permutation of variables already discussed. But any overloading of the discourse with specificity will have the same effect: by presenting the reader with more details than he can synthesize into a whole, the discourse affirms the resistance of the world to interpretation. The immensely detailed, scientifically exact and metaphor-free description of objects in Robbe-Grillet's writing actually prevents us from visualizing them. That this possibility was inherent in the metonymic method was demonstrated a long time ago by some of the late nineteenth-century realists. Jakobson cites the example of the Russian novelist Gleb Ivanovic Uspenskij, quoting the observation of Kamegulov that in his characterization, 'the reader is crushed by the multiplicity of detail unloaded on him in a limited verbal space, and is physically unable to grasp the whole, so that the portrait is often lost.'[62] The celebrated description of Charles Bovary's school cap in the first chapter of *Madame Bovary* is a more familiar example of what might be called 'metonymic overkill'. Robbe-

Grillet not only overwhelms the reader with more detail than he wants or can handle, but also (I strongly suspect) ensures that the details will not cohere. Consider, for example, this description of the harbour which Mattias is approaching in the first chapter of *Le Voyeur*:

> La jetée, maintenant toute proche, dominait le pont d'une hauteur de plusiers mètres; la marée devait être basse. La cale qui allait servir pour l'accostage montrait à sa partie inférieure une surface plus lisse, brunie par l'eau et couverte a moitié de mousses verdâtres. En regardant avec plus d'attention, on voyait le bord de pierre qui se rapprochait insensiblement.
>
> Le bord de pierre—une arrête vive, oblique, à l'intersection de deux plans perpendiculaires: la paroi verticale fuyant tout droit vers le quai et la rampe qui rejoint le haut de la digue—se prolonge à son extrémité supérieure, en haut de la digue, par une ligne horizontale fuyant tout droit vers le quai.
>
> Le quai, rendu plus lointain par l'effet de perspective, émet de part et d'autre de cette ligne principale un faisceau de parallèles qui délimitent, avec une netteté encore accentuée par l'éclairage du matin, une série de plans allongés, alternativement horizontaux et verticaux: le sommet du parapet massif protégeant le passage du côté du large, la paroi intérieure du parapet, la chaussée sur le haut de la digue, le flanc sans garde-fou qui plonge dans l'eau du port. Les deux surfaces verticales sont dans l'ombre, les deux autres sont vivement éclairées par le soleil—le haut du parapet dans toute sa largeur et la chaussée à l'exception d'une étroite blande obscure: l'ombre portée du parapet. Théorétiquement on devrait voir encore dans l'eau du port l'image renversée de l'ensemble et, à la surface, toujours dans le même jeu de parallèles, l'ombre portée de la haute paroi verticale qui filterait tout droit vers le quai.
>
> Vers le bout de la jetée, la construction se complique . . .[63]

But this already sufficiently *compliqué* to make the point. The published English translation of this passage is as follows:

> The pier, now quite close, towered several yards above the deck. The tide must have been out. The landing slip from which the ship would be boarded revealed the smoother surface of its lower section, darkened by the water and half-covered with greenish moss. On closer inspection, the stone rim drew almost imperceptibly closer.
>
> The stone rim—an oblique, sharp edge formed by two intersecting perpendicular planes: the vertical embankment perpendicular to the quay and the ramp leading to the top of the pier—was continued along its upper side at the top of the pier by a horizontal line extending straight toward the quay.
>
> The pier, which seemed longer than it actually was as an effect of perspective, extended from both sides of this base line in a cluster of parallels describing, with a precision accentuated even more sharply by the morning light, a series of elongated planes alternately horizontal and vertical: the crest of the massive parapet that protected the tidal basin from the open sea, the inner wall of the parapet, the jetty along the top of the pier, and the vertical embankment that plunged straight into the water of the harbor. The two vertical surfaces were in shadow, the other two brilliantly lit by the sun—the whole breadth of the parapet and all of the jetty save for one

dark narrow strip: the shadow cast by the parapet. Theoretically, the reversed image of the entire group could be seen reflected in the harbor water, and, on the surface, still within the same play of parallels, the shadow cast by the vertical embankment extending straight toward the quay.[64]

The translator has not made things easier for us by translating *plus lointain* as 'longer', and by using only three English words (*pier*, *quay* and *jetty*) to translate four French words (*jettée, quai, digue, chausée*)— and not using them consistently, either, translating *jettée* as both 'pier' and 'jetty', and *quai* as both 'pier' and 'quay'. But one can only sympathize with anyone engaged on this task. An obvious procedure for a translator would be to make a sketch or diagram of the harbour, but when I invited students, and subsequently some colleagues in the French Department of my university, to do this, none of them succeeded. The description simply doesn't come together into a visualizable whole.

The last word on metonymic excess may be left to Jorge Luis Borges, who in his story 'Funes, the Memorious', describes a man who, after the shock of an accident, is able to perceive everything that is happening around him and unable to forget anything.

> We, at one glance, can perceive three glasses on a table; Funes, all the leaves and tendrils and fruit that make up a grape vine. He knew by heart the forms of the southern clouds at dawn on 30 April 1882, and could compare them in his memory with the mottled streaks on a book in Spanish binding he had only seen once and with the outlines of the foam raised by an oar in the Rio Negro the night before the Quebracho uprising.[65]

Funes inhabits a world of intolerable specificity and his time and energy are wholly absorbed by the interminable and futile task of classifying all the data of his experience without omission or generalization:

> He was the solitary and lucid spectator of a multiform world which was instantaneously and almost intolerably exact ... I suspect, nevertheless, that he was not very capable of thought. To think is to forget a difference, to generalize, to abstract. In the overly replete world of Funes there were nothing but details, almost contiguous details.[66]

Short Circuit

In Part Two I suggested that at the highest level of generality at which we can apply the metaphor/metonymy distinction, literature itself is metaphoric and nonliterature is metonymic. The literary text is always metaphoric in the sense that when we interpret it we apply it to the world as a total metaphor. This process of interpretation assumes a gap between the text and the world, between art and life, which postmodernist writing characteristically tries to short-circuit in order to administer a shock to the reader and thus resist assimilation into conventional categories of the literary. Ways of doing this include: combining in one work violently contrasting modes—the obviously fictive and the apparently factual; introducing the author and the question of authorship into the text; and exposing conventions in the act of using them. These ploys are not in themselves discoveries of the postmodernist writers—they are to be found in prose fiction as far back as *Don Quixote* and *Tristram Shandy*—but they appear so frequently in postmodernist writing, and are pursued to such lengths as to constitute, in combination with the other devices we have surveyed, a distinctively new development.

Vladimir Nabokov, a transitional figure between modernism and postmodernism, teasingly introduced himself (and his wife) on the perimeter of his fictions as early as his second novel *King, Queen, Knave*, originally published in Russian in 1928. As the coils of the intrigue tighten around the distracted hero, Franz, at a German seaside resort, he notices a vacationing couple talking a language he does not understand and carrying a butterfly net (something of a private joke, this, in 1928, when Nabokov was not yet the world's most famous lepidopterist):

> He thought that they glanced at him and fell silent for an instant. After passing him they began talking again; he had the impression they were discussing him, and even pronouncing his name. It embarrassed, it incensed him, that this damned happy foreigner hastening to the beach with his tanned, pale-haired, lovely companion, knew absolutely everything about his predicament. . . .[67]

In *Pale Fire* (1962) Nabokov plays off the metaphoric and metonymic modes against each other with typical cunning. The novel consists of a poem and a commentary. Normally a poem is fictional and a commentary factual, as verse is a metaphorical and prose a metonymic medium. In *Pale Fire*, however, the prose commentary is more obviously fictive than the poem, in the sense that the commentator Kinbote is a madman suffering from the delusion that he is the exiled monarch of a Ruritanian kingdom called Zembla, while John Shade's poem is a meditation upon entirely credible personal experience. A measure of Kinbote's insanity is the way he perversely and absurdly interprets Shade's poem as a tissue of allusions to his own fantasy; but it would be an oversimplification to say that Nabokov demonstrates the difference between illusion and reality by this opposition between Kinbote and Shade. For one thing, Kinbote's evocation of Zembla has an imaginative power and eloquence which makes us all too eager to suspend our disbelief, and beside it Shade's world seems less interesting. For another, Shade himself is a fiction, an illusion created by a 'real' author, Nabokov, whose well-known personal history corresponds far more closely to Kinbote's than to Shade's. Even the murder of Shade, which, within the limits of the book was 'in fact' committed by an escaped criminal who mistook Shade for the judge who sentenced him, but which Kinbote represents as the error of an assassin sent to kill the exiled king of Zembla, has an origin in Nabokov's own experience, for his father was murdered by political assassins who were attacking someone else.[68] Teasing allusions to the author persist in Nabokov's subsequent novels.

In the last but one of J. D. Salinger's stories about the Glass family, 'Seymour: an Introduction', the narrator, Buddy Glass, mentions that he has written two other stories about his brother Seymour—'Raise High the Roofbeam, Carpenters' (which is no surprise to the reader of the sequence) and 'A Nice Day for Bananafish', which I think *is* a surprise. For 'Bananafish' had no identified narrator, and appeared years before in a collection of *Nine Stories* (1953) by J. D. Salinger, seven of which did not concern the Glass family. Buddy goes on to claim authorship of one of these seven stories, and to refer to a novel of his that sounds very like Salinger's best-seller, *The Catcher in the Rye* (1951). Further on, Buddy refers to criticism of his work and rumours about his private life that are much the same as those provoked by Salinger himself. These revelations have a disorientating effect on the reader. The fiction that Buddy Glass is the author of 'Seymour: an Introduction' is made logically dependent upon the supposition that the J. D. Salinger who we thought wrote 'Bananafish' was the pen name of Buddy Glass, but of course J. D. Salinger's name appears on the title page of both books. Compelled to face the question, who is real, Buddy Glass or J. D. Salinger, common sense tells us the answer, but the rhetoric works in the opposite direction. This deliberate entangling of the myths of the Glass family and the Caulfield family with Salinger's personal history is typical of his later work, where he plays sly games with the reader's assent, stepping up the fictionality of the events as he damps down the literariness of the manner in which he describes them. Purporting to tell us a 'true' family history, and dropping heavy hints that he is the same person as J. D. Salinger, Buddy yet insists again and again on the autonomy of art and the irrelevance of biographical criticism. An extravagantly transcendental philosophy of life involving the endorsement of miracles and extra-sensory perception is put forward in terms of studied homeliness, wrapped around with elaborate qualifications, disclaimers, nods and winks, and mediated in a style that, for all its restless rhetorical mannerism, is strikingly lacking in any kind of 'poetic' resonances. As Ihab Hassan, one of the few critics to have placed Salinger in a postmodernist context, has observed: 'Ungainly, prolix, allusive, convoluted, tolerant of chance, whimsy, and disorder, these narratives define a kind of anti-form. Their impertinent exhortations of reader and writer undercut the authority of the artistic act.'[69]

In their play with the ideas of illusion, authorship and literary convention, however, Nabokov and Salinger maintain a precarious poise. Their narratives wobble on the edge of the aesthetic, but never quite fall off. Modes are mixed, but a certain balance, or symmetry, is preserved. The same is true of Doris Lessing, whose *The Golden Notebook* (1962) and *Briefing For a Descent into Hell* (1971) have certain features in common with their work—the Chinese-box authorship puzzle, for instance, and the reality/fantasy contrast in which the fantasy is more potent than the reality. Present-day American writers are often more slapdash, or less inhibited, in mixing up fact and fiction, life and art. Brautigan's *Trout Fishing in America*, for instance, has many signs of being an unstructured autobiography. The text frequently refers us to the photograph of the author on the front cover, and includes a great many factual documents—letters, recipes, bibliographies, etc. But it also contains extravagantly fictitious episodes such as the one in which the narrator buys a used trout stream from the Cleveland Wrecking Yard:

> It was stacked in piles of various lengths: ten, fifteen, twenty feet, etc. There was one pile of hundred foot lengths. There was also a box of scraps. . . . I went up close and looked at the lengths of stream. I could see some trout in them . . . It looked like a fine stream. I put my hand in the water. It was cold and felt good.[70]

This fantastic event is narrated in a style of sober realism, just as the more banal events in the book are elaborated with fantastic similes. Brautigan leaves to the reader the task of integrating these totally disparate modes of writing. Plainly, he is not bothered.

Kurt Vonnegut uses an apparently artless, improvised mixing of modes to more deliberate thematic effect in *Slaughterhouse 5* (1969). Vonnegut happened to be a prisoner of war in Dresden at the time of the air raid which destroyed it at the end of World War II, and was employed in digging some of the 130,000 incinerated corpses out of the rubble. For years, he confides in his first chapter, he has been trying to make this lump of raw experience into a novel; but such novels have a way of covertly celebrating what they outwardly deplore and being turned into movies with parts for Frank Sinatra and John Wayne. The only way to write an anti-war novel is to write an anti-novel. 'It has to be so short and jumbled and jangled . . . because there is nothing intelligent to say about a massacre.'[71] *Slaughterhouse 5* is a *bricolage* of fragments, short passages that are grim, grotesque and whimsical by turns, which describe the experiences of the very two-dimensional hero, Billy Pilgrim: his war-experiences (which bear a close resemblance to Vonnegut's) his civilian life as a married man and successful optometrist (domestic and social comedy) and his delusions of having been abducted by aliens from the planet Tralfamadore (science-fiction parody). Billy finds the Tralfamadorian concept of time as a field of simultaneous events, from which we are free to select, an answer to the problem of meaningless death which is instanced on almost every page of *Slaughterhouse 5* (invariably accompanied by the laconic comment, 'So it goes') for according to this doctrine (perhaps a parody of Christianity) 'we will all live for ever no matter how dead we may sometimes seem to be.' This concept also provides a justification for the drastic dislocation of chronology in the book, which prevents the reader from locating himself on a narrative line or settling into a single mood, and jumbles together disparate experiences in a way that imitates the incongruities and disjunctions of modern history. Nor are the various planes of the narrative—autobiographical, fictional, fantastic—kept insulated from each other. At his first German prison camp, for instance, Billy Pilgrim and his fellow American POWs are welcomed by a contingent of British veterans who provide a feast that makes the half-starved Americans violently ill. The latrine is crammed with these unfortunates.

> An American near Billy wailed that he had excreted everything but his brains. Moments later he said, 'There they go, there they go.' He meant his brains.
>
> That was I. That was me. That was the author of this book.[72]

This statement has an interesting double effect. On the one hand it reminds us that the story has an autobiographical, documentary origin, that the author 'was there', and therefore that the narrative is 'true'. On the other hand it simultaneously reminds us that Billy Pilgrim and the author belong to different planes of reality, that we are reading a book, a story, which (whatever its specific proportions of fiction to fact) is necessarily a highly conventionalized, highly artificial construction, and necessarily at a considerable distance from 'the way it was'.

In *Breakfast of Champions*, Vonnegut brings himself as composing author into the 'time present' of the narrative—for example:

> 'Give me a Black and White and water,' [Wayne] heard the waitress say, and Wayne should have pricked up his ears at that. That particular drink wasn't for any ordinary person. That drink was for the person who had created all Wayne's misery to date, who could kill him or make him a millionaire or send him back to prison or do whatever he damn well pleased with Wayne. That drink was for me.[73]

This is what the Russian Formalists called 'baring the device' carried to an extreme, and it is a persistent feature of postmodernist writing.

> The droplets rain from the eaves. The shadow of a cloud dims the snow dazzle. George Washington crosses the Delaware on the walls. I sit at my desk, making this up. . . .

Thus Ronald Sukenick, in 'What's Your Story?'[74] 'I wander the island, inventing it,' begins Robert Coover's story 'The Magic Poker', in which his skill in evoking scenery and generating mystery and suspense is constantly undermined by declarations of his own manipulating presence—the narrator revealed as author:

> Bedded deep in the grass, near the path up to the first guest cabin, lies a wrought-iron poker. It is long and slender with an intricately worked handle, and it is orange with rust. It lies shadowed, not by trees, but by the grass that has grown up wildly around it. I put it there.[75]

'Another story about a writer writing a story! Another regressus ad infinitum! Who doesn't prefer art that at least overtly imitates something other than its own processes? That doesn't continually proclaim, "Don't forget I'm an artifice!" That takes for granted its mimetic nature instead of asserting it in order (not so slyly after all) to deny it, or vice versa?' That is a quite common complaint about the kind of writing I have surveyed in this chapter (especially among British reviewers and critics) but this particular expression of it occurs in a text by one of the most elaborately and ingeniously selfconscious of all postmodernist writers, John Barth;[76] and in context will give little comfort to partisans of traditional realism, one variety of which is amusingly parodied in the following passage:

> C flung away the whining manuscript and pushed impatiently through the french windows leading to the terrace from his oak-wainscotted study. Pausing at the stone balustrade to light his briar he remarked through a lavendar cascade of wisteria that lithe-limbed Gloria, Gloria of timorous eye and militant breast, had once again chosen his boat wharf as her basking place.[77]

The way the narrative tracks its subject through spatial and temporal contiguities with obsessive attention to redundant detail is well-caught, and the characterization of Gloria makes effective fun of the realistic writer's reliance on synecdoche.

The 'manuscript' in this passage is the story itself, entitled 'Life-Story', the trace of a writer's attempts to write a story about a writer who has come to suspect that the world is a fiction in which he is a character—a hypothesis which, if confirmed, would affect both writers, indeed all writers, including Barth. The process of trying to make a story out of this *donnée* provokes various pronouncements about the theory of fiction such as the one quoted above, which seem to be comments upon the fiction but which prove to be part of the fiction. 'Life-Story' is a metafiction cleverly constructed to outmanoeuvre critics of metafiction, since the metafictional frame is continually being absorbed into the picture. This 'regressus in infinitum' is finally arrested by the device of the short-circuit:

> To what conclusion will he come? He'd been about to append to his own tale inasmuch as the old analogy between Author and God, novel and world, can no longer be employed unless deliberately as a false analogy, certain things follow: 1) fiction must acknowledge its fictitiousness and metaphoric invalidity or 2) choose to ignore the question or deny its relevance or 3) establish some other, acceptable relation between itself, its author, its reader. Just as he finished doing so, however, his real life and imaginary

mistresses entered his study; 'It's a little past midnight' she announced with a smile; 'do you know what that means?'[78]

The interruption reveals to him that 'he could not after all be a character in a work of fiction inasmuch as such a fiction would be of an entirely different character from what he thought of as fiction', and the birthday kiss his wife bestows upon him obscures his view of his manuscript and makes him 'end his ending story endless by interruption, cap his pen'.[79] Barth himself has referred to postmodernist writing as 'the literature of exhausted possibility'—or, more chicly, 'the literature of exhaustion',[80] and has praised Borges for demonstrating 'how an artist may paradoxically turn the felt ultimacies of our time into material and means for his work—*paradoxically* because by doing so he transcends what had appeared to be his refutation'.[81] Certainly, in seeking 'some other . . . relation between itself, its author, its reader' than that of previous literary traditions, postmodernist writing takes enormous risks—risks of abolishing itself, if ultimately successful, in silence, incoherence or what Fiedler calls 'the reader's passionate [i.e. non-aesthetic] apprehension and response'.[82] I would certainly not claim that all the texts surveyed in this chapter are equally interesting and rewarding: postmodernist writing tends to be very much a hit-or-miss affair. But many of these books and stories are imaginatively liberating to a high degree, and have done much to keep the possibilities of writing open in the very process of asserting that the most familiar ones are closed. If this assertion were really made good, however—if postmodernism really succeeded in expelling the idea of order (whether expressed in metonymic or metaphoric form) from modern writing, then it would truly abolish itself, by destroying the norms against which we perceive its deviations. A foreground without a background inevitably becomes the background for something else. Postmodernism cannot rely upon the historical memory of modernist and antimodernist writing for its background, because it is essentially a rule-breaking kind of art, and unless people are still trying to keep the rules there is no point in breaking them, and no interest in seeing them broken.

Appendix A

'A Hanging' By George Orwell

[1] It was in Burma, a sodden morning of the rains. A sickly light, like yellow tinfoil, was slanting over the high walls into the jail yard. We were waiting outside the condemned cells, a row of sheds fronted with double bars, like small animal cages. Each cell measured about ten feet by ten and was quite bare within except for a plank bed and a pot of drinking water. In some of them brown silent men were squatting at the inner bars, with their blankets draped round them. These were the condemned men, due to be hanged within the next week or two.

[2] One prisoner had been brought out of his cell. He was a Hindu, a puny wisp of a man, with a shaven head and vague liquid eyes. He had a thick, sprouting moustache, absurdly too big for his body, rather like the moustache of a comic man on the films. Six tall Indian warders were guarding him and getting him ready for the gallows. Two of them stood by with rifles and fixed bayonets, while the others handcuffed him, passed a chain through his handcuffs and fixed it to their belts, and lashed his arms tight to his sides. They crowded very close about him, with their hands always on him in a careful, caressing grip, as though all the while feeling him to make sure he was there. It was like men handling a fish which is still alive and may jump back into the water. But he stood quite unresisting, yielding his arms limply to the ropes, as though he hardly noticed what was happening.

[3] Eight o'clock struck and a bugle call, desolately thin in the wet air, floated from the distant barracks. The superintendent of the jail, who was standing apart from the rest of us, moodily prodding the gravel with his stick, raised his head at the sound. He was an army doctor, with a grey toothbrush moustache and a gruff voice. 'For God's sake hurry up, Francis,' he said irritably. 'The man ought to have been dead by this time. Aren't you ready yet?'

[4] Francis, the head jailer, a fat Dravidian in a white drill suit and gold spectacles, waved his black hand. 'Yes sir, yes sir,' he bubbled. 'All iss satisfactorily prepared. The hangman iss waiting. We shall proceed.'

[5] 'Well, quick march, then. The prisoners can't get their breakfast till this job's over.'

[6] We set out for the gallows. Two warders marched on either side of the prisoner, with their rifles at the slope; two others marched close against him, gripping him by arm and shoulder, as though at once pushing and supporting him. The rest of us, magistrates and the like, followed behind. Suddenly, when we had gone ten yards, the

procession stopped short without any order or warning. A dreadful thing had happened—a dog, come goodness knows whence, had appeared in the yard. It came bounding among us with a loud volley of barks, and leapt round us wagging its whole body, wild with glee at finding so many human beings together. It was a large woolly dog, half Airedale, half pariah. For a moment it pranced round us, and then, before anyone could stop it, it had made a dash for the prisoner, and jumping up tried to lick his face. Everyone stood aghast, too taken aback even to grab at the dog.

[7]   'Who let that bloody brute in here?' said the superintendent angrily. 'Catch it, someone!'

[8]   A warder, detached from the escort, charged clumsily after the dog, but it danced and gambolled just out of his reach, taking everything as part of the game. A young Eurasian jailer picked up a handful of gravel and tried to stone the dog away, but it dodged the stones and came after us again. Its yaps echoed from the jail walls. The prisoner, in the grasp of the two warders, looked on incuriously, as though this was another formality of the hanging. It was several minutes before someone managed to catch the dog. Then we put my handkerchief through its collar and moved off once more, with the dog still straining and whimpering.

[9]   It was about forty yards to the gallows. I watched the bare brown back of the prisoner marching in front of me. He walked clumsily with his bound arms, but quite steadily, with that bobbing gait of the Indian who never straightens his knees. At each step his muscles slid neatly into place, the lock of hair on his scalp danced up and down, his feet printed themselves on the wet gravel. And once, in spite of the men who gripped him by each shoulder, he stepped slightly aside to avoid a puddle on the path.

[10]   It is curious, but till that moment I had never realized what it means to destroy a healthy, conscious man. When I saw the prisoner step aside to avoid the puddle, I saw the mystery, the unspeakable wrongness, of cutting a life short when it is in full tide. This man was not dying, he was alive just as we were alive. All the organs of his body were working— bowels digesting food, skin renewing itself, nails growing, tissues forming—all toiling away in solemn foolery. His nails would still be growing when he stood on the drop, when he was falling through the air with a tenth of a second to live. His eyes saw the yellow gravel and the grey walls, and his brain still remembered, foresaw, reasoned—reasoned even about puddles. He and we were a party of men walking together, seeing, hearing, feeling, understanding the same world; and in two minutes, with a sudden snap, one of us would be gone—one mind less, one world less.

[11]   The gallows stood in a small yard, separate from the main grounds of the prison, and overgrown with tall prickly weeds. It was a brick erection like three sides of a shed, with planking on top, and above that two beams and a crossbar with the rope dangling. The hangman, a grey-haired convict in the white uniform of the prison, was waiting beside his machine. He greeted us with a servile crouch as we entered. At a word from Francis the two warders, gripping the prisoner more closely than ever, half led, half pushed him to the gallows and helped him clumsily up the ladder. Then the hangman climbed up and fixed the rope round the prisoner's neck.

[12]   We stood waiting, five yards away. The warders had formed in a rough circle round the gallows. And then, when the noose was fixed, the prisoner began crying out on his god. It was a high, reiterated cry of 'Ram! Ram! Ram! Ram!', not urgent and fearful like a prayer or a cry for help, but steady, rhythmical, almost like the tolling of a bell. The dog answered the sound with a whine. The hangman, still standing on the gallows, produced a small cotton bag like a flour bag and drew it down over the prisoner's face. But the sound, muffled by the cloth, still persisted, over and over again: 'Ram! Ram! Ram! Ram! Ram!'

[13]   The hangman climbed down and stood ready, holding the lever. Minutes seemed to pass. The steady, muffled crying from the prisoner went on and on, 'Ram! Ram! Ram!' never faltering for an instant. The superintendent, his head on his chest, was slowly poking the ground with his stick; perhaps he was counting the cries, allowing the prisoner a fixed number—fifty, perhaps, or a hundred. Everyone had changed colour. The Indians had gone grey like bad coffee, and one or two of the bayonets were wavering. We looked at the lashed, hooded man on the drop, and listened to his cries—each cry another second of life; the same thought was in all our minds: oh, kill him quickly, get it over, stop that abominable noise!

[14]   Suddenly the superintendent made up his mind. Throwing up his head he made a swift motion with his stick. 'Chalo!' he shouted almost fiercely.

[15]   There was a clanking noise, and then dead silence. The prisoner had vanished, and the rope was twisting on itself. I let go of the dog, and it galloped immediately to the back of the gallows; but when it got there it stopped short, barked, and then retreated into a corner of the yard, where it stood among the weeds, looking timorously out at us. We went round the gallows to inspect the prisoner's body. He was dangling with his toes pointed straight downwards, very slowly revolving, as dead as a stone.

[16]   The superintendent reached out with his stick and poked the bare body; it oscillated, slightly, '*He's* all right,' said the superintendent. He backed out from under the gallows, and blew out a deep breath. The moody look had gone out of his face quite suddenly. He glanced at his wrist-watch. 'Eight minutes past eight. Well, that's all for this morning, thank God.'

[17]   The warders unfixed bayonets and marched away. The dog, sobered and conscious of having misbehaved itself, slipped after them. We walked out of the gallows yard, past the condemned cells with their waiting prisoners, into the big central yard of the prison. The convicts, under the command of warders armed with lathis, were already receiving their breakfast. They squatted in long rows, each man holding a tin pannikin, while two warders with buckets marched round ladling out rice; it seemed quite a homely, jolly scene, after the hanging. An enormous relief had come upon us now that the job was done. One felt an impulse to sing, to break into a run, to snigger. All at once everyone began chattering gaily.

[18]   The Eurasian boy walking beside me nodded towards the way we had come, with a knowing smile: 'Do you know, sir, our friend (he meant the dead man), when he heard his appeal had been dismissed, he pissed on the floor of his cell. From fright.—Kindly take one of my cigarettes, sir. Do you not admire my new silver case, sir? From the boxwallah, two rupees eight annas. Classy European style.'

[19]   Several people laughed—at what, nobody seemed certain.

[20]   Francis was walking by the superintendent, talking garrulously: 'Well, sir, all hass passed off with the utmost satisfactoriness. It wass all finished—flick! like that. It iss not always so—oah, no! I have known cases where the doctor wass obliged to go beneath the gallows and pull the prisoner's legs to ensure decease. Most disagreeable!'

[21]   'Wriggling about, eh? That's bad,' said the superintendent.

[22]   'Ach, sir, it iss worse when they become refractory! One man, I recall, clung to the bars of hiss cage when we went to take him out. You will scarcely credit, sir, that it took six warders to dislodge him, three pulling at each leg. We reasoned with him. "My dear fellow," we said, "think of all the pain and trouble you are causing to us!" But no, he would not listen! Ach, he wass very troublesome!'

[23]   I found that I was laughing quite loudly. Everyone was laughing. Even the superintendent grinned in a tolerant way. 'You'd better all come out and have a drink,' he said quite genially. 'I've got a bottle of whisky in the car. We could do with it.'

[24]   We went through the big double gates of the prison, into the road. 'Pulling at his legs!' exclaimed a Burmese magistrate suddenly, and burst into a loud chuckling. We all began laughing again. At that moment Francis's anecdote seemed extraordinarily funny. We all had a drink together, native and European alike, quite amicably. The dead man was a hundred yards away.

Appendix B

'Michael Lake Describes What the Executioner Actually Faces,'
Guardian 9 April, 1973

[1]   It is doubtful if those who seek the reintroduction of capital punishment have ever seen a hanging. It is a grim business, far removed from the hurly burly of Parliament, from the dusty gloom of the Old Bailey and a million light years away from the murder.

[2]   In New Zealand hangings were always in the evening. There were never any crowds, but three journalists were always summoned to witness the hanging. Their names were published later that night, along with those of the sheriff, the coroner and others, in the Official Gazette. I watched the last hanging in New Zealand.

[3]   Walter James Bolton was a farmer from the west coast of the North Island. He had poisoned his wife. He was 62, and the oldest and heaviest man ever hanged in New Zealand. They had to make sure they got the length of rope right so the drop wouldn't tear off his head.

[4]   I arrived at Mt Eden Gaol, Auckland, at 6 o'clock on a Monday evening. With the other witnesses I was led through the main administrative block, down some steps, and along a wing which it turned out, was a sort of Death Row.

[5]   We were led to the foot of the scaffold in a yard immediately at the end of the wing. The sky was darkening and a canvas canopy over the yard flapped gently in the breeze.

[6]   After a long time, there was a murmuring. Into view came a strange procession; the deputy governor of the prison, leading four warders and among them, walked or rather shambled the hulking figure of Bolton. His arms were pinioned by ropes to his trunk.

[7]   Behind him walked a parson reading aloud. It was with disbelief and shock that I recognised the Burial Service from the Book of Common Prayer.

[8]   High upon the scaffold, 17 steps away, the executioner stood immobile. He wore a black broad-brimmed hat, a black trench coat, and heavy boots, and he was masked. Only the slit for his eyes and his white hands gleamed in the light.

[9]   Bolton was helped up the steps by the warders, who bound his ankles together. The sheriff then asked him if he had anything to say before sentence was carried out.

[10]   Bolton mumbled. After a few seconds mumbling the parson, apparently unaware that the prisoner was talking, interrupted with further readings from the Burial Service.

[11]   I checked my shorthand notes with the other reporters. One, an elderly man who had witnessed 19 hangings, had heard nothing. The other man's shorthand outlines matched my own. He had said: 'The only thing I want to say is . . . .'

[12]   The warders did all the work. They bound him and put a white canvas hood over his head as he stood there, swaying in their grasp. Then they dropped the loop over his head, with the traditional hangman's knot, tidied it up, and stepped back.

[13]   The sheriff lifted his hand and lowered it. The executioner moved for the first and only time. He pulled a lever, and stepped back. Bolton dropped behind a canvas screen. The rope ran fast through the pulley at the top, and then when the Turk's Head knotted in the end jammed in the pulley, the block clanged loudly up against the beam to which it was fixed. The rope quivered, and that was the end of Walter James Bolton.

[14]   A doctor repaired behind the screen which hid the body from us. A hanged man usually ejaculates and evacuates his bowels. In New Zealand, at any rate he also hanged for an hour. Bolton hung while we sat back in the deputy governor's office drinking the whisky traditionally provided by the Government for these occasions—'Who's for a long drop,' asked some macabre wit.

[15]   The city coroner, Mr Alf Addison, an old friend of mine, called us across to his office where we duly swore we had seen the sentence of the court carried out.

[16]   I went back to my newspaper office and wrote three paragraphs. No sensations, I told the night editor, the bloke hadn't made a fuss. Then I went home with a sense of loss and corruption I have never quite shed.

Appendix C

An extract from The Naked Lunch, by William Burroughs

Room like gymnasium. . . . The floor is foam rubber, covered in white silk. . . . One wall is glass. . . . The rising sun fills the room with pink light. Johnny is led in, hands tied, between Mary and Mark. Johnny sees the gallows and sags with a great 'Ohhhhhhhhhhh!' his chin pulling down towards his cock, his legs bending at the knees. Sperm spurts, arching almost vertical in front of his face. Mark and Mary are suddenly impatient and hot. . . . They push Johnny forward onto the gallows platform covered with moldy jockstraps and sweat shirts. Mark is adjusting the noose.

'Well, here you go.' Mark starts to push Johnny off the platform.

Mary: 'No, let me.' She locks her hands behind Johnny's buttocks, puts her forehead against him, smiling into his eyes she moves back, pulling him off the platform into space. . . . His face swells with blood. . . . Mark reaches up with one lithe movement and snaps Johnny's neck . . . sound like a stick broken in wet towels. A shudder runs down Johnny's body . . . one foot flutters like a trapped bird. . . . Mark has draped himself over a swing and mimics Johnny's twitches, closes his eyes and sticks his tongue out. . . . Johnny's cock springs up and Mary guides it up her cunt, writhing against him in a fluid belly dance, groaning and shrieking with delight . . . sweat pours down her body, hair hangs over her face in wet strands. 'Cut him down, Mark,' she screams. Mark reaches over with a snap knife and cuts the rope, catching Johnny as he falls, easing him onto his back with Mary still impaled and writhing. . . . She bites away Johnny's lips and nose and sucks out his eyes with a pop. . . . She tears off great hunks of cheek. . . . Now she lunches on his prick. . . . Mark walks over to her and she looks up from Johnny's half-eaten genitals, her face covered with blood, eyes phosphorescent. . . . Mark puts his foot on her shoulder and kicks her over on her back. . . . He leaps on her, fucking her insanely . . . they roll from one end of the room to the other, pinwheel end-over-end and leap high in the air like great hooked fish.

'Let me hang you, Mark. . . . Let me hang you. . . . Please, Mark, let me hang you!'

'Sure baby.' He pulls her brutally to her feet and pins her hands behind her.

'No, Mark!! No! No! No,' she screams, shitting and pissing in terror as he drags her to the platform. He leaves her tied on the platform in a pile of old used condoms, while he adjusts the rope across the room . . . and comes back carrying the noose on a silver tray. He jerks her to her feet and tightens the noose. He sticks his cock up her and waltzes around the platform and off into space swinging in a great arc. . . . 'Wheeeeee!' he screams, turning into

Johnny. Her neck snaps. A great fluid wave undulates through her body. Johnny drops to the floor and stands poised and alert like a young animal.

He leaps about the room. With a scream of longing that shatters the glass wall he leaps out into space. Masturbating end-over-end, three thousand feet down, his sperm floating beside him, he screams all the way against the shattering blue of the sky, the rising sun burning over his body like gasoline, down past great oaks and persimmons, swamp cypress and mahogany, to shatter in liquid relief in a ruined square paved with limestone. Weeds and vines grow between the stones, and rusty iron bolts three feet thick penetrate the white stone, stain it shit-brown of rust.

Notes and References

All page references are to editions actually cited. Where a first edition has not been used, and its date is significant, this is given in square brackets unless already given in the main text. Place of publication is London unless otherwise indicated. 'Harmondsworth' denotes a Penguin edition; other paperback imprints are usually named.

Part One

1 What is Literature?

1. Anthony O'Hear, commenting in *The New Review*, II/13 (1975) p. 66, on an earlier and longer version of this chapter ('A Despatch From The Front', *TNR* I/11 (1975) pp. 54–60). For my reply see *TNR* II/14 (1975) pp. 60–1.
2. For example, John R. Searle, at the beginning of his article 'The Logical Status of Fictional Discourse', *New Literary History* VI (1975) pp. 319–32. See Wittgenstein, *Philosophical Investigations*, I. 66–7.
3. Tzvetan Todorov, 'The Notion of Literature', *New Literary History* V (1973) p. 8.
4. See particularly Richard Ohmann, 'Speech Acts and the Definition of Literature', *Philosophy and Rhetoric* IV (1971) pp. 1–19. Austin discriminates between three kinds of acts that one performs as a speaker: the locutionary (which is simply to say what one says), the illocutionary (which is to use the conventions of a given speech community to perform a specific kind of speech act, e.g. to state, to command, to question etc.) and the perlocutionary (which is to produce a specific effect or consequence by speaking). Ohmann shows that literary texts are abnormal on the illocutionary level, that they appear to work without satisfying Austin's criteria of 'illocutionary felicity'. He therefore proposes that 'A literary work is discourse whose sentences lack the illocutionary forces that would normally attach to them. Its illocutionary force is *mimetic* . . . a literary work *purportedly imitates* (or reports) a series of speech acts, which in fact have no other existence. By doing so, it leads the reader to imagine a speaker, a situation, a set of ancillary events, and so on.' However, Ohmann explicitly limits his definition to 'imaginative' literature, excluding history, science, biography, etc. from his discussion, and is obliged to say that Truman Capote's 'non-fiction novel' *In Cold Blood* is

not a work of literature because it meets all Austin's criteria. John Searle, in the article cited above, uses essentially the same terminology to distinguish between fictional and non-fictional discourse, maintaining that it is impossible to distinguish formally between literary and non-literary discourse.

5. Ruqaiya Hasan, 'Rime and Reason in Literature', *Literary Style*, ed. Seymour Chatman (1971) p. 308.
6. Paul L. Garvin (ed.) *A Prague School Reader on Aesthetics, Literary Structure and Style* (Washington, 1964) pp. vii–viii.
7 Jan Mukařovský, 'Standard Language and Poetic Language' in Garvin, *op. cit.*, pp. 20–3.
8. Hasan *op. cit.* pp. 309–10.
9. Roland Barthes, *Mythologies* trans. Annette Lavers (Paladin edn. St Albans, 1973) p. 36.
10. Ian Watt, *The Rise of the Novel* (1957) pp. 86–96.
11. Garvin, *op. cit.* p. 23.
12. *Ibid.* p. 20.
13. *Ibid.* p. 24.
14. Roman Jakobson, 'Closing Satement: Linguistics and Poetics' in *Style in Language* ed. Thomas E. Sebeok (Cambridge, Mass., 1960) pp. 350–77.
15. For example, of the Russian Futurist poets Jakobson said: 'A number of poetic devices found their application in urbanism.' Quoted by Victor Erlich, *Russian Formalism: History Doctrine* (The Hague, 1965) p. 195.
16. Stanley Fish, 'How Ordinary is Ordinary Language?' *New Literary History*, V (1973) pp. 46ff.
17. Todorov, *op. cit.* pp. 15–16.
18. Fish, *op. cit.* p. 52.
19. *Ibid.* p. 49.
20. Fish's argument begins to falter somewhat as he sees precisely this difficulty looming up:

'Everything I have said in this paper commits me to saying that literature is language . . . but it is language around which we have drawn a frame, a frame that indicates a decision to regard with a particular self-consciousness the resources that language has always possessed. (I am aware that this may sound very much like Jakobson's definition of the poetic function as *the set towards the message*; but this set is exclusive and aesthetic—towards the message *for its own sake*—while my set is towards the message for the sake of the human and moral content all messages necessarily convey.' (p. 52)

Literature, here, is identified by a decision to pay particular attention to linguistic form; in order to dissociate this position from Jakobson's (message-minus) position, Fish hastens to say that attention is paid to literary messages for the sake of the kind of content *all* messages necessarily convey. But if all messages are alike in this respect, the only distinguishing characteristic of literary messages must be the attention-worthy form in which the content is expressed: literature as message-plus. Fish cannot in the end find a position outside the message-minus and message-plus definitions he has rejected. It would seem that literature must be *either* one *or* the other.

21. H. G. Widdowson, *Stylistics and the Teaching of Literature* (1975) p. 47.

22. *Ibid.* p. 46.
23. Dell Hymes, 'An Ethnographic Perspective', *New Literary History* V (1973) p. 196.
24. J. M. Cameron, *The Night Battle* (1962) p. 137. I have described Cameron's argument at greater length in *Language of Fiction* (1966) pp. 33–8. Cf. Widdowson, *op. cit.* p. 54: 'Literary discourse is independent of normal interaction, has no links with any preceding discourse and anticipates no subsequent activity either verbal or otherwise. Its interpretation does not depend on its being placed in a context of situation or on our recognition of the role of the sender or of our own role as receiver. It is a self-contained whole, interpretable internally, as it were, as a self-contained unit of communication, and in suspense from the immediate reality of social life.' This incidentally explains why advertisements that use fictional narrative are not axiomatically literary texts—they depend for their interpretation as advertisements on the prior existence of the product and the possibility of purchasing it. There is, however, no reason in principle why advertisements should not acquire the status of literature in the same way as other nonliterary texts, by responding satisfactorily to a literary reading.
25. Northrop Frye, *Anatomy of Criticism* (Princeton, 1957) p. 268.
26. Jonathan Culler, *Structuralist Poetics* (1975) p. 128.
27. Jean-Paul Sartre, *What is Literature?* trans. Bernard Frechtman (New York, 1965) p. 37.

2   George Orwell's 'A Hanging' and 'Michael Lake Describes . . .'

1. Peter Stansky and William Abrahams, *The Unknown Orwell* (1972) p. 224.
2. *Ibid.* pp. 163–4.
3. George Orwell, *The Road To Wigan Pier* (Harmondsworth, 1962) p. 128.
4. Stansky and Abrahams, *op. cit.* p. 205.
5. For a perceptive discussion of this point, see 'The Language Field of Nazism', *Times Literary Supplement*, 5 April 1974, pp. 353–4.
6. Victor Shklovsky, 'Art as Technique', quoted by Robert Scholes, *Structuralism in Literature* (1974) pp. 83–4. Scholes follows the translation of Lee T. Lemon and Marion J. Reis, *Russian Formalist Criticism* (Lincoln, Nebraska, 1965), but emends the final sentences (italicized) for reasons explained in a note.
7. Victor Shklovsky, 'Tristram Shandy: Stylistic Commentary', Lemon and Reis, *op. cit.* p. 57.
8. 'Coming Apart' by James Griffin & Robb Royes of 'Bread'.
9. Ludwig Wittgenstein, *Tractatus Logico-Philosophicus* (1922) 6.4311.

3   Oscar Wilde: 'The Ballad of Reading Gaol'

1. Quotations from 'The Ballad of Reading Gaol' are from Oscar Wilde, *De Profundis and Other Writings* (Harmondsworth, 1973) pp. 231–52.
2. Northrop Frye, *Anatomy of Criticism* p. 195.

3. George Orwell, 'Politics and the English Language' *Collected Essays, Journalism and Letters* (Harmondsworth, 1970) vol. 4, p. 168.

4 What is Realism?

1. See Roman Jakobson, 'On Realism in Art' in *Readings in Russian Poetics* ed. L. Matejka and K. Pormorska (Cambridge, Mass., 1971) pp. 38 ff, for a brilliant demonstration of the relativity of the concept. In his later writings, however, Jakobson's own use of the term implies that it has some kind of stable meaning.
2. *Sunday Times*, 30 June 1974.
3. Quoted in *The Age of Realism*, ed. F. W. Hemmings (Harmondsworth, 1974) p. 166.
4. Hayden White, *Metahistory: the Historical Imagination in Nineteenth Century Europe* (1973) p. 3n.
5. *Ibid.* p. 274.
6. *Ibid.* p. 275.
7. See Tom Wolfe, *The New Journalism; with an anthology edited by Tom Wolfe and E. W. Johnson* (New York, 1973); and my review-article 'The New Journalism?', *The New Review* II/4 (1975) pp. 67–71.

5 Arnold Bennett: 'The Old Wives' Tale'

1. All quotations from *The Old Wives' Tale* [1908] are from the Pan edition (1964).
2. Henry James, 'The New Novel' in *The Future of the Novel* ed. Leon Edel (Vintage edn. New York, 1956) p. 270.
3. Roland Barthes, *Writing Degree Zero*, trans. Annette Lavers and Colin Smith (1967) p. 39.

6 William Burroughs: 'The Naked Lunch'

1. William Burroughs, *The Naked Lunch* (1965) p. 7.
2. David Lodge, 'Objections to William Burroughs', *The Novelist at the Crossroads* (1971) p. 165.

7 The Realistic Tradition

1. Hegel's phrase, applied by Lionel Trilling to Jane Austen's fiction in 'Jane Austen and Mansfield Park', *Pelican Guide to English Literature* 5 (Harmondsworth, 1957) p. 128.
2. Gustave Flaubert, *Madame Bovary*, trans. Alan Russell (Harmondsworth, 1950) p. 140.
3. Roland Barthes, 'To Write: an Intransitive Verb?', in *The Structuralist Controversy* ed. R. Macksey and E. Donato (Baltimore, 1972) p. 140.

8 Two Kinds of Modern Fiction

1. Henry James, 'The New Novel' in *The Future of the Novel* p. 271.
2. *Ibid.* p. 273.
3. *Ibid.* pp. 263–4.
4. 'The New Novel' was originally published in two articles entitled 'The Younger Generation' in the *Times Literary Supplement* for 14 March and 2 April 1914.
5. *Ibid.* p. 260.
6. See C. K. Stead, *The New Poetic* (1964) and Cyril Connolly, *Enemies of Promise* (1938).
7. Quoted by Richard Ellmann in *James Joyce* (1959) pp. 360–1.
8. Letter to Hugh Walpole, *The Letters of Henry James*, ed. Percy Lubbock (1922) vol. II p. 246.
9. Virginia Woolf, 'Modern Fiction', *Collected Essays* (1966) vol. II p. 105.
10. Henry James, 'The New Novel' *op. cit.* p. 267.
11. Virginia Woolf, *op. cit* p. 108.
12. See E. M. Forster, *Aspects of the Novel* (1927) Chap. 8; Stuart Gilbert, *James Joyce's 'Ulysses'* (rev. edn., 1957) Part I, chap. 2; and Joseph Frank, 'Spatial Form in Modern Literature', *Sewanee Review*, 1945.
13. Rubin Rabinowitz, *The Reaction Against Experiment in the English Novel, 1950–1960* (1968).
14. Quoted by John Lehmann, *New Writing in Europe* (Harmondsworth, 1940) p. 27.
15. Quoted by George Orwell in 'Inside the Whale', *Collected Essays, Journalism and Letters* (Harmondsworth, 1970) vol. I p. 560.
16. Christopher Isherwood, *Lions and Shadows* (Signet edn., 1968) pp. 159–60.
17. George Orwell, 'Inside the Whale', *op. cit.* I p. 557.
18. John Lehmann, *op. cit.* p. 134.
19. Graham Greene, *Collected Essays* (1969) pp. 115–16.
20. See Greene, *Collected Essays* pp. 23–74.
21. Virginia Woolf, 'Mr Bennett and Mrs Brown' in *Criticism* ed. M. Schorer, J. Miles and G. McKenzie (rev. edn., New York 1958) p. 69.
22. Gordon Haight, *George Eliot* (Oxford, 1968) p. 464
23. See my introduction to George Eliot, *Scenes of Clerical Life* (Harmondsworth, 1973) p. 8.
24. C. P. Snow, *Sunday Times*, 27 December 1953; quoted by Rabinowitz *op. cit.* p. 98.
25. B. S. Johnson, *Aren't You Rather Young To Be Writing Your Memoirs?* (1973) p. 14.
26. Virginia Woolf, 'Mr Bennett and Mrs Brown' *op. cit.* p. 72.
27. Northrop Frye, *Anatomy of Criticism* pp. 26–7.

9 Criticism and Realism

1. Clara Reeve, *The Progress of Romance* (1875) vol. I, Evening vii. Cited in Miriam Allott, *Novelists on the Novel* (1959) p. 47.
2. David Lodge (ed). *Jane Austen's 'Emma': a Casebook* (1968) p. 35.

3. John Bayley, 'Against a New Formalism', *The Word in the Desert (Critical Quarterly* 10th Anniversary No.) ed. C. B. Cox and A. E. Dyson (1968) pp. 66–7.

4. Calvin Bedient, '*Middlemarch*; Touching Down', *Hudson Review* xxii (1969) p. 84.

5. Bedient *op. cit.* p. 71.

6. Mark Schorer, 'Fiction and the Analogical Matrix', *Kenyon Review* 1949. Reprinted in *Critiques and Essays on Modern Fiction 1920–1951* ed. J. W. Aldridge (New York, 1952) p. 91.

7. Malcolm Bradbury, 'Towards a Poetics of Fiction (1) An Approach Through Structure', *Novel* I (1967) p. 50. Mark Schorer's article 'The Humiliation of Emma Woodhouse' is alluded to.

8. Schorer, 'Fiction and the Analogical Matrix' *op. cit.* p. 83.

9. See my 'Crosscurrents in Modern English Criticism' in *The Novelist at the Crossroads* (1971).

10. Schorer, 'Technique as Discovery', *Hudson Review* (1948). Reprinted in David Lodge, ed., *Twentieth Century Literary Criticism* (1972) p. 387.

11. *Ibid.* p. 391.

12. Bayley, *op. cit.* p. 60.

13. *Ibid.*

14. *Ibid.* p. 63.

15. I discuss Kermode's book at greater length in *The Novelist at the Crossroads* pp. 42–5.

10   The Novel and the Nouvelle Critique

1. John Sturrock, 'Roland Barthes—A Profile', *The New Review* I/2 (1974) p. 16.

2. Jean-Paul Sartre, *What is Literature?* Trans. Bernard Frechtman (New York, 1965) pp. 14 and 20.

3. Roland Barthes, *Writing Degree Zero*, trans. Annette Lavers and Colin Smith (1967) p. 66.

4. *Ibid.* p. 69.

5. *Ibid.* p. 72.

6. *Ibid.* p. 84.

7. Roland Barthes, 'To Write: An Intransitive Verb?', *The Structuralist Controversy* ed. R. Macksey and E. Donato (Baltimore, 1972) p. 135.

8. *Ibid.* p. 138.

9. *Ibid.* p. 144.

10. George Orwell, 'Inside the Whale', *op. cit.* p. 557.

11. Barthes, 'To Write: An Intransitive Verb?' p. 141.

12. Eugenio Donato, 'Of Structuralism and Literature', *Modern Language Notes*, LXXXII (1967) p. 571.

13. See G. D. Martin's 'Structures in Space; an account of the *Tel Quel*'s Attitude to Meaning', *New Blackfriars* LII (1971) pp. 541–52 and Chapter 10, ' "Beyond Structuralism": *Tel Quel*', of Jonathan Culler's *Structuralist Poetics* (1974) for an informed discussion of this school.

14. See Ian Watt's *The Rise of the Novel* (1957) for the classic exposition of this view.

15. Peter Caws, 'What is Structuralism?' *Partisan Review* XXXV (1968) p. 82.

16. *Ibid.* p. 85.

17. Roland Barthes, *Critique et Verité* (1966) quoted by Gabriel Josipovici, *The World and the Book* (1971) p. 271.

18. Roland Barthes, 'Criticism as Language', *The Critical Moment* (1964), reprinted in David Lodge. ed. *Twentieth Century Literary Criticism* (1972) pp. 650–1.

19. Eugenio Donato, 'The Two Languages of Criticism', *The Structuralist Controversy* pp. 95–6.

20. Edward W. Said, 'Abcedarium Culturae: Structuralism, Absence, Writing', *Tri-Quarterly* XIX/XXI (1970–71) p. 41.

21. Roland Barthes, 'Style and its Image', *Literary Style* ed. Seymour Chatman (1971) p. 10.

22. *Ibid.* p. 11.

23. Vladimir Propp, *Morphology of the Folktale* (Bloomington, Indiana, 1958). See also his 'Fairy Tale Transformations' in *Readings in Russian Poetics*, ed. L. Matejka and K. Pormorska (Cambridge, Mass., 1971).

24. Tzvetan Todorov, 'The Structural Analysis of Narrative', *Novel*, III (1969) p. 70.

25. Claude Lévi-Strauss, *Structural Anthropology* (New York, 1963) p. 130. Quoted by Neville Dyson-Hudson in *The Structuralist Controversy* p. 232.

26. Claude Lévi-Strauss, *Tristes Tropiques* (New York, 1961) Quoted by Eugenio Donato, *The Structuralist Controversy* p. 90.

27. Philip Young, *Ernest Hemingway: A Reconsideration* (rev. edn., 1966) pp. 1–21.

28. Gabriel Josipovici, *The World and the Book* (1971) p. 309.

29. *Ibid.* p. 133.

30. *Ibid.* p. 139.

31. *Ibid.* p. 307.

32. David Lodge, 'Onions and Apricots; or, Was the Rise of the Novel a Fall From Grace? Serious Reflections on Gabriel Josipovici's *The World and the Book*', *Critical Quarterly* XIV (1972) pp. 171–85.

33. Josipovici, *op. cit.* pp. 260–1.

34. Roland Barthes, *S/Z*, trans. Richard Miller (1975) pp. 5–6.

35. *Ibid.* p. 30.

36. *Ibid.* p. 4.

37. *Ibid.* p. 137.

38. *Ibid.* p. 153.

39. Roland Barthes, 'Style and its Image', *Literary Style* p. 5.

40. Barthes, *S/Z* p. 120.

41. *Ibid.* pp. 54–5.

42. *Ibid.* pp. 80–1.

11 Conclusion to Part One

1. Oscar Wilde, 'The Decay of Lying', *De Profundis and Other Writings* p. 74.

2. *Ibid.* p. 78.

Part Two

1 Jakobson's Theory

1. Victor Erlich, *Russian Formalism* p. 231.
2. Roman Jakobson and Morris Halle, *Fundamentals of Language* (The Hague, 1956) p. 78n.
3. René Wellek and Austin Warren, *Theory of Literature* (Harmondsworth, 1963) p. 195.
4. Roman Jakobson, 'Closing Statement: Linguistics and Poetics', *Style in Language*, ed. Thomas A. Sebeok (Cambridge, Mass., 1960) pp. 350–77.
5. Roman Jakobson, 'Two Aspects of Language and Two Types of Linguistic Disturbances', in Jakobson and Halle, *Fundamentals of Language* p. 58.
6. Roland Barthes, *Elements of Semiology*, trans. Annette Lavers and Colin Smith (1967) p. 63.
7. Stephen Ullmann, *Style in the French Novel* (Cambridge, 1957) p. 214.
8. Richard A. Lanham, *A Handlist of Rhetorical Terms* (Berkeley, 1969) pp. 67 and 97.
9. Jakobson, 'Two Aspects of Language' p. 60.
10. *Ibid.* p. 61.

2 Two Types of Aphasia

1. Jakobson, 'Two Aspects of Language' p. 63.
2. *Ibid.* p. 64.
3. *Ibid.* p. 69.
4. *Ibid.* p. 72.

3 The Metaphoric and Metonymic Poles

1. Jakobson, *op. cit.* p. 76.
2. *Ibid.* p. 78.

4 Drama and Film

1. Stephen Booth, 'On the Value of Hamlet', *Reinterpretations of Elizabethan Drama* (New York, 1969) pp. 137–76.
2. Marshall McLuhan describes some of the relevant research in *The Gutenberg Galaxy* (1962) pp. 36ff.
3. John Harrington, *The Rhetoric of Film* (New York, 1973) p. 138.
4. Sergei Eisenstein, *The Film Sense* (1938); reprinted in *The Modern Tradition: Backgrounds of Modern Literature*, ed. R. Ellmann and C. Feidelson Jnr. (New York, 1965) pp. 163–4.
5. *Ibid.* p. 165.
6. Harrington, *op. cit.* p. 139.
7. Roy Armes, *Film and Reality* (Harmondsworth, 1974) p. 51.

8. George Eliot, *Scenes of Clerical Life*, (Harmondsworth, 1973) p. 53.
9. See chapter 17 of *Adam Bede*.

5   Poetry, Prose and the Poetic

1. Jonathan Culler, *Structuralist Poetics* (1975) p. 161.
2. W. K. Wimsatt, 'One Relation of Rhyme to Reason', *The Verbal Icon* [1954] (1970) pp. 152–66.
3. Roland Barthes, *Elements of Semiology* p. 87.
4. W. B. Yeats, 'Adam's Curse'.
5. Roman Jakobson, 'Closing Statement: Linguistics and Poetics' *op. cit.* p. 358.
6. *Ibid.* pp. 350 and 356.
7. *Ibid.*
8. *Ibid.* p. 358.
9. *Ibid.* pp. 374–5.
10. Jakobson, 'Two Types of Language' pp. 81–2.

6   Types of Description

1. *The Columbia-Viking Desk Encyclopaedia* (New York, 1964).
2. 'The University of Birmingham', *The Guardian* 9 October 1967, p. 4.
3. E. M. Forster, *A Passage to India* [1924] (Harmondsworth, 1959) p. 9.
4. Jakobson, 'Linguistics and Poetics' p. 356.
5. Charles Dickens, *Bleak House* [1852–3] (1892) p. 1.
6. *Ibid.* p. 7.
7. Philip Collins, ed., *Charles Dickens: the Critical Heritage* (1971) p. 273.
8. *Ibid.* p. 272.
9. Charles Dickens, *Oliver Twist* [1837–9] (Harmondsworth, 1966) p. 442.
10. *Ibid.*
11. *Ibid.* p. 443.
12. Quoted by John Carey, *The Violent Effigy: a study of Dickens's Imagination* (1973) p. 130.

8   The Metonymic Text as Metaphor

1. Guy Rosolato, 'The Voice and the Literary Myth', *The Structuralist Controversy* ed. Macksey and Donato p. 202.
2. Ian Gregor, 'Criticism as an Individual Activity: the Approach through Reading', *Contemporary Criticism*, ed. Malcolm Bradbury and David Palmer (1970) p. 195.
3. Arnold Kettle, 'Emma', in *An Introduction to the English Novel* (1951); reprinted in David Lodge, ed. *Jane Austen's 'Emma': a Casebook* (1968) p. 89.

9   Metaphor and Context

1. Richard A. Lanham, *A Handlist of Rhetorical Terms* p. 66.
2. Northrop Frye, *Anatomy of Criticism* p. 136.
3. Aristotle, *Rhetoric* III, 1410b. Quoted by Lanham, *op. cit.* p. 66.
4. Winifred Nowottny, *The Language Poets Use* (1962) p. 68.

5. Graham Greene, *In Search of a Character* [1961] (Harmondsworth, 1968) p. 18.
6. Virginia Woolf, *The Waves* [1931] (Harmondsworth, 1964) p. 94.
7. Gerard Genette, 'Metonymie Chez Proust', *Figures III* (Paris, 1972) p. 53.
8. *Ibid.* pp. 42–3.
9. *Ibid.* p. 45.
10. T. S. Eliot, 'The Love Song of J. Alfred Prufrock'.
11. *Poetry* (Chicago), XXIX (1926). Reprinted in *The Modern Tradition* ed. Ellmann and Feidelson pp. 158–62.
12. Thomas Gray, 'Sonnet on the Death of Mr Richard West', quoted by Wordsworth in Preface to *Lyrical Ballads*.
13. William Wordsworth, Preface to *Lyrical Ballads. The Lyrical Ballads 1798–1805*, ed. George Sampson (1959) p. 8.
14. *Ibid.*
15. William Wordsworth, 'Lines written at a small distance from my house, and sent by my little boy to the person to whom they are addressed.' *The Lyrical Ballads* p. 84.
16. Christopher Ricks, 'Wordsworth: "A Pure Organic Pleasure from the Lines"', *William Wordsworth; a Critical Anthology*, ed. Graham McMaster (Harmondsworth, 1972) p. 513.
17. Samuel Taylor Coleridge, *Biographia Literaria*, chap. 22.
18. Wordsworth, Preface to *Poems* (1815).
19. Lewis Carroll, *Alice Through The Looking-Glass* (1872), Chap. 8.

Part Three

1 **James Joyce**

1. Barthes, *S/Z* p. 156.
2. *Ibid.* p. 140.
3. *Ibid.* p. 200.
4. James Joyce, *Dubliners* [1914] (Harmondsworth, 1966) p. 7.
5. *Ibid.* p. 9.
6. Richard Ellmann, *James Joyce* (1959) p. 169.
7. Joyce, *Dubliners* pp. 7–9.
8. *Ibid.* p. 13.
9. *Ibid.* p. 10.
10. *Ibid.* p. 11.
11. *Ibid.* p. 15.
12. *Ibid.*
13. *Ibid.*
14. James Joyce, *A Portrait of the Artist as a Young Man* [1916] (Viking Critical edn., New York, 1968) p. 27.
15. *Ibid.* p. 7.
16. *Ibid.* p. 171.
17. *Ibid.* p. 228.
18. Ellmann, *op. cit.* p. 729.
19. Ian Watt, *The Rise of the Novel* (Harmondsworth, 1963) p. 13.
20. Ellmann, *op. cit.* p. 729.

21. Anthony Burgess (ed.) *A Shorter Finnegans Wake* (1966) pp. 7–8.

22. James Joyce, *Finnegans Wake* [1939] (Viking edn., New York, 1962) pp. 213–14.

23. See Edmund Wilson, *Axel's Castle* [1931] (Fontana edn., 1961) p. 188 and A. Walton Litz. *The Art of James Joyce* (1961) p. 113.

24. Hayden White, *Metahistory* p. 372.

25. Joyce, *Finnegans Wake* p. 3. I am heavily indebted to Anthony Burgess's Introduction to *A Shorter Finnegans Wake* pp. 22–3, and vicariously to the several scholars he draws on, for the parenthetical glosses.

26. T. S. Eliot, '*Ulysses*, Order and Myth', *The Dial* November 1923, Reprinted in *Criticism*, ed. Schorer, Miles & McKenzie (New York, 1958) p. 270.

27. *Ibid.*

28. Virginia Woolf, 'Modern Fiction', *Collected Essays* II, p. 106.

29. T. S. Eliot, 'The Metaphysical Poets', *Selected Essays* (1961) p. 289.

30. E. H. Gombrich, *The Story of Art* (1952) p. 406.

31. Eliot, '*Ulysses*, Order and Myth' pp. 270–1.

32. *Ibid.* p. 270.

33. Walton A. Litz, *The Art of James Joyce* (1961).

34. Stuart Gilbert, *James Joyce's 'Ulysses'* (1930; rev. 1952).

35. Lawrence Sterne, *Tristram Shandy*, Book I, chap. 4.

36. Virginia Woolf, 'Modern Fiction' p. 107.

37. James Joyce, *Ulysses* [1922] (Bodley Head edn., 1954) p. 34.

38. *Ibid.* pp. 34–5.

39. I am indebted to Stuart Gilbert, *op. cit.* (Harmondsworth, 1963) for this gloss.

40. *Ulysses* p. 52.

41. See p. 75 above and note.

42. *Ulysses*, p. 57.

43. *Ibid.* p. 704.

44. *Ibid.* p. 701.

45. Stuart Gilbert, *op. cit.* p. 341.

46. *Ulysses* p. 698.

47. *Ibid.* p. 699.

2   Gertrude Stein

1. Gertrude Stein, *Look at Me Now and Here I am: Writings and Lectures, 1911–45*, ed. Patricia Meyerowitz (Harmondsworth, 1971) p. 21.

2. John Passmore, *A Hundred Years of Philosophy* (Harmondsworth, 1968) p. 105.

3. Gertrude Stein, *Look At Me Now* p. 110.

4. Gertrude Stein, *The Making of Americans* (Harcourt Brace edn. [1934] reprinted 1966) p. 37.

5. *Ibid.* p. 122.

6. *Ibid.* p. 123.

7. *Ibid.* p. 124.

8. *Ibid.* p. 207.

9. *Ibid.* p. 232.

10. *Look At Me Now* p. 102.

11. *Ibid.* p. 25.
12. See Stephen Ullmann, *Style in the French Novel* (Cambridge, 1957) chap. III.
13. See Seymour Chatman, *The Late Style of Henry James* (New York, 1972) and my review in *Novel* VII (1974) pp. 187–9.
14. Roman Jakobson, 'Two Types of Language etc.' pp. 64–5.
15. *Look At Me Now* pp. 124ff.
16. *The Making of Americans* p. 355.
17. *Look At Me Now* p. 109.
18. *Ibid.* pp. 108–9.
19. *Ibid.* p. 105.
20. *The Making of Americans* p. 218.
21. *Look At Me Now* pp. 105–6.
22. *Ibid.* p. 96.
23. *Ibid.* p. 213.
24. *Ibid.* p. 113.
25. *Ibid.*
26. *Ibid.* p. 130.
27. *Ibid.* p. 137.
28. *Ibid.* pp. 161, 163, 170, 171 and 187.
29. *Ibid.* p. 115.
30. *Ibid.* p. 142.
31. *Ibid.* p. 138.
32. Jakobson, *op. cit.* pp. 71–2.
33. Ortega y Gasset, *The Dehumanization of Art and Other Writings on Art and Culture* (New York, 1956) p. 22.
34. Allegra Stewart, *Gertrude Stein and the Present* (Cambridge, Mass., 1967).
35. *The Modern Tradition: backgrounds of modern literature*, ed. R. Ellmann and C. Feidelson Jr. (New York, 1965) pp. 111–12.
36. Ezra Pound, 'A Retrospect', *Twentieth Century Literary Criticism* ed. David Lodge (1972) p. 59.
37. See T. S. Eliot's essays 'Hamlet' and 'Tradition and the Individual Talent' in *Selected Essays*.
38. See Joseph Frank's classic study, 'Spatial Form in Modern Literature' first published in the *Sewannee Review* in 1945.

3 Ernest Hemingway

1. Ernest Hemingway, *A Moveable Feast* (Harmondsworth, 1966) p. 20.
2. Hemingway, *Green Hills of Africa* [1935] (Harmondsworth, 1966) p. 26.
3. Hemingway, *Death in the Afternoon* [1932] (Harmondsworth, 1966) p. 6.
4. Hemingway, *A Farewell to Arms* [1929] (Harmondsworth, 1968) p. 144.
5. Hemingway, *Men Without Women* [1928] (Harmondsworth, 1972) pp. 51–4.
6. *Green Hills of Africa* p. 26.
7. Quoted by Charles A. Fenton, *The Apprenticeship of Ernest Hemingway: the early years* [1954] (New York, 1961) p. 35.
8. *Men Without Women* p. 44.

4   D. H. Lawrence

1. See D. H. Lawrence, *Studies in Classic American Literature* (1924) and Ernest Hemingway, *Green Hills of Africa* pp. 24–5.
2. Lawrence, *Lady Chatterley's Lover*, chap. 9.
3. Lawrence, 'Why the Novel Matters', *Selected Literary Criticism*, ed. Anthony Beal (Mercury edn., 1961) p. 105.
4. Lawrence, *Women in Love* [1921] (Harmondsworth, 1960) p. 126.
5. *Ibid.* p. 123.
6. *Ibid.* p. 209.
7. *Lady Chatterley's Lover* was originally published in Florence in 1928. The first version of the novel was published as *The First Lady Chatterley* in New York in 1944 and the second version, entitled *John Thomas and Lady Jane* was published in London by Heinemann in 1971.
8. Harry T. Moore, *The Intelligent Heart: the Story of D. H. Lawrence* [1955] (rev. edn. Harmondsworth, 1960) pp. 238–9.
9. Barbara Lucas, 'Apropos of *England, My England*', *The Twentieth Century*, March 1961, pp. 288–93.
10. This would correspond to Egbert's weekend leave as described in *England, My England* (Harmondsworth, 1973) p. 35.
11. This passage is deleted (without any indication to that effect) from the relevant letter in D. H. Lawrence, *Collected Letters* ed. Harry T. Moore (1962), vol. 1, pp. 465–9, though Moore quotes part of it in *The Intelligent Heart*, pp. 284–5. It is reproduced here by permission of Yale University, which owns the manuscript. The letter will be printed in full in the complete edition of Lawrence's letters to be published by Cambridge University Press, under the general editorship of James T. Boulton.
12. Emile Delavenay, *D. H. Lawrence: the Man and His Work. The Formative Years: 1885–1919*, trans. Katharine M. Delavenay (1972) pp. 431–4.
13. Letter to Lady Cynthia Asquith, *Collected Letters* ed. Moore, I, p. 364.
14. Lawrence, *England, My England* (Harmondsworth, 1973) p. 7.
15. *Ibid.* pp. 7–8.
16. *The English Review*, October 1915, pp. 238–9.
17. *England, My England* p. 8.
18. *Ibid.* p. 10.
19. *The English Review*, October 1915, p. 239.
20. *England, My England* pp. 10–11.
21. *Ibid.* pp. 12–13.
22. *Ibid.* p. 13.
23. *Ibid.* p. 14.
24. *Ibid.* p. 15.
25. *Ibid.* pp. 15–16.
26. *Ibid.* p. 17.
27. *Ibid.* p. 18.
28. *Ibid.*
29. *Ibid.* pp. 19–20.
30. *Ibid.* p. 19.
31. *Ibid.* p. 20.
32. *Ibid.* pp. 20–1.
33. *Ibid.* p. 31.

34. *Ibid.* pp. 29–30.
35. *Ibid.* p. 7.
36. Graham Hough, *The Dark Sun* [1956] (Harmondsworth, 1961) p. 202.
37. *England, My England* p. 11.
38. *Ibid.* p. 30.
39. Frank Kermode, *Lawrence* (1973) p. 53.
40. Lawrence, *Phoenix II* ed. Warren Roberts and Harry T. Moore (1968) p. 407.
41. *Ibid.* p. 408.
42. *Ibid.*
43. *Ibid.* p. 402.
44. *The English Review*, October 1915, p. 243.
45. *England, My England* p. 32.
46. *Ibid.* p. 33.
47. *Ibid.*
48. W. E. Henley, *For England's Sake* iii, 'Pro Rege Nostro'.
49. Stephen Spender, 'D. H. Lawrence, England and the War' in *D. H. Lawrence, Novelist, Poet, Prophet* ed. Stephen Spender (1973) p. 76.
50. *England, My England* p. 16.
51. *Phoenix II* p. 400.
52. *England, My England* p. 36.
53. *Ibid.* p. 36.
54. *Ibid.* p. 37.
55. *Ibid.*
56. *Ibid.*
57. *Revelation* chap. VI.
58. *England, My England* p. 40.
59. *Ibid.* p. 38.
60. *Ibid.* p. 39.
61. *Phoenix* II p. 383.

5 Virginia Woolf

1. Virginia Woolf, *To The Lighthouse* (1960) p. 225.
2. *Ibid.* pp. 162–3.
3. Richard Ellmann, *James Joyce* p. 87.
4. *To The Lighthouse* p. 249.
5. *Ibid.* pp. 248–9.
6. *The Waves* (Harmondsworth, 1964) p. 248.
7. *The Voyage Out* (Harmondsworth, 1970) p. 123.
8. *Ibid.* p. 301.
9. *Ibid.* p. 215.
10. Quentin Bell, *Virginia Woolf, A Biography; volume II, Mrs Woolf 1912–1941* (1972) p. 72.
11. Virginia Woolf, *A Haunted House and Other Stories* (1943) p. 12.
12. *Jacob's Room* (Harmondsworth, 1965) p. 148.
13. *Ibid.* p. 69.
14. *Ibid.* p. 46.
15. *Ibid.* p. 167.
16. *Ibid.* p. 168.

17. Quentin Bell *op. cit.* p. 106.
18. *Ibid.* p. 107.
19. *Ibid.*
20. Carl Woodring, *Virginia Woolf* (New York, 1966) p. 19.
21. *Mrs Dalloway* (1960) p. 5.
22. *To the Lighthouse* p. 76.
23. *Mrs Dalloway* p. 6.
24. *Ibid.* p. 11.
25. *Ibid.*
26. *Ibid.* p. 33.
27. *Ibid.* p. 35.
28. *Ibid.* p. 36.
29. *Ibid.* pp. 55–6.
30. *Ibid.* pp. 202–3.
31. *Ibid.* p. 201.
32. *Ibid.* p. 203.
33. *Ibid.*
34. *Ibid.* p. 204.
35. Virginia Woolf's Introduction to the Modern Library edn. of *Mrs Dalloway* (New York, 1928), quoted by Jeremy Hawthorn, *Virginia Woolf's Mrs Dalloway* (1975) p. 29.

6   In the Thirties

1. Graham Greene, *The Confidential Agent* (Harmondsworth, 1963) pp. 47–8.
2. *Ibid.* p. 51.
3. George Orwell, *Keep The Aspidistra Flying* (Harmondsworth, 1962).
4. George Orwell, *Coming Up For Air* [1939] (Harmondsworth, 1967) p. 224.
5. Stephen Spender, *The New Realism* (1939) p. 8.
6. Samuel Hynes, *The Auden Generation: Literature and Politics in England in the 1930s* (1976) p. 211.
7. 'Full Moon at Tierz: Before the Storming of Huesca', in *Poetry of the Thirties* ed. Robin Skelton (Harmondsworth, 1964) p. 137.
8. *Coming Up For Air* p. 33.
9. *Ibid.* p. 65.
10. *Ibid.* p. 73.
11. *Ibid.* p. 74.
12. *Ibid.* p. 79.
13. *Ibid.* p. 105.
14. *Ibid.* p. 222.
15. *Ibid.* p. 74.
16. Quoted in Hynes, *op. cit.* p. 271.
17. Christopher Isherwood, *Goodbye to Berlin* [1939] (Harmondsworth, 1965) p. 7.
18. Christopher Isherwood, *Lions and Shadows: An Education In The Twenties* (Signet edn., 1968) pp. 52–3.
19. *Goodbye to Berlin* p. 27.
20. Graham Greene, *The Confidential Agent* p. 111.
21. *Ibid.* p. 142.

22. *Ibid.* pp. 152–3.
23. Richard Hoggart, 'The Force of Caricature' [1953], *Speaking to Each Other* (1970) II p. 49.
24. *Ibid.*
25. *Poetry of the Thirties* pp. 133–6.
26. George Orwell, 'Inside the Whale' [1940], *Collected Essays, Journalism and Letters,* ed. Sonia Orwell and Ian Angus (Harmondsworth, 1970) I, p. 566.
27. Bernard Bergonzi, 'Auden and the Audenesque', *Encounter* XLIV (February 1975) pp. 65–75.
28. *Poetry of the Thirties* pp. 142–3.
29. 'Autumn Journal', *Poetry of the Thirties* pp. 160–1.
30. Rex Warner, 'Hymn', *Poetry of the Thirties* p. 59.
31. 'Musée des Beaux Arts', *W. H. Auden: a selection by the author* (Harmondsworth, 1962) p. 61.
32. *Ibid.*
33. Bergonzi, *op. cit.* p. 70.
34. Hynes, *op. cit.* p. 152.
35. Edward Upward, *The Railway Accident and Other Stories* (Harmondsworth, 1972) p. 83.
36. Graham Greene, *Journey Without Maps* [1936] (Pan edn., 1948) p. 228.
37. Graham Greene, *Brighton Rock* [1938] (Harmondsworth, 1951) p. 128.
38. Graham Greene, *The Power and the Glory* [1940] (Compass Books, New York, 1958) p. 108.
39. Isherwood, *Goodbye to Berlin* p. 7.
40. *Ibid.* p. 8.
41. Graham Greene, *England Made Me* [1935] (Harmondsworth, 1945) p. 9.
42. Graham Greene, *Brighton Rock* (1947) p. 117.
43. Greene, *Brighton Rock* (Harmondsworth, 1951) p. 23.
44. Greene, *The Power and The Glory.* Quoted by Richard Hoggart *op. cit.* p. 48.
45. *Ibid.*
46. *Ibid.*
47. *Ibid.* pp. 47–8.
48. Collected in *The Railway Accident and Other Stories.*
49. See W. H. Sellers' Introduction to *The Railway Accident and Other Stories* pp. 11–12.
50. Isherwood, *Lions and Shadows* p. 12.
51. *Ibid.* p. 43.
52. Isherwood, Foreword to 'The Railway Accident' in *The Railway Accident and Other Stories* pp. 33–4.
53. *Lions and Shadows* p. 43.
54. André Breton, 'What is Surrealism' *The Modern Tradition* ed. R. Ellmann and C. Feidelson Jr. (New York, 1965) p. 606.
55. A. L. Lloyd in *Left Review.* Quoted by Julian Symons, *The Thirties: A Dream Revolved* (1960) p. 94.
56. Breton, *op. cit.* p. 602.
57. I am indebted to William Gaunt for this idea. See his note on 'Time Transfixed' in *Painters of Fantasy* (1974).
58. *The Railway Accident* p. 39.
59. *Ibid.*

60. *Ibid.* p. 40.
61. *Ibid.* p. 61.
62. *Ibid.* p. 13.
63. *Lions and Shadows* pp. 168–9.
64. See Hynes, *op. cit.* pp. 14–15.
65. Quoted in Hynes, *op. cit.* p. 207.
66. 'Journey to the Border' in *The Railway Accident and Other Stories,* p. 125.
67. *Ibid.* p. 151.
68. *Ibid.* pp. 141–2.
69. *Ibid.* p. 171.
70. *Ibid.* p. 138.
71. *Ibid.* p. 193.
72. *Ibid.* p. 195.
73. *Ibid.* p. 197.
74. *Ibid.* p. 204.
75. *Ibid.* p. 200.
76. *Ibid.* p. 220.
77. 'Inside the Whale', *Collected Essays, Journalism and Letters* I, p. 572.
78. Northrop Frye, *T. S. Eliot* (1963); David Lodge, *Evelyn Waugh* (1971).
79. See Evelyn Waugh, 'Ronald Firbank', *Life and Letters* March 1929 (pp. 191–6).
80. Brian Wicker has commented perceptively on this aspect of *A Handful of Dust* in *The Story-Shaped World* (1975) pp. 160–1.
81. Christopher Sykes (*Evelyn Waugh: a biography* (1975) p. 63) records a fascinating passage from Waugh's diaries about the composition of one of his first stories (never reprinted) called 'The Balance': 'I am making the first Chapter a Cinema film and have been working furiously ever since.'

7 Philip Larkin

1. 'The Modern, The Contemporary and The Importance of Being Amis', *Language of Fiction* (1966) pp. 243–67.
2. Quoted in David Timms, *Philip Larkin* (Edinburgh, 1973) p. 60.
3. *Ibid.* p. 109.
4. *Ibid.* p. 21.
5. *Ibid.* p. 62.
6. *The Whitsun Weddings* [1964] (Faber paperback edn., 1971) p. 28.
7. Timms, *op. cit.* p. 112.
8. 'Coming' in *The Less Deceived* [1955] (1973 edn.) p. 17.
9. Quoted in Timms, *op. cit.* p. 61.
10. 'I Remember, I Remember' in *The Less Deceived* p. 38.
11. 'Mr Bleaney' in *The Whitson Weddings* p. 10.
12. 'High Windows' in *High Windows* (1974) p. 17.
13. Wordsworth, Preface to *Lyrical Ballads. The Lyrical Ballads 1798–1805* ed. George Samson (1959) p. 8.
14. 'The Large Cool Store' in *The Whitsun Weddings* p. 30.
15. 'The Building' in *High Windows* pp. 25–6.
16. *The Less Deceived* p. 13.
17. *Ibid.* p. 45.
18. 'Here' in *The Whitsun Weddings* p. 9.

19. 'Show Saturday' in *High Windows* p. 38.
20. *The Whitsun Weddings* pp. 21–3.
21. *The Less Deceived* pp. 28–9.
22. *The Whitsun Weddings* p. 10.
23. *Ibid.* p. 32.
24. 'Ignorance' in *The Whitsun Weddings* p. 39.
25. 'Nothing to be Said' in *The Whitsun Weddings* p. 11.
26. *High Windows* p. 17.

8 Postmodernist Fiction

1. Samuel Beckett, *More Pricks Than Kicks* (Picador edn., 1974) p. 18.
2. *Ibid.* pp. 18–19.
3. *Ibid.* p. 16.
4. *Ibid.* p. 17. The allusion is to the use of the fish as a symbol for Christ by the early Christians.
5. *Ibid.* p. 11.
6. *Ibid.* p. 13.
7. *Ibid.* p. 19.
8. See above p. 138.
9. Beckett, *Murphy* (1963) p. 5.
10. *Ibid.* pp. 52–3.
11. Beckett, *Watt* (1963) p. 67.
12. *Ibid.* pp. 71–2.
13. *The Unnamable* in *Three Novels By Samuel Beckett* (New York, 1965) pp. 394–5.
14. Donald Barthelme, *Snow White* (Bantam edn. New York, 1968) p. 129.
15. Hugh Kenner, *A Reader's Guide to Samuel Beckett* (1973) p. 94.
16. Joseph Conrad, 'Henry James: an appreciation', quoted by Alan Friedman *The Turn of the Novel* (New York, 1966) p. 77.
17. Muriel Spark, *Not To Disturb* (1971) p. 61.
18. John Barth, *Lost in the Funhouse* (Harmondsworth, 1972) p. 117.
19. Richard Brautigan, *A Confederate General from Big Sur* (Picador edn., 1973) p. 116.
20. Richard Brautigan, *Trout Fishing In America* (Picador edn., 1972) p. 150.
21. *Ibid.* p. 151.
22. See Leslie Fiedler. *The New Mutants, Partisan Review* Autumn 1956. Reprinted in Bernard Bergonzi, ed. *Innovations* (1900) pp. 23–45 and the same author's 'Cross The Border—Close That Gap; Postmodernism', *American Literature Since 1900* (1975) ed. Marcus Cunliffe. pp. 344–66.
23. Frank Kermode, 'Objects, Jokes and Art' in *Continuities* (New York, 1968) p. 23.
24. Fiedler, 'Cross the Border etc.' p. 348.
25. Kermode, *op. cit.* p. 20.
26. Samuel Beckett, *The Unnamable, op. cit.* p. 357.
27. Leonard Michaels, *I Would Have Saved Them If I Could* (New York, 1975) p. 137.
28. Quoted by Tony Tanner in *City of Words: American Fiction 1950–1970* (1971) p. 191.
29. Gore Vidal, *Myra Breckinridge* (1968) and *Myron* (1975).

30. John Barth, *Giles Goat-Boy* (1967) p. 672.
31. Jorge Luis Borges, *Labyrinths* (Harmondsworth, 1970) p. 37.
32. *Ibid.* p. 51.
33. Beckett, *Watt* p. 200.
34. Beckett, *Molloy* (1966) pp. 73–9.
35. Beckett, *Murphy* p. 68.
36. *Ibid.* pp. 43–4.
37. Joseph Heller, *Catch 22* (Corgi edn. 1964) p. 16.
38. Ronald Sukenick, *98.6* (New York, 1975) p. 167.
39. Raymond Federman, *Double or Nothing* (Chicago, 1971) p. 85.
40. Leonard Michaels, *I Would Have Saved Them If I Could* pp. 117–48.
41. *Ibid.* pp. 59–60.
42. Donald Barthelme, 'Edward and Pia', *Unspeakable Practices, Unnatural Acts* (Bantam edn. New York, 1969) p. 75.
43. Barthelme, 'Will You Tell Me?', *Come Back, Dr Caligari* (Boston, 1964) p. 47.
44. In 'See The Moon'. Quoted, and amusingly discussed by the author, in *The New Fiction: Interviews with Innovative American Writers* by Joe David Bellamy (1974) pp. 53–5.
45. Barthelme, *Come Back, Dr Caligari* pp. 90–1.
46. Quoted by Tony Tanner, *op. cit.* p. 126.
47. See *The Novelist at the Crossroads* pp. 13–14 and 166–70.
48. Barthelme, 'A Film', *Sadness* (Bantam edn. New York, 1972) p. 78.
49. Brautigan, *Trout Fishing in America* pp. 7–8.
50. *Ibid.* p. 27.
51. *Ibid.* p. 31.
52. *Ibid.* p. 34.
53. *Ibid.* p. 39.
54. *Ibid.* p. 72.
55. *Ibid.* p. 80.
56. *Ibid.* p. 13.
57. *Ibid.* p. 43.
58. *Ibid.* p. 89.
59. *Ibid.* p. 129.
60. *Ibid.* p. 131.
61. *Ibid.* p. 148.
62. Roman Jakobson, 'Two Aspects of Language' p. 80.
63. Alain Robbe-Grillet, *Le Voyeur* (Paris, 1955) pp. 11–12.
64. Alain Robbe-Grillet, *The Voyeur*, translated by Richard Howard (1959) pp. 6–7.
65. Jorge Louis Borges, *Labyrinths* p. 92.
66. Quoted by Tony Tanner in *City of Words* p. 41. The translation differs slightly from that of the Penguin *Labyrinths*, and I have preferred to quote it in this instance because the word 'contiguous' is used.
67. Vladimir Nabokov, *King, Queen, Knave* (1968) p. 259.
68. Nabokov, *Speak, Memory*, (Pyramid edn., New York, 1968) p. 143.
69. Ihab Hassan, *The Dismemberment of Orpheus: Toward a Postmodernist Literature* (New York, 1971) p. 251.
70. Brautigan, *Trout Fishing in America* pp. 142–3.
71. Kurt Vonnegut, *Slaughterhouse 5* (1970) p. 17.
72. *Ibid.* p. 109.

73. Vonnegut, *Breakfast of Champions* (Panther edn., 1975) p. 179.
74. Reprinted in *Superfiction, or the American Story Transformed,* ed. Joe David Bellamy (New York, 1975) p. 254.
75. Robert Coover, *Pricksongs and Descants* (Picador edn., 1973) p. 15.
76. John Barth, *'Life-Story'*, *Lost in the Funhouse* p. 121.
77. *Ibid.* p. 122.
78. *Ibid.* pp. 131–2.
79. *Ibid.* p. 132.
80. John Barth 'The Literature of Exhaustion', *Atlantic* August 1967, p. 29.
81. *Ibid.* p. 32.
82. Leslie Fiedler, 'Cross the Border—Close That Gap' *op. cit.* p. 346.

Index

This index includes the names of all writers, artists, etc. referred to in the text and notes, and explanatory references to certain literary and linguistic terms. These terms are printed in small capitals. **Bold type** page numbers indicate substantial discussion.

want to meet me too?'

'They did,' said Mum. 'We told them you weren't well.'

'Showed them some video I took one of the many times you were in a stinking mood and not talking to anyone,' Dad said.

'Thought you'd show them my best side, did you?'

'You know how these shows work, Jig. It's not good telly if everyone's all sunny and cuddly. Thought we stood more of a chance of getting picked if our son came across as a surly little git.'

'Did the trick too,' said Mum brightly.

'And there's going to be a party at the end of shooting,' said Dad.

'I hate parties,' I muttered.

Read the rest of
Kid Swap
to find out what happens next!

we knew we'd been selected,' Mum said. 'Wanted it to be a surprise.'

I glared at her. 'Oh, it's that all right.'

'I didn't know about it either till she told me we had to go and meet the producers,' my father added, polishing his e-Bay halo.

I swivelled the glare his way. 'Went along with it then though, didn't you?'

He shrugged. 'Be a crime to turn down the loot they're offering.'

'Anyway, it was all kind of rushed,' Mum said. 'Four of the six episodes have already been filmed apparently, and the fifth is underway. I applied months ago and didn't hear a thing, but one of the families who'd agreed to do the sixth episode pulled out at the last minute, so they had to find a replacement family.'

'And there we were,' I said, 'just waiting for them like three sitting ducks. What's my share?'

'Your share?'

'What do I get out of this lousy deal?'

'You continue to have a roof over your head when you're back in the family fold,' said Dad.

'Oh joy. How come the producers didn't

of filming and that would be it. Could be a long two weeks, though.

I felt something brush my ankles. I looked down. Stallone, our cat, had crept upstairs and joined us. But he wasn't brushing my ankles out of affection. Stallone doesn't do affection. He was doing it because he'd just been outside rolling in something disgusting and wanted to pass it on. He looked up at me and snarled, the way he does.

'Here's a thought,' I said to my unfaithful parents. 'Tell the company you've changed your minds about *Kid Swap* and'll wait for *Pet Swap*. Then we can exchange Stallone and see how we adapt to a terrapin or something.'

'No can do,' Dad said. 'The contract's been signed. And you want to count yourself lucky it's not *Gender Swap* (though they'd probably call it *Sex Swap* to get more viewers). If it was *Gender Swap* or *Sex Swap*, you'd have to become a girl.'

I'd already been there and done that, but that's between me and you.* 'What I want to know,' I said, 'is why I'm the last to hear about this, seeing as I'm the victim.'

'We thought we should keep quiet about it till

---

* See the second Jiggy book, *The Toilet of Doom*.

have to swear sixteen times in every sentence.'

'I can do that,' said Dad.

'That sort of thing happens in *other* shows,' Mum said. 'Carla, the nice girl from the television company, assured us that *Kid Swap* is going to be much classier.'

'And you believed her,' I said pityingly.

Dad smiled. 'She was quite a looker.'

I shook my head again, this time in sorrow. Parents. So easy to con. I should know, I con mine all the time. I explained, as gently as I could, to the feeble-minded old souls.

'Those TV types tell you what they think you want to hear to get you on board,' I said. 'It's only later, when you've invited your friends and relatives round to watch the result while nibbling cheese straws that you realise what a fool you've been made to look, and hear yourself say all the things they promised to leave on the cutting-room floor.'

Mum laughed. 'Jiggy, you're such a cynic. You're going to have a whale of a time. Trust me. But even if you don't, it'll all be over in a couple of weeks, then you're back home again.'

Yes, that was the one plus to all this. Two weeks

CHAPTER TWO

Did you ever see any of those TV programmes where people are swapped to see how they get on with different people or in different situations? Two families switch holidays or homes or wives for a while, and there are all these rows and lots of sulking and talking about one another behind their backs. Well, a new series was being made, and this was what my parents had signed us up for. It was going to be called *Kid Swap*. In *Kid Swap,* two families would exchange one child of about the same age, and cameras would go into each home and record everything.

When I heard that I was going to be in this thing like it or not, which I didn't, I shook my head in a neat combination of horror and amazement. 'Have you seen what *happens* on those shows?' I said.

'What do you mean?' This was Mum.

'People break down. Have tantrums. Throw things. They whisper to camera by torchlight and

'The television company's paying for it.'

'The what?'

'The TV company that's going to film it all.'

'Film what all?'

'If you'll just sit quiet a moment, we'll tell you,' Dad said.

So I sat quiet. Wasn't easy to keep still, though. My elbows flapped like they were battery-operated and my feet Riverdanced like maniacs. (They do this when I'm upset or agitated.)

If you want to hear about the cruel deal my parents had set up for me, drag your eyes to the next page. I wouldn't bother personally, but it's your time you're wasting, not mine.

Probably never did. It's because I can't keep still, isn't it?'

'Oh, Jiggy.'

'And don't "Oh, Jiggy" me either.'

'Calm down, Jig,' Dad said from the door. (He looked like he wanted to make a bolt for it.*) 'We have to talk this through.'

'Talk it through with me?' I said. 'Why? I'm just some unwanted kid who happens to be related to you by a freak of nature.'

He ignored this, probably because it was true. 'It'll be a real experience for you,' he said. 'Chance to see how the other half lives.'

'Other half?'

'The rich half.'

'They're rich?' I said.

'That's the impression we get.'

'Oh, so *they're* paying you. Have they got a son they don't like either then?'

'No, no, the money's not coming from them,' said Mum.

'Who then? The government? Is this some new government initiative to place kids with more loving families?'

---

* Which would have been nice. I wasn't allowed a bolt on my door.

up to see if I'd got used to the idea yet. Those thirty-two minutes included twenty-five for Mum to watch *Home and Away. Home and Away.* Said it all, didn't it? They were staying home and sending me away.

They knocked on my door. Well, one of them did. Dad, I guessed. My mother hardly ever knocks. She barges in, all hours, day or night, usually screeching at me to change my underwear, get a move on, or do stuff I've been trying not to think about, like homework. The knock meant that part two of Sell Your Son to the Nearest Bidder was about to occur.

'Jiggy, we have to explain,' Mum said, flinging the door back when the knock was answered with a leave-me-in-peace-forever-you-pathetic-excuse-for-parents silence. Dad shuffled in after her, looking a bit guilty. So he should.

'There's nothing *to* explain,' I snarled. 'You want to get rid of me, end of saga.'

'It's not that,' she said, plonking herself on the bed beside me and squeezing my shoulder. 'It's not that at *all*, darling.'

'Don't darling me,' I snapped, shrugging her off. 'You don't want me any more and that's that.

'You *think*?'

'I do. It's quite a privilege to be selected. You wouldn't believe the number of applicants.'

'Applicants? You actually *applied* to swap me?'

'It's the way it works, Jig,' my treacherous father explained.

'I don't believe you can make money by swapping kids,' I said feebly. 'I just do *not* believe it.'

'Oh, but you can,' Mum said brightly. 'And by doing so we'll be able to pay the mortgage for six whole months.'

'*And* have enough over for a long weekend on the canal,' said Dad.

'But me!' I cried. 'Your number one son! Your only child so far!'

Mum looked at Dad. Dad looked at Mum.

'Maybe he should hear the details,' she said to him.

'I thought he was hearing them,' said he to her.

'I don't *want* the details!' I yelled, and ran out, slammed the door, pounded up to my room, slammed that door too, and punched Roger, my toy monkey.

They gave it thirty-two minutes before coming

back on essentials like my favourite biscuits, fizzy drinks, the tasty little packet snacks that Mum keeps threatening to ban. There was even talk of 'looking at my pocket money', which you could already count on the fingers of half a hand.

'Dad could get another job,' I said.

'He *could*,' said Mum. 'But you're talking about someone who's proud to wear a T-shirt with "WORK-SHY" in big EasyJet letters across the chest.'

'All right, that's him. But why will you be off work?'

'Why? I'm expecting a baby. Your little sister. Had you forgotten?'

I glanced at her stomach, which was almost as big as the downstairs cloakroom. No chance of forgetting that. 'But you've got two months yet. And what's the big deal anyway? You go to the hospital one afternoon, have her and a cup of tea, back at work next morning. Dad and I can look after her.'

Mum sighed. 'Jiggy, you're being swapped, and that's that. You should look upon it as an experience. Most kids would jump at it.'

'You're going to swap me for another *boy*?'

'It was your mother's idea,' Dad said, trying to shift the blame and failing.

I gawped some more, at both of them. What kind of parents would swap their own son?

'What kind of parents would swap their own son?' I asked.

'The kind that need the money,' said Mum. 'As you know, we had to cancel the week's touring holiday we were so looking forward to.'

'Whoa,' I said. 'Back a bit. You're swapping me for *money*?'

'Well, you don't think we'd just *give* you away, do you?' said Dad.

'Your dad's out of work,' Mum said.

'So what's new?' I said.

'So I can't pay the mortgage on my wages alone. And I'll be off work myself in a couple of months too, so no more overtime for a while. In other words, there's going to be a bit of a cash-flow problem.'

The Dad/work thing was true enough. He'd lost his job a few weeks earlier. He's always losing something, my dad. Keys, temper, hair. But his job. So selfish. Thanks to him we'd already had to cut

'I'll leave it to you, Peg,' said Dad, getting up.

'Oh no you won't,' said Mum. 'Sit down.'

Dad sank back in his chair. This was starting to sound serious.

'What's going on?' I asked, trying not to seem nervous.

Mum took a deep breath, which made me even more nervous. Deep breaths before speaking in my house mean Heavy Subjects are about to zoom Jigward. Had I been expelled from school while I was filing my nails? Was my pathetic chocolate ration going to be reduced to zero? Was Mum leaving Dad for a man?

But even though it was my mother's deep breath, it was my father who got in first with the news. The first bit of it anyway.

'Jig,' he said. 'We're going to swap you for another kid.'

I gawped at him. He was joking, of course.

'You're joking, of course.'

He smiled. 'Nope. Perfectly serious.'

'You're going to swap me for another kid?' I said.

'Another boy.' This was Mum. She was smiling too now.

CHAPTER ONE

Have you ever wished you lived under a different roof? I mean in a different house, flat, basement, with different people, wallpaper, toilets? Course you have. Who hasn't? But I bet you've never been traded for another kid, have you? Well, guess who has. Yes, the one and only Jiggy McCue. And by my own *parents* would you believe!

The first I heard about it was one Wednesday, towards the end of my mother's idea of an evening meal – the latest vegetable dish she'd failed to learn how to make from a celebrity chef with a stupid haircut.

'Jiggy,' said Mum.

'Mother,' I replied, pressing the pain in my chest.

'We have something to tell you,' she said.

'Text me,' I said. 'I'm going to my room to lie down.'

'You'll stay right there while I talk to you,' said she.

Don't miss
the next exciting
JIGGY adventure...

TURN THE PAGE
TO READ THE BEGINNING...

Look out for more JiGGY in 2010!

A new drama teacher arrives at Ranting Lane School.
Is Jiggy really going to have to play Bottom in the
school production of *A Midsummer Night's Dream?*

And introducing a brand-new series...

...in which we meet a whole host of Jiggy's ancestors
and discover that, through centuries past,
there have *always* been Jiggy McCues!

Don't miss the first book,

where we meet a 13th century Jiggy...

And I'll watch over her while she's growing up, and read to her at bedtime, and maybe even make her bed sometimes.

And I'll tell her all the insane things that happen to me, and she'll believe me right off, without any argument, because that's the sort of person she's going to be.

And she'll call me Joseph. The only person I'll allow to do that. Everyone else – and that includes you – would still have to call me Jiggy.

Jiggy McCue

CHAPTER ONE

I was woken by the jolly sound of my mother throwing up in the bathroom. Good job too. That she was throwing up in the bathroom, I mean. It would have taken her ages to get it out of the carpet on the landing. Naturally, I would have preferred to be woken by the tweet-tweet of dear little birdies in the trees that aren't outside my window, but I never get any say in these things.

'Is it me?' I asked, sliding out of bed and peeking round my bedroom door as she staggered out to the landing.

'Is what you?' she gurgled.

'Well, you're always saying I make you sick…'

She smiled feebly – 'Remind me to avoid prawn curries' – and tottered downstairs.

Before I go any further I'd better tell you my name. It's McCue, Jiggy McCue, double-o-nothing, stirred, not shaken. You might know that already. If you don't know it already, it's still Jiggy McCue.

That's Jiggy, not Ziggy or Biggy or Piggy, or Wuggy or Muggy or Buggy – and *definitely* not Juggy. You have to get that straight because of the stuff I'm going to tell you about.*

Now that I think of it, there are one or two other things I ought to get out of the way first. Here they are. I go to a school called Ranting Lane and live with my parents and cat (Mel, Peg and Stallone) in a house called *The Dorks* (yes, really) on a housing development called the Brook Farm Estate, which was built on what used to be a farm (Brook Farm). We live on the cheapo side. The really terrific houses, the ones with double garages and designer poodles and columns holding up the porches, are over on Hillary Clinton Walk, Hannibal Lector Way, and a few other streets named after someone's heroes. The not-so-upmarket streets on our side have names like Crack End and Snit Close. *The Dorks* has three bedrooms and two toilets, though we only use two of the bedrooms. My next-door neighbour is a cement-head from my class called Eejit Atkins, and just across the road is the house where Pete Garrett and Angie Mint live. Pete and Angie are my best buds. We call ourselves the Three Musketeers and

---

* Actually my real first name's Joseph, but the only people who use it are Golden Oldie teachers you can't educate. Jiggy's been a sort of nickname since I was knee-high to our garden gnome. I got it because I have this complete inability to keep still when I'm agitated or upset or scared, which means I'm as jumpy as two frogs on a bed of nails quite a lot of the time.

we're a sort of gang. Not a bad gang, we don't trip up old ladies and stuff, but when there's three of you and you hang together you have to call yourselves something.

I'd better start by telling you what happened the evening before the morning my mother chucked up in the bathroom and woke me so thoughtlessly. I was working on the Musketeer Rule Book in my room. It was a little red notebook I'd bought out of my pathetic excuse for pocket money. On the cover I'd printed our heroic battle-cry, 'One for all and all for lunch', and inside I'd written the rules that I'd been laying out for a year. It's hard work dreaming up rules, but I was already up to Rule Four, which was…

Rule 4: Musketeers must not hug (specially one another).

This was mainly for Angie. Angie's a female, but she's always saying it's not her fault. She's more boy than Pete and me put together most of the time, even though she doesn't have our dangly bits, but she forgets herself occasionally and comes over all soppy and flings her arms round you. Let me tell you, it's

9

no fun inside a Mint bear-hug.

'Jiggy!'

That was my mum, calling from downstairs. She's always doing that, calling me from some part of the house I'm not in. Sometimes we're in the same room together and she hardly speaks, then she goes out and shouts for me, and I answer, and she says 'Pardon me?' and I repeat myself, and she says, 'Will you come here please?' and I sigh, and heave myself out of my chair or off my bed, and go to wherever she is, and she says something like, 'Hold the other end of this sheet,' like it's really urgent. There's quite a lot I don't get about my mother. Her whole generation in fact. The Golden Oldie universe is fifteen-point-four light years away from mine.

'Jiggy!'

'What?'

'Will you come down here please?'

'What for?'

'Because I'm asking you to.'

I tutted and passed through my bedroom door (which was open, I'm not a flaming ghost) and went out to the landing. I looked down the stairs. Mum wasn't there any more, which meant I couldn't

interrogate her further without trudging down.

Trudge, trudge, trudge.

'Where are you?' I yell from the bottom (of the stairs).

'Who?' Dad yells back from the living room, where he's watching something sporty on TV as usual.

'Not you!' I yell back.

'I'm in the kitchen!' yells Mum.

I go into the kitchen. My mother is standing there with her ironing board.

'What?' I say.

'Will you stop saying "What?",' she says.

'I'll stop saying what if you stop calling me.'

'I'm calling you because I want to show you how to iron.'

'What?'

'I'm going to show you how to iron.'

'What?'

'Clothes. It's about time you learnt.'

'Why?' I said.

'Because if anything happened to me, you wouldn't know what to do.'

'I would. I'd go for the wrinkled look. What brought this on?'

'What brought it on is that I have so much ironing to do all the time, and get no help from you or your father.'

'Why would you? Ironing is women's work, well-known fact since the dawn of Men's Lib.'

'Jiggy, this is the twenty-first century,' Mum says.

'And this is Wednesday,' I reply.

She frowns. 'What's that got to do with anything?'

I frown back. 'Haven't a clue. Can I go now?'

'No. You'll stay here and learn to iron.'

'Mother,' I said. 'I have homework.'

'Yes,' she said. 'You do,' she said. '*This* homework. Come round here.'

I went round there. I always do as I'm told when I run out of excuses or Mum gets bossy.

Now I'm going to tell you something about ironing. What I'm going to tell you is that it isn't as easy as it looks, specially when the point of the iron gets stuck in the gusset of a pair of underpants. A handkerchief would have been easier. I suggested this, but Mum said anyone could iron a handkerchief, which was why I wasn't.

'But why underpants?' I enquired.

'Underpants are just the start,' she replied. 'You take it for granted when you open your drawer and see them lying there neatly pressed. Well, now you're going to learn how they get that way.'

'Mum.'

'What?'

'It doesn't matter to me if my underpants aren't neatly pressed.'

'Well, it should.'

'Well, it doesn't. It wouldn't matter to me if they were as wrinkled as a pair of prunes. I don't care if my underpants are pressed, tied in a bow, or have tyre marks. No one in their right mind *would* care.'

'I care,' said Mum.

'My point exactly,' I said.

'Whatever you say, Jiggy, whether you like it or not, from now on you're pressing your own underpants.'

'These aren't my underpants.'

'No, they're your father's. We're using his things to practice on. If you make a mess of your dad's clothes he won't notice. He has no pride *whatever* in his appearance.'

'Well nor do I.'

'No, but just in case you develop some eventually I'm going to show you how to look smart. You'll thank me one day.'

'I'll visit the Home specially,' I said.

It wasn't just underpants either. She also tried to show me how to iron T-shirts, and shirts that weren't teed, and pyjamas, and quite a few other things. I grumbled a bit more, naturally, but after a while it got kind of interesting. Kind of a challenge to make everything smooth. I felt like I'd failed when I made a crease where there wasn't one before.

Dad strolled in while I was struggling with one of his shirt collars. 'This I do not believe,' he said, stopping in his tracks and grabbing the door to support himself.

I scowled at him so he wouldn't know it wasn't as bad as it looked. 'You don't have to believe it. I'm going to wake up in a minute and tell you all about it. Then we can both crack up.'

'I'm teaching your son to appreciate the things that are done for him,' Mum explained.

'You don't plan on teaching me too, do you?' said Dad, worried.

'Oh no, you're past saving. Lost cause, you.'

'Whew,' he said, and scooted back to the telly.

As it happened, my mother did me a favour, showing me how to iron. Why was that a favour? Because of what was coming, that's why. If you want to hear what that was, stick around. If you don't, go and press someone's underpants. And watch that gusset!

CHAPTER TWO

Thursday. The morning I was woken from my sweet dreams by my old dear throwing up in the bathroom. I was down in the kitchen gulping my cereal when I heard the post drop through the letterbox.[1] I went out to the hall and picked the envelopes up from the mat, hoping there was one for me.[2] There wasn't, never is, but I live in hope. I'm thinking of sending myself a letter so I'll have one to open like everyone else. The reason I haven't done that so far is that it wouldn't be much of a surprise, even if I disguised the handwriting. There were three envelopes today, including a couple of long ones with windows, which Dad snatched off me only to drop them right away like they were on fire.

'Bills!' he snarled. 'Why do I only ever get *bills*?'

'Look on the bright side,' I said. 'Bill probably gets yours.'

There was also one for Mum, with the name of the

---

[1] Post as in letters, not a long bit of wood.

[2] Envelope, not mat.

local hospital in small print in the top left-hand corner. When she came down she opened it and read the page inside.

'Monday afternoon,' she said to Dad.

'Bit short-notice,' he replied.

'Has to be, I suppose.'

'I'll take the day off,' he said.

'You don't have to, I can still drive.'

'Give up an excuse for not going to work? No chance.'

'You don't have to take the whole day. The appointment's not till two.'

'Oh, it's hardly worth going in just for the morning.'

'You know, Mel, your dedication to work is like Jiggy's to school.'

'What's going on?' I asked them.

Mum glanced at me. 'Going on?'

'This hospital appointment.'

'I'm just having something checked,' she said, slotting the letter back in the envelope and dropping it in the shoulder bag she wears to work.

'Having what checked?'

'Don't go on, Jiggy, it's nothing, here's your lunch

box, you'll find some sardine-and-tomato paste sandwiches in there.'

'Sardine-and-tomato paste sandwiches?'

'And some new-flavour crisps I came across in SmartSave.'

'Mum. I don't like sardine-and-tomato paste sandwiches.'

'Oh, you're always saying that.'

'Yes,' I said. 'I am,' I said. 'And guess why,' I said. 'BECAUSE I DON'T LIKE THEM!'

'There's no need to shout,' she said, and left the kitchen, which meant I'd still be getting sardine-and-tomato paste sandwiches when I'm forty-three. I don't know what you have to do to get through to Golden Oldies, I really don't.

I met Angie and Pete outside as usual and we set off with lead in our socks like we do most school mornings. Halfway along the street, Angie shuddered. I asked her why.

'I just walked on the paving stone Dawn Overton was mugged on.'

'How do you know it was that one?'

'She showed me.'

'How does she remember the exact paving stone?'

'There's still a mark – look.'

Dawn Overton and her mother Mrs Overton (Janet) are my next-door neighbours on the side that doesn't contain the Atkins family. Dawn's a nurse.* Not long ago she and her mum got a dog, a big hairy beast called Charlie Farnsbarns. Every evening that it's not raining, Mrs Overton kicks Charlie F into the back garden and says, so loudly the whole estate can hear without straining, 'Do your business, Charlie Farnsbarns!' She says this over and over – 'Do your business, Charlie Farnsbarns! Do your business, Charlie Farnsbarns!' – until the critter's done it. Mum and Dad and I realised what a regular event this was on a few evenings in the summer when we had tea in the back garden, just over the fence from the Overtons'. When you're tucking into something that could be anything, like most of the food my mother dishes up, one thing you don't want to hear over the fence, repeated with every swallow, is, 'Do your business, Charlie Farnsbarns!' because you know what that business is and it's hard not to think of the dog doing it.

Anyway. The night Dawn Overton was mugged, Charlie Farnsbarns had got out of their front gate,

---

* The same Dawn Overton who got a panoramic view of my bare behind in *Nudie Dudie* after it was attacked by a seagull.

mooched along a bit, and done his business on the pavement for a change. Mrs Overton came looking for him, found him, ordered him back into the garden, and Dawn went out to shovel the doggy biz into a small carrier bag. She'd just finished and straightened up when a boy on a mountain bike snatched the bag and rode off with it.

'Wonder what he said when he opened the bag?' Pete said.

'My guess is he described the contents in a single word not beginning with J,' said Angie.

'J?' I said.

'Joy,' she snapped. 'Not everything's about you, you know.'

'Wotcher, you free!' bawled a croaky little voice behind us.

We groaned. Eejit Atkins. Eejit talks like no one else except his brother Jolyon, Sir Hooligan of the Brook Farm Estate. No one else we know speaks like those two, including their parents. Mystery where they got it from as they grew up in the same streets as the rest of us and have been to the same school as us. Atkins-speak is kind of like measles. After a minute with Eejit or being sworn at by Jolyon, you're

talking like them yourself, and then your mother tells you off like it's your fault. Even if he didn't talk that way Eejit wouldn't be the brightest candle on the cake, but I sometimes get the idea that he works at it because in his tiny mind he thinks it's cool to be a moron.

'Lo, Eejit,' I said wearily.

'Get lost, Atkins,' said Pete. Pete's not as kind to the mentally challenged as I am.

'I wuz talkin' ta me bruvver yesterdy,' Eejit said, frowning at his feet as he tried to get them to walk in step with ours. When he managed it, Pete did a little skip and got straight out of step.

'Musta bin excitin',' said Angie, dropping into Atkins-speak right away.

'Yer,' said Eejit.

And that seemed to be it.

Fifteen skippy steps on, absolutely stuffed with curiosity, I said, 'Wot wuz ya talkin' abaat?'

'Oo?' said Atkins.

'You an' Jolyon.'

'When?'

'Yesterdy.'

He shrugged. 'Search me.'

'Well why'd ya menshun it?'

'Menshun wot?'

'That you wuz talkin' to him.'

'Talkin' to oo?'

'Yer bruvver.'

'Wuz I?'

'Said ya wuz.'

'Did I?'

'Yes. You did.'

'Oh. Right.'

And that wuz it. Fairly standard conversation with Atkins. Angie, Pete and I sighed at one another.

On the other side of the main road that separates the estate from town, Eejit spied some of his idiot buds doing kangaroo impressions round a man in a wheelchair. 'Be seein' ya!' he cried, and scooted off to join in.

Then someone else came by. Mr Rice, jogging. Mr Rice is our Pointless Exercises teacher. He used to jog to school with Miss Weeks, the Deputy Head, but she'd been off having a baby and wasn't back yet. The Sugar Ricicle is about as famous as Eejit Atkins, but not for the way he talks. He doesn't actually talk anyway, he shouts – at us kids anyway – but it's not

the shouting that he's famous for either, it's for always wearing a tracksuit during school-time, on the sports field, in the gym, even on the stage in Assembly, which I think is pretty sad. And it's always a red tracksuit, maybe even the same one, year in, year out. We're not great pals, Mr Rice and me. He's always trying to get me to run faster or jump higher or kick balls into giant hairnets – things that don't even make the bottom of my list of top million things I like to do.

'Hope you three are all set for the weekend!' he boomed as he jogged by in his stupid red tracksuit.

Another three-person groan. We'd been trying not to think about the weekend, when our least favourite sporty type was taking two classes from our year on a survival course in some hills.

'Why, what happens at the weekend?' I asked innocently.

He swung round to face me, jogging backwards now, holding on to his hair like it would take off if he didn't.

'You know very well what happens at the weekend, McCue, and if you're not waiting for the bus with everyone else at seven-forty-five on

23

Saturday morning I'll come round and personally drag you out of your pit!'

'You won't get in,' I said. 'Our door's triple locked against strange men in red. We even block the chimney to stop Father Christmas getting into our house.'

Still jogging backwards, he gave me one of his fiercest glares.

'Watch it, lad! I've got my eye on you!'

'Hey, you're not so bad yourself, sir!'

He might have said something else if his spine hadn't slammed into a lamp-post at full jog. We hurried by, covering our sniggers while he was still bouncing off the nearest rubbish bin.

CHAPTER THREE

Most of that Thursday was like any other Thursday during term time — so yawny our toes almost dropped off with boredom. The only slightly unusual thing occurred first thing, at Assembly, because of what one of us had done the day before in History.

We didn't have History in the usual room that day because men with smears and blobs all over their white overalls were painting it. As they were painting it the same fantastically monotonous colour as before, the only difference when they finished would be that it would stink for weeks. The usual room had a blackboard because our history teacher, Mr Hurley, was old and preferred a blackboard, but the borrowed classroom had a big whiteboard whether he liked it or not. There were a couple of other differences too. As well as its own full wad of desks and chairs, the desks and chairs from the usual history room had been stacked in there, which

made it kind of hard to get from A to B, or even C to P. To give us even less space, the giant photocopier from Miss Prince's office had been wheeled in because her office and the Head's were also being painted.

Now Mr Hurley is a serious man. Serious as in seriously boring. He's short and square and thick-necked, and he always wears the same check jacket, brown trousers and maroon tie, and he doesn't seem to like us much. A smile on the Hurley features in our lessons is about as rare as a pilchard quacking, and he never makes jokes. I mean he *never* makes jokes. He also doesn't have a clue most of the time when we're jerking him around. Example. A week or two before the day I'm telling you about, he came in, coughed loudly to silence us, and wrote 'Henry VIII' on the board. Then he turned to us, waited for the last of the noise to fade, and said, 'A spot of recapping today, class, starting with the six wives of Henry the Eighth. I would like their names please.'

'Bet you would,' someone muttered.

'Henry the eighth what?' someone else asked.

'He was a *king*,' Mr H said. 'Of *England*.'

'You mean he was the eighth king of England?'

'No, I mean the eighth king called Henry.'

'The eighth king called Henry? What did he call him for, sir? And what did they talk about?'

Hurley took a deep breath and started again, speaking very slowly.

'I would like this class to tell me the names of the six wives of the eighth King Henry of England. The very wives we discussed in two periods just the other week.'

'What did he want six wives for?' someone asked. 'My dad says one's one too many.'

'Don't be silly, boy, he was married to them one at a time, not all at once. Oh, you can't have forgotten their names already. Not *all* of them.'

Silence in class.

'Anyone?' he said, glaring gloomily around.

More silence.

'Can't you at least take a *stab* at this?' he asked. 'Come on, give me some names. I only want six. Is that so hard?'

Well, put like that...

Here are the six names he got before he held his hand up to stop us.

'Kirsty.'

'Saffron.'

'Kylie.'

'Sharon.'

'Jade.'

'Bert.'

Everyone except Eejit Atkins knew these weren't right, of course, but classes as boring as Hurley's have to be juiced up somehow.

But that was another day. The Wednesday I'm coming to, the Wednesday in the temporary History room, also started with a Hurley baiting session. The class was still yelling and throwing stuff and running over the extra desks when he came in with a grin on his chops – a sight which caused everyone to freeze for at least ten seconds because chop-grinning wasn't something Hurley did, ever.

'You'll be thrilled to hear that we're going to have a history test today,' he said when we were sitting down and looking his way.

Foreheads smacked desks and a hearty chorus of 'Noooooo!' went up.

'Knew you'd be keen,' he said with something worryingly like a giggle. 'It will be a test with a

difference, however,' he went on. 'The difference being that you'll choose your own questions.'

Some of us looked at others of us with puzzled expressions. Choose our own questions?

'Do they have to be questions about history?' someone asked.

'Of course they have to be about history,' H beamed. 'This is a history *lesson*. But for every question you get right you'll receive a gobstopper.'

'You mean if one of us gets a right answer we all get a gobstopper?' someone asked.

'No, I mean that the *person* who gets a right answer will get a gobstopper.'

'That'll shut some of us up,' said Holly Gilder, glaring around. Holly never plays up in class.

'To eat out of school, or at home,' H added.

'Bad for your teeth, gobstoppers,' said Pitwell.

'Since when did you care?' said Hislop.

'I don't, I'm just saying,' Pitwell replied.

'How does choosing our own questions work?' Angie asked Mr Hurley.

'I'll tell you if you'll kindly pay attention,' he answered cheerfully.

'Sir, I've got one for you,' Pete said.

'One what?'

'A question. Why isn't your nose twelve inches long?'

'My nose?'

'BECAUSE THEN IT WOULD BE A FOOT!' chorused half the class.

'That one was doing the rounds when I was a boy,' said Mr H.

'Back in Roman Times?' someone asked, to show he knew his history.

'Though I'd have thought you'd be using centimetres these days.'

Pete shook his head. 'Doesn't work. The answer to "Why isn't your nose thirty centimetres long?" would have to be "Because then it would be thirty centimetres long". How funny is that?'

'How funny is it anyway?' I said.

'Tell you what would be funny,' said Mr Hurley. 'If, just for a change, you paid me some of that attention I asked for.'

We paid attention, sort of, mainly because looking like we were paying attention to Mr Hurley was a habit we hadn't kicked yet. Things would change if he went on like this, though.

Someone had to ask why he was being so nice.

'Sir?'

'Yes, Mr McCue?'

'What's with the sun-has-got-his-hat-on mood?' He looked puzzled. 'The larky behaviour,' I explained. 'The big fat grin. Not like you at all.' The big fat grin withered a smidgen. 'I mean has something happened? You get the job as Maria the singing nun or something?'

'If you must know,' he replied happily, 'I'm going on a cruise.'

'A cruise?' said Martin Skinner. 'You mean like on a boat, sir?'

'No, he means on a bike, snail-brain,' said Ryan.

'A very large boat,' said Hurley. 'Next month, for thirteen weeks. My acceptance arrived this very morning.'

'Have you told Mother?'

'My mother?'

'Mr Hubbard.' (Mother Hubbard is Head of Ranting Lane School.)

'I sought Mr Hubbard's permission for leave of absence before applying for the position. He was all in favour.'

'Couldn't wait to get rid of you,' said Majid Aziz behind his hand.

'It won't be all pleasure, though,' Hurley said. 'I'll be there to work.'

'Scrubbing the decks?' said Neil Downey.

'Giving lectures and talks.'

'What, like you do here?' said Sami Safadi.

'Like I do here, yes, but for paying guests keen to know something of the history of the places we'll be visiting.'

'What places?'

'Well, there'll actually be several cruises, one after the other, in and around the Mediterranean. We'll be docking at Messina, Alexandria, Malta, Archenland, Dubrovnik, and many other wonderful places.'

'And you'll be talking all the way?' said Pete.

'Speaking, yes, much of it.'

'And people will stop their sunbathing to listen to you?'

'Hopefully. Though I expect that some of my talks will take place on deck, or even at the sites themselves.'

'Do you know the history of all those places

then?' Milo Dakin asked, winking at me. We both knew – everyone knew except the man himself – that we were milking this for every last drop so there'd be less time for his stupid test.

'No, in all honesty I can't say I do, yet,' Hurley admitted. 'I'll have quite a bit of swatting to do.'

'Bet you will,' someone said. 'Lotta flies out there.'

'Now what do you say we get on with our test?' he asked.

Before any of us could think of a good answer to that there was a knock on the door and the Head's secretary looked in.

'Mr Hurley, would you mind if I made a few quick photocopies?'

'Of course not, Miss Prince,' he said, flashing his manky choppers at her. 'Go right ahead.'

'I won't be a minute,' she said, ignoring the class whose eagerly-awaited history test she'd interrupted.

Miss Prince is a very large lady who almost always wears black leggings and always seems to be trying to forget that kids exist. While she got to work on the copier, Mr Hurley dug into his

33

briefcase and came up with…a pack of playing cards.

'Anyone good at shuffling?' he asked.

'Yer, me!' cried Eejit, jumping to his feet.

'Here then, please, Mr Atkins.'

And Eejit *shuffled* to the front of the class.

Mr H groaned. 'I was referring to shuffling cards,' he said.

'Cards?' said Eejit.

'These,' Hurley-Burley said, holding up the pack.

Atkins thought abaat this. 'Well, I could give 'em a go.'

He took the cards from the history man and started shuffling them. Half of them shot straight up into the air, another half shot to the floor, and half slapped him in the face. Mr Hurley asked him to kindly return to his seat. Eejit kindly did so.

'Thank you, Mr Hurley,' Miss Prince said, heading for the door with her photocopies.

'My pleasure,' he said, stooping to pick up the playing cards.

'What are the cards for, sir?' Julia Frame asked.

'These are Trivial History cards,' Hurley said,

shuffling them himself. 'They contain the questions I want you to try and answer. What I'd like you all to do, in turn, is choose a card at random and answer the question that's printed on it, simple as that. And here are the prizes for those who give the right answers.' He held up a bag of gobstoppers. 'Who wants to go first?'

No one answered, even for a chance to stop their gobs.

'All right,' he said. 'Who wants to be last?'

Fifteen hands hit the ceiling.

'Tell you what,' he said, 'seeing as you're all so eager, why don't we do it in seating order? No need to get up. I'll come to you. That way we won't be deafened by a cacophony of deliberately scraped chairs.'

And that's what he did, starting at the desk nearest the door and working up that aisle and down the next, the cards fanned out in his hand for us each to choose one as he got to us. We weren't allowed to take the card, just touch the one we picked, then he read the question on it and we gave him an answer. We got as much fun as we could out of it, but it was still quite a slog. Here's the way it went, card

questions first, some of our answers second.

Question. What caused the Great Depression of 1929-1933?
Answer. Too much History homework.

Question. What were Julius Caesar's famous last words?
Answer. 'Is that a sword in your hand?'

Question. What happened at Custer's Last Stand?
Answer. Someone gave him a chair.

Question. The Ancient Greeks were very fond of myths. What is a myth?
Answer. A female moth.

Question. What was Sir Francis Drake famous for?
Answer. He circumcised the world with a 100 foot clipper.

'There's a phone call for you in the office.' This was Miss Prince, poking her unsmiling head in again.

'Thanks,' said Pete, standing up.

Miss P scowled at him. 'Mr Hurley,' she said. Pete sat down again.

Mr Hurley went to the door. 'While I'm away,' he said to us, 'perhaps one of you will carry on circulating with the cards. Julia, I think.'

'Why me?' said Julia Frame.

'Because you're a responsible person.'

'I am?' she said, like it was news to her.

He handed her the Trivial History cards. 'If anyone should actually get a question right, make a note of their name on the board please.'

'How will I know if they've got one right?' Julia asked.

'The answers are upside down on the back of the cards.'

'Are they?'

'They are. But don't let anyone see them.'

'I won't!' Julia said, instantly taking charge. Loves power, that girl.

Hurley left us. Not a very clever move, leaving us alone in a classroom without a guard, but teachers never learn. Julia showed the backs of the cards to one of the girls, but even before the girl

picked one, things were being thrown about, boys were making rude noises, and the spare desks were being moved into the aisles. While all this was going on, Harry Potter went to the photocopier Miss Prince had used. Potter had been trying to make a name for himself – his own name – since he started at Ranting Lane the term before. He climbed up on the photocopier, tugged his trousers and underpants down, pressed a button, and turned this way and that while the machine reproduced his backside from different angles. Most of the boys loved this. Most of the girls pulled faces. But then there was the sound of something breaking and everyone went quiet. Potter isn't a big kid, but even a smallish kid wriggling on the glass of a photocopier must have been weighty enough to break it, because that's what he'd done. He jumped off, hauled his togs up, grabbed the prints he'd made, and started back over the desks that were now jamming the aisles.

'Let's see, let's see!' cried Pitwell, snatching the photocopies as Potter climbed by.

Several others said the same thing, but before Pitwell could pass them round the door opened

and Mr Hurley shimmied in. The big fat grin didn't last long this time, maybe because of all the yelling and people clambering over or standing on the desks. The shrill little voice of Julia Frame shouting, 'Stop it, stop it, take a card!' didn't help, specially when he saw the state of the photocopier. We denied everything, naturally, and just for once no one pointed fingers. We tried jollying him along with friendly stuff like, 'Bet you're looking forward to sending those passengers to sleep with History, eh, sir?' but we'd blown it. He was Surly Hurley again until the aisles had been cleared of desks, and there wasn't much lesson time left after that.

He didn't see the photocopies, though. Not till next morning anyway, when Pitwell and a couple of his mates hung them all round the main hall just in time for Assembly. Mother Hubbard was hopping mad when he saw them. He knew that the bum in the prints belonged to someone in our class because Hurley had told him that it was in his lesson that the copier got broken. He also knew it was a boy's behind, don't ask me how, I've never studied the difference. He kept the boys of our class *behind* (ho-ho!) and asked the culprit to step

39

forward. No one moved. Potter was at the back, near me and Pete, almost wetting himself. I got the feeling that he didn't want to make his name any more. But he might as well have signed each print because on every left buttock in every one there was a wart like you'd expect to see on a hog, and he was the only boy in our class with a wart just there. (The teachers didn't know this, but you can't hide bum warts in the showers after Games, so even if we hadn't seen him butt the copier every boy would have known it was Potter's.) Gradually, all eyes found their way to him. They couldn't help it. It was like they were drawn to him by magnets. Hubbard finally got the message and looked directly at Harry (pretty red in the face by this time) as he said:

'For the last time before I suspend the lot of you for a very long time, who is responsible for this *childish* act?'

And Potter stepped forward. 'Me, sir,' he said in a trembly little voice.

'You did this?' Mother Hubbard said.

'Yes, sir.'

'Oh.'

It was obvious what that 'Oh' meant. It meant that Potter would get a detention and a note to his parents but nothing more major. If it had been me or Pete or Ryan or Atkins, or almost any other boy, we'd have been suspended from the school battlements if there were any, but not Harry Potter. If they'd suspended him, local radio might have picked it up, then TV, then the big national papers. The tabloids would have had a field day. Reporters would be hanging round the school gates for a week. Why? Why do you think? Because of the poor sap's *name*, of course!

CHAPTER FOUR

Like I said, most of the rest of that school day was pretty average. Average as in dull. There wasn't the teensiest hint that everything was going to go banana-shaped by home-time. I didn't pay attention to most of the day anyway. Other things than school on my mind. At lunch in the Concrete Garden, where the Musketeers have a private bench and swap crisps and sandwiches every weekday, Ange asked me what was up.

'What makes you think something's up?'

'Well, you're not your usual self today.'

'What's my usual self?'

'Oh, I don't know. Chirpy, sarcastic, critical…'

What I didn't tell her, or Pete, was that I was worried about my mum. Just a bit, you understand, nothing major. Did I mention that she threw up that morning and blamed it on last night's prawn curry? Who did she think she was kidding? Well I know who she *thought* she was kidding, but she'd hardly

touched that curry so who did she think believed that was what had made her sick? Then I remembered that she hadn't been eating much of anything lately, and she wasn't looking so hot either. I also remembered the hospital appointment that she and my father didn't want to talk about in front of me. She was going there to have 'something checked', she said. What something? Dad was even taking the day off work to go with her, so it had to be serious. And what about last night's ironing lesson? Mum had never tried to show me how to iron before. And the reason she gave for showing me?

'If anything happened to me, you wouldn't know what to do.'

If anything happened to me. Like she thought it might – soon!

As the day trudged on, and me with it, I got more and more worried. We don't always see eye to eye, Mum and me, or even nose to nose. We have rows. We shout at one another. She tells me off for being sarky, or lazy, for not doing my homework or tidying my room, or making my bed like she asked, all sorts of stuff, and I make fun of her hair, her clothes, her suicidally depressing TV soaps. But she's my mum.

43

The only one I've got. I can't go to IKEA for a replacement. Mothers don't come in flat packs. They're flesh and blood and nail polish. They have to be there from the start, so they can be trained in the ways of the real world (slowly in my mother's case) by their super-smart kids.

The final lesson of the afternoon was RE. We had a newish teacher for this. Our previous RE teacher, Mr Prior, finally gave up after his third nervous breakdown and went off to do something less stressful than try and ram superstition into our disbelieving skulls.* His replacement – Mr Staples – was just as bald as Mr Prior, but he grew his hair extra long on one side and combed it over his dome to try and kid the world he was fully thatched. Mr Staples wore a dark-blue blazer with silver buttons, and he had holiday-camp-type badges all down both lapels, except they weren't holiday camp badges, they were badges for religions. I only knew one of them, the fishy one, because some people have it on the back of their cars alongside CLEAN ME. When we asked about the badges on his lapels during his first lesson, Mr Staples said, 'Each of these badges represents a different faith.'

---

* Rowing forwards across the Pacific, the rumour was.

So we got started. Well, you have to test the water with new teachers, don't you? See how far you can prod them before they burst.

'What's a faith, sir?'

'It's a religion. Surely you know that.'

'How many religions are there, sir?'

'Quite a lot.'

'Why so many, sir?'

'Oh, you know, different cultures...'

'Do you believe in all the religions you've got badges for, sir?'

'My personal beliefs have no bearing on this lesson, but no, I wouldn't go so far as to say that I believe in all of them.'

'So why are you wearing their badges?'

'Because this lesson is about comparative religion, not just one.'

'What's comparative religion, sir?'

'It's the study of many religions.'

'Why are we doing that, sir?'

'Because the curriculum says we must.'

'Why does it say that, sir?'

'Because it's been decided.'

'Who by, sir – God?'

'No, not by God, by the people who make such rulings.'

'Do you know these people, sir?'

'I don't know them personally, no.'

'But you're still doing what they tell you.'

'Yes, it's my job to do so. Now please stop asking questions and let's get started.'

'Do all these religions have different gods, sir?'

'Well, no, most of them have the same god, though some know him by a different name.'

'Why doesn't God stick to just one name, sir?'

'It's not God who decides which name he's known by, it's Man.'

'Is that the same man who tells you to talk about all your badges?'

'I mean Man in general.'

'You mean a man who's a general, sir?'

'No, I don't mean that at all, don't be silly.'

'What does God think about that, sir?'

'What does God think about what?'

'About people calling him different names.'

'I really can't say, I haven't asked him.'

'Why don't you send him an email?'

'I don't think God has an email address.'

'Oh, he must have. Everyone has an email address.'

'I don't, and I don't want one.' (Julia Frame.)

'If all these religions have the same god, sir, why are they different?'

'That's quite a complicated subject, which we'll get to another day.'

'Which day's that then?'

'I mean some future lesson.'

'Oh, goody. Give us something to really look forward to.'

That was our first session with Mr Staples. Two or three lessons later, the Thursday I'm rattling on about, I stuck my hand up because I needed to go for a tinkle. I hadn't gone at lunch-time, hadn't thought of it, probably because I was worried about my mum, but my legs had been in a knot for the past twenty minutes. Another five and there'd have been a puddle on the floor that I'd never live down.

'Very well, Joseph, but be as quick as you can.'

'Jiggy, sir.'

'I'm sorry?'

'Jiggy, not Joseph. You want a badge for that too?'

Teachers. Such hard work.

I scooted along the corridor to the Boys, spurted

my orangeade with a gasp, washed the McCue hands like my mother's always yelling at me to, and stepped into the corridor. I'd just started the return to the RE room when I heard a voice from the other side of an approaching corner — Mr Rice's, which you can't miss even with cotton wool in your ears. I didn't want to bump into him just then. He'd probably have a go at me for chortling when he jogged into the lamp post on the way to school. I needed to hide till he went by. But where? The lavs were too far behind me now and there were no other corners to dive round. The only door in view was the one attached to the caretaker's broom cupboard, so I ran to it, hoping it was unlocked and there was no one on the other side of it. I turned the handle. The door opened. I looked in. Dark, great, no one at home. I stepped in. Closed the door smartly but quietly behind me.

I couldn't see a thing in there, but I'd got a glimpse of the interior as I jumped in and had a mental snapshot of brooms, mops, sponges, polish, and industrial-sized cans of spray to massacre the flies we get in herds at Ranting Lane. There was

also a bucket to trip over, but my mental snapshot hadn't included that, so I tripped over it. When I tripped – not quite as silently as I would have liked – Mr Rice, who'd just reached the other side of the door, stopped talking. My mouth turned to sawdust. Maybe the person he was chatting to was Mr Heathcliff, the miserable broom honcho who never had much to say, which meant the door could open any sec and I would be discovered and lugged out by the scruff of whatever.

I felt my way through the blackness behind me, very carefully so as to not to fall over anything else or make any more noise, and hid in a row of smelly old workcoats hanging at the back. If the door opened now they'd only see me if they looked down and saw my lower legs and feet.

And I heard it, the door opening, but it closed again almost at once. Relief. I was safe. I waited for Rice to start talking loudly again in the corridor, but he didn't. He must have moved on without saying anything else. But to be on the safe side I decided to give it half a minute and stayed where I was amidst the smelly old workcoats.

When the half minute was up I started forward, step by careful step, hands raised like paws in front of my eyes in case something sharp felt like skewering eyeballs in the dark. I was still walking when I sensed that I wasn't alone in there. I stopped, spine tingling. I couldn't see anyone, of course, and there hadn't been a sound, but...

'Hello?'

This was me, but as I said it I thought I heard a kind of echo of it, like someone else had said the same thing at the very same instant. I was so spooked by this that I didn't care what I crashed into or tripped over or whose arms I ran into in the corridor. I rushed forward, and as I did so...

...I felt someone rush by me!

'Eeeek.'

I know for *certain* that two voices said this. I charged through the dark, slapped the door, tore it open, and shot out into the deserted corridor, blinking like a maniac. From there I looked back to see who'd been in the broom cupboard with me. Apart from the brooms themselves, and the mops, the tripping bucket, the tins of polish, the cans of

industrial fly spray, the dusters, boxes, jars of screws, the brown workcoats at the back, and all the other stuff that school caretakers seem to need, it was empty.

CHAPTER FIVE

I strolled back to my RE lesson. Felt I ought to, seeing as there was still a quarter of an hour to go before home-time. Reaching the classroom I noticed a plaque on the door that I couldn't remember seeing before.

SPIRITUAL TECHNOLOGY

Spiritual Technology? Was that what they called it now? Must have missed that. Still, same old prehistoric mumbo-jumbo, whatever name it travelled under. I opened the door.

'Ah, Juggy, good of you to take the trouble to return to us,' said a voice as I entered the classroom.

'Eh?' I said.

This seemed a pretty good question in the circs. Why? Five reasons.

1. It was Mr Hubbard who'd spoken to me. Hubbard the Head, not Mr Staples, who'd been hosting the lesson when I went to water the pony.

2. Mother Hubbard had known me for more years that I wanted to think about, and unless my ears had deceived me he'd got my name wrong.

3. Eejit Atkins was sitting in the seat next to mine at the back, where Pete Garrett belonged.

4. Pete was sitting next to Martin Skinner, down the front.

5. Pete was wearing glasses – which he doesn't!

It was all very weird, but I didn't want to get into some big fat dialogue about what had gone down in my absence, so I mooched to my desk at the back like nothing was out of order.

'Face front, everyone!' Mr Hubbard said sternly when every eye in every head watched me go. Most of them faced front, though a few couldn't seem to tear their orbs off me. 'You'll have to

catch up, Juggy,' he said to me as I sat down.

'Do my best,' I said. 'And it's Jiggy.'

'Excuse me?'

'I'll write it on the board for you if you like, so you can practise saying it till it sinks in.'

He looked kind of puzzled, but went back to talking about whatever it was he'd been talking about while I was out. I turned to Atkins, who like I said was sitting next to me without my say-so.

'What are you doing in Garrett's seat?' I whispered.

'What?' he whispered back.

'I said what are you doing in Garrett's seat?'

'What do you mean?'

'I mean what are you doing in Garrett's seat?'

'I always sit here. Garrett sits with Skinner. What have you done to your ears?'

'My ears? What about them?'

'They're not sticking out.'

'I didn't know they were supposed to.'

'But they *always* stick out.'

'Have you two finished at the back there?' Mr Hubbard asked.

I looked in his direction. Noticed that the whole

class had turned to gawp at me again.

'Almost,' I said. 'Give us a minute, will you?'

'I'm just filling McCue in on what he's been missing,' Atkins lied.

'Well fill him in afterwards,' Hubbard said. 'Turn *round*, everyone!'

There was quite a lot of whispering as everyone turned round a second time. Mr Hubbard waited impatiently for the last whisper to die, then carried on from where he'd broken off.

'What happened to Mr Staples?' I asked Eejit behind my hand.

'Who?'

'The comb-over king. I know he's not very memorable, but you can't have forgotten him already.'

'Jug, did you take something while you were out?'

'Take something?'

'And please explain those *ears*.'

'What is this ear fixation?' I said, touching one of my perfectly normal lugs. 'And who are you to ask questions anyway, talking like that?'

'Like what?'

'Like an ordinary human being.'

'I'm talking the way I always talk,' he said.

'No, you're not.'

'I am.'

'Atkins, you are definitely not talking the way you— '

'You two!' Mr Hubbard shouted. 'One more word and it's detention.'

We buttoned the lips.

Mr H glanced at the clock on the wall. Still a bunch of ticks to go. Maybe he was struggling, I thought. Counting the minutes to the end of the lesson because RE wasn't his subject. Spiritual Technology, I mean. Staples must have been called away and Hubbard had had to stand in for him and was just waffling his way to the bell.

'As today's session is almost up,' he said, 'I think we'll have a quick Q-and-A to see what we've learned to date.'

And then he started asking this string of questions I wouldn't have believed any teacher could dream up, and the class – including Atkins, in his new voice – gave answers you wouldn't believe either. All the questions and answers were

given in dead seriousness, like everyone actually believed what they were saying, which they couldn't possibly. The scene went like this, starting with Mr Hubbard's first question, which was:

'Who was Xenu?'

And the first answer: 'The ruler of the Galactic Confederacy.'

'When was this?'

'Seventy-five million years ago.'

'And the Galactic Confederacy was...?'

'A union of stellar systems.'

'How many stars and planets were contained within those stellar systems?'

'Twenty-six stars, seventy-six planets.'

'One of those planets was Earth. What was the name of Earth in Xenu's time?'

'Teegeeack.'

'Apart from being the omnipotent ruler of the GC, what is Xenu's primary claim to fame?'

'He paralysed billions of people and brought them to Teegeeack.'

'Why did he do that?'

'Because his corner of the galaxy was overpopulated, and he was a meany.'

'How did Xenu bring the people here?'

'In a fleet of spaceships.'

'Space *planes*, Gemma. The Founder has written that they resembled 1960s aeroplanes. What did Xenu do with the prisoners once they landed?'

'He positioned the planes round volcanoes and put bombs in them. In the volcanoes, not the planes.'

'Sir?'

'Yes, Martin?'

'If Xenu wanted to kill all the people why didn't he just throw them out on the way to Teegeeack?'

'Xenu's thinking on this has not been passed down to us,' Mr Hubbard said. 'Were there any survivors after the bombs went off? Bryan, how about you?'

Ryan looked up from the football mag he was reading under cover of his desk. 'How about me what?'

'Were there any survivors of Xenu's bombs?'

He shrugged. 'Dunno. Don't care.' (Ryan, the Voice of *Sanity*?)

'Anyone else?' Mr Hubbard asked.

There was, but I didn't see who, just saw a hand

in the air behind some heads. 'No one knows how many survived,' this person said.

'The figure is indeed unknown,' said the man 'but a considerable number did survive. The physical forms of the majority perished, of course, but not their souls. Who can tell me the proper name for those souls?'

'Thetans, sir!'

'Well done, Julia. What happened to the thetans?'

'I know! I know!'

This was Pete, wriggling in the seat next to Skinner with his hand in the air. Pete Garrett was speaking up in *class*? Pete Garrett had an answer to a question like *that*?

'Yes, Peter?'

'They were taken to huge cinemas in the Canary Isles and Hawaii and places.'

'That's right. Where they watched…?'

'3D films for twenty-six days.'

'*Thirty*-six!' Holly Gilder cried.

'Correct, Holly!' Mr Hubbard turned to her. 'Can you tell me what kind of material the thetans were subjected to during those thirty-six days?'

'Propaganda, sir. Phoney religious stuff.'

'Excellent! And what happened to the thetans once they'd absorbed all this false information?'

Pete jerked his hand up again. 'They were put into the bodies that'd survived the explosions!'

'And that means...what exactly?'

'That everyone walking the Earth today has thousands of souls loaded with total crap,' muttered Ryan.

'Everyone except True Believers like us,' Mr Hubbard said. 'Now, just one more before we— '

Too late. The bell went. Just in time too. One more question and answer like the ones I'd just heard and my head would have pinged off my neck and bounced out the window to be pecked to pieces by pigeons.

I was in a bit of a daze as I grabbed my school bag and dragged it towards the door. Something had happened here while I was admiring my reflection in the urinal and hiding in the broom cupboard. Something that didn't make any kind of sense.

'Are you all right, Juggy?' Mother Hubbard asked as I reeled by.

'Is anyone?' I said. 'And it's Jiggy. Jiggy, OK?'

Close up, I noticed that he wore a little badge. Just one badge, shaped like a volcano. Whatever loopy religion he'd been banging on about, it wasn't one of the ones on Mr Staples' lapels.

CHAPTER SIX

Everyone else left the classroom like normal kids – pushing, shouting, laying life-threatening hexes on one another – but me, I left like I'd just stepped off the scariest roller-coaster at the fair. Atkins was waiting for me outside.

'What is *wrong* with you?' he said.

'Wrong with *me*!' I cried.

'What do you mean?'

'You. You're like a different person.'

'Jug,' said a voice. Angie's. She'd got tangled up with some of the others in the corridor, broken free, was coming towards us.

'Hang on,' I said, shoving a finger in each ear and looking at both tips. (No wax.) 'My name. What is it again?'

'Which one?' said Ange.

'Which one? How many have I got?'

'Well, you've got Jug, Juggy, McCue, and right now Wallybrain.'

'What's this Jug-Juggy stuff?' I said.

'And your ears,' said Angie. 'How did you do that?'

'Do *what*? They're just my *ears*.'

I barged through the doors to the playground, where the throng of kids were trying to trip one another up on the way to the school gates. I saw Pete a little way off. His shirt wasn't hanging out for a change and his tie was done up properly, also for a change, and he was still wearing those glasses. I went over to him.

'What's with the specs?'

He scowled at me. 'What?'

'The bottle-tops. Where'd you get 'em, Zappa's Joke shop?'

'What's wrong with them?'

'What's wrong with them, Garrett, is that you don't wear glasses.'

'I do. I've worn glasses for years.'

'No, you haven't.'

'I have, haven't I?' he said to Angie, who'd joined us with Atkins.

'Never noticed,' she answered.

'Obviously you haven't either till now,' he said

63

to me. 'Why the sudden interest?'

'Well, we're buds.'

'Buds? You and me? Since when?'

'Since the three of us were bumps in our mothers' dodgy dungarees from Help the Pregnant.'

'The three of us? Which three?'

'You, me and Ange, who else?'

He looked at Angie. She looked at him. They looked at me.

'What are you on about?' they said together.

Before I could answer, we were interrupted – by Skinner.

'Come on, PG. Tea round mine tonight, remember.'

Pete (*PG*?) glared at me one last time, then went off arm-in-arm with Skinner. Skinner, who he's always saying is the kind of creep he wouldn't even use as a boot-scraper. I was still trying to get over this when I felt a finger and thumb on my left ear. I jerked my head away.

'What are you *doing*?'

'Trying to find out how you did it,' said Angie.

'Did what?'

She peered behind the ear. 'There's nothing there,' she said in a voice of wonder.

I shook her off and headed for the gates, but couldn't get through in a hurry because of the eager escape committee still filling the gap. When I finally made it I found that Angie was right behind me. With Atkins.

'Don't you have some monkey chums to go home with?' I asked him as we walked away.

'Only you two,' he replied in his weird new human voice.

It wasn't only his voice that was human either. He wasn't walking the Atkins walk: hunched over, dragging his fists, lower lip a landing strip for bluebottles. How come?

And then it came to me. The truth. My heels carved a dent in the pavement.

'OK, who came up with all this?'

They skidded to a couple of other halts on either side of me.

'All what?'

'The unnatural behaviour, the ear references, the name game, Garrett pretending to be pals with Skinner, the loony class about aliens – how did you

65

get Staples and Hubbard to go along with *that*?!'

They stared at me like I was a plughole salesman from Mars. The stares of people who weren't going to admit they were fooling around. That did it. I can take a joke as well as the next kid, and probably the kid next to him, but enough was enough. They could milk their stupid gag as much as they liked, but without me. I stormed off. Walked the rest of the way alone.

When I reached the estate, and my street, and finally my house I would have gone in the front door but I'd forgotten the key Mum and Dad presented me with in a special box when I got out of hospital after my thirteenth birthday.* Because I couldn't get in the front door, I nipped up the alley a few houses along and round the back of the row. Our back gate is always kept bolted, so I had to haul myself up and reach over the top to get in. I did this, but couldn't feel the bolt. I reached further down. There it was. Must have misjudged the position. I yanked the bolt, swung in on the gate, jumped off it to rebolt it behind me, walked round the L-shape of our garden fence and saw something that made me almost trip over my

---

* If you don't already know why I spent my thirteenth birthday in hospital you'll have to read a thing called *Ryan's Brain*. You need your frontal lobes examined if you think I'm going through all that again here.

toes. My kennel wasn't there. The kennel I'd made so lovingly in woodwork for the dog we didn't have, never wanted, had no plans to get. The fact that I'd made it for a non-existent dog didn't give anyone the right to chuck it. I'd have some strong words for the parental types when they got in from work.

Next stop, the garden gnome that stands beside the step. He was the next stop because the key to the back door is stored in the hole Dad drilled in his little red bottom. But...

No gnome. I glanced around. No sign of him. They'd dumped him too? When? Overnight, while I was asleep?

I looked around in case they'd only moved the gnome, but he wasn't anywhere. That left me with a problem. How could I get in the house if there was no garden gnome with a hole in its backside?

But then I noticed something else. Quite close to where our trusty old gnome has stood since Dad won it in a raffle stood a fairy. A stone fairy, with stone wings. So my parents had swapped our fat, scowling, hairy old gnome for a soppy, smirking, unhairy fairy. Well, I wouldn't miss him much, but

I hoped Dad had run a drill into the fairy's behind too. I got down and peered under her little stone skirt. No hole.

I got up and kicked the fairy. Tinkle. No, that wasn't its name, it was the sound of a key dropping from under one of its sickeningly cute little wings. I picked the key up and shoved it in the lock. I turned it. The door opened. I went in, miffed that no one had told me they'd dumped my beautiful kennel and traded in the gnome. For that I was going to empty the entire biscuit tin into my trap, and if my mother got uppity at tea-time because I didn't eat the lousy processed food she put in front of me, I'd let her have it. I would not be treated like this. Who did these parents think they *were*?

I slammed the door and lobbed my school bag into the corner where it spends most of its life. Thought the house smelt slightly unusual, but shrugged. My old lady's always experimenting with smells. I was halfway through the kitchen door when I skidded to a halt like a flying haddock had socked me in the kisser. The cupboards, the phoney quarry tiles, the aprons on a hook, none of them were the same as the ones I'd ignored at

breakfast. Even the fridge magnets were different. Even the calendar. The calendar (Mum's choice) should have shown famous paintings I didn't know. This one didn't have famous unknown paintings. It had photos of muscle-men and muscle-women with sparkly grins. Dad might have chosen one like that – the muscle-women anyway – but if he'd tried to hang it Mum would have hung him there instead.

I just stared, stared and stared some more. Could they have had workmen in to totally remake the kitchen while I was at school? Was that even *possible*? I felt a worry coming on. My legs starting to twitch. Then my feet started to soft-shoe. Then my elbows started to flap. In twenty seconds I was jigging round the kitchen like a ballet dancer with ants in her knickers.

I forced myself to stand still. Wasn't easy, but I managed it. I rubbed my eyes, hoping I'd imagined all this. When I stopped rubbing, I looked again. No change. This was crazy. I knew my own house. Ought to, I'd been told off in it enough times, done enough rotten homework in it. But this didn't look like my house, even though the rooms and walls

and doors were in the right place. Was it possible that I could have walked into the wrong one by mistake? I went out to the hall, opened the front door. The broken street lamp was still by the gate where it should be. It was my house all right. So what *was* this?

Because I couldn't make sense of any of this, I felt a sudden need to hide myself away while my brain unsteamed. I staired it up to my room, went in, shut the door, leant against it with my eyes closed. What an afternoon. First, Mother Hubbard talking seriously about aliens. Then Pete being friends with Skinner but not me. Now this. I took a bunch of long, slow breaths, eyes still closed, and started to feel better. Whenever the world does one of its back flips and a fresh batch of weirdness starts up, I always have my bedroom, my sanctuary. Nothing can touch me there. I opened my eyes, smiling, and…

That wasn't my wallpaper!

That wasn't my chest of drawers!

That wasn't my anything!

And where was my bed? There wasn't any kind of bed. Unless you counted the cot.

Yes, a cot. A baby's cot. I rushed to it. A little brown teddy-bear stared up at me, all glassy-eyed like it had been drinking.

I had never seen that teddy in my life!

I flung myself at the door, tore it open, and tottered downstairs like a Really Golden Oldie. I returned to the back door and whipped my mobile out of my bag. I don't usually take my phone to school because they don't like us using them in class for some reason, but I had that day, don't remember why. I punched digits. A voice answered.

'Ange,' I said. 'I think I've lost it.'

'Yes…' she said, like this wasn't something new.

'I'm at my house. Except that it's not.'

'I don't get you.'

'The house I lived in when I left this morning, number 23, seems to have other people living in it.'

'Number 23? Since when have you lived with Mr Rice and Miss Weeks?'

'Uh?'

'When you say you're there,' Angie said, 'you mean outside, right?'

'No, I mean in the back hall.'

There was a pause. Then she said, 'How'd you get in?'

'The stone fairy in the garden.'

'Mr Rice has a stone fairy?'

'I don't know what Mr Rice has. What I do know is there's a fairy where my gnome should be and everything in the house is different too.'

'Juggy,' said Angie.

'Jiggy,' I said.

'What's going on?' she said.

'You tell me,' I said. 'Ange. Do me a favour. Come over. This is turning into an all-for-lunch emergency.'

'A what?'

'Just get here. Please.'

She sighed heavily, but said, 'Oh, very well. Stay there. But outside. I'll be there in ten.'

'Ten? Ten minutes? Angie, this is a crisis. I need you now!'

'Yes, well it takes eight minutes walking fast to get to you from my side of the estate and I'm not working up a sweat for you when I know you're messing me about.'

'What do you mean, your side of the—?'

She clicked off before I could complete the question.

My cheeks puffed themselves out. My head shook itself. I'd never been great at maths, but suddenly nothing, I mean *nothing*, added up. I had a feeling that even two and two might have a struggle making it to four right now.

CHAPTER SEVEN

I needed something to lean against, so I spined the busted street lamp outside the front gate and gazed across the road to where Angie had lived almost as long as I'd lived at *The Dorks*. That very morning I'd seen her and Pete shove one another off the step before joining me in the street to drag our bags to school like we do every morning except Saturdays, Sundays, holidays, and anytime we can con our parents that we're not well enough to go.

I also knew where I lived, but suddenly my insane PE teacher, the Deputy Head and a glassy-eyed brown bear seemed to be living there instead. Not only that, but there was a stone fairy in the back garden and no dog kennel for the dog we didn't have. There were even different aprons and a different calendar in the kitchen. Crazy or what? Crazy or not, it wasn't until Angie finally dawdled along the street that my jaw hit my chest.

'What's with the fancy dress?' I gasped.

'She looked down at herself. 'It's just an ordinary dress.'

'Yeah, but it's pretty. It's all…girly.'

'I am a girl,' she said. 'I like pretty things.'

It was the first time Angie had ever said that, but I shook myself. More important things to talk about.

'Is Pete coming?'

'Pete?'

'Thought you'd have brought him. He likes to be in on these things.'

'Do you mean Pete Garrett?'

'What other Pete do you know?'

'I don't. Why would I bring Pete Garrett with me?'

'Because he lives with you?' I prompted.

'He what?'

'Because he lives with you.'

She scowled. 'Look, I've got things to do at home. If you're living out some fantasy here, let's get it over with, shall we – inside?'

'Inside?'

'Your skanky peasant house.'

'That's just it,' I said. 'I don't know which

is my skanky peasant house.'

'You were serious about that?'

I kicked the wall of number 23. 'This morning I lived here. Now I don't. Care to explain that?'

'Have you got your front door key?' she asked.

I ground my teeth patiently. 'If I had my front door key, why would I have gone round the back and looked up a fairy's skirt?'

'How would I know? Maybe it's your hobby. Come with me.'

'Where to?'

She didn't answer, so I followed her a couple of doors along, then down the alley I'd gone down earlier, then to the back gate of number 25, Mrs Overton's.

'Up you go,' she said.

'Up I go what?'

'The gate.'

'I can't do that.'

'Course you can. Used to do it all the time before you got the front door key you don't have today.'

'I went up *that* gate all the time,' I said, pointing to the next one along.

She sighed. 'Have it your way, but get up this one now.'

So I climbed the Overtons' gate. Climbed it, threw my arm over the top, found the bolt, no trouble, yanked it, swung in, jumped down.

'After you,' I said, standing aside because I'm such a gentleman. She was just walking through when I noticed something I'd missed before. 'Ange, how long's your hair been that colour?'

'What colour?'

'That reddish tint.'

'About a month.'

'I never noticed.'

'Why would you? You're a boy.'

She walked along the path. I closed the gate quietly behind me but didn't bolt it. I didn't feel right about this. We were trespassing on someone else's property. Suppose Mrs O or Dawn were in and saw us from a window? Would they call the cops? Would we end up in some cellar having lights shone in our eyes while men in braces threatened to tear our toenails out if we didn't talk?

The Overtons' house was just like ours – I'd been inside it a couple of times with Mum – but their

back garden wasn't the same shape. You still had to go round a bit of fence to get to the house, though. I followed Angie round the bit of fence, and saw…

'My kennel!'

Yes, there it was, my woodwork project dog kennel.*

'Hey, some guard-dog you are,' Angie said.

'What do you mean some guard-dog I am?'

'Not you, toggle-brain – Stallone.'

'Stallone? My cat?'

'Your cat?'

'Yes, my cat, my cat.'

'Woof.'

That wasn't me. Wasn't Angie either. It was this big black beast that had just looked out at us.

'There's a dog in my kennel!' I cried, freezing to the spot.

Dogs do that to me, freeze me to spots. All dogs except china ones, plastic ones and the long hot ones you get in rolls with onions. Big black ones that flash their munchers as they lurch towards me are the worst. That's what the dog from my kennel was doing right now. When this enormous stunt double for the Hound of

---

* The kennel woodwork project happens in *The Meanest Genie*.

the Baskerwillies reached me, it — well of course!
— sniffed my crotch.

'Get it off me!' I yelled, reaching for the clouds.

'He's not doing anything,' Angie said.

'He's sniffing my zip!'

'He always does that.'

'Now he's licking it!'

'That's because he loves you.'

'I never saw this monster in my life before! It's
sure not Charlie Farnsbarns, and I don't like him
either.'

'Charlie who?'

'Farnsbarns. Who lives here. In the house, not
my kennel.'

Angie laughed. 'Here, Stallone, come to someone
who likes you.'

The hound turned to her and licked her
outstretched hand.

'Stallone?' I said.

'His name,' she said. 'Haven't we been over that?'

'But Stallone's a cat.'

'Quiet, you'll give him an identity crisis.'

'He's licking your hand,' I said.

'Yes. Sweet.'

'Sweet? How can you stand all that gloop running down your wrist? And that tongue could have been anywhere.'

'Not anywhere,' Angie said. 'It's been here with him in the garden all day.'

'It's been at my zip.'

'Apart from that.'

'Before that it was probably licking *his* zip.'

Her face twisted like an old rag and she pulled her hand away from the mutt's gleaming tongue. 'That's one image I did *not* need.'

She wiped her hand on my arm. I shuddered and took my jacket off. Held it by the loop in the collar as far away from me as I could get it.

Angie carried on along the path and I stepped carefully round the dog to follow her. The thing growled at me. Once they get the zip-love out of their system dogs always growl at me. They probably sense that I'm not a massive fan.

As I went after Angie I saw something familiar beside the back step.

'Our garden gnome!'

'Oh, something you recognise,' she said sarcastically.

When I reached the gnome I stooped, felt his bottom, found his hole, pulled the key out.

'Now what?'

'Now open the door,' said Angie.

'But it's not my door,' I protested.

She snatched the key, shoved it in the lock, turned it, flipped the handle, opened the door. When she handed the key back, I re-inserted it in the gnome's rear end and followed her inside, along the hall, into the kitchen. My feet locked just inside the doorway. I gaped around. It was my house's kitchen. My kitchen's cupboards and blinds and phoney quarry-tile floor. My mother's famous unknown paintings calendar was on the wall. Even the fridge magnets looked right.

'I...I...I...' I said, pronouncing all the vowels very carefully.

Angie leant against a cupboard and folded her arms, waiting to see if I could go on to construct a full sentence.

'Ange,' I said, taking a stab at it. 'I've lived next door to this house ever since we moved to the estate, but...'

'But?'

'I gotta check upstairs.'

I scampered up the stairs, too agitated to remove my shoes, like Mum insists whenever anyone goes upstairs. Angie followed more slowly.

On the landing, I pushed back the door of what would have been my room if this had been my house. Pushed it kind of timidly, no idea what to expect. I looked in. It was my room all right, but it was so much neater and tidier than my room knew how to be except after one of Mum's blitzes. And the bed. When I left it that morning, the pillows were in knots and the duvet was half on the floor. This bed was made. Perfectly made. How come? Mum wouldn't have had time to make it before going to work. *So who had made my bed?*

I was about to go in when I noticed that the third bedroom door on the landing was open. In my house, my actual house, that's the room we chuck all our junk in so no one can come to stay. I couldn't see any junk through the bit of open door, but I could see something else, something that shouldn't be there. I went to the door and pushed it back. No junk. Not one bit. But...

'Whose is that?' I said in amazement.

Angie joined me at the door. 'Whose is what?'

'That bed. Who's using this room?'

She didn't tell me. She said, 'Oh, this is getting too boring. You don't want my help, you want to just string me along some more. I have better ways of wasting my time than playing some stupid game with *you* boys.'

This annoyed me as much as she was pretending to be annoyed by me. I gave her a heavy scowl.

'I am not,' I said firmly, 'playing some stupid game.'

'Is that a fact?' she said, starting downstairs.

'Yes, it's a fact,' I replied, going after her.

She was halfway down when the front door bell rang. It rang again, for a bit longer, before she'd quite reached the bottom. Then the letterflap opened and a little kid's voice shouted through.

'Joseph! Joseph, I know you're in, I can see your bag down the hall! Let me in, I need a weeeeee!'

'Joseph?' I said. 'Is whoever that is calling me?'

'Who else calls you Joseph?' said Angie. 'Who else is *allowed* to?'

She opened the door. A little girl in a green school uniform rushed in from the step. 'Hi, Ange!'

the girl said, scampering past her and into the downstairs cloakroom.

'And I suppose you don't remember her,' Angie said.

I stared at the closed khazi door. 'Remember her? I never saw her in my life.'

'Better not try that one on her. She'll be most upset.'

'Why would she be upset?'

Angie glared at me. 'Because she's your little SISTER, Jug. Who thinks the sun shines out of your armpits!'

And she went, slamming the front door behind her.

CHAPTER EIGHT

I was kind of stuck for a minute. Couldn't move, couldn't think. There I am in the house next door, which all of a sudden seems to be my house, and we have a mangy dog called Stallone instead of a mangy cat called Stallone, and someone I don't know uses the junk room as a bedroom, and there's this little kid, this girl I'm supposed to believe is my sister, in the downstairs toilet that my mother calls the 'cloakroom', even though none of us hangs a cloak in there, or even has one. Some wild things had happened to me in my time, but whatever was happening here was shaping up to be the wildest yet. When I heard the toilet flush, my toes started to twitch. One more second and my feet would be dancing me up the wall. I had to give them something useful to do, so I ordered them to run me back up to the bedroom that looked like mine only tidier. I closed the door behind me, and, because there was no lock on it, jammed the chair

under the handle to stop anyone coming in. With the chair in place my feet started to calm down. I sat on the bed. Safe!

But then...

Footsteps. Coming up the stairs. My spine shot me to attention.

'Joseph?'

The girl. Calling me. By the name no one gets away with.

Then she was knocking on the door.

I didn't answer.

She knocked again. Said 'Joseph' again.

I still didn't answer. I felt trapped. This small but total stranger was knocking and calling me by the forbidden name and there was nowhere to go except—

I looked at the window. All I had to do was open it and...

No. It would hurt.

The girl turned the handle, but the door stayed shut. To make extra sure it would hold, I jerked my lower portions off the bed and jammed my feet against the chair. I was now lying with the top half of my back on the bed and my legs stretched out

like a bridge between it and the chair.

'Joseph, let me in!'

I said nothing. The door handle rattled.

'JOSEPH! STOP MESSING ABOUT!'

I continued to say nothing, but I was getting more nervous by the minute. It might only be a little kid on the other side of that door, but it was a little kid who was making out that she knew me and expected to be let in. I eyed the window again. If I whipped my foot off the chair, would I make it down to my mother's favourite rose bush before the kid pushed the door in? All right, I might break an arm or leg, but I still had another one of each. Of course, if I broke my neck I didn't have a spare, but maybe I—

'JOSEPH McCUE, I WON'T SPEAK TO YOU EVER AGAIN IF YOU DON'T OPEN THIS DOOR RIGHT *NOW*!'

This was followed by some kicks on the wood. I suddenly wished Angie hadn't shoved off. This wasn't a situation for one lone Musketeer, specially a male one. Be even better if Pete had been there too. Then I could have stood behind them, peering between them. But they weren't there, either of

them. It was just me, under siege from this pint-sized brat who didn't sound like she was going to give up and leave quietly any time soon. There was no alternative. I had to face this. Face the little person on the other side of the door. Find out why she was in my house, pretending to be my sister, calling me by *that* name.

Heart all thumpety-thump, I took my feet off the chair and slid off the bed. I went to the door. She was still kicking it, still shouting to be let in. I took the chair away, but kept the toes of one foot against the door.

'Whaddayawant?'

'I want to come in and talk about school!' the kid said.

'Why?'

'Why? Because it's what we always do!'

'No, we don't.'

'We do. Always!'

'Who are you?' I asked through the door.

'What?' she said on the other side of it.

'I said who are you?'

'What do you mean who am I?'

'I mean who are you?'

'Who am I?'

'Yes! Who are you?'

There was a pause. Then she shouted again – 'Joseph McCue, let me iiiiiiiiiiiiiiiiiiiiiiin!' – and kicked the door again. And again. And again.

Pint-sized or not, the kid was obviously a violent type. I couldn't take any chances with someone like that. I looked around for something to bash her with when I opened the door. The only thing that wasn't attached to something else and could be lifted was a table-tennis bat I keep for bouncing ping-pong balls up and down on when I'm really, really bored. But to get to the table-tennis bat I would have to take my foot off the door, and if I took my foot of the door the kid might choose that moment to try the handle again, and if she tried the handle again she'd be able to open the door and come in, which I didn't want her to do before I had a good grip on that bat. But I had to chance it. So I took my foot off the door and made a dash for the bat. And while I was dashing…

…the kid tried the handle. Opened the door. Came in.

I grabbed the bat. I whirled. I stood there, a lean,

muscular, terrifically macho fighting man, ready for anything, even terrifying small girls.

'Come any closer and I'll whack you!!!' I shrieked manfully.

And she…put her little fists on her little hips.

'What is wrong with you?' she demanded. 'What have *I* done?'

'How about trespassing, for starters?' I boomed heroically.

'Trespassing? In your room? You never minded before.'

'Before? I never laid eyes on you before!'

'Joseph,' she said, removing the terrifying fists from the terrifying hips, 'what is it? Are you in trouble at school? Tell me about it.'

'What?' I said.

'Tell me about it,' she repeated.

'You tell me,' I said.

'Tell you what?'

'What you're doing here and who you are. Also, while you're at it, why I'm suddenly living in the house next door.'

She pulled a puzzled face, but I wasn't fooled. This was a set-up, no doubt about it. She took a step

towards me. I raised the table-tennis bat. One swipe would ping-pong her out the door. She reached up, closed her little hand round my muscular wrist like someone stupid enough to imagine they had the strength to stop a person as dynamic as me – and lowered my arm. Yes, she lowered my arm. Not with superhuman strength, not with any strength much, but just by doing it. When it came to it, I couldn't ping-pong her. Why not? Because of the way she was looking at me. Because of her big blue eyes and her little worried face, and her spiky all-over-the-place hair.

'Joseph,' she said, as gently as someone twice her height and four times her age, 'sit down and talk to me.'

I sat down on the bed. She sat down beside me. Took my hand. Held on to it. Listened while I said that I didn't know what was going on, didn't know why my bedroom and everything else was in this house instead of the one next door, or why my cat was a dog, or why there was a fairy in the garden instead of a gnome, or why Garrett was chums with Skinner instead of me, or why Eejit Atkins spoke like a human being, and that I didn't know

her from a daughter of Eve.

'I see,' she said when it was all out.

'You do?' I said.

'No, but it's very interesting.'

'Interesting? It might be to you. To me it's plain crazy.'

'Yes, that too. You really don't know me?'

'I really don't. Who's behind this?'

'Behind it?'

'Well, it's obviously someone's warped idea of humour at my expense.'

'Do you really believe that?' the little girl said.

'I don't know what I believe.' I never said a truer six words.

She let go of my hand and rolled her sleeves up.

'What are you doing?' I asked, thinking that she was going to try and slap some sense into me or something.

'Just getting comfortable,' she said. 'We have some serious sorting out to do here. First, tell me about your ears.'

'Why does everyone keep asking about my ears?'

'Because they're not the ears we're used to seeing on that head. Mind if I look behind them?'

'What for?'

'May I?'

'Well…OK.'

I leaned my head down. She cleared the hair away and inspected the area behind my lugs. I was glad I'd washed back there only last month.

'Have you done something to them?' she asked.

'Like what?'

'Well, they're not right.'

'No, one's left, it's the way ears are.'

'I mean they're not the way my brother's ears should look.'

'Why should they? I'm not your brother.'

'But you look like him in all other ways.'

I shook her off my ears. 'I do?'

'You want me to show you?'

'I think you'd better.'

She got off the bed and went to the door. 'Don't go away.'

'Where would I go?' I said.

'And keep that door open!' she shouted as she ran downstairs.

I didn't move the whole time she was gone. Just

sat there, mind as empty as a footless shoe.

When she came back she was carrying a framed picture that she kept turned away so I couldn't see it.

'What's that?'

'A photo of my brother, who everyone except me calls Juggy.'

'Juggy,' I said. 'People keep calling me that. My name's Jiggy.'

'Jiggy?' she said. 'Funny name.'

'And Juggy isn't? Why does everyone except you call your brother Juggy?'

'I don't call him it because I think it's insulting. Even when I was little I wouldn't call him it. And Joseph's such a nice name.'

'Matter of opinion. Why is he Juggy to everyone else?'

She turned the picture she'd gone down for. I leaned forward to look at it. An enlarged holiday-type snap of her and her brother. Couldn't have been taken more than a year ago, because she didn't look much different. And her brother...

Was me.

Almost.

There was one thing about him that wasn't like me. The ears. My ears lie pretty flat, like the ears of most people who aren't royalty. The ears of the Jiggy in the photo didn't lie flat. They stuck out like they were held by invisible hands. They looked like jug-handles.

'Juggy...' I murmured, staring at those hefty lugs.

And then I murmured it again. 'Juggy...'

And then I said, 'Holy ear-holes.'

CHAPTER NINE

I couldn't get my head round it, but the thought that someone was pulling one or more of my legs was fading. This little girl didn't look like she knew how to pull legs. She was so serious about all this. So sincere. And those big eyes of hers!

'But if you're not Joseph,' she said, 'who are you?'

'I am Joseph,' I confessed. 'It's just that no one calls me it.'

'I would if you were my brother.'

'Yeah, well I'm not. I'm nobody's brother.'

'But you look just like him. *Exactly* like him apart from the ears.'

I chinned the photo. 'He's welcome to those.'

'I can see why you're not called Juggy,' she said. 'But why Jiggy?'

'Because I jig about sometimes.'

'Jig about?'

'It's something that kicks in when I get nervous.

Doesn't your brother jig?'

'No more than anyone else.'

'That must be it then. I got the jigginess, he got ears.'

'And you're here instead of him,' the girl said.

'Yes, I was kind of getting that too.'

'So where's my brother?'

I said I wished I knew. Then I asked her what her name was.

'Swoozie,' she said.

'Swoozie?'

'My parents named me Suzie, but when I started to talk it came out as Swoozie, and that's who I've been ever since.'

I had a blood-freezing thought.

'If I'm not who I'm supposed to be, it must mean that no one's who I thought they were either. Now I know why Mr Hubbard was hosting the mumbo-jumbo class. And that that wasn't the Pete Garrett I know. Or my Eejit Atkins. Or Angie. And you, you're really who you say you are.'

'Of course I am,' said Swoozie McCue.

'But...how did it happen?'

'Good question. Another good one is where's my Joseph?'

'Maybe he's still here,' I said. 'Maybe he's on his way home from school and is just a bit late.'

'You think?'

'No, not really. He wasn't around when I left school with Atkins and Angie. Which means that right now, this minute, he's in my house, where he doesn't have a sister or a dog.'

Swoozie's eyes welled up with water. Her face crumpled.

'But that's terrible! Poor Joseph! He'll be so confused!'

'He's not the only one.'

'And lonely.'

'He'll get used to that. You do when you're an only child.'

'But he hasn't been an only child for years! There's no one to look after him if I'm not there.'

'Well, there'll be my mum and d...' I stopped. 'Woh! It's your mum and dad who live here, not mine.'

'I certainly hope so,' she said.

Then she plonked herself on the bed beside me.

The worried look was gone. She was all excited now, keen to get a handle on the situation. That's girls for you. They get used to stuff with a snap of a finger and thumb. Must be a gene thing. The get-over-it gene that only females have.

'What we've got to do,' she said, 'is try and work out how to switch you and Joseph back before anyone catches on.'

'Yes,' I said. 'Absolutely.'

'Looks like a job for the Three Cavaleiros.'

'The what?'

'The Three Cavaleiros. Joseph's gang. Don't you have Three Cavaleiros where you're from?'

'No. I've got Three Musketeers. Who are they, these Cavaloorolls?'

'Leiros. Joseph, Angie and Eejit.'

'Eejit? Eejit Atkins is a member of your brother's gang?'

'Of course. He's his best friend. Him and Ange.'

'Atkins is a moron,' I said. 'No McCue would be best friends with him.'

'Eejit isn't a moron. He's very bright. Joseph says he has to practically gag him in class to stop him answering every question.'

I thought about this. The Eejit I'd talked to earlier certainly hadn't seemed dumb. He was like a different species of Eejit. An Eejit that had survived evolution. Atkins Erecticus.

'So why do they call him Eejit?' I asked. 'I know why we call our Eejit 'Eejit' – he's as thick as a breeze block – but why would you call a bright person Eejit?'

'It's a joke,' said Swoozie McCue, the sister I didn't have.

'And he doesn't mind?'

'Doesn't seem to. Shall I phone them?'

I wasn't sure about that. They weren't my Angie and Eejit, and this place's Angie hadn't been very happy with me when she left and might not want to come back. I told Swoozie this. She grinned.

'I'll talk her round. You three need to put your heads together.'

'Seems like you're doing the job of three heads yourself,' I said.

She flashed me a big, pleased smile. 'Thanks, Joseph!' Then she remembered that I wasn't her brother. 'Is it all right to call you that?'

'I prefer Jiggy.'

'Doesn't sound right. And I can't call you Juggy, because people would wonder why I was doing it when I never do.'

'OK. Joseph. Just you.'

She beamed again. 'That's what my brother says. Just me.'

She started for the door. 'Where are you going?' I asked.

'To call Angie. My mobile's in my room.'

She didn't come back with her phone, but I heard her speaking in the room I was used to seeing junk in next door. When she returned, she said, 'Angie says she'll be round later if she's stopped crying, and she'll collect Eejit on the way.'

'Why's she crying?'

'She's chopping onions for tea because her dad's working late.'

'Her dad?'

'Yes, her dad. Why did your eyebrows just shoot up?'

'My eyebrows just shot up because where I'm from Angie's mum and dad split up aeons ago. Her

mum's been living with Pete Garrett's dad since we were ten.'

'Pete Garrett's dad? Mr Garrett the boozer?'

'Boozer? Ollie likes his beer, but I wouldn't call him a *boozer*.'

'Well this one would live in a pub if they didn't keep chucking him out for being drunk and disorderly,' Swoozie said.

Suddenly I heard the front door slam. My body twitched, head to toe.

'Anyone at home?' a voice called from downstairs.

My mother's voice!

Swoozie went to the door and leant out. 'We're in Joseph's room.'

'All right. Just so I know.'

'I can't deal with this,' I whispered as she pushed the door to.

'You'll have to,' she said.

'How? She'll know I'm not her son. We'll have to tell her everything.'

She shook her head. 'She's a Golden Oldie. Think of all the kid-hours we could waste not being believed.'

She was right. Try and tell the GOs some slightly unusual fact and you might as well go back to bed and stuff your face in a pillow.

'She's bound to notice the ears,' I pointed out.

'Mmm, yes,' Swoozie said. 'The ears are a bit of a giveaway.'

'Bet he wishes he could,' I said.

'Bet who wishes he could what?'

'Your brother. Give his ears away.'

'He's used to them. We all are. When he was little, Mum taped them back, but the kids in the Infants made fun of him and he kept coming home in tears, so she had to stop. I wasn't born then, of course. I heard about it later. There was one boy in particular who really got on his case about the ear tape. Bryan Ryan. They've been arch-enemies ever since.'

'Good to know some things don't change,' I said.

'Oh, I know what we can do!'

She fell to her knees and felt under the bed. When she found what she was after she gave it a tug and came up with a ball of fluff-covered chewing-gum the size of a large plum. I had one under my bed just like it. I add more gum to it all

the time. I have an ambition to get it as big as a grapefruit and eBay it to the highest bidder.

'Put it in your mouth,' Swoozie said.

I reared back. 'No chance. It's not mine.'

'Oh, you Josephs!' she said, and jammed it in her own little mouth. It was such a big gumball that it made her cheeks bulge. Can't have been easy to move it around but she did her best, and after a while forced it out again. Then she squeezed the gum with one hand while she picked fluff off her tongue with the other. The gum wasn't as solid any more.

I eyed it suspiciously. 'What are you going to do with it?'

She broke two bits off the gumball and pinched them to make them even softer. 'Turn round,' she said.

I turned round and, in no time at all, my faithful lugs were so much like sticky-out handles that my name could have been *Juggy* McCue.

CHAPTER TEN

Let me tell you, that was one strange tea-time. I sat across from my borrowed sister, with my borrowed father at one end of the table and my borrowed mother at the other. The mother and father were like mine in almost every way. *Almost* every way. This mother's hair was a bit shorter than my mum's, and it had a green streak in it, and the father wore a little gold ring in his right ear. The hair I could cope with, but I couldn't help staring at the earring. Yeah, I know, a lot of men wear earrings, but the Melvin McCue I know would never have a hole drilled in his lobe and stick a ring through it.

And the way they spoke to me. My parents have this completely false idea that I'm going to do something childish or stupid every minute of the day and they're always on guard for when it happens so they can tell me off or ground me or deprive me of something till I apologise. But those two, they talked to me like I was a human being

instead of a thirteen-year-old boy. I wasn't used to that, but to tell you the truth I kind of liked it. I still had to watch my mouth in case I put my feet in it, but Swoozie was always there to cover my tracks when I said something that seemed a bit odd to them. The thing is, this was a McCue family of four and I was used to a McCue family of three. Families of four have done things that families of three haven't, and it stands to reason that when there's an extra kid, and the extra kid's a girl, some of the things they've done are with her, and I wouldn't know about those things. A good example of something they did with her occurred that evening. Her mum was taking Swoozie for a ballet lesson. My mum never took me to ballet lessons. Normally, Swoozie went to ballet right after school, she told me, but the lessons had become so popular that some of the older students (which included her even though she was only eight) had been asked to take the later one. She didn't mind because it meant she could have her tea first.

The other Angie Mint arrived just after half-six. She'd phoned Eejit on the way and met him

outside. This Eejit lived in the same house as my Eejit, only where I come from it's just over the fence, not next-door-but-one. When the dad-who-wasn't-mine let them in, they kicked their shoes off like people have to in my real home, and trotted upstairs. Swoozie only had a few minutes before she went to ballet, but she filled them in on the basics. When they didn't believe her right off she stood in front of them with her little hands on her little hips, and said, 'It's true! He's not Juggy, he's *Jiggy*!'

'What sort of name is Jiggy?' said Atkins.

I pulled a face at him. 'What sort of name's Juggy? Better still, what sort of name's Eejit? You have to be a prize-winning cretin to let people call you Eejit if you're not one.'

'He has a point,' Angie said to him.

Atkins grinned. 'Yeah, guess he has.'

To make sure they got it that I wasn't her brother, Swoozie showed them the chewing gum she'd wedged behind my ears. She even took one piece out so they could see how flat the ear went without a prop, and waggled it back and forth to prove that it wouldn't stay out when she let go.

After that they had to believe. When Swoozie left, they threw question after question at me. I won't bore you with them all because they were mostly the same ones Swoozie had asked after I let her into the bedroom, but there were two I couldn't answer.

1. 'How?'
2. 'When?'

'I'm guessing that the "when" was during Spiritual Technology,' the other Eejit Atkins said.

'Why then?' the other Angie asked.

'Because he was his usual self when he headed for the bogatorium, but when he returned his ears were flat and he wondered why I was sitting in Garrett's seat.' He looked at me. 'Wherever you're from, I can't believe you're friends with that bonehead.'

'Can't believe it myself sometimes,' I said. 'But it's Atkins who's the real bonehead there. How long have you and Juggy hung out together?'

'Couple of years. Since we realised we were better than anyone else at EI.'

'EI?'

'Then we started practising together, thinking up ideas, working out strategies, and here we

are today, representing the school.'

'Representing the school in what?'

'Look, can we leave the background info till we've sorted out what happened here?' Angie said. 'We need to find out where Juggy went and how come his clone took his place.'

This got me. 'Hey,' I said. 'Get this straight. I'm nobody's clone. I'm a total original. A one-off. There is no other Jiggy McCue.'

'Maybe not,' she said, 'but there's a Juggy McCue, and only two obvious differences, both of them on the side of your head. You want to push that one out, by the way? Looks kind of weird, one ear like a wing, the other like a flapjack.'

My ears were that way because Swoozie had forgotten to rejam the gum behind the one she'd waggled for them. I replaced it and wiped my hand because it had been in two other mouths.*

'What's your pal like?' I asked when Ear Two was back in handle mode.

'Juggy?' Angie said. 'Except for the ears he's exactly like you.'

'No, I mean as a person. Is he loaded with character, charisma, charm, stuff like that?'

---

* The gum, not my hand

'Not that I've noticed.'

'But he's very witty, yes? Good with the one-liners, the rapid come-backs?'

'Not especially, no.'

I was shocked. This Juggy person was like me but he didn't have these essential McCue characteristics? But there was one thing my almost-double had to share with me.

'Tell me some of the insane things that have happened to him.'

The other Eejit Atkins and the other Angie Mint looked at one another like I was suddenly talking backwards in Swedish.

'Insane things? Like what?'

'Well, like…'

I took a long sorrowful breath, then ticked off the list, one tragic event after another.

'Like his mother buying him underpants that take over his life.' [1]

'Like switching bodies with a girl and having to wear green knickers in netball practice.' [2]

'Like peeing a thousand and one times and conjuring up a teenage genie with dreadlocks who makes him eat maggots.' [3]

---

[1] *The Killer Underpants*

[2] *The Toilet of Doom*

[3] *The Meanest Genie*

'Like discovering a small green creature on the council tip that lives on human nose-juice.' [4]

'Like being haunted by a dead goose.' [5]

'Like having all his clothes disappear in public places whenever he writes with a certain pen.' [6]

'Like sprouting a tail after being blackmailed by a puppet in a red bowler hat.' [7]

'Like wading through the slime in a giant slug's gut because he stepped aside in football practice.' [8]

'Are you talking about your nightmares?' Atkins asked when I'd finished.

'Wish I was,' I said. 'They're things that have happened to me.'

'You're not serious.'

'Wish I wasn't. Please tell me I'm not alone in the universe. Tell me that stuff like that also happens to Juggy.'

'If it does, he's been keeping it to himself,' said Angie.

Amazing. 'So there's absolutely nothing that makes your version of me stand out from the crowd apart from the ears.'

'Well, he's got us.'

'You?'

---

[4] *The Snottle*

[5] *The Curse of the Poltergoose*

[6] *Nudie Dudie*

[7] *Neville the Devil*

[8] *Ryan's Brain*

'We're a sort of gang. Juggy, Eejit and me.'

'Oh yeah, I forgot. The Three Camelearoles.'

'Cavaleiros,' said Atkins.

'I've got a gang too.' I managed a smile. 'You could say I have a doppelgang.'

'Why would we say that?'

'Well, "doppelganger" is German for someone's double, and you have a gang and I have a gang, and…'

I fizzled out. They were looking at me strangely. I knew those looks. I get them quite often when I say terrifically intelligent things. People can't keep up.

'What's yours called?' Angie asked at the end of the silence that followed.

'My what?'

'Your gang.'

'The Three Musketeers.'

'The Three Musketeers? How boring.'

'Boring?'

'So obvious. So predictable. I bet that all over the world, whenever three kids want to form a gang, the first name they think of is the Three Musketeers. Except us. What's your motto?'

'We don't have a motto, we have a battle cry.'

'Oh, you go into battle, do you?' said Atkins with a smirk.

'Well, no, not exactly. We just sort of band together in times of stress and face the world shoulder to shoulder, toe to toe and back to back.'

'Contortionists then, are you?'

I glared at him.

'What's this battle cry?' Angie asked.

'You wouldn't be interested,' I said. I was quite miffed about the Musketeers being trashed like this.

'Why wouldn't we be interested?'

'Because you think the Three Commodes is a better name than the Three Musketeers.'

'Cavaleiros,' said Atkins.

'We don't think it's *better*,' Angie said. 'The Three Musketeers isn't a bad name, just an over-used one. Tell us your battle cry.'

I looked from one of them to the other. They seemed like they really wanted to hear our battle cry.

'All right.' I took a deep breath, puffed my chest out, and uttered it, slowly, in my deepest, most heroic voice. 'One for all and all for lunch!'

'What?' said Angie.

I repeated it for the hard of hearing. 'One for all and all for lunch!'

'One more time,' said Atkins.

'One for all and all for lunch.'

'That's your battle cry?'

'Yes.'

They fell to the carpet, chortling merrily. 'One for all and all for lunch!' they gasped. 'One for all and all for lunch! One for all and all for lunch!'

I scowled down at them. 'OK, so what's your brilliant battle cry?'

'Motto,' said Angie, staggering to her feet and deactivating the chortle.

'What's the Three Catatonics' motto then?'

'Cavaleiros,' said Atkins. 'And it's kind of a secret.'

'I promise not to tell anyone,' I assured him, thinking that maybe I'd spray-paint it on every wall in sight, first chance I got.

They looked at one another like two people who weren't sure they wanted to share their secret motto with a stranger who looked exactly like their best boring friend except for the ears.

But then they said:

'Well…all right…'

They crossed very serious arms over their chests so that each of their left hands rested on each of their right shoulders and each of their right hands rested on each of their left shoulders.

'The Three Cavalieros' secret motto is…' Angie said, and looked one more time at Atkins. He nodded, and together they spake their big deal motto.

'Hola! Hola! Hola!'

I waited for a minute for the dust to settle, then cleared my throat.

'Would you mind saying it again?'

They said it again.

'Hola! Hola! Hola!'

'Hola! Hola! Hola!?' I said.

'Yes.'

'You know what hola, hola, hola means?'

Angie removed her hands from her shoulders. 'Hello, hello, hello.' She looked kind of embarrassed, I thought.

'What are you, secret policemen?' I asked.

'We were young when we came up with it,' said

Atkins, shoving his hands in his pockets and drawing a circle on the carpet with his toe.

'Here's a thought,' I said. They looked at me expectantly. 'What do you say we don't mention your motto or my battle cry ever again as long as we live? At least while we're all in the same room together.'

They agreed.

'Maybe we could be a new gang with a new motto or battle cry while we figure out how to switch Juggy and Jiggy back,' Eejit said.

We agreed on this too and sat down on the floor, where we spent the next hour failing to decide on a new gang name. In the end, in desperation, we just called ourselves The Three. And our battle-cry-motto?

'Bam-kerchow!'

It takes a bunch of real geniuses to think up something like that.

CHAPTER ELEVEN

'Let's go back to Spiritual Technology,' the other Eejit Atkins said when the name of our gang was settled.

'Back to school?' said the other Angie Mint.

'I mean to what happened between the time Juggy left ST and Jiggy came back.'

'It's RE where I come from,' I said.

'What is?'

'ST. Was last time I checked the door anyway.'

'What does RE stand for?'

'Religious Entertainment. Your ST beats anything Mr Staples bangs on about though. Do you believe all that stuff that went down in class today?'

'That the human race was brought to Earth by an alien dictator and stacked around volcanoes while he blew them up and that the souls of the dead went to the pictures afterwards?' Angie said. 'What do you think?'

'You were pretty convincing.'

'It's a quiet-life thing. If we don't act willing, or give too many wrong answers, Hubbard says the Spirit of Xenu is in us or gives us detention where we have to read about all that twaddle, silently.'

'Ryan didn't seem bothered about that.'

'Yeah, well that's Ryan.'

'And Pete Garrett seemed genuinely interested.'

'Garrett and his pal Skinner are among the converts. They wear the badge, attend the voluntary after-school "spiritual expansion" chats, and cross their backsides every time they say the name Xenu. They're as crazy as Ronnie Hubbard himself.'

'We were talking about what happened today,' said Atkins impatiently.

It was still hard to look at him the way he was and get used to proper words coming out of his mouth. Eejit Atkins talking sense and behaving like something that didn't scratch its armpits in trees? What an unbelievable world this was. World. Yes. It was a different world all right, no doubt about it, and I had no idea how I'd got to it. Or had I...?

'Mr Heathcliff's broom cupboard!' I said suddenly.

'What about it?' Angie asked.

'Before I went in there everything was normal. When I came out it was like this.'

'This is normal.'

'Not to me it isn't.'

'What were you doing in Heathcliff's broom cupboard?' Atkins said.

'Hiding from Mr Rice. Hey, you haven't got a Mr Rice too, have you?'

'Sure we have. He's the Power Jogging and EI coach.'

I clutched my head. There was even a bozo in red here? Angie asked why I was hiding from Mr Rice. I declutched the head.

'He's always got it in for me because I'm not a sports nut. I try and keep out of his way. When I heard him coming, Heathcliff's broom cupboard was the nearest thing with a door to put between us.'

'What happened in there?' Eejit asked.

'I don't know if anything happened in there, but…'

'But what?'

'But now that I think of it…'

'Yes? What? Stop breaking off in the middle of sentences.'

'It was too dark to see, but I had a feeling I wasn't alone.'

'You think Heathcliff was in there too?'

'No, not Heathcliff. If he'd been in there the light would've been on. Besides, it didn't feel like him.'

'How could you tell if it felt like him if he wasn't there?' Eejit asked.

'I mean I sensed him. Not Heathcliff, someone else.'

But then it came to me. I stared at them both.

'You said your mate Juggy left your alien religion lesson, didn't you?'

'Yes.'

'Well, who's to say that while he was out he didn't pop into your Mr Heathcliff's broom cupboard when I popped into mine?'

'Why would he do that?'

'Same reason I did, to hide from a teacher. Yes, that must be it. We switched places, schools,

homes, mates, the whole bunch of wahooley, because we're alternative versions of the same person who happened to go into Heathcliff's broom cupboard during the same pee break.'

'And you think the two of you passed in the dark and stepped out of one another's school broom cupboard,' Angie said.

'Exactly!'

Eejit stroked his beardless chin. 'That could be it,' he murmured.

'It *has* to be,' I said. 'And right now, this minute, your eary chum could be sitting in my bedroom with the remaining two Musketeers trying to work out the same things we're trying to work out here.'

'But things like that don't happen in real life!' Angie exclaimed.

I looked at her sadly. Enviously. 'Not in your life maybe.'

When Swoozie came home from ballet she rushed straight upstairs and threw back the door. 'What have I missed?' she demanded, standing there in her cute little pink ballet outfit.

We told her where we'd got to and she rolled her bright blue eyes in amazement. But then

she came over all troubled.

'So right now my Joseph's in another room like this?' she said, looking around as if expecting to see him sitting in a corner or somewhere.

'Could be,' I answered. 'But next door.'

'I hope he's all right there.'

'He'll probably be as all right there as I am here.'

'Oh!' she said.

'What?' I said.

'School.'

'What about it?'

'He'll have to go to yours tomorrow.'

'Yes, and I'll have to go back to an alternative Ranting Lane.'

'Ranting Lane?' said Angie and Eejit together.

'Isn't that the name of your school?' I asked.

'No, ours is called Arnold Snit Compulsory,' Angie said.

'Arnold Snit? As in Councillor Snit?' She nodded. 'He's done well here then,' I said. 'He only got a park and a cul-de-sac named after him where I come from.'

'Lucky you. Here, half the town's got his moniker on it. There's Arnold Snit Parkway,

Arnie Snit Boulevard, the A.F. Snit Theatre of Contemporary Issues, The Snit Centre for Cheap Immigrant Labour, and Xenu knows what else.'

'He's popular then.'

'No, he's just good at blackmail. My dad says old Snitty's got every influential person in town in his pocket.'

Swoozie wasn't listening to any of this. She was still thinking about her brother. Worrying about him. Must be nice having a little sister who cares that much about you, I thought. When she heard that we'd formed a new gang to deal with the problem of me being there instead of her brother, she wanted to join us.

'You can't,' Angie told her. 'We're called The Three. You can't have four people in a gang called The Three.'

'We could change the name,' I said.

'We are not,' she said, 'sitting on this floor for a further hour to work out another name for our gang!'

'No need. We just call ourselves The Four.'

'The Four...' she said, chewing this over. 'Do you think it works without "Fantastic" or

"Famous" in the middle?'

'It works fine. And it's only for a while after all.'

'We don't know how long it'll be,' Eejit said. 'You might be stuck here forever.'

'Don't say that!' cried Swoozie. 'I want my brother back!' Then she realised what she'd said and turned to me. 'Sorry. I don't mean I want to get rid of you. If I could, I'd keep you as well.'

'It's OK,' I said. 'I want to get back to my family too.' And I'd never said *that* before. 'Look,' I said to the other two of The Four. 'If I got here via my school caretaker's broom cupboard, doesn't it stand to reason that to get back I have to go through the broom cupboard in your school?'

'Ye-es...' they said, though they didn't sound too sure.

'So that's what I'm doing at morning break tomorrow. I'm going into your Mr Heathcliff's broom cupboard and I'm walking out of my Mr Heathcliff's broom cupboard. Then all this will be behind us and we can get back to normal. Well, you can. Normal isn't in my vocabulary, except as a word.' I sighed. 'It's not fair, y'know.'

'What isn't?' the other Angie Mint asked.

'Some kids get nice old wardrobes, fur coats, snowy woods, fauns. But me, Jiggy McCue? Oh no. I get a caretaker's broom cupboard, stinky old workcoats, cans of fly-spray, and another school with Mr Rice!'

CHAPTER TWELVE

It was a long night. A very long night. A night so long that I started to think that daytime had been cancelled. I did an awful lot of turning and tossing and sitting up in bed saying, 'Whaaaat?' but I must have slept eventually because I woke from something in the morning. And when I woke I realised that it had all been a dream. One bleary-eyed glance around was proof of that. Still, because it had been such a vivid dream I slid out of bed and looked for something extra to prove that I wasn't just in a very similar room. When I spotted my little Musketeer Rule Book on the desk I chuckled quietly with relief. I picked the book up fondly. On the cover, where I'd written our heroic battle cry 'One for all and all for lunch', were the immortal words...

'Hola! Hola! Hola!'

My knees sagged so fast I almost broke my jaw on the way down. I gripped the desk to steady

myself. My feet started moving. My arms flapped. I would have yelled for Mum, but it wasn't my mum snoring in the room along the landing. Not my dad either. I was in the house next door to the one that would have been mine if I hadn't been here. This was probably the very room where Dawn Overton put on her bra in my world. I felt my eyes brighten. But then I felt them go dull again. Less interesting but more important things to think about. In this world Angie Mint lived in one of the rich people's houses on the other side of the estate, I was best friends with Eejit Atkins, and I had a little sister. Sister. Weird to think that I had a sister, even a borrowed one. But here's a funny thing. When I thought of Swoozie I calmed down right away. Stopped fox-trotting and flapping round the room. She was the only McCue in the house apart from me who knew I didn't belong there. I needed someone like that. Needed to speak to her. I crept to the door in the pyjamas I'd got out of the drawer the night before – even if the boy who slept in that bed was another me, I wasn't wearing his unwashed PJs – and went out to the landing.

The resident Golden Oldies' bedroom door was still closed, but Swoozie's was open just a bit. I tiptoed to her room and looked in. She was fast asleep.* She didn't actually have her thumb in her mouth, but it sort of sat there on her pillow, a few inches away like it really wanted to go in. I was thinking how sweet she looked lying there when she opened her eyes. Maybe she sensed me or something. She blinked the sleep out of her eyes and smiled.

'Hi, Joseph.'

'No, it's me,' I said. 'Jiggy.'

'I know.' She sat up. 'But still Joseph.'

'Can I come in?'

'Course.'

She patted her duvet. I sat down on it.

'Thought I might have dreamed everything,' I said.

'Well, you didn't,' she said.

'No. And...' My shoulders slumped. I went all feeble and helpless. 'And I don't know what to do about it.'

'Yes you do,' she said.

'I do?'

---

* Can anyone tell me why you have to be *fast* asleep? What's fast about sleep? The sleep I'd just come out of had been about as fast as a snail crossing Antarctica on crutches.

'Yes. You said it yourself last night. You're going to school and you're going into the caretaker's broom cupboard, and when you walk out you'll be back where you belong.'

'I don't know if it'll work.'

'No, but you have to try it.'

'If it does work, it won't automatically bring your brother back.'

'Maybe not, but when you get there you'll have to find him and tell him to do what you did, only the other way round.'

My knees puckered. 'You mean I have to talk to him?'

'Well, you could try signing, but talking might get the idea across more quickly.'

'It'll be like talking to myself,' I said. 'So... weird.'

'It probably will, but it has to be done.'

She was right. It had to be done.

'Morning!'

We turned to the door. Her mum was looking in.

'One of your early-morning chats?' she said.

'Joseph had a bad dream,' Swoozie told her.

'Oh, no.' She gave me a small concerned frown.

'You over it now?'

'Getting there,' I said.

But then: 'Juggy!'

'What?'

'Your ears!'

'What about them?'

'Well, they're... flat?'

The 'flat' came as a question, like she couldn't believe she was saying it. I felt my ears. I'd forgotten to put the gum behind them. How could I get out of this? But I needn't have worried. Swoozie was there.

'He must have been lying on them,' she said.

'You think that's it?' her mother said.

'Of course. They're often flat first thing. Haven't you noticed?'

'No, can't say I have. Fancy that. Now don't spend all morning chatting!' she said as she left us.

I turned gratefully to Swoozie. I obviously needed someone like her to watch my back. And my ears.

'Go on,' she said. 'Shoo. Big morning ahead of you.'

I went back to the bedroom that wasn't quite mine and mouthed the earballs to soften them. I stuck them where they had to be and fluffed out some hair to cover them. As I checked myself in the mirror to make sure I'd got the ear angles right I got to wondering how it would have been for Juggy if he'd done what I reckoned he had: stepped into my school when I stepped into his. From the broom cupboard he would have gone to the class he thought was his, and been puzzled to find Mr Staples chuntering about a bunch of fruit and nut religions instead of Mr Hubbard chuntering about just one. He would have been surprised to find Pete Garrett sitting next to him, and to hear that they were best friends. And what about Atkins? The Eejit Atkins of Ranting Lane was quite a different kettle of crabs to the one at A.S. Compulsory. Then, when school was out, this other McCue would have gone round the back of Janet and Dawn Overton's and not found a fairy with a key up her backside, and eventually realised that he lived next door, in the house he expected Mr Rice and Miss Weeks and their glassy-eyed

teddy-bear to be living in. Finally, he would learn that Angie Mint didn't live on the rich side of the estate but just across the road, with Garrett and his dad, and that he was a member of the Three Musketeers instead of the Three Cranberries. And what would the kids in my class think when they saw those flapping lugs? What would my parents think? I mean, those things couldn't exactly be *disguised*.

But I had enough worries of my own without getting into his. The main one was putting the first lesson of the day behind me before I could sneak into the broom cupboard and home again. Unless...

Unless I could get to school before class. Getting to school before class isn't something I go out of my way to do as a rule – question of principle – but this was an emergency. I phoned the other Angie Mint to ask her to come in early with me.

'I can't,' she said. 'I'm straightening my hair.'

'Isn't it already straight?'

'It's got kinks.'

'Doesn't it usually have kinks?'

'Don't rub it in,' she said.

'I'm not rubbing anything in. I've got kinks. My hair is all kinks. I can live with them, why can't you?'

'You can live with them cos you're a boy,' she said, and hung up.

I was still standing there with the mobile in my mitt when it rang again.

'I forgot,' Angie said when I put it to my sticky-out ear. 'You're not Juggy.'

'No. So will you come to school early with me?'

'I can't. I'm straightening my hair.'

She hung up again.

At home I usually go down to breakfast in my PJs and dressing gown, but this wasn't my house any more than the school was my school and I'd have felt undressed around Golden Oldies who looked like my parents but weren't. I put on the same clothes as yesterday (because they were my own) and went downstairs. In the kitchen, the mother-who-wasn't lobbed me a big surprised smile and said how unusual it was to see me dressed before breakfast.

'Gotta go in early,' I told her. I could hardly meet her eye. Either one of them. Apart from the

hair, she was a dead-ringer for my mum right down to the last varicose vein, but she wasn't her.

'Why have you got to go in early?' she asked.

My mind blanked. Best I could come up with was that one of the teachers had asked for my help before class.

'Which teacher?'

'Mr Rice.' Tragically, this was the first name that came to me.

'Oh, you'll be getting the gear ready for tomorrow then.'

'Gear ready? Tomorrow?'

'For the big weekend.'

'The big...?' With all this going on I'd forgotten the Rice Krispies Survival Weekend. So the same thing was set to occur here. There were absolutely no pluses to switching worlds. 'Yeah, that's it,' I said. 'He needs help with the gear.'

'Well, have a bowl of cereal before you go.'

'Thanks, Mum.' Smooth, eh?

'Good to see that your ears are back where they should be,' she said as I went to the cupboard where the cereals are kept at home, hoping they were also kept there here.

'Yes,' I said. 'Got me kind of worried for a minute when you said they were flat like normal people's.' The cereals were in the same place, but I couldn't find my new favourite. 'No Choco Nuggets?'

'Since when did you like chocolate cereals?' Mum 2 asked.

'Um…' Had to be careful here. 'How about always?'

'News to me,' she said. 'Whenever I've brought a chocolate cereal home you've asked me to get something healthier next time.'

'Healthier? Me?'

'Don't tell me you've gone off the Super-Nutritious All-Swiss Muesli with Extra Fruit and Vitamins.'

This caused me to lose the use of my mouth for a minute. What sort of alien language was this woman speaking? Nutritious? Muesli? Extra Fruit? Vitamins? Didn't she know her son was a teenage boy?

While I was still trying to reactivate the mouth flap, she reached past me and took out the packet of Super-Nutritious All-Swiss Muesli with Extra

Fruit and Vits and carried it to the table. She tipped a small mountain of this unnatural stuff into a bowl, went to the fridge for a carton of milk, poured some on to the stuff, and handed me a spoon.

I sat down at the table and stared into the bowl while she did other things in another part of the kitchen. I, Jiggy McCue, was expected to eat muesli? Super-Nutritious muesli? Super-Nutritious All-Swiss Muesli with Extra Fruit and Vitamins? But I had to. I didn't dare run the risk of letting her think I might not be her son. If she even suspected that, a huge round of questions might start flying. If she was like my real mum she wouldn't let me out of the door until she knew everything. School might be cancelled for the day, and that would be terrible.*

I dipped into the bowl, closed my eyes, and plunged the loaded spoon into my muesli hole. My mouth was immediately full of sawdust, wood chippings and squashed beetles. And that wasn't all.

'The milk's off,' I gasped, spitting the Swiss muck back into the bowl.

---

* I can't believe I just said that.

'It can't be,' Mum 2 said. 'I only bought it yesterday.'

But she went to the fridge and took the carton out again.

'It's nowhere near its sell-by,' she said, squinting at the small print along the top. She brought the carton to the table and showed me the date. She was right. But then I saw the printing below it.

'That's semi-skimmed soya milk.'

'Well, of course it is,' she said.

'Why have you given me semi-skimmed soya milk?

'Because it's your favourite. You wouldn't drink any other milk, you've said so many a time.'

'I have?'

'You have, Juggy. It's the healthy option, you're always saying so.'

Juggy. Of course. Different kid. But *that* different? A McCue male who was into healthy options? This other world was even more insane than I thought. But I had to cover myself.

'It could be me,' I said. 'I've been thinking for a while that maybe I don't like soya milk and muesli

so much any more. Is there any bread for toast?'

'Yes, of course. But you'll have to do it yourself, I must get ready for work.'

She was on her way out of the kitchen when Dad 2 came in. They wrestled in the doorway to get past one another, then she was out and he was in.

'Hey, Jug.'

'Hey...Dad.'

He went to the bread bin and took out a loaf, sawed a couple of wedges off, dropped them in the toaster. When I saw the kind of bread it was I wasn't hungry any more. It was brown, very grainy, with loose bits on top. My real father would never have eaten bread like that. Nor would the real me. I felt in my pocket. There was some change in there. Maybe I'd get some proper food on the way to school.

Five minutes later, after going to the bathroom and cleaning my teeth with a finger like I had the night before (I wasn't using someone else's toothbrush even if his teeth were identical to mine), I was almost ready to leave. I looked in the fridge for my lunch box. Mum usually does my

school lunches the night before and puts the box in the fridge, but there was no lunch box in this fridge. I went to the bottom of the stairs. It didn't feel right doing this, but I was trying to seem normal, so I yelled up.

'Mum!'

A pause.

'Mu-um!'

The bathroom door opened. She looked down.

'Yes?'

'Where's my lunch box?'

'Lunch box?'

'Yeah, where is it?'

'That's tomorrow,' she said.

'What's tomorrow?'

'When you take a lunch box.'

'What about today?'

'What do you want one today for? You did pay in your dinner money on Monday, didn't you?'

'Er...ye-es...'

What else could I say? So this Juggy character was forced to have school dinners? Poor kid. No wonder his ears stuck out.

I put on my jacket, shouted 'Bye!' to anyone

who cared, grabbed the school bag I'd brought home yesterday, and was about to close the door on myself when I heard a voice.

'Well, thank you *very* much,' it said.

I turned. Swoozie stood there in her green uniform – green for a school other than Arnold Snit Compulsory. She was frowning.

'What's up?' I asked.

'If you go back through the broom cupboard I'll never see you again,' she said. 'You know that and you don't even bother to say goodbye?'

Put like that it did sound a bit mean. Fact is, I hadn't thought of it.

'Didn't think of it,' I admitted.

'That makes it even worse,' she said.

'Sorry.'

'So you should be.'

'You want your brother back, don't you?'

'Course I do, but I thought we were friends.'

Friends. We'd only known each other since yesterday and this little girl already thought of me as a friend. Now I felt *really* bad.

'We are,' I said feebly.

'Well friends say goodbye when they're

going away,' she said.

'Yeah. Right. Bye then.'

She stuck her jaw out and scowled up at me.

'They say it *properly*.'

She reached up with both hands, grabbed my shoulders, and pulled me down to her level. Then...she kissed me, once on each cheek.

'And don't you dare forget me, Jiggy McCue!' she said, and closed the door.

CHAPTER THIRTEEN

I was just closing the front gate when I remembered that there was someone apart from Angie who might go to school early with me. I walked past the house that should be mine, trying not to look like I was peering sideways into the windows, and reached Eejit's gate.

At home, the Atkins' garden is never up to much. Mr and Mrs A are nice enough, but they don't bother with their garden at all, front or back, so imagine my surprise when I saw that these Atkins' front garden was quite well looked after. There were nice flowers, the grass was short, and there were no beer cans all over the place. In my world, the cans are lobbed by Eejit's brother Jolyon when he's finished with them. Maybe this world's Jolyon had been sent to an institution for young offenders, where he belonged.

I opened the gate, walked up the path, and rang the bell. A tall, neat person with neat hair opened

the door. He wore a neat suit and tie and a really neat shirt. He smiled at me. A very neat smile.

'Hi, Jug. Early, aren't you?'

It was an almost unrecognisable Jolyon. I looked at the slice of neck above the neat collar. No barbed-wire tattoo. I looked at his hands. No H.A.T.E. on the four left fingers, no H.A.T.E. on the four right ones. Here was a Jolyon who didn't hate. A Jolyon who looked like he wouldn't bad-mouth anyone and said grace before meals. A Jolyon who didn't drink too much or hang out with other hooligans, and changed his socks every day.

'What?' he said. 'My tie crooked?'

'No, I…'

'You're early.'

Eejit, who was quite a bit smaller than his brother, had appeared in Jolyon's armpit. He was still in his pyjamas.

'That's what I said.' Still smiling neatly, Jolyon stepped back to let Eejit through.

'I want to try the broom cupboard before school,' I explained when we were alone. 'Wondered if you'd come with me.'

143

'Early to school?' Eejit said. It obviously wasn't something he did a lot of either. 'I'm not dressed and I'm still having my breakfast.'

'It's OK,' I said. 'Just thought I'd ask.'

'Give me ten minutes.'

'Don't worry.' I turned away. 'See you later – or not, if it works.'

He said something as I headed for the gate, but I didn't catch it.

Once the estate was behind me I saw a few other kids dawdling or playing the fool so they wouldn't get to school too soon, but none of them wore faces I knew well enough to talk to, so I didn't have to get into anything with them. I zipped through the shopping arcade and from there to school. The name on the big board attached to the fence that runs round half the school was the one Angie and Eejit had told me about. It was there yesterday, of course, but I hadn't noticed it as I was leaving. Apart from the name everything looked about the same as at Ranting Lane. There were even a couple of younger kids playing hopscotch in a corner of the playground, like there often is when I get to school. Probably dumped

there by their parents on the way to work.

I didn't hang about. The odd early teacher might be behind the windows that overlook the playground. Running low (because no one notices you when you run low) I reached the double doors of the main building and pushed the bar. It didn't budge. I tried the other door, which did. I opened it a fraction and peeked in. No one beyond. I stepped inside. I closed the door by hand. If I'd just let it go, like I usually do, it would have clanged all round the building. Mr Heathcliff's broom cupboard was just around the corner up ahead, and a little way along. I trotted to the corner and peered round. The way was clear all the way to the broom cupboard, but the door was open. Heathcliff was reaching in for something.

I waited, hoping he would go. He backed out with a pair of step ladders, which he propped against the wall while he went back in for something else. This time when he came out he was holding an old tin box of tools. Oh good, I thought, he'll go now. And he did. He hoisted the ladders under his arm and walked off with the toolbox in his other hand. But not before he'd locked the door.

'Bummer,' said a voice behind me.

I whirled. 'Atkins, what are you doing here?'

'I said I'd come with you, didn't I?'

'No. You said you weren't dressed and hadn't finished your breakfast.'

'I also said I'd get a move on, but you wouldn't wait.'

'I didn't get that, I was in a hurry.'

'What for, to see Heathcliff carry a ladder down the corridor?'

'He's ruined everything,' I said.

'You mean the key thing?'

'Yes, I mean the key thing. Key things turned in lock things kind of prevent people from getting into broom cupboard things, savvy?'

'You don't have to talk to me like I'm a moron,' he said.

'I'm used to talking to you like you're a moron.'

'Well get un-used to it. I'm the best friend you have here. And I can get you into that cupboard.'

'You can? How? Got an axe or crowbar in your school bag?'

'No, something a bit more portable.'

He took a bunch of keys out of his pocket and

dangled them in my face.

'You think one of those'll fit the lock?' I said.

'Sure of it.'

When we reached the broom cupboard, Atkins inspected the lock, then started going through the keys. 'Keep a lookout,' he whispered.

'Lookout?' I said. 'We're in the middle of a corridor that goes both ways. At the end of both ways there's a corner. I can only keep a lookout at one of those corners, and I'm not at either of them.'

'So keep a lookout both ways.'

'But what if a teacher or someone comes?'

'Then you tell me.'

'I won't need to tell you. They'll have seen us by then.'

He glared at me. 'D'you want my help or don't you?'

'Course I want your help. I'm just stating the obvious, that's all.'

'Well don't.'

He slotted one of the keys in the lock and turned it, but not far.

'Doesn't work,' I said.

He tried another key. Same result.

'Still no good,' I said.

He glared at me again.

'I'm just saying that it's another wrong key,' I said.

'I know that.'

'So why use it?'

'I didn't know till I tried it. I won't know which key fits till it turns the lock.'

'What makes you think any of them will turn it?'

'They're skeleton keys. I just have to find the right one.'

'What are you doing with skeleton keys?'

'They're my dad's.'

'What's your dad doing with skeleton keys?'

He put another key in. 'Not a lot since they caught him.'

'Who caught him?'

'The police.'

'Caught him what?'

'Breaking and entering.'

'Breaking and...?'

He tried a fourth key. 'The chemists in the shopping arcade. He spray-painted the CCTV-cam but the lens had been treated with an anti-spray

148

agent, so they were still able to record his every movement.'

'Hold on,' I said. 'Are you saying your dad's a burglar?'

'No, I'm saying he's a guest of His Majesty's Prison Service.' He took the fourth useless key out of the lock. 'Hey,' he said. 'If my family lives next door to you in your world and your Eejit's dad's line of work isn't common knowledge, he must still be free there.'

'He is. We thought Mr Atkins was a landscape gardener who didn't bring his work home.'

'Well, if he's still free when you get back, you could warn him to steer clear of the shopping centre cameras.'

'Oh sure. I'll ring his doorbell one evening and say, "Listen, Mr Atkins, whatever you do when you break into another shop, choose one that's not near any cameras."'

Eejit shoved another key in the lock. Yet another that might as well have been a chocolate éclair for all the good it did.

'I thought skeleton keys fitted every lock,' I said.

He sorted through the bunch of keys again. 'You

thought wrong. You need a good range to cover every kind of lock. One of these'll do it.'

He tried another key. And...

'And there we are,' he said.

He turned the doorknob. The door opened.

'Hello, what are you two up to?'

We turned. It was Mr Rice. The other Mr Rice. The one who lived in the house that should have been mine. And he was coming towards us.

CHAPTER FOURTEEN

At first, I thought that the other Mr Rice was like my Mr Rice in every way except the way he dressed. Like I said back there somewhere, the Mr Rice I know is never seen without his red tracksuit. Just as well if it's the only thing he owns, I suppose, but this one wasn't wearing a red tracksuit. He was wearing a saggy red romper suit that he might have picked up at a Teletubbies' car boot sale. 'Does he always dress like that?' I asked Atkins as the other Mr Rice came towards us. He didn't answer. Too busy closing the door, fiddling with the keys behind his back, and trying to look like his halo would be delivered by courier any minute.

'What's so darned fascinating about Mr Heathcliff's hidey-hole?' Mr Rice asked as he joined us.

'Jug and I were just saying that you'd think he'd wipe the grubby marks off his door seeing

as he's the caretaker,' Eejit said.

Mr Rice held out one of his enormous palms. 'May I see?'

'See what, Coach?'

'Whatever it is you have behind your back.'

'Behind my back? The only thing behind my back is the door.'

'Well in that case you won't mind showing me, will you?'

'No problem,' Eejit stepped aside so Rice could see the door better.

'I mean your hands, Ralph.'

'Oh, my *hands*,' Eejit said.

He held out one of his hands. It was empty.

'And the other one?'

He showed his other hand. Also empty.

Mr Rice grinned. 'I pulled the same trick when I was your age.'

'Trick, sir?'

Mr Rice reached behind Eejit's collar. 'Always keep your keys here, do you?' he said, lifting out the bunch.

Atkins smiled. Fair cop. 'Doesn't everyone?'

'I'll hang on to them for now,' Rice said. 'Collect

them from the staff room at the end of the day. Now, outside, the pair of you.'

'He didn't shout,' I said to Atkins as we went. 'Why would he shout?'

'Well, my Mr Rice always shouts, whether you've done something wrong or not.'

'Really? Ours doesn't. Not often. He's OK, Mr Rice.'

'So what do we do now?' I said when we were outside again.

'About what?' said Atkins.

'About getting into the broom cupboard.'

'Have to try again at morning break.'

'We won't have your keys at morning break.'

'Maybe it won't be locked then. Mr Heathcliffs obviously don't always lock their doors or you wouldn't be here now.'

'Yes. Curse them.'

We hung around the playground while it slowly filled up with kids. When Angie arrived with her straightened hair, she didn't spend much time with us because she had stuff to talk about with some girls. That was almost as weird as Mr Rice not shouting or wearing a tracksuit. My Angie prefers

to hang out with the boys and agrees with me and Pete that she was short-changed when she got the female bits instead of our manly gear. But this Angie was different. She seemed to actually like being female! Even in school uniform she looked more girlie than my Angie ever did in anything. As well as her hair, she'd taken trouble with the way her face looked, and her nails were neatly filed and polished, and she walked like she had books on her head. She even had bigger chest bumps, so I guessed she'd discovered inflatable bras. If my Angie ever wore one of those I'd have to stick a pin in it. Two pins.

The first lesson of the day turned out to be Highland Dancing with Mrs Porterhouse. Yes, Highland Dancing. In the real world, my world, Mrs Porterhouse teaches Geography. I guessed that this Mrs P did too, only she'd decided to liven the subject up a bit, like my Mrs P does occasionally without any success whatever. Highland Dancing, though? We were nowhere near any highlands. But maybe you had to be trained in it at school here because when you grew up you were expected to Highland Dance every weekend instead of

download music and anything else you can think of. Perhaps adults here Highland Danced every free hour of their stupid lives until it was time to apply for the Zimmer.

I stuck my hand up. 'Miss!'

'Yes, Juggy?'

'Miss, can't we just do Geography?'

'Geography?'

'Yes. Can't we be bored out of our cranial cavities with that instead of poncing about to the sound of squealing cats?'

'Well, you could if I actually *took* Geography,' she chirruped. 'Come on, Juggy, you did very well last week.'

'I did?'

'You know you did. You're a natural dancer. Why else would I have asked you to show the others how it was done?'

So this Mrs Porterhouse didn't teach Geography, and Juggy McCue was the High King of Highland Dancing. I had to be careful not to say the wrong thing here.

'Miss, can you answer another question for me?'

'If I can, certainly.'

'Can you tell me what use Highland Dancing is to anyone with a single brain cell left who doesn't live in the Highlands or wear a kilt?'

This seemed to floor her a bit. 'Well,' she said after a pause, 'you never know when you'll be called upon to do it, I suppose.'

'I do,' I said. 'Never.'

'There's always the off-chance, Juggy.'

'Yeah, well off-chances don't usually come in bundles, miss. Maybe you never noticed that.'

'The fact remains,' she said more firmly, 'that we'll be doing Highland Dancing every Friday till the end of term as part of the government's Physical Activity Nurtured Through Schools initiative.'

'You're teaching Highland Dancing for the whole term?' I gasped.

'It's only one period a week,' she replied. Then she grinned brightly all around. 'Next term, we'll be getting into shape with something rather different. We'll be studying Liposuction, Face-lifting and Body-hair Sculpture. Won't that be exciting?'

Damn. And I was going to miss it.

We spent the five or six years till morning break with our knees and arms in the air, hopping from one toe to the other to avoid plastic swords while the Porterhouse played shrieky bagpipes through the speakers of her tiny eardrum-busting music machine. When this ordeal was over and we'd Highland Danced out of her presence, I had just twenty minutes to get into Mr Heathcliff's broom cupboard and not come out again. Angie knew what I planned to do, so she didn't go off with her girlie chums this time, but loitered with Eejit and me as close to the broom cupboard as we could get while we waited for the corridor to empty. I started this loiter with a grumble.

'Dunno why we're standing here. Might as well go outside and make daisy-chains or draw something rude on a wall.'

'Why?' said Atkins.

'It'll be locked. That's the way my luck goes. And Mr Rice took your skeleton keys.'

'I've got it covered,' he said.

'Got what covered?'

'If you remember, the door was unlocked when I handed over the keys.'

'Yes, but Heathcliff's bound to have been back and locked it again since then.'

'Maybe, maybe not.'

When the corridor emptied we snuck to the broom cupboard. I turned the handle. 'Told you,' I said when the door didn't open.

'Try this,' said Eejit, opening his hand. There was a key in it.

'Where'd you get that?'

He popped the key into the lock, turned it, opened the door a tad.

'It's the one I used earlier.'

'It can't be. It was on the ring Mr Rice confiscated.'

'I slipped it off before he took it.'

'I didn't see you do that.'

'You were beside me, not behind my back where the action was.'

'He's good at sleight-of-hand,' Angie said. 'Comes of having a burglar in the family.'

'My dad prefers Private Entry Executive,' Eejit said. 'But yes, I've learnt a lot from him. If I don't make it to Uni at least I'll never starve, thanks to all the stuff Dad's shown me.' He held the door

open for me. 'Over to you.'

I stepped inside a little way. 'Hola, hola, hola,' I said in parting.

'One for all and all for one,' Angie replied.

'Lunch,' I said.

'What?'

'It's "one for all and all for lunch".'

'Oh yeah. Shows how memorable it is, doesn't it?'

I closed the door on them. The smell of polish and dust and caretakery sweat hit me as I felt my way through the deep darkness. I wasn't sure how it worked, but I imagined I'd have to go right through this cupboard to get to the door of the Ranting Lane one. My left foot touched something. I reached down. It was the tripping bucket. I made my way round the bucket before standing up straight again – and banged my shoulder on a shelf. I knew it was a shelf because something about the size of a tin of polish fell off it and cracked me on the side of the head on its way to the floor. I kicked it aside and carried on groping forward, wishing I'd thought to turn the light on – the switch

was probably just inside the door – because in darkness that lightless I couldn't tell how far it was to the back. I felt my way round boxes and pots and things, bumped into a chair, fingered the smelly old workcoats, and after a while touched something flat that had to be a door. I felt for a handle, and found one. I turned it, opened the door, and blinked at the light of a school corridor just like the one I'd left a few minutes before.

I'd made it! I was back where I belonged!

As I stepped out of the broom cupboard, a voice said, 'Hello! You, lad! What business do you have in there?'

It was Mother Hubbard, Ranting Lane's beloved Head. I closed the door with relief as he came towards me.

'Looking for Mr Heathcliff, sir.'

'Why, pray?'

'Why pray?' I said. 'My dad's always saying that. Prayers are a waste of time, he says. Never work for him.'

Mr H frowned. 'Are you trying to be funny?' he asked sternly.

As he said this my eyes drifted down to the left lapel of his jacket, and a little badge shaped like a volcano.

I was still at Arnold Snit Compulsory!

CHAPTER FIFTEEN

I was pretty fed up when I joined Eejit and Angie in the playground. They didn't get it right away because the wads of chewing gum were still behind my ears. Eejit held his hand up to be slapped.

'Good to have you back, Cavaleiro!'

I didn't slap it. Wouldn't have been time anyway, because Angie jumped between us and threw her arms round my neck.

'We thought we'd lost you!' she squealed girlishly.

'Wish you had,' I said, spitting straightened hair out of my mouth. 'Dump the hugs, willya? I have rules about this stuff.'

She let go of me with a puzzled expression. Obviously, hugs weren't off-limits between the Three Carveries.

'What was it like there?' Eejit asked.

'It's a broom cupboard,' I said sourly. 'What do you think it was like?'

'I mean in Jiggy's world.'

'Fantastic. Oceans better than here.'

This seemed to interest him. 'In what way?'

'In every way,' I snapped.

He frowned up at me. 'What happened?'

'Take a flying guess.'

'It's not him,' said Angie. She'd gone round the back of me to check the lug supports. 'He's still the pathetic copy.'

Atkins gaped. 'But he went into the broom cupboard!'

'And came out again.'

'You turned round and came straight out again?' he said to me.

'No, I didn't turn round and come straight out again. It was too dark to go straight in any direction.'

'But you must have known which way you were going.'

'I did, but something fell on me, obviously threw me off course.'

'Well, why didn't you turn the light on?'

'I didn't think of it till it was too late.'

He groaned. 'You're really brilliant, aren't you?'

It wasn't a compliment.

'You'll have to try again at lunchtime,' said Angie.

'Same thing might happen then,' I mumbled.

'Don't be so defeatist. You won't know till you try.'

'And if I fail again?'

'You try again after school if there's no one about.'

'And if there is someone about?'

'You try again on Monday.'

'Monday? A whole Survival Weekend away?'

'Survival Weekend?'

'The legendary Jiggy McCue sense of humour,' Atkins muttered.

'It'll be a very interesting weekend,' Angie said.

'For you maybe,' I said. 'You're not stuck in the wrong world, wrong house, with the wrong friends, wrong parents, and a sister.'

'What's wrong with Swoozie?'

'Nothing's wrong with Swoozie. Swoozie's OK. I'm just saying.'

Angie came to stand in front of me. She looked serious.

'You want to count yourself lucky you've got us,' she said. 'You want to also count yourself lucky that we believe you're who you say you are.'

'You have to,' I said, and waggled my ears. One of the blobs of gum fell out. I picked it up, licked the dirt off, stuck it back.

'On top of that you want to count yourself lucky we're prepared to go out of our way to help you,' she said.

'Some help,' I grouched. 'I'm still here, aren't I?'

'Eej,' she said to Atkins. 'I don't think we're appreciated here.'

'I think you're right,' he said.

With that, they span round and walked away. I watched them go, feeling suddenly very friendless. And lonely.

When I saw Pete Garrett across the playground I suddenly wanted to talk to him. Garrett had been there to chew the cud with and give Chinese burns to all my life. I needed that right now. He wasn't with Skinner this time, he was with Sami Safadi and Milo Dakin. That wasn't so bad. Sami and Milo are OK in my world. I went over.

'Hey,' I said.

'Hey, Jug,' said Milo.

'Hey, Jug,' said Sami.

'Hey, Pete,' I repeated to the one who hadn't answered.

He scowled at me. 'What do you want?'

'Want? I don't want anything. Being friendly, is all.'

'Friendly? We're not friends, McCue. Never will be.'

That hurt. My lifelong bud Pete Garrett was telling me he wasn't my friend. I know he wasn't actually my Pete, but he was the nearest thing to him that there was around here. Garrett and I had fallen out occasionally, but we'd known one another longer than anyone except Angie because our three mothers were in each other's houses from day one until his mum legged it with the podium-dancing osteopath with Tourette's and his dad moved in with Angie's mother Audrey.

'Give us a minute, willya?' I said to Sami and Milo.

'What for?' Sami asked.

'Wanna talk to Garrett.'

'What do you want to talk to me about?' Pete said suspiciously.

'I'll tell you when these two put a couple of gaps between us.'

'We have nothing to say to one another.'

'We might have.'

'We haven't, McCue. We haven't had anything to say to one another since we were six. Now get away from me. Scoot.'

He sounded like he meant it. Looked it too. I scooted. Sadly. Thought I heard him and the others chuckling as I went.

It was a long morning. Longer than most because it was History with Hurley, which I could certainly have done without. They must have had a different timetable there, because by Friday at Ranting Lane History's behind us. This Mr Hurley wasn't as cheerful as mine the last time I saw him either. He didn't crack a smile once, so I guessed he had no immediate plans to bore people senseless on a cruise ship. He spent the whole period writing stuff about some industrial resolution on the board for us to copy down and memorise because he'd be testing us next week.

I hoped he wouldn't be testing me next week.

Atkins sat next to me, like he had in Spiritual Technology. Maybe he sat next to me in most lessons, the way Pete did at home, but he didn't seem to want to talk to me to fight the boredom, like Pete would. I didn't make any effort to talk to him either. If he and the other Angie Mint were going to be like that, I could be like it too.

But then it was lunchtime. Time for another stab at the broom cupboard. Only trouble was…

'Atkins,' I whispered as we packed up at the end of the lesson.

He put a hand to his ear, like someone listening for distant thunder.

'Did I hear my name spoken by some complete stranger who doesn't value the few friends he has?'

'I need the key,' I said.

He stuffed his books into his bag. 'What key?'

'The one we opened the broom cupboard with earlier. Did you take it out of the lock when I went in?'

'Maybe I did, maybe I didn't,' he said, moving away.

'If I don't get in,' I said, a bit louder so others could hear, 'you'll never get your pal back.'

He stopped. Came back. Hissed at me.

'That's blackmail.'

'It's not blackmail, it's a fact. You want him back or don't you?'

'Given the choice between him and you? Hmm, tough one.'

He dipped into his pocket, handed me the key, and was about to leave when I asked him something that had been bothering me since morning break.

'Have you got any idea why Pete Garrett doesn't like Juggy?'

'Sure,' he said. 'Common knowledge.'

'Not to me.'

'Until they were six, the two of them were best pals. Then, one day when they were playing marbles in the playground, they got into a scrap about who had the best marbles and Jug dropped Garrett's down a drain.'

'And that's it?'

'Garrett was very proud of those marbles.'

'Well, he's not the only one who's lost his

marbles round here.'

Atkins shoved off.

Desperate as I was to get back to my proper world and my true friends, it was that time of day when chow is wolfed, and I was hungry. I didn't have my usual packed lunch, but the mother-who-wasn't had asked me if her son had paid his dinner money in, which must mean he was entitled to eat in the canteen. I'd never stayed for school dinners at Ranting Lane. Nor had Pete and Angie. Packed lunches in the Concrete Garden, that was our routine. We preferred it that way. More freedom.

Even if the canteen had been in a different part of the building here, I would have known where it was because half the school was scrambling in a direction that wasn't the playground. I didn't have time to go with the flow and saunter at slug speed towards the dishing-up counters while kids with an hour to kill tried to decide whether to have the beans or the chips. I pushed my way through the crowd, stuck elbows in ribs, took every short cut in town, and when the canteen doors were opened I was among the first eleven food disciples.

'How'd you get up there, McCue?' a voice rang out.

'Cos I'm quick, Ryan,' I shouted back.

'I never noticed before,' he replied.

'That's because you're so slow, bung-head.'

'Watch it McCue.'

'Watch it yourself, Ryan.'

I couldn't believe what I saw when I got to the row of food counters. At Ranting Lane they serve the chips and burgers and sausages and stuff that packed lunchers aren't allowed near. Here there wasn't a chip or burger or sausage in sight. It was all pasta and salad and vegetables and rice with bits in. The sort of low-fat chow that would make my dad turn in his grave if he was dead. I almost turned in my own and went off to starve in the broom cupboard, but then I thought, 'Suppose I don't make it past the brooms again and I stay stuck here? I'll starve all afternoon.' Better to shove a spoonful of school pasta down me than shove nothing at all. I could always close my eyes and hold my nose.

So that's what I did, except for the eye-closing and nose-holding. I even had a little bowl of fruit

salad afterwards so all the gaps would be filled. I wolfed the whole lot in five minutes flat. I sat on my own while I did this. I didn't want to talk to anyone. These weren't kids I knew. Even faces that I could draw on the back of someone's hand didn't belong to people I knew.

I was just jamming the last organic pineapple chunk in my trap when I caught Pete Garrett's eye. I forgot for a sec that we weren't friends here and raised my hand. Maybe if the pineapple chunk hadn't just found a parking place behind my teeth I might have thrown him a friendly grin as well, but a grin wasn't possible without firing the p. chunk at Gemma Kausa and Holly Gilder on the next table. It could be that because of the grin famine my raised hand didn't look so much like a friendly greeting, because the hand Garrett raised in reply was definitely not.

From the canteen I zipped to the corridor where the broom cupboard was. A couple of lady teachers were chatting near it. I went past them and loitered just round the corner, constantly looking back to see if they'd gone yet. After a

while, when it started to look like they'd be there till Doomsday – they were in full-frontal natter mode – I went back to them.

'Scuse me, Miss,' I said, meaning both of them at once. You can't really say 'Scuse me, Misses'.

They stopped speaking. Asked me what I wanted.

'Some trouble in the playground,' I lied with a worried expression.

'What kind of trouble?'

'You have to see it. Some kids over the far side.'

'I'll attend to it,' one of them said to the other, and she stormed in the direction of the playground.

I followed her, slowly, until, glancing back, I saw the other teacher go off in the opposite direction and disappear round the corner. I returned to the broom cupboard and tried the handle. The door opened. Great, no need for the key after all. I'd jumped inside and closed the door before I realised the light was on.

'Help you?'

Mr Heathcliff was in there, chomping on a sandwich in a deckchair and drawing moustaches

on the faces above the bosoms and bottoms in his favourite paper.

'Sorry,' I said. 'Wrong door.'

I went out again.

Things just were *not* going my way!

CHAPTER SIXTEEN

Eejit and Angie eyed me with a mixture of hope and suspicion as I walked over to them towards the end of lunch. As I still hadn't removed the gum from behind my ears they had to ask which McCue I was. When I told them about the latest failed attempt their faces sagged.

The next lesson turned out to be Science. The science teacher at Ranting Lane was Mr Flowerdew, but at Arnold Snit Compulsory it was a bloke called Mr Numnuts. I asked Eejit behind my hand if that was his real name. He said he wasn't sure, but Mr N was such a character that he wouldn't put it past him to call himself that for a joke.

Mr Numnuts wasn't all that ancient by Golden Oldie standards, about thirty maybe, and he had a pointy little beard that he'd dyed bright green, and a mass of curly hair that he hadn't. He wore this suit that was too small for him – a hairy fawn thing – and he had the tiniest feet I ever saw on

someone over eight years old. Eejit said that Mr Numnuts liked to make Science fun. He told me that at the end of one lesson he filled a white balloon with hydrogen and let it float to the ceiling, then lit this long taper and touched the balloon with it. There was this ffffffffffft sound, then the balloon exploded. Everybody jumped like maniacs, and then all these little bits of white rubber drifted down like snowflakes. 'What was that for?' someone gasped. 'I just wanted to end the lesson with a bang,' said Mr Numnuts.

The science lesson I had with Mr Numnuts started out like any other − pretty dull − but once he'd run through the heavy stuff he took a small box out of the bag he'd brought with him. He didn't have a leather briefcase like most teachers. He had a big green canvas bag with the words WHY DO THE WEIRDOES ALWAYS SIT NEXT TO ME? on the side. The box he took out of the bag contained Turkish Delight, twenty pink cubes and twenty blue ones, all covered in this sugary coating that made every tongue immediately jerk out and lick lips.

'Ooh, is that for us, sir?' someone asked.

'Gordon,' he replied, unwrapping the box. He liked the kids to call him Gordon. 'And it is for you, but not to eat.'

'Can we have some anyway?'

'You can have a nibble in a minute if you're still up for it, after we've conducted our little experiment.'

'What's the experiment, Gordon?'

'Well, there'll be two. It's a comparison thing.'

He'd also brought along a pair of small transparent boxes. He put the blue cubes in one of these, which he called Group B (for blue), and the pink cubes in the other box (Group P). Then he told us to spit on the Group P cubes.

'Spit on them, sir?'

'Yes, spit on them, and will you *please* call me Gordon, I can't get be doing with all this "sir" stuff. I want you to drench every pink cube with phlegm, saliva, sputum, or whatever you want to call it.'

'What happens then?'

'Then we turn to the blue Turkish Delight.'

'And spit on that too?'

'No, we'll do something different with Group B.

Now gather round and get ready to hurl. Have to get a move on because we've wasted so much of this lesson on National Curriculum bilge and the bell'll go any minute.'

'Do we all have to spit, Gordon?'

'No, Julia. Only those who'd like to.'

'Only my nan says spitting's rude.'

'So it is, unless it's part of a supervised experiment by a qualified science teacher who plays keyboards in a rock band at weekends. Now gather round, those of you who want to participate.'

So we gathered round the box of pink cubes, hawked for an Oscar, and spat. Mostly it was the boys who did this. Julia Frame wasn't the only girl who stood back with a sour expression. We spat and spat and spat until all the cubes of pink Turkish Delight were dripping and shiny. When we were all spat out, Mr Numnuts put the lid on the box and we wiped our chins and grinned at one another. You don't get permission to gob your guts out in many lessons.

'Why did we have to spit on the pink Turkish Delight?' Angie asked.

'You mean why the pink instead of the blue?' said Mr Numnuts.

'Yes.'

'Worry not, Angie, it's not a gender issue. We could have spat on the blue cubes just as well.'

Someone asked what we had to do with the blue cubes.

'We're going to drench them with urine,' Mr Numnuts said.

'Urine, sir?'

'Urine, widdle, piddle, wee, pee, take your pick.'

'I'll start if you like, Gord,' said Ryan.

'Start what?'

'The spraying.'

'No need, I've come prepared. Put it away please, Bryan.'

He dipped into his WHY DO THE WEIRDOES ALWAYS SIT NEXT TO ME? bag and took out a bottle of yellow stuff.

'Sir, that isn't what I think it is…?'

'Yes, Pete, the very liquid.'

'Is it… yours?'

'No, I paid some homeless people to fill it for me. Who wants to be mother?'

'I'll do it!' said Eejit.

'I think our friend's taking the piss,' Mr N said, handing him the bottle.

When Eejit dribbled the bladder-dew over Group B there were quite a few groans, but most of us – even the girls – leaned forward to see what happened to the cubes. We were disappointed. The sugar coating cracked here and there and tried to dissolve, but that was it.

'Now what?' we asked.

'Now the bell goes,' Mr Numnuts said. (It just had.) 'And we gather here this time next week to see what's happened to the cubes over the past seven days. I'll put the boxes in this cupboard and hope Queenie doesn't come across them.* If she finds them she'll probably think we're breeding a rare form of intelligent school life and dump them. Oh – anyone fancy that nibble before we go?'

No one did.

We were about to leave when the door opened and Mr Rice looked in. He still wore the saggy red romper suit.

'May I have a word, Mr Numnuts?' he said.

'Have as many as you like as long as it's not with

---

* I found out later that Queenie was Mrs Sidaj, head cleaning lady at Arnold Snit Compulsory. I've no idea who runs the cleaning at Ranting Lane, but here it was Queenie Sidaj. Eejit told me that they called her Queenie because she acted like she ran the joint. No one – even the teachers, he said – dared cross Queenie Sidaj.

me,' Mr N replied. 'I have an appointment with a bungee-jumping instructor.'

Mr Rice looked impressed. 'You're doing bungee-jumping?'

'No, I just have an appointment with her.' Mr Numnuts grabbed his WHY DO THE WEIRDOES ALWAYS SIT NEXT TO ME? bag and waggled his hips at us. 'She's rather lovely.'

When he'd gone, Mr Rice closed the door so we couldn't escape till he said so. 'I hope the two team members in this class have been training hard for the big weekend,' he said.

'Sure have, Coach,' said Atkins.

'Good. Because I for one would love to see that trophy in a bullet-proof glass cabinet in the main hall for the next twelve months. We all would, I'm sure.'

A rumble of agreement from a few kids.

'And those of you accompanying the team, I want you to give your full support during their heats. That's why you're going, remember, to cheer them on, not to stand around observing quietly. Understood?'

Another rumble of agreement, then he said that

that was all and that we could go. As I walked past him, he touched me on the shoulder.

'Juggy.'

I paused. '...Yes?'

'I'm counting on you most of all.'

'Eh?'

What was the big wazoo on about? Since when did a Mr Rice count on a J. McCue for anything?

'Whether we bring that trophy home or not could be your call.'

'Mine?'

'Just do your very best when the time comes — OK?'

'Riiiiight,' I said, and skidded out the door.

What had a trophy to do with a Survival Weekend, for Pete's sake? Or even Eejit's sake? And why was he counting on me? Juggy, I mean. Not that I really cared. I wouldn't be Surviving with him. I'd be back in my own mad world, with my own Mr Rice, probably hiding behind a tree hoping he'd forget I existed.

Eejit and Angie went with me to the broom cupboard. There were still a few kids in the corridor, so they covered me while I tried the door.

It was locked. I popped the skeleton key in, turned it, and opened the door just enough to slip in sideways.

'In case I don't see you again...' I said to the other two of The Four.

'Yeah, yeah,' said Atkins, turning away.

'Just go,' said Angie.

This time I flipped the light switch before closing the door. It seemed so much smaller in there when you could see everything. I stepped round the tripping bucket, avoided Heathcliff's deckchair, didn't knock anything off a shelf, and in a stride or two was parting the old brown workcoats to see what was behind them. What was behind them was a wall. I pushed at the wall. It was solid. Brick solid.

Puzzle. What had been different that first time? All I could remember doing was darting into the Ranting Lane broom cupboard and walking out of the Arnie Snit Compulsory version. Oh, wait. Of course. Juggy had been in there too, on his way to my world. So did that mean that we always had to be there at the same time to swap places? If that was the case, it might

never happen again. When I thought about it, it was pretty amazing that we'd gone into our respective school broom cupboards at the same time once. To do it twice would be stretching coincidence to ripping point.

Unlikely as it was that Juggy would go into the Ranting Lane broom cupboard a second time while I was there, I hung in there, hoping – until the knocks on the door started. At first I thought it was him trying to get in, but then I heard the door on the other side of the workcoats open and looked through to see Eejit and Angie peering in.

'How's it going?' one of them asked.

'It's not.'

'Still you then, are you?'

'Yeah, sorry.'

We might have talked some more, but they closed the door suddenly and I heard them answering the questions of some nosy teacher who'd charged onto the scene. Then a little rap of fingernails told me they'd been moved along. I waited a minute before cracking the door. The corridor was deserted. I slipped out and locked up

after me. That was it then. I was going to be stuck here till Monday, which meant that I'd have to go on the Survival Weekend with the wrong Mr Rice after all.

Hallay-flaming-looyah.

CHAPTER SEVENTEEN

At the end of the afternoon, Eejit collected the rest of his keys from Mr Rice in the staff room and the three of us started for home. (That's Eejit, me and Angie, not Eejit, me and Mr Rice.) Just before we reached the estate I told them to go on without me.

'Why, where are you going?'

'Nowhere. Just don't want to go home yet.'

'Because it's not your home exactly?'

'Probably.'

'It's somewhere to sleep,' said Angie.

'I'm not tired.'

'And eat.'

'Not hungry.'

I walked off, dragging the school bag that wasn't mine.

I didn't pay much attention to where I went. Vaguely noticed a boarded-up café, a vandalised Age Concern shop, The Jacqueline Wilson Tattoo Parlour, and that was about it. There weren't

many differences between this town and mine, but I didn't need to remind myself that however familiar everything looked I'd never seen it before. I felt pretty helpless actually. Pretty hopeless. I needed my friends. My real friends. But there were no Musketeers here to gallop to the rescue at the punch of some buttons. I was absolutely alone.

'Hi, kid, how ya doin'?'

'Eh?'

I'd been mooching with my eyes on the pavement. I looked up. It was Pete Garrett's dad.

'Hi, Ollie,' I said.

He screwed his eyes up. 'Do I know you?'

I mentally slapped myself round the face, twice. The sight of him had thrown me. I'd known this man all my life. I was round his house all the time with Pete and Angie. He'd even been on holiday with us. But this wasn't the Oliver Garrett I knew. He looked a lot rougher than my Oliver, couldn't have shaved for days, there were bags under his eyes, and his hair was long and greasy.

'I'm a friend of Pete's,' I said. Well, it was partly true.

I realised where we were. *The King's Arms* pub. Except it wasn't called *The King's Arms* here. The old wooden sign swinging high up on the wall told me that in this wonky world it was called *The Queen's Legs*.

'Got any money?' the other Oliver Garrett asked.

So that was why he'd called to me.

'Money? No. Sorry.'

I had a few coins in my pocket, but I might need them. I started to go. But then I felt guilty about leaving him there without saying something friendly. He might not be the Ollie I knew, but he was sort of the same person, and he looked like he might be glad of a spot of lively conversation.

'What are you up to then?' I asked with a friendly smile.

'Up to?'

'I mean what are you doing?'

'Doing?' He scowled. 'Whatja think I'm doing? I'm waiting for *The Queen's Legs* to open so I can get a drink.'

I moved on.

Eventually I had to admit I was a bit peckish.

I took another route to the estate, and as I still didn't have a front door key, went round the back of the house that wasn't mine. I opened the gate – cautiously – and peeked round the fence. Stallone the dog stuck his snout out of the kennel and started towards me with a growl. I jumped back, slammed the gate, and went round to the front to wait for Juggy's mum or dad to get home from work. I flopped down on the step, wishing I'd stashed some chocolate bars or crisps in the bag I'd been dragging round all day.

'Joseph?'

I hadn't heard the door open behind me. I turned. Swoozie.

'No,' I said.

'Are you sure?' she asked, looking me in the ears.

'If you mean your brother, yeah, definitely sure.'

'Didn't you go back into the broom cupboard?'

'Three times,' I said. 'Didn't work once.'

'Oh dear. But why are you sitting on the step?'

'Because I didn't think anyone was in.'

'I'm always in by this time. I go to my friend Penny's for half an hour after school and come home when I know you're in. I mean when Joseph's

in. But no one was in today.'

'So how did you get in?'

'With the key under the front step.'

'Your mum puts a back door key under the front step?'

'A front door key. In case Joseph's late.'

'My mum doesn't put any kind of key under the front step,' I said.

'You don't have a sister,' said Swoozie.

She was right, I didn't have a sister, but now that I thought of it, if my mum had put a front door key under the front step when we moved to the Brook Farm Estate instead of a back door key up the garden gnome's bum, I could have got in so much more easily all this time.

I went into the house. Swoozie closed the door.

'Sorry to disappoint you,' I said.

'Disappoint me?'

'Not being your brother.'

'Well, I expect we'll get him back sooner or later,' she said. 'And it's nice to have you here.'

'You're just saying that.'

She beamed me a colossal smile that told me

that she wasn't just saying it, she really meant it. Then she gripped one of my elbows and pulled me into the kitchen.

'Bet you're hungry,' she said.

'How'd you guess?'

'You're a growing boy. Shall I make you a Vegemite sandwich?'

'No, I'll just have a batch of bickies.'

She got out the biscuit tin and opened it for me. I grabbed a handful.

'Better?' she said when I'd rammed half of them past my teeth.

'Yeah.'

'Got any homework?'

'Homework? Should I have?'

'Sometimes Joseph does, sometimes he doesn't. I help him with it. Well, I do most of it really. He just copies it out.'

'Get away. You're too young for a thirteen year old's homework.'

She beamed again. 'Young but bright.'

'Brighter than him?'

'No, it's just that I like doing homework and he doesn't. In return he makes my bed and stuff.'

'He makes your bed?'

'Yes. He's so much better at bed-making than I am.'

'But – but – but he's a boy!' I stammered.

'He's my brother,' said Swoozie happily. 'He loves me.'

That evening I picked up some more weird info about this world. Not only did Juggy make his own bed and his sister's, but his dad did most of the cooking, washing, vacuuming, and just about every other thing that my mum complains about doing without help. He wasn't the only dad either. Housework was Man's Work here. And what did the women do? The women earned the big money, checked the oil and tyres of the cars, and went to football matches. Yep. Went to football. And the football was played by…women!

I got most of this from Swoozie, but one piece of news came from her dad after he'd loaded the dishwasher following the meal he cooked when he got in from work.

'Better get one last practice in, Jug,' he said.

'Practice?'

'Come on, let's see how you do.'

He took the ironing board from its cupboard and set it up in the kitchen. While the iron was warming up he brought a big plastic basket in. The basket contained a heap of clothes he'd put through the washing machine and tumble dryer last night or the night before.

'What do you want to try first?' he asked.

'First?'

'Shirt, trousers, pants?'

'You choose.'

'OK, let's ease into it with your mother's undies.'

He found a pair of little blue things and laid them out on the ironing board. Then we both stood there looking at them like we were waiting for them to get up and dance.

'Go on then,' Dad 2 said. 'The iron should be warm enough by now.'

I stared. At the pants. At him. At the pants again. 'You want me to iron these things?'

'Of course.' When I went right on staring at them, he laughed. 'Come on, son, you want to win that trophy, don't you?'

'Trophy?'

He closed my fingers round the handle of the

iron. He actually expected me to press his wife's knickers. And because I had to act like he thought I would, I bit the bullet, spat it out, and got stuck in.

But after a few seconds he asked why I was doing it like that.

'Like what?'

'Well, the way you're going about it, you'd think you'd never ironed women's underwear before.'

'Oh, really?'

'Stretch that section between your thumb and fingers and ease the point of the iron in. That's it. Don't press, the iron'll do that. Just ease it in and follow the contour… yes… and withdraw, and go smoothly over the stern… oh, that's more like it.' He chuckled. 'Had me worried there, lad!'

After the little knickers I had to iron the other clothes in the basket, clothe after clothe. Just as well my mother had given me that bit of tutoring a couple of nights back or I'd have been really stuck. I think I did a pretty neat job actually. My real father would have been ashamed of me.

I'd just ironed the last thing in the basket when Swoozie's mother wandered in.

'How did he do?' she asked her husband.

'He's done better. Still, I guess it won't be about quality so much as content.' He looked at me. 'Feel like going to hang upside down from a tree in the park?'

Mum 2 got in before I could get my lips round an answer to this.

'He's put in enough practice over the past few weeks, Mel. He'll either do well at the weekend or he won't. It's in the lap of the gods.'

'Or Xenu,' said Dad 2 with a sigh.

'What he needs is an early night, to be fresh for tomorrow. Go on, Juggy, up you go, get a good night's sleep.'

'But it's only nine o'clock,' I said.

'Yes,' she said. 'And you're about to pass the watershed. Upstairs.'

I didn't dare appear too clueless, so up I went.

Swoozie's light was on. I knocked on her door.

'Come in, Joseph.'

I looked in. 'Your parents are insane,' I said.

'Bit heavy with the ironing practice, were they?'

'A bit and a half.'

'Just go along with it,' she said. 'You've taken

my brother's place, so you have to be him while you're here if you don't want tricky questions.'

'Yes, but what's ironing got to do with this weekend?'

She looked surprised at this. 'It has everything to do with it.'

It was on the tip of my tongue to ask her to explain that, but then I thought that maybe it wasn't only her parents who were out of their minds. Maybe out of your mind was normal here.

I went to the bathroom, squeezed toothpaste onto a finger, swiped my teeth with it, spat, rinsed, went to the bedroom that wasn't mine, got into the pyjamas that weren't mine either, and the bed (ditto) for my second night in the room that should have been Dawn Overton's. But I couldn't get to sleep. Kept thinking that along the landing was the little sister I didn't have. That downstairs were someone else's parents who thought I was their son. From there I got to thinking about Mum. My real mum. Who was going to the hospital on Monday about something so bad she and Dad wouldn't

tell me. And I couldn't even be with her over the weekend, when she might need me.

Don't tell anyone or I'll set Stallone the dog on you, but I think I cried myself to sleep.

CHAPTER EIGHTEEN

Saturday morning. Early. So early I didn't want to think about it, certainly didn't want to be awake in it, and wouldn't have been if Swoozie hadn't set her alarm to make sure I got up. I rolled out of my borrowed bed in my borrowed pyjamas, softened the gummy earballs, and popped them in place behind the McCue lugs. When I went down for some of the junk they called breakfast in that household I noticed the ironing board leaning against the wall by the front door and felt quite envious. I wanted to lean against a wall myself, but I had to go out there and Survive the Weekend.

Swoozie's dad had also got up early. He'd made me a packed lunch.

'What's in it?' I asked. 'Lettuce?'

'And celery.'

'Really pushed the boat out, didn't you.'

'There's also a vegetable pasty and some sesame seed crackers, some goats' cheese and

a natural raspberry yogurt.'

'Ooh, can't wait.'

'I've polished your EI boots,' he said.

'My Eee-eye boots?'

He pointed to a pair of shiny orange walking boots. The kind of boots I wouldn't even wear in the dark. The sooner I got off this planet the better.

As well as the lunch box, Dad 2 had packed a sports bag full of things he thought I'd need for the weekend. I looked inside. Everything was so *neat*! If my dad packs a bag he grabs everything with his eyes shut, crams it in, and calls for me to sit on it while he tries to close the zip.

'I've put your costume at the bottom,' Dad 2 said.

'Costume?'

'Wrapped in tissue paper to protect it.' The doorbell rang before I could ask for more info on this. 'Get that, will you, Jug?' he said.

I went out to the hall and opened the front door. Eejit stood on the step with a lunch box and a sports bag like the one that had been packed for me. There was also something strapped on his back.

I scowled at him. 'What time do you call this?'

'Six-fifteen.'

'Well, go home, come back in twenty minutes.'

'We have to do a detour to Angie's.'

'What for?'

'She needs help.'

'What with?'

'I don't know. Stuff. She phones, we go, that's the way it works.'

'What's that on your back?'

'What do you think it is?'

I turned him round for a better look. It was an ironing board.

'Why are you taking that?'

'Well, I'd look pretty silly going without it,' he said.

'Silly *without* it?' I said.

'Come on. It's ten minutes' to Angie's and we have a bus to catch afterwards.'

I shoved something vaguely foodish in my gob, paid the bathroom a farewell visit, came down again, and laced my shiny orange boots. Eejit was in the hall now, chatting with Dad 2 and Swoozie.

'Ready?' he said to me.

I grunted and he reached for the ironing board

that was leaning against the wall.

'I'll give you a hand,' said Swoozie.

Then the two of them began strapping the ironing board to my back while I stood with my arms hanging and my jaw going up and down silently. What was *this* all about?

'Now you two be careful,' said Dad 2.

'That's right,' Mum 2 agreed, joining us in her dressing gown, hair standing up like she'd had a fright. 'Be creative, but don't take silly risks. We'll be proud of you even if you don't bring the trophy home.'

The father-who-wasn't-mine put the unnaturally healthy lunch box in one of my hands and the ultra-neat sports bag in the other, and Eejit and I were about to go when Swoozie reached up, pulled my head down, and kissed me on the forehead.

'Don't worry,' she whispered in one of my gum-enhanced ears. 'It's only a sport.'

With the things in our hands and on our backs, Atkins and I shouldn't have tried to get through the gate at the same time, but we did, and we ended up going through sideways, chest to chest.

As we set off across the estate I asked him why we were wearing ironing boards.

'You don't know?' he said.

'Would I ask if I did?'

'But I thought you were doing the same weekend with your Mr Rice.'

'Why would we take ironing boards on a Survival Weekend?'

'Survival Weekend? I thought you were joking about that.'

'A Survival Weekend's no joke,' I said. 'You think I wouldn't rather be at home reading comics with my feet up the wall? What's this one of yours about if it's not to teach us how to survive it?'

'It's the Nationwide Extreme Ironing Challenge.'

'The what?'

'The Nationwide Extreme Ironing Challenge.'

'The *what*?'

'The Nationwide Extreme Ironing Challenge. Teams from schools all over the country are gathering to compete for the trophy this weekend.'

'It's an *ironing* trophy?' I gasped in disbelief.

'I thought you knew.'

'Well I didn't. And we'll be ironing out of doors?'

'Yes. Before quite a big audience, I expect.'

'Ironing in front of a horde of absolute strangers?'

'And the judges.'

'Our ironing's going to be *judged*?'

'And marked accordingly. But the quality of the ironing will only be a part of it. It's *how* we iron that'll win us the big points.'

'How many ways are there to iron clothes?' I asked.

He frowned. 'We obviously should have gone over this with you.'

'That would've been nice,' I said.

So that's what last night's ironing practice had been about: to prepare me for what I had to do this weekend. Something came back to me that Mr Rice had said – thinking I was Juggy – as I was leaving Mr Numnuts' science lesson.

'I'm counting on you most of all. Whether we bring that trophy home or not could be your call.'

I supposed that meant that Juggy was pretty nifty with the iron. But he wasn't there. I was going to be taking his place. And I'd only held

an iron twice in my life.

Angie lived on Richard Branson Crescent, where the houses had pillars and solid wooden doors instead of no pillars and white plastic doors.

'Which is hers?' I asked.

'The one with the lion on the gatepost.'

I growled at the lion as we pushed the gate back and hunched up the path with our ironing boards, lunch boxes and sports bags. I didn't feel right going to a house like this, but Eejit didn't seem bothered. He climbed the step and rang the bell while I climbed the step and stood listening to it echoing through the en-suites. When the door eventually cranked back I expected to see a butler on the welcome mat. It wasn't a butler. It was Angie's dad, Bill, who I hadn't seen since I was eight. He looked the same as I remembered only a bit fatter, with a moustache and a flashy gold medallion round his neck.*

'Hi, you two.'

'Angie asked us to come over,' Eejit told him. 'Said she needs help with something.'

'She's got you well trained,' Bill said, widening the door.

---

* Only the medallion was round his neck. The moustache filled the gap between his top lip and his nose.

We went into the hall. The house was much bigger inside than the ones on our patch. Probably because it was also bigger on the outside.

'Angie, your slaves are here!' her dad yelled up the stairs.

A distant reply from somewhere above. 'Tell 'em to wait!'

'You get that?' he said to us. Eejit said that we had, and Bill strolled down the tiled hallway to wherever it was he'd been before he came to answer the door.

I stared about me. What was an Angie Mint doing in a house like this? It didn't seem right. Not that I envied her, you understand. My house was as good as this – my real house, I mean, not Mrs Overton's. As good but a bit smaller, that's all, with fewer fancy touches and no chandeliers. All right, so some of our cupboard doors fell off occasionally, and our lights flickered every time a bike went by, and the downstairs toilet leaked, and there were cracks down a couple of the walls, and we had a burglar for a neighbour, but apart from that it was as good as this.

'Hi, Juggy, hi, Ralph,' said Angie's mum, coming

down the stairs in a black silk kimono with dragons all over it.

'Hi, Aud,' I said.

This seemed to surprise her, but she smiled anyway and went the same way Bill had, to the kitchen, I guessed. I get on great with the Audrey Mint of my world, but maybe this Audrey and Juggy weren't as close because they didn't see one another all the time. She might not be best buds with his mum either. Maybe this was the way things would have worked out at home if Bill and Audrey had stayed together. If my world's Bill had made money and he and Angie's mum hadn't split, they might also have moved to a house on Richard Branson Crescent.

When Angie came down she looked like she was going to a fancy hotel for the weekend instead of a couple of days' open-air ironing. I told her this.

'One must look one's best,' she said.

'Must one?' I said.

'Of course. If one doesn't, one might as well stay at home.'

'One wishes one could.' I turned to Eejit. 'Is she always like this on her own turf?'

'Oh, no,' he said. 'Sometimes she puts on airs and graces. What do you want help with?' he asked Angie.

'I need a hand to pull my case.'

'Do we look like we've got spare hands?' I said, raising my two full ones and nodding at Eejit's pair of also full ones.

'What case?' said Eejit.

Angie pointed at something by the door. One of those folding trolleys with handles that Really Golden Oldies wheel their shopping home on. Except this one didn't have shopping on it. It had an expensive-looking suitcase.

'You're not taking that,' Eejit said.

'I need a few things,' Angie replied.

'Well so do we, but we're only taking what we can manage ourselves.'

'That's because you're not girls.'

'Why can't you pull it?' I asked her.

'Because I've done my nails,' she said, like this should be obvious even to a flat-eared knucklehead like me.

She flounced off and Eejit and I looked at one another.

'Isn't your Angie like that?' he asked.

'My Angie bites her nails. And if you try and help her with anything she thumps you.'

'Sounds like heaven.'

When she came back Angie was wearing white fur-topped boots, a matching hat, and a colour-coordinated cagoule.

'What's with the winter snow gear?' I said. 'It's not cold.'

'It might be later. We'll be out all night, remember.'

'We'll be undercover,' said Eejit.

'In tents. Tents don't have walls and central heating. Shall we go?'

She swept towards the door like a pop diva.

'Where's your ironing board?' I asked as she went.

She half turned and looked down her nose at me.

'What would I be doing with an ironing board?'

'You mean me and Atkins are ironing and you're not?'

'Atkins and I,' she corrected, and added loftily,

'I wouldn't soil my hands. Extreme Ironing's a *male* sport.'

She yelled 'Byeee!' to her parents, ordered us outside, closed the door, and started up the path with her polished nails standing out from her hips like flippers. Me and Eejit (Eejit and I) followed with our ironing boards, lunch boxes and overnight bags. As he was also pulling the suitcase trolley Eejit had a bit of a struggle. When he bounced the trolley off the fifth or sixth kerb on the way to school, Angie told him to watch out, which didn't help his mood all that much.

'If you don't like the way I'm pulling it, pull it yourself,' he snapped.

'All I'm saying is, be careful,' Her Royal Hoightyness said. 'There's some delicate stuff in there.'

'Like what?' he snarled. 'Frilly pink underwear?'

'No, *not* frilly pink underwear,' she retorted. 'I'm not a pink person.'

About a dozen kids were already hanging around a green-and-yellow minibus in the car park when we got to Arnie Snit Compulsory. The driver sat behind the wheel cleaning out an ear and

reading a magazine with the door shut, so no one could get in till he was ready.

'I hope this isn't the only bus,' I said.

'Why wouldn't it be?' said Angie.

'Well, you won't get two whole classes in that.'

'Two classes? It's only for the EI Team and the lottery winners.'

'Lottery winners?'

'There were just ten places for cheerers-on,' said Eejit. 'Those who wanted to come drew lots. Angie was one of the winners from our class.'

'How many are in the team?'

'Six.'

'Six? Just you, me and four others?'

'Hang on, let me count. Yes, four fingers and two thumbs make six.'

'And we're the only two from your class?'

I said this because there were three other ironing board wearers present and I didn't recognise any of them. One of them had a constant sniff that could really get to you if you stood near him for more than five seconds. 'That's Fuseli, Shenoy and Smee,' Eejit said when I asked who they were. 'We practise with them sometimes.'

'Here come the chiefs,' Angie said.

She meant Mr Rice and a woman I didn't know. They were carrying large sports bags with the word NASAL on the side. NASAL? Were they the bags they kept their lifetime supply of nose-drops in? More likely, it was this world's version of ADIDAS or NIKE, though for all I knew it could have been the initials of the National Association of Sweaty Armpitted Losers.

'Who's the one with the pudding?' I asked Eejit.

'Pudding?'

'Mr Rice.'

'That's Mrs Bevoir. She's here to look after the girls. Standing in for Miss Weeks while she gets over having Mr Rice's baby.'

'She's had a Rice baby as *well* as Miss Weeks?'

'No, I mean she's here in Miss Weeks's pl— '

I held my hand up to stop him. 'Kidding.'

Mrs Bevoir was dressed in normal clothes, but Mr Rice was in another of those romper suits he seemed to be so fond of in this world – a purple one today. As well as carrying his NASAL bag, he was pulling a trolley, quite a bit larger than Angie's, with a big box on top.

211

'Morning all!' he cried.

'Morning!' a handful of wide-awake voices cried back.

'Raring to go, team?' he asked those of us doing turtle impressions with ironing boards.

Atkins and the three I didn't know said, 'Yo, Coach!'

Rice noticed that I'd given the Yo a miss. 'Juggy?'

'What?'

'Raring to go?'

'Oh, I'm raring to go all right. Home.'

My usual Mr Rice would have barked at me for talking back that way, but this wasn't my usual Mr Rice. He came up to me, laid a giant mitt on my shoulder, and said, quietly, so no one else could hear, 'I know this is a nerve-wracking time for you, Jug, but if we don't win we don't win, simple as that. Just give it your best shot, eh?' Then he inspected the faces waiting for the bus.

'Where's Eric?'

'Here!'

Heads turned. Another boy I didn't know was hurrying towards us, lunch box in one hand,

sports bag in the other, ironing board on his back. The team was complete. The bus doors clunked open. Everyone started to get on board. Time to go and make a lollipop of myself while people booed.

CHAPTER NINETEEN

Don't ask me where the bus took us. The wilds, is all I know. There were some hills and some woods and a river, all that country-type stuff that's so bad for you, about two hours' journey from the school. Three other buses were there before us and two more turned up soon after. They left when everyone had got off and unloaded their gear. None of the school parties seemed keen to mix with any of the others, though some of the teachers marched up to one another and shook hands and chatted a bit. I asked Eejit how many schools were taking part. He said six. Six teams of six then, all competing to see who could do the best ironing. My mind boggled. Never again would I mock tattooed airheads who kick balls into nets and become millionaires with surgically-enhanced wives.

'This is the final,' Eejit told me. 'It's quite something to make it this far. Hundreds of schools

were eliminated along the way.'

'Has your school ever done this well before?'

'No, first time. If we win, the school shoots up the league tables and the Head gets on the list of nobodies queuing to buy a knighthood.'

'So out of all the kids from all the schools who tried for this, your pal Juggy's one of the thirty-six best ironers in the country?'

'Yes. And it's iron-*ists*, not iron-*ers*.'

'And I'm expected to take his place. I, who have only used an iron twice in my life.'

'Twice? Come on. Don't you take turns with your dad at home?'

'Take turns?'

'With the ironing.'

I smirked. 'My dad doesn't know one end of an iron from the other, and I didn't myself till last Wednesday.'

'Who does the ironing where you come from then?' This was Angie, who'd just torn herself away from a heavy girlie chat about nail polish.

'The women, who else?'

'The *women*?' She reeled. 'Whoever heard of women ironing?'

'Except when they live alone and there's no man around,' Eejit put in.

'Except then. What sort of mad world do you *live* in, Jiggy McCue?'

'I used to wonder that myself,' I said. 'Not any more!'

'Well, all I hope,' said Eejit, 'is that on the two occasions you did the ironing you did a good job. I can stand not winning, but I'd hate us to come last after getting this far.'

'Take my advice,' I said. 'Get used to the coming last scenario.'

'You might be able to avoid that if the team puts on some really imaginative displays,' said Angie.

'What's imagination got to do with ironing?' I asked her.

She glanced at Eejit. 'He doesn't know?' He raised his hands helplessly. 'Looks like you should have dreamt up some routines for him,' she said.

He nodded gloomily. 'Yeah. A whole year of planning, training, additional weekend EI courses, all for nothing.'

'Come on, people,' said Mr Rice, jogging by. 'Get the tents up.' He jogged on to say the same thing to

the other members of our team and support group.

There were five Snit Compulsory tents, three biggish ones and two single-person ones. The single-person tents were for Mr Rice and Mrs Bevoir, two of the bigger ones were for the supporters (boys in one, girls in the other) and the third was for the team. The other schools had similar arrangements and soon there were tents everywhere, in six groups. Everyone had to put their own tents up, even the teachers, or at least help in some way, even if it only meant holding a pole or moving the gear to make room for a groundsheet. My job turned out to be securing the guy-ropes.

'Why do I have to do the guy-ropes?' I asked Eejit.

'Because you're the guy-rope wizard,' he said.

'Me? I've never even tripped over a guy-rope.'

'You might not have, but Juggy has. There's a school camping trip most terms.'

'Holy macaroni.' School camping trips: one of my many visions of Hell. I looked at the ropes. 'How do you work these things?'

'You tie them to the ground pegs,' he said, a bit

sharply I thought, and left me to it.

I couldn't ask advice from anyone else – no one else in our team had even spoken to me yet – so I did the best I could and hoped it was OK for the ropes to be tied in bows.

'Why d'you think they're called guy-ropes?' I asked Eejit when he strolled back my way.

'What else would they be called?'

'Well, they could be called cricket bats, table mats or digital cameras, but I mean why "guy" ropes? If they have to be male why not man-ropes? Or boy-ropes? Or bloke-ropes, mate-ropes, even geezer-ropes?'

'You have a very weird mind, you know that?' Atkins said, and left me again.

When the tents were up, the teachers from the six schools emptied their NASAL bags. They all had them. Some also had big boxes like Mr Rice's, and they emptied these too. The bags and boxes contained the equipment the teams planned to use over the weekend. They laid all the stuff out for the judges to check that it complied with EIO* rules. I saw underwater goggles, crash helmets, coils of rope, lengths of chain, planks of wood, drills,

---

* The Extreme Ironing Organisation, which was running the show.

screwdrivers, and quite a bit more. One school had brought a couple of pushbikes, another a surfboard.

'As I'm sure you're aware,' the chief judge said when the equipment had been inspected and the teams were lined up for the Big Welcome Speech, 'any of the approved items may be used or adapted as aids to your displays. Natural objects found in the vicinity may also be used. In all heats but the first and last, two or more team-members may participate. The irons and heat pellets will be supplied by the EIO. You may use more than one iron at a time if you require it.'

'Heat pellets?' I said to Eejit.

He didn't answer. He was listening to the BW Speech.

'In the interests of safety,' the chief judge went on, 'I am required to stress that— ' He broke off when an ambulance pulled in where the buses had been. 'Perfect timing,' he said as a couple of medics got out. 'I was about to remind the contestants that in tournaments such as this, accidents can happen. Do not, whatever you do, teams, sacrifice care for the sake of effect. We do

219

not want a repetition of last year.'

'What happened last year?' I asked Eejit.

'One boy broke an arm, another landed on his head and spent three months in hospital wondering who he was, a third went over a cliff.'

'Over a cliff? Was he hurt?'

'Dunno, our school wasn't in competition, but from what I heard the last anyone saw of him was his heels.'

'Now it only remains for me to wish you all the very best of luck,' the chief judge said. 'But remember, only one team can win The Golden Iron!'

'That's the trophy,' Eejit said.

'An iron made of gold?'

'Gold's the colour, doesn't matter what it's made of, it's such an honour to win it. The winning school keeps it until next year's tournament.'

I shook my head. This was sooooo sad.

'Mr Trumpkin, the irons, if you please!' the chief judge cried.

A very short Golden Oldie in a blazer threw back the lid of an old wooden box the CJ was standing behind. Everyone craned forward to see what was

inside – a stack of old-fashioned irons, the non-electric kind, like the one my mother uses for a doorstop. A cheer went up like they were something special.

Finally the chief judge told us that there would be six rounds of six heats (six was obviously the magic number round here), three today, three tomorrow, and that the first would commence at mid-day, so we had two hours to check out the terrain.

'Look for ways of using our surroundings,' Eejit explained. 'Making the most of the environment is a big part of the challenge.'

'Team – to me!' (Mr Rice.)

The six members of our team, including me, went to him as ordered.

'Are you all right to go first with your speciality turn, Hot Stuff?' he asked one of the boys I didn't know.

'Sure am, Coach,' the boy answered with a cocky grin.

'*Hot Stuff*?' I rasped in Eejit's ear. 'Did he call him *Hot Stuff*?'

'That's his ironist name,' he whispered back.

'We all have one.'

Mr R told us to be back by half-eleven, in time to change for the first heat. What we had to do now, he said, was explore and make notes. Eejit said that I'd better go with him. We were just leaving when I heard Mr Rice say 'De-Wrinkle Man', which I ignored, but when he said it again, louder, Eejit tapped my arm.

'Coach wants you.'

'He does?'

'He called your name.'

'I didn't hear.'

'De-Wrinkle Man. Your ironist name.'

'De-Wrinkle Man? That's me? De-Wrinkle Man is the best anyone could come up with?'

'It's the name Juggy came up with.'

I was amazed. 'Why would he choose a name like De-Wrinkle Man? Why would *anybody*?'

'It's not easy finding a name that has something to do with ironing,' Eejit said. 'So many have been taken, and no ironist is allowed the same name as another.'

'I just wanted to see if you're all right,' Mr Rice said to me when we turned to him. 'You seem

a mite distracted today.'

'Distracted,' I said. 'Yeah, that covers it pretty well.'

Eejit stepped in. 'He's having trouble deciding on the best manoeuvre for his solo tomorrow.'

'Well, whatever you do decide,' Rice said, again to me, 'make sure all safety aspects are covered,' and he added, with a chuckle, 'We want to be able to find *your* body, don't we?'

I flipped to Eejit. 'When you say "solo"…'

He grinned at Mr Rice. 'He's kidding. He knows that as our most daring and creative ironist he'll be doing the final heat tomorrow' – he glanced at me – '*alone.*'

'A-a-alone?' I stammered.

'Alone is how solos work,' said Atkins.

'Tell me,' I said in a surprisingly high-pitched voice. 'Are we anywhere near the cliff that kid from last year went over?'

Mr Rice guffawed at that. I was hilarious without even trying today.

While members of the six teams strolled in twos and threes around the local rocks, holes, water and cow dung, Atkins led the way past some straggly

old woods. To take my mind off the news that I was our team's star turn, I asked him what his ironist name was.

'Iron King,' he said.

'Iron King? You're Iron King and I'm De-Wrinkle Man?'

'Yep.'

'Whaddayasay we swap?'

'I say go iron your ears.'

He had a notebook with him, which he kept stopping to write or sketch something in. I asked him what. He said he was looking for places that might be good for an ironing display, and that when we met up with the rest of the team we'd pool info and work out some strategies for the four multiple-ironist entries.

'Strategies?'

'We have to demonstrate the most unusual ways we can think of to iron things,' he said. 'The idea is to show how adventurous ironing can be in the natural environment.'

'The natural environment for ironing is inside a building,' I said.

'That's domestic ironing, not the extreme sport

variety. EI is about taking the activity as far as you can. Points are awarded for originality. The more unusual the display, the more points you stand to get.' He showed me some of his sketches. 'I'm making notes in words and pictures of trees and rock formations and anything else that might provide something to hang from, climb inside, that sort of thing.'

'Hang from? Climb inside?'

'Like the bough of this tree. See how it sticks out across the ravine? A competitor could be roped to his ironing board and hold on to the branch with one hand while pressing a shirt with the other.'

'That's insane.'

He grinned. 'Insanity's the name of the game.'

'What's the drawing of the nose all about?'

'That's not a nose, it's a pair of caves. I only drew them because...' He saw what I meant. 'Hey.' He went back a few paces and looked up at the hill we'd just passed. 'I didn't notice when I was drawing it.'

About two-thirds of the way up, there was a big rocky bump almost exactly like a colossal broken nose. The hill sort of leaned out at that point so the

tip of the 'nose' hung over nothing. The two caves Eejit had drawn were underneath the bump, which made them look like its nostrils. He laughed when he saw this. I didn't. I didn't see *anything* funny in being here today.

When we'd done all the exploring and note-taking we could in the time, we headed back. When we met the rest of our team we squatted with them and swapped ideas. Well, they swapped and Eejit swapped, I kept my gap shut. I didn't get how these people could be so serious about ironing out of doors in the maddest ways possible. But serious they were, all five of them, discussing what stunts might gain the most points. Unbelievable.

'No thoughts from you, De-Wrinkle Man?' one of them asked.

He said it kind of sarcastically, I thought. The other strangers also looked my way like they weren't going to trade high-fives with me any time soon. The one with the snuffle – Smee – gave an especially noisy sniff as he looked at me, like it was me who'd given him that cold.

'Thoughts?' I said. 'Oh, you wouldn't believe the thoughts I'm getting.'

I was saved from sharing my true thoughts by Mr Rice, who bounced up and asked how it was going. He was behind me when he asked this, so I didn't see him at first, but when the others started telling him what they had in mind for the events he came round and squatted with us. When he did this, my eyes almost ignited. He'd changed out of the purple romper suit into a one-piece, neck-to-ankle, sky-blue costume with a yellow stripe down one leg. This might have been hard to take if it had been a loose garment, but it wasn't a loose garment, it was so tight that nothing, like *nothing*, inside it was hidden. You could see the outline of every rib, vein, nipple and wart, plus one or two other bits I definitely didn't want outlined for me. A squawk like a hen being strangled came from nearby.

'What was that, De-Wrinkle Man?' Mr Rice asked.

'Nothing. Just squawking.'

To keep my eyes from dropping below Rice waist-level, I forced them to stare without blinking at the little shield with the letters EIO on his skin-

tight blue chest. When Atkins and I were alone again I asked him why our coach was dressed like that.

'How else would he be dressed?'

'How else?' I said. 'Well, jeans and shirt, say, or even the Teletubby romper suit, seeing as this is slap-me-senseless land. Anything but what he's got on now.'

'All the coaches dress like that,' Eejit said. 'Look around you.'

I looked around me. Saw three of the other male teachers in outfits just like Mr Rice's except they were different colours.

'We'd better get changed too,' Eejit said.

'Into what?'

'Our suits.'

I felt something in my throat. I think it was a tank. But I followed him to the tent. The other four team-members were already there, inside it, pouring themselves into a quartet of blue costumes with yellow leg stripes. I was still gulping like a goldfish down to its last gill when the Fantastic Four left – scowling at me, for some reason – until I realised something. I gasped with relief.

'I haven't got a suit like theirs!'

'Course you have,' said Atkins.

I grinned happily. 'I don't think I have.'

He dropped to his knees and unzipped the overnight bag Juggy's dad had packed for me. He rummaged, found what he was looking for at the very bottom, unwrapped the tissue paper, and held up a sky-blue one-piece that could only fit a five-year-old.

I laughed. 'I won't be able to get into that.'

He handed it to me anyway. 'Sure you will.'

I held the dinky little suit against my chest. Its ankles just reached my waist. 'I would if I was a doll,' I smirked.

'It's the same as mine,' Eejit said, pulling his shirt off. 'Same as the rest of the team's – and Mr Rice's. One size fits all. They stretch.'

My feet started to move.

'What are you doing?' Atkins asked.

'I'm jigging. It's what I do when I'm agitated.'

'If you say so.' He dropped his jeans. 'Come on, we're a bit behind.'

'We'll be all behind in these things,' I said.

He dropped his underpants and before I could

229

cover my eyes reached for the teensy little blue outfit he'd taken out of his bag. He shot a foot through a leghole, shoved his other foot in the other leghole, and pulled upward. The material stretched, just like he said it would.

'Aren't you going to wear anything underneath?'

'We're not allowed,' he replied. 'You can lose points for VPL.'

'VPL?'

'Visible Pant Line.'

He hauled the super-stretchy one-piece up his top half and jammed his arms in. I watched with a mixture of amazement and dismay as the material flattened across his chest and shoulders like it had been ironed there.

'Now you,' said Eejit Atkins, my Extreme Ironing team-mate.

CHAPTER TWENTY

When I'd squeezed the totally starkers McCue bod into the super-stretch costume I looked down at myself in horror. How could one person have so many bulges in unmissable places? I'd worn the odd pair of huggy underpants in my time, but never a skin-tight neck-to-ankle one-piece – and underpants at least have the decency to hide under something else.

'I might as well be nude!' I cried.

'If you were nude you wouldn't be blue,' said Atkins.

'I would if I was cold.'

'With a yellow stripe down your leg?'

'I might have had an accident in a high wind.'

When we left the tent it was just me that was holding one hand over his hind-quarters and the other over his front.*

'You can't walk around like that,' Eejit said. 'People will stare.'

---

* When I say 'his' I mean my hind-quarters, my front, not Eejit's.

'You mean they won't if I don't?'

'Look at the others. Are people staring at them?'

I glanced at the thirty-four other team-members and the six coaches, all standing around in costumes as skin-tight as ours.

'Yes,' I said.

'Only because they're the centre of attraction,' said Eejit.

'Oh, they're that all right. You can see everything they've got, back, front and sideways. Why else do you think those girls over there are giggling behind their hands?'

'They're just happy to be here.'

'Good to know someone is.'

When we joined the rest of our team and Mr Rice, I dived into the midst of them so the spectators would get an eyeful of them rather than me. I didn't really listen to what Mr R and the boys were whispering (and sniffing in Smee's case) but I think it was something to do with what Hot Stuff was going to do in the first round. When the chief judge blew a whistle the teams had to go and stand in six separate lines, hands behind backs, feet spread, which believe me is not the way to stand if

you're wearing a costume like that and don't want to be noticed. When I saw Angie waving from the mob of cheerers-on I did not wave back.

To decide the order the teams would go in, the six contestants who'd prepared for the first round's solo displays dipped into the pocket of an official shirt on a coat-hanger and took out a button. Each button had a number on it: one, two, three, four, five or six. Hot Stuff got the number four button. A bearded man in an Extreme Ironing Organisation T-shirt and track bottoms (lucky devil!) handed one of the official irons to the boy who'd picked the number one button. Just before he handed it over he slotted a heat pellet into the iron's base. The pellets kept their heat for about twenty minutes, Eejit said. Just long enough for each heat, you might say. Then, to encouraging wolf-whistles from his supporters, the first contestant – whose costume was emerald green with a red zigzag down the back – stepped forward with his ironing board.

'Ironing boards must be used in the opening heat,' Eejit whispered. 'After this we can iron on anything we like.'

'What else would you iron on?'

'Anything at all. Though ironing boards are used most of the time.'

Although the boy in green used his ironing board he didn't put it up. He placed it flat on the ground with its legs folded under it, threw his own legs up in the air, and, balancing on one hand, pressed a T-shirt with the iron in the other. There wasn't a sound while he did this. Silence was expected, Eejit said, so he wouldn't lose his concentration. When he'd finished he jumped right-way-up and his supporters shouted and whistled and stamped their feet while everyone else clapped politely. When an adjudicator examined the pressed T-shirt (only one side had to be ironed) he held up a card with a number 5 on it.

'Five out of ten for standard of ironing coupled with delivery,' Eejit said. 'Not bad, not great.'

Contestant number two was a thin blond kid with streaks in his hair from a school called Slitheen, Snivelling, Slytherin or something. His costume colour was black – handy, because it stopped the light picking out every nook and cranny of his body. Like the first contestant he left his ironing board on the ground instead of putting

it up. When he was standing over it, a team-mate put a blindfold on him and the Extreme Ironing Org man gave him his heated iron. Then he spread his feet, tested his balance, bent over backwards, and started ironing a pair of boxer shorts like he always ironed upside down. When he was done he flipped upright, whipped his blindfold off, and saw that he'd missed a bit of the shorts – 'Not a good idea, the blindfold,' Eejit said – and, like the first contestant, was given five points. His supporters still applauded and stomped like crazy, though.

I won't describe what every contestant did, but our boy, Hot Stuff, pressed an apron as he roller-skated past his board, jerked himself around, and pressed more of it on the way back. He made four passes, ironing a bit more each time. He was awarded six points, which at the end of the heat put us neck-and-neck with the fifth contestant, who'd requested an extra iron so he could press a short-sleeved shirt on his grounded board with an iron on each foot and his arms folded.

As I hadn't gone out of my way to include myself in our team's chat about who was going to do what

in which heat, the stuff they did in the second and third rounds that afternoon was as much of a surprise to me as what the other teams did. Some of the stunts looked quite dangerous while some were just plain nutty. The ironists had names like Crease Wizard, Steamer, Shirt Stuff, The Human Press, Laundry Basket, and The Scorcher. Here are some of the things that were done by various contestants and teams in the second and third rounds that day.

Ironing on a board held up by a team-mate lying on the ground.

Ironing in a hammock between trees, board across lap.

Hanging over the edge of a table to press something with an iron fixed to the top of the contestant's head.

Ironing while running between two team-mates on bikes, an ironing board stretched between them.

Ironing board suspended between the branches of a tree, contestant reaching down to iron from a higher branch.

Ironing the shirt on a friend's back while he lay

face down in a stream breathing through a straw.

When the points were totted up at the end of the afternoon, our team was in third place. The lead team was from a school called Telmar Senior and the team a few points ahead of us was Lantenwaist Court. Mr Rice seemed pretty chuffed about our position.

'This is just Day One,' he said, rubbing his hands, 'and already we're third out of six. We're in with a chance, lads!'

'They're a bit strict on ironing quality,' said a boy who went by the name of Smooth Dude.

Mr Rice agreed. 'Those of you who'll be ironing tomorrow must pay special attention to the standard of your crease-work.' He turned to me. 'I hope your ironing's up to scratch, De-Wrinkle Man. If we're lucky enough to make it to second place in the fifth round your closing solo could be the decider. All our eyes and hopes will be on you with the spectacular finale you've been keeping so quiet about.'

'Spectacular finale?' I said faintly.

He laughed. He thought I was pretending. The

others seemed to think that too, though they weren't laughing. Only Iron King Atkins knew that I had absolutely no idea what I was going to do tomorrow – or that I had almost zero ironing skills.

CHAPTER TWENTY-ONE

That evening everyone except the EIO judges (who'd shot off in taxis to a luxury hotel the moment the day's heats were over) gathered round a big bonfire well away from the tents. No luxuries for us. Sleeping bags, hard ground, and food burnt in the flames by the teachers. All this was bad enough, but then a couple of brain-lites with a guitar started singing *Old MacDonald Had a Farm* and quite a few others joined in. They seemed to have chosen this song because of the chorus line: 'Eee-eye-eee-eye-oh' — EIO, Extreme Ironing Organisation, geddit? They followed this with *One Man Went to Mow*, except their version was *One Man Went to Iron* (a T-shirt, some Y-fronts, a tablecloth, etc). By the time they started on *He'll be Coming Round the Mountain with an Iron*, I was sitting with my head covered, wishing I was on the Ranting Lane Survival Weekend. No jolly singsongs round camp-fires there, bet your life.

239

The supporters were allowed to mingle with the teams now the day's events were over, so Angie joined Eejit and me in the firelight. The teams and coaches were back in civvies, which was a relief for me if no one else, after a day's walking round with my hand over my front bits.

'This is unreal,' I said.

'What is?' Angie asked.

'Whatever the turkey in this burger is made of.'

'It's Quorn,' she said when I opened it to show her.

'Corn?'

'Quorn.'

I slammed the bun shut. 'In other words it's made of nothing faintly resembling poultry.'

'It's vegetarian.'

'The bun might be, but I'm not.'

To tell you the truth, I was pretty fed up. I was the only one of our team who'd not been asked to help out in the second or third heat of the afternoon, so I'd done nothing but stand around trying not to bulge in my blue prat suit. I'd never been so bored.*

'What's the plan for tomorrow?' Angie asked

---

* Apart from every single day at school. Or when doing homework. Or shopping with my mum.

Eejit while I nibbled round the edge of the bun to avoid the fake turkey.

'You know we can't discuss team plans with outsiders,' he replied.

'I'm not an outsider, I'm a friend, a school-mate and a supporter.'

'An outsider is anyone who's not in the team.'

'Whisper to me,' she said.

'No. Wait and see.'

She turned to me. 'You'll tell me what's lined up for tomorrow, won't you?'

'I would if I could,' I said. The fact was, I hadn't paid much attention when the team talked about what they were going to do in the fourth and fifth rounds. 'Hey, it's getting a bit windy.'

'You mean you're not going to tell me either.'

'No, I mean it's getting a bit windy.'

It was too. And soon it was more than a bit. Inside of a minute the light breeze that ruffled hair became a gale trying to rip it out of our skulls. The fire flared like a huge pair of bellows had been rammed up it, pots and pans clanked without human hands attached, and there was a sort of billowing sound in the far darkness, like an enormous bird winging it

241

for the hills. Then it started to rain. There were just a few little drops at first, but they were followed almost immediately by bigger drops that felt like they were seriously thinking of forming a society and becoming a downpour.

'To the tents!' a teacher bawled.

Oh dear, and I hadn't finished my phoney turkey burger.

Everyone jumped up and scrambled in different directions. Angie went to the girls' tent while Eejit and I headed for ours, which was one of the furthest from the fire and the terrific food. The rest of our team got there ahead of us, but they hadn't dived inside the tent like you might expect. They were standing in the wind and rain staring at the sports bags and ironing boards that weren't out in the open last time they looked.

'Where's the tent?'

'Are we sure this is where it was?'

'Course. That's our gear.'

'Anyway, look, the pegs are still in the ground.'

'It must have been carried off by the wind.'

'Must've. The guy-ropes can't have been secure enough.'

Everyone looked at me.

'Don't look at me,' I said.

'Who else would we look at?' one kid said. 'You tied them.'

If there'd been a high horse within arm's reach I'd have climbed up on it and galloped away, but there wasn't, so I went for indignant.

'Yes, I did,' I said. 'And who's the best guy-roper in this team? Juggy McCue, that's who. No, there was nothing wrong with those ropes,' I added, stooping to examine a rope-free tent peg. 'My guess is sabotage.'

All eyes popped. 'Sabotage?'

I raised an ultra-serious, solved-it eyebrow. 'What else could it be?'

'But who'd sabotage a tent?'

'This is a competition,' I explained. 'There are five other groups of people who might want to put the best of the opposition off their stroke.'

'But why us? We're not in the lead.'

Something flew at me on the wind and splatted round my face. I tore it off. 'Not yet we're not. But we could be by the end of tomorrow. Someone could have realised that.'

I looked at the thing in my hand. It wasn't easy to make out details in the darkness and wetness and windness, but it looked kind of furry, which is how it felt too. I realised what it was when Mr Rice ran up in his purple romper suit, snatched it off me, and jammed it on his head.

He was bald! Mr Rice wore a toupee!*

'I don't know what happened here,' he said, straightening his rug, 'but we must get you lads under cover before you get soaked and catch a chill. Let's go to my tent while we think what to do. Bring your gear!'

So we grabbed our bags and ironing boards and ran after him to his tent and stuffed ourselves and our things inside. As it was a one-person tent and that one was Mr Rice it was quite a tight fit – the half dozen ironing boards didn't help – and there was a honk of rain on steaming bodies that would have been a perfect target for one of my mother's so-called fresh-air sprays. While we steamed and cuddled our ironing boards, the rain hammered the canvas and the wind thumped it, and what-to-do-next type chat got started.

---

* It suddenly made sense that my own Mr Rice was one of those who exposed his skull to public gaze on Sponsored Baldness for Charity Day a while back (see *Ryan's Brain*). I don't know how he made it look like it was growing back afterwards, though. Must have speckled the bristles in with a felt pen or something until they looked thick enough to slam the horse blanket on again.

'We can't stay here, that's for sure,' said Smooth Dude.

Everyone mumbled amen to that.

'De-Wrinkle Man and I saw a couple of caves earlier,' said Atkins.

'Caves?' Mr Rice said.

'Up on the hill out there.'

'Are they accessible?'

'Think so. Bit of a climb, that's all.'

'We can't spend the night in a cave,' said Smee, the one with the drive-you-bonkers sniff.

'Anyone got a better idea?' Mr Rice asked. I suggested phoning for taxies to run us to the luxury hotel the judges had stashed themselves in for the night, but our secretly bald coach wouldn't have it. 'The ethos of these competitions is that they take place *away* from comfortable amenities,' he said.

'Wonder what sadist thought that up?' I muttered.

'We'll give the rain a minute to ease off,' Mr Rice said. 'Then check out those caves.'

We gave the rain a minute. Then we gave it five more.

'How's it looking?' Mr R said to Eejit, who was nearest the flaps.

Eejit peeked out. 'Like it's never going to stop.'

'Well then, we'd better make a dash for it. Agreed?'

Five people agreed. I wasn't one of them.

'Are you coming too, Coach?' Starch Fiend asked.

'Of course. I can't let my team spend the night alone in a cave, can I?'

I pointed out that if he went his tent would be empty.

'Yes,' he said. 'And?'

'Well, if you're not using it, one of us could.'

He looked around. 'De-Wrinkle Man's right. One of you could stay here...' But he said it like he'd be disappointed if anyone stuck a hand up and cried 'Me! Me!', so I didn't. When no one else did either, he said, 'I'd better tell Mrs Bevoir what's happening,' and we all leaned back so he could crawl over us and break our legs on his way out.

When he came back a couple of minutes later his rented hair was running into his eyes. 'Leave your

boards but bring your overnight bags,' he commanded.

We left the tent hugging our bags to our chests or balancing them on our heads. It was raining as hard as ever and twice as windy. Perfect weather for six extreme ironists and their coach to jog up a hill in the dark. There was a path up the hill, which helped, and every so often we came across a skinny little tree to shelter under for a second or two, but we were still pretty drowned and windswept when we finally trotted into the nearest of the two caves Eejit and I had seen from the ground that morning. At first it looked like a very shallow cave, but as our eyes got used to the dark we saw that it went back a bit. If there'd been a light switch we might have gone further in, but there wasn't, and the only torch was the tiny one Mr Rice took out of a pocket in his Teletubby suit.

'Could be worse,' he said, pencilling the mini-beam around the rocky walls and ceiling.

'Could also be a modern house with central heating and fridge magnets,' I said.

Our bags contained all the usual overnight stuff, but Mr Rice had an extra item in his. He showed it

to us in the narrow beam of the torch. 'My practice iron,' he said. 'As the judges are so strict on quality, those of you who'll be ironing tomorrow might want to get some last minute smoothing in.'

'I'll be OK,' sniffed Smee, wiping his nose on his sleeve.

'So will I,' said one of the others – Fuseli, I think.

'De-Wrinkle Man?' said Mr Rice.

'What?'

'Even if you've worked out a fantastic routine for your solo you could still lose vital points if your ironing's not perfect.'

He held up the iron, expecting me to take it.

'I'll think about it,' I said, shoving my wet hands in my windy pockets.

The truth was I had no plans to think about it. Not even one. The wally I was going to make of myself tomorrow was not terrifically high on my agenda of things to think about during a stormy night in a cave with a skinhead Mr Rice and five boys who thought of ironing as a sport and sang songs about it round camp-fires.

CHAPTER TWENTY-TWO

The rain had stopped and the wind had died, and everyone but me was snoozing. I'd unrolled my sleeping bag near the back of the cave, a bit away from the others, and lay inside it with my hands under my head looking towards the cave mouth, which was chocka with stars. I swear I never saw so many stars. Some other time, another place, I might have really appreciated them, but now that it was so quiet all I could think about was tomorrow, when I was going to have to make an exhibition of myself in a figure-hugging suit before the wide eyes of strangers. Worse still, I was supposed to be the team's star ironist, but worse even than that was that I hadn't the faintest idea what I would do in my solo spot when my turn came.

I could just make out Mr Rice's practice iron from there. It stood where he'd left it, rimmed by starlight, like it was inviting me to pick it up. Maybe I ought to get some practice in after all. Maybe while I was

ironing I would get an idea for my solo that wouldn't show me up too much. I wouldn't win the kind of points everyone expected me to, but I could always say the rubbish food had given me guts-ache or something.

I jemmied myself out of my sleeping bag and started forward. The stars were bright enough for me to pick my way between the other bags without tripping. I reached the practice iron. Mr Rice, snorting nearby like an old steam train, had left his little torch out too, and a heat pellet in case anyone changed their mind. I put the pellet and the torch in my pyjama pocket and was about to carry the iron off when I remembered that I needed some clothes to use it on. Mr Rice had slung some of his over a big stone. They'll do, I thought. He wouldn't miss them because as soon as I'd pressed them I'd return them. I bundled his togs under my arm and crept back to my sleeping bag, and past it, into the depths of the cave.

It was pitch black there and the torchlight didn't reach very far, but I found a boulder with an almost flat top and stretched one of Mr Rice's things out on it – a T-shirt with the words 'Extreme Ironing Coach'

across the chest. I pressed the heat button on the pellet, the way I'd seen others do it, and slotted it into the base of the iron. Thirty seconds later the iron was hot. I stuck the torch in a rocky hollow so I could see what I was doing, and got to work. I pressed the T-shirt very carefully, and when I'd finished I swapped it for the top half of Mr Rice's romper suit. The material of this was thicker than the T-shirt and it kept ruffling up under the iron, so I had to go even more carefully with it.

While I was working, my mind wandered to the first time I'd held an iron, in the kitchen of *The Dorks* three nights ago, under my mum's command, and I felt myself get kind of misty-eyed. Then I remembered the medical condition of hers she was going to the hospital about on Monday, and my mind kicked up its spurs and galloped into worst-case scenario territory. Even worse than the worse-case scenario was that I wasn't there with her, and maybe never would be again. Maybe, if I ever did get back, it would be too late, and there'd be just me, Dad and Stallone (the cat version).

I shook myself. Stop thinking like that! Stop thinking anything but what to do tomorrow. I tried

that, but nothing came. I pressed on.

The last piece of clothing was Mr Rice's skin-tight one-piece. It was much smaller without him inside it, of course, but not as small as the ones Eejit and I had put on. If it was true that all the suits started out the same size, Rice's bigger body must have permanently added extra centimetres to his in every direction. I laid the thing across the boulder and got stuck in. The seconds tiptoed by, until—

'Jiggy?'

I whirled round with the iron behind my back, so whoever it was wouldn't see what I was doing.

'Who's there?'

He came closer. 'Me. Eejit. What are you up to?'

'I thought that if I got some practice in, some ideas might come for my solo tomorrow.'

'Anything so far?'

'Not a stuffed dicky-bird.'

'Maybe we could work something out between us.'

'I could do with some input.'

I flipped the little suit over and started on the back. Eejit watched by torchlight.

'You sure do need the practice,' he said almost immediately.

'Oh, I thought I was doing quite a good job.'

'Not by competition standards. If the others saw the quality of your ironing, they'd tell Mr Rice that we might as well go home tonight.'

'If he agreed I'd be first in line.'

'They'd probably vote to leave you behind.'

'The others don't seem to like me much,' I said.

'They're jealous.'

'Jealous? Of me?'

'Of Juggy. Him being Mr Rice's star ironist and all. They think they're just as good. Looks like you're going to prove them right. More than right. Poor old Jug. If he ever returns, his reputation will be shot to pieces.'

'If this is an attempt to boost my confidence,' I said, 'maybe you should try harder.'

'Hey, what's that?'

'What's what?'

He whipped the torch from the hollow in the rock and trailed the light over the cave behind us.

'Woh,' he said.

I told him to keep his voice down and asked him

253

what he'd seen. He didn't answer, but went further into the cave, taking the light with him.

'Come and look at this,' he whispered when he was a dim outline against the rock.

I put the iron down and went after him. He was running the light over something long and thin that hung from the ceiling.

'Ever see one of these before?' he asked.

'Course. In pictures. It's a stalacmite.'

'If it was sticking up from the floor it would probably be a stalagmite,' he said. 'That's "g" as in ground. From the ceiling, like this one, it would usually be a stalactite – "c" for ceiling. Everyone knows that.'

'Stalactite,' I said. 'That's what I meant.'

'Only this isn't a stalactite.' He poked the thing with the end of the torch. 'A stalactite would be hard. This is quite soft.'

'So what is it?'

'A snottite.'

'A wottite?'

'A snottite. Look closely. What does it remind you of?'

I looked closely. It reminded me of a long

thick strand of nose-juice.

'Is it really called a snottite,' I said, 'or did you make it up?'

'It's really called that. I don't know much about them, but I think I read somewhere that snottites are bacteria that just grow and grow in the right conditions. I didn't know they grew in this country, so I've learnt some… Oh, look!'

The torch had picked out more snottites further on. He went to examine them. I followed. The deeper we went the more there were and the longer and thicker they got. Some reached all the way from the roof of the cave to the ground.

'There are dozens of them,' Eejit said excitedly. 'If this cave is really deep there could be *hundreds*.'

He went on. Seeing as he had the light, I went on too. We passed a spider hanging by a thread from one of the snottites, but Eejit was more interested in the snottites themselves than what lived on them. The cave was like a tunnel, but not a straight one, so we had to keep ducking and stooping and turning this way and that, always avoiding the snottites.

'How far are we going?' I asked.

'I want to see how deep the cave is,' Eejit said.

'It might go on forever.'

'Just a bit further.'

That bit further made the difference. The snottites started to thin out and the darkness got a little less dark. Then we saw stars.

'Another cave entrance!' Atkins said. He went ahead of me to the mouth of the cave. 'And guess which one. The other nostril.'

'Nostril?'

'You were the one who pointed it out. The way the hill bulged around the two caves like a broken nose?'

'Oh, yeah.'

I went and stood beside him. Far below were the tents that didn't include ours and the dull embers of the rained-on fire.

'We could take the short cut back,' Eejit suggested, meaning the narrow ridge that ran along the hill between the two caves.

'We could if we wanted to risk falling to pulp while screaming,' I said.

'OK. Back the long way, through the snott...'

He broke off.

'What?' I said.

'The spider we saw dangling from the snottite back there has given me an idea for your solo heat.'

'Oh yes?' I already didn't like the sound of this.

'From the ground these caves look like nostrils under a huge nose,' Eejit said. 'Well, imagine swinging from one of them like that spider.'

'Imagine swinging from a cave on a spider's thread?' I cried in horror.

'Not a thread, a rope. We dangle your ironing board from one cave-nostril and dangle you from the other. You swing across to the board and press an item of clothing while everyone down below shades their eyes to stare up in wonder. It'll be fantastic! A real show-stopper!'

'Heart-stopper, more like. Mine.'

'Those extra points'll be in the bag!' he said excitedly.

'Yes, and me along with them, zipped up on a stretcher. You're out of your mind, Atkins. Forget it.'

'I thought you said you wanted input.' He sounded kind of offended.

'I did. I do. What I don't want is to do spider impressions while hanging from a giant nostril in the sky.'

I snatched the torch off him and charged to the back of the cave and beyond, ducking and weaving round all the snottites. Eejit rode my heels, not wanting to be left alone in the dark, yammering his crazy idea all the way. Drawing near to our cave, I smelt something.

'Oh, no.'

I remembered that when I'd put the hot iron down to go and look at the first of the snottites Atkins had discovered, I'd intended to go back to it – and hadn't. I rushed to the boulder and seized the iron. The heat pellet was cooling now, but too late, the damage was done. I'd set it down on Mr Rice's all-in-one coaching outfit, and…

I stuck the torch between my teeth and held up the little suit. There was an iron-shaped hole in its posterior. A hole that would stretch and stretch when Mr Rice put the suit on. A hole that covered (or uncovered) the very place where he would slot his bare rump in the morning.

CHAPTER TWENTY-THREE

It dawned. The Sunday I was to make a public prat of myself. It started a bit nippy, which I wasn't sorry about because when Mr Rice emerged from the depths of the cave in the costume he'd changed into in the dark, he also wore the top half of his romper suit, which covered the gaping burn in the backside.

'Let's hope it stays cold all day,' I whispered to Eejit. 'Are my ears straight?'

He reached behind my left ear and reshaped the piece of gum I'd stuck there.

The heats started earlier that day. The fourth round kicked off at ten, the fifth was due to start two hours later, and the final round, the solo heats, was set for 2pm. The judges looked like being even more strict than yesterday, telling us that if a team took too long to get started it would be eliminated from that round and the next team would be asked to step up.*

Eejit told me that because it was day two the

---

* This happened almost right away, when Telmar Senior, the lead team, couldn't get a piece of machinery to work – some weird contraption they'd cobbled together from chains and bits of metal to help with their display. Getting no points in that heat set them back a bit, but they were still in the lead because they'd done so well yesterday.

teams would be putting on more ambitious displays in the hope of earning more points – bad news for someone who hadn't thought of anything even slightly ambitious. Nothing at all, in fact. As time grew short and the ideas failed to pop into my head, I realised I had no choice but to go for Atkins's mad scheme. He was thrilled when I told him, but said we had to put it to Mr Rice. He also said we should make it sound like it was my idea, so we did. When he heard, the coach's features cracked into the kind of grin you'd expect to see on a lunatic who's just downed his second bottle of rum in ten minutes.

'I love it! I knew you had something up that blue sleeve of yours, De-Wrinkle Man!'

The coaches weren't allowed to help their teams during a heat, only advise them, and Mr Rice's advice was to take whatever equipment we needed up to the caves and get everything ready well in advance. The only equipment we needed were two long lengths of rope, one shorter length and my ironing board. The two of us carried them up to the first cave, where Atkins outlined a ten-point plan he'd devised to make the most of my display. While he told me the plan I leant against a rock wishing he

was the other Eejit, who never had a bright idea in his miserable little life. Here are the ten points.

1: In Cave One, tie the two long ropes round the ironing board, one at each end to balance it.

2: Peg an item of clothing to the ironing board.

3: In Cave Two, tie the shorter rope round an ankle of the solo contestant (me).

4: Just before the start of the display, lower the ironing board out of Cave One so that it hangs in space.

5: When the starter whistle goes, lower the contestant out of Cave Two by his ankle. When he and the ironing board are level they will look to the spectators below like they're hanging on snot-strings from a big nose.

6: The contestant swings to the ironing board and holds on to it.

7: The contestant does some serious upside-down ironing for about thirty seconds.

8: The contestant swings away from the ironing board and is hauled up into Cave Two.

9: The ironing board is carefully lowered to the ground for the judges to inspect the quality of the ironing.

10: Wild cheers break out and the contestant (in a coma) wins a massive amount of points.

Because there was still quite a bit of time before it was my turn to hit the fan, we went back down for the sandwiches that were on offer. Veggie sandwiches. 'You know, this is an obsession,' I said, peering at the wad of foliage inside my two planks of granary. But I bit into it because it might be the last thing I ever tasted.

Today, there was something new in the middle of the central space where most of the ironing displays took place: an ironing board that didn't belong to any of the teams. Its legs had been painted black, a

piece of red cloth was draped over it, and sitting on the cloth was the trophy we were competing for. The Golden Iron was pretty much like the competition irons, just a bit bigger, and of course gold-coloured. Team-members and coaches kept going up to it and touching it for luck. I didn't bother. Luck had never worked for me before, so why would it change its rotten ways now that I was going to come flying out of a giant hooter in the sky with a rope round my ankle?

Because the day was slow to warm up, almost all the team-members and coaches wore something extra over their top halves till the second round of heats. Eejit thought this was because the judges were wearing coats and didn't like to ask us to strip when they had no plans to. He was probably right, because when they eventually took their coats off they ordered us to lose ours too. The only people puzzled by the crowd-wide gasp and the titters as the sun smacked Mr Rice's bare kazoo were those who were facing the other way. These were the judges, Mrs Bevoir and Mr Rice himself. Eejit and I walked smartly from the scene, urgently inspecting our fingernails and

whistling unknown tunes.

We managed to keep out of Mr Rice's way after that until just before the final round, when he came across us down the far end of the central display area.

'What a result!' he crowed. 'The superb efforts of Starch Fiend and Smooth Dude have put us in second place, just five points behind Telmar!'

'It helped that Lantenwaist Court made such a mess of ironing under that waterfall,' Eejit reminded him.

'It helped, but without our boys' efforts we still wouldn't be this close to taking the Golden Iron home.'

'That's not gonna happen,' I muttered.

'Now I don't want to hear that kind of talk,' he said, still smiling. 'You'll do a grand job, Juggy, I know you will.'

'I'll do a grand job of breaking my neck or some other part I'm quite attached to,' I said. 'I have no experience of hanging upside down from high places by an ankle.'*

'Well, I'll be happy if you keep us in second place,' Mr Rice said. 'To come second in a

---

* This wasn't quite true. Not so long before, I'd hung out of a high window in nothing but a musical jock-strap while my father held my ankles. I still shudder when I think of that, but if you must hear all the embarrassing details you can tick them off one by one in a tale of woe called *Neville the Devil*.

tournament as prestigious as this is a heck of an achievement. Look, even the press have turned out for it.' He waved at a bunch of reporters and photographers, who waved back. 'They must think our team's got something. They keep snapping me. Asking me to do press-ups, knee-bends, flex my muscles with my back to them. They're not asking anyone else to do things like that.'

'Bummer,' said Eejit.

Mr Rice glanced at him. 'Sorry?'

'Bare-faced cheek. Taking so many pictures of you.'

'Mm, yes, s'pose so.'

'Have you arsed them?'

'Asked them?'

'Why you and no one else?'

'Well, not in so many words, no.'

'Maybe they got wind of what a great coach you are.'

'Oh, surely not.' But he blushed as he said it.

'Any flashing? Of their cameras.'

'Not that I noticed. The sun's quite bright now.'

'Well, try not to crack, sir.'

'Crack?'

'Under the strain of all the exposure. We need you behind us.' Eejit shivered suddenly. 'Still a bit breezy down the bottom here, isn't it?'

'I was thinking the same thing myself,' said Mr Rice. 'I'd better be getting back. Good luck, De-Wrinkle Man. Knock 'em dead up there!'

'Sooner them than me,' I said.

He headed back to the men from the press, his cargo hold bobbing cheekily in the sunshine. The photographers grinned at one another and hoisted their cameras. They were having a peach of a time.

Some of the displays in the first two rounds of the day had been quite clever and some had been seriously bananas. Most had taken place in the central space, but some of the more imaginative ones hadn't, so the crowd was constantly moving to see them. Here are some of the ones I saw.

A contestant folded over the bough of a tree ironing a hanky on a fellow team-member's head. Six points.

A contestant with an ironing board on a surfboard (on the river), ironing an apron. Awarded just one point because he toppled in

and his apron drowned.

A contestant ironing on top of a human pyramid formed by his team-mates. Eight points.

Synchronised ironing with dance steps by four team-members to *Hit Me Baby One More Time*. Seven points.

Ironing on a board while windsurfing. The wind fell. So did the contestant. Two points.

A giant catapult made from tree branches and heavy-duty elastic. Contestant fired at ironing board, broke his nose when he smashed into it but awarded three points for effort.

Ironing while doing the splits, irons on both feet, two ironing boards set quite a way apart. Contestant almost lost his gooseberries on a passing hedgehog but gained seven points.

The six contestants for the final round stood to get double points if their solos really impressed the judges. And wouldn't you know it, when we took our order buttons from the Official Shirt pocket I got number six, which meant I was going last. My nerves were already in rags, and now I had to wait to the very end to get it over with. Angie popped

out of the crowd to make me feel better.

'We're all counting on you, so you'd better be good,' she said. Like everyone else except Atkins and Mr Rice, she had no idea what I was going to do.

'Get ready to be disappointed,' I scowled.

'If you were Juggy,' she said, 'I'd give you a good-luck hug.'

'Just as well I'm not then. Musketeers don't do hugs.'

'You're not a Musketeer now, you're one of The Four.'

'I'm starting a rule book for us. Zero hugs are Rule One.'

She went back to the crowd.

I didn't watch any of the other heats in that round. Didn't want to know what the competition did. If they were really good, I would look even more pathetic that I expected to. I went up to Cave One and sat chewing my nails alone. Eejit joined me about 2:45 with the iron and heat pellet he'd collected from the organisers. He also brought another kid from our team to help out – Smee, the one that hadn't stopped sniffing since we started

out. His ironist name was Board Stiff, but Board Sniff would have suited him better. He wasn't just sniffing now either. He'd been sneezing since he woke up, and he had sneezes like no one else except my dad's, which are so sudden and table-rattling that it takes your heart ten minutes to settle down after each one. Getting soaked in last night's rain had brought his cold to a head, he said.

'Just keep your lousy germs to yourself,' I said to him. 'It's going to be bad enough hanging over nothing by a rope without sneezing what's left of my brains out.'

But then I had a thought. I switched on the famous McCue charm.

'Tell you what, you're about my height. No one'll notice all the way down there at the centre of the earth if you take my place. How about it? The glory will be all yours.'

'If I take your place,' Board Stiff sniffed, 'everyone'll think I'm you from a distance, which means you'll get the glory, not me, so thanks hugely for the offer but bog off.'

'Tie that end, will you?' Atkins said to him.

The two of them got to work fixing the pair of

long ropes round the ends of the ironing board while I stood in the cave's gloom and my own, thinking that this was it. My time had almost come.

'Instead of just standing there,' Eejit said, 'why don't you go next door and take some deep breaths before jumping head-first to your death?'

I gulped.

'Joking,' he said with the kind of chirpy little laugh that makes you want to smash faces in with mallets.

'Where's the torch?' I growled.

'I forgot it.'

'You * it? You mean I've got to walk through all those snottites in total darkness?'

'Yeah. Mind your head.'

I started towards the back of the cave.

'Take the third rope,' he called. 'And the iron. And the heat pellet.'

I grabbed the rope, the iron and the heat pellet, barged into the deep darkness at the back of the cave, and banged my head on a snottite.

CHAPTER TWENTY-FOUR

When I got to the approximate snottite where we'd seen the spider that had put this whole stupid idea into Atkins's head I thought that here was one spider that deserved to have its thread snapped. The reason I didn't snap it was that I couldn't find it in the dark. Also, snapping the spider's thread might have tempted fate. Mine. In a few minutes I was going to be swinging on a thread of my own, with a looooong way to fall.

When I reached the second cave, I sat just back from the mouth and tied the rope in a triple knot round my left ankle. Then I leaned out, very cautiously. Way below, dozens of little blobs were watching the last-but-one solo heat. I could just make out what they were seeing. The competitor, standing on the parallel crossbars of two bikes with an ironing board fixed across them, was pressing a piece of material or clothing while somehow steering the bikes in figures-of-eight.

Clever. Could earn a bunch of points, enough to win maybe, but even if he messed up and fell off he wouldn't have far to drop. Unlike me. With all that empty space between me and the ground, I suddenly realised that I wasn't terrifically fond of heights. Well, no, heights are fine. What I'm not terrifically fond of is being up on them. Especially when the plan is for me to be thrown off them to iron something upside down in mid-air. My mother's hair would have immediately turned white if she'd known about this.

'Better tie the rope round your ankle,' Atkins said, emerging from the dark at the back of the cave.

'Already have.'

'Yes, well I seem to remember that you also tied some guy-ropes to some pegs and a breeze puffed the tent away, so I think I'd better check, don't you?'

With a flick of the wrist he undid the rope I'd triple-knotted so tightly and started again. When he'd finished, it felt like I'd need a blowtorch to get me out of it. He looped some of the loose rope round a pillar of rock at the back of the cave.

I asked if he was sure it would hold.

'Pretty much,' he said. 'With the two of us on the end you should be fairly safe if you don't wriggle about too much.'

'I won't move a millimetre,' I assured him.

He went to the mouth of the cave and looked down. 'They'll be ready for us in a minute.'

'Us? You're coming too then, are you?'

He laughed. Well he would, wouldn't he? He was going to be safe and sound up here while I was... I tried to blank my mind.

'I'll go and give Board Stiff a hand to lower the board,' Eejit said. 'We have to get it in place before you go out.'

'Don't forget to come back, will you?' I said.

'If I forgot to come back,' he said as he vanished into the snottite-filled darkness, 'there'd be no one to lower you out of the cave.'

'Correction!' I shouted. 'Forget to come back!'

I went once more to the cave mouth and looked over. If anything went wrong – like if the rope round my ankle snapped, say – five minutes from now I'd be Spam. I saw my ironing board being lowered from the neighbouring cave and Eejit and

Smee leaning out a little. When the board caught on a bit of rock they twitched the ropes to work it free. Then it was clear of the hill, turning a little this way, a little that, with nothing except a big bunch of air between it and the earth way below – just as I was going to be very, very soon.

In a minute I heard a loud sneeze echoing through the snottites behind me and Atkins and Board Stiff stumbled out of the darkness.

'Ready for the off?' Eejit asked me.

'No.'

He went to the edge and looked over.

'They seem to be ready for us down there. Better get in position. Once the whistle goes we'll have to lower you right away. If we're too slow starting we could be eliminated from the round, which, with the way the points are stacking up, means we could be back in third place, maybe even fourth.'

'I'm happy with fifth,' I said.

'Well, no one'll be happy with you,' he said. 'What you have to do...' – he put his mouth to one of my sticky-out ears so Smee wouldn't

hear – '...is get out there and iron as only De-Wrinkle Man can, and make the school proud of him.'

'Why would I care if the school's proud of him?' I whispered back.

'You don't have to care. Just remember who's holding the rope.'

'You wouldn't.'

He twisted his mouth at me. 'Tempt me.'

I was staring at him, wondering what he might do if I let his team down, when Board Stiff sneezed so loudly we almost flattened our haircuts on the cave roof.

'You ought to take something for that,' I said, jamming my spine back where it belonged.

'I will,' he said. 'Right after your funeral.'

'Talking of which...' Eejit said.

It was time.

I got down on my knees like I was about to pray, inched to the edge of the cave mouth, and looked down through all the empty nothingness that ended with very solid somethingness. My audience was staring up at me, eagerly waiting to see what I would do.

And then the whistle went.

'Move out a bit further,' Eejit said behind me. 'It's OK, we've got the rope, you won't fall.'

'Could I have that in writing please?'

'Later,' said Smee. 'While they're scraping you off the ground.'

'Atkins,' I said, 'why did you choose that sniffy little ray of sunshine to help you?'

'He's the only little ray of sunshine who would,' he answered. 'The rest blame you for losing the tent.'

'So do I,' sniffed Smee. 'I just wanted to be in at the kill.'

The rope round my ankle jerked suddenly. My heart smacked me under the chin.

'*What did you do?*' I cried in italics.

'Just checking the tension,' said Atkins.

'You don't need to check it, just ask.'

'Go on, De-Wrinkle Man, over you go.'

And over I went. Slowly, slowly, the front part of my skin-tight pratsuit scraping rock as I slithered out and down, head first. I heard a sound nearby. 'OooooOOOOOOOO,' it went. It was me.

Now I was completely out of the cave, upside down against the rock, going down bit by bit by bit, the rope squeezing the blood and bone out of my ankle.

'You're heavier than you look!' Eejit shouted from somewhere above me.

'Don't say that!' I yelled back.

'Don't worry, we've still got a grip – just! Say when. you're level with the top of the ironing board! Can't see from in here!'

The board hung three or four metres away, from the other nostril.

'I'm level!' I shouted.

'Good! Now push yourself towards it!'

I bent my knee – the one that wasn't attached to the leg whose ankle had a rope round it – and shoved myself away from the hill. Not hard enough, though, because I went less than a metre before crashing back.

'What was that jerk?' Eejit shouted.

'It was me!' I replied.

'At last he admits it!' Smee said.

'Did you make it to the ironing board?!' Eejit asked.

'No! Gotta try again! Get ready for another jerk!'

'One's enough!' Smee again.

I prepared to kick harder at the hillside. If I got it right this time, I would swing across and grab hold of the ironing board and start to press the pair of boxer shorts Eejit had pinned to...

Oh no.

'Atkins!' I called.

'What?!'

'I've forgotten the iron!'

'What?!'

'You'll have to pass it down on another rope!'

'We hadn't got another rope, you twonk!'

'There's no need to be insulting!'

'There's *every* need to be insulting! How could you forget the iron?! Ironing's what this is all *about*!'

'You might not have noticed,' I shouted back, 'but I had a couple of other things on my mind when I left the cave!'

'Hey, look at this.'

Smee said this. Not to me, though I heard him. I wanted to know what was so interesting up

there that they had to look at it rather than concentrate on keeping me from decorating the ground. 'Look at what?' I demanded, spinning slowly round while the blood rushed to my hair.

'The rope!' This time it was Atkins.

'What about the rope?'

'The one round your ankle's one of the long ones! It should be the short one!'

'What difference does the length make?'

'It makes ALL the difference! It means that in the dark we got them mixed up! It means that someone who wasn't me...'

'Don't blame me,' Board Stiff said.

'I do blame you!' Atkins yelled at him. 'I checked the rope I tied round my end of the ironing board!'

'I checked mine too, but it was dark.'

'And in the dark you used the *short* one!'

'Like I said' – this was me – 'what difference does it make if I've got one of the long ropes round my ankle instead of the short one?'

'It doesn't make any difference to you!' bawled Atkins. 'But it'll make a hell of a difference when it comes to lowering the board to the ground for

the judges to check the quality of the ironing! It'll make that difference because one of the ropes it's hanging from ISN'T LONG ENOUGH TO GO THAT FAR!' He was getting quite worked up by the sound of it. 'What a disaster,' he wailed. 'My carefully-thought-out plan ruined by you two. McCue forgets his iron and one of the board's ropes is too short. And they call *me* Eejit!'

'I'm going to sneeze,' said Board Stiff.

'Well don't do it over me,' Eejit snapped.

'Uh… uh… uh…'

And then it came. The biggest, most cave-shaking, most echoey sneeze I ever heard while roped upside down in mid-air. Such an ear-shattering sneeze that the sneezer couldn't possibly have kept a grip on a rope he was holding.

And he didn't.

I knew the rope had lost one of its grippers when it went a little slack. When it went a lot slack I knew that Eejit hadn't been able to hold me on his own. As the rope started to unreel I headed earthward, and because dive-bombing through nothing isn't one of those things I do for pleasure

my feet started jigging about. During one of the jigs I kicked the hill, which pushed me clear of it, into a big wide arc. As I swung across the arc, the rope got longer and longer, and when I reached the end of the arc I started back, in another arc, and when I reached the end of this one I started on yet another, and all the time I was getting nearer and nearer to the ground and closer and closer to the eyeballs staring up at me. I would like to say that I kept bravely quiet during this little adventure, but it wouldn't be true. Waving my arms and kicking wildly all the way, I bawled, at the top of my voice:

Mummmeeeeeeee!!!

I was vaguely aware of my audience leaning back from the central arena I was heading towards. I was just as vaguely aware of Mr Rice running forward: to my rescue? I never found out. I was two metres from the ground when I reached for something – anything – that might stop me swinging into the orbit of Mars. My hands closed

on two things, though I didn't pause to check what they were. In one hand there was something hairy. In the other there was something that felt like a handle of some sort. The something hairy felt so weird that I let go of it immediately – it soared away from me and disappeared into the trees – but I held on to the handle thing. A handle couldn't stop me flying through the air, but handles are usually attached to something, and that was promising, even if the only thing it was attached to was me.

So, holding the handle, I swept upside down over the space where many of the ironing displays had been staged. Over it and back, and over it again, on the end of the long rope. I should have been even closer to the ground by now, and not swinging, but (I heard this later) the end of the rope up in the cave had caught on something, and held. If I'd known this I would have thrown an immediate party, with balloons and paper hats and cake, because it stopped me just in time from standing on my brain in a McCue-sized molehill. The handle I was holding was quite heavy, but it was all I had to hold on to, so I just let it hang at

the end of my arm, but each time I reached the middle of the open space there was a jolt and a flash of red, like blood. I dreaded to think what the jolt and the red flash were all about. Had I killed something? Someone?

CHAPTER TWENTY-FIVE

It was Angie who told me how it had looked from the ground.

'We saw the ironing board hanging from the cave,' she said. 'Then we saw you dropping from the other cave on the end of a rope. (Hey, did you know those caves and that bit of hill look like a nose from below?) Then we saw you pretending to be too feeble to push yourself to the ironing board. Then you waved your hands to show that you hadn't actually got an iron. Then we heard this signal*, and next thing we knew you were falling and falling, and honestly, I thought you'd had it. But then you were swinging in these great sweeps like Tarzan in the jungle, but upside down, screaming like a madman as you grabbed Mr Rice's wig in one hand, the Golden Iron in the other. Then you tossed the wig into the trees and swung back to press the red cloth on the Iron's board — with the Golden Iron itself! Then you swung

---

* The almighty sneeze in the cave that had caused Board Stiff to let go of the rope and start my dive to the ground from the nose on the hill (you could call it my nose-dive).

forward again, then back again, and forward again, ironing more of the cloth each time, until you stopped swinging and the rope round your ankle loosened and you dropped into the inflatable paddling pool used by the last team but one. I tell you, McCue, I never saw anything so mad or brilliant. Nor had the judges, you could tell. For what you did, they could even forgive you using the trophy to iron its own cloth – great bit of ironing too! – and even for cracking its ironing board on the last swoop. Incredible!'

And then she hugged me, even though I was still dripping from the paddling pool. And I let her. It was the nearest I could get to a Mum-hug, which I badly needed after the most terrifying experience of my life, especially as I had to make out that what everyone had seen had been my carefully-planned ironing display.

You may not be surprised to hear that because of the way it looked from the ground I got such a load of points that I won the tournament for Arnold Snit Compulsory. Yes, me, yours truly, I, Jiggy McCue, with my 'extremely daring and skilful ironing display', as the judges put it when they

handed our team the Golden Iron.

As we started for home, Eejit and Angie phoned their parents to tell them when to expect them back, and Angie told me to phone Juggy's parents with the same info. Once I'd done that I scrunched up in a corner of the bus and shut the world out. The part of the world I most wanted to shut out was the bit with Mr Rice in it. He sat at the back in Mrs Bevoir's bright yellow folding rain hat, not speaking to anyone, me most of all. He wasn't speaking to me for two reasons. The first was that I'd exposed his baldness to the whole wide world by throwing his wig into the trees, where a fierce bird had instantly made a nest of it and refused to let him have it back. The other reason was that right after the wig incident someone finally told him that he'd been flashing his raw tomato all afternoon, then someone from our team – not sure who – slipped him the word that he'd seen me sneaking into the back of the cave with his practice iron and costume the night before, which meant that it had to be me who'd caused him to hang out in public all afternoon. When Mr Rice realised why

the photographers had been snapping him in all those macho poses, the blood drained from all four of his cheeks.

It was almost dark when the bus pulled in at the school. Parents were waiting for some of us, including Eejit's and Angie's and Juggy's dads. Miss Weeks was there too, with her baby strapped to her chest, and she'd brought a spare wig for Mr R, which he put on under cover of an umbrella. He smiled a bit once it was in place, but not at me. Wouldn't come anywhere near me, even though I was the hero of the hour, the day, the weekend, the year.

Back at the house Janet and Dawn Overton should have been living in, there was a lot of typical Golden Oldie fussing – 'You must be starving, now tell us all about it, every last detail' – and when all that was out of the way (I only told them what I thought they'd want to hear) the parental types went off and watched telly, leaving Juggy's little sister and me sitting at the kitchen table.

'Now how did it *really* go?' Swoozie asked.

I told her. The truth, not the official version. She rolled her eyes a few times, dropped in the odd question, said 'Holy ironing boards,' twice, and when we were done...

'We missed you.'

'Missed Juggy, you mean,' I said.

'Same thing.'

'Not quite.' I waggled my gum-enhanced ears at her.

'When are you going to try the broom cupboard again?' she asked.

'Tomorrow at school, if I can get in there.'

'What if it doesn't work again?'

'It's got to.'

'But what if it doesn't?'

We just looked at one another across the table. She was probably thinking the same as me. Like, if I didn't get back through the broom cupboard I could be stuck here forever, in the wrong house, with the wrong parents, at the wrong school. I would always have to wear chewing gum behind my ears, Pete Garrett would never be my friend again, and Swoozie would always have to pretend to be my sister. It didn't bear thinking about. Well,

most of it. Maybe I could live with the last bit.

Next morning, as I was leaving for school, Swoozie slipped something into my jacket pocket when her parents weren't looking.

'What's that?' I asked.

'Some biscuits so you don't go hungry before lunch.'

It was such a nice thought that I didn't know what to say. Then she threw her arms round my waist and squeezed.

'And what's this for?'

She smiled up at me, a bit sadly I thought. 'It's for in case you make it through the broom cupboard and I never see you again.'

At school that morning we only had half a lesson before first break – Maths, no loss – because the Head had called a Special Assembly. When a Special Assembly's called at Ranting Lane it usually means we're going to be told off for something, or given bad news, or warned about some dodgy character hanging round the school gates. But this wasn't that kind of Special Assembly. As you know, the Head at Ranting Lane is Mr Hubbard, but the Mr Hubbard

of Arnie Snit taught a potty religion about aliens, and the Head was an old geezer in a tweed jacket with leather elbows called Professor Kirke.* The Prof wanted to show the Golden Iron to the whole school and say a few words about our efforts over the weekend. He said the few words, then called me and the rest of the Extreme Ironing team onto the stage to shake our hands and give the Specially Assembled kids a chance to cheer us. It felt strange being cheered on stage. The only other time it ever happened to me was when I was in the Infants. I was playing a Heavily-Bearded Wise Man in a Christmas nativity play and I accidentally dropped my little sack of chocolate coins and jumped off the stage to get it back. That wasn't when they cheered, though. On the way back up the steps I fingernailed one of the gold wrappers off and shoved the coin in my infant trap. Then I screwed my face up and turned to the audience, and said 'This is wubbish,' which covered the play pretty well too. That's when they cheered.

After the Special Assembly and the cut-down Maths it was morning break, and time for another shot at getting home. Eejit and Angie went to the

---

* The *Head* was called Professor Kirke. The leather elbows were called Leather Elbows.

broom cupboard with me, but it wouldn't have mattered if I'd gone alone because the door was open and Mr Heathcliff was there, talking to Mrs Bevoir about dusters or something. All we could do was slide by and hang around the corner, looking round every minute or two to see if they'd gone yet.

While we were waiting I took out the biscuits Swoozie had dropped in my pocket. She'd put five chocolate digestives in a little plastic box that was just big enough for them. The box was pink and it had ponies all over it. Sweet. Eejit smirked until I told him that Swoozie had given it to me because she didn't want me to be hungry. Then he said he wished he had a sister, and I gave him one of the biscuits. I offered Angie one too but she said she was watching her figure.

I was just slotting the last choc dige into my gap when Angie said: 'I think they're going.'

She was right. Mr Heathcliff was locking the broom cupboard door and strolling away with Mrs Bevoir. I put the empty biscuit box back in my pocket and asked Eejit if he'd got his skeleton keys.

'Yes.'

'Remember which one fits?'

'Yes.'

'Come on then. This could be the time it happens.'

We pushed the door back – just as the bell went. I said something unprintable as all the really keen students ran to the doors and stampeded over us in their eagerness to get back to their lessons.

'This is never going to work,' I wailed as we picked ourselves up and went with the flow.

'Yes, fate doesn't seem to be on your side, does it?' said Atkins.

'Nor yours if you want the third Crapologist back,' I pointed out.

'*Cavaleiro!*' he snarled.

'Still, if that's the way it has to be,' Angie chipped in, 'we could do worse than be stuck with you.'

This was one of the few kind things she'd said to me in the three or four days we'd known one another. 'Thanks,' I said.

'Not a lot worse, though,' she added. 'You being such a whinger and defeatist with such a warped sense of humour and all. But I suppose you *could* be worse.'

The next lesson was English. I wouldn't have minded that if I wasn't so disappointed about not being at Ranting Lane.* The English teacher was Mrs Gamble, the same as at RL, and she smiled at me whenever I gave the right answers (every time) to her questions about grammar and punctuation, but looked kind of surprised too, so maybe Juggy wasn't the wiz at her subject that I was. Getting things right in English made me feel a bit better about being in the wrong world, and I got to thinking that maybe I could make a go of it there if I really had to. Eejit might become a proper friend in time, Angie too maybe, even though she was a bit more girly than I liked, and now that I was the Extreme Ironing king I was somebody for the first time ever. I kind of liked being somebody. Naturally, there would be a few problems if I had to stay. Like the food. If they thought I was going to eat leaves for the rest of my life they were thinking of the wrong bunny. But there were good things there too. Swoozie, for one. That little kid would be a definite bonus.

We were only about a third of the way into the

---

* And I never thought I'd say *that* in this lifetime!

lesson when Mrs Gamble decided to stop talking without notes and opened a paperback to read something to us. I thought I heard her say a word under her breath that teachers aren't supposed to say, specially old teachers with wrinkles, but then she looked up and told us that she'd forgotten her reading glasses.

'Don't worry about it, Miss,' said Wapshott. 'You just rest your ancient eyes and we'll go for early dinner.'

'Kind of you, Ian,' she said, 'but I'll try and soldier on. I must have left them in the science lab.' She said the last bit more to herself than us.

'What were you doing in the science lab, Miss?' Sami asked.

'Mr Numnuts is off sick today,' Mrs Gamble replied, 'and and other teachers are taking turns to mind his classes in his absence.'

'Know much about science, do you?' Marlene Bronson asked. Anything to throw a teacher off their stride, even teachers we like. It's the principle of the thing.

'Next to nothing,' Mrs G admitted. 'I did half a crossword while the students got on with some

revision. Look, while I'm struggling to see this ridiculously small print I wonder if one of you would be so kind as to go to the science lab and look for my glasses?'

She peered round the suddenly blank faces before her, and finally slapped her orbs onto her best student.

'Juggy, would you go? They'll probably be on the desk.'

'What's it worth?' I enquired, the way you do.

'How about not getting a thick ear for cheeking a beloved teacher?'

'If McCue's ears got any thicker,' said Ryan, 'he'd never get out the door.'

'They helped me fly through the air and win the Golden Iron,' I said as I shunted to the front. 'Something you couldn't have done, dirt-box.'

'You'll have to fetch the key to the lab from the office,' Mrs Gamble said. 'I'll give you a note for Miss Prince.'

She scribbled something on a pad and tore the sheet out. I folded it into my top pocket and went out sideways like a popular actor leaving the stage. This fame thing is cool.

I collected the key from Miss Prince without any trouble, except a bit of misery-mouth — 'Bring it back the moment you're done there!' — and went to the science lab, where I found that I didn't need the key after all because the door was open. The head cleaning lady, Queenie Sidaj, was in there, dropping anything she didn't like the look of into a bin on wheels. I saw a glasses case on the desk, but didn't like to go in uninvited. I cleared my throat in the doorway. Mrs Sidaj glanced my way, saw that I wasn't a grown up, and scowled.

'You want something?'

'My teacher left her glasses here and sent me to fetch them.'

'Well *I* don't know where they are!' she snapped, like I'd accused her of nicking them.

'No, I think that's them on the— '

'Just don't disturb me while you look for them,' she said, hauling cupboard doors open and looking inside for things to feed to her wheelie. 'Some of us have work to do.'

'I won't say another word,' I said.

'What?'

'I said I won't say another word.'

'Make sure you don't. What's this?'

I would have said 'What's what?' if I hadn't just made two promises never to speak again. Queenie was wearing rubber gloves, but even with them on she didn't seem keen to handle what it was she took out of the cupboard. I went over. She'd found Mr Numnuts' two boxes of Turkish Delight with added flavouring. Because the boxes were transparent you could see the changes that had already started to occur inside. The pink cubes were redder now and the blue cubes were closer to purple. But it was the sugary coating that had changed most. On the pink cubes the sugar had started to crack, like they'd been left out in the sun too long. On the blue cubes it was going furry.

'It's one of Mr Numnuts' experiments,' I said, blowing the vow of silence in eleven-point-two seconds.

'Experiments!' she snorted, and dropped the two boxes in her bin.

I was so shocked by this that I forgot to be scared of her. 'But we wanted to see what happened to the cubes!' I cried.

'Did you now?' she growled. 'Well, I'll not have

rotting food in my school, so you'll have to see it somewhere else!'

She slammed the cupboard door and went to the next one, hauled another something out, chucked it in the bin, and was on her way to the one after that when the theme tune for *The Simpsons* started up. She tore a phone from a pocket of her dungarees, and began giving instructions to her old man, who from the sound of it was ringing from a supermarket. 'No, the chicken-flavoured ones, it was on the list, wasn't it? And you know what cheese to get, I've told you a thousand times. What do you mean you can't find any of the— '

I stopped listening because now that she'd turned away to have this private conversation about shopping I saw my chance to save some of the Turkish Delight to show Mr Numnuts and the class if I had to stay here till our next lesson with him. I couldn't take the boxes, because Queenie might rugby-tackle me if she saw bulges in my pockets that hadn't been there before, but I thought I might get away with a couple of sample cubes if I was quick – and I had just the thing to put them in. I bent over the bin, flipped the lids of Mr N's two

boxes, and popped one pink cube and one blue cube into Swoozie's little pink pony box. I dropped the pony box back in my pocket, licked my fingers, and stepped away from the bin just as Queenie switched her husband off and turned round.

'Ah, there they are!' I said, scurrying to the desk and picking up Mrs Gamble's glasses case.

'You got what you came for then?' the Queen of Charm barked.

'Yes.'

'Well get outta here and let me get on with my work.'

I got outta there.

CHAPTER TWENTY-SIX

I returned the unused key to Miss Prince, who was about as grateful that I'd been so quick as Queenie had been for my company, and started back to class. To get to Mrs Gamble's from the office you had to pass the gym. I walked past the gym the same way I'd passed it on the way to the office, with bent knees, so only the top half of my head would be seen if anyone inside glanced my way. Just enough height to chortle at the bunch of saps doing the pointless exercises that give the lesson its bad name. Better this side of the glass than theirs, I thought, until a voice shouted a name too much like my own for comfort, and the door sprang back and Mr Rice stood there. The very Mr Rice I'd managed to avoid all morning and wanted to carry on avoiding.

'Juggy,' he said again. 'A word.'

'Sorry, sir, can't stop,' I replied. 'Urgent mission for Mrs…' – No, don't tell him whose class I'm in,

he might come for me there – '… for a teacher!'

I scuttled round the nearest corner, then the next, hoping he wasn't hoofing after me. But he was.

'Just a minute, Juggy, please!'

Panic. Hide. But where? There was only one door in sight. Was it unlocked? Was there anyone the other side of it? I turned the handle, opened the door – no light on, good sign – and plunged in. I closed the door, stepped backwards in the darkness, and bumped into something that made me sit down hard. The tumble made a bit of a clatter, so I sat absolutely still, fingers and toes crossed that Mr Rice hadn't heard and would fling the door back and find me sitting on… what? I felt below me. Something hard and cold, like a bucket. A bucket? Hey. Of course. I hadn't thought where I was going in my panic, but here I was in Mr Heathcliff's broom cupboard!

I was still realising this when light splurged briefly behind me and I heard a small click like a door closing. Hang on. The door was in front of me. The last thing before the back wall was the row of workcoats…

I heard something moving back there. I jumped to my feet.

'Hello? Anyone there?'

But it wasn't me who said this. It was someone else. Someone using my voice.

'Er...' (*This* was me.)

'Who are you?' the other voice whispered.

'Who are *you*?' I whispered back.

'It's not... Jiggy, is it?'

My heart bounced around my ribs for a while and came to rest in my throat. 'Juggy?' I said.

'At last!' he cried.

'At last?' Me again. 'What do you mean, at last? I've practically taken up residence in this crummy cupboard trying to get back.'

'*You* have!' he said. 'I've been in here every chance I got.'

'Oh. Really. Different times to me then, obviously.'

'Obviously.'

'Well now that we've finally made it at the same time,' I said, 'maybe we can get back where we belong.'

'Can't be soon enough for me,' he said. 'Did you

take my place like I took yours?'

'Had to, no choice. How did you get on?'

'I managed. Even if it was like going from a starring role in *Hamlet* to an outtake from *Home and Away*.'

'How were my friends?'

'Some friends. Garrett, of all people. Give me Eejit any day. My Eejit. Yours is a cretin.'

'Yeah, well your Angie's a bit girlie.'

'I like her that way. Yours might as well be a boy.'

'I like *her* that way. How'd you manage with the physical thing?'

'Physical thing?'

'The ear situation.'

'Double-sided tape. Extra-adhesive.'

'Who thought of that?'

'Angie. What did you do about yours?'

'Put wads of chewing gum behind them. Your sister's idea.'

'Not the chewing gum under my bed?'

'Yes, why?'

He groaned. 'I was building that gumball into a record-breaker!'

'Well you'll have to rebuild it, won't you? It took

some hefty lumps to stack my ears like yours. How do *sleep* with those things? Can you lie flat? Do you have to sit up all night?'

'Are you making fun of my ears?' he asked.

'Fun?' I said. 'Ears like that are no fun. I speak from experience.'

'How would you like it if I made fun of your jigginess?'

'You can't make fun of my jigginess. You haven't seen it at work.'

'Oh no? I got action replays wherever I went. People kept asking why I wasn't flapping my arms and dancing whenever the slightest thing went wrong. You wouldn't believe the number of impressions of you I had to put up with. Quite an act you have there.'

'It's not an act. It's me, I can't help it. If I didn't do all that stuff I wouldn't be Jiggy McCue.'

'Like if I didn't have these ears I wouldn't be *Juggy* McCue.'

Put like that we were about even.

'Why did you come in here in the first place?' I asked.

'What, just now?'

'Last Thursday.'

'Mr Lubelski was coming. I keep out of his way as much as possible.'

'Why? Mr Lubelski's one of the nicest teachers at Ranting Lane.'

'Lucky you. The one at ASC isn't nice – to me anyway. It's because I can't see the point of art. He shouts at me in Polish all the time.'

I'd never heard my Mr Lubelski even raise his voice, in any language, so this was a surprise, but hearing that my double wasn't into art surprised me even more. Art's one of my two best subjects.

'Why did you come in here?' Juggy asked.

'Last time or this time?'

'This time.'

'Mrs Gamble sent me to fetch her glasses from the science lab.'

'What was she doing in the science lab?'

'Minding Mr Numnuts' class. He's off sick.'

'Well, your Mrs G asked me to fetch her glasses too, but from the staff room. We'd better swap in case their eyesight's slightly different or the frames aren't the same.'

We groped for one another to exchange the

glasses. I shuddered when our hands touched. Think he did too. Touching yourself in another body is not a terrifically comfortable experience. When we'd made the switch, he asked me if I'd taken his place in the EI tournament. I said that I had.

'And?' He sounded kind of nervous about my answer.

'And I brought home the Golden Iron.'

I heard him gasp. 'You won the trophy?'

'Almost single-handed. Juggy McCue's the big cheese at Arnie Snit.'

'Whew. I was scared you'd ruin my rep.'

'Ruin it? I made you a hero. How was the Survival Weekend?'

'I didn't go.'

'You didn't go? But you had to. Everyone did whose parents sneakily signed the permission form when we weren't looking.'

'Made out I had a sore throat. You think I wanted to go on a two-day endurance course with my ears taped back? It's because I didn't go that I dodged in here just now. Mr Rice saw me from the gym and was coming after me, yelling. Probably wants to

have a go at me for skipping his rotten weekend. Your Mr Rice is terrifying.'

'Oh, I can handle him.'

'You're welcome to him. Come on, let's do this. The Mrs Gs will be wondering where we've got to.'

'Fine by me. Just make sure you go past me and not back to Ranting Lane.'

'No problem. All I have to do is keep going forward. Make sure you do the same or there could be two of us at my school.'

'You know, this is pretty amazing, isn't it?' I said.

'What is?'

'All this, us, everything. This is a perfectly ordinary broom cupboard except when we're both in it at the same time, then it's got a door at each end, each one leading to an alternative version of the school.'

'I wonder if it's just us?' he said.

'Just us?'

'Well, suppose, say, your Eejit Atkins and my Eejit Atkins also went into their school broom cupboards at the same time. Would they switch?'

That made me smile. Alternative Atkins's might

be even harder to disguise than alternative McCues.

'Let's go,' said Juggy. 'Ooh, I can't wait to get back to proper food!'

'You call what you eat *proper* food?' I said.

'Thousand times better than the high-fat unhealthy garbage you like.'

'Thanks for your opinion. Watch how you go, there's a bucket h—'

Clang.

He'd kicked the bucket.

Clang.

He'd kicked it again, deliberately this time.

I pushed my way through the smelly old workcoats and felt for the back wall. I found it, except that it was no longer a wall.

'I'm at my door,' I said.

And, from beyond the coats: 'And me.'

'So. This is it.'

'Yes. None too soon either.'

I turned the door handle. 'Say goodbye to Swoozie for me. I'll miss her.'

He didn't answer. He was back in Arnold Snit Compulsory. And I—

'McCue! There you are! What the devil do you mean, running off when I call you?! And what are you doing in that cupboard?! Why aren't you in class?!'

I laughed. I couldn't help it. I closed the broom cupboard door for the last time. I was *never* going in there again.

'And what's so flaming funny?!' Mr Rice demanded, marching up to me in his stupid red tracksuit.

CHAPTER TWENTY-SEVEN

'Explain!' Mr Rice bawled, glaring down at me from the summit of Everest.

'Mrs Gamble asked me to get her specs from the staff room,' I said, pulling the glasses case from my pocket to prove it.

'Mr Heathcliff's broom cupboard is nowhere near the staff room!' he bellowed.

'I got lost.'

'Lost?! In a cupboard?! What kind of fool do you take me for, boy?!'

I put my fingers to my chin. 'You'll have to give me a minute on that one, sir.'

'And what's happened to your ears?!'

'Oops, forgot.' I took the gum from behind my lugs. 'I was trying something.'

'Trying something?! Trying what?!'

'To see if I could cruise in high winds.'

'Are you trying to take me for a ride, McCue?!'

'Would if I could, sir, but you need a licence

for hauling men in red.'

'Less of the lip! Why weren't you with us at the weekend!'

I remembered Juggy's excuse, made a phlegmy sound in the tonsil area, tried to speak huskily. 'Sore throat. Very bad. My mum kept me in from Friday night till this morning.'

'Do you really expect me to believe that?!'

'No, course not. You wouldn't be you if you believed me.'

'What's that in your pocket?!'

'My pocket? I showed you. Mrs Gamble's glasses.'

'The other one!'

I looked at my other jacket pocket. It bulged.

'Oh, that's nothing.'

He snorted. 'Nothing! I catch you in the caretaker's cupboard with a bulging pocket and you say it's *nothing*?! Show me!'

He held his enormous hand out, fingers twitching fiercely.

'It's just a little box,' I explained.

He wasn't having it. 'Let me see!'

I took Swoozie's biscuit box out. He scowled at it.

'That's *yours*?'

'It is now.'

'But it's… pink!'

'So?'

'Well, not very masculine, is it!'

'I know. I'm working on that.'

'Open it!'

'You don't really think I stole a little pink biscuit box from the school caretaker?' I said. 'What would Mr Heathcliff be doing with a box like this?'

'Open it!'

'You'll wake the school if you keep shouting like that,' I told him.*

'OPEN IT!' he screamed. 'AT ONCE!'

I opened the box. He bent over it to peer inside.

'Uh?!' he said intelligently.

'It's Turkish Delight,' I said.

'It's like no Turkish Delight I ever saw!'

'This is special. My mum has it sent from Turkey. You can't buy it here.'

He studied the two little cubes up close. 'This blue one, it's… furry!'

'That's the secret Turkish ingredient.'

'Looks like the beginnings of mould to me!' he boomed.

'It is mould,' I said. 'Didn't you know that real

---

* Oh, it was good to be back!

blue Turkish Delight always has mould? Edible mould, of course. Like you get on those stinky blue-veined cheeses.'

He looked up at me from his crouch over the box. 'You mean Stilton?! Gorgonzola?! Camembert?! I love those cheeses!'

'Well, you'd probably love this then.'

'Where can I get some?'

'Try Turkey. If you're quick, you could get a one-way flight today.'

His eyes flipped back to Swoozie's box. 'Does your mother have any to spare?! Just a sample, so I can see if I like it!'

'No. Sorry. This is the last.'

'Oh. Pity.'

He stood up straight, towered over me again, obviously disappointed that he couldn't get his jaws round some mouldy Turkish Delight.

'Tell you what,' I said. 'Why don't I give you this piece?'

'Eh?!'

'Yeah, why not? Go on, help yourself. Just the blue one, though.'

'But it's yours!'

He was so surprised that I would give him

something for free that he looked quite shaky for a sec. I switched on my most endearing smile (the one I melt my mother's heart with when she's in a lather with me).

'My way of saying sorry I couldn't make the weekend,' I said. 'I was so looking forward to it too.'

'You were?!' he said in disbelief.

'I should say. Learn to survive? Top of my list of things to do, survive.'

I offered the little box. He hesitated – still a bit suspicious, probably – but then picked up the mouldy blue cube and popped it in the Rice fodder gap. He started chewing immediately, and a second later pulled the kind of face people pull when they're thinking of spitting something out, and his neck started to glow, and the glow spread up to his cheeks, and his eyes went round like something out of this world had just reached his inner taste buds (which it had in a way). When he gulped the last of the cube down, his Adam's apple bobbed, and his lips spread across his face like a bad accident. When they reared back to make way for a grin, I saw that his teeth were blue. And furry.

'Now that's what I *call* Turkish Delight!' he said.

'All you need now is the flying rug,' I said, 'and you're off.'

One of his hands started towards his hair, but stopped half way. Was his secret out? Did everyone *know*?

'F-flying rug?' he stammered, for once not booming.

'I mean flying carpet,' I said. 'Turkish Delight, flying carpets, they kinda go together.'

'Oh! Yes! See what you mean! Ha-ha!'

And he swung round and jogged off like his feet were on springs. I watched him go, shaking my head in amazement. Who would have thought that peed-on Turkish Delight could have such an effect?

I was just approaching Mrs Gamble's room when the lunch bell went. People were jumping up from their desks and streaming towards the door as I streamed in.

'At last!' Mrs G said. 'I could have got them myself if I'd known you were going to be this long.'

'Sorry, miss. Got laywaid by Mr Rice.'

'Laywaid?'

'Waylaid. I kept telling him I had to get back, but I couldn't stop him banging on about sporty stuff.' I handed over her glasses. 'Did I miss much?'

She shook her grizzled old head. 'Nothing you can't catch up on.'

'OK. Bye, miss.' I went to the door. 'Good to see you again!'

She looked surprised at this, but I went out before she could ask what I meant.

Angie was waiting for me in the corridor. 'You want to have another go at the broom cupboard?'

'Are you kidding?' I said. 'I'm never going near that cupboard again.'

'What? After all you've been saying about wanting to get home?'

'No. Think I'll stay. I like it better here.'

'Since when?'

'Since now.'

'But you don't *belong* here!'

'Who's to know?'

'Well, I will for starters.'

'Yeah, but you won't tell.'

'I will! I want my Jiggy back!'

I felt my eyebrows lift. '*Your* Jiggy?'

'I mean the McCue that belongs to this school.'

'What do you want that loser back for?'

She scowled. 'Jiggy McCue might be a loser. He might be pain in the bum. He might make my life

316

a misery because of the things that happen to him. But he's my friend. Our friend. Pete's and mine. You're not. I want you gone and him returned.'

It was hard to keep a straight face. 'You'll get used to me.'

'I won't,' she said. 'You'll never take Jig's place. Jiggy hates healthy food. His bedroom's a tip. He has a wonky way of looking at things. He cheeks the teachers. He gets detentions like you probably get badges for good behaviour. He's... unpredictable.'

'And these are *good* things?'

'No, but they're him.'

It sounded like this was as near to praise as I was going to get.

'Do me a favour, will you?' I said. 'The tape behind my ears feels loose. Will you check it for me?'

I turned round so she could look behind my ears. She cleared the hair away to get a good decko.

'Where is it?'

'Where's what?'

'The tape.'

'Can't you see it?'

'No.'

'Well, it should be there,' I said. 'If they were Juggy's ears.'

'Yes, but it's...not.'

There was a longish pause, during which I could almost hear the cogs of her brain passing one another. I smoothed down the hair behind my ears and turned round. Waited for her to realise.

'Jiggy?' she said, finally.

I spread my hands. 'The one and only.'

And she thumped me. Hard, on the shoulder. Then she gripped me by the armpit and frog-marched me to the lockers to collect our lunch boxes. I looked at mine with affection. Real food again!

'How long have you been back?' she asked as we went outside.

'Since just before the end of English.'

'You came from the broom cupboard?'

'Where else?'

'And Juggy?'

'We passed in the dark.'

'In the dark of the broom cupboard?'

'No, in the dark of the icecream parlour in the shopping arcade.'

She squinted at me. 'You haven't changed. Still a smart-arse.'

'It's my trademark. Wasn't he a smart-arse too?'

'Not so much, no.'

'I hear he managed to skip the Survival Weekend. You and Pete go?'

'Oh yes, we went.'

'Have a good time?'

'Good time? It was the most miserable weekend of my life so far.'

'That go for Pete too?'

'Pretty much. He's not talking to you, by the way.'

'Why, what have I done?'

'He didn't believe Juggy wasn't you.'

'How could he think he was me with those ears?'

'He thought you'd done something to make them stick out and got all uppity when the joke went on and on.'

'Some joke. Didn't you put him right?'

'Try and put Garrett right when he gets a fixed idea in his feeble brain? You know how far that gets you.'

We were almost at our private bench in the Concrete Garden when I spotted Atkins trading punches with a couple of pals. I went over to him.

'Hi, Eej, how's it hanging?'

He paused mid-punch. 'Whatcha, Jig. 'Ow's yerself?'

'Not so bad. Yer dad knocked over any good chemists lately?'

He jaw hit his kneecaps. 'Wot?'

I took him by the arm and walked him away from his thump-buddies.

'I know he's not a landscape gardener,' I whispered.

'Oo said he was?'

'That's what everyone thinks he is. Atkins, I know your secret.'

'Wot secret's 'at then?'

'That you're not really as stupid as you make out.'

'Er?'

'I've often thought that no one could be as thick as you *and* comb his hair.'

'I don't comb me 'air.'

'Figure of speech. Just wanted you to know that it won't go any further.'

'Wot won't?'

'Your secret.'

'Wot secret?'

I winked at him. 'OK, Eej. Got it. Between ourselves, eh?'

He went even blanker. When he puts his little mind to it, my version of Eejit Atkins can be blanker than an ungraffitied wall.

'Jig…' he said.

'Wot?'

'You ent 'alf bin pecoolia these last foo days.'

''Ave I?'

'Yer. But don' worry abaat it.'

He tapped a finger against the side of his nose. Then he skipped away to fump his mates some more.

CHAPTER TWENTY-EIGHT

Angie wasn't kidding about Pete not talking to me. He even swapped seats with other boys in a couple of classes so he wouldn't have to sit next to me. I could live with that. I was back, that was the main thing. Home ground, familiar territory, faces I knew on people I knew. You won't believe how comforting it is to know that the person you're talking to is the person he or she looks like. I was even pleased to see my teachers' features.

After school, Angie grabbed Pete and made him take a slow stroll round town with us while we tried to convince him about what had happened and that I hadn't been pulling his doodah. He still didn't seem too sure by the time we'd finished, but that was Pete all over. He never likes to back down or give in.

From town we headed for the real Brook Farm Estate. When we reached our street I gratefully watched P and A fighting on the step of the house

across the road to try and be first inside, then went round the back of my house – number 23! I hauled myself up the gate, reached over, slipped the bolt, swung in, shot the bolt again, and started along the path. Round the fence corner I saw my kennel, and this time no lousy dog stuck its muzzle out to snarl at me. Better still, the good old garden gnome was beside the back step. I went to it, bent down, slipped the key out of its behind, and kissed it. The key, that is.

I unlocked the back door and was treating my senses to the genuine McCue atmosphere of the once and future house, when I saw Stallone slinking towards me, glaring at me with those mean green eyes of his. I dropped my bag – my own bag, which Juggy had left by my desk in English – fell to my knees, and reached for him.

'Come here, you mangy critter!'

Stallone snarled, reached for me in return, and scratched my hand. But I didn't mind. I was so happy to be home.

Without even bothering to take my jacket off and chuck it at the wall, or even dart into the kitchen to plug my face, I ran up to my room. My real room. My sanctuary. I threw the door back – and froze,

staring. It was so tidy it looked like someone else's. But of course it *had* been someone else's. For four nights it had been the resting place of a neat freak. I went in. Opened my wardrobe. My shirts hung so perfectly they could have been in a window display. I opened my underwear drawer. It should have been all over the place because I spend so much time rooting around in there for pairs of pants I can stand being seen dead in. But today every pant and T-shirt was stacked in perfect alignment with all the others, and there wasn't a crease in one of them, except where there should be.

I looked around some more. My slippers stood to attention behind the door, toes facing the wall. My chair was placed just-so under my desk. The desk was shinier than it had been when Mum assembled it from the flat-pack. I spotted the Musketeer Rule Book. At least that wouldn't have been tampered with. I picked it up, read the stirring words 'One for all and all for lunch', flipped the cover to read the four rules I'd laboured so hard over, and found... a fifth rule! It was in my own handwriting, underlined just like the others.

Rule 5: Musketeers must keep their rooms tidy at all times!

I closed the book with a growl, wishing I'd thought to add a rule to the Three Carrotlovers Rule Book.

'Jiggy? That you up there?'

My mother, calling from downstairs. I hadn't heard her come in. Maybe she'd been in all the time, in the kitchen or living room. But what was she doing at home at this time of...?

I remembered. It was the day of the hospital appointment. The appointment I'd been dreading because I just knew there was going to be bad news. Probably the worst news imaginable.

'No, it's the burglar from next door,' I called.

'Would you come down here please?'

I went out to the landing, still in my school uniform, and was about to go downstairs when I thought of the room Swoozie used as a bedroom in the house that wasn't Mrs Overton's. I pushed the junk room door back. It was chock-a-block in there, no room to move, no bed, no dolls, games, books about fairies and ponies, and all the other cute little things Swoozie had. Welcome back to the real world, Jiggy McCue. The world of no sister and a mother who'd got this terrible thing wrong with her.

I went back to the head of the stairs and leaned

there for a minute. I didn't want to go down. As long as I stayed up here I couldn't hear the bad news. Here, there wasn't even a Swoozie to help me get through it.

'Are you coming, Jig?'

Dad's voice. He should also be at work at this time. Oh, wait. He'd said he was going to the hospital with Mum because it was such a big deal.

I went down.

'In here,' Mum said.

I went into the living room. They were sitting on the couch, very close together, holding hands. My mother and father never hold hands, so it had to be serious. I took an especially deep breath and tried to feel like a Musketeer. Bold, I mean, afraid of nothing, ready for anything. I wanted to go to Mum and give her a big hug, in spite of Rule 4. This was because I hadn't seen her for a while, you understand. The real her, I mean. I even sort of wanted to hug Dad, and that would have surprised him.

'Come and sit down, son.'

Son. My father hardly ever calls me son. When he does he's usually either fooling around or trying to play the heavy father. He didn't sound like he was trying to be heavy now, or like he was fooling.

They looked very tense sitting there. Nervous about giving me the bad news.

I was about to sit down in the chair facing the couch when I felt Swoozie's little biscuit box in my jacket pocket and remembered the effect the piece of Turkish Delight had had on Mr Rice. The Turkish Delight with the special ingredient from another world that had put such a spring in his step. Maybe, I thought, maybe if Mum was ill, the remaining piece of TD (with the second special ingredient for another world) would give her a lift too. Such a lift that she'd be cured of whatever it was she'd got. Could other-world widdle and spit be a sort of magic potion? I couldn't sure, but it was worth a try. I took the box out of my pocket.

'Before you say anything, Mum, this is for you.'

I opened the box. She looked in.

'What is it?'

'Turkish Delight.'

'Where'd you get it?'

'A friend. I've been saving it for you.'

'It looks a bit... old.'

'It's meant to look that way. It's the real stuff, authentic Delight all the way from Turkey. Eat it. Please.'

'Can I save it for later?'

'No!'

I almost shouted this. She had to have it now, before she told me what was wrong. That way she might be cured before she said it and we could all forget how close she'd come to whatever it was.

'Where did the box come from?' she asked, picking up the pink cube.

'Same friend who gave me the TD.'

I stood there while she nibbled a corner of the cube. I think she tried not to pull a face. 'The best medicine doesn't always taste nice.' She used to say that to me when I was little and screwing my face up because she was trying to get me to swallow something to get me over some illness. I didn't say it to her, though.

'Are you sure it's all right?' she said.

'Absolutely. And I'm not listening to you till you've swallowed it.'

She made a square of her lips, popped the cube in, chewed rapidly a few times, and swallowed hard. She gave a little shudder as it went down. Not a great one for sweet things, my mum. There was no immediate effect, like there'd been with Mr Rice, but maybe other-world spit took longer to do

its work than other-world wee.

I put the little box away and went to the armchair. There was a pause. Mum and Dad used the pause to look at one another. I don't think I ever saw them so nervous.

'Jiggy,' Mum said eventually.

'Here,' I said. It was coming. The bad news I'd been dreading.

'Darling, you obviously suspect that something's up,' she began.

Darling. Now I knew I was in for the worst. I folded my arms so no one would see my hands shaking. Come on, Turkish Delight, do your stuff, do your stuff.

'What makes you think that?' I asked innocently.

'Well, the fact that you brought me a present, for one thing. Also, you've been so good these past few days. Tidying your room, cooking last night's meal, insisting on doing the ironing…'

'I cooked last night's meal?'

'And very good it was too.'

'Bit on the healthy side for me,' Dad muttered.

'You even stayed at home over the weekend rather than go off and enjoy yourself with your friends,' Mum said.

'I had a sore throat,' I reminded her.

She smiled like she knew better. But then she went all serious again.

'We can't keep it from you any longer,' she said.

I unfolded my arms and put my hands on my flat ears. 'I don't want to know.'

I saw Dad's mouth move. I took my hands away. 'What?'

'You'll have to know sooner or later,' he repeated.

'Later works for me,' I said, getting up.

'Jig.' Dad again. His stern voice. 'Your mother and I decided it would be best to keep it to ourselves until we saw the scan this afternoon. That was our deadline.'

'Deadline?' I sank back into the chair in horror.

'What your dad means,' Mum said, 'is that we planned to tell you once we knew what it was. Afraid you might take it badly, you see.'

'And now you're not?' I said.

'Now you must know. There's no way out.'

'Let me go to my room,' I pleaded.

I didn't want to hear this. Didn't want to know about it. Maybe I'd go out later, break into the school and Mr Heathcliff's broom cupboard, try and get back to Juggy's world,

where his mother wasn't sick and everything was fine. Yes, I know, I wasn't thinking straight. It was a pretty sure thing that I couldn't return to Juggy's unless he was in Arnie Snit's broom cupboard at the same time, and why would he be, out of school hours – or ever again, in fact? Also, what would I do if I got through? I couldn't just waltz in and join his family? I mean, where would I *sleep*?

Mum got off the couch and came over to me. Sat on the arm of my chair. Put a hand on one of my shoulders.

'Jiggy, it's going to happen and there's nothing to be done about it,' she said. 'Now let's get it over with, shall we?'

I clenched my fists and closed my eyes. One for all and all for lunch, I thought. 'Go on then,' I said. 'If you really must.'

I heard her take a deep breath. Then she said:

'I'm going to have a baby.'

My eyes flew open. 'What!'

'I'm going to have a baby.'

'WHAT!'

'She's going to have a baby, Jig,' said Dad from the couch.

331

'A baby?'

'I know how hard it must be for you to accept at your age,' Mum said, 'but, well, there you are, it's a fact. An incontrovertible fact.'

'A baby?' I said, gawping up at her.

'Little human-type creature without a lot of hair,' Dad said. 'Fond of stinking the house out.'

'Yes, but… a baby?!'

'This is what we were afraid of,' Mum said.

'Afraid of?'

'That you'd take it badly.'

'I'm not taking it badly, I'm just….' I started again. 'So you're not ill.'

'Ill? Well, I wouldn't call it *ill* exactly.'

'Do you know what kind?'

'What kind?'

'Boy, girl, or alien like its parents.'

'Today's scan revealed all,' Dad said. 'Because your mum's cracking on a bit, we couldn't be certain everything would be as it should, but the scan cleared that up – she's fine – and told us what to expect.'

'And?' I said.

He looked at Mum. It was up to her to tell me. So she did.

'Jiggy, you're going to have a baby sister.'

'A sister?'

'Yes.'

'A sister?'

'Yes.'

'A sister!'

'How d'you feel about that?' Dad asked me.

I hauled myself out of the chair. I needed time to think. Solo time.

'Dunno,' I said, heading for the door.

'You're not upset?'

'Why would I be upset?'

'Well.' This was Mum. 'A boy, just into his teens, suddenly hears he's not going to be an only child any more…'

I stopped. Turned to face them.

'I promise not to be upset on one condition.'

'Condition?' said Dad.

'That you call her Suzie.'

'Suzie?'

'Suzie.'

'Why Suzie?'

I went to the door. 'I like it.'

Dad raised his eyebrows at Mum.

Mum smiled. 'Suzie's fine with me…'

Dad nodded, slowly. 'Suzie. Suzie McCue. Mm.'

'Do we have a deal?' I said.

They both looked at me. Happily. We had a deal.

'Good.'

I went out and closed the door behind me – just in time or they would have noticed the water in my eyes. I started upstairs.

Half way up, I turned and sat on the step.

Wooh.

I was going to have a baby sister.

I *am* going to have a baby sister.

A sister called Suzie.

Who's going to be the sweetest little girl you ever saw, with the biggest, bluest eyes, the spikiest hair, the nicest ways.

And because she won't be able to say Suzie exactly right when she starts to talk, she'll call herself Swoozie. Then everyone will call her that, and before you know it, it'll stick, like Jiggy has to me.

I'm going to be Swoozie McCue's big brother!

I am. I really am.

And she'll love me.

And look up to me, and not just because I'm taller than her.

*I would like to dedicate this book to
Penny Morris, long-suffering editor of it and
a variety of others that we've somehow managed
to produce between lively lunches, strolls in
literary gardens, and casual forays
into days gone by.*

ORCHARD BOOKS
338 Euston Road, London NW1 3BH
Orchard Books Australia
Level 17/207 Kent Street, Sydney, NSW 2000

First published in 2007 by Orchard Books
This revised edition first published in 2009

ISBN 978 1 40830 405 1

2 3 4 5 6 7 8 9 10

Printed in Great Britain

Orchard Books is a division of Hachette Children's Books,
an Hachette UK company.

www.hachette.co.uk

A JIGGY McCUE STORY

THE IRON,
THE SWITCH AND
THE BROOM CUPBOARD

MICHAEL LAWRENCE

ORCHARD

The Jiggy McCue books can be read in any order, but to get the most out of them (Jiggy and Co are a wee bit older in each one) we suggest you read them in the following order:

Visit Michael Lawrence's website:
www.wordybug.com

And find loads of Jiggy fun at:
www.jiggymccue.co.uk

THE iRON,
THE SWiTCH AND
THE BROOM CUPBOARD

WHITE HEAT

WHITE HEAT

Paul D. Marks

Published by Timeless Skies Publishing

WHITE HEAT

Copyright © 2012 by Paul D. Marks

ISBN-10: 098507602X
ISBN-13: 978-0-9850760-2-3

Published by Timeless Skies Publishing

Visit Paul at: www.PaulDMarks.com
www.whiteheatnovel.blogspot.com

Book and cover design by Timeless Skies Publishing.
Cover photo © by Paul D. Marks

Timeless Skies Publishing

TIMELESS SKIES
PUBLISHING

For

Amy

and

Norma and Norm

Author's note:

Some of the language in the novel may be offensive. But please consider it in the context of the time, place and characters.

This place [Los Angeles] was a lot friendlier and a lot nicer when I came here twenty-six years ago. There are still pockets of civility here, but they are rapidly disappearing as neighborhoods and ethnic groups get more and more polarized, and as the city gets more and more crowded. I think the violence and the ruthlessness is going to increase...

—Don Henley
(musician and former
Eagles band leader)

APRIL 1992

April is the cruelest month.

The Waste Land
—T.S. Eliot

CHAPTER 1

My father always said I was a fuckup, that the only reason we get along is 'cause he keeps his mouth shut. Maybe he's right: I fucked up high school.

Fucked up college.

Fucked up my marriage.

Fucked up my life by leaving the service.

And now I've fucked up a case.

Fucked it up real bad.

Teddie Matson was different. She had a golden life, until her path had the misfortune of crossing mine. I sat staring out the window of my office, k.d. lang playing in the background. It was a while till the sun would set, that *golden* hour when everything takes on a gilded glow.

Golden hour is the time when the light hits just right in the early morning or late afternoon. The time when movie cinematographers most like to shoot. The light is tawny and warm. Gentle. It makes the stars shine brighter.

Golden hour is the time when Teddie Matson was killed.

◈ ◈ ◈

"Duke Rogers?"

"What can I do for you?"

The Weasel shifted back and forth. Left foot to right. Right to left. Nervous. Fidgety. Blue eyes so pale they almost lacked color darted back and forth across the room.

"I, I want you to find a friend of mine," he said, voice cracking. He slapped a snapshot on the desk, a sleek chrome and smoked-glass job that I'd picked up at auction. A greasy lock of hair dropped over his eye. He shooed it away.

She was a beautiful girl. Woman? No. Hardly more than a girl. Smile was warm and inviting. Dark almond shaped eyes. Long dark tresses curling around her neck. They looked like they were ready to strangle her.

"Who is she?"

"W'we went to school together. I heard she was in town and I–" He sucked in his already-sunken cheeks.

Who was I to argue with him? Just because he looked ten years older than her. Maybe he'd had a rough life. Just because she was black and he was white? That didn't mean they couldn't have gone to school together.

"How much is your fee?" he said. Lit a cigarette. I pointed to the universal "No Smoking" sign over my desk. I needed the gig, but I didn't need it that bad. He grunted. Stubbed it out on the linoleum floor.

"Two-fifty. Sounds simple enough." The words came out by rote. My mind was somewhere else. At the moment, thinking about redecorating the office. Getting rid of the orange crate art, replacing it with Hopper prints, *Rooms by the Sea* and *Chop Suey.* They seemed to go with the building. A little more classic. But I knew I could use the cash for an overdue plumbing bill. Redecorating would have to wait.

The Weasel pulled out a wad of sweaty bills, peeled off a handful. Sucker. The job would take me all of an hour, if that. He was also a dweeb. He deserved to be fleeced.

"Here, write down her name, any other information you might have on her, age, height, scars, that kind of thing. Where she was born." I handed him a piece of paper and watched him scribble in an unsteady hand. He shoved the paper back at me. He had scrawled her name: "Teddie/Theodora Matson".

"How long will it take?"

"Couple-a days. What's your phone number?"

"I'll come by on Thursday."

"Around ten."

He headed for the door.

"Hey, what's your name?"

"Jim, Jim Talbot."

"See ya Thursday, Jim."

He left. I opened the window wider to let in some fresh air. I inhaled deeply, taking in the whiff of orange and lemon blossoms outside the window.

◈ ◈ ◈

I wondered how the dweeb would spend the time between Monday and Thursday at ten a.m. Didn't look like he had many friends. Maybe not any. If he was from out of town he might go to Disneyland. Nah. Not a place you go to by yourself. He might go down to the Santa Monica pier and throw a line off. Sure, the beach. That's where they all go. Isn't that why people come to Southern California anyway? So the beach would be one place for sure. He might take in a museum, but dweeby as he was, he didn't look the museum type. Might go on the Universal Studio Tour. Sure. He could see all the papier-mâché and phony fronts that make Hollywood what it is. Yeah, that was his kind of place all right. Maybe he'd check out Griffith Park or the Observatory or Farmers' Market. He had to eat. Well, what did I care how he spent those days in between?

I called Lou Waters at the DMV. We'd been friends since we went to Fairfax High together a decade or two ago. Seemed more like a century. I'd aged. She hadn't. She was one of those people who actually looked better the older she got – aging like a fine wine, she'd say.

"What's on today, Duke?" she asked.

"Can you run a name for me?"

"You know I'm not supposed to."

"Never stopped you before."

"And it won't stop me this time."

"Why do we always have to play this game, Lou?"

"It brightens my day."

"I thought the sound of my voice alone did that."

"You're not the fair-haired boy anymore."

I never was. But if being a second rate P.I. is success, I guess I've succeeded beyond my wildest dreams. But in the land of Beamers and Benzes, I'm just a Camry.

I gave Lou the info the dweeb had given me. I could hear the clicking of her computer keys over the phone. She had an address for me in a few seconds.

"Thanks, Lou. I owe you one."

"You owe me a ton."

"I'm good for it."

"Yeah, sure." She hung up. I knew she was smiling. We'd dated briefly in our sophomore year of high school. She'd left me for an older, more sophisticated guy – a junior, with a car.

I had to figure out what I'd do between now and the time the dweeb came back. I had a couple other scut cases I was working. Might as well check out some leads on them.

Later that day, while I was trying to decipher a new software program for billing my clients, new business walked in the door.

"Marion Rogers?"

"Yes." She was attractive in a plain sort of way. An all-American way. Open face, cute smile. Natural blond hair. She didn't have the sultry appeal of Teddie Matson, that's for sure.

"You don't look like a Marion."

"Maybe that's why my friends call me Duke."

She introduced herself as Laurie Hoffman, sat down and crossed her legs. I could tell she wanted to get to the point. And she did.

"Someone's following me. I went out with him once and now he won't leave me alone."

"Get a restraining order."

"I have. It doesn't do any good. And by the time the police arrive he's gone."

"Has he threatened you?"

"Not in so many words. He just tells me how much he wants me, things like that."

"I'm not really sure what I could do for you. Surveil him maybe, but—"

"I think he's dangerous."

"He hasn't done anything."

"Yet."

"Problem is I don't really have the time right now. I'm a one man office and I've got more than I can handle already."

"You don't need the money?"

"It's not that. But I honestly don't think I'd be able to devote the necessary time and that wouldn't be good for either of us." I wrote Harvey Zenobia's name and number on a piece of paper. Handed it to her. "This is a colleague of mine. Give him a call. Maybe he can help."

Truth is, I did need the money. I had a second mortgage on the house my dad left me and I could barely make the payments. What I didn't need was another short term shit job that was more trouble than it was worth. Domestic cases, stalking cases are hell. I landed in jail on one once when I tried to intervene between a husband and wife. I got between them when he was coming after her, slugged him, hard. He filed assault charges and I got three days in jail. The fact that he had a knife in his hand didn't seem to matter to the judge.

She stood to leave, looking defiant. Angry. But too proud to say anything.

"I'm sorry," I said as she disappeared through the door.

◈ ◈ ◈

The dweeb showed up at ten on the nose. I knew he would. You can tell these things about a person.

"Didja get it?" He was almost breathless. A bubble formed at his lips when he talked.

I handed him a slip of paper. He looked down at it. His mouth didn't move. But his eyes smiled. He stared at the paper an awfully long time. He was wearing a good suit. English cut. Expensive. Then I noticed his shoes: old. Scuffy. Didn't quite fit.

He turned and left. Didn't say a word. He had paid so I didn't care. He was a happy man. And I was happy to have him out of my life. I'd wish later that I'd never met the lousy dweeb.

CHAPTER 2

I'd gone out of town for about a week on a case. My buddy Jack had collected the mail and taken care of my dog, Baron. I came home, greeted by Baron in his usual overzealous manner. There was a message from Lou on the answering machine. She didn't say what she wanted and I couldn't reach her. Everything else was in order. I went to the office, was sitting in my chair, listening to k.d. lang, catching up on a week's worth of newspapers and taking my lunch break of gin-laced lemonade. I'd cut down on the alcohol. Cut down, not out. I could handle it in small doses. The article I was reading said that a verdict in the Rodney King beating case was expected any day now. But it was another headline that slammed me in the gut.

Another photo.

Made me want to vomit.

Through force of will, I was able to control it.

I crumpled the paper.

Tossed it in the can.

Kicked the can with such force that the metal sides caved in.

Fucked up a case.

Fucked it up real bad.

"Promising Actress Shot by Rabid Fan" the headline read. "Teddie Matson, the 26 year old second lead of such Hollywood sitcom hits as *Day Timers* and *Holier Than Thou* was on her way to becoming one of Hollywood's lights. The, some say naive, young actress answered the door to her apartment building yesterday afternoon expecting a script delivery from the studio. Instead an unknown assailant delivered a .32 slug to her abdomen. Police surmise that it was a berserk fan who fired the gun, but don't have a clue as to who he is."

I knew it was my client. It was a Weasel named Jim Talbot, if that was really his name. But it was how I knew that made me want to split a gut. And it had taken only a few minutes' work, still I had charged Talbot a full day's fee. Talbot didn't mind. He was happy to pay. He had walked out of my office with the biggest shit-eating grin on his face that I'd seen since I left the service.

I didn't know what to do, if there was anything I could do? Should do. I bottomed another glass of the saucy lemonade. Before I could get toasted the phone rang.

"Hello, Duke. Lou."

"Hey, Lou. Sorry I didn't get back to you sooner. I was out of town for a few days." Did she know? We talked a couple times a month, so maybe this was just a friendly call. At any rate, neither one of us brought up Teddie right now.

"Listen," she said, "how 'bout we have dinner tonight?"

"Okay. Usual place." The roar of a Harley chewed up the street below as she affirmed the usual place at seven. She must have known because we normally had dinner about once a year and we'd already met our quota this year. I was about to dive back into the lemonade, when the door opened and Jack Riggs walked in, looking like a Hell's Angel in heat. Tossed his kit bag on my desk and sat down like he owned the place.

I'd known Jack since we went through boot camp together. We'd split up or been split up after that, but we both ended up in the Teams. There was definitely a bond there – after he got over the fact that my name was Marion – though I couldn't say what it was exactly. I had to join the Teams to counter a name like Marion. That's where I got the nickname Duke. Who would name a boy Marion, especially in this day and age? My parents, that's who. They both loved John Wayne and his real name was Marion Michael Morrison. And his nickname was Duke. If it was good enough for him it was good enough for me, on both counts. Only right now I felt more like a knave than a duke.

The first words out of his mouth were, "What's that shit you're playing?"

"k.d. lang. I like it."

"Hell, man, don't'cha know she's lez?"

"I'd heard something about it," I said, "but I don't see how it matters."

Jack poured himself a lacy lemonade. He knew what was in it. "When you listen to a song, a love song, don't you sit there an' think they're singin' t' you? Or if it's a man, that it's you singin' to a girl? But how can you get into that fantasy when you know she's AC-DC, so t' speak?"

I didn't know what to say. I never knew what to say to Jack when he came on like this. How could I argue with that logic? Besides, no matter what I said, he wouldn't buy it. So I said, "I don't know, Jack. It's just a song."

"Man, it's no song. It's a political statement. It's–"

I wanted to shut him up, or off, or something, so I flipped the switch from CD to radio. Eric Clapton was on singing the MTV *Unplugged* version of *Layla*. Tell you the truth, I liked it better than the harder, faster version. But I didn't say that to Jack. It would have brought another lecture in pretzelogic.

He saw the newspaper sitting on the desk. "This Rodney King thing's gonna blow wide open. Whole town's gonna go up in smoke."

"You're crazy," I said, but somewhere inside me I thought maybe he was right. I didn't want to admit it. Not to him. Not to myself. I'm a multi-generation native of Los Angeles, which makes me a rare bird. And I love my home town, not so much as it is, but as it was when I was a kid. I grew up in a real *Leave it to Beaver* neighborhood. No one locked their doors. No one worried about getting shot on the freeways. Of course, my relationship with my dad was no Beaver and Ward thing, but I survived, after a fashion.

He looked down at the paper, saw the headline about Teddie Matson. "She was hot. I wouldn'ta minded havin' a hormone fix with her."

"She was black."

"I make exceptions on occasion. I would've made one for her."

"How *white* of you." I don't know if he caught the sarcasm. If he did he didn't say anything. I was just as glad. 'Cause a mad Jack was crazier than a mad dog. I'd bet on him against five pro boxers at the same time, when he was mad, three when he wasn't. His washboard stomach rippled under the t-shirt that was always at least one size too small. Even if it wasn't, his arms were too big for the sleeves. Had to have his shirts custom made to accommodate them. He'd stayed in shape. I hadn't.

On the other hand I'm not very large to begin with. But wiry and determined.

"Hey, I'm not as bad as you think," he said. "'Sides, I just say what everyone else is thinkin'."

"Not everyone."

"Hell, almost everyone. Especially the damn limousine liberals that wanna baby everyone, make 'em victims. Make 'em dependent on 'em and on ol' Uncle Sam. That's their power base. Hell, the liberals and the–"

"Cut it out, Jack. Segue." It was a command. An order. I didn't want to talk about that shit anymore. Jack stopped. Looked at me. Hurt. He loved to expound. We had a deal. Segue was the end of it. Change of subject. Worked either way, for me or him. We tried not to exercise it too frequently.

"Hell, I'm only saying out loud what you're too afraid to even think. What everyone's afraid to think. 'Cept the niggers. It's okay for them to think it about us. Change history."

I told him to shut up again. But I didn't kick him out. The problem is that Jack's too open. Doesn't even try to hide his prejudices. No veneer of civilization there. Makes me face my own prejudices and fears. Makes me see what I could be and helps me to avoid it. Sometimes I'm successful. Sometimes not. But it's also one of the things I like about him. You know where he's at. So you know where you're at with him.

Jack and I go back a long way and I do like him. But I don't like all of him.

◈ ◈ ◈

The lobby was crowded. Lou's strawberry hair glinted in the lights, accenting a still-perfect complexion. Her Anne Taylor dress highlighted her figure, flaring at the waist. Stunning, as usual. ▪

She knew. Her eyes said it. The corners of her mouth said it. And her weak handshake instead of a hug said it. She knew.

El Coyote was an old restaurant from the old neighborhood, a few blocks west of La Brea on Beverly Boulevard. It attracted an eclectic clientele. Tonight was no different. Teens in hip-hop drag mixed with elderly couples and homosexual couples and young hetero couples on dates. All inside a restaurant that had been here since before the war – the Big War. Lou particularly liked the decor, paintings made out of seashells. "Interesting," she always said, as if that was enough. And she loved the food. So did I. But I knew a lot of people who didn't. You either loved it or hated it, there was no in between. That's the kind of place it was. I liked their margaritas. They weren't those slushy crushed ice new fangled things you find in most restaurants. They were just tequila, triple sec, lime juice and salt around the rim. Damn good.

"Interesting," Lou said looking at a shell painting, after we were seated. I nodded. There was an awkward feeling between us, a gulf of turbulent air that we were trying to negotiate. There was nothing for me to say in response. This wasn't a social call. She leaned forward, talking quietly. "You know why I wanted to have dinner, don't you?"

I nodded.

"I didn't want to leave any specifics on the answering machine or call a bunch of times."

"In case the cops were on us already."

She nodded. "I shouldn't have run it for you. I didn't know who Teddie Matson was. I don't watch television, especially sitcoms. How was I to know you were asking me to look up a TV star?"

Lou did watch television. Lots of it. She watched old movies. What she meant was she didn't watch sitcoms or dramatic series. Made for TV junk.

"I don't watch sitcoms either," I said. "I had no idea who she was. The headline hit me like a hurricane." What did Lou want from me?

"You know I run these things for you 'cause you're an old friend. But I shouldn't. I could catch hell."

"Does anyone know you did it?"

"I don't think so. There's no record. But you're an accessory. So am I." She looked into my eyes. A searing, guilt-edged gaze that tore into me. She looked away. "Who'd you get the information for?"

"I don't know." My face flushed red. It hadn't done that in years. I was embarrassed. I had fucked up – bad, just like my father always said: *"You're as dumb as the Mexicans at the plant." "Why dad? Because I wasn't a carbon copy of you."* "He paid in cash, up front. I'm sure the name he gave me's a phony."

"You've got to find him."

"I know. I will."

"I should go to the police. They should know everything. It would help them solve it."

"Don't, at least not yet. Give me a few days."

She said she would. Neither of us ordered food. We left a good tip and split.

CHAPTER 3

The light was mellow, soft. It grazed across the row of Spanish style stucco duplexes and apartments, reflected off leaded picture windows and prismed onto the street. Each had a driveway to one side or the other. Gardeners worked the neatly manicured greenery of every other building. It was a nice old neighborhood in the Fairfax district, one of the better parts of town. My old stomping grounds.

The same time of day Teddie Matson had been murdered. I planned it that way, hoping the same people would be around that might have been around that day.

I walked up the street, my eyes darting back and forth, up and down, aware of everything around me – radar eyes – looking at the addresses on the buildings. The number was emblazoned in my brain. I could see it before my eyes, but it was only a phantom. I passed a gardener at 627, coming to a halt at 625. I stared at the building.

A typical stucco fourplex from the '20s. Even though I hadn't been inside yet I knew the layout – I'd seen enough of them. Two units upstairs, two down. A main front door that would lead to a small, probably tiled hall, with an apartment on either side and a stairway heading to the two upstairs apartments. I walked up the tiled walk, stuck my hands through the remnants of yellow crime scene tape, tried to open the front door. Locked. I rang the bell. No response. I felt as if I was being watched. Still no one answered the buzzer.

A silver 1970s era Buick pulled into the driveway, slowing. A gray haired man with wrinkled skin leaned out the window.

"Who are you? What do you want?" There wasn't even the slightest hint of friendliness in his voice.

I started to approach his car. The electric window shot up. He held up a cellular car phone, finger poised over the 9 of, I assumed, 9-1-1. I backed off, holding my hands out in front of me so he could see them. He wasn't dialing 9-1-1 – yet.

"I'm here about Teddie Matson." I had to shout so he could hear me through the rolled up window. I'm sure the gardener next door could also hear.

"You the police?"

"I'm a private detective, looking for her murderer."

"How do I know?" It was hard to tell, but it sounded like he had a trace of an accent. Today, the Fairfax area is home to a lot of people from Eastern Europe.

Gingerly, I pulled my I.D. from my pocket. Held it up for him. He squinted trying to read it, motioning me closer, until I was almost pressed up against the glass. The window zoomed down to the halfway mark. Progress.

He took the card from me and spent three full minutes glaring at it, before giving it back.

"We already talked to the police," he said. "What can you do that they can't?"

"I can help them."

"Who're you working for?"

"That's confidential information." I could hardly tell him I was working for myself, that I'd given the killer the address.

He gunned the engine and the car lurched past me, down the driveway into one of the four garages at the end. I stayed at the front of the building. It looked like he was going to go in the back door, then he walked toward me.

"What do you want? We've been questioned so many times already, the police, the news people. Even her family. It's bad enough to go through something like this, but to have to relive it every day is torture. My wife hasn't slept since the, the–"

"I'm sorry. We're all just trying to help. Just a few questions?"

He nodded warily.

"Was anyone else home when it happened?"

"My wife. She's always home. She's an invalid. But she didn't see nuthin'."

"Might she have heard something?" Was she the person who I felt watching me as I had rung the doorbell.

He shrugged. I asked to see the entry hall of the building where it happened. He was reluctant to show me, but gave in. From the info Lou had given me and looking at the doors in the downstairs entry hall I knew Teddie's apartment had to be upstairs.

Tiled red floor. A large antiqued mirror. Walls a dirty plaster that had once been white. A black wrought iron chandelier hung overhead, showering a dull yellow light on the ashen walls.

"This is where she fell." He pointed to the stairs leading to the second floor. "Her apartment was up there. Number four. We think she came down to answer the door for–"

"Why would she open the door to a stranger?"

"If you'll just let me finish, the intercom was broken and she was expecting a script delivery from the studio. Must've thought it was them."

A heavily carved wooden door off the hall opened a crack. It was to unit number two.

"That's really about all we know."

"You didn't see him?"

He shook his head.

"Or your wife?"

Before he could answer the door swung open and a tiny blue-haired woman stood engulfed in its frame. Blue and white polka dots blurted from her dress. Her hair was neatly done. She hardly looked like an invalid. Her husband, who still hadn't told me his name, looked miffed that she'd come out.

"It was unseasonably hot that day," she said in a strong, grandmotherly voice. "Teddie was a–"

"You don't even know who you're talking to," her husband barked.

"You're talking to him. And I seen him show his card to you outside."

"He's not a policeman. He's a private detective."

"Like Jim Rockford," she smiled. I nodded. Her smile grew. "He's so handsome. I watch him every day in the reruns." She looked me up and down, appraising whether or not I met Rockford or James Garner's good looks. The smile remained, but since it didn't grow I figured I lost to the actor.

"It was terrible," she said, the smile falling off her face.

"Tell me about it."

The old man's mouth turned down. He wanted no part of this. But his wife was in her element, repelled by the horror and drawn to it. Reveling in it.

"Terrible," she said. "He knocked, quietly at first, as if he was afraid of disturbing someone. When no one answered he knocked louder. Then he walked out to the sidewalk."

"You saw him?"

"Only through the curtains. He came back and rang her buzzer. I heard the door lock open on her apartment upstairs and Teddie coming down the stairs. She asked if he was here to deliver the script. He mumbled something. She opened the front door. We always keep the front entry door locked these days. And she asked what he wanted. She was frightened. Then he approached her–"

"You saw this through the crack in the door?"

"No, no. I could hear it. I heard it."

She didn't seem nervous, but I felt that she was holding something back. Looking at her husband I figured she didn't want to deal with him later. He had enjoyed telling me what he knew, even though he would never admit it. But now he wasn't the star anymore. The spotlight was on her and he didn't like that. I pictured him lambasting her after I left. She went on:

"She was scared. I could hear it in her voice. She usually talked smooth and quiet. But her voice was shrill, loud. He kept moving towards her, and finally, finally–"

"Enough," the old man said, cradling her in his arms. "Get out of here." He motioned toward the door with his hand. I thanked them and left, butterflies, no moths, churning in my gut.

"Mrs. Perlman," she shouted behind me.

Yellow streaks of sun pierced the stucco and glass buildings, melting everything in a golden hour glow.

"Hey."

I looked around. The Salvador Dali-mustached gardener next door motioned me with his hose. Was he gonna spray me? It was hot. Not that hot.

"You a cop?" he said.

"Private."

"Didn't think you were the L.A.P.D. type." He took a swig from the gushing hose, then sprayed a flower bed. "I seen 'im. He walked right past me."

"Who?"

"Don't play this shit with me."

"Okay, what'd you see?"

"You gettin' paid?"

I couldn't tell him the truth so I told him I was. I put a twenty in his hand. Disappointment shattered his placid face. I gave him another twenty and a ten. That was more to his liking.

"Brown hair, dark brown. And blue eyes. Pale. Man, they didn't have no passion behind 'em. Nothin'. Steely. Spooky. He didn't look like he belonged in this neighborhood. Kind of seedy looking, white trashy, but tryin', you know, to dress up or look like he was better 'an he was."

The Weasel.

"Did you see him get into a car?"

"No, man. No car. He come from up there, diddy-boppin' along the sidewalk. He stops here and there, checkin' addresses I guess. Then he goes up to that place," he pointed to Teddie's building. I noticed Mrs. Perlman parting the curtains. If only Moses had had her talents. "Guess I don't give you much to go on." He pulled one of the twenties, thrust it back at me. I couldn't tell him I had also seen the Weasel. I shoved it back in his hand, headed to my car.

When the gardener used the term diddy-boppin' I recognized him as a Viet Nam vet. I thought about saying something, brother-to-brother, Desert Storm vet to Viet Nam vet, and all that and normally I would have, but I didn't want to get sidetracked. I was on a mission – the most important of my life, find Teddie's killer – and I didn't want to waste even one second on small talk. I went over to the studio where Teddie's series was filmed. Couldn't get past the guard at the gate. On the way home, I stopped at a payphone and tried to make an appointment to see the producers of her show. They're in mourning, I was told. They just didn't want to talk, for whatever reasons.

The sun was beginning to set. Another Golden Hour – dead.

I pulled up to the house, a Spanish-Colonial built in the twenties. The driveway ran alongside the house back to the garage, which like a lot of people in L.A. I never used as a garage, even though I had a classic Firebird. The stucco was beige, though it might have been lighter at one time. A small courtyard in front was fenced off from the street with a wooden gate. At the back of the courtyard was the front door. I pulled about halfway down the driveway to where the back door was, parked. Baron, my tan and black German Shepherd was waiting for me with a green tennis ball in his mouth. We played catch. He loved running after tennis balls. Seeing him, playing with him, gave me a feeling of normalcy again. Made me forget about things for just a moment. After half an hour it was time to cool off:

Most L.A. pools are small and kidney shaped. Of course some are shaped like guitars or cars or whatever ego trip the ego tripper building them was involved in. And most aren't built for swimming. One of the good things my dad did was build a pool that was lean and mean, long and skinny. Built for swimming, not just skinny dipping. It was wide enough to play around in, but long enough to get a good workout. Problem was, he'd get mad when I'd use it: *"Why aren't you doing something constructive? You never do anything around here. Can't even change a light bulb."* Of course, I changed more light bulbs than you could count, but he never saw it.

Screw the workout.

I floated on a raft, staring up at the afternoon sun, watching a dragonfly dip down toward the water, then retreat. Over and over. Dip and run. Fascinating.

Then he got too much water on his wings. The weight pulled him down. Under. He drowned. I thought it was a dream, or I would have tried to save him. I was too late.

It wasn't the first time:

I was too late in high school when I finally decided to buckle down and study. If I had I might have been able to get into a good college.

I was too late in college to graduate, took too much time getting through the required course work. Spent too much time drinking and fooling around. And I quit early to join the service. At least I'd learned enough in school to allow me to pass the math and diving physics for the Teams. That was saying something.

I was too late to get a real job instead of working for my dad or being a second-rate P.I.

I was too late in my marriage to notice my wife drifting away from me. Slowly. Surely. Anyone would have seen it. Anyone but me.

I was too late in realizing that I should have stayed in the service instead of listening to my dad. I felt at home there. Doing my twenty would have been easy. Life on the outside was hard. I went into my dad's wholesale meat business but it didn't last. We couldn't get along.

It wasn't that I wasn't smart. I was too smart – for my own good. It's okay to fuck yourself, but when you fuck with someone else's life you have to pay. I'm paying now.

◈ ◈ ◈

He walks up the street.

One hand thrust into pockets filled with lint and grime.

Sweaty coins.

The other clutching a crumpled piece of paper.

With an address from a detective scribbled on it.

Passes 625 North.

Turns around.

Heads back.

Gardener at 627 looks up.

Smiles.

He doesn't return it.

He steps onto the walk leading up to the door of 625.

Tries the door.

Locked.

Looks at the names next to the buzzer.

Knocks tentatively.

Louder.

No one comes.

Retreats down the sidewalk.

A whirlpool of thoughts buzz his head.

Can't pick any one out.

A fingerpainting swirl:

Green here.

Yellow there.

Purple

Orange.

Blue.

Red and golden.

Especially red.

Everywhere.

If he doesn't do it now, he never will.

Turns around, heads back to 625.

Walks up to the door, buzzes number four.

Waits.

And waits.

Sun sliver hits the back of his neck.
Speckles of sweat form.
Running down his back.
Shivers.
In the middle of a hot day:
Shivering.
Thinking of it makes him chuckle.
What does the gardener think seeing this man standing here, laughing out loud?
Thinks he's crazy.
But he's not crazy.
Just smitten.

He knows she's the one.
Knew it from the first time he saw her.
Meant to be.
The only one.
There could be no one else.
She has the look:
The smile in her eyes,
as well as on her lips.
The curly dark hair.
Turned up nose.
Skin as smooth as cream.
Cafe au lait.
When she talks, she talks to him.
There's no one else for her to talk to.
She asked him to come out to the Coast – to see her.
So why does he feel funny standing here?
Why should he worry about what the gardener next door thinks?
Why should he worry about what she'll think?

The door opens.
It's her.
Looks just like she does on TV.

The smile.
The hair.
The eyes.

"Yes," she says.
She's speaking to him. Really speaking to him.
"Are you dropping off the script from the studio?"
He doesn't know what to say. Stutters. Nothing
comes out.
"Look," she says, "if you're selling something–"
"I, I'm not selling anything. I c'came t'to see
y'you."
"I'm sorry, but you'll have to go."
The door drives toward him, an implacable force,
meeting an unmovable object – his foot. The smile's
gone from her face. She isn't dissin' him anymore. She
respects him. His strength. His power.
He walks her back into the entry hall, closing the
door behind them. The slightly parted curtains in the
nearby window also close.
Light beams in through the leaded glass door. Yet
it's dark. The red tile floor swallows the light like a
black hole. She backs towards the stairs.
"I'm not going to hurt you."
"What do you want?"
"I, I just want to be f'friends."
"Listen, I'd like to be your friend–"
"Really?"
"Yes, but, but I have a boyfriend."
"But you asked me to come out here."
"I did?" Her eyes open wide. Anyone else would
see the terror in them. He sees only love.
"Yes."
"Have we met before?"
She's playing coy.

"You asked me to come out. F'from the TV, you were looking right at me."

"From the TV?" She tries to remember what she'd been told to do in a situation like this. Stars are always being hounded by admirers. Most of them are harmless. There's always a few who aren't. What was he?

She backs into an apartment door on the ground floor. Discreetly putting her left hand behind her back, she tries the knob. Locked. Her heart flutters. He moves closer.

"I, I just want to talk. Be friends."

There's a faraway look in his eyes. He isn't looking at her. Through her. What does he see? If she knew she might be able to talk him out of here. But she doesn't.

"Sure, we can be friends."

His eyes draw narrower. Even in the dark light, the pupils close down.

"You don't mean it. I can tell. You don't want m'me here."

"But I do. I invited you, didn't I?"

"Fuck you. I thought you were different. But you're not. You're just like all the rest."

He balls his hand into a fist. Slams it into his head. She jumps back.

"Why?"

"Why what?"

"Why are you backing away from me? You think I'm crazy. You think I'm going to hurt you? You think–"

"No, of course not." She tries to still her trembling voice. She backs up the stairs. If only she could dash for her apartment. The door is thick. These old buildings were built solid. She could hide behind it and call the police. Damn, why hadn't the intercom been fixed yet? Why did she have to be home when he showed up? How did he get her address anyway? From a Movie Stars'

Home Map? The DMV? How? Her mind races. That's not important. The only thing now is to get away.

She turns and runs up the stairs. If only she can make it to the first landing and around the corner she might have a chance. She hopes he doesn't have a gun.

The crack of the pistol shot reverberates in the tiled hall. Bouncing off the walls, ricocheting. Like being stuck in a metal drum when a construction ball hits. Her scream is swallowed by the shot's report echoing through the black hole. Everything is swallowed by the black hole, light, sound, sight. Only the black is left.

And the red. Red everywhere. Blood.

Her blood.

He looks at her crumpled on the stairs, brushes his hand across her hair. Sounds come from upstairs. People. He runs toward the door. Sees a face in the antique mirror. Disfigured. Grisly. Melting in front of him. Fading away. He runs out the door. The gardener looks at him. Fuck the gardener. He runs down the street. It's Golden Hour. He's heard of it. He's conscious of it. He doesn't care. He remembers the face in the mirror. The face of Duke Rogers.

◈ ◈ ◈

I woke up, my hand dragging in the water next to the raft, splashed water on my face. It'd been a long time since I'd dreamt. I missed it. Now I wasn't so sure about that. It was only a dream – a nightmare. One that I had caused. How much of it was true? The gist of it, if not the details.

I swam to the edge of the pool, climbed out, toweled off and went into the house, Baron trailing behind me. I grabbed a phone book from a kitchen cabinet, found the Perlmans' number. Mrs. Perlman answered. I told her who I was.

"I can talk for a minute only, my husband's in the bathroom," she whispered.

"Is there anything you forgot to tell me? Anything you couldn't–"

"I probably shouldn't tell you this, but you seem like a nice young man–"

Yeah, right lady. A fuckup. A major fuckup, just like my dad said: *"Marion, if we get divorced, it'll be your fault." They argue. They fight. He's mad at the world, but if they get divorced it'll be my fault.*

"I didn't tell the police. They're so, well you know. Anyway, I picked up a piece of paper from the hall. I didn't give it to them. I know I should have. Will you give it to them for me?"

CHAPTER 4

I dressed – short sleeved shirt, jeans, windbreaker – and outta there before hanging up the receiver. When I got to the Perlman's, I wasn't the only one there. Several people were packing Teddie's things up, loading them into a beatup blue van. The usual stuff, posters from movies she'd had bit roles in, stuffed animals, clothes.

Mrs. Perlman waved from the porch. No hiding behind curtains now. The paper curled in her scrawny hand. I made my way up the walk.

Cold eyes turned on me. He was smaller than me, but those eyes spoke of death. Teddie's? Mine? I didn't know.

"What'chu want?" he said. He was wearing blue jeans and a Public Enemy T-shirt. His face was dark. Round. Short hair in a fade. He was a little man. Lean and mean as a pit bull. And I didn't have to talk to him to see the wells of anger behind his tombstone eyes. Didn't have to get close to feel that anger shooting out at me. Where did he keep it all? How did he live with it?

Discretion is the better part of valor. Small as he was he looked tough. Wiry, like me. I could probably take him, but if he was one of Teddie's friends or family I didn't want to antagonize him. Might need him. Hell, he might even need me.

Ignoring him, I went up to Mrs. Perlman. She held out her arms, greeting me like a long lost son, grabbing my hand with hers, pressing the paper into it. She whispered: "I don't want the *schvartzes* to see." She turned to the short man, beaming with pride:

"This is Mr. Rogers. He's a detective."

The man's eyes widened. "What're you doin' hangin' 'round here?"

I ignored him again. He went back to his work. Two other men came down the stairs, carrying a large oak trunk. Both of them were large, over six feet. Mrs. P. and I had to step back into her apartment to clear a path. I backed into Mrs. Perlman, felt her unsteady hand on my back. Was it due to her age or her fear of these black men, I wondered. Still, she had rented to a black woman. Jack would have advised her not to, regardless of the laws prohibiting discrimination.

Her apartment reminded me of my grandmother's. It had been only a mile or so from here. The Wilshire District, east of Fairfax. Doilies on the arms of the couches. Little porcelain knickknacks everywhere. Crystal bowls filled with candies – I left a business card in one. Hardly a sign of Mr. P.'s input or existence.

Mrs. P. and I went out to the lawn. Watched the men loading the van. The short one came up to me. Stood four inches from my nose; stared into my eyes. "I don't know what'chure hangin' 'round here for, but you stay outta my sister's life. Get it?"

He expected me to back off. I didn't. He expected me to dis him. I didn't. I didn't do anything. Just stared back.

"C'mon Warren. Why you wastin' your time an' energy on that shit?" the larger of the other two men said. "Ain't gonna bring her back."

Warren ignored him, still staring at me: "Who hired you? What'chu nosin' 'round here for?" He inched closer. I held my ground. "Don't need no honky motherfuckers nosin'–"

The larger of the other two men walked over. Put his arm on Warren's shoulder, pulled him back a step. Warren's feet were still planted a foot closer to me; the upper part of his body jerked back, followed by his feet. He looked humiliated.

"They call me Tiny," the larger man said more to Mrs. P. than to me. "Don't mind Warren. His mind's not in the right place. You know, Teddie an' all. I'm sorry." He pulled Warren back to the van. I thought about following them, but figured Warren'd be watching for that. I wrote down the license, thinking I'd have Lou run it for me.

"Who were they?"

"The little one is Teddie's brother. Never saw the other two before. Maybe his friends. Maybe other brothers."

"They don't look like family."

"You know how it is with *these* people. None of them have the same father."

There was nothing to say to that, though I knew what Jack would say. He'd probably slap Mrs. P. on the back and compliment her on her astuteness. Tensions were high in the city. A verdict in the Rodney King beating trial was due any day now. Maybe even today. The mayor was blaming the chief of police. Blacks were blaming whites. Whites were blaming blacks. Koreans were blaming blacks. Blacks were blaming Mexicans. The town was ready to explode. Everyone knew it, but everyone was in one degree of denial or another. The biggest problem: no one was talking about the issue that really mattered – race.

My family goes back several generations in L.A. and it's not the same town I grew up in. It used to be a large small town. Now it's a big city, with all the problems of a big city. Some parts of town are hell. You take your life in your hands just by walking down the streets.

People shouldn't have to live like that. Too many rats in a maze.

I don't have the answers for this city, but I try to stay out of trouble. Jack looks for it. I used to get pissed at people in cars, flip 'em off. I hold my tongue today. Today they don't yell back. They shoot. I wondered what would happen if Jack and Warren ever met on a dark street. I wouldn't want to be there.

I thanked Mrs. P. for the paper. Asked her if there was anything else she could tell me. No. I asked for Teddie's family's address and phone number. She gave me the index card and application that Teddie had filled out. Both had been kept in the same folder and both were illegible. Something had spilled on the folder causing the ink to run and blur. I didn't even take them with me.

In the car, I checked out the paper. Thought it would be the sheet I handed the Weasel in my office. It wasn't. It had the address scribbled on it in his hand, not mine. And the name of a motel printed at the top – The William Tell Motel in West Hollywood. The motel where he had stayed?

Orange trim around the windows and dumpy cheap stucco from the '60s defined the William Tell Motel. Real classy. Perfect for the Weasel. Desk clerk's hair was razor cut, short, except for one long strand on the right side of her head. Cute. She didn't look up when I entered. Didn't smile when I rang the bell. Didn't seem to give a damn if I wanted a room or a rape. Just watched Geraldo on the tube.

"Yeah," she said finally getting off her ass and plodding over to the counter. "Can I help you?"

When I didn't smile, when I gave her my hostile face, she tried a smile. I didn't break the corners of my mouth. Hell, if she wanted to play tough mama, I'd play tough too. The customer's always right.

"Wanna room?" she said, softening her voice. Worried that maybe she was scaring a customer away.

"Information."

"Dial 4-1-1."

"Cute."

"This ain't information central."

"Where're you from?"

"That's the information you want?"

"Just trying to make small talk."

"It ain't gonna work."

"I'd say Arkansas. Maybe Alabama or Louisiana."

She couldn't keep her lips from curling into a slight smile. She tried though. "How'd you know. I thought I'd lost my accent."

"I know a lotta people from down that way. Got some former in-laws from around Selma. I hear them in your voice."

"I dunno if that's a compliment or not."

"Neutral." She looked at me funny. "It's neutral."

"You the heat?"

"I'm looking for a friend."

"Yeah, right."

"Squirrelly kinda guy. Nervous. Pale blue eyes you can almost see through. Dart back and forth a lot. Dark brown hair."

"You gotta name on him, your friend?"

"Jim Talbot."

"'s almost as bad as John Smith, ain't it?"

I grinned. She looked through a box of cards behind the counter. No computers for William Tell. Crossbows?

"No Jim Talbot. When did he stay here?"

"A few days ago, within the last week."

"Guy was here a few days ago, might be him." She riffled through the cards. "Here he is. Talbot Sparks."

She handed me the card. I wrote Sparks' vitals down in my notebook. If Jim Talbot was a phony name, Talbot Sparks might be too. So could his address and all. What the hell. A lead's a lead. 'Sides, a lotta these guys do a turn on their real name, so even if Jim Talbot or Talbot Sparks weren't his real name, the overlapping Talbot might be a clue. Of course, he might also be smart enough to play the alias game and not get caught.

"Did he give you a credit card?"

"Paid cash." She pointed to a spot on the card. Gave us a hundred dollar deposit for a few nights. Then split without paying the last night's rent. I had to pay it outta my paycheck since I signed him in."

"Tough."

"Yeah, man. Tough shit." She turned back to Geraldo and transsexuals who were about to have an operation to make them what they were in the first place: "Women Who Used to be Men Who Want to be Men Again" was the subject. Then a promo for the news. The King verdict might come in today. Stay tuned.

She tossed me the keys to a room. "Check it out."

The room was bleak. Motel cheapo. I tossed it. Nothing. Besides, how many other people were in here since he left? It hadn't been that long, but in this kind of place– I returned the keys to the clerk. I dropped a twenty on the counter.

"What's that for?"

"What do you think?"

"I ain't no prostie."

"Get yourself a new barber."

"Why don't you get yourself a life?"

She meant it to hurt. And it did. "Will it cover Sparks' room?"

"More than. But I–"

"You provided a service. Information. I'm giving you a fee for that service. That's how the world works. Capitalism, you know. Don't make a big thing out of it."

"Hey, he said somethin' about he was only stayin' here till his apartment was ready."

"In L.A.?"

"Yeah, maybe, I dunno for sure." She talked to me, but I could tell her heart was with Geraldo. "Maybe I shouldn'ta talked to you. Maybe–"

I let her ramble on as I hit the street and my car. Two men walked by arm in arm. One had a goatee and short, close-cropped hair. The other a moustache and long straight hair almost to his shoulders. They stopped at the corner waiting for the light to change – French kissing. Jack would've blown them away. Hell, he wouldn't even listen to k.d. lang.

CHAPTER 5

Next morning, I phoned the number Sparks-Talbot had left on his room card. 415 area code – San Francisco. A nice old lady answered. Said she'd had that number for several years. Never heard of Sparks or Talbot. I figured the address was a phony, punched it and the phone number into the computer and threw out my spiral notebook page. The guy was a Weasel, but Weasels are smart. Cagey. My respect for him began to grow. Not much. A little.

Where'd that leave me? Dead in the water – like the dragonfly. I called Lou.

"You're outta your fucking mind," she said in a loud whisper after I told her what I wanted. "Look what happened the last time I ran someone for you."

"I know, Lou. But this is the yang of that yin. I'm trying to right the situation."

"When are you going to the police? Your few days are running out."

"I need some more time. It's only been a couple days. Give me a week."

"So the trail'll grow cold."

"No, damn it. So I can clean up my own mess. Run the damn plate for me."

She finally agreed. I gave her the tag number on the blue van. The address was on Florence, near downtown, close to the area known as South Central.

My car is a '69 Pontiac Firebird. Orange paint. Black vinyl top. Black interior. Man, she flies. State of the art sound system. Four on the floor. They don't make 'em like that anymore. They don't guzzle gas like this baby anymore either, but you gotta make some sacrifices. I hit the CD button. My indulgences were my car and my stereos, home and for the car. When times were good that's where my money went. My player scrambled among six CDs loaded in a cartridge in the trunk. Time-Life '60s series. *Get Together* by the Youngbloods blasted out.

I hit a Taco Bell on La Cienega. I was sitting in the driveway, waiting to get into the street when some slime-muffin cut across two lanes of traffic to pull into the driveway. The way he cut across, his car almost nosed into mine. He pulled up alongside me:

"Hey, fuck you," he said.

I smiled at him. Hell, I was in the right place. He was the lunatic. That's the problem today. City's filled with 'em. I could've pulled the Firestar 9mm that was nudged under my right thigh. Normally I wouldn't have a gun under my thigh, after all it is illegal, and I didn't really expect the worst, but it never hurts to be prepared. The verdict in the Rodney King cop trial was due any day now. And he might have had a gun, might not have. But who needed the fucking paperwork? I might have gotten off, might have gone to jail. Hell, it wasn't worth the trouble. He pulled into the driveway, barely missing my car. I let it go, pulled out and headed towards Florence. A comfortable April L.A. day.

The address for the van was a truck rental facility on Florence near Normandie. The building looked as if it had been there since the '40s or before, but had gone through a lot of different uses. This week it rented blue vans to friends and family of Teddie Matson.

Strange looks intercepted me as I debarked the Bird. Locked the door with the electronic lock I'd had installed. Set the alarm. I was out of my territory, on foreign soil – Indian country. The only white face on the street. A few might be driving by; none on the pavement. The Firestar was tucked inside my in-the-belt conceal-carry holster. Hollow points in the mag, an extra mag tucked in next to the holster. Several sets of eyes followed me into the office. Is this what it feels like for blacks in a white neighborhood? Knowing everyone's wondering what the hell you're doing there. Are you going to rob them? Are you a cop? A junkie? What the hell's going on? Eerie.

I walked into the office like I didn't notice any of it, but my eyes and ears were fine tuned, radar and sonar. SEAL training. I didn't like to think of myself as being like Jack. Maybe I was more like him than I cared to admit. Maybe some of these folks were also more like him than they cared to admit, but coming from the yang side instead of the yin.

The man behind the counter was large, black: unsmiling. I could almost see the chip on his shoulder. A small TV was on in the corner behind him. The news gurus were still waiting for a verdict in the King case.

"You lose yo' way?"

"I don't think so. I'm pretty good with directions." I thought I'd try to lighten things up.

"A comedian."

Two other men came in from the lot. "Don't look like no Richard Pryor. Not even Eddie Murphy."

"M'be he Slappy White."

"Sho' is white."

"Mus' be all that white milk his mama feed him. We like chocolate, don' we?"

They laughed. I didn't. They obviously didn't think I was a cop, or didn't care.

"Okay, you've had your fun, can we get down to business now?"

"*Yussah, massah.* What'chu be wantin' me a do fer you, White Boss Man?" one of the men who'd followed me in said in his best Stepin Fetchit dialect. If I didn't know better, I would have thought he was committing a hate crime against me. He sounded like Jack. And I was sounding more and more like him too. Spooky. I found myself thinking of jokes I could say back. Of course the odds were against me. And The Powers That Be probably *would* prosecute me for a hate crime. Instead, I stood my ground. Didn't say anything. They kept on for a couple minutes until the guy behind the counter finally spoke:

"Awright. You ain't lost, so what'chu want?"

Someone was moving around in the small room behind the counter. Might have been a petite little accountant or receptionist, but I didn't think so. I moved to the side of the doorway. Some might consider that a racist action. I considered it a move to possibly save my life.

"I'm looking for some people who rented one of your vans."

"An' why should I help you?"

"So maybe I can help them?"

"Big White Brothah gonna help us y'all," one of the men behind me said. It didn't seem like the situation was easing up at all. I was nervous, fingering my belt near the concealment holster.

"Okay, never mind." I backed toward the door. The man behind the counter called out.

"Why you wanna be helpin' them?"

"Forget it."

The two men behind me moved in closer. "Brother asked you a question honky."

"Don'tchu mean Mistah Honky?"

"Massah Honky."

The two behind me kept at it. They hadn't touched me yet. But I was waiting for it. Hell, I hadn't done anything to them. I was a symbol. And I didn't like it. Not one fucking bit. I pivoted on my heel and backed into a corner that didn't have any windows or doors. They were in front of me now, not behind. I might have been backed into a corner, but no one could come at me from behind now. I could see them. And if I could see them, I might be able to get away. I was well trained. I doubted they were. I didn't want to use the gun. That was a last resort. Put my hands in front of me in a defensive position.

"All right. Let's cut the crap. You want me, come get me. You don't want me, leave me the fuck alone."

"Big talk, white boy," said the man nearer me. "He think he Mohammed Ali dancin' like that. You ain't no butterfly, boy. An' I'm sure you don' sting like no bee."

"Queen bee, mehbe."

"Ye-eeeeh."

I'd thought maybe his partner in crime had given up, but I was wrong. The guy behind the counter just stood there, watching me, the TV. Back and forth. I was still aware of someone in the back room. Were they toying with me for fun, or were they toying with me before moving in for the kill? I didn't know. I didn't really care either. I wanted things to come to a head. This game playing was bullshit. There was no point in trying to reason with them. They were pissed off at white people. Didn't matter who you were. And I was on their turf. They might not have been planning to harm me, but they sure as hell wanted to let me know that I was in the wrong part of town. Didn't matter what I was there for. Get the hell out and don't come back. That was their message.

I didn't care anymore about finding out who rented the van and where they lived. I was happy to get out with my pride, as long as the rest of me was in one piece. If that meant fighting my way out, so be it.

I jabbed at the dude closest to me. He feinted. Good move. Crack. A baseball bat slammed into the counter. The man behind the counter had slammed the bat into the Formica top, splintering it. All three of us on the other side jumped, looked at him.

"Cut the shit," he said to all of us. "Go on. Get out."

His word was boss around there. The other two parted to let me pass. I walked carefully, checking all sides. Making sure no one was waiting for me on the outside. Looked clear.

Before I got out the door, the guy behind the counter turned up the volume on the TV. The four cops who were caught on home video beating Rodney King had been acquitted. I knew I had to get the hell out of there pronto. People were already filling the streets.

CHAPTER 6

What I didn't know when I stepped out into the abyss that day was that the night before Laurie Hoffman's unwanted admirer had called her again:

The phone rang at eight p.m. sharp. She knew who it was. He'd called the last three nights in a row – at eight sharp. The same guy she'd told me about. Last night she didn't answer the phone. She let the answering machine pick up. Her incoming message tape could take sixty minutes of messages. That was his first call.

"Laurie, I know we only went out once, but I know we're right for each other. It's meant to be. Does that sound corny? Jeez, that's not me. That's what you do to me."

After that message, she turned off the machine and unplugged the phone. When she plugged it back in an hour later, it was still ringing off the hook. She unplugged it for the rest of the night.

She pulled all the shades down, closed the curtains and hunkered on the floor of her living room, all-night *Gilligan's Island* reruns on Nick at Nite in the background for company. She didn't know who to call. There was no way to prove it was him after the first call. The restraining order only specified he couldn't get within a hundred feet of her. So unless he came in through the window, there was nothing the police could do.

Their first date had been rather ordinary. He had responded to her ad in the back of a magazine:

Looking for love in all the right places. Feminine lady, fun and frolicsome, looking for a fairytale love. Candlelight dinners, sunset walks on beach. Let others romance the stone, I'll romance the man. 5'7" tall, 120 pounds. Curly blonde hair. Cute smile. Non-smoker. UB2. Looking for intelligent, humorous, caring man for serious, long-term relationship. SASE and photo to Laurie, P.O. Box 986321, Los Angeles, Calif.

◈ ◈ ◈

"Hello, is this Laurie?" the man's voice smooth and cool. Confident.

"Yes."

"This is Gary Craylock. You sent me your phone number, in response to my answering your ad."

"Yes, I remember. How are you, Gary?"

"Now that I've met you, so to speak, fine, just fine. I don't want you to think I'm just a physical kind of guy, but, wow, judging from your photo, you are truly gorgeous."

"Thank you. You're very kind."

"And you make me blush."

Laurie laughed. She liked a sensitive man, even if he was only joking.

◈ ◈ ◈

Kate's was one of those trendy places, here today, gone tomorrow. Today it was the hottest place in town. Laurie had never been there. She doubted she'd ever go again, unless she and Gary hit it off. She'd called in sick to work. Spent most of the day primping and preening. She looked as good as she would ever look, blond hair glinting in the light. Jade eyes clean and clear.

She didn't want to appear star struck on their first date, but the fact that Patrick Swayze was at the next table was hard to avoid. She'd never considered herself impressed by the surface glitz that movie stars possessed, but being so close one could really feel it.

"I don't normally answer personal ads," Gary said after ordering Courvoisier for both of them. "But yours sounded so genuine that I couldn't resist."

"Thank you," she said, hoping she wasn't blushing. Her face grew hot.

"It's so hard to meet people these days. I guess the in place is the gym."

"Or laundromat."

"Yes, I've heard that. But what kind of people are you going to meet there? And I don't have time to take classes where you might have a better chance of meeting, um, a higher class of people."

She laughed at his pun; he smiled. In her grandfather's words it was a "million dollar smile." Who was this knight in shining armor and could he really be as good as his first impression? She hoped so.

Their drinks came and he toasted their relationship. He could have toasted her health, others had. He could have toasted her future or her looks. But he had toasted their relationship. She liked that.

He had picked her up in his BMW. She normally wouldn't give a stranger her address on the phone, would have met him at the restaurant. But he had sounded warm and sincere and, truth be told, she was feeling a little desperate after a string of frogs. The drive to the restaurant was smooth and filled with small talk: what music do you like, which movies, do you go to art galleries? Pleasant enough. Non-threatening.

He had opened the car door and the door to the restaurant for her. Did all the right things. That was rare today. Some men were afraid women would think they were wusses. Some women wanted doors opened for them. And some women didn't. So some men stopped doing it. Laurie didn't care one way or the other. That's not how she judged men, or anyone else. Still, when he did it, it felt good.

All the way to the restaurant, she had fondled the single long-stemmed rose he had brought her. Other men had done the same or similar things. With him it was different. More elegant. More exciting. He was dashing in a way the others hadn't been.

"In this age of AIDS you've really got to be careful," he said, sipping his drink. "That's one of the reasons I don't date very often. Besides, there's not very many good women out there." He winked at her.

"Or men." She winked back.

They hadn't planned on dinner, only a drink or two to see if they were "companionable." Then Gary had asked her if she'd like to eat.

"Of course," she said.

They ordered steak and blackened red snapper. The conversation continued genially. Mostly small talk and small jokes. Entertainment Light. He was a psychologist. Made good money. Had good looks, almost movie star looks. Could this be love at first sight? She thought Gary felt the same about her.

"What is this?" Gary blared when the waiter brought their order, interrupting Laurie from her reverie. "I ordered the two inch steak, medium rare. This is overcooked shoe leather."

People at other tables turned to look. The waiter took the plate away. Laurie put her hand on Gary's to calm him. He looked at her, realized what he was doing and cooled off.

"I'm sorry. I guess it doesn't make a good impression on the first date, but I'm very particular.

When I pay a lot of money for something, I expect to get what I ordered."

"I don't blame you." She squeezed his hand.

◈ ◈ ◈

A chill breeze sliced through Laurie and Gary as they walked to her front door.

"I didn't know it would be so cold tonight."

"It's that time of year. Warm days, cool nights."

They stood at the door while she fumbled in her purse for her keys.

"Thank you, I had a lovely evening."

"Aren't you going to invite me in?"

"There'll be plenty of time for that."

"What's the matter? Don't you like me?" An edge in his voice.

"It's our first date. I like to get to know someone a little better."

"I'm not saying we have to, you know. But maybe just a cup of coffee and some good conversation. Besides, let's talk about our plans. Friday, I have tickets for the Dodgers. Then Saturday I've got two tickets to the Music Center, but I didn't know who I'd go with. Now I do. And Sunday I thought we could drive up to Santa Barbara. I know this great place for brunch and–"

"Listen, Gary, I like you. But it's late and I have to go to work tomorrow."

"You're sure you're not just making excuses."

"I'm sure."

She gave him a peck on the cheek. He tried to move around to her lips. She slid away and in through the door. He trudged back down the walk. What did he have to be so incensed about, she thought as she bolted the front door.

The next morning, he was waiting for her, bouquet in hand, as she came out to her car. Wanted to take her to breakfast. When she declined, he followed her to work. Up to her office. The receptionist thought he was cute. Laurie thought he was scary.

The pattern continued. A few days later she came to see me for the first time.

◈ ◈ ◈

The morning after he had let the phone ring all night, she woke up to find a stuffed teddy bear on her front porch, a small heart shaped necklace clutched in the bear's hand. The note from Gary quoted lines from *And I Love Her*, an old Beatles' song. She called me and left a message on my machine. I was already on my way to South Central. She said she wanted to talk to me again. She'd heard I was a good detective – I should've told her my dad's opinion of me. Should've told her about Teddie Matson. She wanted to try again with me before looking for another private dick. Besides, Harv was out of town on a case and wouldn't be back for several weeks.

CHAPTER 7

*S*un shoots streaks of blinding light into my
eyes.
I squint.
Put on my shades.
Head for the Firebird.
People running down the street.
Suspicious looks shoot my way.
Already they've got armloads of loot.
TVs. Stereos.
A huge mattress.
Some have smaller things, more practical things:
Food. Diapers. Baby formula.
Running.
Jostling.
Accosting people in their way.
Not everyone loots.
Some have just come out to watch the show.
Several gang bangers heading my way.
I have a gun.
I can protect myself.
But this isn't the time.
I duck behind a low wall.
One of the bangers sees my car.
Rushes to it.
He breaks the driver's window.
Glass shatters.

The cacophony of shattering glass fused with blaring
sirens, droning chopper blades. People shouting.

When he couldn't hot wire the car, he started smashing all the windows. His friends joined in, slashing the seats and tires. Great, how was I going to get out of there? I thought about using the gun to scare them off. What was the point? The damage was done. Besides, they were probably better armed than me.

The smoke from fires hadn't blotted out the sun and sky yet. A large shadow hovered over me from behind. I turned around to see a huge barrel-chested black man standing over me. My hand was already on the gun. He looked familiar. Tiny, the man helping to move Teddie Matson's things out of her apartment. I had to assess the situation quickly. Go for his knees? Groin? I was crouching. Even if I were standing, he'd have a great height advantage over me. I felt confident. Not that confident. Not when I was so outnumbered.

He stuck a hand out. I didn't take it. Got up on my own.

"Relax," he said.

Sure. I fingered the trigger with my other hand.

The bangers saw us. Headed our way. Caught between a gang and a Tiny. I almost saw my life passing before me. I wasn't a big guy. Sort of compact like a mortar shell – powerful like one, I hoped. And if the body was a Volkswagen, under the hood was a Porsche engine. I had the training and a gun, but what good would it do if it was twenty against one? This wasn't a Hollywood movie, after all.

"This yo' car?" the leader said. He wore a red bandana on his head. Bloods.

"Yeah."

"We customized it fo' yo'."

"Thanks. I was getting tired of it always looking the same."

"Ha ha. Very funny."

They moved closer. Tiny didn't move. Neither did I. I figured if it was over it was over. But I wouldn't go down without a fight.

The leader lifted his shirt, revealing a semi-auto pistol underneath. Another banger pulled an Uzi from under a jacket.

"Now we gonna customize you." He took a step closer. Tiny didn't move.

He put his hand on my shoulder, gripped tight. I was about to make an evasive move when he shoved me aside. He stepped between the bangers and me. "Why you wanna do this shit?"

"Fo' Rodney, man."

"Yeah, fo' Rodney."

"This boy ain't done nothin' to Rodney. Not to you either," Tiny said in a deep baritone.

I didn't want to be protected. I thought I could take care of myself. But, as they say, discretion is the better part of valor. I held off. This was probably the better way.

"His people done it to Rodney."

"Yeah, man, white people."

"Aw go on," Tiny said. "You boys wanna loot, get a free TV, go on. Hurtin' on someone's different."

"Who gonna stop us? You?"

"Yeah, man. Me."

"There's six a us. One a you. An' him, if he can even fight fo' himself."

"Yeah, whyn't you let him speak fo' hisself?"

"He's my friend. Now you done wrecked his car. Go on. Party. Get outta here."

The bangers stood there a moment. Anything could have happened. I was still standing behind Tiny. I moved next to him. The leader turned to me.

"What'chu think about this verdict?"

"Don't answer, man," Tiny said. "These guys don't know 'bout Rodney. Don't give a fuck 'bout Rodney. They're just lookin' for an excuse to party."

"We don' need no excuses. We gonna take this city down." He turned, followed by his comrades. Headed out to the street.

"Thanks."

"I don't want no killings on my head. Not on my property either."

"This is your company? That was you walking around, looking out from the backroom?"

"Yeah. Maybe I shouldn't have let my employees get on you like that. C'mon." He led me into the back door, to the back office. It was cluttered with papers, folders, notebooks. Girly calendars. The desk was old, wooden, stained brown. He sat behind it. I moved a stack of papers, sat on a spotted couch. He gave me a cup of coffee. "This city's going to burn." He leaned back, let out a huge sigh. Sipped his coffee. His voice softened, his manner relaxed. He didn't have to put it on for the bangers anymore. "Not a smart move coming down here today."

"I didn't know the verdict would be coming in. Probably wouldn't have made a difference anyway. I've got a job to do." I drank the coffee. It was cold. Bitter.

"And what is that?"

"I need to find Teddie Matson's family?"

"Seems her brother didn't want to talk to you."

"Look, what is this resistance? I'm trying to help find her killer."

"Nobody trusts you."

"'Cause I'm white. Jesus, what difference does it make?"

"To me it doesn't. To Warren it obviously does."

"Hell, Teddie didn't live down here. She lived in a white neighborhood. I don't see–"

"Maybe that's one of the reasons Warren's so pissed. Maybe he didn't like her living uptown, so to speak. Maybe he felt she had some success, then abandoned her own. Maybe–"

It wasn't a maybe for him. He knew what he was talking about.

"Will you tell me where her family lives?"

He leaned back so far in his chair it looked like he was going to fall over. It looked like the chair could hardly hold his bulk. But it did. He leaned back farther, till the back of the chair hit the wood paneled wall. The panels were dark with grease stains. It was like that in just about all the automotive businesses I'd ever been in. Grime everywhere.

"You can't drive home in your car. I'll loan you a truck. No charge. Well, I have to charge you a buck just to make it legal."

"I appreciate that. But I don't want to go home. I want to find her family."

"Man, you're the end. Like my mother used to say, you're a persistent little cuss. Why do you have such a bug up your ass? And don't tell me it's your job. You can come tomorrow or the next day, when things quiet down."

"The longer I wait, the colder the trail gets. I'm already down here."

"Your white face is gonna act like a trouble-magnet."

"I'll take that risk."

"Are you stupid or gutsy?"

"A little of both, I guess."

"Man, I just don't get it. What is this, some kind of white guilt?"

It was guilt, but not the way he was thinking of it. Not white man's guilt. I felt guilty about Teddie. More than guilty. Sick. I couldn't bring her back, but I could do what I could to help bring her killer to justice. Noble thoughts? Lofty? Maybe. I couldn't help it. I wanted the Weasel. I wanted to kill him. Maybe that's why I didn't pull the gun on the bangers. I was saving my bullets. But a quick gunshot death would be too easy for him. Maybe I'd tear him apart with my hands. Maybe I'd slice the layers of his skin off one at a time with the razor sharp Gerber dagger I always carried strapped to my boot. Yeah, a gun was too quick. Let the bastard suffer.

I didn't like myself much for thinking like that. It seemed so primitive. But what the hell. The son-of-a-bitch deserved it, and it hardly looked like a civilized society anymore. Not just the day of the riot, but for a long time before.

"Not guilt. Duty."

"But you're not going to tell me who you're working for or why this person is so concerned about finding Teddie's killer." Before I could speak, he put his hand up. "Don't give me that crap about client confidentiality either. Let me see your investigator's license."

He took it from me, perused it for a couple minutes. I guess it passed inspection. He got up, tossing what was left of his coffee cup in the wastebasket.

"Let's go."

He locked the back door. Went to the front turned off the lights, took the cash from the register, stuffed it in his pants. He grabbed a .38 revolver from behind the counter, put it in his belt and covered it with his shirt.

"Help me with this."

We pulled a large, hand painted sign from behind the counter. It was awkward. Bulky. We taped it across the front window. In two foot high red letters it read "Black Owned and Operated."

CHAPTER 8

We stepped outside, squinting into the sun. People were running by, in both directions. Police cars, sirens wailing, sped by. No one stopped to help a man laying in the street. Tiny looked around, surveying the situation: "The good life is just a dream a way," he said.

He went to the cab of one of his trucks, started the engine. Motioned for me to get in as I was about to head for the man bleeding at the curb. I went to the downed man. He was Asian. Korean? A gash was leaking blood over his right eye.

"You all right?" I started to reach for him.

"Lemme 'lone," he said, pushing himself up off the curb. He staggered away. I started to go after him when Tiny called out.

"Let's go, man."

I jogged back to Tiny's van, got in. He eased it toward the street. A rock cracked the windshield. Thrown by a boy who couldn't have been more than nine or ten. Tiny didn't make any attempt to chase him down. He killed the engine.

"This is shit," he said, surveying the street up and down. "We better walk." He looked at me. Studying my face. No emotion in his eyes. "You're gonna stick out like a sore thumb. At least in the van you couldda ridden in back."

"Got some shoe polish? I can go in blackface."

"Not funny."

But he didn't seem to take offense. I wasn't trying to be racist or offend, only to make light of a bad situation. The humor may have been in bad taste, but that's how I deal with tense situations. Bad jokes.

Tiny and I closed the wrought iron gate that led to his lot, locking it with the biggest padlock I'd ever seen. The rusty chain that he triple wrapped around the two sections of fence had to be almost an inch thick.

"Hell, this won't keep 'em out," he said, clasping the lock shut. Tugging on it. "Nothing will." He spun the cylinder of his revolver, snapping it back in place. "Let's go. No use keeping the vultures waiting."

We started off down the street. The acrid smell of smoke blanched my nostrils. He pulled out a green kerchief and held it over his nose. Not red or blue. No identifying with Bloods or Crips. A neutral green. But hell, that was probably somebody's colors. Somebody's signal to go to war too. I coughed. Tiny ripped his kerchief in half, handing me a ragged end. I flashed him the OK sign. I wanted to say thanks, couldn't talk. The green cloth made a fair smoke screen. But hey, fireman, how 'bout one of those oxygen bottles you've got on your back? That's something I'd be tempted to loot for.

Running, jostling bodies sprinted up and down the street, loaded with booty. VCRs. TVs. Even mattresses. It was as if there was a giant sign hanging over L.A., being pulled along by the Goodyear blimp, that said: "Free Shopping Day."

A police car pulled up in front of a stereo store. The window had been bashed in, the door pulled from its hinges. People were running in and out, taking anything they could carry. Going back for seconds. Thirds. The cops jumped out of their car, pounding batons on a low wall. People zipped off. The cops headed back for their car. Three young men came out, loaded for bear. They started chanting: "Rodney King. Rodney King. Rodney

King." It lasted about five seconds. They laughed self-consciously. Gave up the chant. Ran off with their loot. The cops didn't give chase.

"This isn't about race anymore," Tiny said. "Got nothing to do with Rodney King."

A mob of kids ran toward us. We ducked into the doorway of a book store. No looting there. It didn't seem to interest them as they kept running. If I had been at home, I'd probably be shouting at the TV for the police to "shoot the looters," like Jack was, no doubt, doing now. But down there on the streets, it was different. They were just people. Maybe doing things they shouldn't. But still people. Still Americans. At least most of them. There were, we learned later, a lot of illegal aliens taking part in the Big Party.

And it was a party. Giddiness run rampant. These people acted as if they didn't have a care in the world. Most of them grabbed stereos. The brand didn't matter. They'd keep the ones they liked best. Sell the rest. Some of their situations were a little sadder, though the people were just as giddy. They were taking cartons of Frosted Flakes, diapers and Tide. Whole families participating together. Real family values.

Tiny and I bolted from the doorway, ran down the street, ducking for cover by low walls, doorways, shrubs all along the way. We weren't out to party. We were on a mission. He was taking me to Warren, to Teddie's family. I didn't know why, but I was curious about it. Warren obviously wanted nothing to do with me. Yet here was Tiny taking me to him. What was this all about? Was it a setup? Were they going to beat some confession out of me when we hooked up with Warren? Was I being paranoid? Were my own prejudices coloring my thoughts? Was I scared shitless to be one of the few white faces down there when the fires of hell were breaking out all over? I didn't know. I didn't care. I just wanted to find Teddie's family.

Maybe I should have gone home. Watched the whole conflagration on the tube with a gun in one hand, a beer in the other. Hell, we could've had a party. Like a Super Bowl party, only this would have been a Hellfire party. Everything's burning. Get out the violins and fiddle while the city turns to dust.

But my car was trashed. And though Tiny would have let me borrow a van, something told me not to go. Maybe it was the same crazy something that had made me join the Navy. Maybe it was the same something that had made me fuck up my marriage? My life? Maybe my dad was right. Maybe I was a fuckup. Maybe I'd fuck myself for good down here – *Marion you're always going out of your way to hurt yourself. Mixing where you don't belong.* – in the middle of this inferno?

Maybe that's what I wanted.

A group of men came out of a trashed beauty shop with armloads of blow dryers. What were they gonna do with all those?

We came to Florence and Normandie. Half a block away the cops were regrouping. Or retreating. Or hiding out. It was hard to tell. There was a swarm of them, but they weren't doing much of anything. People were looting, throwing rocks, bottles and the like right under their noses. As we left the intersection, I glanced back. A large semi was pulling into the intersection. We continued away from the intersection. Later I learned that this was where Reginald Denny, the driver of the semi, was pulled from the truck. Beaten within an inch of his life. We were gone before it happened. But I still have pangs of guilt for having been so close and having done so little. Now I know how lucky we were.

In a sense it was a *quid pro quo* situation. Tiny's black face was my passport among his people. My white face was his insurance that the cops might just leave him alone – if they knew he was with me. That might have been why he wanted to help me out. Protection. But it wasn't an uneasy truce. I felt comfortable with him. Like we'd known each other all our lives. Maybe we had. The last thirty minutes had been a lifetime.

We crouched behind a low wall at a service station, surveying the situation. He watched two sides. I watched the other two, covering each other's backs. We were both armed; neither of us wanted to use our guns.

Noise barked from every direction. Sirens. Shouts. Choppers hovering. Shots. Too many shots. It all blended into a cacophony of confusion. The din was ear shattering and lifeless, inert, all at the same time.

"Why're you helping me?" I asked Tiny as we scoped the street out. He never answered my question, though I asked several more times.

There was an explosion in the distance, then the shock wave. A new column of black smoke appeared every few minutes. Slow-motion funnel clouds.

"Man, don't they know they're tearing down their own goddamn neighborhoods," he said, scanning the horizon. "Where're they gonna get food and clothes when all this burns to the ground?"

We were on the move again, ducking in and out of doorways. We ducked into a mom and pop grocery. The owner came at us with a thirteen round semi-auto pistol. He was Korean. He wasn't shouting at me when, in pidgin, he said: "Get out. Get out now. Don't come back. Don't never come back. I don't need your business. Animal. Animals. You peoples are all animals."

The Korean racked the slide of his pistol. Tiny and I split, two jackrabbits in a hunter's sights. Tiny never said a word about the Korean. About the animosity between blacks and Koreans. It was hard to tell if he didn't care. If he'd made peace with it in his own mind. Or if he was storing up a reserve of rage that would explode sooner or later.

For the moment, Teddie had become lost under a pile of ashes – the ashes of Los Angeles, my home town. I wasn't concerned about her now. I was worried about getting out alive. Part of me wondered if I didn't want to make it out at all. The rest of me would have done anything to survive.

We turned down a sidestreet. It was quieter than the main drags had been. A pretty young woman was sitting on the porch steps of an old California bungalow. She held a large black cat in a cardboard carton, soothing its eyes with a damp cloth. There were tears in her eyes. In ours. The smoke stung. Our nostrils were dry, our throats raw.

"He saved my life," she said. "One night three men were coming over the fence in our backyard. He woke us up before the men got inside." She tore a fresh piece of cloth from a large strip, dipped it in a bowl of water and put it on the cat's eyes. She offered us each a strip. We declined. We hadn't said anything to her. Hadn't asked what she was doing with the cat. She had just started talking to us. She needed someone to talk to. We all did.

"Will you be okay?" I asked.

"I think so. The fun's up that way," she said, pointing to the main drag.

I wanted to offer her something. Anything. I had nothing to offer. Except a gun and a knife. If she didn't know how to use them they would be useless. We wished her the best and headed off, eventually making our way back to Normandie.

People were still running every which way, carrying home the desserts of their shopping spree. The cops continued to do next to nothing. A security gate at Wherehouse Records was breached. A black man turned to a young white kid and invited him to join the celebration. He did.

Two other men stood outside talking.

"I don't steal," one said, palming his hands upwards, almost embarrassed.

"Neither do I," said the other, "but–" He showed a large canvas bag he'd brought to haul stuff way. "This is different. Society's rules don't apply no more. There is no society here. No civilization. Not today. Anarchy is king."

A black and white pulled up, wailed its siren. Throngs of looters dispersed. The cops drove off. The looters were back within seconds, picking up the goodies they had set down on the street. Two women argued over an electric piano someone had put down when the cops came. One snapped out a switchblade. Slashed the other. She fell, bleeding. A melee ensued. No one knew anymore what started it. Everyone just piled on for the fun. The Big Party.

We asked some people if they knew if there was a curfew on the city? No, they told us. The mayor hadn't done anything yet. We moved out. In the crowd. Swirling. Sucking us in. Down. Under. We moved along with the flow. My hand kept checking my gun. Was it there? Would it be there when I needed it? I didn't take my hand off it.

The crowd surged toward another small grocery/liquor store. We were caught in it. No escape. The store owner, shotgun in hand, hard-charged someone who'd broken off from the crowd. He waved the gun wildly, maybe at the man who'd broken from the crowd. But we were all in his kill zone. Through the smoke it was hard to tell if he was Mexican, Korean, Armenian – didn't matter anyway. He was shouting. I couldn't understand what he was saying. Neither could anyone else it appeared. It wasn't English, and the din was too loud to figure out what it was. No one was listening anyway. He jacked the slide of his twelve gauge. People hit the deck, dispersed, fell all over each other. A blast rang out. A young woman fell. I rushed to her, tearing my belt off, making a tourniquet on her arm that was bleeding profusely. Tiny pulled me off.

"It's no use. We got business. Leave her be."

"Somebody's got to."

"She's dead," Tiny said. Get it? She's dead. Doesn't matter what you do."

I didn't move. He lifted her head. The side that had been facing away from me was a mess of bloody hamburger. How could I not have seen it? Maybe I didn't want to.

He pulled me away. I let him.

We dashed across a gas station where two men were lighting a Molotov cocktail. Behind us the sound of shattering glass. I slid beneath a car on the street. Tiny hugged a wall. The gas station went up in an overwhelming fireball of light and heat. White heat. And it seemed as if the Post Modern Age had gone up with it.

Welcome to the Apocalypse.

CHAPTER 9

People on the sidestreets were mostly hunkered behind closed doors or heading for the main boulevards. Not many people sitting around shooting the breeze. Gang graffiti littered walls and sidewalks. Some cars. Broken glass everywhere. I noticed a couple bullet holes – at least that's what I thought they were – in one of the houses. I thought I stood out like a Dodger fan at a Reds game on their home turf. But no one seemed to pay us much mind. A short, small boned very black man whacked a teenager across the cheek. The boy lurched back. He was twice the man's size, three times his weight. The boy looked frightened. He dropped the 25" TV he was holding.

"You don't steal," the man said.

"It ain't stealin'. They's Ko-reans."

"Don't matter. Stealin's wrong."

"Ev'erbody's doin' it."

Whack. The man slapped the boy again. He looked at the TV. "If that TV's broken, you gonna pay for it."

"Fuck that shit." The boy spun on his heel, walked off – toward the main drag. The man stood watching. Trembling.

The boy strutted towards us. Tiny and I took up the whole sidewalk. The boy didn't care. He headed straight for us. He wasn't about to step off the sidewalk either. He barged into us. Right into Tiny's uplifted forearm. A forearm that looked like it was reinforced with steel.

"Honky pig," he said to me as he pitched backwards from Tiny's arm. I didn't mind a good fight now and then, but down here the odds just didn't seem to favor it. I was about to say something when Tiny spoke:

"Seems this boy's colorblind. Boy, the arm that hit you is black. Black as the night sky. Ain't white." Tiny was back into his tough-guy mode.

The boy stood up. Glared at Tiny. At me. "Why you bringin' a cracker fuck down here, Tiny."

"Listen, Maurice, why you gotta dis yo' daddy?"

"I ain't dissin' no one. I thought he'd be proud havin' a big TV like that."

"He would be proud. But he be proud if you earn it for him. Not if you steal it."

"Ever'one's doin' it."

"Don't make it right."

Maurice fixed his gaze on me. His eyes were narrow slits, his pupils tiny bullets – aimed at me.

"'s his fault. All this shit's his fault."

"What'chu talkin' 'bout?"

"What'chu doin' bringin' the man down here?" Maurice turned to me again: "What'chu doin' here, white man? Come to see all the bad niggers? See why they shoudda never let us off the plantation?" He spit at my feet. "I ain't no slave no more."

"None of us are. That was over 'hundred years ago."

"He keeps us down. He–"

"He don' do shit. You keep yo'self down. Nobody does it to you but you."

"She-it." Maurice went around us, heading for the boulevard.

Tiny turned to me, "Used to be a good kid. Got in with the gangs. He doesn't dis me though."

"You in a gang?" I said.

"Used to. I got out. I'm a lucky one." Tiny resumed the march up the street. "Hey, man, what's your name?"

"Everyone calls me Duke."

"Like in Duke Wayne?"

"Exactly."

"Well, everyone calls me Tiny. My real name's Tee-won. Sounds Ko-rean, doesn't it?" We laughed. "It doesn't mean anything. I guess my mama and daddy just thought it sounded good. That was before we had all these problems with the Koreans. I guess they wouldn't have known it sounded anything, one way or the other." He coughed. The smoke was heading our way. "Duke your given name?"

"No." It blurted out. I didn't like talking about my real name. And down here I thought it would only make things worse. I was waiting. It came:

"What is? Your real name that is."

I would have given anything for a gang fight at that moment. We were the only people on the street now so there was no one to rescue me. I tried to ignore him, pretend I didn't hear the question. It was no use.

"Must be a pretty bad one," he said. "Can't be as bad as Tee-won though."

"Marion. It's Marion."

His eyes sparkled and a big grin rode across his wide face. "I was wrong. That's pretty bad."

An explosion in the distance. A plume of smoke hit the sky.

"They don't realize that they're only wrecking their own backyard. One of the first things my daddy taught me was never to piss in the wind and don't shit in your own backyard. Problem is, too many of 'em just don't have daddies," he said wistfully. He stopped, turned up a walk. "Here we are, Teddie's family's house."

The house was a Craftsman bungalow. It had a low-pitched roof, a stone fireplace that was also seen from the outside, exposed struts and a wide porch. It wasn't big. It wasn't small either. Comfortable might have been the word. It looked almost rural with its magnolia trees, shrubs and wood and stone exterior. Looked like a nice place to grow up. In fact, the whole street was clean and well tended except for the graffiti and broken glass. I assumed the broken glass was from that day. I hoped it was.

We walked up the walk. Someone moved about inside. The door opened. A woman in her fifties stood behind a screen door. She wore a flowered house dress and slippers. Her hair was in a bun. Her eyes were splotchy, red. She'd been crying.

"Hello, Tiny." She forced a smile. We walked up the steps to the porch. Her face was striking, very angular, high cheekbones, smooth caramel-colored skin. The housedress was on the frumpy side. Under it was a slender figure that still looked pretty good. "Won't you come in? I'd ask you to sit on the porch – I used to love to sit on the porch and swing – but the smoke is so thick I think it's better inside."

We followed her in, past the swinging love seat. We sat on a well used but comfortable sofa. The room was dark. The shades drawn down to within half an inch of the window sill. The floors were hardwood. Highly polished. Throw rugs were scattered about. The mantle was filled with photographs, Teddie, Warren, other children, teens and adults I didn't recognize. An antique coffee table was in front of the sofa. Mrs. Matson poured us all iced tea. It had an odd taste. A good odd taste. As if there were raspberries mixed in with it. It went down easy on my parched throat.

"Mrs. Matson, this is my friend Duke."

"Pleased to meet you."

"Same here, Mrs. Matson." We shook hands. Her grip was firm.

"Forgive the way I look. I haven't been feeling too well lately. Just sort of staying home and keeping to myself so I don't get much dressed up."

Of course she was staying home mourning because her daughter had been killed – murdered. And I fired the bullet. If not in reality, real enough for me. I wasn't about to tell her or Tiny that reality. I was the fuckup.

"Isn't it terrible what's happening outside?"

"Yes, ma'am." Tiny said. He seemed deferential towards her.

She talked about the riot, the kids rushing back and forth earlier, empty-handed one way, full of goodies coming back.

"This isn't such a bad neighborhood. We got nice homes and yards. Can even afford a new TV every once in a while. I don't see why they got to go crazy. The Rodney King verdict isn't no excuse to be crazy. If they only knew what things were like before. Thirty years ago. If they only knew how far we come. Maybe we ain't there yet, ain't where we wanna be, but nothing happens overnight."

"They'd call you an Uncle Tom, Auntie Tom for talking like that."

"My own son thinks I'm a Tom. Makes me cry." She sniffled, wiped her nose with a tissue. "I'm sorry. What brings you two gentlemen here today?"

"Duke's been wanting to meet you. He got stuck at my place, waylaid is more like it. Car annihilated. But he was looking for you. I didn't know if I should bring him, but I figured for all his trouble, maybe I should."

"Yes."

"It's about your daughter, Mrs. Matson."

She stifled a cry.

"I'm terribly sorry about what happened to her." More sorry than she would ever know. "I'm a private detective. I've been hired to help track down her killer."

I waited a moment while Mrs. Matson gathered herself together. It was painful to watch. Watching any mother mourn the loss of a child would have been painful. This was a lance through my gut. If I could have traded places with Teddie, I would have. Gladly. I would have done anything. I was doing what I could.

"Who are you working for?"

The guillotine blade was dropping. "I'd like to tell you, Mrs. Matson. But I can't. I know it sounds corny as all get out, you've seen it on TV over and over, but it's client privilege. All I can say is it's someone close to her."

"From the studio?"

"It's someone she worked with."

"Then they do care. I thought the studio wasn't going to do anything. She gave so much to them, and I know she was paid for it, but it seemed like after the funeral, after the flowers and all that they didn't care anymore." Her smile brightened the entire dark room. What I'd told her was a lie. As far as I knew the studio didn't give a shit. It made her feel better though and that was enough. Now I'd never tell her the truth. "What can I do for you, Mr. Duke?" It wasn't worth correcting her.

I proffered my I.D. wallet. Showed her that I was truly a licensed private detective. "We believe the man was a fan, a deranged fan. I thought maybe if you have any fan letters that I could look at. Other correspondence. It might give me a lead."

The tears welled up in her eyes again. "The police were here. They also asked about the fan letters. They're so busy though. It's just another case to them. To you too?"

"No ma'am. It's the only case I'm working right now. I can give it my full time."

She got up, went to an ornately carved chest. "I gave the police all her letters I had here and they took what was in her apartment. But I got my lawyer to have them photocopy all the letters so I could keep the originals. The police already checked them for fingerprints." She opened the chest. It was filled with letters, from top to bottom, side to side. "These are all to Teddie."

The pile was intimidating and black here and there with fingerprint powder..

"You can sit at the breakfast table and go through them if you like."

"I'd appreciate that. Before I do though, can you tell me, do you know if she got any calls or if there's someone from her past that might have been more, um, interested in her than she might have realized."

Mrs. Matson thought a moment. "She was always getting calls. She had an unlisted number. Somehow people would find it out. I even took a couple calls for her here."

"Did they leave a name? Phone number."

"No. I wish they would have. Even if they did I would have thrown it out by now."

"Well, thank you. I think I would like to go through these."

She showed me to the breakfast table. It was beautiful. Inlaid wood in lighter and darker shades. Flower pattern. The kind of piece about which you'd say "they don't make 'em like that anymore." There was a faux Tiffany shade on the lamp over the table. The letters were neatly bundled and rubber banded together. I started with the most recent bundle, figuring the Weasel was probably in touch with her right before he came to me. He had to tell her how much he loved her. How he'd sacrifice for her. Do anything for her. And, of course, how much she loved him. How they were meant to be. I lost myself in the piles.

Tiny fell asleep on the couch in the living room. I don't know what happened to Mrs. Matson. I hadn't seen her for at least an hour when the back door swung open. If Maurice had stared bullets in my direction, Warren was staring missiles.

"What're you doin' here?"

I stood up.

"Get outta my mother's house."

"She invited me in."

"You musta deceived her. What she want with you?"

"Listen pal–"

"–I ain't your pal. An' don't be dissin' me."

"Listen Warren, I'm trying to help."

"I want you out of here."

"I'm not leaving. Unless your mother asks me to go."

He looked at the piles of letters sitting on the table. Grabbed one. "This's my sister's stuff. Pers'nal."

"Yeah, real personal. Fan mail."

"Well you got no right to be lookin' at it."

"Listen, man, what's your problem? I haven't done anything to you? Where'd you get that chip on your shoulder?"

He stormed out the kitchen door. I went back to the piles.

A few minutes later, the door burst open again. Two young black men charged in. Low rider pants, prison style. Unlaced tennis shoes, also adapted from prison garb. Backwards Raiders caps. Tats up and down their arms. Bangers from top to bottom. Two angry young black men. Two angry young black men with guns. I had already reached for my gun. It was a standoff. There was noise in the front of the house. Seconds later, Warren and Maurice marched Tiny into the breakfast nook at gunpoint. They'd already relieved him of his revolver. He didn't look any too happy about it either.

They shoved him in a corner, forced him down into a chair. Sweat beaded on his forehead. I took that to mean that he knew these guys would use their guns, especially today.

Where the hell was Mrs. Matson? I still had my gun in my hand. Maurice put a short-barreled Uzi to Tiny's throbbing temple.

"Gimme the gun," Warren said to me, "or Maurice'll blow this niggah's fat head off."

"Don't do it," Tiny said. "Don't give in to these hardhead punks."

I took a step back. Eyeing down the barrel of the Firestar.

"You boys should–"

"Don' lecture me. I don't need no lectures from Mr. White-man."

Maurice jacked the bolt on the Uzi. Short barreled Uzis were illegal, even before the ban on certain semi-auto rifles. I guess these guys didn't know the law. Maurice jammed the gun into Tiny's temple. The raw metal bit his skin, blood trickled down. Maurice smiled. There was a bit of the sadist in him. I put my pistol on the table. One of the others snatched it – slapped it across my cheek. Blood dribbled from me. I didn't fall though. Held my ground.

Warren approached.

"What's your name, boy?"

"Duke."

"Got a last name?"

"Rogers."

"Duke Rogers. Man, we got royalty in this house to-day."

CHAPTER 10

Warren shoved me into the corner, knocking several clusters of envelopes to the floor, started rifling my pockets. Didn't come up with much. My wallet. Extra pistol mag. Spiral pad and pen. Some change. He looked disappointed. He opened the wallet, checked my I.D. Both my driver's license and P.I. license are in the proper name Marion, not Duke. If he noticed he didn't say anything. He forgot to frisk me, missed my boot knife.

With my training in hand-to-hand combat and martial arts, I thought I might be able to fight my way out of there. Might get hurt in the process, but hell, I might have gotten hurt anyway. Problem was, I didn't want to endanger Tiny. He was big and he looked tough, but looks can be deceiving. Some of the toughest guys I know are some of the smallest. And vice versa. He had, of course, clotheslined Maurice, so he might be okay in a fight.

Warren grabbed my gun from his buddy, buried its nose in my ribs. Jammed it in. Twisting and turning it.

"Why'n't we prone him out?" his buddy said.

Maurice grinned. "Why don't we prone out this mother-fuckah white niggah? Shit, he can't help bein' white," he waved the Uzi in my direction, turned back to Tiny: "this niggah can." The muzzle of the Uzi whipped across Tiny's face leaving a trail of blood. The big man didn't make a sound. Hardly flinched. He didn't need to say anything. His eyes said it all, burning with contempt. Indignation. Maurice saw the anger in Tiny's eyes. Shoved the barrel of the Uzi in Tiny's mouth. He gagged. Maurice liked that. He drove the Uzi in deeper, down Tiny's throat. Blood oozed out the corner's of his mouth.

Warren had me backed into the corner, my own pistol tickling my ribs. I was biding time. Waiting for the right moment. Time was running out. Maurice was ready to play. Chomping to get out of the starting gate.

"Now tell me who you workin' for?" Warren said. "Tell me now, tell it all, tell it clean or I'll let my friend there rip into yo' friend Tiny. An' when that Jew-zi's done with him, he'll be like his name, *tiny* strips-a flesh hangin' out to dry." Warren and his cuzzes laughed.

"Different sense of humor down here," I said.

"Different sense of everything. Now tell me."

"In your mother's house. You'd–"

"Don't lecture me, white boy. I've had enough lectures to fill a lifetime."

There was no point arguing with him. Tiny must have done that in the past to no avail. He was into his speech, into an almost trance-like state of mind, ready to reel off all the indignities that had been done him by the white man. Ready to make me pay.

I was ready to kill him.

Warren was left handed. I'm a righty. I was primed to thrash him in the neck with my left, seize the pistol with my right. Failing that, I'd reach for my knife. As he prattled on, Maurice smirked, gouging the Uzi deeper into Tiny's throat. Tiny kept gagging. Blood and saliva foamed around his mouth. The other two watched. A voice broke into the room like an ice breaker smashing through the Arctic. Everyone stopped. Turned.

Standing at the back door, hands on her hips, was Mrs. Matson. "I can't believe what I'm seeing. I just can't believe it."

Warren let the gun drop to the floor. Maurice eased off of Tiny. The other two boys lowered their heads. Mrs. Matson took two steps deeper into the room. She glared at each of them in turn. She walked to Maurice. He didn't move. She put a weathered brown hand on top of the Uzi, stepped between Maurice and Tiny. Removed Maurice's hand from the gun. He stepped back. Tiny reached up to take the weapon. She gently pulled it from his mouth. She held onto it; he dropped his hands. Raised them again to wipe his mouth. His breath was short and raspy.

"This thing loaded?" she said, grasping the Uzi. "I'm sure it is. You boys don't play with toy guns no more."

"Listen, mother–"

"No, you listen to me, these men are my guests and this is my house. You got a problem with that? 'Cause if you do you can find your own place to live. And the rest of you. I know all your mothers. Do you think they'd be proud of you? Do you think this is what they want for you? Do you think–"

"This dude's got no business here."

"If I say he got business here, he got business here. I don't want to have to say it again."

"First Teddie, now you," Warren said.

"What'chu talkin' 'bout, boy."

"Sellin' your soul to the white man. Sellin' your soul to be white."

Slap. The sound reverberated in the small kitchen and breakfast nook. Must've stung Warren pretty bad. He winced. Tried not to show it. It showed.

"I'm black and I'm proud. I'm also proud to be an American. Maybe there's problems, but you got a nice house. You never wanted for anything, you–"

"My people want."

"My people. My people. What do you know about your people? What have you struggled? What have you–"

Before she finished, Warren was out the door. His three *cuzzes* followed. Mrs. Matson did not give up the Uzi. She laid the gun on the breakfast table, went over to Tiny to see how he was doing. I dropped the magazine from the Uzi, and ejected the shell from the chamber. Put my pistol back in my belt holster.

"I'm sorry," she was saying to Tiny. He couldn't talk. Was still gagging. Spitting blood. I was about to try to help him when the back door opened again. I spun 'round on my heels, reaching for the Firestar. The safety was off. It was aiming at the back door when she walked through.

For a split second, I thought maybe Warren had done more to me than I'd realized. Maybe I was dead, dreaming. The young woman in the doorway was stunning. A stunning beauty and a stunning twin for Teddie Matson. Same eyes. Same smile and glowing caramel skin.

Tiny spit up blood, said with almost a smile: "Looks like you seen a ghost."

It might have been in bad taste any other time. Now it was a good tension breaker. Mrs. Matson laughed, then Tiny. Then me. Only the vision in the doorway didn't laugh. She was late to the party. Didn't know what was going on. We laughed for over a minute, that uncontrollable laughter where you've forgotten why you're laughing in the first place, but the laughing is self-contagious. And self-perpetuating. You're laughing because you're laughing.

"What's going on? I just saw Warren, Maurice and a couple others charge out of here like they're on their way to a–"

"–riot." Tiny finished the sentence for her, laughing even harder. Spitting up more blood and sucking down air with a wheeze. He stood up, wobbly.

"We need to get you to the hospital."

"I'm okay." He waved us off with his hands.

The woman in the door still wasn't laughing, but the other three of us began all over again. The young woman saw the Uzi on the table. The gun in my hand. The blood at Tiny's mouth. What must she have been thinking? All of that horror and there we were, laughing like naughty kids at the back of the classroom.

"This is my daughter LaRita Matson. I'm sorry, I've forgotten your name in all the excitement."

"Duke. Duke Rogers."

"People just call me Rita."

"Rita." We shook hands. Hers was soft and smooth. The opposite of her mother's hard, crisp hands. She was Teddie's older sister – twenty-nine. Teddie had been twenty-six. I had never seen Teddie in person, but from her pictures, I figured they were both about the same size, petite, same coloring, same soft hair. She had full lips and perfect teeth. She could've been a star too. I wondered what she did.

"What's going on here?" Rita asked, explaining she had been at work when the rioting began and they'd let her go early. She had made her way through the flying bottles, rocks, bullets and flaming cocktails and had gotten to her mother's safely. Mrs. Matson told Rita why Tiny and I were there. Explained that while I was looking at the letters in the kitchen and Tiny was sleeping on the couch, she had seen some neighbors out front and gone to talk with them, then had joined them for coffee in one of their houses.

She left the room. There was an uneasy silence between Tiny, Rita and me. Mrs. Matson returned with a bottle of Listerine, poured some in a glass full strength and asked, no ordered, Tiny to gargle with it to kill the germs from the gun. Tiny did as he was told.

"We better get you to the hospital, just to be sure," Mrs. Matson said.

"I don't need no hospital." He had trouble getting the words out. Each movement of his mouth looked measured. Painful.

"You know you won't win with her," Rita said.

Tiny nodded. His head began to loll. Mrs. Matson and I caught him, eased him back into the chair.

"Rita, if you and Mr. Rogers would be so kind as to drive Tiny to the hospital. Then loan him your car so he can get back to his neighborhood."

Rita didn't seem to like that idea, but she didn't say anything. At least not about that. "Which hospital?"

"MLK."

Having just sat Tiny down, we helped him up. I wanted to ask Mrs. Matson if I could take some of the letters home with me. Read them and return them. It seemed inappropriate with Tiny the way he was. We took him outside and laid him in the backseat of Rita's dark gray Dodge Shadow. It was a small backseat and the car was only a two-door. It was decided that I'd ride up front with the gun in case there was trouble on the way. It was no easy task getting Tiny into the small backseat.

As we pulled down the driveway, Warren slammed a fist into the passenger side of Rita's car. He leaned in, glaring at us. Nothing needed to be said. He knew where we were taking Tiny. He didn't approve. Didn't seem to approve of much of anything. I was sure he didn't like a *honky mothuh-fucker* driving with his sister. Might even be dangerous, if there were others like him about – and there were – by the bushel.

He leaned into my window. "You will never understand. Never."

Rita drove off. I rode shotgun, literally.

CHAPTER 11

The night Rita Matson and I took Tiny to the hospital, Laurie Hoffman came home to find a letter tucked in her front door. Not in her mailbox. Jammed between the door and the molding. One way or another she knew it was junkmail, she told me later. Either some company advertising a product or service she didn't need. Or a man – a man named Gary Craylock – also advertising goods and services she didn't need, didn't want and would have preferred to forget about all together.

She debated whether or not to open it. Whether or not to call me again, or another detective. Or the police. She took it into her living room, set it on the glass-topped coffee table. She turned on the television and watched the riot news. Fires everywhere. Gunshots. The conflict heading north and west, out of South Central, towards Hollywood and West Los Angeles. Even Beverly Hills. Scary. She'd never owned a gun. Never even held one. Didn't know how to use one. She wished she knew now. Wished she had one. Was it for the looters or for Gary Craylock that she wished it? She didn't know. Maybe both, she thought. But guns were out of bounds. Even if she could buy one that night, she'd have to wait two weeks to pick it up. That was no good.

Laurie went to all four windows in the living room, closing them, dropping blinds, closing the slats tightly, hoping no air, let alone light would escape them. She did the same for the rest of the small house. The phone rang. A jagged sound startling her. She was afraid to pick it up. Afraid it was Craylock. She had left the answering machine off when she went to work because the day before Craylock had called several times, filling up the entire sixty minute tape. Some of the messages were short, not sweet: "Just calling to see if you're home." "Just calling to see if you got home safely." "Just calling to see if we might have dinner tonight."

Others were long dissertations on this and that. Mostly on how much he loved her. How the hell could he love me, she asked me later, when he didn't even know me? That's why she was afraid to open the letter. She knew it was from him. There was no return address. No stamp. It was thick. For a minute she almost thought she could see his greasy fingerprints on the envelope. She imagined him sitting in his house, under a small desk lamp throwing off yellowish light, writing feverishly. Making sure every word was perfect, every letter perfectly formed. He was obsessed. She was scared.

The riots didn't help.

Every channel she turned to: fire engines screaming, smoke rising, choppers hovering, people running. She turned off the TV. Sirens still wailed all over the place, choppers crisscrossed the skies. Anne Tyler's *Dinner at the Homesick Restaurant* sat open on the coffee table next to the letter. It was a good book. Not what she wanted to read right now.

The phone continued to ring. It had to be him. She unplugged it. She thought it wasn't a good night to unplug the phone. She didn't feel she had a choice.

The walls seemed to grow closer together. The room was hot with the windows closed. It was funny, the neighbors were probably terrified by the riots, and here she was more terrified by one man than the mass violence going on around her. Should she go outside, see what the neighbors thought, what they were doing to protect themselves? She decided not to. They didn't know each other. Didn't give a damn about each other; as long as your avocado tree wasn't hanging into my yard, no problem. Typical L.A. neighborhood of the '90s.

Laurie checked the kitchen door. Locked. She opened a drawer, stared at the steak knives. Too small. Opened another drawer. The carving knives, butcher knives. More like it. Butterflies raced through her stomach. She placed a hand on the wooden handle of a knife she'd held a thousand times. It felt different. She felt different. She wasn't pulling it out to carve a roast. She didn't want to think about why she felt the need to keep it nearby. A foolish feeling passed through her. She was overreacting. Craylock wouldn't come over. Wouldn't break in. The riots were far enough away. She put the knife back in the drawer.

As long as the electricity didn't go out, she felt she'd be okay. She had a flashlight in her earthquake kit and was pretty sure she'd kept updating the batteries for it. She pulled the kit out of the hall closet. Set it near the coffee table in the living room. Stared at the letter again. What harm could a letter do? It wasn't a letter bomb, she hoped. She thought she was being paranoid. Crazy. It wasn't like her. She was a down to earth, logical person. She picked up the letter. Hefted it in her left hand. Then the right. She tore open the end and pulled out the contents.

The top sheet was a letter that began: "I dreamt about you last night. All night long. Ever since we met, you are the only vision in my dreams. A vision of beauty. Of loveliness. Sincerity and hope. And I do sincerely hope that we'll be together for the longest time. The longest time is eternity."

That frightened her. She stopped reading. Her hand trembled slightly. She let the top two pages fall to the floor. Below them were pen and ink drawings. He wasn't a bad artist. She saw herself in the woman's face in the various pictures. His in the man's. That made it even more frightening. One was of a wedding cake. The bride and groom on top – you guessed it. Another was of Gary and Laurie in bed. Fully clothed. Staring amorously into each other's eyes. There was one of them on the beach, another in front of a Vegas style wedding chapel. They made her gag. She crumpled the wad and threw it to the floor.

There was a noise outside. Sounded like footsteps. Was she being paranoid? Was it one of the neighbors checking things out? The rioting and looting hadn't spread to her neighborhood yet. Was it now? She went back to the kitchen for the butcher knife. Picked out the one with the largest blade. Made sure it was sharp. It was. She was good about those things. She plugged in the kitchen phone. It wasn't ringing. Helicopters and sirens wailed in the distance. People hunkered behind their doors. And she was alone. All alone.

She picked up the receiver, relieved to hear a dial tone. She dialed her mother. The line was busy. Who could she call? She called my office. Left a message on the answering machine. Asked me to call as soon as possible. I was incommunicado at the moment, making sure Tiny would get some kind of care in the damn hospital. She started to call a couple of friends. Put the phone down when she heard another noise outside.

From previous experience, she knew the blinds weren't light-tight. They gave her a certain amount of privacy. Still, if the lights inside were on, people outside could tell. The living room was quiet and she hoped her shadow couldn't be seen moving around from the outside. She sat on the floor in the center of the room.

There was a knock on the door. She jumped, letting out a little gasp. Her hand shot to her mouth in an automatic response to stifle herself. She clutched the knife and shifted to a prone position on the floor.

The knocking continued. Louder. Persistent. It had to be him. Looters don't knock. It might have been a neighbor, checking on her. The neighbors didn't care. No. It had to be him.

Her heart fluttered, racing along. Beads of sweat broke out on her forehead, her back. She ran her finger across the blade of the knife. She almost cut herself.

She chided herself for worrying too much. He hadn't actually done anything to her. Hadn't threatened her. The pictures were hardly obscene. He was just obsessed with her. Her mother thought she should be happy. She thought her mother was crazy. Her best friend, Sue, thought she was making too big a deal out of it when she had told her about the earlier incidents. What would Sue think now? Where was Sue now? Was she okay? No time for that. She had to worry about herself.

"Laurie, are you in there?" Him. Her hands shook as she flattened herself as flush with the floor as she possibly could.

"Laurie, it's Gary. With all this rioting going on I wanted to see if you were okay. Your car's at the end of the driveway, but maybe you're with friends or neighbors. Are you in there? Let me know. I'm worried. I care about you."

She didn't know what to do. He seemed genuinely concerned. He was also crazy. She decided to stay flat on the floor. She wanted to turn the lights off. That would have been a giveaway. She hoped he'd leave soon.

He went around to the kitchen door. Knocked again. It sounded like he was trying the windows. God please. No! It was impossible to meld with the floor any further. That didn't stop her from trying.

"Laurie, if you're in there, open the door. I want to protect you. I love you. Don't be scared. It's only me."

He sounded like they'd known each other for ages, instead of having only been on one date together. He sounded like she'd reciprocated his feelings. She never had. That date had been okay, barely. There was no need to see him again. How did he get this idea that he loved her – and that she loved him back? It was crazy. He was crazy.

She crawled to the still-unplugged living room phone. Plugged it back in, dialed 9-1-1. The line was busy. She hit the redial button. Still busy. What good was a restraining order? She couldn't get through to the police. Even if she could have gotten through that night, they probably had other things to do.

"Laurie, I don't know if you're in there. I'll sit in my car for a while to make sure nothing happens."

Footsteps padded away. She crawled to the window, peeked under the blinds. He got in his car, rested his head against the headrest. She crawled back to the center of the room, lay on her back, staring at the ceiling. Wide eyed, for hours.

At 5:30 the next morning, the footsteps came back to the front door. "Laurie, I have to go home and shower for work. You didn't come home. Maybe you're in there, maybe not. I have to go. I'll call you later. Things shouldn't be so bad in the daylight." He started to walk off. Walked back. "I love you."

The footsteps receded again. She crawled to the window and looked out under the blinds. Watched him drive off. Her heart finally began to return to its normal rate. She was tired, but wired on adrenaline. She waited a few minutes. When he didn't return she went out the front door to get the morning paper. There was an audio cassette on the mat. A red rose was attached to it. She picked it up, looked at it, a compilation Beatles album: *Love Songs*.

CHAPTER 12

The streets were on fire. If I was a user – drug user – this would have been the worst bad trip of my life. It was anyway. We raced through Dante's inferno. Demons appearing on all sides of us. My pistol was in my lap, ready. Was I? That was the real question.

Geysers of flame shot up on all sides of Martin Luther King Hospital. It was almost pretty. Almost. It wasn't almost hot – it was blistering. We were all coughing. Rita and I started to pull Tiny from the backseat. It wasn't easy. We had to roll him this way and that to get him out of the car. He tried to help as best he could. He wasn't doing well, having trouble breathing, not from the smoke but from the damage the Uzi jammed down his throat did. We finally got him out, standing between us, and walked him into the emergency room. You'd have thought the Dodgers and Giants were in the playoffs. We had to take a ticket. A nurse practitioner went around triaging the incoming patients. She looked down Tiny's throat, took his pulse. He was stuck somewhere in the middle, after the gunshot, knife and burn victims, before the broken fingers. He signaled us to leave. We didn't want to.

"It's best if you do leave. He'll be all right," the nurse said. Her arm swept across the no-longer sterile hospital hall. Now it was a mass of bloody brown, black and white bodies.

"What do you want to do?" Rita said.

"Let's stay."

Tiny looked up, forced a smile, still having trouble breathing.

"You really must go," said the nurse. "We don't have room for any extraneous people."

Tiny tried to talk, squeaked out: "Go on. I'll be okay. I'm feelin' better now." His voice was weak. He looked around, scanning the hall. Was he checking to see if Maurice was there? "All these people–" He put his hand out for me to shake. I did. But we didn't go. Until he had seen the doctor and been assigned a bed.

"We'll check up on you," I said as he was being wheeled down the hall.

"Take care of yourselves. It's murder out there." This time he wrote instead of trying to talk. He leaned his head back against the pillow.

Rita and I walked a gauntlet of crying mothers, screaming babies, hurting men and boys, out of the hospital to her car. Her car wasn't dark gray anymore. A thin mist of light gray ash covered it. She opened the trunk, took a spray bottle with blue liquid in it and a roll of paper towels and cleaned the front and rear windows. Even in this mess, she didn't litter, throwing the used paper towels in a small plastic bag in the back seat.

Traffic moved slowly along Compton Avenue. There weren't many cars out. Everyone drove cautiously. No one wanted to antagonize another driver and get blown away for no good reason. Hell, why should this night be different from any other in the Big Orange? City of Angels. City of Dreams. And like most dreams this one was going up in smoke.

We were silent. The tension wasn't between us. It was outside, a steady stream of ash and smoke, sirens and thudding choppers. Bangers banging, people running. Looters looting. Anarchy. I think neither of us knew just what to say. Rita started to laugh.

"I don't even know where I'm heading. I'm taking you home, right?"

"You don't have to."

"Mama said I should loan you my car. If you don't mind, I'd rather just drive you there so I can have access to it."

"I don't mind. But if you just get me out of this area, I can make my way home."

"Am I heading in the right direction?"

She was heading north. I nodded.

"Of course. North and west."

The better L.A. neighborhoods were north and west of South Central. I didn't know if she was being snide or just stating a fact. White people – most of them – lived north and west. Plain and simple.

"How do you know Tiny?" I said, trying to change the subject.

"He's a friend of the family, grew up in the same neighborhood."

People ran in front of us, causing Rita to slam on the brakes more than once. And more than once they were carrying TVs, VCRs, anything they could get their hands on. One couple had a six foot tall refrigerator they were moving across the street in starts and stops.

I looked across to Rita, a face of calm silhouetted by flame and smoke. It was hard to think about Teddie during the fracas in the house with Warren, Maurice and their cuzzes. Hard to think about her while we were taking Tiny to the hospital, hard to now, with the ruckus outside the Shadow – I wished it was a shadow, slipping silently and unnoticed along the street. Looking at Rita reminded me of Teddie, of why I'd been in South Central in the first place. Teddie was cute. Rita was beautiful. She definitely had it over her sister in the looks department. Why wasn't she a star?

"What do you do?"

"Huh?" She looked at me, then turned back to the road. "Oh, yeah. I'm a draftsman."

"Architect?"

"No, draftsman. The architect designs. I draw lines. Only today I do it on a computer. Some day I might go back to school, become a full-fledged Frank Lloyd Rita."

"I like that, Frank Lloyd Rita. I'll just call you Frank from now on."

"And I'll call you Johnnie."

I looked at her quizzically. She saw from the corner of her eye. "Frankie and Johnnie," she said.

It felt like flirting. I wasn't sure. In the middle of a riot that had to do largely with race, two of the major protagonists of color, black and white, were flirting. It was more surreal than the motion picture flashing by outside the car's windows.

"Should be a lot of work for you when this is over, Frankie."

"Unfortunately. This makes me very sad."

Lucy's, the taco stand at La Brea and Pico was still standing. The fires hadn't gotten that far – yet. And we were closer to home, my home. Not much traffic on the streets. Not many people about up there either.

"Are you hungry?"

"A little. But I don't think we should stop out here," she said. I gave her directions to my place from there. Keep heading north on La Brea. Turn left at Beverly Boulevard. Then it's only a few blocks and a right.

We pulled into my driveway. Everything was quiet in the immediate vicinity, except for Baron's anxious barking. There was the now ever-present sound of sirens and choppers in the distance. The smell of smoke. But my little piece of heaven seemed just fine.

The light from my security lights hit her just right through the car window. She was half in silhouette, half in the dusky light. She could have been a model. Should have.

"Would you like to come in?"

She thought about it. "I'd like to call my mother, tell her I'm okay."

"No problem, assuming the phones are working. I'll even fix you up something to eat, if I have anything to fix."

Baron greeted us, jumping on me to say hello, then on Rita, checking her out. I pulled him off.

"It's okay, I love dogs. What's his name?"

"Baron."

"Good boy. He looks like a handful to take care of."

"Hell, he takes care of me."

Her mother's line was busy, or out of order. I fixed a healthy high cholesterol meal of eggs and bacon. The pistol sat on the table next to us while we ate in silence. I wanted to talk to her. Didn't know what to say. I didn't want to talk about Warren, Teddie, Maurice or her mother. Not about her job, or mine either. I wanted to talk about us. Was it because she reminded me of Teddie? I hardly knew Rita well enough to fall for her so strongly, even if she was beautiful. I didn't know anything about Teddie either. Maybe it was just the fuckup part of me looking for trouble. I didn't know. Didn't care. What I did know was that I wanted her.

I put on the little TV in my breakfast room. Every channel had the riots. I'd figured they would. Hell was breaking out all over L.A. Maybe Rita would see it and not want to drive home. But where would she stay? No point staying in a motel. Why spend the money? Why chance driving on the streets anymore? I had a spare bedroom.

I hated myself for being so insidious. Not enough to stop:

"Pretty bad out there," I said.

"It's terrible, really terrible."

"Still can't get through to your mother?"

"No." She looked bleak. "And Warren's probably out doing who knows what?"

She dialed the phone again. It was a few minutes after 11:00 p.m. Her mother picked up. "Mama, I was worried about you. You're line's been busy." She waited while her mother talked. "Yes, I'm okay. I'm at Duke's house. Tiny's being taken care of at MLK. Yes, there were a lot of people out. Lots of fires....I'm sorry, I thought I should keep my car and drop him off home....No, we made it here in one piece, no trouble....His neighborhood's kind of quiet. At least right around us....Mama, I hardly know him....Okay." She turned to me. "She wonders if it will be safe to drive home this late."

"You're welcome to stay here." More than welcome. I had nothing nasty on my mind. I wouldn't force anything. If it happened, I wouldn't fight it either. If it didn't happen, we could stay up watching the City Fireworks Show or an old movie.

"Yes, yes, mama, that's what he said." Mrs. Matson had obviously heard my invitation.

"I have a spare bedroom. It'd be no problem."

Mama heard that too. It was settled. Rita was staying. She was worried about what she'd wear to work the next day. That was quickly gotten over.

Baron followed us as I showed her the spare bedroom. It was in the middle of the house, halfway between the front and rear. A good size. The walls were eggshell white. Levelor blinds covered the windows. A never-used desk sat in one corner. A double bed across from it. One wall was lined with bookshelves, filled with books. My library. Two windows that didn't get much light since they were on the north side of the house. Rita approved. It was comfortable enough.

She headed back, out of the room. I was blocking the doorway. She stopped, three feet in front of me. I didn't move. It was awkward. She looked at me. Didn't avoid my eyes. I looked into hers. It lasted only a fraction of a second. I backed out. She walked through. We ended up in the den, at opposite ends of the couch. The TV droned in the background. I thought about offering her one of my special lacey lemonades. Thought better of it.

It didn't feel right to make a move. She had just lost her sister. Her brother was walking around with a chip on his shoulder that someone was bound to knock off and shove in his mouth sooner or later – might even be me – and here she was in a strange man's house – a white man's house – in the middle of a major riot. I wanted to talk to her, if nothing else. Didn't know what to say.

"I'll give you some pajamas or a T-shirt to sleep in. You can also have my robe."

"I'm not sleepy."

"Who would be tonight? I don't think anyone's going to sleep well." I shifted to face her better. "I can put a tape in, comedy or something. Maybe that'll help."

"No thanks. I think I'd like to leave the news on."

"Afraid of seeing Warren?" I knew I shouldn't have said it as soon as it sprung from my mouth. I thought she'd be pissed. She wasn't.

"I do worry about him. He's so angry."

"How come you're not?"

"How do you know I'm not?"

"You don't seem to be."

"There are things that upset me, sure. Some of the same that upset Warren. But why go around being mad all the time? You just got to pick yourself up and go about your life. You can do it if you want to. I have a good job. There are still some problems, but when I hear my mother talk about how it was when she was my age, or my grandmother. I don't expect things to change overnight."

"You know what I think, I think life's hard for everybody. Doesn't matter what color."

"It is. But it's still harder for black folks."

"Maybe. Maybe not. People do make it."

"It's a struggle."

"For all of us."

"At least you're honest. The one thing that does make me mad are these white liberals who don't speak the truth about their own prejudices. They patronize. They're hypocrites. What I'd like to know is what schools do they send their kids to, public or private? I'd rather know a bigot and know where he stands for real than some of these phonies who smile to your face, then stick a knife in your back."

"You'd love my friend Jack. He says what he thinks and means what he says. Sometimes he's not such a nice guy, but he's loyal."

"Like a dog? I guess we all have a friend Jack. They're mean and nasty, but they tell the truth."

"He speaks his mind, that's for sure."

She got up. "I think I'll wash up now. Maybe try and get some sleep."

I showed her to the guest bathroom, gave her a new toothbrush, my robe and an old pair of pajamas. I hadn't slept in anything but the buff in years. "If you need anything just let me know. If not, I'll see you in the morning."

I went to my own bathroom, washed, put on a pair of old pajama bottoms. I walked through the house, turning off lights, locking doors and windows. Walking down the hall, I came to Rita's room. The door was half open. The light on. She was sitting at the desk looking through musty notebooks of my butterfly collection. I hadn't collected since I was a kid. Hadn't looked at the books since I went into the service. She saw me in the doorway. Looked up. The smile that crossed her lips was a slight one. Barely a smile at all. It was beautiful.

"Did you collect these?" she said.

I took a step inside the room. "When I was younger. I haven't looked at them in years."

"I know," she said, brushing dust off the cover. "It's hard to imagine you collecting butterflies."

"It was a phase." I was embarrassed.

"Don't be embarrassed. I used to collect them myself."

"Really?"

"What made you start?" she said.

"One of the first memories I had as a child was being in my grandmother's yard, seeing a Monarch butterfly. It flitted about. It was beautiful. I didn't know what it was. My grandmother told me."

"In L.A.? Did your grandmother live in L.A.?"

"On Fuller, near Beverly. Not too far from here."

"I haven't collected in a long time either. Maybe we can compare collections some time."

"I'd like that."

◈ ◈ ◈

It wasn't planned on either of our parts. We'd both been thinking about it. Somehow we ended up in the guest bed together. Her naked body was sleek and taut. Perfectly proportioned. It didn't seem like a one night stand to me. I wondered if that's what it was to her. Two people coming together in the midst of crisis, letting off some pent up emotion. I hoped not.

We fell asleep wrapped up in each other, a tangle of limbs. My dreams were nightmares. Back to the Inferno. I woke up in the middle of the night, sweating.

The light from the hall fell across her body in a chiaroscuro of light and dark. She woke up.

"Is anything wrong?" she said.

"Nothing, just a bad dream."

CHAPTER 13

Sun streaked the windows. It bled through the blinds casting *film noir* shadows across our naked bodies. Rita lay soft and warm next to me, taking long, quiet breaths. Baron was on the floor next to the bed, laying on his back, feet in the air. The sirens and chopper blades had died down somewhat. We had made love again, long and hot. Didn't take any precautions. In the heat of passion, you don't always do what's right. At least I don't. We didn't talk much. What was there to say?

We had the same thing for breakfast that we'd had for dinner the night before.

"Lots of variety around here."

"Heinz 57. Fifty-seven ways to cook eggs, as long as they're not runny. I do have a variation on the bacon routine. I can heat up some tortillas. You put on some mustard or hot sauce, wrap the bacon in the tortillas. And–"

"Hmm hmm good." The expression on her face didn't believe it. Hey, I'm a bachelor. We're inventive. It was better than eating Doritos all the time – or tofu. "I better shower and get out of here."

"Going where?"

"To work."

The TV droned on in the background. The city was still on fire. It didn't seem like a good day for going to work, or anywhere else for that matter.

"I think it's a good day for taking off."

She wanted to smile. Wouldn't let it show. "I still have to call them. And I want to call my mother."

While she made her calls, I showered. Got dressed. She was still on the phone with her mother when I came out. She hung up.

"How's your mother?"

"She's fine. Their street's okay. Next street over a house caught on fire."

"Molotov cocktail?"

"They think it was from flying embers."

"What about work?"

She turned away from me. I thought she was trying to hide another smile. "I have to go in."

Wrong. "Where are they, your offices?"

"On La Cienega, down near Pico."

"That's pretty close to the–"

"I know."

I turned to the TV. The sun was still ascending. The all night party was never-ending. "Don't they ever sleep?" I said.

"I suppose not." She burst out laughing.

"What is it?"

Uncontrollable laughter. She couldn't stop and she couldn't tell me what was so funny. So I started laughing too. We were almost rolling on the floor.

She fell into my arms, looked me in the eyes. Her eyes were a deep shade of chestnut. Large and clear. She may have known pain; it didn't show in her eyes. Not now. She was still laughing.

"What is it?" I said, finally, hoarse from all the gaiety.

"I don't have to go to work. I was just kidding."

I looked at her. "That's what was so funny?"

"I guess it really isn't. But it sure felt good to laugh."

That it did.

It also felt good to kiss her again. Until the back door opened. She jerked back, out of my arms. I didn't blame her for being scared. With all the shit flying, people bustin' other people, the door bursting open would make anyone jump. The man in it: slitty, squinting eyes. Stringy long blond hair. Three days unshaven beard. Six foot two of solid muscle in dirty jeans and workshirt. Jungle boots. Looked like a white trash nightmare. I almost jumped myself, except that I recognized the beast as Jack. I'd heard the roar of his Harley. Felt the house vibrate. Didn't want to break the mood with Rita, so I hadn't said anything. Baron greeted him with a sloppy kiss on his cheek. Jack wasn't a dog lover, but he liked Baron.

He had a key to my place; came and went when he felt like it. He had fierce eyes, of a color I can't describe. They were almost black in a certain light. He stood in the doorway staring. We had never talked about it, but I was sure he didn't approve of interracial romance. Unless it was a one-night stand. I wondered if it was.

I introduced Rita and Jack. They shook hands tentatively. He tossed his kit bag on the table. He carried it with him all the time. I guess he thought he had to be prepared for Armageddon. I guess he was right.

We sat at the breakfast table, the TV still droning. I was worried about what Jack would say. He had definite opinions about the riot, I was sure. He had them about everything else.

He pierced the set with his eyes. Watching intently. Then it came:

"This is all crazy. Damn looters should be shot on sight. No questions. No second chances. No chances to cry how oppressed they are. Hell, next thing you know they'll be inviting gang bangers to the White House."

He looked at Rita. What was he thinking? I would have given the proverbial anything to know.

What was she thinking?

He looked at her. At me. Back to her. She squirmed. I was uncomfortable. He was never uncomfortable.

"Hey, don't get me wrong. It's not a race thing. Don't matter if they're white. Looters should be shot."

That didn't help.

"But you know what I just don't get. The system worked. The four cops were tried, by a jury of their peers. They got justice. I mean, what do these people want? A jury of junkies and homos? Bangers. That ain't a jury of their peers. We don't know all what went on in the trial. We don't know. And King, man, he was stoned on something. A stone-ass criminal to boot. And if you watch the entire tape, he got up. He charged the cops. I know what I wouldda done in their situation. And ol' Rodney King Cole wouldn't be here to talk about it today. Someone charges me. One of us dies. Doesn't matter which one. But one of us eats the cheese. They got justice. What else do they want?"

Rita didn't say anything. She didn't avert her eyes. Didn't shift position. But she didn't respond. I thought the beating had gone too far, but I agreed with Jack in part. If King had come toward me, what would I have done in the heat of the moment? I might have gone crazy and killed him. The cops didn't do that.

Jack and Warren were opposite sides of the same coin. I was in the middle, I hoped. But it was a hard balancing act. I wondered where Rita fit. She loved Warren, even with his positions and attitude. And I loved Jack.

"I guess you guys don't have opinions," he said. It was a challenge. He was looking for a fight. Rita knew it too.

"Oh we got 'em, least I do," she said. He glared at her, challenging. "What's going on out on the streets is wrong. What happened to King is wrong. Cops do treat blacks differently. I wonder what would have happened if he was white."

"I'll tell you what would've happened if I was the cop. I wouldda killed him. Color don't matter. He's not special 'cause he's black. Another guy wouldn't be special 'cause he's white. Someone comes after me, I–"

"You really think he went after the cops."

"Hell, he was tased twice. Didn't go down. All he had to do was lie down on the ground."

"He should have. I'll admit that. Still, the cops went too far."

"Maybe," Jack said. That was victory enough for Rita.

He turned to me: "Hey, buddy, I only came to see if the house was still here. I called last night, but no one answered, no answering machine. Nothing."

"Yeah, I forgot to turn it on. Must've slept like a log."

Jack panned from me to Rita. His look said, "Yeah, right. Slept."

I had purposely left the machine off, turned the bells on the phones off. I wanted privacy.

A sly grin formed at the corners of Jack's mouth. "Hey, he play k.d. lang for you?"

I had.

"I think so. I think it was her."

Jack snorted a laugh. "Well, I hope it's not contagious." He got up, headed for the door. "Don't forget, don't you dare capitalize her initials or name. It ain't PC."

"Where're you going?"

"You know what they say, two's company, three don't fit with family values. Besides, some of us have to work."

Work, I thought. Jack worked about every third day. He was an antiques refinisher. Could have made a good living at it if he put more effort into it. It was more important for him to be able to ride his Harley up and down the coast. Come and go as he pleased. On leaving the Navy, he promised himself he'd never work a nine to five job. He never did.

"Today?"

"Yup."

He grabbed his kit bag and was gone.

"Don't let him bother you," I said to Rita as we cleared the breakfast plates. "He'd give his life for you."

"For you. I'm not so sure about me."

"He'd give it for you too. I'd bet my own life on it. But he has a certain way of looking at the world."

"We all do. I have a friend just like him. If he knew I'd slept with a white man last night he'd slit my throat."

"What would he do to me?"

"Nothing."

"Nothing?"

"You're not a black woman."

After breakfast, we didn't know what to do with ourselves. It wasn't a great day for doing the touristy spots. We went back to bed.

◈ ◈ ◈

We lay in bed, wrapped in each other's arms. No TV. k.d. lang spilling from the five disc CD player, which had speaker outlets in almost every room.

"Why doesn't Jack like her?"

"She's a lesbian."

"I bet he'd give his life for her," she said with a mocking smile. Was she baiting me?

"I believe he would." I really did. "But that doesn't mean he has to support her lifestyle."

"Oh, he's one of those 'I-may-not-agree-with-you-but-I'll-fight-to-the-death-for-your-right-to-say-anything' guys."

"You got it." I sat up.

"What's wrong?"

"I think I'm feeling guilty."

"Guilty – for sleeping with a black woman?" There was a hint of seriousness under her joking demeanor.

"Guilty that I should be pursuing Teddie's case."

"Today?"

"Yeah, even today."

"Can you tell me who you're working for?"

Was that the only reason she'd slept with me? There were so many things to consider. So many layers. So many possible ulterior motives. For both of us.

"I can't. You know that." And I couldn't tell her where the guilt really came from. "You wanna go down to my office with me? I want to make sure it hasn't been broken into, check the mail. Then we can go to lunch."

"How far away is it?"

"Not far. Over on Beverly."

She agreed to go. I fed Baron on the way out. We talked about Teddie on the way there. She had been a normal little girl. Closer in age to Warren. Had helped to bring him up. Liked dolls and baseball as a kid. Outgrew the dolls, not the baseball. She decided to become an actress when an Englishman had brought a rag tag group of actors to her junior high school and put on a play of Shakespeare's. Then he did workshops with the students, where they did Romeo and Juliet. Instead of the Montagues and Capulets, the warring *families* were the Crips and Bloods. That was Teddie's introduction to acting. She had a small part in the play, but longed to be Juliet.

I told Rita about going to Teddie's after the murder, seeing Warren. His attitude, which she knew quite well. About heading down to Tiny's, reading Teddie's letters, which, I informed her, I still wanted to do. I told her I had come across a possible suspect I was calling the Weasel – I didn't tell her how. I described the Weasel to her. She didn't have much to add about who he might have been. Rita and Teddie hadn't been close since they were kids because of the age difference. While Rita had been away at college Teddie and Warren had gotten closer. He'd be the one who might know something.

There wasn't much traffic on the streets. Some looters along La Brea. Police were out now. No sign of the National Guard. Not in this area. Not yet.

No problem finding a parking place in front of the office. I didn't bother putting a quarter in the meter. It was an older two story building. Stunning red brick, with leaded glass windows. At golden hour, when the light falls just right, it looks like something out of Edward Hopper.

My office was on the second floor. The mail hadn't come yet. There was an urgent message from Laurie Hoffman on the answering machine. She wasn't home when I called her back. We called the hospital. The nurse said Tiny was in good condition but his throat was swollen from having the gun stuck in it. She wanted to know who'd done it. Tiny wouldn't tell and neither would we. He wouldn't be allowed to talk for a couple of days she told us. They were keeping him there for observation. She'd relay our message.

We started to leave the office to go and get some lunch. As we were leaving, we ran into Laurie on the stairs. There were dark circles under her eyes. She was fidgety. We went back to the office.

CHAPTER 14

Back in the office, I introduced Laurie and Rita.

"Are you Mr. Rogers' secretary?" Laurie asked innocently. Rita chose to ignore her. I intervened, escorting Laurie into the private office, while Rita waited out front. I closed the door.

"I need your help, Mr. Rogers."

I gazed out the window. Smoke and ash rose from all points south. The symphony of sirens and choppers continued from all directions. The city was on fire. I felt like Nero. It's not that I didn't care about Laurie Hoffman's problems. I cared more about finding Teddie's killer. I owed her and her family that much. I also cared about what was happening to my home town. And had no idea what I could do about it. Yet here was this woman in need. She looked like she hadn't slept in days, and I didn't really want to help her. More important things on my mind.

I suggested she call Kevin Tracy, another good private detective. I started to write his name on a piece of paper.

"Please, Mr. Rogers. I can't go calling every detective in the book. I know you're busy, but can't you just check into it for me."

"I'm not sure what there is to check into. I can take a photo of your stalker coming within a hundred feet of your house so you can possibly have a judge throw the guy in jail."

She looked like she had something to say. She didn't want to say it. What was she afraid of? She finally spoke: "Maybe you could, uh, talk to him." She said *talk* to him; she didn't mean with my mouth. She might have meant with fists or a club. I didn't think she meant I should let my trigger finger do the walking or talking. "I'll pay you double your rate. Just go and talk to him one time, let him know that I'm not in this alone."

One silky leg crossed the other. Was she really uncomfortable or was she shifting to give me a better view? To entice me? Or was I being totally sexist by even thinking it? It didn't matter. I decided to talk to the guy for her. If I could help her that might be a little payback for Teddie too.

"I'll talk to him, one time. At my normal rate. I charge by the day, one day minimum."

"Agreed." A wave of relief washed over her face. The muscles around her eyes and mouth unknotted. A hint of a sparkle flashed across her hazel green eyes. She was pretty. I guessed her age to be mid-thirties, a very attractive mid-thirties. She'd lost ten years in ten minutes.

She handed me a piece of paper with Gary Craylock's name, address and phone number already written on it. She had come prepared. I smiled at her, trying to let her know that it would be all right. It wasn't easy. It didn't come immediately. She smiled back. I felt good knowing that I might be able to help her.

"I have to be honest with you," I said, feeling good to be honest with someone, "but I don't know how the riot will affect things. I'll try to get to him today or tomorrow. I don't make any promises. This mess throws everything out of kilter. If he harasses you, call me." I handed her my card. "If I'm not in, I'll get back to you as soon as possible. Also fill out this contract and make sure both your work and home addresses are correct. Also in the 'other' section at the bottom, put down your normal home, work and other activity hours. I know it seems like prying–"

"Hardly. I'll be happy for someone to know my whereabouts. Someone besides him. All my friends think I'm crazy, making too much out of nothing. Some even think I should be flattered." She looked me in the eyes. "I was at first. It wore off quickly."

"I imagine it would."

◈ ◈ ◈

It dawned on me after she left that I didn't have a car to get around in. We had come to the office in Rita's car. I hardly knew her well enough to ask to borrow it. She took me to a car rental place. I rented the cheapest car they had available, a fire engine red Toyota Corolla, and hoped that it wouldn't get damaged in the riot. Normally, I wouldn't have bought the extra insurance the rental companies offer. I did that day.

Some places were closed, others open. It was real hit and miss. El Coyote was open. Rita and I met there for lunch after she took me to get the car. It wasn't very crowded.

"This way, senor," the hostess said. She wore a multicolored dress of green, white and red. The skirt billowed out for miles in every direction. We were seated in the No Smoking section. Chips and salsa were brought. We dipped in. I could tell the salsa was too hot for Rita. I liked it that way.

Awkward. Neither of us knew what to say to the other. We'd spent a night of heat and passion in the middle of a night of heat and passion in the larger city. She was black. I was white. Blacks were pulling whites out of cars and beating on them for no reason other than that they were white. If certain of her friends or family knew, they might have beat on me. If one friend of mine in particular knew, he might look at me differently from then on. And he knew. If people saw us driving together, they might pull us both out of the car and put a brick, or worse, through our heads. It was the best of times, it was the shittiest of times.

Was it the heat of the moment that brought us together intimately and lustfully, just as the heat of the moment had led to our initial meeting at Rita's mom's house? Or was there more? I wanted to know. Was afraid to ask. I wondered what she was thinking. What the people in the restaurant around us thought of this *zebra-striped* couple. Did they notice? I was sure they did, especially today. Did they care? I didn't know.

"What're you thinking?" she said, not looking at me.

"Will the city still be here tomorrow?"

"The question is, will the National Guard be here tomorrow?" she said. It was a good question. The Guard had been delayed. The police didn't have enough manpower and seemed to lack a plan. It was a damned good question. But it wasn't what I was thinking about.

"What will you do the rest of the day?"

"Guess I'll try and work the case."

"Did that woman we met on the stairs hire you?"

"Yeah, but it's a quick job. Some dude's stalking her. Just gotta put the fear of God – or someone – in him."

"I imagine you could do that quite well."

I wasn't sure if it was a compliment or not. "What about you? What'll you do?" I was hoping she'd say she wanted to stay with me. Of course, I hadn't said that I wanted to spend the afternoon with her, so it was probably asking too much. Maybe we were both scared.

"I need to check on my mom. See if she's all right. Then I want to check on my apartment."

"I'd like to come by your mom's again, look at those letters."

"I don't think today's a good day."

"No, you're probably right." I had fucked myself, for a change. I didn't know if I'd ever see her again. At least socially. I knew I might run into her at her mother's. We never did order food.

◈ ◈ ◈

Craylock's house was in Rancho Park, on Tennessee, a block west of the Twentieth Century-Fox studios. It was an expensive one story Spanish job, not unlike my own house. A new jet black BMW sat in the driveway. Pickup car, I thought. She hadn't mentioned what he did for a living; it must have been something where he could charge people more than he was worth, Hollywood. A doctor. Plumber maybe.

The riots hadn't stretched this far west, yet. It was a good neighborhood, if there was still such a thing in L.A. I used to live only a couple blocks from Craylock's before I moved back into my folks' house. The first street north of Pico. The Olympic Marathon runners had run down Pico just across the alley behind my apartment. I watched from my breakfast area window. It was a different L.A. then. It wasn't that long ago.

I walked to Craylock's front door. Rang the bell. A pretty-boy handsome man in his late thirties or early forties answered. His dark hair was slicked back, the way Tyrone Power used to wear his. I guess the fashion had returned. He wore a polo shirt with an alligator, naturally. Dockers pants and Gucci loafers. Dressed to kill. I perished the thought.

"Gary Craylock?"

"Yes."

"Laurie Hoffman asked me to come see you."

His eyes lit up at her name, but he still blocked the doorway. I didn't want to go inside anyway. I thought it best to keep things formal and let him know I wasn't his pal. I stood my ground.

"Ms. Hoffman–"

"–Ms. Hoffman. Laurie."

"Ms. Hoffman asked me to ask you to leave her alone." The lighthouse in his eyes began to flicker. "She doesn't want you coming by her house, leaving her notes, calling her. She doesn't want you showing up at her work or any other place she might be." The beacon died. He did a tactical retreat in his head. I could almost see the wheels spinning.

"You can't mean Laurie. My Laurie."

"Listen, pal, she isn't your Laurie. She doesn't want to be. Lay off. Stay away. I can't make it any plainer."

"Or what? Maybe I should call the police. You're threatening me."

I was threatening him.

"Go ahead. But I think they might have better things to do today."

He knew they did. Besides, he didn't need the police on his tail. I'd tell them about Laurie. About the restraining order. He may have been a pest. He didn't appear to be an idiot.

"There's already a restraining order in place. You could be in a lot of trouble."

"Don't threaten me. I don't like being threatened." His voice quivered. He was nervous. He knew he didn't have a leg to stand on. Had to save face. It was a pretty face, too. One I'd just as soon have punched in the nose as looked at. I didn't know the S.O.B. Didn't need to. I knew the type. God's gift to women. Hell, God's gift to the world. Everyone should like him. Especially if he liked them. And get out of the way if they didn't return it.

It wasn't that he really thought he was so wonderful. It was that he doubted it. Doubting yourself can make you crazy. Make you look for love and reassurance and respect in every quarter. When you don't get it, you get pissed. Maybe punch someone out. Maybe yell at strangers on the freeway. Maybe yell at the people closest to you and push them away. Maybe if you're crazy enough you go into a McDonald's or a schoolroom and open fire with a semi-auto rifle.

I knew all about wanting respect from every quarter.

CHAPTER 15

I left Craylock standing in his doorway. He had the forlorn look of a lost puppy. I went home. Tried calling my insurance company about the Firebird. Constant busy signal. Played catch with Baron a while. I threw a tennis ball across the yard, Baron fetched it. When he was tired of the game, he gnawed on the ball. He went through five or six balls a week. Maybe one a day. I crashed on the raft in the pool. Baron crashed next to the pool, after a short swim. Sun glared down at me through the smoky haze. Ugly. Angry. Squinting. Me. It.

The water was cool. The raft cut through a layer of gray ash on the water's surface. No dragonflies. Dead? Scared off by the smoke? Siren bleat. Music. L.A. in the '90s. Wasn't the town I grew up in. Wasn't the town anyone grew up in.

Get on with it. I had a case to solve. A client to please. The worst client in the world – me. Where to turn? I needed to see those letters again. Timing wasn't right to go to South Central. I didn't know if I could get down there with the National Guard arriving and the police staking out turf. The roads might have been closed. Wanted to see Rita again. Warren was another story. I didn't think he could hurt me. I didn't want to hurt him. If it came to it, I knew I would. Thought of Tiny. Call him when I get out of the pool.

Stainless steel jabbed into the raft's cupholder. Better than mountain spring water on a brisk L.A.

spring day like today. Seven rounds in the mag. One in the chamber. Wet and wild. California funtime. Will a gun work after it's been in the water? Ask the SEALs.

Leads. None. Nothing. *Nada* – there's a '90s L.A. word for you. Hip. Flip. Hip Hop.

Where to turn? Letters. The William Tell Motel. Weasel. Grinning. Like he's about to drool spit. Paid me cash. Paid the motel cash.

Why the William Tell? Did he know it? Did he like the overture? Like the Lone Ranger? Chance? Significance? Nothing came to mind.

The Perlmans. Maybe the old lady would remember something else. Maybe she wasn't telling all to begin with.

Damn riot. Cramps my style. Already too much time lost on Teddie's case. Trail getting colder with each passing day. Nothing like a riot to make a Weasel's day. Drool dribbling, must be laughing to himself.

Black chicks? That his gig? Black movie stars? TV stars? Check into it. See if any other good looking black actresses got harassed. Scary letters. Calls. Followed. If that doesn't work spread the search wide.

Go back to Mama Matson's. Those letters. The only tangible piece of anything so far; hardly enough to warrant calling it evidence.

Sun glaring. Squinting.

Drive by shooters laughing at silly boys and girls playing in the street.

How stupid of them.

Crack.

It wasn't meant for you.

For your older brother.

Bang.

You're dead.

My little girl was killed–

My sister raped.

Mother shot.
Father strongarmed, robbed.
Son murdered.
Spanish.
Korean.
Chinese. How many dialects?
Japanese.
Tagalog.
Polish.
Yiddish.
Street jive. A language to itself. Only for the initiated.
English?
Tears streaming.
Hate burning.
Getting a hamburger is an exercise in survival.
Driving – forget it.
Armed. Better be.
Fear.
Anxiety.
Alarm.
Panic.
Terror.
Frenzy.
Hysteria.
Rampage.
Riot.

Riot.

Chaos.
Confusion.
Commotion.
Pandemonium.
Mayhem.
Anarchy.

Riot.

*Never Never Land: Kids who'll never grow up. Lost
to a bullet. Lost to a gang. Lost to themselves.*

Scared?
Scared shitless. Scared to death–
L.A. for the '90s. La La Land.
California dreamin'.

◈ ◈ ◈

"Murder City U.S.A.," Jack said after I told him
about my dream. "Animals. They're all fuckin' animals.
I don't care what the fucking bleeding hearts say. These
people are responsible for themselves. Hell, half of 'em
don't even belong here. Goddamn illegal aliens."

The dream: a kaleidoscope of images. Flashes.
Light. Dark. Brown. Yellow. White. Black. Missing
blue. Heart pounding, sweating dream. Shouldn't have
told Jack. Had to tell someone. He popped by. Harley
lullaby charging down the driveway, waking me not so
gently. Do not go gently into that good night. I
promised myself I wouldn't.

"Segue." I wasn't in the mood. Teddie filled my
waking dreams, if not the sleeping ones.

I told Jack about my lack of leads while I got
dressed.

"Brown babes. Don't forget the brown babes.
They're not a subgenre of black. They're separate
entities. Coconuts. Not Oreos."

"Shut up."

"These fucks are burning your hometown down.
Don't you care?"

"I care about finding this girl's killer."

"Hey, bud, if you're so damn sensitive you better get it right. She ain't a girl. She's a woman. Don't wanna be politically incorrect."

"Sometimes you give me a pain in the–"

"Sometimes I save your ass blind."

Touché. I had no comeback for that. Sometimes he did.

We had roast beef sandwiches for lunch. The meat was deli-cut thin, the bagels onion, a couple days old. I thought about asking him how come he ate bagels. What was the point? Mustard oozed out the sides of his bagel.

"I heard 'bout this Mex actress." Nothing else came. He chomped on his sandwich.

"Yeah, so."

"So lemme eat, will ya?" He spooned more mustard on the edge of the sandwich. A bright yellow moustache instantly grew on his upper lip. A Chia moustache. Just add water. "I heard 'bout this Mex bitch, or to be politically correct, *puta*. Got her ass whupped good."

"I don't remember hearing about anything like that."

"Was hushed up. I don't remember why."

"What show was she in?"

"Don't remember."

"You're a big help."

"Hey, man, I don't need the sarcasm. I'm tryin' to help you. Mighta been a small story on some back page of the Times. About a year or two ago. Check it out. All I remember is she wanted some part, it was going to a Caucasian. She protested, along with a bunch-a her sisters. I mean, hell, acting's acting right? So any actress should be able to play the part. But no, they gotta make a stink."

"Get to the point."

"She got beat one night after the protest. That's all I remember. 'Bout a year ago. Maybe longer."

A few minutes later, a plume of gunmetal gray smoke belched out of the Harley lullaby machine, wafting skyward, joining the ever-present smog and riot smoke.

Would the libraries be open? A phone call would have sufficed. I was itchy. Had to get outta there. Hopped in the car and went to the John C. Freemont branch. Open. I searched the L.A. Times on microfilm. What a pain. Checked all of '91. Nothing. Should I go back as far as '90? What else did I have to do?

The library was closing early. I had about an hour left. I didn't have that much patience. I had started with December of '91, working my way backwards. I was at July. About to give up. Something caught my eye.

A photo. An actress. Kind of cute. Dark skinned. Originally from Mexico City. A fan had tried to get close to her. Too close. He was in love with her. He thought she was in love with him.

Coincidence?

How'd he find her? Found her family. Told them he was an old friend?

Sound familiar?

Coincidence?

Probably an M.O. used by a lot of Weasels. Could it be my Weasel?

Another article a month or so later, which I'd missed the first time around, said she'd split town. No trace. No trace of the suspect either. A white male. No firm description. But about my Weasel's age?

Coincidence?

CHAPTER 16

The girl's family wasn't hard to trace. East L.A. I could hit El Tepeyac on the way home. By the time I got there I figured there wouldn't be a line half way around the block. I drove across the Macy Street bridge, over the L.A. River. It was like going to another country. Thinking like that made me think of Jack. I didn't want to think like him. Sometimes I couldn't help it. Signs were in Spanish and English, some not even in English. Street vendors sold tacos, not hot dogs, Jalisco, not Good Humor ice cream. All that's not what got me. The streets were filthy. Trash everywhere. Empty garbage cans. Trash piled up under bus stop benches, solid. Graffiti on the walls, dirt and litter, everywhere.

It didn't matter then though. What did matter was getting through roadblocks and not getting my rental car or myself smashed. It wasn't as hard as I'd figured. The National Guard still wasn't fully deployed. Most of the rioting was happening farther south and farther west.

I pulled up in front of a ticky-tacky house on Folsom Street. Parked. A couple punks eyeballed me. I glanced their way, went about my business. Headed to the door. Small white frame house. Paint peeling in places. Overall in pretty good shape. New Honda Accord in the driveway. Knock-knock.

A small man opened the door. Henna colored skin, sagging at the edges. Small white moustache. Zinc gray hair. Half moons under his eyes you could drop a penny into and it wouldn't fall. Baggy brown pants, cuffs. Yellow, viscous eyes. Huaraches. Looked like he was just off the farm. Looked old. Tired.

"Yes," he said. No trace of accent. I felt foolish for thinking he looked like a recent arrival.

"My name's Duke Rogers. I want to talk to Pilar Cruz's family."

"Who are you?" Teary eyes. Because of the smoke and smog? Because of what I asked?

"I'm a private detective. I'm looking–" I handed him my card.

"–For Pilar's attacker?"

"No, I'm sorry."

"For Pilar herself? Someone has hired you to find her."

"No. She's only peripherally involved."

He peered around me. "Your car?"

I nodded.

"Be careful. Damn *pachucos*'ll take everything but the car alarm if you're not careful," he said using the argot of his day.

"Why don't they just take the whole car?"

"They'll do that too. Pull it into my driveway."

After I did, he invited me into the house. He had just fixed lunch. Invited me to join him. We sat in the kitchen, eating chorizo and beans. Fresh salsa with cilantro. Homemade. I wouldn't be stopping at El Tepeyac on the way home.

"Eat. *Mas*?"

He reminded me of my grandmother. He reminded me of all grandmothers.

"Pilar was my daughter. I am Ben Cruz."

I stopped chewing. He saw.

"You are thinking I look old. How does this old man have such a lovely young daughter? I am not that old, *senor*. I am older than my years. Losing my daughter, losing my wife, that will do it to you."

I didn't know what to say. I had some feeling for his loss. Not much. I didn't know him. Didn't know his wife or daughter. What do you say in a situation like this? "I'm sorry."

"The police don't care. She's Mexican. They put her case in some file cabinet or computer somewhere. Low priority. They don't care. You're the first person's come around here asking me about her in over a year. At first there were a few fans. They came by – I don't know how they knew where to find me – or they sent cards. She could have made it big."

Teddie Matson had made it big and was on the road to making it bigger. It was no protection for her. It might have been her downfall, along with me.

"I'm trying to find the man who killed Teddie Matson."

"A terrible thing. Similar to the attack on Pilar."

"That's what I was thinking. I was wondering if there was anything you could tell me. Anything at all that might help me in my search. You said that some fans came by after she left."

"Yes. There was a handful."

"Who were they?"

"Some were from a Latina actress group. They wanted to find her. Help her. I couldn't help them. I didn't know where she went myself. They didn't believe me. After a couple of visits they gave up."

"Anyone else?"

"There were a couple of young men that came by. Maybe three or four. It is hard to remember."

"You've got to try. Tell me about them. Were any of them white?"

"Two were Mexicans. I think the other two were white."

I asked him to describe the white ones to me. One of them sounded like he might fit the Weasel's description. "Do you have any idea how to find them? Did they leave anything?"

"I will give you everything. She was not a very big star. Not a star at all. She had a couple of bit parts on TV and did a couple plays. She was known in the Hispanic community more than the general community."

He led me to her bedroom. A Mexican flag hung over the bed, Mexican pottery and a brightly colored shawl decorated the dresser. He pulled a small box, little bigger than a shoebox, from under the bed. Put it in my hands.

"Take it."

I hesitated.

"You wonder, how I can trust you? I don't know you. Maybe you are the one who attacked her. Maybe you had cards printed saying you are private detective."

I didn't say anything. I was too busy thinking that, while I had nothing to do with Pilar's attack, I might just as well have been the one who attacked and killed Teddie.

"You have an open, honest face. But that is not why I am willing to trust you with these things. I do not think you are the attacker. He would be nervous. You are not. Maybe you are a very good actor. I don't think so. So maybe you will find Teddie Matson's killer. And maybe along the way you will look for and find my Pilar. I have some money I can give you." He reached for his wallet.

"Later." I would look. I wouldn't take his money. I didn't tell him then. I would if I found anything.

"And you tell her to come home. It is not me she is hiding from. I will protect her." He sat on the edge of the bed. Didn't care if I saw him weeping openly.

"Do you have any idea where she might be? An old girlfriend she might have gone to stay with. Anything?"

He kept weeping as he pulled another box from under the bed. This one was bigger. Stuffed to the gills with letters and cards. "These are her personal mails, from friends, not fans. Maybe there is something in there. I read through everything after she left but couldn't come up with anything. I called her friends. They didn't know anything or wouldn't tell." He went to her desk, opened the center drawer, pulled out a small address book. Handed it to me. "These are her friends. Her best friend Anna Martinez."

"Boyfriend?"

"No good punk. *Se llama* Ramon Martinez."

"Related to Anna?"

"*Si, her brother.*"

I left Cruz in Pilar's bedroom. Found my own way out. The punks were waiting for me in Cruz's driveway.

"Get lost, *amigo?*" One of them grinned, a gold frame sparkling around one tooth.

"You need a sunburn to be in this neighborhood."

"Who writes your dialogue? You need a rewrite man."

"Very funny. Very funny."

Tom Bond, my buddy in the L.A. Sheriff's, had more occasion than I to come down to this part of town. He said these kids would just as soon kill you as look at you. These two didn't have weapons showing. I thought I saw a bulge in one of their waistbands. That's what flashed my brain at that moment.

"What'chu doin' here, man? Lookin' for some dark meat?" They laughed.

"Don' white boys like white meat?" Gold frame leaned on my car.

"Get off my car. Get outta my way."

"Tough guy."

"It ain't no time to be doin' your thing here, man. You're outnumbered. Might be only two of us here, but everywhere you turn you gonna see people look like us."

"I don't give a shit what you look like. Get off my car." I stepped toward the driver's door. Gold frame didn't budge. I pushed him aside. His *amigo* dove for my knees. I was ready, lurching out of the way. My own leg came up kneeing the diver in the nose. He careened back into the car, sliding to the pavement. Blood spilled from his nose. Pivoting on my heel, I heard the unmistakable racking of an automatic slide. Turned to face down a blue steel 9mm semi auto.

"What now, *gringo*? Might be your country, but it's my street. My gun." He was only a couple feet away from me and he was in love with his tough talk. While he savored the words, I swung my foot high. High enough to broadside his face – hard. It shook him up. He didn't drop the gun, until I rammed my finger into his eye. That did the trick. I stuck the gun in my belt. I'd get rid of it later, where no one would ever find it.

"Tell the ACLU you were just an innocent victim." I got in the car. Drove off. I wondered if he'd slap me with a suit. I thought I was sounding more like Jack than ever.

◈ ◈ ◈

Drove by Craylock's on the way home. Not sure why. It wasn't on the way. A thought zapped me, Craylock a stalker. I wondered if the Weasel was a stalker, not just a celebrity stalker, but a plain-old-brown-paper-bag-vanilla-flavored stalker. Thought I might call Tom Bond, check out stalkers.

Knocked on Craylock's door. Not happy to see me.

"Get the fuck outta here. I'll get a restraining order on you."

I strongarmed him into the foyer of his house. I hadn't seen the inside before. Crummy art on the wall. Streaks of paint, mostly black, white, gray – how politically incorrect, where's brown, black, red, yellow? – that didn't make any sense. Ponderous. Someone like Craylock figures he doesn't understand it, it must, therefore, be meaningful.

"Whadda you want?"

"I want to talk."

"About what?"

"Stalking."

CHAPTER 17

I started through the entry hall toward the living room or den. He cut me off, steering me toward the kitchen. Expensive tastes. Real hard wood cabinets. None of that paste on stuff. Newly tiled counters it looked like. Hazy sun streaks shot in through a window box filled with green stuff. A mini herb and vegetable garden right there in the kitchen. He motioned for me to sit at the counter that divided the kitchen from the breakfast room. I chose to stand. So did he. A siren whizzed by outside. The first one I'd heard in a long time, say about five minutes.

He offered me orange juice. He started: "I'm not a stalker."

"Some people have other opinions."

"Some people lead people on. I may be in love, but I'm no stalker. I'm just a romantic guy, like to make my woman feel special." He smiled a slight smile, trying to be friendly. Trying to disarm me. I wasn't about to be disarmed. "Laurie and I are friends."

Yeah, right. Friends.

"If you're friends, why don't you leave her alone when she wants to be left alone?"

"She doesn't want to be left alone."

"That's not the way I hear it."

"She's playing hard to get."

I was trying to figure out how to get direct answers to questions about stalking. But it was impossible. He was smitten. In his mind, she was playing hard to get. He wouldn't take no for an answer.

"We're friends."

"You think that by giving her gifts you can win her?"

"I would never buy a woman's love, or interest. I give them to her to show my affection."

Affection? Affectation.

"How'd you meet her?" I knew the answer. I wanted his version.

"I answered her personal ad in the back of Los Angeles Magazine."

I never could understand people placing those ads. Every man is an intellectual hunk with a good sense of humor. Hung, no doubt. Every woman is into long walks on the beach, reading, and gorgeous. Hung up, no doubt. There should be truth in advertising laws about personal ads.

Was he dangerous? The kitchen didn't seem to have anything unusual about it. Carving knife set. Everybody has one. I started through the breakfast room to the dining room, hoping to get to the rest of the house. He cut me off again. It wasn't the time to push it.

"I should call the cops on you. But I'm fascinated."

"Guess I'm not the usual stiff you hang with."

"Definitely not. Much more unpolished. More real."

"Thanks. I wouldn't wanna hang with the automatons you hang with."

"Oh, I don't hang with anyone in particular. I'm a self-starter."

"Loner."

"Not a word I prefer."

But a good word to describe you. And maybe the Weasel. That limited the possibilities.

"Besides, why do I need friends when I have Laurie?"

Fantasy Island. Goof's living in a parallel universe.

There was a glint in his eyes. A tiny speck of light, sparkling at the inside corners. Hard to tell if it was coming from the sun or somewhere inside him. Made him look demoniac. Possessed. Which I was sure he was, if not by the Devil then by devils within himself.

He started toward me. I wheeled aside, ready. He went past me to the sink. Rinsed his glass.

"Are you done psychoanalyzing me now?"

"Sure, I'll bill you."

He didn't laugh. Didn't crack a smile. The glint in his eyes grew steely. "I'm not used to being a guinea pig."

You smell like one. I didn't tell him. I wanted to see the rest of his crib. Figured I'd do it when he wasn't there. Might be of some interest. Tell me more about the Weasel. I could've strongarmed the goof. Probably wouldn't have helped me get anymore info from him. Would've helped me vent some bile though.

I was about to leave, turned back: "Did it ever occur to you that Laurie may not be playing a game with you? That maybe she really doesn't want you."

"You just don't understand, do you?"

What could I say to that? It was the second time in as many days that someone had said something like that to me. But he was right. I didn't understand.

◈ ◈ ◈

I cut down to Pico, heading east. Things were pretty calm down here in Rancho Park. By about Fairfax, people were running wild in the street. Party Time! *Sales* in almost every store.

Turned north on Fairfax. Traffic commotion, tie up, near Wilshire. Cars blocking the intersection. Others going around them. No one paying attention to lights.

Crash. Plate glass shattering.

Get whitey.
Get whitey.
Screams.
People rushing.
Angry black faces.
Shouting.
Mad brown faces.
Shrieks of terror.
Scared white faces
Dodging.
No cops in sight.
Squeal of brakes.
Mine.
Stop now or hit the damn car in front of me.
Nowhere to turn.
No way to get around.
Nissan 300-ZX mid intersection.
Lights change.
No one moves. Cars anyway.
People scrambling.
Woman screaming.
Dragged from car.
Help. Someone help me.
Power kick to the belly.
Grab her purse.
Rifle it.
Out of my car.
Running.
Hand on Firestar.
Two men and a woman on her.
People here and there on the sidewalk.
Looking.
Gaping.
Gawking.
No one helping.
Some cheering muggers on.

Stomp to the face.
Blood.
Glasses broken.
Moaning.
Blood.
Safety off.
No words.
Why bother.

Blam.

Blam.

Blam.

I could have shot them.
I fired over their heads.
Crowds scatter.
No cops in sight.
Three rounds off. Four to go.
Gun in right hand.
Woman in left.
Grab her license, credit cards. Keys.
Drag her back to my car.
Jam in reverse.
Bumper kiss car behind me.
Driver's startled.
Too scared to get out of his car.
Pushing him back. My tires slipping on the asphalt.
He jams it into reverse. Hits car behind him.
Everyone's trying to backup. Not a lot of room. Finally
enough for me to back up, ease car to make U turn.
Cars on other side of road. But not as bad as my
side.
Make the turn.
Got a ticket for pulling a U-ey once.

No ticket this time.
Woman coughs blood.
Rented seat. Rented rug of rented car. Bloody.
Jam it down Fairfax. Back the way I came.
Double park across street from Westside Hospital.
Pistol in belt.
Take woman with both hands.
Dodge traffic across Fairfax.
Honking at me. At my parked car.
Pull her inside hospital.
Nobody helps.
"We don't have an emergency doctor on duty. No emergency room," bitch at front desk says.
"This woman's dying."
Set her down on lobby couch.
Melodramatic. Only way to get action.
Still no response.
"Does she have insurance?"
Gun flies from belt.
Smells recently fired.
Bitch notices.
Safety still off.
Barrel jammed on receptionist's forehead.
"Best insurance in the world."
"I'I'll call a doctor."
Life during wartime.

◈ ◈ ◈

I left the woman at the hospital, a doctor looking at her. At the very least, he said, her nose was busted and she'd have to have her jaw wired. Some fun. Not only free TVs, free-for-all. I didn't hang around to tell them who I was. No need to get tied to the shooting at Fairfax and Wilshire, even if I didn't shoot anyone. Probably would have gotten off. Though you don't know these days. No need to hassle the paperwork. An

Alice In Wonderland World, where the good guys are the bad guys and the bad guys good.

I started thinking about Teddie. I felt numb. Pushed the guilt down inside, in a black hole where the rest of my guilt hid. Where the bile for my father lived. A seething reservoir inside me, waiting to explode.

I pushed down hard on the accelerator, heading farther west. There wasn't much traffic and no sign of cops. I could have gone ninety and gotten away with it.

The office was quiet. No messages. No mail. No nothing. Called Tom Bond at home. His wife said he was on duty. She was worried. I tried to calm her fears. Told her that he'd be all right. That it looked worse on TV.

I lied.

She said she'd have him call me if he called her.

I sat back in my ergonomically correct desk chair, feet on the desk. Which probably defeated the ergonomic design of the chair. Thought about Craylock and the Weasel. Teddie Matson and Pilar Cruz.

What was there to tie them all together? Both women had been in show biz. High profile targets. Even if Pilar hadn't quite made it, she had been seen. I sued someone once. Made it to *People's Court*. My Fifteen Minutes of Fame. Segment lasted all of ten minutes. People recognized me for weeks afterward. If Pilar was on a couple of commercials that aired constantly, she'd be easily recognizable, especially if someone were looking. Teddie was on a hit TV series. Millions of people all over the country would know her.

A thought hit me. What if Pilar's commercials were local? If they weren't national spots, I could narrow down the search geographically. Of course, that still didn't mean that her stalker was the same as Teddie's. It wasn't much. It was all I had.

Pulled the Firestar from my belt. Dropped the magazine and replaced it with a fresh, fully loaded one. I wouldn't have minded shooting those people, but I didn't need the paperwork. I also didn't want to be like Jack in that way. I would have felt justified in killing them, but there's still a part of you that smarts. It's never easy killing someone. Some people get used to it. Some have no conscience. Don't even have to get used to it. It's just another high.

I had brought up the box with Pilar's letters and skimmed through them. Nothing out of the ordinary. Fan mail. Puppy love sentiments. No threats. Nothing bordering on harassment. I was dying to compare notes with Teddie's fan letters. Then I might be able to make some comparisons that would be helpful. That would have to wait. I turned on the Call Forwarding on my phone so my calls would be routed to the house. Hit the stairs. Thinking:

I'd have to talk with Ramon and Anna Martinez. I wasn't looking forward to meeting them. I didn't think they'd appreciate being questioned by a white man. Especially now. But judging from some of Anna's personal correspondence with Pilar, I figured if anyone knew her whereabouts it was Anna. Their letters were deep, introspective. Intimate. Almost sexual. Ramon's notes were scribbled in a near-illegible hand. Talked of love and body parts. Of course, I didn't have Pilar's responses to them. Nor her responses to Anna. But it seemed to me that the real relationship here was not Ramon+Pilar, but Anna+Pilar. It was hard to tell if it had ever been sexually consummated. If it wasn't, I was sure it came close.

I wanted to find Pilar. Find Teddie's killer. Keep Craylock off Laurie's back.

I wanted penance. Needed it.

My first act of penance already completed: I didn't kill those scumbags when I could have and gotten away with it.

◈ ◈ ◈

Except for Baron's raucous greeting, my place was quiet when I got there. Smoke loomed in three directions. The sky was hazy. Gray. Dialed Martin Luther King Hospital. Tiny couldn't talk. The nurse said he was improving. He'd be able to talk in a day or two.

I wasn't home long when the doorbell rang. Who the hell could it be?

Rita was framed by the door. I was glad to see her. More glad than I showed. I invited her in. We collapsed into each other's arms.

CHAPTER 18

We didn't say anything. The sun was still high in the sky when we went to bed. Was it love or tension release? We glided in and out of each other in easy, smooth motions. Practiced motions. A thought shot through my mind: what was she doing here? Why had she come back? In the middle of a riot.

What was I doing here, making love – if that's what it was – to a black woman when blacks and whites were at war with each other? Were we like Teddie in her school play, Romeo and Juliet, Capulet and Montague?

Would we end up like Romeo and Juliet?

I put it out of my mind, concentrating instead on the moment. Her eyes, her lips, her skin.

Her eyes were heavy lidded. Sultry. Heat-simmered brown embers. What was she thinking? It didn't matter. We continued our cruise into the sea of *Terra Incognita*. Black heat. White heat. Until we were both spent.

My fingers gently drifted across her caramel-colored skin. Would I be making love to her if her skin was ebony? Black.

We lay wrapped in each other's arms, cradling each other tight. Holding strong against the storm raging outside. She my protection, me hers. k.d. lang singing her crystal clear voice out on the CD player, helping to muffle the outside world even more.

No riots.

No Teddie.
No Warren.
No Jack.
No Pilar.
No Laurie.
No father.
No black.
No white.

"What're you thinking?"

"I'm wondering what I'm doing here. Why I came back."

"I was wondering that too."

"Maybe it's best not to think about it," she said.

"Maybe it's best not to think about anything." I bit into her neck. She pulled away.

"I don't want to be an ostrich. I hardly know you. Hell is breaking out all over. But do I stay with my mother? Do I go to a friend's? Do I go home? No. I go to the house of a man I hardly know. A white man. Something's missing."

"You're being too analytical. Who was it who said 'don't be too profound in analyzing history, for often the causes are superficial.' Maybe you just like me."

She tried to stifle a laugh. Couldn't. "Maybe I do." This time she didn't pull away. We drew closer together, if that was possible. No kissing. No anything. Just holding each other tight.

"I like your house," she said, finally.

"It's solid."

"It's beautiful. Hardwood floors, real plaster walls. Spanish tile in the hall. Tile in the bathroom. Scrollwork along the ceiling." She knocked on the wall. "Solid? That's all you can say about it?"

"Hell, if it wasn't for my parents, I wouldn't have this house. Might even be living in a cardboard box or under a freeway offramp." I paused, stared at the walls: "This was their house."

She heard the guilt in my voice. "They're gone?"

I didn't respond. Looked away.

"I'm sorry," she said.

"Don't be. You didn't know them."

"Not very nice people, huh?"

I pulled back. Separated now by a sea of blue sheets. She sat up on one elbow, looking into my eyes.

"I guess I shouldn't be talking about that. But my father was no great shakes either. He left when I was fourteen. I was glad to see him go. Used to beat Warren to a pulp just for the fun of it. He was unhappy with his own life, his station in life – couldn't hold a job. Mom worked. Worked hard. But daddy couldn't cut it, so he took it out on poor Warren."

"Maybe that's where some of his anger comes from."

"He doesn't blame daddy."

"He blames whitey."

"Says that if the white man hadn't held us down none of it would've happened."

"Why don't you blame whitey?"

"Maybe I do." She looked at me intensely, the brown coals of her eyes challenging me.

"If you did you wouldn't be here."

There was a long silence, as if she was debating whether or not to come clean, to tell me something. Then: "What's the point of blaming anyone else? We each of us have to live our own lives. Be responsible for ourselves. No one else can be responsible for us. No one else gives a damn. I'm a black woman trying to make it in a white man's world. It's not easy. I've seen prejudice. So what should I do? Holler racist. KKK. Wait for a lynching?"

"What do you do?"

"The best damn job I can. Not because I'm black. Not because I'm trying to prove something. Because I'm me. And I have to do the best I can for me. No more. No less. And you know what?"

"What?"

"I always get by. Still, I suppose it's easier for you."

"Why, 'cause I'm white? You don't know anything about me. Nothing at all."

"Maybe more than you think."

"Nothing."

"Then why don't you tell me."

"You sit here spouting off how you don't care about this and that, about the KKK or racism and all. And then what do you come back with? 'It's easier for you.'"

"I shouldn't have said it. You're right and I'm sorry. I would like to know you better. Tell me something you never told anyone else."

It took me a while to respond. Took me a while to get the courage up, not just to say it, to admit it out loud: "I'm a fuckup," I said. "Excuse my language. No, don't excuse my language. It's what I am. Might as well call a sp–"

She laughed. So did I. We moved a little closer again. Not too close, but closer. Less ocean of blue between us.

"That's what I am, a fuckup. I've fucked up almost everything I've tried in my life."

"I've seen you. You're a hard working private detective."

"Not a very good one." I was thinking of Teddie more than anything. I didn't want to tell her. Couldn't.

"I see you working your cases – hard."

"I try."

"You make the mortgage on the house."

"Barely. Okay, I'm an okay private dick."

"You said 'almost,' you fucked up almost everything in your life."

"I didn't fuck up the Navy. In fact, I was damned good there."

"Why didn't you stay in?"

"My father. He thought I fucked up just by joining the service. Thought I could do better. Like him. Wanted me to be a businessman. But a nine-to-fiver wasn't for me."

"Your heart wasn't in it."

"Damn straight. I did spend some time after college working as an investigator for an insurance company. That's what gave me the background to become a P.I. But then I decided to go into the Navy."

"Why don't you go back to the Navy?"

"Too late now. I've lost the fire. I could never do what I was doing, at least I don't think so."

"And what was that?"

"SEAL Team. You know, join the Navy, see the world."

"Pretty heavy duty stuff. Does it help you in being a detective?"

"There's some crossover stuff and if there is any strongarming that needs getting done, I can do it."

"Before the Navy, did you have a goal?"

"*Razor's Edge*"

"What?"

"*The Razor's Edge*, I wanted to explore the world like Larry Darrell in *The Razor's Edge.*"

"Why didn't you ?"

"My dad thought it was a waste of time. I figured a good compromise was the Navy. Thought he'd think I was finally a man."

"Why'd you care so much about what he thought? Why are you rebelling so hard?"

"Nothing I ever did was right. Everything was my fault. Hell, I couldn't even go to school without a hassle. He wanted me to work for him. When I told him school was my job he beat the shit out of me." I could feel the veins in my neck sticking out, the blood rushing in my head. My tone got angrier. Louder. Couldn't control it. "But hell, he was never there when I needed him. He hated the fact that I collected butterflies."

"Can't go on blaming him forever."

There was a silence. I was thinking about the Navy. Finally said: "I liked the Navy. Did see a lot of the world. Saw a lot of shit too. I shouldda done my twenty."

"You can still see the world."

"It's not so easy. I've got the house now. Gotten used to creature comforts. I'm not twenty-one anymore."

"Who is? Then be the best damned detective you can be."

I didn't say anything. After several minutes of silence, I turned to her: "I'll tell you something I haven't told anyone, not even Jack." Another silence. Then: "My father's not dead. He's in a rest home. Alzheimers. I had to put him there two years ago." I paused, collecting myself. "I never visit him, never call. I just pay the bills."

She took me in her arms, holding me close to her breast, stroking my hair. It was comforting. Baron loped back and forth a couple feet away.

"I always hoped my father would die first. Didn't happen that way. Mom died in a car accident. Always hoped they'd get divorced. I'd lay in my bedroom and listen to them arguing at night. Bitch this and fuck that. Every bad word I knew I learned from him calling it to my mom. I'd pray they'd get divorced. They never did. And he laid the blame for everything that went wrong on me. I was the cause of all their troubles. Never took any responsibility for himself. Never even gave a thought that his temper, his perfectionism, his insecurity, might be the cause of it all. Had to blame someone else. Always. We never got along, my dad and I."

"He made you think you're a fuckup."

"What else could I believe? He was my dad."

"But that was a long time ago." She took my hand in hers. "You're not a fuckup, Duke. I know."

She pulled me closer yet, if that was possible. Didn't say anything, just let me know she was there. I made a promise to myself to be the best damned detective I could be. I made a stronger vow to get Teddie's killer, no matter what it took, including my own life.

CHAPTER 19

R ita didn't stay long. Just long enough. Soon after she left, I heard someone coming up my walk. Gun in belt, I headed outside. It was Sing, the mailman.

"Good morning, Mister Rogers," he said. Baron barked from inside the house, held back by my hand. Sing saw the gun in my waistband. His eyes narrowed, as if he was X-raying it to see if it was loaded.

"I didn't think the mail would be delivered today."

"Through sleet and snow and L.A. riot," he grinned. "Actually in some parts of city if they want mail they have go to post office. No delivery. We dedicated. Not *loco*," he said in Spanish-tinged Korean-pidgin English and laughed out loud.

"Multicultural humor," I said.

He handed me the mail, which had to be sniffed and approved by Baron. It was pretty thin. Not the usual lot of junk mail and other fun stuff. Mostly bills. I flipped through them as he walked to the next house to bring mail and mirth on a pretty mirthless day. There was one item that wasn't a bill. A plain white envelope. No return address. My address was neatly typed on it, correct down to the last zip plus four digits. I sliced it open as soon as I got inside with my downsized Ka-bar look-alike letter opener that Jack had given me. It didn't say much:

"Lay off. I know where you live. Let sleeping dogs lie. Or they will lie. You too."

That's all it said. It could have been from anyone. A former client, not all of whom were quite reputable? Someone I'd found for a client? My first thought was the Weasel. But how would he know where I lived? How would he know I was even after him? It wasn't exactly making the headlines. Next thought was Craylock. They were the two most recent cases. Neither was exactly a goody-two-shoes. I didn't give it much thought other than to tell myself I'd have a *chat* with Craylock one of these days. He hadn't been violent with Laurie yet. I doubted he'd get violent with me. And I just couldn't believe the Weasel could find me. Still, if the Weasel had found Teddie what was to say he couldn't find me?

The phone rang. I jumped half a foot into the air. Was it the riots, the threat letter? The days of rage? I didn't know. What I did know was that my nerves were on edge. A glass of straight Scotch would help that.

"Duke, Duke, Duke, Duke of Earl, Earl, Earl," the tired voice sang over the phone.

"Hey Tom when're you gonna get it right? It's Duke, Duke, Duke, Duke of Rogers, man."

Tommy tried hard to laugh. All that came out was a small choke.

"Having fun?" I said.

"Hey, the ads said the Sheriffs would be an adventure."

"Kinda like Disneyland?"

"For the young at heart. Too bad I ain't so young anymore. Jenny said you called, important."

"Could've waited till Disneyland closed. I'm on a stalker case. Couple of 'em actually. Wanted to see if you could run some stats for me."

"No problem. But you'll have to wait till the South Central Olympics're over. Computers are all tied up now and much as I'd like to help you and take some stalkers off the streets, it's low priority now."

Crack!

"What was that?" I said.

"Gunshot."

"I knew that. What's going on?"

"Gotta go. I'm at a CP, shouldn't even be on the phone. Talk to you in a couple days, if I don't get my ass shot off." He hung up. I lit out. Wasn't really sure where I was headed. Didn't have a plan. I could try to track down the Martinezes. Or I could bring Pilar's letters down to Mrs. Matson's and compare and contrast them. That's what I decided to do. The Martinezes would happen tomorrow. Maybe the riots would cool off by then. I knew the situation at the Matson's: unpleasant. But I could handle it. The Martinezes were an unknown. They would have to wait.

◈ ◈ ◈

Mrs. Matson didn't seem particularly glad to see me. She also wasn't particularly unglad. She sat me at the dining room table this time, with a glass of lemonade, and gave me the boxes of Teddie's correspondence, including the personal stuff. She hadn't seen Warren since the day before. I was just as glad about that. I had hoped that Rita might be there. She wasn't.

The ride down had been uneventful. Still, it seemed like all there was in the city anymore was smoke, sirens and some gunshots, but the police and National Guard were better organized now. It wasn't like it had been the first day of the riots.

I poured over the letters, first Pilar's box – it was smaller. Then Teddie's boxes. Anything that seemed similar to something in one of the letters to Pilar I put aside. After three or four hours, the double check pile was beginning to grow. There were about a dozen letters or cards in it. And I still had three other boxes of Teddie's to go through. My eyes were starting to blur. My temples ached. It was after curfew. I didn't think I'd have much trouble getting home. I'd tell the cops I was stuck somewhere, afraid to come out, and now that I had the chance I was heading home. There were a million things I could make up to tell them. I decided what the hell, I'll just stay the night, if Mrs. Matson would let me. I didn't ask her. I just kept working.

Lots of mash notes. Lots of hearts and flowers and "you're the one for me" stuff, from both men and women. A few gifts: some flowers, long dead, dried and rotted. Brittle to the touch and falling back to the earth, dust to dust style, when I did touch them. Most of the flowers were roses or carnations. But there were two with what looked like orchids, one for each woman. Could they be from the same guy? And was he a big spender? I put those cards aside.

Teddie's said: "Only being with you can put out the fire in my heart. Sparks fly whenever I see you."

Pilar's, attached to a Smokey the Bear teddy bear, said: "You'll need Smokey to put out the fire when the sparks start flying between us."

Close enough for me. The signatures on each were illegible. Neither had a return address or envelope. I had a friend who did forensic work for the city on occasion. I made a note to call her, stuck these two cards and orchids in my coat pocket.

Mrs. Matson, in a flowery robe now, poked her head in: "It's late. Would you like to curl up on the couch, Mr. Rogers?"

"Maybe in a while. I think I'd like to keep working."

"I hope you find something."

"Me too."

She walked off. "Me too." She couldn't know how much. It was my atonement. Atonement for being a lousy detective. For not having my heart in my job. Not doing what I wanted to do. For not living my own life.

A few minutes later the back door flew open. Warren, gritty with sweat and ash, charged in. He looked at me from the corner of his eye as he barged past, off to some other part of the house. Not a word. Not a grunt. No kind of acknowledgement for the white devil in his dining room.

I kept at my work until I fell asleep around 3:00 a.m. I had tried to stay awake as I didn't want Warren sneaking up on me. He didn't. When I awoke again around seven, my gun was still on me. The letters hadn't been touched. It was only four hours' sleep. It felt wonderful.

Mrs. Matson was already in the kitchen. Glorious smells permeated the house. The smells of food that we're not supposed to eat anymore – real food: bacon, eggs, hash browns, nice and greasy. Love is the food that you put on the table. I wondered why it hadn't worked for Warren. She came into the dining room: "Breakfast's almost ready," she said.

I was more than ready. Famished. Couldn't remember the last time I had eaten. She put plates and glasses out on the breakfast room table. I set the silverware. Three places. Mrs. Matson, Warren and me. I squeezed fresh oranges in an electric juicer as she finished up the bacon, eggs and spuds. The bouquet of smells made my stomach growl something fierce. Mrs. Matson smiled at me. I smiled back sheepishly.

Everything was ready and on the table, enough to feed an army of private detectives.

"Come and get it," Mrs. Matson shouted.

Footsteps echoed throughout the house. Warren padded towards us. Mrs. Matson and I were already seated. Waiting for him before we dug in. He bounded into the room, stopping in his tracks. The expression on his face went from satisfaction to malice. His mother looked at him: "Warren, please," imploringly.

He shoved his hand deep in a pocket. Instinctively, I reached for the gun in my belt. Didn't pull it out, just let my hand rest on it. Warren's eyes smoldered with hate. For me. For himself? He charged through the room, out the back door. A thick silence hung in the air. Then:

"I'm sorry, Mrs. Matson. I'll go. He'll come back when he sees me leave." I started to get up. She laid a firm hand on my arm.

"This is not how we treat guests, Mr. Rogers. Especially guests who are trying to help us. Please sit down and enjoy your breakfast. It isn't often that I go to all this trouble. If he wants to eat he'll come back."

We ate in silence except for the sounds of silverware clinking on china plates.

"It's delicious." It was. The best breakfast I'd had in years. Filling and tasty. Not in that order.

"Thank you." It was just something for her to say. I'm sure she meant it, but her mind was in another place. I cleared the table, rinsed the dishes, put them in the dishwasher. Soft sobbing came from the next room. When it subsided, I went in.

"I'll pack everything up now and leave in a few minutes."

"You don't have to." Her eyes said otherwise. She appreciated what I was doing in trying to find her daughter's killer. Of course, she didn't know the whole truth and nothing but. She also would be just as glad to have me out of there and get her son back, if it wasn't too late. Not because of me, but because of where life had taken him.

I wondered about Warren. Where was he coming from? Why all the anger directed at me? Just a symbol of the white man? Or was there more? I hoped to see him on my way out.

Didn't take long to pack up. I took several of Teddie's letters, put everything else back the way I'd found them. Packed up Pilar's letters and took those. Mrs. Matson walked me out to my rental car.

"I won't come back. I held up a handful of Teddie's letters. I'll either mail them back or send them with Rita."

Her eyes smiled. "I thought you and Rita might be seeing each other. She didn't say. But I figured—"

I was almost ready to ask her permission. What was the point? Rita could make her own decisions. So could I.

"I'm sorry for any trouble I've caused."

"Isn't you. He's been goin' bad for a long time. Nothin' I can do about it." She put her arms around me. "If I don't see you again, I thank you from my heart for what you're doing trying to find my daughter's killer."

What could I say? Guilt stabbed at my gut. I felt nauseous. Hoped I could hold breakfast down. As I drove out toward the main drag, I scanned for Warren. No sign. I pulled into an alley and vomited my guts out. It wasn't breakfast. It was my life.

I didn't know what the Weasel had wanted the info for. Didn't even know who Teddie Matson was when he'd come to me. What was I to do? But I was also stupid. Hadn't even made the Weasel fill out the standard contract forms 'cause it seemed like such an easy cash case – no forms, no IRS report, the better to pay the mortgage or the plumber with.

My dad was right. I was a fuckup. Never took things seriously. I was paying for it now. I wasn't the only one. That was the killer.

◈ ◈ ◈

Pockets of rioting flared and exploded on the way home. It wasn't confined to South Central as the Watts riots of '65 had been. These fires engulfed large parts of the city. Ugly. Very ugly.

I waited in a long line of cars at one of the few open gas stations for a fill up. The radio blared riot news. Everyone was blaming everyone else. Mayor Bradley blamed Police Chief Gates, who blamed Bradley. The city council blamed both of them. No one took responsibility.

I was glad to pull into my driveway. Something was wrong. I could sense it. Baron's familiar greeting wasn't there. I threw it in park; jumped out before it stopped moving.

The backyard gate was locked from the inside. I jumped it. No time for the latch. No Baron. No barking. No nothing.

Heart beating double time.
Firestar in hand.
Safety off.
Why am I acting this way?
Paranoid?
Crazy?
Check Baron's favorite spots.
Behind the garage.
Nothing.
Run on the other side of the house.
Nothing.
Smell something funny.
Burnt almonds.
Silence.
Deafening, deadening silence.
Check the trashcans.
There, behind the cans.
A paw.
Bloody.

Jesus!
Baron.
Dead.
Mangled.
Slit across the throat.
Ice cream.
Smells like burnt almonds.
Cyanide.
Must've been one hell of a lot to smell up the yard.
Melted ice cream on Baron's jaw.
Cyanide laced ice cream.
Blood on his paws.
His?
His killer's?
Goddamn it.
Goddamn you God.
Do you exist?
Are you the Devil?
Evil?
Why?
Damn.
Damn.
Damn.
A note stuck into Baron's hide with a nail.
"'Let sleeping dogs lie – who wants to rouse 'em?'
—David Copperfield / C. Dickens."

CHAPTER 20

Checked out the garage first. No sign of the killer. I covered Baron with a tarp from the garage. Gun in hand, I went in the backdoor. Service porch – nothing. Kitchen. No sign he'd been there. Breakfast room, living room, den, bedrooms. Nothing. Bathrooms. *Nada*. Didn't look like he'd come into the house. I was glad of that.

He was toying with me. Teasing me. The question was, who was he? Was it a *he*? Craylock – I wouldn't put it past him. Besides, the Weasel wouldn't know the Dickens quote. Or would he? I'd underestimated him once. Shouldn't do it again.

House secure, I went to talk with the neighbors.

"Didn't see a thing," Mrs. Fraley said. "I wouldn't even be home if not for the *troubles*." If Mrs. Fraley didn't see anything, I doubted any of the other neighbors would have. She knew everything about everyone in the neighborhood. Probably knew I was shacking up with Rita. It was there in her eyes, if not on her tongue. Even when she wasn't home she had antennae out that gave her the lowdown on everyone's lives. Hers was the first house north of mine. After checking with her, I went to the Timmerman's on the south. They hadn't seen or heard anything either. Neither had anyone else.

Three fourths of the neighborhood were home due to the riots and no one had seen or heard a thing. Maybe it was the Invisible Man.

I picked up the ice cream container with a Kleenex, only touching one small part of the rim and slipped it into a plastic bag. I put it in the outside freezer, careful how I opened the door so all the bottles I was saving on top of it wouldn't topple. Grabbed a shovel from the garage and dug a hole behind it for Baron. Wrapped in the tarp, I laid him in the hole and stood over it for a few moments of silence. My eyes teared – something that didn't happen often. I loved that dog and he loved me, in a way no person ever had. I didn't know if anyone ever would. Now I had two missions: find Teddie's killer, and find Baron's.

Burying him in the yard probably wasn't legal. But I knew the response I'd get from any city authorities – can't come out. The riots. I tried a couple of vets' offices. Closed. The riots. What else could I do? I wasn't about to let him rot behind the garage until sanity returned.

I went back in the house, grabbed the gin-laced lemonade from the fridge. I needed a drink and it was the handiest thing. I picked up the phone. Dialed. It rang and rang. I was just about to hang up. Then:

"Lab."

"Yeah, hello," I said, polishing off a lacey lemonade. "Is Mary Kopeck there?"

"Not in today."

"Is she home?"

"She's out in the field."

"Today?" I didn't mean to sound surprised. It just came out that way.

"She's dedicated."

"Can you tell me where she is? I need to talk to her."

"Who is this? Is this official business?"

"It's Duke Rogers, I'm a–"

"Duke Rogers, yeah, I remember her talking about you. I guess it'd be okay. You know that last major turn before Coldwater turns down into the valley?"

"Yeah."

"There's a little arroyo on the west side of Coldwater. That's where she is."

"Thanks, I know the place."

Grabbed my keys, headed for the door. Near it, on the floor, was a chewed green tennis ball. Baron's favorite chew toy. I was about to pass it by, head out the door. Instead, I bent down. Picked it up. It was still moist from his chewing. I didn't throw it out. Set it on the hall table. I hadn't cried since I was eleven years old – since I stopped collecting butterflies. I bent my head and sobbed for the second time in an hour.

◈ ◈ ◈

Traffic was light. Not a lot of people venturing out. It took me about twenty minutes to get there. Cars were parked up and down Coldwater where cars didn't normally park. People sifted dirt in screened boxes. Others scooped at it with spoons or soft brushes. A uniformed cop stopped me.

"Are you part of the forensic team?"

"I'm here to see Mary Kopeck."

"That doesn't answer my question." He looked nervous. Itchy. Hoping for some action. Hey, the action was somewhere else today. I was the only one he'd get to have fun with. Before I could respond, Mary saw me. Saw my distress. She let me wriggle a moment longer, then came over, half eaten sandwich in hand.

"It's okay, officer. He's got big feet, but I don't think he'll mess anything up." Mary's face was covered with soot and grime, the badge of her profession. Her long brown hair was pulled into a bun on top of her head, a couple wisps dangling on each side, and buried in a funny looking green Robin Hood hat.

"Very funny," I said, as she led me to the site she was working.

"Wood rats built a nest out of twigs, leaves and bits of human bone." She took a bite of her sandwich. Crunched it gleefully. "Looks like the bums, er, excuse me, the homeless individuals that lived here had dinner one night – feasting on one of their own." She dug dirt from her fingernails. They were medium length, black top and bottom. Almost looked in fashion. When I'd first met her I asked her why she didn't keep her nails shorter. "Got to be able to pick up those bone fragments," she had said.

She showed me the charred bones and badly decomposed body of a man, flesh ripped from his arms and thighs. She turned him over for me to get a better view.

"They would have felt at home with the Donner Party."

"Passionate society we're living in. Legacy of the Sixties," she said, taking another bite of her sandwich. "No one's responsible for anything. There are no moral laws. Everything's relative."

She must have seen the look in my eyes.

"I'm sorry. I get on my soapbox every once in a while. I see too much." She sat down, so did I. She offered me a sandwich out of a cooler.

"No thanks. How can you eat with him staring up at you?"

"You get used to it. Hell, I don't even wash my hands."

I supposed if I'd had to I could do it too. But I wasn't out in the bush. Didn't need to. And I wasn't that hungry.

"What brings you out here, Duke? Slumming?"

"Someone killed my dog. Poisoned, I think."

"Baron. No. He was the greatest dog. He–"

"I–"

"I'm sorry. You must be in a lot of pain."

"Enough."

"Remember though that life goes on."

I winced.

"I know it's a corny cliché. But people talk in clichés. Keeps their lives normal." She put the sandwich down, put her arm around me. "You want me to take a look at him."

"I buried him. There was ice cream on his mouth. A half eaten container on the ground near him."

"You think that held the poison?"

"What else? Wasn't my brand of ice cream. I thought maybe you could come look at the container. I didn't bring it with me. Thought it would melt and maybe change composition." I handed her the piece of paper with the sleeping dogs message. She studied it.

"Looks like it came off a laser printer. Probably a Panasonic – the kind a lot of libraries use. But it's hard to tell here. Mind if I hang onto it."

"Go ahead."

"There's also another couple notes maybe you can look at. Another case – I think."

"Sure, I can look 'em over."

I searched my pockets. Realized I didn't bring Teddie's and Pilar's notes. "I don't have them with me." My heart started thudding harder. I could feel the blood rush through my veins. In my eagerness to get to Mary I hadn't thought to bring the evidence. I'd fucked up again.

"I can drop by after I'm done here, look at the ice cream and the notes. Sometime this evening."

I took the garage key off my ring. "If I'm not home, the container's in the outside freezer. In the garage."

"Where'll you be, out bracing the bad guy no doubt."

"No doubt. Except I don't know who the bad guy is."

I thanked her and started heading back to the road.

"I'm sorry, Duke, really sorry," her voice trailed off after me.

◈ ◈ ◈

Craylock's black Beamer wasn't in the driveway. I pulled around the corner. Walked back to his house and nonchalantly down the driveway, past a security company's sign. Alarm system. My Navy training would help here. I'd brought a set of tools from the car. It was easy to jimmy the lock on the alarm box. The system looked pretty rudimentary. As long as it wasn't a pulse system that would send a signal to the alarm company if the phone line was cut it wouldn't be a problem. It didn't appear to be that kind. He didn't want to spring for the cost. Sweat beaded on my forehead as I played with wires. Snip-snip. A done deal.

Getting inside was a cinch. I had the seen the kitchen before. Nothing new to report. Made my way through the house. Quiet. I could hear my own breathing. The blood rushing in my ears.

The living room was a sight. Photos of Laurie everywhere. Huge blowups. Some framed. Some poster sized, unframed. Laurie walking down the aisle of a market. Laurie getting into her car in the morning. Laurie sunbathing in her backyard.

Boxes of negligees from Neiman Marcus. Dresses from Robinson's. His and Hers T-shirts: Gary Loves Laurie. Laurie Loves Gary. Future gifts.

Laurie.

Laurie.

Laurie.

A shrine to Laurie Hoffman.

A frilly quill pen sat in a holder on a blotter on an antique desk in the corner. On phony parchment paper, he'd written, calligraphy style, the lyrics to *Got to Get You into My Life*, an old Beatles love song. He was in love all right. Also crazy.

Looking at his paean to Laurie made me sick. Angry. I hoped he wouldn't come home now. I didn't know what I'd do. I knew what I was capable of. I thought about turning him into the cops, but I knew they wouldn't do anything – couldn't, until Craylock made his move. And then it would be too late. It's a great system we've got.

I gently tossed the whole house, making sure to put everything back as I'd found it and keeping an ear out for a car pulling into the driveway. A thought dawned on me. I checked the freezer. No ice cream of any kind. Looked around the house for poisons. No cyanide. No insecticides that used the stuff. Didn't mean anything. He could be clever enough to hide the stuff.

One bathroom had been turned into a darkroom. Pictures of Laurie hung to dry. I pulled them down. Ripped them up. I didn't care anymore about covering my trail. I tossed the darkroom harder than I had the rest of the house. Put a match to the negatives and let them burn down to my fingers. Then tossed them on the floor. Watching all that fire glazed my eyes. Fixed me in a trance. It was cathartic. After a few seconds I stomped the fire out, but I was tempted to let it burn the whole damn house down.

The only camera I found was a Polaroid? He must have had his other camera with the telephoto lens with him. What did that mean? He was out shooting pictures of Laurie now? His true love. Thinking about it made me crazy. I wished he'd come home. Prayed for it.

My prayers were answered. A car drove up. I couldn't tell if it was in his driveway, next door or out on the street. When I heard the back door open, I knew.

Footsteps quickly padded through the house. He probably smelled smoke. I stepped behind the tub curtain in the darkroom-bathroom. The door popped open. A backhanded fist swung out from behind the curtain and busted him in the jaw. He dropped the small red fire extinguisher he'd brought to save his precious artworks. The blow jolted him back into the doorjamb. Son-of-a-bitch didn't know what hit him.

I jumped out of the tub, the shower curtain derailing around me. He tried swinging at me. It was hard for me to defend myself, wrapped in the curtain. His swings were weak. Ineffectual. He popped me in the jaw, a glancing hit. Hardly hurt. I came back at him, both fists flying. He didn't put up much of a defense. Kept falling back. Out the door, into the hall. Against the wall. I pummeled his belly. He gasped for air. Doubled over. I didn't stop. Grabbed his hair in my left hand, pulled him up. Kept pounding away. Blood trickled from his nose and the corners of his mouth.

I broke contact. He was almost smiling. I socked him in the mouth. He stopped smiling. I let him fall to the floor. He curled up, fetal-like. Got to his knees and vomited on the lush hall carpet. When he was done he sat back against the hall wall, knees to his chest. He was white. His eyes weren't focused. Hands were shaking. He was just how I wanted him: scared.

"How 'bout some dessert?" I said, yanking him down the hall, into the kitchen. Opened the freezer door as he fell to his knees. His unfocused eyes looked at me, questioning as best they could.

"What's your favorite brand of ice cream?" I landed a kick on the side of his head. He fell over. Righted himself.

"I, I don't eat ice cream. Too much cholesterol. I eat yogurt."

"What brand?"

"Dannielle's Proprietary."

That wasn't the brand of the ice cream. Not that it mattered anyway.

"Y'you're crazy." His voice shook. Hands trembled. Fear radiated out of him. I pulled him up. Walked him to the living room, pushed him down on an uncomfortable looking chair.

"You like pets?"

He wrinkled his brow? What was this crazy man talking about now? I walked up and down his bookshelves, looking for Dickens. Or even Bartlett's.

"Pets? You like 'em?"

"Sure. They're fine."

"Dogs?"

"Yeah."

"How come you don't have one?"

"No one to take care of it. I'm out a lot. Working."

"Taking pictures of people who don't want their pictures taken. When they don't know you're doing it." I swept my hand across the room. Went to a wall. Pulled a framed 8X10 of Laurie off, crashed it to the ground. Shattering glass. He jerked back in the ugly chair.

"Whadda you want? I haven't hurt anyone."

"Leave Laurie alone." I crashed another picture to the ground.

"I'll call the cops."

"No you won't." I picked up the camera with the foot long telephoto lens on it that he'd left on the desk when he came home and smelled the fire. There was a 50mm lens in a case. I switched it with the telephoto. Snapped pictures of the room. Proof, if the cops ever asked. When the roll of film was finished, I rewound it, put it in my pocket.

"Leave Laurie alone." I slapped him across the cheek. "She's not interested in you."

"Okay. Okay." He covered his face with his hands, cowering back in the chair.

"Have you ever been arrested?"

"No."

"Tell me the truth. It's easy enough for me to find out."

"No, goddamnit. No."

"How long have you been stalking? Is Laurie your first?" Jeez, it sounded like a first date. First kiss. First lay. First stalk. Society was crumbling around me. And Nero fiddled on.

I grabbed his collar. Shook him.

"No, she's not the first one."

"How many others?"

"I'I don't know. Two. Three." He paused. Took a deep breath. "Women like me. I can't help it. They like it when I shower them with affection. It's just part of their act, playing hard to get, to pretend like they don't want it."

"When was the first one?"

"About four years ago."

"What made you do it?"

He looked at me like he didn't know what I was talking about. Do what? You could see it in his eyes.

"What makes you do it? Why do you hound these women? What about the first one?"

"Hound them?" His hands covered his face. Rubbed his temples. His eyes were red. Teary. A revelation hit him: "I'I don't know. She didn't really like me I guess. I wanted her to so bad I made it up. I believed it. It didn't seem made up to me."

"What happened?"

"She moved away."

"'Cause of you?"

"Yes, I think so." His voice shook. Reality breakthrough. The truth was hard to take.

"Why? Why do you do it?"

"I don't know." He gulped air. "I guess 'cause no one likes me." His whole face seemed to drop when he said it. Shattered. Reality infused with his dream world. He didn't like the reality.

"You know any other stalkers?"

He laughed. "What, do you think we have a society? Stalkers Anonymous?" His laughter was uncontrollable. I shoved a picture of Pilar Cruz in his face. He wiped his eyes.

"You know her?"

"Never seen her."

"Her?" I put a picture of Teddie down for him to look at. He picked it up. Held it close. Recognition crossed his eyes.

"I, I've seen her before. Movies. TV. Can't remember." He held it closer. Pulled a pair of glasses from his pocket. Looked at it again. "Didn't she get–"

"Yeah."

"Shit. I don't know anything about it."

I believed him. He was scared enough at this point to tell the truth.

"Stay away from Laurie."

"Yeah."

"And don't harass anyone else either." I headed for the door.

He was muttering behind me: "It's not stalking. It's–"

I was too far out of range to hear what he said.

The drive home was uneventful, cruise control smooth, except for a thought that kept roiling my mind: Was I any better than the rioters? I also used force to get what I wanted. I figured mine was for a better cause. I was trying to help someone. A couple of people. The looters just wanted free candy. They may have had some legit grievances. Looting wasn't the way. Was bracing Craylock? I don't think he would have talked otherwise.

CHAPTER 21

The answering machine light flashed. One message. Rita. I didn't call her back. Crashed on the living room sofa, strands of golden hour sun beaming in through the Levelors. It was quiet. Every part of me ached with exhaustion. I wasn't a SEAL anymore.

Dancing sunlight.
Candlelight dinners.
Dinner with Rita.
Dinner with Lou.
Breakfast with Mrs. Matson.
Ice cream.
Baron.
Mary.
Craylock.
Lou.
Jack.
Firefight.
Firestar.
Blam.
Blam.
Blam.
Warren.
Warren?
Weasel.
Cruise control smooth.
Cruz, Pilar.
Cruz, Ben.

Martinez, Ramon.
Martinez, Anna.
Teddy bears.
Teddie Matson.
Teddie.
Teddie.
Teddie.
Image shards crash my brain.
Dreaming.
The good life is just a dream away.

◈ ◈ ◈

Door slamming. Startled awake. Grabbed the Star off the couch. Walked noiselessly to the back of the house. Press against the walls, peek out windows. Room to room, ready to fire. No one. Nothing. Unlocked the backdoor, drove it open with a foot. Charged out. Aim left. Aim right.

Noise.
Straight arm the gun at the noise.
Trigger.
Squeeze.
Shit.
Heart stop.
Lay off.

Mary came out of the garage holding a crinkled bag. Seeing the pistol aimed at her gut wiped the smile off her face – fast. I'd forgotten about her, or thought she'd already come and gone.

"It's only me. Friend. Not foe. The wind slammed the garage door shut." Her voice was cheery. Her eyes were scared. I lowered the gun. Some people have been known to pull a trigger unintentionally in a moment of crisis from the tension in their finger. I was relieved I wasn't one of them.

"I heard a noise. I'm a little jumpy."

"Who isn't?" She lowered the sack, revealing a chrome-plated .32 automatic aimed at my heart. I wondered if fearful eyes betrayed my cheery voice, as she slipped the gun into the black leather purse that hung on her shoulder.

"I'm pretty sure it's cyanide," she said, opening the bag for me to see the ice cream container. "But I'll run it to make sure. I'll also run the laser note you gave me. Don't think it'll be much help though."

"Why not?"

"There's a million laser printers in the naked city. How you gonna track one down? Sure, I can tell you the brand and model number most likely. But after that it's almost impossible to find whose it is. It's not like the old movies. Unless you have access to the machines and can compare them, there's no way."

We sat on a bright white wood-slat bench in the yard. Birds sang. I remember thinking about them singing, thinking it was corny. I liked it anyway.

"I don't have a lot of friends," I said. It just came out. I wasn't sure why.

"You know people all over."

"Close friends."

She was silent a moment. Then: "I know what you mean. People you can bare your soul to. People who, if you haven't seen or talked to them in years, you can pick up right where you left off." She put her hand on my knee. "People like Baron."

It was a silly thought, thinking of Baron as a person. It made perfect sense to me. Maybe that's why I kept Jack on as a friend, I thought. No pretenses there. No bullshit. He said what he thought. I said what I thought. No judging. Other people may think he's a bigot and worse. But he was a good friend. That's what counted. Same with Mary. I'd known her a long time. And we'd gone for long periods when we hadn't talked or seen each other. But we always drifted back together, our friendship undiminished by the time gap. And here she was now, doing me a favor, her hand on my knee. A good friend.

◈ ◈ ◈

In the heat of the moment with Mary, thinking about Baron and cyanide, I'd again forgotten to give her the notes to Teddie and Pilar. It was a stupid oversight, one that I hit myself for, but one that I wouldn't let stand long.

By now, the riots were officially over. You wouldn't know it by the troops on the street and the fights breaking out everywhere. And the looting that continued. And the name calling from politicos covering their fetid asses. It was such a nice L.A. day, I decided to go for a drive. To East L.A.

Over the river and through the dale to ganger's house we go. To Indian country. Another world. Signs in Spanish. Graffiti everywhere. The rental car rambled down the last street Pilar Cruz had written in her address book for Anna Martinez. Above it, her address had been crossed out and rewritten seven times. Took up a whole page in the book.

Some newer Toyotas and Nissans mixed in with plenty of faded yellow or shit brown or bright orange junkers, ancient Oldsmobiles, Chryslers, Fords, and more Toyotas and Nissans. I pulled up in front of an old stucco house. One story. Small. Locked the car, walked to the front door. Before I got there, someone popped out of the driveway.

"*Que quiere?*"

Someone else to deal with. On the one hand this was getting old, on the other I could understand people being wary of outsiders in their neighborhood. Mine was the same.

"Hi." My Spanish wasn't very good. I think he wanted to know what I was doing there. He wore a white tank top and lowrider pants. Had nervous hands, moving this way and that, stringy biceps flexing as he did. Coal colored eyes. Solid. Steely. No emotion in them. A raggedy black moustache adorned his upper lip. "I'm looking for Ramon and Anna Martinez."

"*Quien?*"

"Ramon and Anna Martinez?"

"*Ramon y Anna Martinez? No los conozco.*" He shrugged.

I thought he was giving me a line. Not so much from what he said, but how he said it. He was playing me. I wasn't in the mood to be played. I also knew better than to try anything. I was out of my turf. Couldn't speak Spanish. At least not well enough to talk to him. I needed something. Something I didn't have. I used what I did have:

"I'm looking for Pilar Cruz?"

His eyes showed nothing. They were as dead as the Dead Sea. I backed away from him. Headed for the front door. Rang the bell. A haggard Mexican woman opened the door.

"*Habla Ingles?*" My Spanish was rusty but I could get that much out.

"*Poquito.*"

"I'm looking for Pilar Cruz, or her friends Anna and Ramon Martinez."

The woman's dark eyes became liquid. Almost young. Before she could say anything the boy from the driveway stepped between her and me.

"*No Mama, Ramon sera enojado.*"

"*No me dices que hacer. Soy tu Madre.*"

"*Yo decire a Ramon que usted hable con este gringo. Le decire todo.*"

"*Ya vaya a decirle. Que mas puede hacerme?*"

I thought I understood the gist of it. Junior was threatening to tell Ramon if Mama blabbed. Mama didn't intimidate easily."

"Why," she said, pleading in her eyes, "why you want Ramon? *Policia?*"

"No, *no policia. Yo estoy* looking for Pilar Cruz. I thought Ramon could tell me where she is."

"What do you want with Pilar?"

I could understand her reluctance. If things went down the way I figured Pilar might have had a stalker. To her family I might look like another one. I showed her my PI's license, told her I was looking into Teddie Matson's murder. She was quiet a few moments, then finally spoke.

"Pilar." The liquid in her eyes spilled over, running down her cheeks. You can fill a pool only so high, then one ice cube and it's over the edge. My guess was that the old lady – Ramon and Anna's mother? – had been holding a lot in. Wanted to talk to someone. She was clearly afraid of her younger son, who stood menacingly in the background, flashing gang signs with his hands to no one.

"*Ramon es un muchacho bueno, pero* he, how do you say, gets off on the wrong foot. He comes home only when he wants. Not when his mother wishes to see him."

"What about Anna?"

"I have not seen her since Pilar has left."

"Are they together."

"I do not know."

"*Callase Mama.*"

She shoved him aside with a strong forearm. He didn't stand aside long.

"I'm not after Ramon or Anna. I want to find Pilar Cruz. To help her."

"*Gringos* don't help *Mejicanos. Bastardos,*" the kid said.

I understood that. I wanted to slug the kid. Jack would've slugged the kid, then told him to go back to Mexico if that's how he feels. He needed someone to discipline him. I figured his mother tried to no avail. Not her fault really. He needed a father. Of course, I'd had a father, and it wasn't a lot of fun growing up around him. There are no pat answers I guess.

"I've talked with Pilar's father, Ben. That's how I found you. He trusts me. He gave me Pilar's address book. He wants me to help. *Ayudar.*" I pulled it out of my pocket, showed it to her. She clutched it in her hands, then gently flipped through the pages, stopping at her daughter's name. Staring. Lost in a past that wouldn't come again, and a hoped-for future that wasn't ever going to come.

"Where can I find Ramon?"

"*No le dice nada, Mama, o yo dicere a Ramon.*"

"*Mira en que manera tu tratas a tu Mama. Sinverguenza. Si estuvimos en Mejico, no pudieres desgraciarme asi.*"

"*Mejico, Mejico. Si le quiere tanto, porque no le vuelve alli.*"

That stung Mrs. Martinez. She had probably come here for her kids, a better life for them, and this was her younger son's gratitude. She wasn't looking as old now. The lines around her eyes and mouth were softening. Even her hands appeared more supple. Thinking about the way things might have been, thinking about how it was when her kids were young and happy and carefree. Innocent. It was the power of memory. The power of love. Her own private fountain of youth. I had nothing to base this thesis on. It just seemed right.

She handed back the address book, looked squarely in my eyes: "Ramon goes *to una cantina, La Revolucion,* on Whittier Boulevard. He is there a lot."

"*Muchas Gracias.*"

"*Cuidado.* Be careful. Lots of bad people there."

I tipped my non-existent hat to her, retreated to my car to the sounds of yelling from her younger son. The front door closed, muffling the sounds.

◈ ◈ ◈

I drove by the bar. It was a nasty neighborhood. Rough. Dirty. Even the rats were afraid to come out at night. Not a *gringo* in sight. Not on the streets, not driving by in cars. Nowhere. What did they know that I didn't? I drove to a payphone, parked close and put my quarter in. Suspicious eyes followed me, from the gas station, from the street. I put on a look that I hoped said, don't mess with me.

"Jack."

"Yo, old buddy. Where are you? Sounds like you're calling from a sewer."

"I'm in East L.A."

"Didn't I say sewer?"

Whether or not one considers East L.A. a sewer, it was uncanny how Jack could sniff these things out.

"How'd you like to party this afternoon? I found a great bar."

"Not down there, I hope."

"Hell no. Pick you up in half an hour."

"Thirteen hundred. Check."

CHAPTER 22

P arty time," Jack said, gruffly. I didn't think he had believed me about the bar. But he was wearing dress slacks, a black silk shirt and snake skin cowboy boots. "I need somethin' to relieve the tension after the past few days-a this shit."

Beethoven's Ninth blasted from the CD player. The volume made my ear drums cringe. I felt sorry for his neighbors. Jack's apartment was microscopic, cramped – the iron lung he called it. One room with a kitchen and dining area off to one side, a small bathroom on the other. A Murphy bed, now folded away. Busts of Beethoven and Mozart on end tables. Posters of Dewey Weber, from the glory days of surfing, and Hobie boards, on the walls. A picture of the old Team on a small desk. In one corner, a six foot board and a mini, twin 38 SCUBA tanks and a weight belt. Stacks of books in the other corners. He read everything from trashy romance novels to Kafka to How-To books on just about anything. A small 9" television sat on the dining table, hooked up for cable TV.

Jack's kit bag sat on the dining table. "Let's go," I said, picking it up to toss to him. It was heavier than usual. I wasn't prepared for the weight and almost dropped it. "Jeez, what do you have in there, a cannon?"

Jack pulled out a Colt .45 Officer's model. Grinned at me.

"You never carry a piece, man."

"Nobody's gonna Reginald Denny me. They might get me, but I'll take a few of them with me on my way down. 'Sides, I hear hell ain't so bad. 'at's where all the fun people go." He said it with a straight face. No irony there. "Segue, man. Segue." He didn't want to talk about the gun. I tossed him the bag and we jammed out the door.

We pulled away from the curb. He took a cassette out of the kit bag. Stuck it in the player. *Peer Gynt: In the Hall of the Mountain King.* He cranked up the volume. We sat at a light between competing blasts of Nirvana and Ice T. Hell, it all melded together like an artillery barrage of sound. We won.

We headed downtown: The streets looked bombed out. Charred skeletons of buildings hulking over dead sidewalks. Ravaged. War torn. Was this really the U.S.A.?

"Hey, where is this great club?"

"Party time, Jack."

"Yeah, but if I knew it was gonna be this kinda party I wouldda worn a different shirt."

"Maybe you can take it off and ask some pretty young lady at ringside to hold it for you."

He snorted. "Will there be any pretty young ladies where we're going?"

"Doubt it."

"Well, you owe me bro. A hot time on the old town one night." He sounded pissed. I knew he wasn't serious. Jack loved a good fight. I was hoping we'd avoid one. But if it couldn't be helped I wanted him there.

I filled Jack in on the mission. We got lost east of downtown.

"Man, it was easier in the bush or in the sandbox than finding your way around these damned city streets."

I needed directions and the tank needed filling. Pulled into a gas station. Jack pumped while I fumbled with a map.

"How do you get to Whittier?" he asked the attendant after topping off the tank.

"No hablo Ingles."

As soon as I heard those words, I slid a touch lower in my seat. Didn't want to look in Jack's direction. Didn't have to. I knew what he looked like when he got this way – the veins in his neck sticking out. His mouth curling. Eyes narrow. Hands balling up into huge fists.

"Well, does anyone here *habla Ingles*?"

"No, no hablo Ingles."

A police black and white drove by.

"Then why don't all you tamale eaters go back to Mexico if you don't want to learn our culture? Our language."

I slunk deeper in the seat. Jack had a way of picking the wrong time and place for things.

He got back in the car, slammed the door, rolled up the window.

"Drive on, James."

The attendant was beating on the window. *"El dinero. El dinero."*

"You haven't paid?"

"They wouldn't give me directions."

"Maybe they really don't speak English."

"Don't gimme that shit. They speak-a da English." He rolled the window down a little. "I'll give you your money when you tell me how to get to Whittier Boulevard."

Jack was right. The attendant had miraculously learned English awfully fast, gave us the directions, and we were on our way.

◈ ◈ ◈

La Revolucion was a dingy place on the outside. Looked like an old industrial building, small machine shop or something. The bottom half of the stucco wall was painted a dark, though chipping, forest green. Top half was white, or used to be. Grime and dirt crept all the way up to the roof. Made you wonder how it got that high. A handful of men stood outside talking, playing dice and drinking. We parked a few doors down. Jack dumped the contents of the kit bag on the floor, swept them under the seat, all except for his credit card, drivers license holder and the .45, of course, which he put back in the kit and stuck under his arm. We walked back to the entrance. Several pairs of intense brown eyes followed us up the sidewalk.

The door was open, sort of. It was blocked by a large Mexican with a round face and rounder belly in a sweat-stained T-shirt. He grinned at us. Held a pool cue across his chest at port arms.

"Wha's he think he is?" Jack said softly. "The Master at Arms."

We stepped into the doorway. Round face took a short step forward. Pushed the cue out a couple inches.

"Stand aside," Jack said.

"You don't order us around down here."

"Nobody's ordering you around," I said. "We just want a couple-a beers."

"No beer in here. No liquor license."

"Don't give us a hard time."

"I ain't. I'm tryin' to help you. This building's been condemned. You could get hurt in there." He shrugged, squinting his face into a fake smile.

"We'll take our chances."

Jack shifted the kit bag from one hand to the other.

"Nice purse."

"Thanks. My boyfriend gave it to me," Jack minced.

The Mexican grinned deeper, baring pointed yellow teeth. He stepped aside. We walked in in front of him.

"You ain't the police," he said. "This guy dresses too good. Like a *vato*." Several others inside overheard and laughed. Seemed they spoke English.

The floor was covered with sawdust. The bar tin, dented. Dull yellow lights flickered across the ceiling. It was dark and yellow inside. Jaundiced.

"We're the hit of the party," Jack said, as we walked up to the bar, leaning in. Eyes followed us. Bodies too. It was hot in there. Sticky. No windows. No air conditioning. You could smell the sweat on the men who played pool and drank all day and all night.

The bartender ignored us. No one else was giving us that much space. Jack laid his kit bag on the counter.

"If you ain't the *policia*, who are you? And how brave you are, coming into the barrio alone? Two *gringos*."

"Two white bread boys," another Mexican said.

"This ain't like the movies. You ain't Eddie Murphy in a pussy redneck bar now."

"Speakin' of pussy." A short Mexican with a stubbly beard grabbed for Jack's kit bag. Jack caught him by the wrist. Twisted. There was a snapping sound. The man winced with pain.

"We're looking for someone," I said.

"This ain't the lost and found."

"Lost *Gringos*, over here."

"Lost Mexicans, this corner." They had a good time, partying and chugging beer.

Jack sat facing the rear. He could also see behind the bar. I sat with my back to him, scanning the front of the dive and the other half of the bar. They might come at us, but we'd see them coming.

"And jus' who might you be lookin' for?"

"Ramon Martinez."

"Man, you know how many Ramon Martinez's there are? Sort of like John Smith."

"Yeah, well this one has a sister named Anna."

"Another uncommon name."

"Look, we know he hangs here."

"Hangs. Cool talk. You been *hangin'* 'round the niggers again? That's how they talk, *hang*. *Gringo's* been *hangin'* with the niggers again."

"Whachu want this Ramon for? Beat 'im up? He rape your sister and you know no Mexican–"

"That's Mexican-American, ain't it?" Jack said.

"Yeah, man, no Mex-American can *hang* with a white bitch."

The circle around us grew tighter. A noose of people, hot sweaty bodies. The liquor on their breath stank.

"White man's law don't count in here."

"In a few years won't even count in Ca-li-forn-aye-a. We're takin' it back."

"Can't wait," Jack said.

"Well we don' know no Ramon Martinez, so you better go. You never know what a *borracho Mejicano* will do."

"We'll wait. We've got plenty of time."

"White men with no job. Didn't think it was possible."

Someone in the back of the crowd put their hands in their pockets. I heard a very soft click. The safety being shifted on a pistol?

Jack jumped off his bar stool. The Port Arms man we'd met in the doorway stepped in front of him. Jack swung his kit bag hard and straight, right into the man's jaw. That .45 hitting him must've stung. He fell back. Jack whipped the gun from the bag, letting the bag fly. The men surrounding us drew back. The man in the back who had slipped the safety off his pistol drew it –

too late. Jack charged through the crowd, which parted
to let the crazy *gringo* with the gun go by. He jammed
the .45 up to the other man's head, disarmed him.
Backed to a side wall. I moved next to him, Firestar
drawn. He handed me the man's .32, which I slipped in
my belt, and held the man in front of him, the .45 still
jammed into his temple.

"Now," Jack said, "We'll do a little talking. Or a
little waiting. Whatever turns you on. *Comprende?*"

"Ramon Martinez," I said. No response. "My friend
here is crazy. That's why I bring him along. He doesn't
mind killing. He doesn't mind doing time. *Loco.*"

"And I don't like Mexicans. 'Specially Mexican-
Americans." Jack spit. "You wanna be American, be
American, goddamnit. Learn our language."

I nudged him: segue. Might not have been bad to
have him spouting off. Might make them think he's
crazy enough to do anything – and he would, if he
thought he could get away with it. But I had lied. Jack
could take anything, but jail time. He'd go crazy in stir.
He would kill if he had to, but not here, not unless it
was truly a matter of life or death. More than anything,
he didn't want to land in jail. Small as the iron lung
was, he could come and go as he pleased. Eat the slop
he wanted and listen to his classical musical all day and
all night. But he wouldn't be able to adjust to being
penned in, taking orders from people he thought were
morons. He didn't have trouble taking orders in the
Navy because, with an exception or two, he thought the
people there were sharp. When he bucked them and
landed in the brig, he nearly tore his eyes out, until our
lieutenant could get him free.

Jack shoved the .45 harder into the other man's
temple.

A large man, not fat, but well toned, pushed through the crowd. "*Ya basta*. Ramon comes in here just about every day."

Murmurs of disapproval shot through the crowd.

"We'll wait," I said. "Nobody leaves."

I made sure the back door was locked. Everyone, including the unfriendly bartender, sat at tables that had now been pushed to the back of the room. Everyone but Jack and his hostage. They stood near the wall inside the front door. A spot where they couldn't be seen until someone had already entered. I sat on a bar stool on the other side of the door, scanning back and forth between our guests and the front door. I guess we could have been brought up on kidnapping charges had anyone complained. But we didn't want anyone getting out and warning Ramon off.

Any time anyone entered, they were escorted to the rear and sat to wait with the rest of us.

And that's what we did. We waited.

CHAPTER 23

We didn't have to wait long. About an hour. It seemed more like a decaying eternity in a condemned house, as we ushered in more guests, seating them in the back of the room.

"Hey, my *mamacita* wants me home," a long-haired man shouted. Jack and I didn't respond. Our eyes fixed on our designated cover spots. I was glad I didn't have to hold that heavy .45 up to someone's head for an hour.

The door opened. A wash of late afternoon sun poured in. I knew it was him as soon as he stood in the doorway. I knew it was him even in silhouette, from the sun bleeding around his shoulders and head. He held himself like he owned the place. His shoulders were powerful, bulging underneath a black short-sleeved skin tight shirt with rolled cuffs at the ends of the sleeves. Tats up and down his arms. If he knew something was wrong, he didn't let on. Stepped inside.

In the dim yellow light of the bar, I could see his face. The same as his younger brother. Harder looking, more creases. More coldness around the eyes, if that was possible. But the same. A little taller. A little more filled out. But the same raggedy black moustache. Acne scars. Another scar. Longer. A thin slit. Knife. Tough *hombre.*

He sauntered in, easy gait. Cool. Blase. I saw it before he cleared the vestibule. The rectangular butt of an automatic pistol outlined in his waistband under his shirt. Our guests in the back of the room were silent. Probably praying that Ramon would have come in blasting, two gun style, like in the old B westerns. No such luck.

He jerked his neck to his left, saw Jack holding his prisoner. Jerked the other way. His hand flew to the open bottom button of his shirt. Before he could pull the gun out, Jack yanked his prisoner in front of him, leveled the .45 at Ramon. The wheels were spinning in Ramon's head. Should he run for it? Shoot it out? Who were these *gringos* anyway? What did they want? He let his hand drop to his side. Walked deeper into the room. Turned around to face Jack and me.

"Looks like what we have here, *amigos*, is what might be called a Mexican standoff," he said with a trace of Mexican accent. Our guests cackled. Even Jack cracked a smile. My face was immobile. I didn't want to give anything away. "My brother said a couple-a *gringos* was lookin' for me. What'd I do, rape your sister?"

"You guys all learn the same script?"

"It's the script we're given, *amigo*."

I didn't like the way he said *amigo*. He sure as hell didn't mean it.

"Let's talk." I motioned him over to my end of the bar." The Firestar was in my lap. He didn't have a chance with his gun and he knew it.

"I don't have time for your *gringo* bullshit."

"You can leave. You can leave now. But aren't you just a little curious about what we're after?"

"Un poquito." He walked toward me at the bar. Didn't lean against it. Stood tall. Hands at his sides. "Somethin' about my sister."

"We're looking for Pilar Cruz. I thought maybe you or your sister could help us find her."

His eyes swam. Debating. "Man, why should I help you? White man been nothing but trouble for both of them."

"What do you mean?"

"Nothin', *amigo*. Nothin'. I'm just a dumb Mexican. Talk when I shouldn't." His voice wasn't very loud, as if he didn't want the others in the rear of the bar to hear what he was saying. I got the feeling the macho act was as much for them as for us. "What can you do for us, *amigo*?"

"I'm a private detective. I'm trying to find someone that might have known Pilar Cruz."

"How's that gonna help Pilar?"

"Same guy that might have been after my client might be after Pilar." I was beginning to believe it.

"Shit. No one's after Pilar."

"Then why is she hiding?"

The cold eyes warmed. Only for a flash. Long enough for me to know he believed what I was getting at.

"'s bullshit, man. 'Sides, I haven't seen Pilar for a couple-a years."

"What about Anna?"

"Don't see her neither."

"Look, if you're not gonna help us, fine. We'll leave."

I handed him a business card. He rolled it in fingers. "*Un hombre grande con un* bees-ness card." His audience laughed on cue. He glanced at the card. Tore it in half.

Jack and I headed to the door. He walked towards it, pulling the hostage with him. I backed to it. We weren't taking any chances. He shoved the hostage forward and we were out the door.

◈ ◈ ◈

"You sho' know how to give a party, bro."

"Stop bitching. You love it."

"Know I do."

"You really took off after that guy."

"I see a gun, I take defensive action."

The tires squealed as we pulled out. No one had followed us from the bar, but I didn't wait around to see what would happen next. I wondered what Ramon had thought of us. Did he expect it to be so simple? Did he expect us to brace him? We'd have had to brace the whole place. It wasn't part of the plan, but we'd had no choice when they came at us.

"Fuckin' Mexicans. Don't know what's good for 'em. You're tryin' to help 'em out. For what? They don't give a shit. You'll never hear from that sucker."

I felt I owed Jack dinner at the least. We went to El Coyote. He may not have liked the people. He loved the food.

◈ ◈ ◈

I made it home in one piece. When I'm out with Jack I never know if that'll be the case. I settled in. The phone felt cold to my touch. I was going to dial Rita. Changed my mind. I needed an evening alone. Time to think. Sort things out, about her. The case. My life. It rang. Mary.

"Duke, I was right. Panasonic Laser printer. Model KX-P4410. No good way to trace them. And the ice cream is definitely laced with cyanide."

"Easy to get?"

"Easy enough? Some rat poisons have it. Some–"

"I get the idea. I appreciate the fast work."

"Only for a friend."

We hung up. I thought about friends. When I first met her, I had considered Mary more of an acquaintance than a real friend. I was wrong. A friend was someone you confided your innermost secrets to. Someone who would accept you faults and all. Jack considered me his best friend. Sometimes I thought I was his only friend. I accepted him. I didn't like the way he thought about certain things or the way he acted. But I let him be himself. He repaid the favor by accepting me. On the rare occasions I confided in someone it was in him. And that wasn't that often. There was no one else. Did that make him my only friend? If so, what was I hiding from?

With that thought roiling around in my brain, I downed a jigger of Scotch and went to sleep.

I woke up the next morning refreshed. The first good night's sleep I'd had in days. The first thought on my mind was Rita. Could she be a good friend? Could I be one to her? Would our racial differences make a difference? Would they get in the way? So far we'd enjoyed a diverting relationship – mostly on the surface. It seemed we were both giving each other safe harbor during the storm. Telling each other, by our presence in bed together, that things weren't so bad. The country wasn't – and wouldn't be – falling apart. That the races could get along with each other some day. We proved it by our mere presence together. Or was it all just surface? Were we still really strangers? Was she just an *acquaintance*?

There were no answers. Not then. I hoped there would be. Soon. I liked her. She was different. And I was probably different to her. It would all have to come to a head. Or it might just fade away. I wouldn't hear from her. She wouldn't hear from me. It would be over. Nothing said. Nothing resolved. I didn't want it to end that way. Didn't want it to end at all. But I wondered if our differences were so great that without fires raging in the street to push us together, nothing else would.

I got up. Showered. Those thoughts kept circling in my head. I had an onion bagel for breakfast with some melted cheddar on it. It was enough to satisfy me. It was seven-thirty in the morning. The whole day lay ahead. I thought about going down to the ocean for a swim. Or laying on the raft in the pool. I sat in the living room and watched the sun streak in through the leaded glass window. Picked up the book I was reading, *L.A. Confidential* by James Ellroy. Couldn't concentrate.

It felt like I was getting closer. Closer to what? Was I trying to trick myself into believing I was onto something? Trying to avoid being the fuckup of my dad's mind? My mind. Ramon had told us nothing. I thought he knew, but if he wouldn't talk then what? The Jack method? Brace him? Beat the shit out of him? The Craylock method. Ply him with candy? Liquor? Drugs?

He knew where Pilar was. I was sure of that. She was hiding. But why? From who? I figured I'd contact him again – maybe – but it couldn't be at the bar. We – I – couldn't risk it again. We'd been lucky that first time. Might not work out so well again.

What was the connection between Pilar and Teddie? Teddie wasn't here to tell. Pilar was. Somewhere. I had to find her. Without her there were nothing but deadends.

They were both actresses. Both women of color. Was that it? The acting thing seemed more likely. Someone liked actresses. Thought they liked him back. Was rejected. That made sense. It was in the letters. Had to be. A beam of light spread across the floor, a favorite spot of Baron's. For a moment I saw him there, then nothing.

I spent the rest of the day scouring the letters again. The only connecting points were the two *sparks* notes.

Had both been attached to a teddy bear? I only had one bear. Should I do the movie thing and see where the teddy bear was made and sold? Track it that way. That seemed as useless as tracking down Panasonic laser printers.

Should I go back to the Perlman's? See if the old lady had forgotten something? See if there was anything I could glean in Teddie's apartment? What about going back to Mrs. Matson's? Not much there, I figured. Except maybe Rita. That would be worth a trip to South Central. What about Ben Cruz? No, he didn't know anything. Back to the motel where the Weasel had stayed. I could ask Tom Bond to look at mug books. I made a note to do that.

Something was missing. The keystone. What the hell was it? The only thing that made any sense was going back to Ramon. He wasn't the keystone. But he could tell me where to find it.

My eyes were glazed over. Too much reading. Too much thinking. The phone rang again.

CHAPTER 24

Laurie read the words from *Got to Get You into My Life* unemotionally, without any of the rhythm of the song. Things weren't going so well for her either – only I didn't know it at the time. Craylock had sent her a note with these Beatle lyrics. The same note I'd seen in his house.

He didn't give a damn. He'd get her into his life whether she wanted it or not.

"He sent me another note."

"Craylock?"

"Who else?"

I saw her point. It was a stupid question. I had a good excuse. Dazed and glazed. I didn't bother explaining.

"He doesn't take a hint," I said. The line was silent. I could hear breathing at the other end. Slight. Even.

"I thought about buying a gun, but they have a moratorium on gun sales." Her voice twisted like two braided power lines turning around each other, sparking off each other. She was pissed.

"I'll lend you one of mine."

"I don't know, I've never used a gun before, I'm scared."

"I can take you to a range. Teach you to shoot."

"I don't know. I guess I probably wouldn't be able to hit the target."

"All the more reason to learn."

"God, I don't believe this. Me, the person who can't stand to watch violence even in a Saturday morning cartoon, and here I am discussing guns with a detective." There was a sob at the other end of the line. "Do you believe how I'm talking? I used to be for gun control, till I realized through painful experience that it only controls the good guys. The bad guys'll always have their weapons."

"You oughta meet my friend Jack." I was serious too.

"I don't think I'm ready for another man right now. Jeez, what am I saying, *another* man. I don't have a man now. Just one who thinks he's mine and I'm his. This is a crazy world."

I picked her up and we drove out to the range in Tujunga. I liked it 'cause it was an outdoor range and I could fire my Ruger Mini 30 rifle there without a problem. We continued our conversation from earlier:

"And it's gonna get crazier." I caught myself sounding like Jack again.

"I think I know what you mean. I'm starting to see things differently. I used to think that the police would protect us and that if you lived in a nice neighborhood you'd be safe. Maybe that sounds naive, but I always felt pretty secure. I mean, to look at Craylock you'd never think he was capable of doing anyone harm. Now I guess I don't trust anyone."

She had planned to buy a short barreled .38 Colt revolver. Not a bad choice for someone unfamiliar with guns. A revolver is good since it's easier to use and clean than a semi-auto. .38's not a bad size bullet, especially if you go with a Plus-P. If she'd asked me, I would have recommended a .357 and maybe a little longer barrel. Short barrel's good for concealability, which she wanted. But less accurate. Everything's a tradeoff.

The flat hard pops of guns being fired startled her at first. She stood well back from the firing line. I didn't like the looks of some of the folks at the end of the range nearest the parking lot. Backwards baseball hats. Lowrider pants. Tats up and down their arms. Looked like bangers. They were firing everything imaginable. Including AKs. I wondered if they were registered. I thought I knew the answer. We moved upwind.

We started with the targets at twenty-five feet. "But," I told her, "you'll most likely be firing at even closer range." She nervously picked up my .38 Smith and Wesson. It was an older gun that had belonged to my dad. I showed her how to load the gun. She tentatively took it, tried for herself. Hefting it first. Then deliberately inserting each bullet. I'd teach her how to use speed-loaders later. She raised it to the target, hands shaking.

"Go ahead. Pull the trigger. Gently. Squeeze."

She fired the first shot. Winced at the kick. Backed up.

"Steady. Both hands now."

She went back to the firing line, capped off the other five shots. Jerked the gun wildly. I took it from her. Showed her how to hold it. How to position herself properly. She reloaded, fired six more times, shaking less with each shot.

"Now imagine that the target's Craylock. He's broken into your house. He's coming toward you."

She tensed the muscles of her face. Clenched her jaw. She fired. One. Two. Three. No bullseyes. Better than before. Four. Five. Six. Not bad. She looked at me. I nodded approval.

She reloaded, spun the cylinder like she'd seen in the movies. Giggled.

I let her run through a Firestar magazine. Four out of seven hit the target.

We played for about two hours. She got a little better. Not much. The biggest improvement came when we switched from bullseye targets to man-silhouette targets. She started hitting about seventy percent. She didn't want to try the Mini 30.

"After I get comfortable with a handgun I might try it," she said. "It's, it's so ugly."

"Looks are only skin deep."

I wanted to stop at Tommy's Hamburgers on the way home for something to eat. She wanted to get home.

"I'll loan you my .38 till the moratorium is over," I said as we pulled up to the curb in front of her house.

"I'd appreciate that." She started to get out of the car. "Why don't you come in? I'll fix you something to eat." Her voice was taut, a stringed instrument tuned too tight.

I wanted to get home, get back on the Teddie and Pilar letters or something. She sounded upset. I agreed to come in for a late lunch-early dinner.

The sun was still up. It was dark inside. All the curtains drawn, the blinds closed tight. A lonely shaft of golden hour sunlight slithered in here and there giving the room an eerie glow. Particles of dust floated on the slivers of light like so many tiny angels pirouetting along the vector.

She grilled hamburgers on the Char-glow. I made a salad. There wasn't much dialogue during the meal. We watched the sun set through the cracks in the blinds and with it her feelings of security and well being. As I rinsed dishes and put them in the dishwasher, I could see her pupils expanding with fear. The fear of the hunted animal. Night was falling. She was the prey. Craylock the hunter.

Dishes done, I reached for my windbreaker.

"Do you have to go?"

I knew what she was getting at. I didn't bite. Maybe I should have. I wasn't trying to make it hard for her. There were other things I wanted to be doing. Rationalizations floated through my head: if you help Laurie you can make amends for Teddie. Didn't work. Nothing would make amends for Teddie. Perhaps I could help avert another tragedy. But I couldn't be with her all the time.

"Maybe I should pay Craylock another visit on my way home."

"Can't you stay a while? We could rent a movie." Her voice was breathy. Desperate.

"If I stay a while, you'll ask me to stay a while longer."

"Won't you stay the night? I haven't slept in days. I'm not trying to blackmail you or make you feel guilty. I'll pay you for your time. I–"

"He hasn't done anything violent yet, probably won't."

"How do I know he won't? He's obsessed. I'm scared."

There wasn't really a choice. I agreed to stay the night. She would sleep on the floor in her bedroom on the far side of the bed from the window. I would sleep on the couch in the living room, weapons at the ready. There was already a pillow and blanket on the couch. She brought fresh ones. I thought of Rita and felt a twinge of guilt, but there was no real attraction between Laurie and me.

"It's awfully quiet in here," I said.

"The bell on the phone's turned off. Answering machine in my office picks it up."

We checked the machine. The tape had run out. Fear ate at her eyes, the corners of her mouth. Craylock's voice wasn't on the tape. Only music. Semi modern torch songs from the Beatles' *Love Songs* album. We knew who it was. It wasn't enough for the police and he obviously knew that.

"Is there a trap on your phone?"

"No."

"You might think about getting one."

"The phone company tells me I need to go to the police. The police tell me I need to talk to the phone company. Nobody wants to help."

"It's not easy, I know. But it can be done."

She said goodnight. Went to bed. I sat on the couch, thumbing through her magazines. Seems she subscribed to just about everything there was, from *Omni* to *Essence*, *Atlantic* to *Spy*. Lonely? One hand flipped pages. The other curled around the Firestar. The safety was on. Good thing. The way I was hugging that piece of metal with my fingers it might have exploded from the pressure. I hardly realized what I was doing, till I cut myself on the trigger guard, something I would have thought impossible. At that moment, I could have started a fire just by rubbing my two fingers together. I wanted Craylock. Wanted him bad. Bad enough to go outside the law? Bad enough to risk jail? Bad enough to live with myself after I'd done it?

I checked the bedroom. Laurie was curled up in a pile of blankets on the floor. Her breath came in short bursts. At least she was sleeping. I sat back on the living room couch, hoping Craylock would show. If I knew how to pray I would have prayed for his arrival. I wanted the son-of-a-bitch. I wanted an excuse to vent all the anger and rage I'd been storing up since the Weasel did his deed. Since my dad had done his deeds. I used her phone to check my answering machine. No messages. No Ramon. No Rita. The room was stifling, everything shut up as it was. I pulled the blinds up a few inches at each window, opened the windows. A gentle cross breeze made the room tolerable. I sat back on the couch, Firestar in hand, and drifted off to sleep in a few minutes. My senses were acute enough that I would have wakened at anyone tramping about outside the house. I slept through the night.

CHAPTER 25

Laurie would have preferred I stay with her the next day. It wasn't a horrible proposition. If I didn't have other things to do, I might have. Guilt and wanting to do penance had made me stay the night. I didn't think Craylock would come at her during the day. Roaches like him hide from the light. I could have been wrong. Nonetheless I couldn't stay with her twenty-four hours a day. I wasn't a bodyguard. Was this a rationalization? Justification for my leaving.

I went home, showered. Didn't know how I would spend the day. I felt Teddie slipping farther and farther away. Or was it Rita? I hadn't heard from her in a couple days. Of course, she hadn't heard from me either. Why? I put it out of my head.

The phone rang.

"Duke, Tommy here."

"I take it the South Central Olympics are over. You sound tired, man."

"Haven't slept in days. And I'm on duty again. At least the riot's over and things are settling down, sort of. Just don't believe what you see on the news. It's a hell of a lot worse out there. They're trying to make it like everything's back to normal. Ain't so. At least tonight I'll get to go home and sleep."

"Sweet dreams."

"Thanks, bud. I'm back at West Hollywood station. C'mon down. I'll look up the stuff you want."

I figured I was just about in my rental car before he hung up. West Hollywood station wasn't far from my house. Would take me ten or fifteen minutes to get there. Traffic was still light. Lots of people staying home behind locked doors.

The station was guarded more like a military installation than a sheriff's station that day. It was hell getting through the heightened security. When I finally did, Tommy could barely raise a smile.

"Glad to see you, bud," he said. Dark circles engulfed his eyes. His uniform looked like it'd been run over by a truck, not the usual crisp look. He pulled out several thick mug books, dumped them unceremoniously on a desk.

"Stalkers. Let me know when you're done with them and I'll get you some more."

I flipped through the dog-eared pages. Black faces. White faces. Brown and yellow faces. No discrimination here. No Weasel either. I wasn't really looking for Craylock, but I kept an eye out for him too. Didn't expect to find him. And didn't. Tommy came back.

"Hey, Tom, how 'bout we look up some stuff on the computer?"

"I shouldn't be doing this for a civilian."

"Aw shut up. You've been watching too many crummy TV shows."

He flicked a button on a keyboard. A computer monitor lit up. He punched some keys. "All right, whadda you want?"

"Check out a guy named Jim Talbot or James Talbot, J. Talbot. Even Talbot James." Hell, the Weasel might have been stupid enough to give me his real name or a variation of it. Several histories, even computerized photos, popped up. None looked like my Weasel.

"Doesn't mean he ain't done nothing. Only that he's not in our system. He local?"

"Yeah. Now anyway. I don't know his background."

"Well, he ain't done nothing in California."

On a whim, I also had him punch up Gary Craylock. He hit more keys. A simple message popped up: "Unknown."

"What a bust," I said.

"Now you know what we go through. Day in. Day out. Hell, even when we find the bastards our hands are tied. Gotta treat 'em real nice. Especially now."

He then ran Talbot and Craylock through the FBI computer. Nothing there either. A couple of ciphers.

"Late bloomers," Tom kidded. It was his way of saying sorry he couldn't be of more help. We promised to go out to dinner soon. He and his wife. Me and my flavor of the month.

Before leaving, I called Martin Luther King Hospital to check on Tiny. He was in X-ray a nurse told me. I left a message of well wishes.

Instead of heading home, I drove Laurel Canyon to Mulholland. Mulholland to Coldwater. The arroyo was crowded with the forensic crew. Same cop as the first time. He recognized me, passed me through. Mary was crawling on her hands and knees in a trough three feet deep. She was pawing at the dirt with a small mesh screen. She found the carcass of a rat. Picked it up in her gloved hands. Examined it. Bagged it. She looked up, a sparkle in her eyes, happy to see me. I gave her a hand up and helped her out of the trough.

She went to a red and white Igloo cooler, pulled a wrinkled brown paper bag out and two Orange Crushes. She handed me a drink. Opened the bag, handed me a sandwich as we headed to a low berm to sit on. She bit into her sandwich with ferocity. Washed it down with the sweet orange soda. I hesitated. Even though the sandwich had been in a plastic bag she touched it with her gloved hands.

"Go ahead. Eat the damn thing. It won't bite you."

"That's not what I'm afraid of."

"Look, I've been doing this how many years now. Haven't got sick once." She ripped another bite out of her sandwich.

"I don't want to take your lunch from you."

"Chicken."

It was a challenge no macho male could ignore. I clamped my teeth on the whole wheat bread, bit off a chunk. Roast beef with mayo. I hated mayo, rat flavored or not. Couldn't put the sandwich down though. She wouldn't believe me about the mayo being the only reason. She would lay it off to the rat. I forced the thing down quickly, washed it all down with Orange Crush and wished for something hot and spicy. The mayo left a pasty taste in my mouth.

"I don't have anything new to report," she said.

"I didn't think you would. Just wanted to run some things by you." I told her about looking for Teddie Matson's killer without the part about my involvement. Told her about Pilar Cruz, possible connections there. Then: "I brought the notes. Can you examine the handwriting?" She took them from me.

"I'm no handwriting expert. I could show them to someone though."

"Yeah."

"They do both say something about 'sparks.' Sparks flying and the like. That makes me think there's something connected with them. You could also call Teddie's family. Maybe they know if she got a teddy bear."

I had thought about calling them. And had avoided it. I didn't want to impose on Mrs. Matson again. I didn't want Warren to impose on me. And if Rita was there, what would I say to her?

We discussed Craylock. I told Mary about his house. His obsession with Beatle lyrics. His knuckling under and obsequiousness when confronted.

"I'd like to help you there, Duke. I'm no shrink though. It's so far out of my area that I don't have any ideas at all. I'd recommend that Ms. Hoffman move."

"She can't do that. Then he wins."

"Why does it always have to be a thing with winning and losing with you men?"

"That's not me talking. It's her."

Mary blushed. She tried not to show it. Couldn't help it. Dead air filled our corner of the arroyo. Finally, she said: "You're feeling guilty, aren't you?"

My head jerked in her direction. She'd hit a nerve. I hadn't told her my part in Teddie's death. What the hell was she talking about?

Fuckup. It raced through my head, swirling, insinuating into every corner.

Fuckup.
Fuckup.
Fuckup.
Did she know something?
Was she a mindreader?
Psychic?
Racing heart.
Sweaty palms.
Tense shoulders.
Constricting veins.
Short breath.
Don't let her see.
Don't let her know.
Don't tell her.
Don't give it away.
Fuckup, pal.

You are a fuckup.

"What're you talking about? What kind of guilt?"

"You think you should have stayed with Ms. Hoffman today?"

"Yeah, part of me does."

"Guilt."

"You can't protect her forever, Duke."

"I know. But she came to me for help. I shouldn't just leave her alone."

"She didn't hire you as a bodyguard. Even if she did, you can't do it twenty-four hours a day."

"I can try. The police sure as hell don't give a damn."

"You have the other case to worry about. Teddie."

"Yeah, Teddie."

"There was a peak in your voice."

"What're you talking about?"

"Sounds like you're taking this Teddie Matson to heart."

"It's just another case." But I knew it wasn't, and she probably figured that out too.

She stared hard into my face. I had to turn away. "Maybe it isn't Ms. Hoffman you're feeling guilty about?"

"Whadda you mean?"

"Maybe it's Teddie."

"You're crazy. I came on that case after she was–"

"Don't mind me. I like to play little puzzle games in my head. Do it all the time. That's how I put together pieces of rat turd and pieces of bone and come up with a murderer."

"Maybe you can market it as a board game."

"It is a good idea, isn't it?"

❖ ❖ ❖

I left Mary wondering if she had more pieces to my puzzle than I knew or wanted her to have. Driving into the city over Coldwater, my mind darted back and forth. I felt like I'd hit a brick wall. Didn't know where to go from here. Everything was turning into a dead end.

There was one message on the answering machine: "*Hola amigo.* Maybe we should talk. Don't try callin' me. An' don' come to the bar. You do and you'll never hear from me again. I'll catch you sooner or later." The caller didn't leave his name. It couldn't have been anyone but Ramon.

The cordless phone sat on the deck by the pool's edge as I floated into a Never Never Land of drowning dragonflies, woodrats and Weasels.

CHAPTER 26

Ramon had said not to come looking for him. What else could I do? I headed to East L.A. Drove by *La Revolucion*. Circled the block several times. Parked across the street and watched the place for hours. I couldn't just sit home waiting for a phone call. When he didn't show at the bar, I drove by his mother's house. No sign of him there either.

I was at wit's end. Didn't know where to turn. Everywhere were deadends and metaphorical streets with no outlets.

"Fuckup," I said to myself as I headed back to the westside. "Fuckup. Fuckup," I shouted. The man in the car next to mine rolled up his window. Did he think I was yelling at him? Did he think I was crazy? Gonna blow him away for breathing. A riot-ravaged citizen who'd lost his marbles?

Start over. That's what I had to do. Retrace my steps. Retrace Teddie's steps. Might she have known the Weasel? Where would they have met? Did he simply see her on TV? It was impossible. I slammed the steering wheel, hard.

Driving the L.A. streets was like driving through Beirut. Soldiers. Bombed out buildings. Debris everywhere. Instead of turning off to head home or to the office, I kept going to Fairfax. It was the only thing I could think to do: start over.

I was in luck – but I certainly wasn't lucky. Mrs. Perlman was home. Her husband wasn't. She was wearing one of those old-lady dresses, a midnight blue number with tropical fish on it. Her blue-gray hair was nicely coiffed. Maybe she'd just come home from the beauty parlor. She was running a hose on the bushes in front of her apartment building.

"Hello, young man." She remembered me. That was a good sign.

"Hello, Mrs. Perlman."

"Did you find Teddie's killer yet?"

The *yet* cut through my heart like a knife.

"No. I'm still looking though."

"I thought you must be or you wouldn't be here. Unless you were coming to tell me that you had solved the case."

"I'm making some progress. Thought I'd check back with you. See if you remembered anything you hadn't told me. Or maybe you came across something in her apartment that her family left behind."

"I can't think of anything."

"You never saw the man that killed her around here before?"

"Not before that day."

"So you don't think they knew each other."

"Not to my knowledge. Anything's possible though. I'm not a nosy neighbor."

I had my doubts about that.

"We did come across some of her things. Put a box in the garage. Her family hasn't come for them yet."

"Mind if I see them?"

"No. Not at all." She turned the hose off, led me down the driveway. "Seems like the police aren't doing much. After the first couple days, they haven't even been back here."

"Why doesn't your husband want you to talk?"

"He's overprotective, the dear."

"Maybe he's afraid you'll get the credit for cracking the case." I grinned. She smiled back.

"I suppose he simply doesn't want us involved in all the hassles with the police, the media. You know what I mean. But I feel it's my civic duty. Not to mention a responsibility to Teddie."

The garage was dusty. Spider webs filled every corner. Mrs. Perlman pointed to a box on a shelf in the rear. I got it down. Started going through it.

The contents were ordinary. A book on acting. A small actress' makeup case. Some stationery. Nothing unusual. Nothing that gave me a hint in any direction. I put the contents back in the box.

"I could bring these to Mrs. Matson."

"Don't get me wrong, young man. I don't think that's a good idea though. It isn't that I don't trust you. I think that the Matson's should get it themselves. That way it's their responsibility in case anything—"

"I understand."

I put the box back on the shelf. We headed up the driveway.

"Thank you again, Mrs. Perlman."

"I'll let you know if I think of anything. I still have your number."

"Can I see her apartment?" Grasping at straws.

"I'm sorry. It's rented again. The new tenant has already moved in. There wasn't anything to see. It was empty. Completely empty."

Teddie's body was hardly cold in the ground and they'd already rented the place again. There might not have been anything to glean from seeing her apartment again. Didn't matter. I wanted to see it. Be there. To tell Teddie that I was sorry. Very sorry. And I wanted to visit Teddie's grave. It would have been cathartic for me. It wasn't going to happen. At least not now. Right now it was more important to find the Weasel.

I was about to open my car door: "Did Teddie have a teddy bear?"

"Oh, why yes. Of course. She had lots of teddy bears. Her fans were always sending them to her. Teddie – Teddy Bear – get it?"

Just what I needed to hear. "This one looked like Smokey the Bear."

"It doesn't ring a bell. I'm sorry."

So was I. I had hoped harder than hell that there'd be some new shred at Teddie's apartment. Nothing. "Fuckup," I thought as I drove away.

◈ ◈ ◈

I stopped at a gas station for a fill-up. I thought that these small foreign cars were supposed to get such good gas mileage. This one didn't seem to be. Or was I driving more than I thought I was?

I needed the fillup because I wasn't going home. I took another trip through Beirut, U.S.A., heading toward South Central. Toward Mrs. Matson. Warren. Rita.

I had told Mary that I didn't want to impose on Mrs. Matson. That wasn't the whole truth. I was afraid of seeing her. Thought she could read something in my face. Guilt. Responsibility for her daughter's death. There was another reason: Rita. I'd been avoiding her. I still wasn't sure why. For some reason, I hadn't returned her calls. Hadn't called her on my own. It kept gnawing at me. Why?

The Matson's neighborhood was peaceful. Quiet. Kids played on front lawns. I parked in front of Mrs. Matson's. Rang her bell. She answered the door, surprised to see me.

"Mr. Rogers."

Pleasantries were exchanged. She invited me in. We sat in the living room, sipping tea. The house was warm. Cozy. A friendly place to be. A strange feeling came over me. I felt safe there. At home. Like it was my home. Not the house I grew up in, but a place where I could run to escape the outside world and find myself in *Leave it to Beaver Land*. In the real world my father had been a manipulative bully. But I always had my room. The same room Rita had used as a guest room. The same room we had made love in.

The conversation with Mrs. Matson was trivial. Surface. A little awkward. She finally looked me in the eye: "Did you think of something else? Something you might want to look at. Talk about?"

"I don't know."

A spiritless silence filled the room. The air hung heavy. The walls closed in on me. Mrs. Matson got up from her chair. Came and sat next to me on the sofa. She put her hand on my forearm.

"We appreciate what you're trying to do."

"I'm not doing it very well."

"You can only do your best. If you're doing that, there is no more."

Was I doing my best? I thought I was. But I kept running into blind alleys and dead-ends. I was a fuckup. My dad had been right.

Right now, Ramon was the only plausible lead I had. And that was probably a dead-end too.

"I'm doing the best I can. Problem is it isn't good enough."

"You're following your leads. Talking to people."

"Yes."

"What else is there to do?"

Noises in another part of the house. Someone padding around. Warren? Rita?

I didn't want to whine and complain. She'd been through enough. "Did Teddie have a teddy bear?"

"Oh yes, many."

"That fans sent her? One that looks like Smokey the Bear."

"I can't recall it. She got so many stuffed animals and other gifts, she used to give them away to the local hospitals."

The light in my eyes went out. Cold.

Mrs. Matson continued: "She might have had some things at her apartment that I never saw. Or she might have kept something like that, a special one."

"What about the things Warren and Tiny brought back from the apartment? Anything in there?"

"To be honest with you, I haven't had the heart to go through all of her things yet. In the boxes I have gone through there were no teddy bears."

There was more shuffling in the back of the house.

"Do you think Warren would talk to me?"

"I don't think so. Please don't take it personally."

No, don't take it personally. He probably treats all white men the same.

"What about looking through the boxes?"

"I'm afraid now is not a good time."

I figured I shouldn't take that personally either. Warren, guardian of the boxes, Guardian of Teddie, was home. Not a good time to look into them. I thanked Mrs. Matson for the tea. Headed out to my car.

Guess who was waiting for me curbside.

"Whyn't you leave my mother alone? Chill, man."

"I'm not bothering you. If she wants to talk to me that's her business. You hear everything or only the good parts?"

"She-it. There waddn't no good parts." He flashed a toothy smile. "Why you gotta be comin' back to my hood all the time? Can't we get no peace from the likes-a you?"

"Free country. Come to my hood sometime. We'll talk." I shoved a business card in his hand.

"I come to your hood, I get busted. Man don't like me in yo' neigh-bo'-hood. Guess it ain't such a free country at that."

"All depends how you see it. Rita doesn't have a problem."

"Rita, she-it."

"Tiny either."

"Fuckin' Oreo, man."

I walked around to the driver's side of my rental. "Talking to you is a waste of time. You wanna help me find your sister's killer, give me a call sometime. You don't wanna help. That's okay too."

◈ ◈ ◈

On the way home, I stopped at a 7-Eleven, bought some magazines, swung by Martin Luther King hospital. Tiny's throat was still swollen, but he could talk a little now. And he wasn't gasping for air.

"Hey, man, wha's happenin'?" Tiny jerked his hand up for a high five. I slapped his palm. Held up the magazines for him to see. "Don't you know niggahs can't read."

"Guess I was misinformed."

"Or maybe you figured I could just look at the pictures."

"Yeah, that's right." I slapped the magazines on his bed. "You're looking pretty good. What're you doing in bed on a nice day like this?"

"Man, it's the nurses. They won't lemme leave. Just love ol' Tiny."

"When are you getting out?"

"Get my parole tomorrow. From what I hear my business is still standing."

"There's a few of 'em."

"Not many. Crazy business all this. "He pointed up to the TV. "Man, I didn't even have to watch it on the tube. All I had to do was look outside my window."

"How's the food?"

Tiny looked at me. Unsmiling. The corners of his mouth and eyes started to bend. He began laughing. Hard. Harder. "It ain't soul food, that's for sure."

◆ ◆ ◆

When I got home, there was another message from Ramon on the machine. "Fuckup," I shouted, pissed at missing the call again, slamming the machine into the wall.

CHAPTER 27

There's always a scene in B westerns where the cowboys or the cavalry are trekking through a craggy ravine or the desert flatlands, a ridge of mountains in the background. It's hot. Dusty. And silent. One tyro always says something like, "Sure is quiet out there. Indians must be miles away." The grizzled old scout comes back with: "Too quiet." He scans the horizon. Sure enough, there's a horde of Indians on the move. Or looking down on the troop from the ridge above. That's how I felt. After picking up the pieces of the answering machine, I sat on the living room sofa. It was too quiet. Much too quiet. None of the usual neighborhood noises. I sat for at least ten minutes. Not a sound. Not the breathing of the wind or the tinkling of windchimes. No music from down the street. No traffic noise. Utter silence. It was eerie. Otherworldly.

Someone was watching, breathing down my neck. I checked the perimeter of the house. Secure. The grounds. Same. It was making me crazy. It felt like *I* was being stalked.

Ribbons of sun bled in through the windows. I thought about Baron. He had been a great companion and friend. I'd raised him from a pup. He had wandered up to my door, cold, hungry. His coat was mangy. I took him in. We adopted each other. I took him to the vet. Took care of him. He also took care of me. The feeling I had now was the same empty feeling I'd had when I discovered Baron's body.

I felt the presence of someone else. I walked the house back and forth, checking every room. Every closet and window. The only sound was my shoes squeaking on the hardwood floors.

I patrolled the yard again, looking in and under bushes, behind everything. In the garage. Even inside the incinerator. Nothing. I was alone. But it didn't feel that way.

◈ ◈ ◈

Deidre Ireland – could it possibly be her real name? – was one of the biggest TV producers in Hollywood. You could tell that by her office – huge. Separate sitting and work areas. Mahogany walls. Plush carpet. Three TVs, four VCRs. I wondered if any were from the recent street sale. My appointment had been at 11:00 a.m.. She was there. Didn't allow me entry till almost noon. If it had been for anything other than learning about Teddie I would have split long ago or I would have barged into her inner sanctum, telling her what a hypocrite I thought she was. But then this was Deidre Ireland. Big TV producer – produced both of Teddie's shows, *Holier Than Thou* and *Day Timers*. Major contributor to the Cause of the Month Club. Major union backer, except on her own set, where she busted the union, kicked them out and hired scabs.

She pursed her thin lips, swept back her limp brown hair and stared at me across the great divide of her table. "Mr. Rogers, as I told you on the phone, I'm not sure I can really offer anything on your investigation."

"Just a few questions."

She sighed loudly. I wanted to pick up the Emmy on her desk. Crash it through her plate glass window. Not only for her hypocritical politics, but for the lousy TV shows she foisted on the public. Remembering what Rita had said, I wanted to ask her if her kids went to public or private schools. I bit my tongue, literally.

"Did Teddie have a fan club?"

"Yes. Most of my stars do."

Her stars. Her property. Another possession like a new Beamer or cellular phone.

"Do you know if there were any fans, in or out of the club, that were, shall we say, getting overly friendly? Overly familiar?"

"I really don't know of anything myself. Perhaps Ralph Clauson, our head of security might know something."

"Had Teddie ever complained about receiving any threatening mail or phone calls?"

"Isn't that the same question as before? You need a good rewrite man."

"You don't seem very interested in helping solve this case."

"Of course, I'm interested." She stood. I stayed put. "But I'm very busy. I think Ralph would be a better bet for you."

I was out of the office after only a couple minutes. My chat with Ralph Clauson didn't last long either and netted the same results.

◈ ◈ ◈

Jack's bike was parked in Laurie's driveway. I had called him earlier to see if he wanted to make a few bucks bodyguarding her at night. He was leaning against the wall, fiddling with an unlit cigarette. Jack had smoked in the Navy. Quit the day he exchanged a uniform for mufti. It was a rare occasion he toyed with a cigarette in his fingers. I hadn't seen him do it for months.

"Hey, Dukie."

"Gonna take up smoking again?"

"One-a these days I just might."

"Tobacco companies'll be glad. Let 'em know. Maybe you can be a poster boy."

He did his Adonis pose for me.

"Uptight about the gig?"

"It ain't the battle or firefight makes me nervous. You know that. It's the waiting. You said you was up most-a the night. Just listening. That's what I hate. The waiting."

"I know what you mean."

"Makes me nervous." He rolled the cigarette between his thumb and forefinger until it tore open, shreds of tobacco plummeting to the ground. He tossed the cigarette, what was left of it, on the ground, crushing it under his heavy black motorcycle boot. Took his kit bag and sleeping bag from the back of the bike. Went to the front of the house, knocked. It didn't take Laurie long to answer.

"Laurie Hoffman, Jack Riggs."

He put out his hand for her to shake. Hers was on delayed action. Her eyes were wide, unfocused. Staring. I should have prepared her for Jack's appearance. I had thought it might scare her off. I was having second thoughts. She finally managed to push her arm away from her body and shook Jack's hand.

"Don't judge a book by its cover."

"Yeah, I'm really a teddy bear inside," Jack said.

Laurie invited us in. We sat in the living room. She and I went over the history of her being stalked. Jack nodded politely, as if he were bored. He probably was.

"Don't worry," I said, "His bite's as bad as his bark."

"And *his* bite's bigger than his bark," he said referring to me. Laurie tried not to laugh. Couldn't help it. I was relieved. The ice was finally broken.

Laurie told us about her latest encounters with Craylock: "He keeps calling me at work, pretending to be a client. Then he won't let me off the phone and if I hang up he calls right back. The receptionist doesn't want to bother with him so she passes him onto me. The boss said if I don't get my personal life in order I won't get a promotion I'm up for. That I've worked hard for." Laurie's eyes danced with fear.

Jack set about unloading his kit bag. Toothbrush, hairbrush, razor sharp Ka-bar knife. Colt .45. 9mm Beretta backup gun. He was ready. Laurie reached for her purse, pulled out the .38 I had loaned her. Jack dived for the deck, rolling, coming up with the .45 aimed point blank at Laurie's mid-section.

"Whoa, boy. A little fast on the trigger."

"See a gun, take defensive action."

The fear returned to Laurie's eyes. Would she be safe with this madman for even one night? I made excuses to leave. She walked me to my car.

"Are you sure you can't stay? Cost isn't a problem."

"I know. I'm sorry, I'm working this other case day and night. It's not fair to you. Jack's a good man. Don't let his looks fool you. He's a little crude on the outside, but he's okay."

"It's not the looks that–"

"He didn't fire at you. He knew what he was doing."

"Yes, but he seems a little–"

"–Insane? If he's insane, so am I. Don't worry."

She looked like she wanted to say something. Her lips curled into talk-mode, then retreated. Again.

"Say it."

"I, I don't even know *you* that well."

"So you don't know who you can trust? Me? Jack?"

She nodded.

"But you know who you can't trust: Craylock. And I'm telling you, the cure – Jack – isn't as bad as the disease – Craylock. If you don't trust him, or me, say the word, he'll leave with me now. And we're outta your life. Or tell him later. He'll leave."

"I guess I'm just not very trusting right now. Because of what's happened."

"I understand."

"I guess I need to learn to fend for myself. Stand on my own two feet."

"You're learning. People aren't born tough."

"I'm going to do this even if it kills me."

"We won't let that happen."

She thanked me.

I drove to Mary's apartment in Santa Monica. The sun was sinking over the horizon. It reminded me of the giant ball that's dropped every New Years in New York. There were no noisemakers or confetti for this descending ball.

The streets hadn't yet come back to their full capacity. There was traffic. Not as much as usual. I still had the feeling I was being followed. I changed lanes. No cars behind me made a move. I continued down Santa Monica Boulevard, toward the beach. The feeling didn't leave. I told myself it was nerves, stress, anxiety. All those good things that people buy paperbacks by doctors and quacks to cure. I changed lanes again. No one made a move. I turned down 26th Street. Several cars followed suit. If I pulled over to the curb, the tail, if there was one, would suspect I knew I was being tailed. I didn't want him to know that. I kept on 26th. Turned right on Washington, left on Princeton. A couple cars followed down Washington. No one turned on Princeton after me. I pulled up in front of Mary's apartment building, parked and waited. After five minutes, with no one suspicious to take my attention, I went up to the front door, rang the buzzer. Mary buzzed me in.

The building was modest. One of those cheap '50s stucco jobs. Of course, the name wasn't so modest: *Le Grand Villa*. The apartment was comfortably, though cheaply furnished. Mary was saving for a house. No sense throwing money away on rent.

She favored prints of classic paintings. Everyone was there, Rembrandt, DaVinci, Gainsborough. She offered me something to drink. I declined and sat at the dining table.

"I showed the notes to my friend, the handwriting expert." She continued on through a merry melange of her history with this guy. I didn't care. I was trying to be polite. My fingers were dancing on my thighs. She finally came to the part that I wanted to hear. "Anyway, he says they're both from the same hand?"

"One hundred percent?" My heart raced. This was the first real breakthrough I had on the case. Something to tie them together. Teddie and Pilar. A definite connection.

"Nothing's a hundred percent," she said. "He said there's a ninety-nine percent probability they're by the same hand."

"Close enough."

She put the two notes on the table side by side. "Notice the way he makes the loops on g's, y's and the like. And the way he crosses his t's, dots his i's. Also, the same slope of the letters. They fall at the same angle. It's very close."

Silence filled the room. She looked at me: "Are you still with me?"

"Yeah. There's a connection now. You proved it. So the Weasel knew them both, or if not knew them, knew of them."

"But there isn't really a connection yet."

"No?"

"You don't know if these notes are from the Weasel."

"I've got something with his writing on it. A piece of paper he dropped in the hallway of Teddie Matson's apartment building."

"Then you'll know for sure."

"I'll still be nowhere. Okay, so I have him tied to the two actresses. What then? It doesn't help me find him."

"Talk to their families."

"Easier said than done. Much easier. They're stonewalling me. Even the ones that talk don't tell all."

"They don't know you."

"It's not that. They're hiding something. I have no idea what."

"It's a start."

"Yeah. Hey, what about that old movie trick of trying to figure out where the paper came from, tracing it that way."

"Unless it's a very unusual specimen that's a waste of time. And I don't think it's that unusual."

"I had to ask. I'm grasping for straws at this point. It does give me a direction to head."

We made small talk for a few more minutes. Jack used to bug me about my friendship with Mary. Why hadn't we clicked? We'd met on a blind date. We went to Yamashiro's, overlooking the city. Then drove up the coast. With anyone else it would have been a very romantic evening. With Mary it was a course in forensics. Checking the sushi for traces of heavy metals. Worrying about the mercury in the ocean. We never even kissed good night. A week later she called me about a little research she needed for a case she was working. We decided we actually did have something in common, even if it wasn't in the romance department. After that we became fast friends. Mary's one of the two people I trust completely. Jack is the other.

Heading out to my car, I scanned the street. It was dark. A street lamp was out at the north end of the block making it even harder to see. Nothing out of the ordinary. No one sitting in a car, waiting. Stalking.

I drove off down the road. I had to find Pilar. Had to find out what the connection was. I was too wired to go home. I could go to the office or get a bite to eat. Wasn't hungry. I wanted news. I needed news. I jammed the pedal to the floor. Burned rubber, heading east on Olympic. Heading back to Beirut.

There were less cars on the road now. I could count them all. I still couldn't see anyone in particular. But I still had the eerie feeling that I was being followed.

CHAPTER 28

La Revolucion was jumping. People in and out. Mostly men. A few women. Whores from their appearance. Ramon would more likely be here than at home. It was dark. I hung low in my front seat, just over the dash. Enough to see who was coming and going. Popular hangout, for everyone but Ramon. Unless he'd gone in before I got there. No way could I check out the bar myself. After the last visit, my company wouldn't be welcome. And I had no backup.

California law says you have to stop serving liquor at 2:00 am. Maybe they did. They sure didn't close the doors. People kept on coming. Still no Ramon. When the sun crested the sooty building across the street, I decided it was time to go home, get some sleep. At that hour, the drive was quiet. No rush hour traffic yet. A few cars here and there. Nothing out of the ordinary. And still I felt a pair of eyes on my shoulders. If I turned right, they turned right. If I slowed, they slowed.

Paranoid visions.

Monsters in the rearview.

Jam on brakes.

Shrill howl.

Brakes squealing.

Lay rubber.

Skid marks.

Hand on Firestar.

Cursing drivers.

Slamming brakes.

Fingers flying.
Flipping off.
Swerve around me.
No guns pointed.
Lucky me.
Accident avoided.
Lucky me.
Suspicious persons.
Everyone.
No one.
Sign of the Weasel?
Nowhere to be found.
Craylock?
No shiny new beamers.
Not down here.

◈ ◈ ◈

By the time I got home, my eyelids were held up by perseverance and muscles that were locked in place. Sugar plum fairies danced on the lids, closing them tighter. Tighter. Park the car. Auto pilot to the house. The bedroom. Crash. Sweet dreams, sweet prince.

◈ ◈ ◈

Ocean waves swim over me.
Schools of fish brush my shin.
Depleted bubbles rise to the surface.
The direction I should be heading.
No.
Nitrogen narcosis.
Diver's disease.
Loss of orientation.
Swim down when you mean to swim up.
Deeper.
Deeper.
Into the abyss.
Dark chasm.

Gaping open.
Bidding: enter,
Sweet prince.
Enter.
Never to return from here again.
Oxygen tank spent.
Muscles exhausted.
Drift.
Drift
Into the darkness.
Where light doesn't penetrate.
Where men fear to tread.
Dark waters.
Cold.
Angry.
Surround you,
Sweet prince.
Suck you down.
Papier mache Neptunes fire spears at you.
Swim for the surface.
Exhaling all the way.
Don't get punished with the bends.
Drop your weight belt.
Clear your mask.
Pop your ears.
Save yourself.
Shoot to the surface.
Exhale.
Exhale.

◈ ◈ ◈

In the Navy I never got tired. Wasn't allowed to be tired. The stress had served me well. I knew how to carry off long operations. This was different.

The ocean had permeated my thoughts on the drive home. Another world. With its own inhabitants. Its own set of laws. An escape. I was always at home in the water, from the time I was a baby. Could swim before I could walk. Fish out of water. Yet when I dove into a deep sleep after the all night stakeout, the ocean of my dreams sucked me in. Under. Couldn't see. Couldn't breathe. Couldn't find the surface. I'd swim up, but I was really swimming down. That had never happened before. Not even in a dream.

The unexamined life may not be worth living, and the unexamined dream may not be worth dreaming. No way was I going to analyze that dream. Not now.

Dropping weight belts.

Nitrogen narcosis.

Papier mache Neptunes.

What a paranoid dream. I was glad to be up.

Paper. I had to find the note the Weasel had scribbled. Compare the handwriting. Shower. Shave. A quickly devoured onion bagel. Daylight streaming in the windows. Nothing unusual. Yet still the feeling. Eyes watching. Was I a puppet on a string being worked by an unseen puppeteer?

No time for that BS now. Where was that damn paper, if I had it at all? Home? The office? My car? Still at Tiny's. The car would be the last place to look. Might not still be a car. Might be an empty charbroiled hulk.

Had I saved the paper?

Last I remembered seeing it was in my car right after Mrs. Perlman had given it to me. Damn car again.

Where had I gone after the Perlman's? The William Tell Motel. If I left it there it was long gone. Did I bring it to my office? Home?

And why wasn't the damn phone ringing? Where was Ramon? Did he have a spy in the sky letting him know when I wasn't home so he could only call then? It was getting to me. The whole case was getting to me.

I tore through the drawers in the kitchen where I sometimes put things when I got lazy. No paper. Began working my way through the rest of the house. In a hurry. I wasn't putting things back. By the time I was finished, it looked like a hurricane had ripped through the house. Make it easy for whoever's spying on me. Everything out in plain sight, including me.

"Come and get me, you bastard," I shouted. "I owe you a little payback for Baron." I shook my head to clear it. Continued through the house. Damn paper wasn't anywhere. I was about to head for the office when I thought I should look in my clothes. Might be in a pocket somewhere.

What was I wearing that day? Couldn't remember. I hadn't sent any clothes to the laundry or done any laundry myself in several days – too busy working the case. That gave me hope.

Jackets. Shirts. Pants.
Tear 'em inside out.
Nothing.
Laundry hamper.
Zilch.
Damn.
Car.

I raced out to the driveway. Jerked open the rental car's door. My windbreaker sat on the front seat. I turned the pockets inside out. Hard candy wrappers. An old piece of paper from the spiral notebook I carry. Paperclip. Shriveled piece of paper. Unfold it carefully. Smooth it out. Eureka!

The notes to Pilar and Teddie were in a large envelope I had with me. I spread them on the hood of the car next to the Weasel's scribbled note. Examined them for several minutes. The letters that looped below the line looked the same. T's and i's crossed and dotted the same. To my untrained eyes it was a match. Mary and her friend could confirm it later.

My heart did somersaults. The case was closing. Things were coming together. Finally. It was a good feeling. It lasted about ten seconds. Until thoughts of Baron flashed my mind. The joy turned to anger, which turned to determination. I'd get the S.O.B. I still wasn't sure if the Weasel or Craylock or someone else had killed Baron. Short of the two of them, there were no major suspects. Possibles: Warren. Ramon. Someone I'd found for a previous client. Someone who hadn't wanted to be found.

I had an unlisted home phone number and address. It wouldn't have been easy for them to find me. But then it shouldn't have been easy for the Weasel to find Teddie Matson. Anything was easy if you knew how to do it, or someone who could do it for you.

There was always the possibility that some maniac had done Baron. That was the least likely possibility. A maniac doesn't go around with cyanide. He would have cut the dog's throat or ripped his eyeballs out with his bare hands. Maniacs were at the low end of the totem pole.

The phone rang. I gathered up the papers, ran inside. Ramon. It had to be Ramon.

"Hello, Duke. This is Lou."

CHAPTER 29

My heart dropped. Almost stopped. Lou could only want one thing.

"Time's up."

"I need a few more days."

"It's always a few more days with you, Duke."

"A couple days. I'm getting close."

"I'm getting uncomfortable. The police should know what's going on."

"Lou, I could lose my license."

"And I could lose my job. You're not getting anywhere."

"I am. It hasn't been easy, but I'm finally making some progress. Don't cut me off now. The police'll always be there."

"The trail'll be cold."

"The stuff I give them will warm it up for them, if it gets to that point." I thought about telling her that I was being stalked now. Get some sympathy. If it were true, I might have said something. Without proof, there was no point. Lying wasn't my forte. Silence. She was softening.

"I don't know why I let you talk me into these things."

"Because I take you to El Coyote."

"That's as good a reason as any. I'll give you a few more days, but I really am getting nervous. The cops are getting nowhere. They might have information you don't. Don't you have a friend on the force?"

"Yeah, but he's been kinda busy lately." My voice trailed off.

"Well, good luck."

"I'll need it."

More silence. "I thought you were getting hot."

"I am, but I ain't there yet. Can always use luck."

We said our goodbyes. I felt as if I'd been reprieved from a jail sentence. Time to get moving.

Should I hire an answering service? They could keep Ramon on the line while they beeped me. Sounded like a good idea. The Yellow Pages were full of them. Eenie meenie miney moe, Larry, Shemp and Curly Joe. I needed one that could take my MasterCard number over the phone, set me up right away. Found it, Diane's Dial. Cute. They'd have me set up within the next couple of hours and I could stop by to pick up a beeper. They were expensive. The Weasel's money would cover it. The plumber would have to wait.

Jack called. "Quiet as a mouse, buddy."

"How's she feeling?"

"Scared."

"You gonna be there tonight?"

"I feel rejected, man. She said she could handle it alone."

"I thought you said she was still scared."

"Yeah, man. I think she wants to try it on her own. Knows she can't have someone babysitting her all the time."

"It's like the toothache that goes away when you go to the dentist's office. Maybe I'll stop by there later. *Adios.*"

"Hey, buddy, sleep with one eye open."

◈ ◈ ◈

Jack always slept with his eyes open. Spooky. He wasn't going to let anyone sneak up on him. To look at him you'd have thought he was dead. To approach him, you could easily have your series canceled.

Dropped by Diane's Dial. A hole in the wall in a medical building in Beverly Hills. Several operators busy taking calls. Jeremiah, he of the blue suede shoes – for real – gave me my beeper, showed me how to use it. There was no Diane. Ever.

For the first time in a couple days it didn't seem like anyone was following. Guy had to sleep sometime. I felt free.

Laurie wasn't home, must have still been at work. Her house looked still. No missives or fancy-wrapped packages on the porch. Of course, she might already have taken them in. Doors secure. Windows locked. Her work wasn't too far away. I found a phone booth in a gas station. The payphone – I needed a car phone – smelled of dried urine and God knows what else. I didn't want to know. The receptionist at Laurie's office put me on hold. Laurie took my call immediately. Insisted she wanted to try it alone that night. I gave her the beeper number and told her if she called my home or office to let it ring at least seven times. If I didn't pick up, it would switch over to the service, who could also ring through to the beeper, saving her an additional call.

Streets almost back to normal. Traffic bursting up to the curbs. People a little more courteous. Afraid to run a red light or cut someone off. Afraid of getting shot.

Beeper beep. Anticipation. I read out the number of the person who called. Familiar digits. Familiar warmth. Rita. Glad I'm in the car. Afraid to call her. Why?

Where to go? Head to East L.A. so that if Ramon calls I'll be close by. No. Heart racing. Hands drumming steering wheel. Driving in circles. Head swimming. Pull over to the side of the road. Relax. Don't forget to breathe.

Don't forget to breathe.
Silver shadows.
Rearview mirror.
Gleaming chrome.
Snarling black enamel.
Pulls to the curb.
Spaces behind me.
Clutch the wheel.
Squeezing tight.
Tail?
Sitting in his car.
Not moving.
View blocked.
Cars inbetween.
Sitting.
Sitting.
Tail.
Angry fingers.
Grasping gritty steel.
Safety off.
Poised.
Delicate balance.
The waiting game.
Make my move.
Let him make his.
Waiting.
Biding time.
Tension fills.
Angry blood.
Coursing veins.
Hold steady.
Steady now.
Ditch the car.
Roll to the street.

Crouching run to his car.
Yank open driver's door.
Startled look.
Wrench him from the car.
Throw him against hood.
Spread eagle.
Frisk.
Who are you?
Who the fuck are you?
Why are you following me?
I'm not following you. Never seen you before in my life.
Relieve him of his wallet.
William D. Kinnear.
What's your business here?
Fuller Brush Man. Are you a cop?
Shut up. This isn't a residential neighborhood.
I'm stopping to pick up a pair of shoes.
Search his pockets. Find the receipt.
Then what were you sitting in your car for?
Since when did that become against the law?
Don't let me catch you behind me again.
Walk away.
Paranoid motherfucker.
Don't take the bait.
Get in the car.
And drive.
Don't forget to breathe.

◈ ◈ ◈

I was getting as paranoid as Laurie. It scared me. There probably wasn't anyone following me. There was nothing objective to support that theory. The case – cases – were getting to me.

C'mon and beep you damn thing.
Beep, Goddamnit.

Beep.
Back to the office. Clean out old files. Dust the desk.
Windex the windows. Keep busy. Nervous energy.
   Someone on the stairs. Heading down the hall.
Shadow cuts across the pebbled glass.
   Ready.
   Waiting.
   Safety off.
   Cocked and locked.
   Weasel?
   Stalker?
   My stalker?
   Front office door swings open.
   Framed by the door:
   Warren.

◈ ◈ ◈

I visually scanned him for weapons. Hands: empty. No baggy pants today. He had dressed for the white man's hood. Slacks and a sport shirt. Shiny black shoes. Overly shiny. I could've used a pair of sunglasses. No jacket. No place to hide a gun, unless it was a small one. I kept my eyes on his hands.

Watch what people do, not what they say.

"I'm clean." He watched me watch him. Held his hands out, palms up. "Left the Uzi in the car." Didn't even crack a smile.

"I see you made it all the way up here without *the man* busting you."

"The man. Chill, man. Don't try to talk like us okay. You'll never keep up. No one talks like that anymore."

"Fine. We'll talk straight English."

"White man's English."

"Call it what you want. We have to settle on something. You don't want me talking your language."

"For one, you don't know it. For another, you steal everything we have. Leave us our language. Hell, Vanilla Ice. That's a rapper? What mean streets he grow up on?"

"I don't know. Plenty of white kids have their own mean streets."

"Ain't no mean streets like nigger mean streets."

"All right. Let's get down to business."

We walked through the outer office and into the inner sanctum. He sat in my chair behind the desk.

"If you're waiting for me to tell you to get out of there, you'll be waiting a long time. That's the most uncomfortable chair in the place." I sat on a wing chair in front of the desk, right where the Weasel had stood. "You're the man now."

"The seat of power." He spun in the chair.

"Not much power here."

"You white. You got power."

"I don't buy it. Not today."

"You're as prejudiced as the rest." His eyes roamed my office. There wasn't much there to scream power or anything else.

"'Cause I don't agree with you? That's an excuse."

"I been hearin' excuses all my life."

"I don't give a shit."

"That's the problem."

"That's not what we're here to talk about."

"What are we here to talk about?"

"I don't know. You tell me. You came to me." I didn't need his BS. If he wanted to talk he would, but I was getting tired of his games.

Silence.

"Why you so interested in my sister's murder?"

"It's a job, man."

"Figures. Tha's all it is to you, man. A job. Wouldn't be helpin' no niggers 'less there's money in it."

"I don't have time for this. Whadda you want?"

"You're tryin' to find out who killed my sister. I want to find out who killed her too."

"A partner."

"Ain't talkin' no partner shit. But you need me to help you."

It's about time is what I wanted to say to him. I held it in.

"But first I want to know why you're so interested. Yeah, it's a job. Who you working for? She's just another dead *Nee-gress*. No big deal."

"Who I'm working for is privileged information."

"So you're doing it just for the money."

"It's more than that."

"Ah, the Great White Knight. Great White Hope."

"Talking to you makes me feel like the Great White Dope. Maybe I should just give up. Let the guy run."

"It don't seem like just the money with you. Seems more. Personal."

I hid behind a veil of chatter and officiousness. His dark brown eyes tore holes in my veil. But he said: "I know, man, it's just a job."

"Listen, Warren, I want justice."

"Noble words, man. So did we when those cops got off."

"You keep coming back to that stuff."

"That stuff is our lot in life. Okay, if you want to help – noblesse oblige and all that – who am I to say no. Didn't know a nigger knew such big words, huh?" He'd lost his street accent.

I hadn't responded to his speech in any way. The veil was still drawn. Then: "You know what your problem is. You can't stand being treated like a human being by a white man. You want to be treated like a nigger so you can go around pissed off all the time."

He jumped from his chair. I didn't get up. I could feel his hate. It grabbed me by the throat and wouldn't let go. I glared back. A Mexican standoff, except neither of us was Mexican.

"You don't have to like me Warren, 'cause I'm white, or 'cause I'm a private dick or 'cause you like the way I part my hair. But we are after the same things. Might as well work with each other instead of against."

"You're right, I don't have to like you," he said and I could see a softening in his eyes. I didn't think we'd ever be friends, but we didn't have to have our knives unsheathed either. He went on, "But we are after the same thing. Sort of."

His eyes were tentative. Debating. His hand shot out for me to shake. We would never be friends. At least we didn't have to be enemies.

"What can I do to help?" His voice cracked. The helpless squeak of a small child who'd held in a ton of hurt not knowing how to express it. He wasn't about to unload on me, not in any meaningful way. At least we'd moved closer together.

It took about five minutes to tell him about the teddy bear, the handwriting. Ramon. Pilar. How I'd like to find her. I didn't tell him I came upon the Weasel's piece of paper.

"Don't remember anyone named Ramon. And she had lots of stuffed animals. Lotta teddy bears. Don't know about Smokey. So many things. I can tell you it wasn't with the stuff we took from her apartment. I'll look around the house, see if there's anything there. Teddy bears. Notes from fans. Anything looks interesting, I'll give you a call."

"Thanks, Warren." For the first time, I felt hope. I gave him the beeper number. "Call any time, day or night. I'll come down and pick the stuff up."

"You don't wanna come to my neighborhood at night. Not even when there ain't no disturbance."

I was waiting for him to bring up Rita. He didn't. We tried for some normal conversation, sports. Movies. It was almost pleasant. So pleasant you could cut the air with a cleaver.

He got up to leave: "Any white guy that would hang around my neighborhood during the rebellion must have balls."

We shook again. It was warmer this time, for both of us. Not friendly. *Detente.*

As he walked through the outer office, I asked: "Do you like dogs?"

"Say what?"

I didn't want to confront him directly. I figured if he was guilty it would show. What showed was that he thought I was out of my mind for bringing it up.

He stepped out into the hall. Turned back: "Did you know Teddie?"

"Never met her."

❖ ❖ ❖

No point in staying at the office. Things were quiet. With the beeper I was in touch everywhere. Next thing I'd have to get was a cellular phone so I could order pizza while driving. On the way to the market, the beeper beeped. It was the answering service; I stopped at the first payphone. They said they had a caller on hold for me. They put me through.

A hazy voice answered.

It was familiar.

CHAPTER 30

H*ola, amigo.*"

❖ ❖ ❖

MacArthur Park is midway between Hancock Park, not a park, but an upper class neighborhood, and downtown L.A., a neighborhood in search of an identity. When I was a boy, my grandparents used to take me to the park. We'd rent rowboats and paddle through the lake, tossing bread crumbs to the birds. The park is a different place today. You can still rent paddle boats – if you want to paddle across the lake while talking to your dealer. Sometimes on Saturdays or Sundays immigrant families still try to use it as a park. Most of the time, it's a haven for pushers, crack addicts, hookers and worse. Even the police don't like treading there. If they were scared, who was I to play Rambo?

The rental car slid easily into a parking place on Alvarado. Click – locked. Of course that wouldn't keep out anyone who wanted to get in. The Firestar was in my belt, under a loose fitting Hawaiian shirt that was left untucked. Wet grass sucked under my feet. As long as it didn't suck me under I was okay.

"Meet me by the statue of *el general,*" Ramon had said. The statue of General Douglas MacArthur is in the northwestern corner of the park where there was, naturally no place to park. Cutting through the park was not a good idea. I walked along Wilshire Boulevard, past garbage and litter and clusters of men, teens really. Some young men in their early twenties, in white tank top undershirts and baggy pants, charcoal hair slicked back off their foreheads. One man danced a nervous jig by himself in a corner of the pavilion building. Crack dancing.

No one approached me to buy or sell drugs. Probably thought I was a narc. Maybe saw the silhouette of the Star. MacArthur had seen better days, both the park and the statue. Graffiti camouflaged the general's stern visage. No one there cared who he was or why there was a park named after him.

No Ramon.

I stood on the corner. Waiting. Trying to look nonchalant. A black-and-white cruised slowly by. Mirrored eyes scrutinizing. What's the white man doing there? Is he buying drugs? Do they see the gun? Were they calling for backup? Fingering their triggers? Seconds passed like hours. The car drove by. Gone. I felt lucky. Luckier than I had walking the length of the park without getting mugged.

"*Amigo.*"

"Ramon."

He stood behind the statue, signaling me to join him.

"We finally connect, uh, man?"

Nod.

"You must be pretty desperate to be lookin' me up."

I was, but I didn't admit it.

"I used ta hang here. No more. That's why I figured i's a good place to meet. Guys I hang with now don't come down here an' I don' want 'em seein' me talkin' with you. Used to be a nice park." His arm swept across sooty gray water and expanse of green lawn covered with multi-colored garbage. For my money it hadn't been a nice park for at least twenty years, maybe more. "Let's make it quick," he said.

"Ball's in your court."

"Wadda ya wanna know? Whachu want with my sister? With Pilar Cruz?"

"I'm looking for Teddie Matson's killer."

His eyes snapped open. Impressed.

"I have reason to believe that Pilar Cruz might be able to help me find him."

His eyes half closed, heavy lids over dull bloodshot eyes. Should he tell me? Was I to be trusted?

"Pilar don' live in L.A. no more."

"Where does she live? Where's Anna?"

"I haven't heard from Anna in more than a year. Could be anywhere by now."

"Is Pilar with her?"

Silence. Thinking.

"I don't know." More silence. "I think so. Prob'ly."

I looked into his eyes. Probing.

"Don' look at me that way. An' it's not what you're thinking."

"What am I thinking?" I said.

"Never mind."

He was probably thinking that I thought his sister and Pilar were lesbian lovers. He was right.

"Where's the last place you had an address for them?"

A piece of wrinkled paper materialized from his pocket. A street address in Calexico, near the Mexican border, on it.

"I haven't heard from her in over a year."

"Are you worried?"

"Yeah, man. We used to write at least once a month. Me an' Anna. Or me an Pilar. At least once a month."

"Why didn't you go with them?"

Silence. I figured they didn't want him. Didn't want to push it.

"What are they running from?" Maybe they were two lesbian girls who felt alienated from their community. Hiding out so they could be alone – together. But then why Calexico – hardly the most tolerant place, I imagined. Maybe there was something else. Still hiding out, but not from their community. Maybe it was from one person.

He was thinking, hard. How much should he tell me? Was he betraying confidences?

"It's better if you tell me, Ramon. Better for–"

"It ain't gonna bring Teddie Matson back."

"True. But maybe your sister and Pilar can stop running. Live a normal life."

"How do I know I can trust you?"

"Would I come down here if I didn't have good intentions?"

"Depends on what's in it for you."

"Look, someone hired me to find Teddie Matson's killer. If it's the same guy that hurt Pilar I'll be doing us both a favor."

That struck something in him. "I don' even know his name. They wouldn't tell me."

"Pilar and Anna wouldn't tell you?"

He nodded.

"Tell me what you know."

"I don' know much. The girls went to stay with relatives in Sparks for a summer."

"Sparks? Sparks, Nevada?" Sparks flying. Teddie's and Pilar's notes.

"Yeah. Stayin' with relatives. I was here. Workin' a summer job when I was stupid enough to do that kinda sucker shit. Somethin' happened. I'm not sure what."

"Rape?" There was no easy way to say it.

"They wouldn' tell me. Something bad. Knew I'd kill him. Didn't want me goin' to jail. Can you believe it? I been to jail four times since then. Before that summer, Pilar and I– It was never the same. I mean, we was only kids anyways. But I loved her. She loved me. We was gonna get married. Have kids. Live the American Dream. The *Gringo* American Dream." He snorted a disgusted laugh. Sarcasm glinted in his eyes. "It was never the same."

"Did Pilar or Anna know Teddie Matson?"

"I don' know. Don't think so. How could they? She's from another world."

"In Sparks maybe."

"Don't know."

"How long were they in Sparks?"

"I don' know, man. A few months. Maybe they were fifteen, sixteen. Somethin' like that."

Teddie was a few years older than Pilar and Anna. She might have been in Sparks at the same time. Seemed like a long shot.

"Were they in any kinds of plays or something when they were in Sparks?"

"I don' know. Yeah, maybe. I can't remember."

"Is there anything else?"

"Here, man." He handed me a picture of Pilar and Anna. "If you find them, tell 'em to write."

"I will."

He started to walk away. "If you find the dude done this to 'em, lemee know. I'll take care-a him. Waste 'im, man. Then you won't have to go to jail."

"No, you will."

"I can do the time standing on my head." He lit a joint. Walked off.

◈ ◈ ◈

I drove home. It was empty without Baron. I grabbed the phone.

Calexico was a long shot. Information didn't have a phone number for either Anna Martinez or Pilar Cruz. Unlisted number? Gone?

I dialed again, Mrs. Matson this time. The phone rang seven times. I was about to hang up:

"Hello."

"Hello, Mrs. Matson, this is Duke Rogers."

"Hi Duke. Any news?"

"I'm making some progress. Wish it could be faster. Do you have a minute?"

"Surely. What can I do for you?"

"Did Teddie ever live in Sparks, Nevada? Visit there?"

"No, not in Sparks. When she was first starting out she lived in Reno though."

"What was she doing?"

"She was in a chorus line at one of the hotels."

"Do you remember which one?"

"No, I'm sorry. I might be able to find it in her things though."

"Would Warren know?"

"He might. They were very close. He isn't home now."

"If he gets in within the next hour will you have him call me."

"I'll ask him. But he, well, you know—"

"I think he might this time." I didn't go into our rapprochement. "Is there anything you remember about her time in Reno? How long she was there? Any friends she might have made? Anything like that."

"I'm afraid I don't. It was several years ago. I think it was rather uneventful. She didn't work there very long. A couple months. Three maybe."

I thanked her and hung up. Packing didn't take long. Ammo for the Star. More ammo. And a toothbrush. A small bag of clean underwear, fresh shirt. The phone didn't ring. Should I call Mrs. Matson again? See if Warren's in. Don't be a pest. Not yet.

Tanked up the car. Ready to go. I hit the road. It was early enough in the afternoon to miss rush hour. These days just about any time is rush hour. Traffic was bad. Could've been worse. I hit the Hollywood Freeway to the 10 and headed out.

Somewhere around San Berdoo, the beeper rang. Hit the first offramp. First gas station. Old fashioned glassed in booth. Greasy finger marks on the glass. Dial.

"Warren. Duke Rogers."

"Yeah, man. What's up? I haven't found the teddy bear yet."

"Keep looking."

"I will."

"Tell me about Teddie's playing Reno." The line was silent. Dead? "Warren?"

"I'm here."

"Reno."

"Yeah, Reno. Hold on."

Bang, the phone hit a hard surface. Shuffling, non-descript noises. Another extension being picked up. "Okay, you can hang up." A reverbed Warren. Click. First extension being hung up. "I'm back." His voice was low, almost a whisper. Conspiratorial.

"What's going on?"

"You wanted to know about Reno. What do you want to know?"

"I'm not sure exactly. Anything unusual about Teddie's time there?"

Silence. "Yeah, man. But my mom doesn't know. If I talk, it's between us."

"It might come out. I'll do my best and I won't tell her. I'll try to keep it quiet."

"That ain't good enough."

"It's the best I can do. Look, I could lie to you. Tell you it won't come out. I'm not lying. I'm being straight. Be straight with me."

"Okay. Guy there saw Teddie in the show, at the Crystal Palace. She was mostly in the chorus, but she also had a couple of bits. A line here, two lines there. He went head over heels for her. Wouldn't leave her alone."

"A stalker?"

"Yeah, I guess. But it was before that word got into vogue, know what I mean? He'd send her flowers and candy backstage. Notes. All kinds-a stuff."

"Teddy bears?"

"Yeah, I think so. I'm lookin' for it. Really. Can't find it." More rustling. "But even before the shit got so heavy I didn't want her seeing him."

"Why not?"

"He wasn't good for her."

"You're being oblique."

"Good whitey word there."

"Cut the shit."

"He wasn't good for her."

I started to say something. Warren cut me off: "He was white." As if that was enough.

"What else?"

"I don't know. It was a long time ago. Teddie and I were close. Real close. But I'm not sure she told me everything."

"You think she might have liked him? Led him on?"

"Get off, man."

"Might he have raped her?"

"She never said so. I thought maybe."

"Maybe?"

"She wouldn't tell me for sure. Knew I'd kill the guy – didn't want me landing in jail. Already been – would have been really hard time." He lowered his voice even more. "Don't you mention none of this to my Mother. It would kill her."

"Any chance you remember the guy's name."

Silence. "I think his first name was Jack. John. Maybe Jim."

"Jim?"

"Yeah, something like that. One-a those J names."

"Last name."

"Can't remember?"

"Talbot?"

"Doesn't ring a bell."

"Did he ever contact her after she made it on TV?"

"Might have. I remember she did get something that upset her. Some kind of gift. I never actually saw it. Might have been the bear. She could've thrown it away."

"Would Rita know anything?"

"Shit, man, this ain't goin' nowhere. Let's get out. Hit the streets."

"You've got to be methodical. We're taking it as best we can. Now, tell me, would Rita know anything?"

"I don't think so. I was closer to Teddie than Rita."

"Did she know a Pilar Cruz?"

"I don't know. Why?"

"Anna Martinez?"

"I hate beaners, man. They're comin' in here, takin' over all our hoods. Grabbin' the power and they won't even speak English."

"I didn't ask your opinion of them. Did Teddie know either of these girls?"

"I don't know. Doesn't ring a bell."

"Anything else you can think of?"

"Not now. If I do, I'll let you know."

"I'm gonna be out of town for a couple days."

"I'm comin' with you."

"I'm going to be hard to reach. Leave any info with my service. Detailed message and tell them to make sure they get it right."

"Yes, sir, massah." There was a silence at his end of the phone. Then: "See you in Reno." He slammed the phone down. I pulled my map box out of the trunk. Nevada. Sparks. Reno.

Bingo.

Sparks was a suburb of Reno.

◈ ◈ ◈

As I was leaving the booth, the beeper beeped again. Read out a number. Familiar. Rita.

I cleared the beeper. Headed for the car.

Something nagged at me. Why was I avoiding Rita?

CHAPTER 31

Dust swirls engulfed the car. Calexico. A desert border town. Like something out of the movies. A cross of cultures. Or maybe a clash of them.

First thing, gas up. While they filled the tank, I checked the phone book. Lotta Cruz's. Lotta Martinez's. No Pilar Cruz's. No Anna Martinez's. Several A. Martinez's. One M. Cruz. Rip. Tore the page out of the book for future reference if the address Ramon gave me turned bust.

Small house. Faded yellow planks. Faded brighter yellow trim. Two car garage at the end of the driveway. Window in front. Sound of the vacuum cleaner shooshing back and forth. Knock-knock.

"Who's there?"

"My name's Duke Rogers, I–"

"Don't need anything."

"I'm not selling anything."

The door jerked open. "Then waddayou want?" Older woman. Red, puffy skin. Mid fifties maybe. Maybe younger. It was the moo-moo and alcohol lines that made her look old. Might have had a figure at some time. Not now. And if she did, who could tell under the cow tent?

"I'm looking for Anna Martinez and Pilar Cruz." I showed her the photograph of the girls.

"Sorry, you must have the wrong address." The smell of alcohol spit from her mouth like fire from a dragon.

"Well, maybe they don't live here now. But they used to."

"I've owned this house for seventeen years. No Anna Cruz or Pilar Martinez ever—"

"Anna Martinez and Pilar Cruz."

"Whoever."

"You never rented a room or—"

"—Or nothin'. I'm busy now, please."

"Thank you."

Hissing sound. Before I reached the curb, sprinklers doused my pant legs with unfriendly water. As an ex-frogman, I'd thought of all water as friendly. Not so this H_2O.

Simon Bolivar rode a magnificent rearing white steed in front of the cheap motel bearing his name. Both he and the steed were covered with magnificent graffiti *art*. The room was small. Clean. Double bed with a tapestry spread. TV had to be fed quarters. A phone in the room cost extra. It was worth it. I started dialing the names from the phonebook pages. No one had heard of Anna or Pilar, at least they claimed not to have. Both had common enough Hispanic surnames. It was possible that none of the Cruz's and Martinez's in the book knew them. It was also possible they were covering up.

After exhausting the phone pages, I fed four quarters into the TV for an hour's worth of mindless pabulum. *A Team* reruns were the only thing I could stomach – best of the lot. With the sound low, I lay back on the bed, hands folded under my head, and stared at the ceiling.

Ramon could have given me the wrong address to send me on a wild goose chase. I didn't think so. He knew I didn't have much to go on. He'd tried too hard to get in touch with me. Meet off his current turf. I believed the address was correct. He might have copied it down wrong. That was a more likely possibility. Another possibility was that the lady of the house, whose name I'd forgotten to get – fuckup – was lying. The garage had a small curtained window in it. The car door looked sealed shut. There was a people door cut into it. A garage apartment?

The question was, were the girls living there now? Had they moved? Had they ever lived there? Using their own names. Aliases? Mental note: go back there.

Night fell, a crisp desert evening. The town kept bustling. Hustlers on the sidewalks selling everything from marijuana to Rolex watches, or "*un bueno* facsimile*,*" as one of the vendors had so honestly put it.

The smell of dope coupled with the reedy desert air burned my nostrils. A sunburned bearded man in a trenchcoat and ratty knee-high moccasins was digging through a garbage can. He turned, standing square in front of me. Smelled like his skin was decomposing on the spot.

"Got any spare change, man?"

"I gave at the office."

He called up a loogy from the back of his throat, ready to spit a projectile in my direction. I pivoted out of the way just in time. The spittle projectile darted past me landing bullseye on a telephone pole. My nature had me wanting to fight. My judgment said no. I didn't want to touch this guy. Lice and diseases he might be carrying were something I didn't need. I'd made a deal with myself several years ago not to hand out money to anyone on the street. It was dangerous and most likely they'd use it for booze or drugs instead of food or shelter. I gave to a couple of the missions in downtown L.A. every year as well as to the Salvation Army. I figured that was the best way to go. I guess my friend in the trenchcoat didn't agree.

Castle's Bar was a dive. A comfortable dive. And apparently the swankiest dive in town. A washed out blond with black roots in a sequined black velvety dress sang and played piano for tips. It was so low cut everything hung out, almost falling onto the keyboard when she leaned over to light a cigarette. I'd only been in the bar half an hour and she'd already played Billy Joel's *Piano Man* twice, changing the words to *piano girl*. Must've meant something personal to her as no one around the piano seemed to be making any requests.

I ordered a light beer and some conversation from the bartender: "Been here long?"

"Does it matter to ya?"

"I'm looking for these two women. Ever seen 'em?"

He perused the photo of Anna and Pilar. Shook his head. "Mex don't come in here."

That was that. On my way out, the blond was singing *Piano Man* for the third time in less than forty-five minutes. It might have been the only song she knew.

There were several bars on the street. There were several bars on every street it seemed. Good business, drinking at the border. No one in any of them, Anglo or Mexican admitted knowing the girls.

It was almost one a.m. by the time I headed back to the Bolivar. The trip down to the border had been uneventful. No feeling of being spied upon. But now it was back. Faint footsteps, several paces behind me. I slowed, they slowed. I sped up. So did they. Pretending to window shop, I stopped in front of a bridal store displaying outlandish bridesmaid costumes in dayglow orange with green trim in the window. The footsteps stopped.

From the corner of my eye, I saw a shadow in a recessed doorway three doors back. I headed in that direction, retracing my footsteps. The shadow pulled deeper into the doorway. Disappeared. I walked past the doorway, not looking to the side. My peripheral vision told me someone was hunched up against the door in the farthest corner. I walked past. Quietly, I turned around. Headed back to the doorway. Didn't step in front of it. If I was as quiet as I thought, he hadn't heard me.

I waited.

After about three minutes, a sigh escaped the doorway. The man stepped forward. Foot out. I tripped him. He fell into me. I grabbed his collar and pulled him back into the darkness of the doorway. A police car cruised by. Didn't see us.

"Who are you?"

He shrugged. He was taller than me by two inches. Skinny as an I-beam. And as muscular. But he didn't know how to fight. I shoved him back against the door.

"Why are you following me?"

His teeth wanted to chatter. He wouldn't let them. Couldn't stop his hands from shaking though.

"La photo."

"Speak English."

"*Si*, this side of the border, English. I saw the picture you are showing in *la cantina*."

"You know those two girls?"

"They used to come in there sometimes, Castle's."

"Used to."

"*Si*. No more."

"How long since you've seen them?"

"Maybe a year. Maybe less."

That jibed with what Ramon had said.

"Where'd they go?"

"*No lo se.* I don't know. I have not seen them in town for that long, not only the bar."

"Were they hurt? Leave town?"

Shrug.

"I know where they live. Lived. I show you for ten dollars."

"You show me first." I pushed him out onto the street. We walked for several blocks, from the main drag to the residential section. He took me to the faded yellow house. Pointed.

"There. In the back." He pointed to the garage. Bingo. Moo-moo was lying. I pulled a ten from my pocket, gave it to him. We walked to the corner.

"How do you know they lived there? How did you know them?"

He shrugged. Backed away, ready to run. I caught his collar. He seemed to shrivel into his shirt. "I, I follow them here one night. I have, how you say, a liking, a–"

"–crush."

"*Si, un* crush on one of them."

I pulled the photo out. "Which one?"

He pointed to Pilar. *"Ella es muy bonita, no?"*

"*Si.* Did you ever talk to her?"

"No."

I believed him. He was wimpy enough to have followed her around and not say anything to her. "Did she have any boyfriends? Talk to anyone else in the bar?"

"There was *un hombre*, Hector. But I have not seen him around either."

"Was Hector married?" Fishing. Were Pilar and Anna lovers? Something else. What was going on?

"Si."

"His wife gone too?"

"Yes."

"Any of the people in Castle's tonight know them, the girls?"

"I do not know. People come and go so much here. Many migrant, is that right word, workers."

Mental note: Check back at Castle's.

I asked for his phone and address. Said he had no phone. Gave me the name of a farm outside of town where he was currently working. He said he was usually in this area, but not necessarily at the same farm or ranch. I gave him ten bucks; he shuffled down the street in the opposite direction of the yellow house. I headed back to it.

The lights were off. House next door was dark too. I nonchalantly, as if I owned the place, walked down the driveway to the back. Couldn't see through the curtain in the garage window. Walked around the side. Two more curtained windows. I pried at them. Didn't budge. Same with the door. No windows in the back. The fourth side, along the border with the neighbor, was walled in. No way to get to it.

What if someone else was renting there now? A little burglary might enliven their life. The windows on the side were big enough to crawl through. I pulled my boot knife and went to work on them. No need to worry about an alarm here. The window was easy. I was inside in less than a minute.

Musty. As if no one'd been in for a while. Dark. No flashlight. I pushed the curtains aside. A sliver of moonlight shot in. I stood silently, waiting for my eyes to adjust to the dark. Moved to the next window. Opened the curtains there. More light. Enough to see silhouettes by. A sofa-bed against the rear wall. Closed. No one on it. I felt my way to the tiny bathroom in the back corner. Turned on the light. The outside walls of the bathroom faced the neighbor's wall and the rear of the property. No one in the main house would see the light on. Gloomy light filtered out to the main room. A kitchenette in one corner. Coffee table in front of the sofa. I closed the curtains I'd opened, just in case. Set about tossing the place.

Drawers: empty. Shelves empty. Low shelves immaculate. Upper shelves dusty enough to write your name in. Open up the sofa-bed. Nothing in the sheets, under the mattress. Nothing in the sofa. Kitchen: clear. Bathroom: one half-full bottle of Suave shampoo. Nothing else. Not even a hair left on the tile. Why the bottle?

The place was empty. Except for the bottle. Did it mean anything? I couldn't fathom a guess. I turned off the bathroom light, put the windows back the way they were. Split.

◈ ◈ ◈

Back at the Bolivar, I fell asleep to *The Philadelphia Story* dubbed into Spanish. I wondered if it lost something in the translation.

I braced Castle's again in the daytime. Again no one owned up to having known Pilar or Anna.

Went back to the yellow house. Vacuum was going again. The woman had a clean fetish. Maybe that was why the guest house had been so spotless except for the bottle of Suave.

Rang the bell.

"You again."

She tried to close the door on me. Too slow. Too late. I was already inside. Ratty furniture. Old Motel 6 stuff that'd seen better days. Creepy floral patterns. By the numbers paintings on the wall. But all as clean as could be.

"You lied to me."

"Get outta here. I'll call the cops."

"I'm tired of being lied to. The wheel spun round and landed on you. You're gonna tell me the truth." I walked up to her. She was my height. Probably outweighed me by twenty pounds. She didn't back off.

We stood eye to eye. Glare contest. She took a step forward. I didn't move. Our noses touched. Hers was warm, greasy. She finally backed away. I thought I'd give her more space. I stepped back too. She reached behind a large upholstered chair, grabbed a baseball bat. Swung it at me. I ducked. Grabbed the bat. Her grip on the bat was tight. She wouldn't let go.

Twisting the bat in her hand, I freed it. Tossed it across the room. Pushed her into a chair.

"Sit."

She did. Neither one of us spoke. I pulled the Star, held it on her, while I peeked into the kitchen, dining area and hall, without leaving the living room. No sign of anyone else.

"Tell me about Pilar and Anna."

"Leave them alone. They just want to be left alone."

"Who do you think I am?"

"I don't know. I do know, they was bothered. Just wanna be left alone."

"From who?"

"Everyone. Wanna do their thing in peace."

"How long since they've been gone?"

"About three, four months, I think."

"You cleaned up their place pretty good."

"Got nothing better to do. 'Sides, a clean house is a–"

"–clean house."

She glared at me.

"I'm a detective. I'm not out to hurt them."

"They wanna be left–"

"I know. Did anyone else come around looking for them?"

"You're the detective."

"Don't get cute. I'm trying to help them."

"Why?"

"Anna's brother, Ramon, gave me this address. He wants me to find them."

"Yeah, I remember him. Came around a few times."

"Who else came around?"

"You're the cop, you ought to know."

"I'm not leaving till I get the information."

We sat in silence for minutes that passed slowly. She picked up a long, slender cigarette holder from the end table next to her. Stuffed a cancer stick in one end. Lit it. Drew in the smoke. She didn't quite fit my image of the cigarette holder type. "I don't know much. They were scared-a something," she exhaled.

"Someone?"

"Yeah."

"Who?"

"Guy that liked Pilar I think. I don't know his name."

The Weasel.

"You ever see him?"

"Nah. But they told me if he comes around tell him they don't live here."

"How would you know who to tell that to?"

"They told me what he looked like." She described the Weasel to a T.

"Did they tell you his name?"

"Sure."

My heart raced. "What is it?"

"It's been a long time."

"Did you write it down?"

"I don't know. Maybe." She stared at me over the end of her cigarette holder. "Maybe you're working for him."

Not anymore, lady.

"I'm not. I'm investigating the murder of Teddie Matson."

"Poor girl. I used to watch her show."

"We have reason to believe that there's a link between her murder and Pilar. The man that killed Teddie could be the same man who's after Pilar. Are you forwarding mail for them?"

She moved to get up. I lowered the gun. She went to a small table near the front door. Handed me an envelope on it. It was from a loan company, addressed to Anna. A line through the address for the yellow house led to a handwritten note: "No forwarding address known." "I was going to send it out with the mail."

She couldn't have thought ahead this far to prepare something like this. Besides, the letter was postmarked only a few days ago. I handed her my card.

"If you think of his name, come across a paper with it, or think of anything, please call me. The girls are in danger."

"I know. I didn't talk to you 'cause I was trying to protect them."

"I'm on their side. I'm licensed." I pointed to my license number on the card. "Bonded. Check me out. If you think of anything, no matter how trivial you think it is, call me. Leave a message with my service." I didn't plan to keep the service forever. Only until I could replace the machine. "Call me."

"I will."

"By the way, what's your name?"

"Mrs. Laren. There is no Mr. Laren anymore. That's another reason I was cold to you. Never know who'll show on your doorstep."

"You're right to be careful. I'm sorry I barged in like this."

"Maybe I'm too distrustful."

"Keep your guard up."

I headed to my rental car parked at the curb.

"Hey, wait a minute. I think his name started with a J. I'm not sure. James, Jeremy. Something like that."

"Thanks."

"Don't hold me to it. It's been a long time. But I think it was a J-name."

I got in the rental, headed back to L.A.

CHAPTER 32

Instead of heading back to L.A., I turned off on 395 and headed for Reno. The road was a roller coaster of up and down hillocks and valleys. Heat waves melted into the asphalt giving it a sleek sheen of black dye.

Copses of Joshua trees meandered off on either side of the road. *Little men,* hunched over their work, tending the desert garden. I felt eyes on the back of my neck. Was I being followed again? Had I ever been followed?

A gaggle of cars pressed around me, front and rear. There was open road about a mile ahead. I decided to run with the wind. Dodging in and out of traffic. Each car a land mine to be avoided.

Honk. Sorry, buddy, didn't mean to cut you off. Thanks for the bird.

Open road. Check the rearview. No one making any sudden lane changes.

Hoboes count ties, I counted broken lines in the road. Hypnotic. Don't drift. The road began to look the same. Same trees, same fast food joints, gas stations and quick-stop stores clustered in bunches. Same white lines.

L.A. Beirut felt as far away as the real Beirut. It might as well have been across an ocean. The sky was clear, no settling ash from the days of fire and firefights. No lines of people waiting for their ration of food and food stamps. No attitude.

Not far outside Reno: Weird dude on a three-wheeled bicycle. Tattered trenchcoat, in the high desert heat. Stubbly beard. Hat. Saddlebags on either side of the rear wheels and a box on top of it. Heat musta got to him. Pedaling along. Rear view: Stopping. Getting off bike. Bending over. What the hell's he doing? Still no sign of a tail.

I made Reno with only one stop for gas. Checked into the Edsel Motel. Gleaming chrome and polish. Ten Edsels lined up, five on each side of the walk to the main office. Edselmania. I hoped the motel had a better history than the car. The room was cramped. Clean. Repro photos of Henry Ford, Edsel on the walls. Various shots of Ford cars from the Model T through the late '50s porthole Thunderbird. A TV you didn't have to put quarters into. Bathroom glasses wrapped in *sanitary* wrap. "Do Not Throw Sanitary Napkins In Toilet" over the tank.

Beat. Wanted to crash. Couldn't do it. Shaved. Showered. Put on clean shirt. Wished I'd brought more clothes. Called Laurie. No answer. Jack. No answer.

The Crystal Palace Hotel and Casino. Look up gaudy in the dictionary: Crystal Palace. Flashing, clashing neon lights. Lit up like a sunny afternoon in the dark of night. No clocks. Always high noon.

Genteel ladies with blue hair feeding hungry slots. Businessmen in Michael Milken toupees and thousand dollar suits playing five card stud and Baccarat. Long-legged women in fishnet stockings and lowcut *uniforms* serving free watered down drinks to the customers to keep them playing past their bedtimes. Past their limits. Big spenders wearing shorts and flipflops. I felt right at home in my jeans and sport shirt.

Neither Warren, Mrs. Matson nor Ramon could tell me any of Teddie's or Pilar's friend's names from their stays in Reno. It would have been so much easier if I'd had a name. Now I had to start questioning people blindly.

"Thanks," I said, taking one of the free drinks offered by a *hostess*. She smiled, started to walk off. "Wait, please."

"Yes."

I maneuvered her to a corner. She looked slightly uncomfortable. It was hard to tell if it was real or part of the show. "There was a young woman who worked here a few years ago. I'm trying to locate anyone who might have known her."

"I'm sorry. I've only been on the job a few months."

"Who's been around a while?"

"Was she a hostess? Dealer?"

"I think she was in the chorus in the show."

"The show's producer is Jeanette Lyon, but I don't think she's been here that long either."

"Can I talk to her?"

"I'm sorry. I wouldn't know. I have to go now. They don't like us spending too much time with any one customer and they watch through the ceiling." She nodded to a row of mirrors above us. She smiled again, walked off. I headed for the showroom.

The first show of Follies Crys-tal was already in progress. It was more than an hour till the midnight show. Between shows seemed like a good time to find Ms. Lyon. I figured the show'd been rehearsed a dozen times, played for an audience a million. It probably ran by itself. Lyon might not even be around.

A stiff tuxedo, pressed and spit-shined, stood at the door to the showroom. When I headed toward it, the tuxedo nodded and smiled a rehearsed smile at me.

"I'm sorry, sir. There's no admittance until a break in the show. If you have tickets for this show I can arrange to exchange them for–"

"I don't want to interrupt such a lovely and well-practiced speech, but I don't have tickets for the show."

A frown overtook his face. He wasn't prepared to ad-lib.

"I'm looking for Jeanette Lyon. Is she here tonight?"

"Do you have an appointment with her?"

"No. But I think she'll want to see me. An old friend said to look her up."

"If you tell me who that is, I'll look and see if she's here."

"No can do. It's got to be a surprise."

"No can do," he said, mimicking. Nodded his head. Before I could blink, three large men surrounded me. None of them smiling.

"Three for the price of one," I said.

"Can I help you, sir?" the largest said in a meek voice that was more Pee-Wee Herman than Hulk Hogan. Still, the *sir* oozed from his tongue like hot oil slithering from a crank case.

"I'm not sure why you gentlemen were called. I merely told this fellow that I was looking for Jeanette Lyon."

"Miss Lyon is a very busy woman. She can't be meeting with just anyone who wants to meet her."

I wanted to talk to Lyon. I didn't particularly want these hulks to know my business with her. The lid had to stay on the can of worms for now.

"It's nothing really. An old friend of hers asked me to look her up. I didn't think it would be this much trouble."

"No trouble. We take care of our people."

Like they did in the Soviet Union.

"If you tell us who the friend is and where you're staying, we'll have her get back to you. In fact, why don't you step back to my office and we'll see if we can reach her right now?"

Out of sight of the public, are you kidding? "No thanks. It's not that important to me. I'm just doing a favor for a friend."

I started to walk off, into the casino. The four of them stood, guarding the entry to the showroom as if I was stalking Jeanette Lyon. I played a few hands of blackjack, figured I'd better quit for the night and headed back to the Edsel. It was about a three block walk. There were plenty of people on the street. I felt followed, didn't turn around. After making a couple of detours, hoping to lose the tail, if there was one, I finally hit the Edsel. Before hitting the bed, I checked the phone book. No Jeanette Lyon. I called information. Nothing there either. The wild hair was making me crazy. What the hell, I figured and called the Palace, asked for Jeanette Lyon. The phone rang seven times. A raspy woman's voice answered:

"Hello."

"Ms. Lyon."

"No, this is her assistant. She's in a meeting now. Can I take a message?"

"I'll try back later," I said. My head hit the pillow and my brain hit dreamland.

◈ ◈ ◈

It wasn't as good as Dreamland on Coney Island, but it was all I had.

Joshua trees.
Cactus plants.
Blue skies.
Clean air.
Smooth breath.
Breathing like a baby.
Crazy dudes on bikes.
Talking tuxedos.
Desert rats.

Need desert cats.
Keep the rat population down.
Spinning wheels.
Red and black.
Put your wad on a number.
Hope it comes back.
The game is rigged.
Nothing to do.
Do the best with what you've got.
Showgirls and showtime.
Kicking high.
Dancing disco dollies.
Fans waiting in the wings.
Eager to lavish their favorites with flowers.
And candy.
And teddy bears.
And–
Never alone.
People following.
From L.A. to Calexico.
Calexico to Reno.
Good at hiding.
Crawling under the woodwork.
But there.
Always there.
Stalking.
Stalked.
Sleep.
Perchance to dream.
Perchance to nightmare.
Sleep.
Sleep.
Sleep.

◈ ◈ ◈

The sun lunged in through a crack in the drapes, piercing my eyes with hot white light. Enough to wake me up. It was after eleven in the morning. I called the front desk, told them I'd be staying another night. My body telegraphed its desire to go back to sleep. The receiving station was down, the wires had been cut by the men in black hats. The brain wouldn't listen. Forced the tired body out of bed and into a cold shower. That put the connections back together in a hurry.

Before I left the motel, I got a shoe box from the desk clerk, put the Star and my private dick's license in it and had them lock it in the safe. The clerk assured me that the safe was secure and had never been broken into or had anything stolen from it. That was good enough for me. Besides, crooks had better places to steal from than the Edsel.

Bright sun belied brisk weather. I couldn't stand my clothes anymore. It felt like I'd slept in them, because I had. I was sure that there were discount places in Reno, shopping malls, department stores. But I wanted to buy my new clothes at the stores in the Crystal Palace. Why spend a hundred bucks for a suit when you could spend three hundred?

The Palace's casino was booming. More little old ladies with blue hair than the night before. None of the tables were empty. I scanned the room for the Three Tuxeteers. Not around. Must be the nightshift. Other Tuxeteers abounded, but I figured they didn't know my face and wouldn't pay it any mind, especially after I got my new outfit.

Jerome's Men's Wear was a pretty good sized ye olde shoppe for a hotel. It had nice big MasterCard and Visa logos on its front window. That made me happy, since I hardly had enough cash for breakfast. Plastic money I could live on till the year 3000.

The man himself helped me. I was the only patron in the store. He was eager and only too happy to please. His hair was neatly trimmed and slicked down above a beak-like nose. His own suit reeked of fine and expensive taste and fine and expensive perfume, er, cologne. Instead of a tie he wore an ascot. What would Jack have thought of that?

Two other salesmen rearranged stock on racks and shelves.

"Hmm, a dark suit," Jerome said, after I told him what I was looking for. "Does it have to be black or might we go with a dark blue or gray?"

"Doesn't matter. But something sharp. No brown."

"Of course not. Brown, no way."

After measuring me, he pulled a couple suits off a rack. Had me try on the jackets. I needed a good suit. Jerome may as well have my business as anyone else. This was quality stuff. Maybe this was where the Weasel got his suit.

Jerome spent over an hour with me. We finally settled on a double breasted gray suit, kinda snazzy, as mom would have said. While we were trying out various ties and shirts with it, another customer came in. Jerome beamed. One of his salesmen attended to the customer, while the other continued with the racks.

"The pants are a tad long. I can have them tailored for you in a couple of hours, I think." He smiled. Happy for the business.

"Sounds good."

He marked the cuffs with chalk and pins. As I was changing, handing clothes to him over the short dressing room saloon door, I asked if he knew Jeanette Lyon. I wished I could have seen his face when he responded.

"She comes in once in a while to buy something."

"She around today?"

"Haven't seen her."

I came out of the dressing room. His expression was calm enough.

"Are you a detective?"

"That's a strange question." It was. It got me thinking. "Hell no. I'm just trying to look her up for an old friend in L.A. But last night when I was asking around, some big dudes got in the way."

"Yes, they're very protective around here."

"Over-protective if you ask me." He handed me the charge receipt to sign. "Listen, don't tell anyone I'm looking for her. I don't need any trouble."

"I won't, unless you want me to tell her."

"Sure."

"I'll see what I can do. Might be a couple days."

Great, a couple more days at the Edsel. "Great." I left him my room number at the motel. The other customer left without buying anything.

◈ ◈ ◈

I spent most of the rest of the day wandering around, trying to nonchalantly ask if anyone had known Teddie. A couple times I even asked about Pilar. She'd been too young to work at the hotel, but it couldn't hurt to ask. I checked messages at the motel. No calls. And the only ones who should have known I was there were Jerome and Jeanette, if he'd reached her.

About 4:00 p.m., I picked up my suit. Changed into it at Jerome's to see how the tailoring had come out.

"Magnificent," he said. I agreed. I looked pretty good. He offered to have my shirt and jeans washed and pressed and sent to the motel the next morning, no charge. It was an offer I couldn't refuse.

He volunteered: "I looked around a bit for Jeanette. She didn't come in today."

"Will she be here tonight?"

"I imagine. She's here most nights. I'll hang around a bit after closing. See if I can latch onto her."

"Thanks, Jerome." I felt like I should have bought another suit. Maybe two. Up the hall from Jerome's was a shoe store. Men's and women's. The selection wasn't the greatest. I needed a pair of shiny black shoes to go with the suit so I bought the cheapest pair of loafers I could find with the shiniest paint job. The kid who waited on me had only been working there a week, his manager a few months. Neither knew Jeanette. Neither cared that I'd asked. And neither would bother to call the Tuxeteers.

◈ ◈ ◈

The hotel's coffee shop hamburger was soggy, but it would do. There was no point trying to get backstage to see Jeanette. Calling her office only got the raspy voice again. Again I left no message. The Tuxeteers spotted me playing blackjack. Kept an eye on me, but kept their distance. I called the motel a couple times to see if Jerome had reached Jeanette. No messages.

An acne-scarred pit boss, in a black suit with a black and white striped bow tie, closed down the blackjack table I was playing at. Everyone, including me, started to disperse.

"Hang loose, buddy," he said.

When the table was clear the dealer picked up cards and money. The pit boss stood behind the table, beady black holes staring at me. "Why you lookin' for Jeanette?"

"News travels fast."

"We're just one big family." He grinned. Two gold teeth gleamed at me from the top of his mouth.

"Happy no doubt."

"No doubt. We don't like strangers comin' and–"

"There is no and. I told your pals last night, I'm looking her up for a friend. That's all. It's not that important to me so I stopped asking and now I'm just playing."

"Cheap stakes blackjack."

"That's my game."

"You're not staying at the hotel."

"I'm sure you like taking my money anyway." How'd he know I wasn't staying there? Had I been followed last night?

"Cop?"

"No. But I'm getting awfully sick of this place."

"The air is a little bad in here. Bad circulation. Maybe you should stay out."

"You mean my money isn't good enough. I like it here."

"Plenty of other casinos. Some with better odds. Try Harrah's or Bally's.

"Hey, all I did was ask to see the lady. I didn't send her a pipe bomb. Didn't follow her home. What is it with you guys?"

"Better odds down the street."

◈ ◈ ◈

The odds weren't that much better down the street. Three to one in fact. The Three Tuxeteers were waiting for me in my motel room. As soon as I opened the door I knew something was wrong. I'd left the bathroom light on and the drapes open. It was off and they were closed. It could have burned out. I didn't think so. They grabbed me, threw me on the bed face down, spread eagled. Frisked me.

"No gun."

"I.D.?"

"Marion Rogers. Los Angeles."

"Business cards?"

"Nope."

"Whadda you do for a living, Mary-un?"

One Tuxeteer held my feet down. Another my arms.

"Hey, man, it's a new suit. Bought at–" I thought better about telling them I bought it at Jerome's. If they knew, they'd come down on him. I shut up. They didn't seem interested.

"Well, we'll try not to wrinkle it," Hulk Wally said. A line of pain ran up my left leg. Then warmth. Wet. He'd slit my trouser leg up to the butt with a razor sharp knife – my own, which they'd taken off me when they frisked me. That wasn't the only thing he slit. "Wanna tell us why you're here?"

"Vacation."

"And don't you like the fringe benefits of your tour plan?"

I was glad I'd put the license and gun in the safe. "Who're you looking up Jeanette for?"

"Shouldn't that be, for whom are you looking up Jeanette? Don't want to end with a preposit–"

The fist with the knife slammed into my mouth. Luckily not the blade end. My mouth began to bleed. I didn't want to think what the other end of the knife would have done.

"We checked your car. Piece-a-shit rental job. We just don't know enough about you. Wanna cut the jokes and be friendly now?"

"I don't know what else to tell you since the truth doesn't cut it."

"Who's the friend in L.A. wants to look up Jeanette."

Blood gurgled out of my mouth. It was hard to talk. I figured that worked in my favor. I also wished I'd called Rita and gone to see her instead. "Jamie. Jamie Tanberg. She asked me to look up Jeanette. See if she's still here. If so, get her number, or give her Jamie's and see if they want to get back together." I didn't know where I pulled that name from, but it sounded familiar.

"Ja-mie Tanberg. One n or two?"

"One."

He wrote in a small pad. "We'll be seeing you, especially if Jeanette doesn't know anyone with this name." He threw two one hundred dollar bills on the bed. "Get yourself a new pair of pants and some mercurochrome. Have a nice day. The Three Tuxeteers left my Edsel of a room, leaving me with the taste of blood in my mouth and the memory of Jamie Tanberg, a girl I'd had a crush on in fourth grade.

CHAPTER 33

The Tuxeteers hadn't found out anything and I wasn't sure they wanted to. They wanted to scare me off of talking to Jeanette Lyon. They hadn't succeeded in that either. The cut on my leg was only surface. The bash on my mouth wasn't bad either. I borrowed alcohol from the front desk, cleaned the wounds. I had a swollen lip. Nothing else noticeable. I also retrieved the Star and my P.I. license from the safe, slept sitting up against the headboard of the bed. Anyone who tried breaking in would get a severe headache.

I overslept the next morning. It'd been several days since I had a full night's sleep. I checked my service. No messages. I kept waiting for Warren to show up. At my door? In the casino? In a dark alley? Called information for Jerome's Men's Wear in the Palace. Before I could call him, the phone rang:

"Mr. Rogers. This is Jerome."

"Jerome's Men's Wear?"

"Yes, of course."

"You have my pants ready?"

"Yes, but—"

The Tuxeteers might have bugged the phone. I didn't want Jerome giving anything away. I interrupted: "Why don't we meet for breakfast. There's a coffee shop across the street from my motel. Arnold's. Bring the pants and breakfast's on me."

"But—"

"See you there in half an hour. No smoking section." It dawned on me: The Tuxeteers had sliced my only other pair of pants. I caught him before he hung up. "Jerome, meet me at the motel. Bring the jeans. Room 106."

I showered. Shaved. Waited. Towel around my waist. Exactly half an hour later: a knock on the door. I grabbed the jeans, started to put them on. He sat in a chair by the front window.

"I talked to–"

My hand clasped over his mouth. I shook my head. Released my hand. "Thanks for bringing the jeans here." I held up the shredded pants. He noticed my lip.

Whispering: "What happened?"

I put my finger across my mouth: ssh. After I dressed, I landed the gun in my pants. Covered it with the windbreaker. His eyes popped on seeing it. I ushered him out.

◈ ◈ ◈

Smoke from the Smoking Section infiltrated the No Smoking Section. The Star could've solved that situation, but it's impolite to shoot smokers in restaurants. We sat in a corner booth in the back. No one was in the booth next to us. We were both quick to order. The Double Breakfast, pancakes, hash browns, bacon and eggs. OJ. And a double side of cholesterol.

"What's going on?" he said, aflutter. He loved every minute of it. The intrigue. The suspense. A chance to do something more exciting than sell suits. "Some of the hotel security men were asking about you?"

"Anything in particular?"

"No. Just what you bought."

I hadn't noticed them watching me there. More two-way mirrors? "Anyone follow you to my hotel?"

"I don't think so."

"Between you and me?"

He nodded.

"I'm trying to find people who knew Teddie Matson."

"The TV star that was just murdered?" His eyes lit up like Vegas after dark. I guess he just wanted to be part of something.

"She worked as a chorus girl at the hotel a few years ago."

"Yes, I remember hearing about that. And that's what you want to talk to Jeanette about?"

"Would she have known Teddie? Seems a lot of people come and go."

"Lotta drifters. Some-a the pit bosses been around a long time. I'm not sure about Jeanette."

"You?"

"Me? I've been in the hotel a couple years. But I never met Teddie."

"At the motel you started to say you'd talked to someone. Who?"

"Jeanette, of course. She was going to call you in your motel room."

"Why didn't you tell me? We might miss the call."

"You didn't want to talk on the phone. Think the lines are bugged?"

"Maybe. I don't know."

"I can call her. Maybe we can go to her place."

I popped a quarter in his hand. He got up, headed for the phone. I hoped he wasn't calling hotel security. What was their interest in all this anyway? He came back just as the breakfasts were being set down.

"She says we can come by."

I jumped up.

"What about breakfast?"

"We'll get it to go."

"She's not dressed yet. She said in an hour."

Long enough to dress. Or long enough to get the Three Tuxeteers over?

"She live near here?"

"Not far. In Sparks. It's a suburb of Reno."

I was hungry. I could hardly keep the food down.

◈ ◈ ◈

Jeanette Lyon's house was one of those flat-roofed, cheap boxes that developers in the '60s seemed so fond of. No ornamentation. A few cactus plants in a gravelly dirt bed around the house. We parked in front. She met us at the door. Bright red hair stood up on her head, cascading down in back. It looked natural. Her skin was peaches and cream perfection. That white-white skin redheads often have. Very striking. She wore a black body suit and high heeled pumps.

Before we entered, I double checked the street. No sign of a tail. There hadn't been one all the way over. The Tuxeteers probably figured they'd scared me off.

The living room was tastefully decorated. A couple Diebenkorn prints. A mock fireplace with mock wood. Sliding glass door opening to a dead-grass plot of land a little larger than a double burial plot. Rusted swing set. No other sign of kids.

Introductions were short and sweet. Then:

"Jerome says you're looking for people who knew Teddie Matson when she worked here."

"Yes." I showed her my license.

"You looking for her killer?"

"Yes, but I can't go into any details." Were the Tuxeteers going to burst from behind a closed door and try to make me?

"What do I get out of it then, if I don't even get to know the dirt?"

"You get the glorious good feeling of knowing you helped someone." I smirked.

"Good feelings don't pay the bills."

"I don't have any money to offer you. If you know something and want to talk, I'm all ears. If not, I'm outta here." That's when I expected the Three Tuxeteers to erupt through the door. Nothing. Maybe they weren't there.

"People are asking about you. Saying to stay away."

"So why'd you invite me here?"

I sat on one end of the couch. Jeanette on the other. Jerome in a chair facing us. His head didn't move. His eyes followed us back and forth, as if he was at Wimbledon.

"Curiosity."

"Curiosity killed the cat."

"Is that a threat?"

"No. It's an attempt at levity."

"It's not funny." She thought a moment, debating whether or not to go on. Then: "I did know one girl who knew Teddie. Eleanor Hildreth. Was in the line when Teddie was. She quit. It was all very weird."

"Weird?"

"Like there was no reason for her to quit. And now the security guys are asking all kinds of questions. Weird. I don't know anything really, but I can give you her name and number."

"I'd appreciate it. I'd also appreciate it if this meeting never happened as far as anyone else is concerned."

"Yes, I agree," Jerome said. "With them asking all those questions, it's better if our involvement isn't known."

"No problem there," said Jeanette. "I like my face." She stared pointedly at my fat lip.

◈ ◈ ◈

Jerome didn't say much on the way to the Crystal Palace. He did offer to replace the slit pants free. Business didn't look good at his place and I told him just to stitch up the pair I had. I went to the lobby. Checked my service. No messages. Called Eleanor Hildreth. She sounded sleepy. It was noon. She invited me to come by.

She lived in a medium sized – maybe thirty or forty units – apartment building. Another of those flat-roofed, flat facaded boxes painted what I can only call shit-brown. The color of an obvious narc car. She lived in the back, next to the laundry room which made a rumble of white noise in her living room, blotting out other outside sounds.

She looked to be in her early forties. Unkempt, greasy strands of hair fell on her face and shoulders. Flowered robe and chain smoker. The lines on her face said it had seen some of life's little *joys.* Jeanette had described Eleanor as being quite a beauty, although she hadn't seen her in a couple of years. Her beauty had seen much kinder days.

I showed her my license. "How do you know Jeanette?"

"I've known her forever." She almost sounded boozy, but she wasn't drinking. "She went to New York, tried out for the Rockettes. Almost made it too. After a few years in the Big Apple, she came back here. I got her a job on the chorus. In less than a year they made her choreographer, then producer of the show."

"Why'd you quit?"

She retreated into a protective blanket, huddled inside her robe. She didn't want to answer.

"Jeanette said she thought you knew Teddie Matson. Worked with her."

Her face was a stone mask. "I knew Teddie. That's what you're here for?"

I nodded.

"What do you know?"

"Nothing. I've traced her back here. Don't know much else."

"Her murder is such a shame. She was a nice girl. But hey, so was I – back then."

"What happened? To you? To Teddie?"

"Jim Colbert happened."

Jim-Talbot/Jim-Colbert. Made sense. He'd kept his first name, a name he'd respond to when called by it. Phonied his last name.

"Tell me about him."

"He was this punk kid. Used to hang around the shows. I guess he was old enough to get in. Had a thing for the girls in the line, especially coloreds, know what I mean?"

"He had his eye on Teddie?"

"More than his eye?"

"Did they go together?"

"For about two weeks. But she thought he was too weird. Broke it off. He wouldn't stop coming around. Kept sending her candy, flowers."

"Orchids?"

"Yes. He liked to impress them by buying expensive things."

"Did he ever give her a teddy bear."

"Yeah, I think so."

"You said he wouldn't stop coming around."

"He'd hang out by the stage door. That kinda thing. Nothing dangerous."

"Did he ever do anything dangerous?"

"Teddie only worked a few months. After she left, he tried to find her. Write her. Couldn't get anyone to give him the information, so he eventually forgot about her, lit on another girl. Domino. That was her real name. Domino, can you imagine? I don't know where black folks get the names of their kids."

I figured when Colbert saw Teddie on TV it rekindled his spark for her, if it had ever truly dimmed. He got the bright idea of hiring a dick. He knew the show was filmed in L.A. She had to be there. So he came to me.

"How long did he go with her?"

"Not long. A little longer than Teddie. Maybe a month. Then she broke it off. He just came on too strong. Anyone could see. He wasn't for her, or Teddie. They were just kids. I was a few years older than them. Hell, I'm only thirty-four now. You wouldn't know it looking at me."

"Do you know where I can reach Domino?"

"Sure do. 1715 Del Gado Boulevard, Sparks."

"Near here?"

"Not too far."

"Phone number."

"She doesn't have one. Doesn't need it. 1715 Del Gado is the Del Gado Cemetery."

CHAPTER 34

W hat was it about him that the girls couldn't stand after a week or two?"

"He was smothering." Her eyes glazed over as she left the present and ran a movie memory of it all from a long time ago.

"In more ways than one," I said, figuring she'd get the implication.

"He wanted all of their time. Day and night. To be with them. It's not like he was evil. At least not then. But he was sort of – nerdy. Nice guy nerdy. They liked him. But he wouldn't let go. Called them all the time. A hundred times a day. At least it seemed like it. Wanted them to spend every minute with him. Just wanted everything they had and more. And he was jealous. I know he asked Teddie to quit the line. He didn't like all those men in the audience looking at her."

"Did he know she was from L.A.?"

"I think so. I'm not sure."

"I'm curious why he didn't follow her if he was so in love with her – follow her to L.A.."

"I don't know." She shifted uncomfortably. "I think he thought he'd try his luck with Domino. I don't know if it was the actual person that counted or the idea of her."

"What happened with Domino?"

"She wanted to break it off. It bruised his fragile male ego I guess. He stalked her, wouldn't leave her alone. He caught her backstage one day. Chased her into the catwalks. They fought. She fell and died – a bloody mess." She drummed a nervous beat with her foot. "Everybody knew it was murder, but because of the way it went down it could be interpreted differently."

"The hotel covered it up?"

"Didn't want the bad publicity. Nice folks."

"So if anyone comes around asking questions–"

"They take it into their own hands."

"It'll come out sooner or later."

"No, not with these people. They keep everything inside the family – if you know what I mean."

"Didn't you or anyone else put two and two together when you heard about Teddie's death?"

"My math isn't very good. 'Sides, you live around here long enough you learn to leave things alone if you want to be left alone."

"What happened with you? Why'd you quit?" I wanted to ask: Why'd you age beyond your years? Didn't.

"Teddie was a friend of mine. So was Domino. It was just too much. That and the pressure. Having to look perfect every goddamn second. Painted on smiles and kissing customers' asses even when they treated you like shit. Made you feel worthless. But I got back at 'em. All of 'em. I'm on disability now. They can pay for me the rest of my life."

I figured her disability was a payoff from the hotel, but there was no point bringing it up.

"Anyone else know Teddie or Domino?"

"Most of the girls are gone and I wouldn't advise you bothering the ones in the line now. 'Sides, I've lost touch with them. No numbers. No nothing. At least they ain't in the Del Gado Cemetery.

"Did the hotel pay off Domino's family?"

"I don't know."

"Why did Colbert like black girls?"

"Black, brown, green. Didn't matter."

"But no whites?"

"Not that I saw. But I don't know why he liked them. Maybe he didn't feel good enough for a white woman." She snorted a laugh. Jack would have appreciated her thought. What did it mean about Colbert?

"He from around here?"

"Colbert. Far as I know. I think he's from Sparks. He left town though. I mean, he could be back, but I don't think so."

"Why not?"

"That was part of the deal. Get outta town, and the cops and D.A. look the other way. Hotel's big enough to pull that kinda weight."

I asked if I could borrow her phone book. Looked up Colbert. There were a handful. I gave her ten bucks and started making calls. None of the Colberts admitted knowing Jim.

"No luck?" she said, offering me a box of saltine crackers.

"No."

"There's an odd dude might know Jim Colbert. Collects bottles and cans and any other junk he can find. I think he used to be a friend of Jim's or something. Funny to call it a *bi*cycle when it has three wheels, but it's hard to imagine a grown man riding a tricycle. That's for three year olds, isn't it?"

"Where does he live?"

"I don't know. But you can't miss him."

I remembered seeing him on my way into Reno. It had to be the same guy.

"Just hit the highways. You're bound to run into him sooner or later."

"Any idea which roads he favors?"

"Nope."

"What's his name?"

"People 'round here just call him Lobo."

◈ ◈ ◈

I gassed up the car. Hit the road. Since I'd seen him on my way into town from the south that's where I headed. After driving two hours out, I turned around and headed back. Made a couple detours on side roads. No luck. Next I ventured east, only going one hour out. That was sixty miles. Hard to imagine Lobo pedaling more than sixty miles in a day. Of course, he might not have lived in Reno, but somewhere outside. Anyway, it was the same thing. No sign of Lobo within an hour of town.

South. East. North. I hit the roads to the north of Reno and Sparks. Heat waves shimmied up from the ground, dancing on air. An hour out of town, I hit a greasy spoon diner, its parking lot filled with trucks. The greaseburger hit the spot. And stayed there. I asked the waitress behind the counter if she knew Lobo. She did. Had she seen him today? She hadn't. A trucker with snakeskin cowboy boots, a ten and a half gallon hat and three day growth of beard turned to me:

"Lookin' for Lobo?"

"Yeah."

"Law?"

"No. Private investigator. I'm trying to see if he's the relative of a client." I flashed my I.D.

"I saw him out on Highway 80 about an hour ago. Heading for the interchange with 95."

"Thanks." I plopped down enough money to pay for my meal and his.

Golden hour hit the desert like a spray of falling rain – bright specks of dust floating in the air. A rainbow of gold dust. Warm jasmine waves of sun lending the scene a soothing surreal quality. No sign of Lobo on 80. I headed out a little farther. Nothing. U-turn. On the way back I saw a silhouette at the junction of 80 and 95. Pulled over. It was the same grizzled guy I'd seen on my way up here. From what people had said it had to be Lobo.

"Howdy," he said. Looked about fifty to fifty-five give or take a handful of years. I wasn't so proud of my age-guessing ability after being so wrong about Eleanor. Hell, Lobo might have been thirty or seventy. I settled for fifty.

"Hi."

"Need directions?"

"Not really. You Lobo?"

"Lookin' for me? Hardly anybody comes lookin' for me. What can I do for you?" He squinted into the setting sun, his hand on his brow, Indian-style.

"I understand that you knew Jim Colbert."

His mouth narrowed to an angry gash. He backed away toward his bike. Opened a saddle bag, tossed in a couple Dos Equis cans he'd been picking out of the scree when I approached him. Closed the bag, straddled the seat. He didn't look in the mood for conversation.

"Don't go, please. I'll only have to follow you and I don't want to wear out my new shoes."

He settled into the seat, resigned to not leaving. "Whadda you want?"

"It's obvious from your reaction that you know him."

"Jim Colbert, Junior or Senior?"

"I don't know. I'd guess he's in his mid to late twenties."

A dejected shake of his head. "Junior. What do you want him for?"

"I need to talk to him."

"I figured someone'd be askin' about him sooner or later." He reached onto the crossbar of his bike, took a plastic bottle filled with green liquid from it. Swigged. He offered the bottle to me. I declined. He got off the bike. Nestled himself into a rock, stared into the sun. It looked almost as if he was trying to burn his retinas.

"Shouldn't look into the sun like that. It'll hurt your eyes."

"Doesn't matter. They've seen too much anyway."

"Tell me about Jim Colbert, Junior."

"He was a good kid. Never got into trouble or anything. I guess he musta been holding it all inside."

"Holding what inside."

"I don't know. Never did learn. Anyway, he liked a couple girls in the chorus over at the Palace. I'm sure you know the story."

"I know a little of it. Why don't you fill me in."

He did, without adding much to what I already knew.

"Why didn't he follow Teddie to L.A.?"

"I don't think he had her L.A. address. Never needed it. She was here. And when she decided to leave she wouldn't give it to him and neither would any of the girls in the chorus. I seem to remember he started out to L.A., got all the way to Bakersfield and then turned around. Came back. Never did know why. That's when he started dating that Domino girl."

"Do you know why he liked women of color?"

"Why are you looking for him?"

"It's confidential."

"If I'm to give you anymore information I think I have the right to know what this is all about. And if you don't give me the truth, I'll clam up. I promise you that."

I decided to tell him. "I think he may have murdered Teddie Matson."

The angry gash opened a tad. The anger replaced by sadness. "When I heard about that, I wondered if it could have been him. Do you have any proof?"

"Someone saw a man fitting his description at the scene. If it's him they can identify him. If not, he's got nothing to worry about." It wasn't necessary to tell him I'd also seen him. Aided and abetted him.

"Is it because of what happened here?"

"I didn't even know about that when I first learned about him." I sat down on a rock across from him, staring at the endless landscape of sage and juniper, figuring it would make him more comfortable if I wasn't standing over him.

"I knew Jim from a long way back. Farther back than most of his friends and such." He took a deep swallow of air. Just watching him made my throat dry. "His mother was black. You wouldn't know it to look at him. Or her. She was very light-skinned. You could hardly tell if you didn't look very closely at her features. She died when he was a kid. Around seven. I think his seeking out black and brown women was his attempt to deal with losing her."

"Tell me about Pilar Cruz."

"She was another of his crushes." His voice was guttural, hoarse. Filled with desert wind and sand. He took another swig of the green liquid. "She came up here for a summer. They met in some summer acting program at the local high school. This was before Teddie even. And it was the same story with her. He fell all over her, head over heels. Suffocated her with good intentions and love. He just couldn't see that it was too much for anyone else to want. He thought they wanted all that attention. He thought if he lavished them with it they would be his forever. He didn't know that people need space. Freedom." He waved his hand at the expanse of high desert valley, surrounded by snow-capped mountains. "I think the rejection, from Pilar, Teddie, Domino, and a couple others, got to him, especially on top of his feeling rejected by his mother. Wasn't her fault. She took ill with pneumonia and died."

The sun began to sink over the mountains in the distance. Red, orange and magenta ribbons of light spread out along the horizon. Golden hour was done for and twilight settled over the highway.

"Do you have a current address for him?"

"I have an address I can give you. Haven't heard from him in some time though."

"How long is that?"

"Several weeks at least. We used to write pretty regularly." He pulled a grimy notebook from the back of his faded corduroy pants. Pulled a piece of paper from it. Copied the address from the paper onto another sheet, tore it out and gave it to me. It was a Santa Barbara address. I'd hit it on the way back to L.A. "Y'know, I used to think it was nice of the hotel to hush things up and get Jimmy off without any trouble. It's Nevada you know. Mob ties and all that. They bought off the girl's family. But I don't think so anymore. At the very least he should have gotten some kind of psychiatric help. I'm sorry about that now."

There was no point in commenting to him that it was too late.

"I hope you find him," he said. "But be gentle. He's a good kid at heart."

"I'll do my best, Mr. Colbert."

He looked up when I said his name. That was confirmation enough. That and the same piercing blue eyes, the nervous demeanor.

It looked like he was crying. It was hard to tell in the dim light.

◇ ◇ ◇

I closed out my account at the Edsel, gathered my things. Met Jerome outside the Crystal Palace. He gave me a new pair of suit pants. Said he'd ruined the others trying to stitch them up. I didn't believe him, offered him money for the new pants. He wouldn't take it. I thanked him and headed out of town.

Stopping at a phone booth about a block from the hotel, I called Eleanor Hildreth. She confirmed my suspicion that Colbert, Sr. had been an executive at the hotel at the time of Domino's death, though she said she never realized he and Lobo were one and the same. I thanked her again and started to get in my car when I noticed one of the Three Tuxeteers on the sidewalk. I came up behind him, bar-armed his throat, dragged him into the shadows.

His hand shot for the shoulder holster under his expensive Armani jacket. It didn't make it. In fact, I grabbed it, twisting, and broke his wrist.

"What the fuck's this all about?" he said. "You're fucking with the wrong people."

I shoved him into the wall. Down to the ground. Slammed my foot into his mouth. A tooth fell to the ground. Blood flowed out. There was a part of me that wanted to keep going. The more sane part said to quit.

"Have a nice day," I said.

CHAPTER 35

The Santa Barbara address was a bust. The apartment manager said Colbert had moved out two months ago without leaving a forwarding address. I felt like I was back to square one. My leads had taken me there. And there was nothing. I called Martin Luther King Hospital from a payphone.

"Hey, dude, or is that Duke? What's happening?"

"You sound good. Better than before."

"Can't keep me shut up forever. Hey, I'm gettin' out."

"When?"

"Today."

"If you can wait a couple hours, I'll pick you up. I'm in Santa Barbara."

"Don't come back to this mess on my account."

"It'd be my pleasure."

I grabbed a cheeseburger at McDonald's and headed out to the 101 and the drive back to L.A. Tiny was glad to see me. Gave me a bear hug.

"Looks like they patched you up pretty good."

"Can't keep me down. I'm too mean," he growled.

"Feeling feisty."

A nurse wheeled Tiny to the curb and my waiting car in a wheelchair. There was nothing wrong with Tiny's legs. Why do hospitals always have to do that? Insurance?

"Glad to be outta that place." He looked around. Blackened buildings. Charred remains of others. "Or am I?"

We drove by his rental company. Still there and untouched. Which is more than I could say for my car. The tires and hubcaps were gone and what remained was a burned out hulk. There wasn't even enough left to tow away. It sent a shot of sadness mixed with anger through me, but nothing like what I felt for the loss of Baron.

"Whew! But I don't think I want to go in today. Tomorrow'll be plenty of time to do that. Let's go have a beer." He directed me to a small restaurant. I felt odd. I was the only white. Whispers floated our way. Were they wondering what a white man was doing here? Now?

I caught him up on the progress of the case. He offered his help. I told him he needed to rest. I asked him about Teddie. He couldn't give me any new information that would have been helpful. Then: "I'll get your car fixed up."

"You don't need to do that."

"Was on my property. I feel responsible. 'Sides, I know some good people who'll do it for a price."

How could I argue? After a couple beers, I dropped him at his house.

◈ ◈ ◈

Before going home, I dropped by Laurie's. Locked up tight. No sign of Jack's bike. I rang the bell. No answer. Rang again.

"Laurie, it's Duke. I want to see if you're okay."

Her car wasn't in the driveway and I couldn't see in the garage. I figured she might have gone out for the evening so I headed home. My answering service beeper was beeping. Turned it off. I didn't care.

The house felt strange. As if I wasn't alone. Everything appeared undisturbed. Still it was an eerie feeling.

I showered and crashed, dreaming that Baron was licking my face awake like he used to.

◈ ◈ ◈

The morning sun was bright as it streamed through window, waking me. Damn L.A. It'd be nice to have seasons. I didn't want sun on a day like this. Half of L.A. was burned to the ground. What right did the sun have to shine?

The message on the beeper was from Jack. I tried him. Couldn't connect. Called the service. Jack had left a message there too: Craylock had gotten to Laurie. She was in Cedars-Sinai Hospital with a swollen cheek and minor lacerations. It felt like déjà vu. I tried the hospital. Laurie was asleep. Jack wasn't there. Wasn't home either. They'd said she was doing fine. I wanted the details. Where? When? How? Were the police involved? No one would tell me anything.

I called Warren. He didn't have anything new to add. No teddy bear and he was as surly as ever.

"I missed you in Reno," I said.

"Yeah, well something came up."

"I thought the Big L.A. Party was over?"

"Man, some parties never end. Some dude caught me on videotape. Cops came and arrested me and I had to be arraigned. Otherwise I wouldda been there. Been on your ass all the way."

Guilt overcame me so I headed for the hospital. I was about to turn into the parking lot when I spotted a black beamer in the rearview. It couldn't be. Pulling over to the side, I let him pass. It was him – Craylock. He pulled into the hospital parking lot. I drove in behind him. He didn't notice me in his rearview mirror.

I followed to where he parked, blocking his car in with mine. He saw me. Knew he couldn't drive out. He got out of the car and ran.

I left my car blocking his. A parking attendant yelled at me to move it.

"Police," I shouted.

Craylock ran down the sidestreet to San Vicente. Dodging traffic, he dashed across the road into the giant Beverly Center shopping mall parking lot. I chased him through the parking lot, zigzagging in and around cars, to the escalators. He headed up, shoving people out of his way. One thing I never understood is why people went up when they were trying to escape. Unless there was a chopper waiting for them, there was always a deadend. I knew that if I ever had to run from someone I'd go straight ahead, full throttle.

We came out into the mall. Innocent shoppers watched two men run down the hall. He pushed a baby in a stroller out of the way. I kept after him. Mall security joined the chase, running and talking into walkie-talkies at the same time. Craylock jumped onto another escalator, heading up again. He stayed on it until he reached the top level where the food stalls were.

We played dodge-the-shopper until there was nowhere else for him to run to. I crashed into him, knocking him against the Hot Dog on a Stick's brightly striped yellow and blue walls. The fresh lemons in their lemonade machine escaped their bondage and crashed down on us, spilling sticky pink lemonade all over us.

Four uniformed guards from mall security had us surrounded. They were already radioing the real cops. I didn't show the Star. No need to hassle that. Craylock was panting. I was in a hell of lot better shape than him and I was panting too. In between gulping air, I tried explaining to the security guard in charge what was going on. "This man's wanted by the police," I said, gasping for air. He didn't care. They hustled us into a back room where we waited for the police. It didn't take them long to show up. An older L.A.P.D. sergeant, who looked like he'd seen it all, twice, and a young female officer. The mall security guys had neglected to frisk us. The cops weren't so lax. I asked Sergeant Webb if I could speak to him alone for a minute. We went into the hall.

"I'm a licensed private detective." I showed him my I.D. "The man inside is wanted for stalking and beating up a client. I saw him at Cedars, where she's recuperating, and gave chase. And I'm carrying a concealed weapon."

"Real easy now," he said, "Lean against the wall. You know the drill."

I did what he said, spreading my arms and legs. He asked where the gun was. I told him. He removed it, patted me down. Didn't find anything else – I never did get my knife back from the Tuxeteers.

"Do you have a permit?"

"No. That's why I was hoping we could work this out. I was chasing him. I felt I needed the gun."

"We'll see how it plays out. Let's go back inside." He asked for a brown paper bag, got one, and put the gun in it. No one else had seen it.

"I don't know why this man is chasing me. He's crazy."

The sergeant called the station. There was a bulletin out on Craylock. He was wanted for questioning in Laurie's beating. The sergeant got my name, address, phone number. He took my statement. "No need to come down to the station now," he said. "We'll be in touch." The woman cop cuffed Craylock, who was still proclaiming his innocence. "Don't forget your lunch," the sergeant said, handing me the brown bag.

"Thanks, sergeant."

He didn't respond, just turned to the business at hand. I told him where Craylock's car was parked, then headed off. Walking back to the parking lot across the street, I, once again, felt as if I was being followed. There were a lot of people around. Many of them had seen the chase. I passed it off to paranoia and figured people were watching me 'cause of the chase.

The parking attendants hadn't had my car towed, but more police were milling around it. I told them what had just happened. After verifying the story, they let me go without frisking me. I felt lucky.

Before getting into my car, I looked in his. Fresh flowers. He'd been bringing her flowers. People never cease to amaze me.

◈ ◈ ◈

Laurie had been off her guard when Craylock came up to her. It was the middle of the day – her lunch hour. She was walking down the street to a sandwich shop when he cut her off at an alley and pulled her into his car. He'd driven towards the freeway onramp, but hadn't made it. She was kicking and screaming the whole way. He'd tried to beat her into submission, thus the hospital stay, but it hadn't worked. She belted him in the mouth and jumped from the car.

She was home from the hospital after only one day. Craylock was safely in jail awaiting arraignment. Jack and I went to visit her.

"What's this?" she said, as I handed her a brown paper bag.

"Chicken soup. From Cantor's Deli."

"Jewish penicillin," Jack said. He had to say something. "You'll get well more quickly."

Laurie put the soup in the fridge. She poured us all diet sodas. We sat in the living room.

"I told Jack not to come around. I wanted to do it on my own. I figured, what was the point, I couldn't have a bodyguard forever."

"You did do it on your own," I said.

"I know," she grinned. "But I still want to take a self defense class and learn to shoot better. Jeez, how much longer do I have to wait to pick up the gun? I got lucky with that one punch that landed on his nose."

She thanked us. Said to keep in touch. I said we would. At the very least we'd be testifying at Craylock's trial. Jack and I split and hit a bar, downing a few beers.

"I can't shake the feeling of being followed," I told him as we downed another.

"It's just these cases, man. Both stalkers. Got you spooked."

"You're right. That and lack of sleep."

◇ ◇ ◇

I went home. Called Rita. No answer at her place. I left a message saying I'd been out of town and saying she could call me or I'd call back again. Either way. I was nervous about talking to her.

Square one.

Square one.

Square one, I kept saying to myself. Chasing all over hell and back and still nowhere. I wasn't about to quit though. Finding the Weasel had become my mission.

I dialed the phone: "Hello, Lou."

"Duke. What's going on?"

"I'm getting closer. I know who the guy is."

"You do?" She responded quickly, with anticipation.

"Yes. Jim or James Colbert, Jr. Originally from Sparks, Nevada. I think he's living here now."

"Oh no. I can see it coming."

"You have to run him, Lou. If you do I'll find him, get the police in on it."

"You're sure it's the right guy."

I told her Colbert, Junior's story.

"Sounds like it's him." There was a long pause. I could hear her breathing. "All right. I'll run him first thing in the morning. And if he's in the computer fine, you find him, turn him in. But if he's not, we go to the police with what we've got now. Deal?"

"Deal."

We made plans to have another dinner at El Coyote and hung up. My whole body ached. Stiff everywhere. All I wanted was to take a hot shower and hit the hay. Then:

A noise.

Outside.

Go to the window.

Can't see anything.

Crouch on the floor.

Peek out.

Nothing.

Wait.

Waiting hurts.

Silence.

No movement.

Am I being followed?

Maybe I'm not so crazy after all.

Still nothing.

The silence of the night.

Silence.

Calm.

Peaceful.

Too damn peaceful

Too damn quiet.

Then:
A shadow.
Moving across the garage wall.

CHAPTER 36

The shadow of a Weasel?
A Craylock who'd made bail?
Warren on the rampage?
Non-descript burglar, variety 27?
The guy who's been tailing me?
Safety off.
Latch off the back door.
Open slowly.
Hinge creak.
Damn.
Been meaning to oil those hinges.
Toe-walk down the stairs.
Creeping.
Shadow inching along edge of garage.
Padding forward.
A target in the light.
Could've turned the outside floods off.
Would've given myself away
Stillness.
No tranquility.
Rustling breeze.
What's that?
Breathing?
A sucking step into mud or wet grass.
Charge the garage.
Running steps.
He's heard me.
Seen me.

Knows I'm here.
Hard charging.
After him.
Around the garage.
Behind the incinerator.
Shadow on the wall.
He's over.
I'm over.
Running through the neighbor's yard.
Who's there? neighbor shouts.
I'm calling the cops.
Bolt down the driveway.
Intruder runs up the block.
Chase him.
Red lights.
Blue lights.
Cop car.
Ditch into the bushes.
Cops ride by to neighbor's house.
Don't see me.
They're gone.
So is intruder.
Damn.
Fuck up.
Fuck up.
Fuck up.
Head home.
Avoid cops.
Curse the night.

◈ ◈ ◈

What would he have done if I hadn't heard him? Spied on me? Broken in? Robbed? Attacked? Killed? L.A. cops are notorious for not catching calls quickly. My luck these guys must have been cruising nearby. Damn.

The phone was ringing as I entered through the back door.

"Yeah." Angry. Out of breath.

"Sounds like you're having a good night," Jack said.

"I'm sure I'm being tailed."

"You're being paranoid again."

"I chased the son-of-a-bitch outta my yard and into the street. Would've caught him if a neighbor hadn't called the cops."

"Should've let the cops catch him for you."

"And deprive me of the pleasure?"

"You're right. Besides, they prob'ly would've busted your sorry ass." He chuckled, pleased with his little joke. "Who do you think it was?"

"I don't know for sure. My guess is the Weasel."

"Seems weas-ly all right. Smart."

"Not smart enough. I'm onto him. I know who he is. And Lou's gonna tell me where he is."

"Well, I guess you don't wanna go out and have a few."

"Not tonight."

"Stick around, see if he'll come back?"

"Something like that."

"Want company?"

"Thanks, but no."

Jack was right. I thought maybe he'd come back, whoever he was. If he did, I wanted to be there. I slept in the hall, halfway between the kitchen and the living room. Figured I could hear anything at either end of the house that way. The Star was my pillow.

Lou's call woke me the next morning. Colbert had, indeed, moved to L.A., to an apartment about ten blocks from where Teddie lived – and died. Walking distance. That's why no one had seen a car. He had some smarts. Thank God for Lou, computers and the DMV, though some people might fault one or the other sometimes. I wondered if he knew I was onto him. Might he have called his dad? Did Colbert, Sr. even have a phone? Had he followed me? Maybe I wasn't so paranoid all along? If he had he was a damned good tail. I might have seen little hints of things out of the corners of my eyes, but I never saw him. Never anything concrete. Did he know about my meeting with Ramon? Trip to Calexico? Reno? Had he seen me with Laurie?

Had he followed me home? Killed Baron?

Lou had gone into work early to run him. She figured if she had to get up early, so did I. As long as I was up, there was no time to lose. I dressed. Headed out. It took about ten minutes to get to the Weasel's apartment. The name was prettier than the building, The Ocean Breeze Palms. There was no ocean. No breeze. And the palms were dead or dying. Just like the street they lived on. Just like the building named after them. Some Russian-speaking children headed off to school, arguing about the merits of the USA over the former USSR. I don't speak Russian, but enough of their interchange was in English for me to get the gist of it.

The water in the courtyard pool was black. Looked like it hadn't been cleaned in years. Mosquitoes might have liked it. No one else.

Number seven was ground floor, rear. The curtain in the front window might once have been white, maybe off-white. Now it was the same color as the pool water. The knocker was loose on its hinge, but it worked.

No answer.

I tried peeking in the window. He had the curtains taped at the edges. What the hell was he doing in there?

Knocked again.

A neighbor came out. "You are looking for Mr. Jim Colbert? Yes?" he said in a thick Russian accent.

"Da," I said. Couldn't resist.

He chuckled. "*Da, da.* Ver-ry good."

"Yeah, I'm looking for Jim."

"He is at working now."

Pretty early for a lot of jobs. "Do you know where he works?"

"Where he is working?"

"*Da,* where he is working?"

"He is working at produce section of market in Beverly Center. Starts to working very early. Ver-ry early."

Before leaving, I learned that Colbert had only been living there a few weeks. That he had a car and was a good neighbor. From the William Tell to here. I didn't know if that was a step up or down. Before the motel, Santa Barbara. Or something in between? Didn't matter. I was onto him now.

"Thank you." I ditched for the street and my car. The Beverly Center – seemed I was spending a lot of time there lately and I hated the place, wouldn't shop there for all the diamonds in South Africa – was only a couple minutes away. The market was at street level, with its own little parking section. I pulled in. It was half full. I parked near the front door, in a loading zone. Someone started yelling at me to move.

"No speak English," I said in an accent from a world of my own making. He threw his hands up and walked away. Inside the store, I headed for the produce section. In the back, someone was putting lettuce out. I could tell it was a man. No more than that.

I approached. Fingering the Star under my windbreaker.

The man turned around. Strike one. Not the Weasel.

"Can I help you?" he said.

"Does Jim Colbert work here?"

"Yes, if there's anything I can–"

"No thank you. Is he in today?"

"He's in back. Are you the friend who's going to help him move?"

"Move?"

"Today's his last day. Didn't even give two weeks' notice. Hell, he only worked here a few weeks. That's like a lot of them today, they just don't got no pride in their work."

Must've killed Teddie on his lunch hour. Plenty of time to do it and get back.

He stuck his hand out. "I'm Terry Lanton, produce manager."

"Nice to meet you." I headed for the "Employees Only" door.

"I'm sorry, but you can't go back there."

Before I got there, a cart pushed the swinging door open. Wider. It was him – pushing the cart. We stood about twenty-five feet apart, staring each other down. It must have lasted all of a half second. Seemed like half an eternity.

Then he bolted. Back the way he came, shoving the cart in the door at an angle that made it hard to push out of the way. I pushed. It didn't go. I flew across it, knocking tomatoes and avocados in every direction.

"What's going on here?" Lanton's voice faded in the background.

The Weasel ran through the backroom, out onto the loading dock. Jumped into the parking lot and ran for his car. I had to make a split-second decision: get in my car to chase or try to stop him from getting to his. The decision was made for me. He was already pulling out of his parking place in his lumbering old Monte Carlo.

I vaulted onto the hood of his car, trying to hold onto the side mirror on the driver's side. He bashed my hand with a large flashlight. I held on. He kept bashing. I rolled off. Got to my feet and ran for my car.

He crashed the wooden gate arm. I silently thanked him for that as that would be one less dent to pay for on the rental car.

He tore out onto La Cienega, heading north. The light changed. I caught the red. I did what so many other L.A. drivers had been doing lately – I ran it. Nearly hit a cross traffic cement mixer. I figured it would have been better than hitting a carload of gang bangers.

At Sunset he turned right, heading for Hollywood. Where were the damn cops now? Nowhere in sight. We dodged in and out of traffic to Western where he headed north, up into the Hollywood Hills and Griffith Park. I didn't know if he knew where he was going, but heading *up* the winding roads of the park wouldn't get him anywhere, except maybe to the Observatory.

He couldn't know where he was going. I think he was trying to hit the freeway and took a wrong turn. We chased up the backroads of the park, past the boy toys sunning themselves on the hoods of their cars, waiting for another boy toy to pick them up.

Finally, we turned into the Observatory parking lot. He headed around one side of the circular driveway. I cut the other way, heading towards him, hoping we'd meet at some point. If not, he just might get all the way around and take the other road down.

I gunned it around the circle. He was coming for me. A school bus was unloading children near the entrance to the building. I stopped, not wanting to hit any kids. The Weasel kept coming from the other side. Shit – I hoped he wouldn't hit anyone. A teacher saw us coming and hurried the kids out of the way.

He came flying around the circle in one direction.

Me in the other.

Engines gunning.

His old Monte Carlo with the big V-8.

Me in my little Toyota rental.

A hair's breadth before we passed, I cut in front of him. He played chicken and ditched onto the sidewalk. He thought he could go around me.

No way.

He bottoms out.

Fishtails.

Hits the statue in front of the Observatory.

People running back.

Trying to get away from us.

I jam on the brakes.

Stick it in park and jump out.

He runs around the building.

I follow.

Star out.

A park ranger comes around the building.

The Weasel barrels into him.

Knocks him down.

I jump over him.

Keep on running.

If the Weasel keeps on this way, he'll circle to the front of the Observatory.

A mother tries to pull her little boy down from a quarter observation telescope.

She yanks the boy hard.

They fall back into the Weasel.

Knock him to one knee.

He gets up.

It's enough time.

I catch him.

He throws a weak right.

I block.

Counter with a left.

Square on the jaw.

He stumbles.

Kicks me in the groin.

I drop to my knees.
He takes off.
I catch his pant leg.
Tumble him.
We roll on the ground.
The ranger limps toward us.
The Weasel throws me.
Jumps the wall.
Into the bush below the Observatory.
I follow.
Jumping.
Rolling.
Down the hill.
He limps a few yards ahead of me.
I run down the hill.
Jump off a rock point.
Dive for him.
If I miss it's the end of me.
He stumbles.
I land on him.
We roll into a tree.
Arms flailing.
Legs kicking.
I'm on top of him.
He's face down.
I'm about to use some of that old SEAL training.
Break his neck.
No. Stop.
The ranger shouts.
I stop.
Pull the Weasel to his feet.
This is your lucky day, pal.
He snorts for air.

◈ ◈ ◈

The ranger took my gun. I tried to proffer my P.I. I.D. to him. He didn't want to see it. Held a gun – my gun – on both of us, while he fished out his cuffs.

"We won't be able to climb up," the Weasel said, out of breath. The ranger looked up toward the Observatory. No trail. Just scree and scrub. Steep. He put the cuffs back in their holster, motioned us forward, upward with the gun. Escorted the Weasel and me up the hill. I helped him drag the Weasel, telling the ranger he was a wanted fugitive. Feigning breathlessness so I wouldn't have to say anymore.

"I'll get you," Colbert said to me. "I can, you know. I'll tell everyone, the papers, TV, everyone what a hero you are."

We climbed over the wall, back onto the Observatory platform. The ranger cuffed the Weasel, held the gun on me. Didn't trust either of us. Sirens wailed in the background. Cops on the way. Never there when you need them.

The ranger, Weasel and I headed toward the front of the Observatory. The ranger had one hand on the Weasel's cuffed left arm, the other holding my own gun on my back. He was pushing us forward. A crowd of children stared at us as we walked by. The Weasel looked down at them. The ranger kept pushing us forward.

The Weasel broke free, ran for the wall. Jumped to it and tottered along until he came to the point where the ground below was farthest from the top of the wall. The ranger and I chased after him. We almost got to him. He jumped. We were too late.

A piercing scream wrenched the air as the body landed on the hard ground below. A snap. We could hear it all the way at the top of the wall.

The ranger and I scurried over the wall to the twisted body below. It was too late.

◈ ◈ ◈

I hoped it didn't make the news before I had a chance to talk to Rita. If she had to find out, I wanted to be the one to tell her.

CHAPTER 37

I had wanted to kill the Weasel, not because I was angry at him, but so he couldn't talk. So Rita wouldn't find out the part I'd played in Teddie's death. The ranger's "no" had stopped me, but I think I would have stopped anyway. I hope so. Killing him would have been the chicken-shit's way out. The Fuck-up's way.

He died of a broken neck. His own making. With his hands cuffed he couldn't break the fall when he jumped and landed on his neck. Was it intentional – a way to escape jail, or was it an accident?

Between Sergeant Webb's and Tom Bond's vouching for me, the cops didn't file a weapons charge for the Star. I was lucky.

Mrs. Perlman and the gardener ID'd the Weasel as the man who had murdered Teddie. People were treating me like a hero. The news media wanted interviews. I declined. They videoed me entering and exiting the police station to give my story. Camped out in front of my house, hoping I'd give them a few words of wisdom. Jack came by and we watched old black and white movies on American Movie Classics and had a few beers. Didn't say much.

The phone was ringing off the hook. Reporters, media people. Hollywood producers. I wasn't answering, letting the service screen the calls. I didn't want to be a hero. Didn't feel like one. I had wanted to make amends to Teddie and her family for having taken a quick two hundred-fifty bucks on a scut job and having fucked up. Nothing would ever bring her back. But I felt I had evened the score somewhat.

When I checked in for messages late in the afternoon, there had been separate messages from Mrs. Matson and Warren, thanking me. Warren even partially apologized for his behavior. Chagrined, the operator read me the message he'd left verbatim: "You didn't do too bad for a white guy. I owe you one, honky." I thought the honky was affectionate. I wanted to believe it was. It sounded almost like an apology. But I didn't want his apology. Didn't need it. He didn't owe me anything. And I hoped I was square with him and his mother now, even though they didn't know the whole story. I hadn't found Anna and Pilar. I hoped they'd see the story in the papers or on TV and feel comfortable enough to come out of hiding.

Lou had also left a message congratulating me and reminding me about El Coyote. The one message I was hoping for wasn't there.

A few minutes later, the phone rang through. It was one of the service operators: "Mr. Rogers, there's a call on the line I thought you might want me to put through. She says she's a close friend of yours. Her name is Rita Matson."

❖ ❖ ❖

The reporters out front didn't realize who she was and let her through the crowd. "Probably thought I was the maid," she said with a hint of bitterness, then a smile. Jack laughed. Too hard. The smile faded from Rita's lips. She stood by the back door, her dark hair silhouetted by the golden hour sun streaming in through the pane at the top of the door. It was awkward. I could say that was because of Jack being there. It wasn't. It would have been awkward anyway.

"It's good to see you again," Jack said, gathering his overweight kit bag.

"Duke told me on the phone that you helped him. Thank you." She put her hand out. Jack took it. Shook.

"Segue," he said, disappearing out the back door. If anyone could handle the media bloodsuckers, Jack could. If they pissed him off enough, he might use them for target practice.

The sound of a Harley revving. He was gone. There was still a pall of uneasiness between us. The air felt heavy.

"Would you like something to drink?"

"No thanks. Where's Baron?" she said, looking around.

I explained what had happened and that I still wasn't sure who had done it.

"I'm sorry. Everybody's losing something these days."

We retreated to the living room, sat on opposite ends of the couch. The room was gloomy. The curtains were closed so I wouldn't have to see the leeches on my front lawn. At least they weren't making a lot of noise.

I wondered if she knew. If my guilt had shown and she'd known all along. I didn't think so. Didn't want to ask.

"My whole family is grateful to you," she said, tentatively.

They shouldn't be.

"I'm glad I could help. Still, it was my job."

"You attacked it with more energy than most people put into a job. Do you treat all your cases that way?"

I didn't want to respond to that. Thought I'd switch subjects: "I'm sorry I didn't return your calls more promptly."

"I thought you might be avoiding me. 'Cause of the black-white thing. I didn't want to believe that, so I made up my mind that you were busy working on the case."

"I was. I've been all over. Calexico. Reno. Santa Barbara."

"I read the police account in the paper. Don't you want to talk to the press?"

"Fifteen minutes of fame just isn't enough," I gave her a half smile. "Besides, they don't want the real story, they want something they can put on *Hard Copy*. Sensational. It was nothing special."

She moved closer, brushed her finger gently along my swollen lip. "Nothing special."

"All part of the job."

"That's what I'm still curious about, who were you working for on this *job*?"

"You know I can't tell you."

"Confidentiality and all that."

"It could just be a friend of hers. Someone who wanted to know."

"It wasn't the studio."

"I never said it was."

She was making me suspicious. There was no way for her to know the truth, of course, but the more she talked the more it seemed like she had figured it out. If not completely, at least partly. I thought I was pretty good at playing poker face. Maybe not as good as I pretended to myself. Or maybe there was so much guilt it couldn't help but show through.

I put my arm around her, tried to pull her closer. She squirmed. Shrugged it off. She grew colder. The warmth was gone from her eyes, mouth. Voice.

"What's wrong?" I stood up.

"Why're you putting your arm around me?"

"I didn't know it was a crime. In fact, I thought you kind of liked it."

"You ignore me for days. Don't respond to my calls."

"I was working the case."

"Bullshit."

"I got the guy, didn't I?"

"Yes, and I am grateful for that. But were you working the case twenty-four hours a day? Didn't you know I wanted to talk to you? Why would I have called so many times?"

"I'm sorry, I–"

"I don't want to hear it. I think I know why you were avoiding me. And now it's all over, and you're acting sweet and all, but distant. The case is over. Why the distance?"

"Just coming down from a rough few days."

"You know what your trouble is, Duke. You're not honest. Not with me. Not even with yourself."

"What're you talking about? What else am I supposed to do?" My voice was tense, anger-filled.

Now she stood. Each of us at opposite ends of the couch. Leaning forward, in near-pugilistic stances.

"Now that it's all over, things are quieting down. Oh never mind."

"What? Tell me what you're talking about."

"Am I your nigger bitch? Was I? Good for a roll in the hay during the riot?"

"You're crazy."

"Am I? I don't hear from you, you don't return calls. Now the riot's over you don't need my– I think it made you feel good to have a nigger-woman during the riots. Made you feel good and liberal. It was also a shelter for you, like Tiny. Hey, if you're walking through Niggertown with Tiny maybe you're okay. Maybe the brothers and sisters won't beat on you. Maybe if you're sleeping with a nigger bitch, same thing. You're okay.

Things aren't as bad as they seem. You can assuage your white guilt."

"I don't have any white guilt. I haven't done anything. But I do think you've been talking to Warren too much."

"Hardly. I've been thinking about this. All those nights when I felt so alone and no return calls from you."

"So this is your response? To lay it down to some racial thing. I'm not your master."

"And I ain't *yo'* slave," she said in poor black dialect. "But you do get your kicks sleeping with a Negress, don't you? Lotta white men do. You'd never bring one home to mommy and daddy though."

"You don't know what you're talking about, you stupid–"

"Stupid what? — Nigger?" She started to cry. The anger had been welling up in me. I could hardly control it. She was partially right, I think. She had been a safe haven in rough waters. It wasn't that I hadn't liked her, or didn't still. But it was a crazy time. I was running on adrenalin overdrive. I did like her. And it was more than the riots. More than shelter in the storm. It was more than Teddie, but she didn't know that. I don't think the word that was welling up was *nigger*. I didn't want to believe that. I didn't know what it was. Whatever, though, I'm glad she cut it off.

I stepped towards her. She put her hand out in front of her chest to hold me off. I stopped.

"That's what this search for Teddie's killer was all about too. White guilt."

"You're right." But I didn't mean it the way she did.

She looked through me with intense brown eyes. It was as if she was shocked that she'd been right. She had been right. But she'd been wrong.

"It isn't white guilt how you mean it. Colbert came to me to find an address for him. He gave me a name, Teddie or Theodora Matson." My voice had softened. She had to ask me to speak louder. "I had never heard of her. Don't watch much TV, except for old movies and news. He told me he was an old friend. Seemed like an easy gig." I told her the whole story, every detail. Sat in a chair facing the couch. I wanted to hide my head, bury it in my hands. I wouldn't let myself. Forced myself to look her in the eye.

She sat on the arm of the couch. She also didn't want to look at me. She forced herself to. "For two hundred fifty dollars. My sister. And then you slept with me." Her voice cracked. She was holding the tears back.

I went on: "I've done jobs like this before. There was no way to know. That's not an excuse. It's just the way it is."

"No. The way it is, is Teddie is dead. No wonder you don't want to talk to the media. The whole time you played me for a fool."

"Are you concerned about Teddie or about how you think I treated you?"

"Both. Warren's right. Even he softened. He shouldn't have."

"I never played you or your family for fools. I wanted to get the killer. If I'd told you the truth, you wouldn't have helped me."

She slunk down into the couch, huddled in the corner. "That's damn for sure. And then you had the nerve to sleep with me. But I guess that's to be expected. I am just a nigger."

"That's your word. Not mine."

"It's the white man's word."

"Your feelings are hurt. But that's not the way it is."

"Then why didn't you return my calls?"

"I was afraid to."

"A big ex-SEAL like you."

"Why don't you cut the crap? Let's have a decent conversation."

"Niggers can't have—"

I jumped out of my seat. She put her hands in front of her face, ready to block a blow. I wasn't going to hit her. I grabbed her. Jerked her up and to me. Held her. She tried to get away. I wouldn't let go.

"You're right. I was confused. I liked you but it was all happening so fast. I still like you, though I'm sure you don't like me anymore. That's okay. I don't blame you. I don't like myself very much when I think about it. I was afraid to call you back. Afraid to hurt you. Afraid to tell you the truth. Debating whether or not I ever should. Wondering if, after the riots, there would be anything for us. Between us. Or was it all just a *wartime romance*? Two people caught up in something bigger than themselves. Would they, we, have anything in common once it was over?"

She broke free, stepped back. I collapsed on the couch. Exhausted. Talking it out. Telling the truth had wiped me out.

"Are you all right?" she said.

"Yeah."

"We can never tell my mother or Warren."

"It's your call." I closed my eyes. "I didn't intend to hurt you or your family. When I did, I tried to make it up by finding him. There's no way to do anymore than that. I won't say I'm sorry again. Not because I'm not. Because it won't help anything."

She sat next me. Let her hand fall to my thigh. We sat like that for about ten minutes. Silent. Someone knocked on the front door. I let them keep knocking. Didn't care who it was. Probably a reporter. I took her hand and led her to the guest bedroom. Pulled out one of my butterfly collection notebooks. Handed it to her.

"I want you to have this."

"What for?"

"I don't know. I think you'll enjoy it."

"So will you. And you don't need to buy me off."

"I'm not trying to. You see, this is the problem. Now that you know, you'll be suspect of everything. I'll never be able to do anything, give you anything without your thinking it's guilt."

She took the notebook. Clutched it in her hand. She even looked beautiful when she cried.

❖ ❖ ❖

She left a few minutes after that. We had decided to wait a while before talking to each other again. No set time. If one of us decided to call the other, then we'd call. Until then, we'd wait.

❖ ❖ ❖

I never did find out if it was the Weasel or Craylock or some crazy person off the street who did Baron. But I would keep looking until I found him or knew he was dead already. And I never found out who was following me, but I'd wager the mortgage it was the Weasel. It would be nice if things were neat and tidy, but they never are. I also wondered what became of Pilar and Anna. Thought I might give Ramon a call some day and see if he was interested in having me find out.

❖ ❖ ❖

I missed Rita. Several times I started to dial her. Each time, I hung up before connecting. A couple times when my phone rang and there was no one on the other end I wondered if she was doing the same thing.

I took time off of work to work around the house. Run at the beach. The city was returning to a semblance of normal. On the surface. Underneath, tension roiled. I tried not to let it bother me. Not that I wasn't concerned. But I figured I'd better work out my own tensions before trying to solve the world's.

One day, I drove down Beverly Boulevard until it turned into Santa Monica Boulevard. I headed toward the beach. A few blocks before the water, I turned up a sidestreet. Parked in front of the Ocean View Rest Home. No ocean view. There was an ocean breeze.

"Mr. Rogers," a nurse said. "It's been ages."

She led me to my father's room. The TV droned. He had been a round, robust man with a ruddy complexion and thick brown hair. He had shrunk to a ghost of himself. His hair was thin and greasy. His cheeks sunken and pale. Eyes dull.

"Hello, dad," I said, taking his hand. It was clammy. He grunted some kind of greeting. But it could have been to anyone. He didn't recognize me. I sat there about an hour. We had never gotten along. He had never been the father I would have picked. I wasn't the son he wanted. If we'd only respected each other on our own terms we might have gotten along. When I left, a sadness hung over my heart. I drove to the ocean. The sun was dying. Golden hour almost over. I watched the sun set over the horizon, a flaming ball of orange amidst bands of magenta, lavender and yellow.

On my way home, a white woman was stopped at a stoplight. A group of black kids, couldn't have been more than ten or eleven years old, were crossing in front of her car. A late model Honda Prelude. She looked nervous. Averting her eyes. The four kids were taking their time crossing the street. When they were in front of her car, the largest of them turned, pounded on the hood three times. "White bitch," he yelled. The others laughed. She looked ready to cry. Rolled her window up all the way. Made sure the doors were locked. I pulled up beside her. The boys moved on.

The light changed. She drove off. On her rear bumper, which the boys couldn't have seen, a sticker said: "If we knew it was going to be this much trouble, we would have picked the cotton ourselves."

Some things never change. And some people never learn.

I remembered Warren's line that I would never understand. I guess I never will.

The End

Coming soon from Paul D. Marks, *Broken Windows*, the sequel to *White Heat*. Read an excerpt:

BROKEN WINDOWS

Prologue

The Hollywood Sign beckoned her like a magnet – or maybe like flame to a moth. The sign glowed golden in the magic hour sun – that time of day around sunrise and sunset when the light falls soft and warm and cinematographers love to shoot. Like so many others, Susan Karubian had come here seeking fame and fortune, hoping to make her mark on the world. And she would do just that, just not quite in the heady way she had anticipated.

She had spent hours deciding what to wear. After all, this wasn't exactly in the etiquette books. She finally decided on a tasteful dress with high heeled sandals.

The young woman drove her Passat down Hollywood Boulevard, turning up Franklin, past the Magic Castle. She turned slowly up Beachwood Canyon, past the low rent area north of Franklin, up through the towering stone gates with their "Welcome to Beachwood Canyon" signs. Past the movie star homes in the hills. She drove in circles, past piles of rubble from the earthquake several months ago, figuring that sooner or later she'd hit the right combination of roads and end up where she wanted to be.

She reached the crest of the mountain – mountain or hill? What was the difference anyway? A small concrete building with an antenna sat just below the road, which crested the mountain. No cars. No one around. It was like the Sherman Oaks Galleria on a Monday morning.

She got out of the car and realized she'd have to hike down to get to the sign. She had thought it would be at the top of the mountain. She rolled up the windows, locked the car, her purse on the floor by the gas pedal. The note that someone was sure to find snug in her pocket.

She treaded toward the edge of the road. The incessant rain of the last couple weeks had broken. The view from up here was incredible. You could almost see Mexico to the south and the Pacific glittering in the west. A beautiful view of the city, shining and bright from up here. Pretty and clean. Millions of ants scurrying this way and that on important business. Oh yes, everyone here had important business all day and all night. Everyone but her. She gazed down at Los Angeles on the cusp of the Millennium. The place to be. Center of the universe.

She hesitated at the edge of the road, her toe kicking some gravel down the hill. It clattered its way down, somehow reminding her of the industrial music in the clubs she liked to frequent.

Should she try to talk to him? What would be the point now? She was talked out. And he wouldn't forgive her. Why should he? She had hurt him. No, it was beyond hurt. There was no way to rationalize it.

She tentatively stepped off the road, pressing on the dirt, testing its firmness. Loose gravel rolled down the hill. After taking off her Jimmy Choo high heels and holding them in one hand, she made her way down. She walked and slid and finally made it to the landing – she didn't know what else to call it – where the sign rested. The city glowed from here, shimmering with hope and desire and people wanting to make their dreams come true. She had come here for the same reason. The Hollywood Dream. The American Dream. She had wanted to be in front of the cameras from the time her parents took her to her first movie-theater movie, The Black Stallion, in 1979 when she was five. After seeing the movie she had wanted a horse, but more than that she wanted to be in a movie. She hadn't yet heard of Hollywood, but by the time she was thirteen she was making plans to come here. And nothing could have stopped her. Everyone told her how hard a career in movies was, how few made it. But she had faith in herself. She was attractive, more than, though she didn't want to be conceited. And she had talent. She had been acting in school plays for years. She was the star, Juliet to popular Paul Bonnefield's Romeo, in middle school. Rave reviews. Fake gold acting awards. What did that mean in the big picture? She had come here gushing with hope and optimism. She still thought she could make it, but what was the point now?

People looked up this way all the time. How many were looking at her now, as she climbed the scaffolding.

Higher and higher.

Her heart pounded through her chest. Her head throbbed.

Was she doing the right thing?

She reached one hand over the other, gripping the steel scaffolding. She held her shoes in her hands and the hard metal bit into her stockinged feet. The pain felt good, like penance.

Would anyone notice? Would anyone care that she was no longer here?

She gripped the scaffolding with all her strength and pulled herself up another rung.

"Don't look down." Her breath came in short bursts. She climbed higher. Warm blood trickled down her right palm.

She worried that the 6.7 quake last January had loosened the sign's footing. Would she fall even before she made it to the top?

Reaching the summit of the 'H,' she pulled herself up and sat on top, balancing as best she could. The wind slammed her, but she maintained her precarious balance. She clutched a piece of scaffolding – warm to the touch. A gust of wind hammered her. She began to topple, holding onto the scaffolding with all her strength. It wouldn't do to fall off. It wasn't deliberate enough.

Her stockings ran. She thought this might happen, but had hoped it wouldn't.

She looked out again – the golden city. Los Angeles. Hollywood. Was that the ocean dancing in the distance?

Sitting on top of the 'H,' a light breeze blew her night-dark hair. She flicked it out of her eyes. She put on her shoes. She talked to God. He didn't respond. If He did, she didn't hear it.

What had she done wrong? Was she just in the wrong place at the wrong time? No, she had chosen her life.

The note she'd written was burning a hole in her pocket. She took it out for one last read. The wind blew up, snatching it away.

"Damn!" There was no time to write a new note and nothing to write it with.

She forced herself into a standing position. The breeze made her unsteady and she billowed in the wind like a sail. Her dress snagged on the scaffolding.

She was scared to death, literally. That wouldn't last long. She held her breath and pushed off as hard as she could. Shrieking. One shoe flew off as she plummeted downward. If she couldn't be famous in life she would be famous in death. But one way or another she'd make her mark. She hoped her fall from grace would be graceful, even if her life had not.

About the Author

Paul D. Marks is the author of over thirty published short stories in a variety genres, ranging from noir to straight mystery, satire to serious fiction, including several award winners. His work has appeared in various anthologies and magazines, including Dime, the Deadly Ink 2010 Short Story Collection, Murder in La La Land, Murder Across the Map, LAndmarked for Murder, Hardboiled magazine and more. He has also published numerous magazine/periodical articles as well as having done film work.

He is also the last person to have shot on the fabled MGM backlot before it bit the dust to make way for housing. According to Steven Bingen, one of the authors of the well-received book MGM: HOLLYWOOD'S GREATEST BACKLOT: "That 40 page chronological list I mentioned of films shot at the studio ends with his [Paul D. Marks'] name on it."

Visit Paul at: www.PaulDMarks.com
www.whiteheatnovel.blogspot.com

CPSIA information can be obtained at www.ICGtesting.com
Printed in the USA
LVOW040521180812

294811LV00010B/6/P